SUBSIDIA BIBLICA

42

ERNST VOGT S.J. (ed.)

A Lexicon of Biblical Aramaic

Clarified by Ancient Documents

Translated and Revised by J.A. Fitzmyer S.J.

GREGORIAN & BIBLICAL PRESS

Original Title *Lexicon Linguae Aramaicae Veteris Testamenti. Documentis Antiquis Illustratum*
Edidit Ernestus Vogt S.J.

© 1971 E.P.I.B. - First Edition
1994 First reprint with corrections
2008 Second Reprint with corrections

Cover: Serena Aureli

© 2011 Gregorian & Biblical Press
Piazza della Pilotta 35, 00187 - Roma
www.gbpress.net - books@biblicum.com

ISBN 978-88-7653-**655**-7

Table of Contents

INTRODUCTION (Original, 1970)

In his *Lexicon Hebraicum Veteris Testamenti,* Franz Zorell aimed at presenting not only the various meanings of words in a general way, but also at explaining specifically their peculiar uses. Since he left behind no notes on the Aramaic part of the Old Testament, a tool is needed to match that part of the purpose and character of the Hebrew part. The principal difficulty in providing such a tool comes from the brevity of the Biblical Aramaic texts, which in the Hebrew Bible hardly fill twenty pages. Moreover, the sense and occurrence of many words appear only rarely, and some terms are used only in a secondary sense. To remedy this situation, the meanings and use of Biblical Aramaic words will be clarified by the quotation of ancient Aramaic documents. Individual words will be listed not by themselves, but in most cases together with their contexts.

Since the Old Testament Aramaic texts were for a long time the only example of pre-Christian Aramaic, they had to be explained either from themselves alone or from ancient translations of them. From the end of the nineteenth century, however, so many Aramaic documents have been discovered and interpreted by the dedicated work and talent of scholars that the Aramaic language, which played an important role in the lives of the people of the ancient Near East, emerged from oblivion, and the long history of this language became known.

Although the language of such documents clearly manifests differences, according to their varied periods, regions, and writers, a basic unity nonetheless appears, at least in the written language, which first emerged in the ninth century B.C. and survived in a remarkable way for at least a thousand years. Into this history of the language, the Biblical Aramaic texts clearly fit, and it is readily seen how many of the documents retrieved can and must contribute to a more thorough understanding of these biblical writings.

Hence this Aramaic part of the *Lexicon* presents in a short space examples of both the individual biblical and extrabiblical words. It thus sets these words in a broader context, shows the similarities and differences, and stimulates the reader to consult the documents themselves. It also presents meaning of words that perhaps do not occur in the Old Testament, and thus it gives a truer picture and a more graphic image of the biblical vocabulary.

Moreover, the words will be quoted in their immediate context, since in a sentence, no matter how short, they become alive and assume a concrete meaning. For this reason, the reader will be able more easily to understand the usage of the words of the biblical writing, pointed with vowels, as different from the nonvocalized extrabiblical words -- more easily than if he or she is confronted with only the bare numbers of chapters and verses. Thus the reader will be forced to derive the relation in each instance, especially where the verse is lengthy or where the Aramaic sentence is an extended syntactical period.

Only those words are listed that occur in the Old Testament Aramaic writings: Ezra 4:6--6:18; 7:12-26; Dan 2:4b--7:28; Jer 10:11; Gen 31:47. Thus all the forms of each word are given according to the Masoretic text (*BHS*^{3}). For some nouns, the probable premasoretic form is added, written in italic characters.[1]

---

[1] Likewise an attempt is made to vocalize some extrabiblical vocabulary. The vowel *é* at the end of a word seems to have been *ę́* (< *-*í*); see K. Beyer, *ZDMG* 120 (1970) 198.

Only those Old Testament passages are listed verbatim that for some reason have the meaning and usage of the word in question, whereas similar passages that hardly have a different meaning are indicated only by numbers. Texts are chosen from the ancient documents, the sense of which is sufficiently clear; but some, especially those drawn from fragmentary documents or those only recently published, will undoubtedly be better understood with the passage of time. To clarify the language of Ezra and Daniel, documents are used that are not too remote from the periods of such writings, but also older texts, and even some more recent ones. Biblical and extrabiblical examples are not quoted either separately or in a historical order, but rather according to their meaning. However, the age and the area, from which the individual texts come, are indicated carefully. That these notes may be understood more easily, a brief historical overview of the main documents is provided below, even if it is disputed.[2]

     I. Old Aramaic (ca. 900-700 B.C.). The first Aramaic documents appeared in the 9th century, when the kingdom of Damascus, called the "Kingdom of Aram," flourished as the most influential of the Aramean states, especially during the reign of Barhadad II and Haza'el.[3] These early documents commemorate the kings of Damascus and attest to the beginning of the characteristic classical form of the language and its orthography. -- 9th century: Stele from Brēdsh (near Aleppo, Syria), on

---

[2] See J.A. Fitzmyer, *Genesis Apocryphon*, p. 18 n.60 [1966 edition]; see H.L. Ginsberg, *TS* 28 (1967) 574, who is in agreement; cf. R. Degen, *Altaramäische Grammatik*, 1969, pp. 1-2.

[3] The inscription on the small altar from Tell Halāf (to the east of the town of Harran) is to be attributed perhaps to the 10th century (see *KAI* §231); it seems to be an attempt to write in Aramaic.

which "Barhadad . . . king of Aram" is named (*KAI* §201); Ivory plate from Arslan Tash (East of the city of Carchemish), on which "our lord Haza'el" is named (*KAI* §232); Inscription *lšqy'* discovered at Ein Gev.[4] -- Ca. 800: Stele of King Zkr, of the kingdom of Ḥamāt, discovered at Āfiṣ (between Aleppo and Ḥama), on which "Barhadad (III). son of Haza'el, king of Aram" (*KAI* §202) is mentioned. -- Ca. 750: Steles of the King of Arpad, discovered at Sefire (near Aleppo). -- Ca. 730: Stele of Barrakib, king of Sam'al, discovered at Zenjirli (west of the city of Carchemish) (*KAI* §216).[5] -- End of the 8th century, beginning of the 7th: Inscriptions on weights found at Nimrud (*CIS* II 1), which, beside other indications, show that the Aramaic language had spread to Assyria too [usually called "Nineveh Lion Weights"].

II. Imperial [Official] Aramaic (ca. 700-300 B.C.). Although the Aramean states in Syria were conquered and absorbed into the Assyrian Empire, the Aramaic language continued to flourish and somehow even became an international language (see 2 Kgs 18:26). -- 7th century: Two steles of priests (*KAI* §225-226) of Nerab (near Aleppo); Letter found in the city of Assur (*KAI* §233) and three contracts (*KAI* §234-236). -- Ca. 600: Papyrus discovered at Saqqāra in northern Egypt, containing a letter sent by King Adon to a Pharaoh (*KAI* §266). -- 571/570: Contract, on which the year is indicated (*KAI* §227), perhaps found at Sefire (near Aleppo).

Aramaic documents abound from the time of the Persian Empire. 5th century: Many ostraca and numerous papyri have

---

[4] On the eastern side of Lake Gennesaret (*IEJ* 14 [1964] 27).
[5] Two inscriptions found at Zenjirli (KAI §214-215) are not recorded here, because their language differs from the classical Aramaic of the other documents.

been found at Elephantine in southern Egypt (*AP, BMAP*), a-mong which is an Aramaic copy of a remarkable text, which Darius I inscribed on a mountain in Bisitun, as well as the story of the sage Aḥiqar.[6] In Hermopolis (between Cairo and Karnak) eight papyrus letters came to light in northern Egypt; they are preserved today in Padua, Italy. Thirteen letters, written on animal-skin toward the end of the 5th century in the bureau of Arsham, a prince of the Persian royal family, were sent to Egypt (*AD*); they show the use of Aramaic in the Persian administration. From Egypt comes also a grave inscription of the 5th/4th century, preserved today in the Museum of Carpentras, France (*KAI* §269).

The spread of the Aramaic language into Asia Minor and Arabia is attested by inscriptions of the 5th/4th centuries: in Cilicia (*KAI* §258-259, 261), Lydia (*KAI* §260), Mysia (*KAI* §263); and three inscriptions in Tēmā, Arabia (*KAI* §228-230).

III. Middle Aramaic (300 B.C.-- A.D. 200). So many documents have come to light from the end of the Persian Empire, that one has to distinguish subdivisions in this period and use proper names for them.

100 B.C.-- A.D. 100: Many Aramaic texts from Qumran in the Judean Desert (DJD 1, 3, 31, 37), especially the rather lengthy *Genesis Apocryphon*, the language of which is remarkably close to that of the Book of Daniel. -- 1st-2d century A.D.:

---

[6] Aḥiqar, mentioned also in the Book of Tobit, is named in the recently discovered cuneiform tablet, published by J. van Dijk in H. J. Lenzen, *18. Vorläufiger Bericht . . . Ausgrabungen von Uruk-Warka*, 1962, p. 45; see also pp. 51-52: "(In the days of) Esarhaddon, the King, Aba-enli-dari (was) Ummānu (i.e., chief of the sages), [whom] Arameans call Aḫuqar." Aba-enli-dari is known elsewhere as a scribe.

Several inscriptions (*KAI* §237-257) from Ḥatra (to the west of the city of Assur). -- 2d century: Two contracts from the Judean Desert (*Bib* 38 [1957] 461-69), and several other texts from Murabbaʻât (DJD 2).[7]

From this rather sparse overview, it is evident how important Aramaic was in ancient times and how widely and constantly it spread, as it was used also in the Old Testament.

Rome, September 1970

E. Vogt, S.J.

---

[7] Of Late Aramaic (A.D. 200-700) and Modern Aramaic, no account is taken in this work.

PREFACE TO ENGLISH FORM

Since 1970, when E. Vogt composed the foregoing Introduction to this lexicon, many new Aramaic texts have been discovered, most of them in the Dead Sea Scrolls from Qumran and other sites in the Judean Desert. As of this writing, unfortunately, one is still awaiting the publication of the last half of the Aramaic texts from Qumran Cave 4. I have tried to add some further references to such Qumran Aramaic texts, when it is possible and pertinent.

It is also evident that some corrections had to be made to Vogt's work, which, excellent though it was, was governed by what was known about the texts cited at that time. For instance, in the case of the *Genesis Apocryphon* of Qumran Cave 1, parts of the fragmentary text were read differently then from the way they are read today.

Two items should be noted especially in this English translation of the lexicon, items that occur in Vogt's Latin form, which he did not explain. First, there are times when a reference is given and a colon (:) follows it, with further references, sometimes followed by a semicolon (;): e.g., Dan 3:28: 3:22; 6:13; Ezra 1:4. The further references in such a case are usually not verbatim the same or identical to that preceding the colon, but only similar in construction. Second, the italicized vocalizations in parentheses following an Aramaic word are of two sorts: (a) those following an unvocalized form suggest a vocalization: e.g., the infinitive מוּבַל (*môbal*) from the root יבל ; (b) those following a vocalized (biblical) form explain the kind of word it is or display the form from which it developed (e.g., יְגַר (*yagr*) indicates that it is a *qatl* type of noun: *yagr* > *yagár* > *yĕgár*. Or it may say simply (*qatl*).

Finally, I have to express my gratitude to Robert Althann, S.J., who so carefully read the manuscript and suggested many corrections.

12

Abbreviations

AD	G.R. Driver, *Aramaic Documents of the Fifth Century B.C., Abridged and Revised Edition* (Oxford: Clarendon, 1957).
AEDH	W. Muss-Arnolt, *Assyrisch-Englisch-Deutsches Handwörterbuch*; also called *A Concise Dictionary of the Assyrian Language*. (Berlin: Reuther & Reichard, 1905).
AGI	R. Degen, *Altaramäische Grammatik der Inschriften des 10.-8. Jh.v.Chr.* (Wiesbaden: F. Steiner, 1969).
AH	F. Rosenthal, *An Aramaic Handbook* (Porta linguarum orientalium ns 10; 2 double parts;Wiesbaden: Harrassowitz, 1967).
AHW	W. von Soden, *Akkadisches Handwörterbuch* (3 vols.; Wiesbaden: Harrassowitz, 1965-81).
Aḥ.	"The Story of Aḥiḳar" (in *AP* pp. 204-48); cf. J.M. Lindenberger, *The Aramaic Proverbs of Ahiqar* Baltimore, MD: Johns Hopkins University Press, 1983).
Amarna	J.A. Knudtzon, *Die El-Amarna-Tafeln* (Leipzig, 1915; repr. Aalen: O. Zeller, 1964).
ANHW	G. Dalman, *Aramäisch-Neuhebräisches Handwörterbuch* (3d ed.; Göttingen: E. Pfeiffer, 1938).
AP	Cowley, A., *Aramaic Papyri of the Fifth Century B.C.* (Oxford: Clarendon Press, 1923; repr. Osnabrück: O. Zeller, 1967).
API	E. Herzfeld, *Altpersische Inschriften* (Berlin: D. Reimer, 1938).
APO	E. Sachau, *Aramäische Papyrus und Ostraka einer jüdischen Militärkolonie zu Elephantine* (Leipzig: J.C. Hinrichs, 1911).

ASA   F. Altheim and R. Stiehl, *Die Aramäische Sprache unter den Achaimeniden: Erster Band, Geschichtliche Untersuchungen* (Frankfurt am M.: V. Klostermann, 1963).

ASAE   *Annales du Service des Antiquités de l'Egypte.*

BA   *Biblical Archaeologist.*

BE   J.T. Milik, *The Books of Enoch: Aramaic Fragments of Qumrân Cave 4* (Oxford: Clarendon, 1976).

BHS   K. Elliger et al., *Biblia Hebraica Stuttgartensia* 4th ed.; Stuttgart: Deutsche Bibelgesellschaft, 1977).

Bib   *Biblica.*

BibOr   Biblica et orientalia.

Bisitun J.C. Greenfield and B. Porten, *The Bisitun Inscription of Darius the Great: Aramaic Version* (Corpus Inscriptionum Iranicarum. I/V/1; London: Lund Humphries, 1982). Cf. "The Behistun Inscription," *AP* pp. 248-71.

BL   H. Bauer and P. Leander, *Grammatik des Biblisch-Aramäischen* (Halle-Saale: M. Niemeyer, 1927); cited according to page numbers and marginal letters.

BMAP   E.G. Kraeling, *The Brooklyn Museum Aramaic Papyri: New Documents of the Fifth Century B.C. from the Jewish Colony of Elephantine* (New Haven, CT: Yale University Press, 1953).

Brock.   C. Brockelmann, *Grundriss der vergleichenden Grammatik der semitischen Sprachen* (2 vols.; Berlin: Reuther & Reichard, 1908, 1913; repr. Hildesheim: G. Olms, 1966).

CAD   *Assyrian Dictionary* (21 vols.; Chicago, IL: University of Chicago, 1956-<2006>).

CIS	L'Académie des Inscriptions et Belles-Lettres, *Corpus Inscriptionum Semiticarum* (19 vols.; Paris: Reipublicae Typographeum, 1881-).
DISO	C.-F. Jean and J. Hoftijzer, *Dictionnaire des Inscriptions Sémitiques de l'Ouest* (Leiden: Brill, 1965).
DJD	Discoveries in the Judaean Desert (39 vols.; Oxford: Clarendon, 1955-2008).
DSD	*Dead Sea Discoveries.*
DTT	M. Jastrow, *A Dictionary of the Targumim, the Talmud Babli and Yerushalmi, and the Midrashic Literature* (2 vols.; New York/Berlin: Choreb, 1926).
GBA	F. Rosenthal, *A Grammar of Biblical Aramaic* (Porta linguarum orientalium ns 5; 7th ed.; Wiesbaden: Harrassowitz, 2006).
HALOT	L. Koehler and W. Baumgartner, *The Hebrew and Aramaic Lexicon of the Old Testament* (2 vols.; rev. W. Baumgartner et al.; tr. M.E.J. Richardson; Leiden: Brill, 2001).
Hermopolis	E. Bresciani and M. Kamil, *Le lettere aramaiche di Hermopoli* (Atti della Accademia Nazionale dei Lincei, Memorie, Classe di Scienze morali . . . , 8/12; Rome: Accademia Nazionale dei Lincei, 1966) 357-428.
HGHS	H. Bauer and P. Leander, *Historische Grammatik der hebräischen Sprache* (Hildesheim: Olms, 1965).
HSSD	D. Winton Thomas and W.D. McHardy (eds.), *Hebrew and Semitic Studies Presented to Godfrey Rolles Driver* (Oxford: Clarendon Press, 1963).
IEJ	*Israel Exploration Journal.*
JBL	*Journal of Biblical Literature.*

JNES	*Journal of Near Eastern Studies.*
KAI	H. Donner and W. Röllig, *Kanaanäische und Aramäische Inschriften* (3 vols.; Wiesbaden: Harrassowitz, 1962-64).
LFAA	P. Leander, *Laut- und Formenlehre des Ägyptisch-Aramäischen* (Hildesheim: G. Olms, 1966); cited according to page numbers and marginal letters.
Mur	*Murabba'ât Texts* (see P. Benoit et al., *Les Grottes de Murabba'ât* (DJD 2; Oxford: Clarendon, 1961).
OP	R.G. Kent, *Old Persian* (2d ed.; New Haven: Yale University Press, 1953).
Or	*Orientalia.*
Padua	E. Bresciani, "Papiri aramaici di epoca persiana presso il Museo Civico di Padova," *RSO* 35 (1960) 11-24.
RB	*Revue Biblique.*
RHR	*Revue de l'Histoire des Religions.*
RSO	*Rivista degli Studi Orientali.*
RSV	*Revised Standard Version* (of the English Bible).
Sefire I,II,III	A. Dupont-Sommer, *Les inscriptions araméennes de Sfiré (Stèles I et II)* (Mémoires présentés . . . à l'Académie des Inscriptions et Belles-Lettres 15; Paris: Imprimerie Nationale, 1958); idem, "Une inscription araméenne inédite de Sfiré," *Bulletin du Musée de Beyrouth* 13 (1956) 23-41 (+ plates I-VI). Cf. J.A. Fitzmyer, *The Aramaic Inscriptions of Sefire: Revised Edition* (BibOr 19/A; Rome: Biblical Institute Press, 1995).
Sem	*Semitica.*
TS	*Theological Studies.*

Warka	A. Dupont-Sommer, "La tablette cunéiforme araméenne de Warka," *Revue d'Assyriologie* 39 (1942-44) 35-42.
ZAW	*Zeitschrift für die Alttestamentiche Wissenschaft.*

GRAMATICAL AND OTHER ABBREVIATIONS

abs.	absolute
acc.	according (to)
accus.	accusative
act.	active
adj.	adjective
adv.	adverb
Akk.	Akkadian
antepos.	antepositive
Aph.	Aphel
Ar./ar	Aramaic
Arab.	Arabic
assimil.	assimilated
asyndet.	asyndetic(ally)
attract.	attraction, attracted
augm.	augment
Babyl.	Babylonian
Can.	Canaanite
cf.	confer (compare)
cl.	clause
collect.	collective(ly)
compos.	composite
conj.	conjunction
consec.	consecutive
cst.	construct
def.	defective(ly)
dem.	demonstrative
denom.	denominative
determ.	determinate
dir. disc.	direct discourse
dissim.	dissimilated
distrib.	distributive

18

dl.	delete
du.	dual
edd.	editions
e.g.	exempli gratia (for example)
Egyp.	Egyptian
El.	Elephantine
emph.	emphatic
f.	feminine
fut.	future
gen.	genitive
Germ.	German
Gk.	Greek
Haph.	Haphel
hapl.	haplography
Hebr.	Hebrew
Hithpa.	Hithpaal
Hithpe.	Hithpeel
Hoph.	Hophal
homoeot.	homoeoteleuton
ibid.	ibidem (in the same place)
impf.	imperfect
impv.	imperative
indef.	indefinite
indep.	independent
indet.	indeterminate
indir.	indirect
infin.	infinitive
inscr.	inscription
interrog.	interrogative
intrans.	intransitive
invar.	invariable
Ithpa.	Ithpaal
Ithpe.	Ithpeel

Jew.	Jewish
juss.	jussive
k.	kĕtīb (written)
lit.	literally
loc.	local
LXX	Septuagint
m.	masculine
Mish.	Mishnaic
MS.	manuscript
MT	Masoretic Text
n.	note
Nab.	Nabatean
neg.	negative
no.	number
nom.	nominative
obj.	object
opp.	opposite
ostr.	ostracon
OT	Old Testament
p.	page
Pa.	Pael
pap.	papyrus, papyri
pass.	passive
Pe.	Peal
perf.	perfect
perh.	perhaps
pers.	personal
pl.	plural
poss.	possessive
pr.	proper
pred.	predicate
prep.	preposition(al)
prob.	probably

prolep.	proleptic
pron.	pronoun
proport.	proportional
ptc.	participle
q.	qĕrē (read!)
rad.	radical
rel.	relative
repr.	reprinted
res.	resumptive
rev.	revised (by)
sec.	secundum (according to)
st.	state
subj.	subject
suff.	suffix
s.v.	sub voce (look under word . . .)
Sym.	Symmachus
syn.	synonym, synonomous
Syr.	Syriac
tg.	targum
temp.	temporal
Theod.	Theodotion
tr.	translated (by)
trans.	transitive
Ug.	Ugaritic
v.	verse
Vg.	Vulgate
v.l.	varia lectio (variant reading)
vocal.	vocalization
vers.	version
viz.	videlicet (namely)
w.	with
wt.	without
*	form or vowels do not occur in Biblical Aramaic

>	becomes
<	developed from
=	equals
||	parallel to
[ ]	lacuna in document
< >	editorially restored
( )	addition in a translation
{ }	omit
/	or
< (superscript)	accented syllable
▲	name, proper noun
ā	long vowel
ă	short vowel, reduced vowel
†	all biblical occurrences indicated
1 (superscript)	hapax legomenon (occurs only once)
+	passim (occurs elsewhere too)

LEXICON

א

אַב* (BL 179e, 247a), suff. אָבִי (Dan 5:13; BL 77l; v.l. אֲבוּהִי
אֲבִי), אֲבוּךְ, (BL 53q) and אבוה (Aḥ. 55); pl. (w. augm. -āh-) suff.
אֲבָהָתִי (v.l. תַי׳, BL 74y, 77n), אבהי ('ăbāhay), אֲבָהָתָנָא, אֲבָהָתָךְ (v.l.
תָנָא׳, BL 73r, 79t), אבהין ('ăbāhaynā), אבהיהם ('ăbāhayhom, AP
71:2): **father, ancestor.** אָבִי "my father" Dan 5:13; אֲבוּךְ "your
father" 5:11(ter), 18; אֲבוּהִי "his father" 5:2; יא אבי ויא מרי "O my
father and my lord" 1QapGen 2:24; Aḥiqar is אבוה זי אתור כלה
"father of all Assyria," i.e., its counsellor Aḥ. 55; הָרְגִזוּ אֲבָהָתָנָא
"our ancestors provoked (God's) anger" Ezra 5:12: 4:15; Dan
2:23; אבהין בנו "our fathers built (this temple)" AP 30:13; אבהי
"my ancestors" Barrakib 16 (KAI 216); האיתי למטרה אב "does
the rain have a father" 11QtgJob (11Q10) 31:5. [Hebr. אָב]. †

אֵב* see אֲנֵב.

אבד, impf. 3 pl. m. יֵאבְדוּן*, juss. יֵאבַדוּ (BL 30a, 89d,
138a): **perish, be lost.** יֵאבַדוּ מֵאַרְעָא "may (false gods) perish
from the earth" Jer 10:11; when rebellion occurred in Egypt, זך
אבד "that one perished" AD 8:2; כל נכסין זי קנה אבדו "all the
property that he had acquired was lost" AP 30:16; אחרתה תאבד
"may his descendants perish" Nerab 10 (KAI 226); חכמתה אבדה
"his wisdom is lost" (ptc.), i.e., is frustrated Aḥ. 94; if a wife
separates from her husband, מהרה יאבד "her dowry will be lost"
BMAP 7:25; מהרה [י]אבד "his bride-price shall be forfeited" AP
15:27.
   Pa. infin. cst.: **destroy.** לאבדת אשמהם "(I shall be able to .
. . or) to destroy their name" Sefire II B 7. [Hebr. אבד].
   Haph. ('bd > wbd, BL 139i), impf. 2 sg. m. תְּהוֹבֵד, 3 pl.
m. יְהֹבְדוּן, infin. הוֹבָדָה (BL 140o): **lose, kill, destroy.** אֲמַר לְהוֹבָדָה

"(the king) gave an order to destroy (all the sages)" Dn 2:12:
2:18, 24a,b; לְהוֹבָדָה "(they shall take away its [the beast's] dominion utterly) to destroy (it)" 7:26; אהאבד ספר[י]א "I will destroy (these) inscriptions" *Sefire II* C 4; יכטלוך ויהאבדו זרעך "may
(the gods) kill you and do away with your offspring" *Nerab* 11
(*KAI* 225).

 Hoph. 3 sg. m. הוּבַד (BL 139j, 141h): **be killed, be destroyed.** וְהוּבַד גִּשְׁמַהּ "and its [the beast's] body was destroyed"
Dan 7:11.

 אֶבֶן (*'abn*) abs./cst., emph. אַבְנָא, only sg. (BL 202m), f.:
stone. אַבְנָא דִי מְחָת "(that) stone which struck (the statue)" Dan
2:35; וְהֵיתָיִת אֶבֶן חֲדָה "and a stone was brought" (6:18); gen. of
material (cf. דִי I 2): אֶבֶן after an indeter. noun, אַבְנָא after a deter.
noun: **made of stone.** לֵאלָהֵי . . . אַבְנָא "(they praised) the gods . . .
made of stone" Dan 5:4, 23; עמודיא זי אבנא "(they broke) the
pillars of stone" *AP* 30:9; תרען זי אבן 5 בנין פסילה זי אבן "5 gates
of stone, built with hewn blocks of stone" *AP* 30:9-10; מִתְבְּנֵא אֶבֶן
גְּלָל "(the temple) is being built with stone blocks" Ezra 5:8; 6:4;
-- **weight.** כסף כרשן 10 באבני מלכא "(a sum of) silver, 10 karshin,
by royal weights," i.e., Persian *BMAP* 4:21-22; שקלן 4 בא[בני]
פתח "[4 shekels by] the weight of (the god) Ptah," i.e., Egyptian
AP 11:2. [Hebr. the same]. †

 אִגְּרָה (< Akk. *egertu*; BL 56c, 241s) abs., אגרת abs. (*AP*
30:7) and cst. (*AD* 12:4); emph. אִגַּרְתָּא; emph. pl. אגרתא
(*'iggarātā'*; *AP* 37:15), f.: **letter, epistle** (cf. סְפַר .אִגַּרְתָּא דִי שְׁלַחוּ
עֲלֹהִי "the letter that they sent to him" Ezra 4:11: 5:6; כְּתַבוּ אִגְּרָה
חֲדָה עַל־יְרוּשְׁלֶם לְאַרְתַּ "they wrote a letter to Artaxerxes against
Jerusalem" 4:8; אגרת חדה בשלמך לא שלחת עלי "you sent no letter
to me about your welfare" *AP* 41:5; [ ] שלח אגרה על דבר כן לצאן
"he sent a letter about it to Ṣa'" *AP* 40:3; בבל לם אגרת מן
"let a letter be sent by my lord to . . ." *AD* 10:2; ארשם יהבת על "a letter from Arsames (see BL 316h) was deliv-

ered in Babylon to . . ." *AD* 12:1; חזי אגרת ארשם זי היתיו על פסמשך
על "Look at Arsames's letter that they brought to Psamshek
about . . ." *AD* 12:4; כזי אגרתא זא [ת]מטא עליך "when this letter
reaches you" *AP* 42:6-7; מטו אגרתא "the letters arrived" *AP*
37:15; כלא מליא באגרה חדה שלחן בשמן על "the whole matter we
have sent in a letter in our name to . . ." *AP* 30:29 (see another ||
construction in 31:28). -- Epistolary Perfect: כתיב ב 5 לאפף
אגרתי ז[א] "on the 5th of Epiphi, this letter of mine has been
written (m.!)" *BMAP* 13:8 (cf. perf. of contract s.v. יהב no. 1 and
perf. of decree s.v. שׂים no. 4). -- For the address of a letter, see על
no. 2a. [Hebr. אִגֶּרֶת]. †

אֱדַיִן (BL 252b) and בֵּאדַיִן, temp. adv.; both forms have the
same meaning: (1) **then, at that time** (= Hebr. אָז). מִן־אֱדַיִן וְעַד־כְּעַן
"from that time until now" Ezra 5:16; בֵּאדַיִן בְּטֵלַת "then stopped
(the work on the temple)" 4:24; אדין אמר עננ"י בר עזריה "then
Anani son of Azariah said. . ." *BMAP* 10:1 + ; אדין מומאה מטאה
עליכי "then an oath came (= was imposed) upon you" *AP* 14:4-5;
כזי מצרין מרדת . . . אדין "when Egypt revolted . . ., then . . ." *AD*
5:6; קדמן כזי מצריא מרדו אדין "previously, when the Egyptians
rebelled, then (Psamshek) . . ." *AD* 7:1; ואברם באדין הוא יתב
בחברון "Abram then was dwelling in Hebron" *1QapGen* 22:2-3.
-- (2) **then, thereupon, on that occasion** (in Ezra, Dan, *1Qap-
Gen* in narratives; in papyri אחר; s.v. ן I 4). Daniel begged for
time . . . , אֱדַיִן . . . לְבַיְתֵהּ אֲזַל "then he went to his house" Dan
2:17 (+ 19 times in Dan); בֵּאדַיִן עֲנֵה דָנִיֵּאל "thereupon Daniel
spoke up" Dan 5:17 (+ 22 times in Dan); וֶאֱדַיִן יְתִיבוּן נִשְׁתְּוָנָא עַל דְּנָה
"and then a written order about it would be returned" Ezra 5:5:
4:23; 5:4-9; 6:13; בֵּאדַיִן דָּרְיָוֶשׁ מַלְכָּא שָׂם טְעֵם "then King Darius
decreed" 6:1: 5:2; in Ezra 4:9 after אֱדַיִן no verb follows; read
prob. אִנּוּן "these (are)" (see הוא no. 2a); לבי עלי אדין אשתני "then
my mind was changed within me" *1Qap-Gen* 2:11; הא באדין
חשבת "then I thought" *1QapGen* 2:1. (3) **then, therefore, infer-**

ential (cf. adv. אחר no. 3 and Hebr. אָז). . . . אנת יה ברי הכצר כל כציר
אדין תאכל . "You, my son, are to gather every harvest . . . , and
then you shall eat . . ." *Aḥ.* 127. [Hebr. אֲזִי, אָז].

אֲדָר (< Akk.): **Adar,** 12th month (= Feb.-Mar.). Ezra
6:15. [Hebr. the same]. [1]

אִדַּר* (cf. Akk. *adru*; BL 56c), אדרן pl. abs. (see below),
cst. אִדְּרֵי : **threshing floor,** where grain is sorted and wind-
blown. עוּר מֶן־אִדְּרֵי־קַיְט "chaff of the summer threshing floors"
(see דִּי I 2a; BL 316h) Dan 2:35; באדרן ינתן "on threshing floors it
will yield" *Letter of Assur* 5 (*KAI* 235). [1]

אֲדַרְגָּזַר* (prob. < Old Persian *handarza-kara* "giver of
advice or command"; emph. pl. אֲדַרְגָּזְרַיָּא (BL 56d; *GBA* p. 62):
counselor. Dan 3:23. Cf. הנדרז יעבדון "they will give counsel"
AD 10:3. Cf. בעל עטתא "master of counsel" *Aḥ.* 42. †

אַדְרַזְדָּא (< Persian *drazdā*-), adv.: **carefully.** Whatever is
ordered by God, יִתְעֲבֵד אַדְרַזְדָּא "let it be done carefully" Ezra
7:23. [1]

אֶדְרָע (*qitāl*, BL 189p, 193o) w. prothetic א; f.: **arm,
upper arm; force** (cf. דְּרָע and יַד). They made them cease בְּאֶדְרָע
וְחָיִל "by force and power" Ezra 4:23; דרעיהא מא שפירן "her
(Sarai's) arms, how beautiful" *1QapGen* 20:4. [Hebr. זְרוֹעַ]. [1]

אַזְדָּא (< Persian *azdā* "noted" or "notice"; cf. אזדכרא =
azdā-kara "herald" *AP*17:5-7), prob. f. adj.: **what was made
known** or **was done.** מִלְּתָא מִנִּי אַזְדָּא "(my) decree is made
known," i.e., I decree that you shall be killed unless you reveal
my dream and its interpretation, Dan 2:5; you are trying to gain
time since you see אַזְדָּא מִנִּי מִלְּתָא "a decree has been made known

26

by me" 2:8. Cf. abs. m. noun אזד : **knowledge**; הן אזד יתעבד מן דיניא "if knowledge (i.e., an investigation) be made by the judges" *AP* 27:8-9. †

אֲזָה * (BL 168c), Peil pass. ptc. m. sg. אֲזֵה (*'azēh*; BL 52o, 67p); Peil infin. מֵזֵא (*mi'zē'*, def. written; BL 138a, 156x), w. suff. מֵזְיֵהּ : **set on fire, heat**. The king gave orders . . . לְמֵזֵא חַד־שִׁבְעָה עַל דִּי חֲזֵה לְמֵזְיֵהּ "to heat (the furnace) seven times more than it used to be heated" Dan 3:19; אַתּוּנָא אֵזֵה יַתִּירָא "the furnace was heated very hot" 3:22. †

אֲזַל, 3 pl. אֲזַלוּ, 1 pl. אֲזַלְנָא; impf. 2 sg. m. תאזל (*ti'zil*; Sefire I B 39); impv. sg. m. אֱזֵל־ (Babyl. vocal. for אֱזֵל* < *'zil*; BL 30b, 66n, 67p, 138d,e; v.l. אֱזֵל); the impf. and infin. are usually taken from the syn. verb הֲךְ*: **go, go away, set out,** w. לְ of place and עַל of person (cf. opp. אֲתָה "come"). לְבַיְתֵהּ אֲזַל "went to his house" Dan 2:17: 6:19-20; Ezra 5:8; אֲזַל Dan 2:24 prob. dl. (BL 351d); אֲזַלוּ . . . לִירוּשְׁלֶם עַל־יְהוּדָיֵא "they went . . . to the Jews in Jerusalem" Ezra 4:23; אזלן עמה מצרין "are going with him to Egypt" *AD* 6:4; כזי ארשם נפק ואזל על מלכא "when Arsames departed and went to the king" *AP* 30:4-5; אזל על ב׳ וינתן לך כתון "go to B. and he will give you a coat" *AP* 42:8; אזל לסון "he went to Syene" *AP* 56:2; אזלת לי לביתי "I went to my house" *Aḥ.* 22; הוית אזל לדרומא "I kept going southward" *1QapGen* 19:9; . . . נגדו וקטלין ואזלין מדינת דרמשק "(the kings) set out . . . killing, and making their way to the city of Damascus" *1QapGen* 22:4-5; גבריא די אזלו עמי "the men who went with me" *1QapGen* 22:23-24; אזלת . . . בנכסין שגיאין "I went forth . . . with many flocks" *1QapGen* 20:33; קום והלך ואזל "rise, walk about, and go (through the land)" *1QapGen* 21:13; הא אנתתך אזל דברה ועדי לך מן כול מדינת מצרין "Here is your wife. Take her away; go, depart from all the provinces of Egypt" *1QapGen* 20:27-28. -- After אזל, another verb often follows asyndet. (BL 351b,c): שָׂא אֱזֵל־אֲחֵת הִמּוֹ בְּהֵיכְלָא

"take (these vessels), go, (and) put (read אֲחֵת) them in the Temple" Ezra 5:15; אזל אזלת אשכחת "I went (and) I found" *Ah.* 76; אזל אמרת אזל חן[ל]יל[א זך קרב "he went (and) drew near" *Ah.* 110; . . . [קטל] "I said, 'Go (and) kill that t[roo]p . . .'" *Bisitun* 19-20; אזל אמר שמע ח' מלי לוט אמר למלכא "Go, tell the king" *1QapGen* 20:23; כדי שמע ח' מלי לוט אזל אמר "when he heard the words of Lot, Ḥ went (and) said" *1QapGen* 20:24. [Hebr. אָזַל].†

אַח *, w. suff. אחי (*'ăḥī*), אחוך (*'ăḥûk*), אחוהי (*'ăḥûhî*), אחוכם (*'ăḥûkōm*), pl. אַחִין *, emph. אחיא; w. suff. אחי (*'ăḥay*), אַחָיךְ k. and אֶחָךְ q. (BL 56b, 77o), אחוה (perh. *'ăḥawah* < *'ăḥayah*), אחיכם (*'ăḥaykōm*): **brother.** חד אחוה "one of his brothers" *Sefire III* 17; לוט בר אחוהי "Lot, son of his brother" *1QapGen* 21:33; cf. 34; תלתת אחיא אמוראא ; "the three Amorite (*'ămôrā'ē'* < *'ămôrāyē'*) brothers" *1QapGen* 21:21; אחיכם "your brothers" *AP* 20:12. -- Transferred: **kinsman, colleague.** מָה דִי עֲלָיךְ וְעַל־אֶחָיךְ יֵיטַב "what seems good to you and to your colleagues" Ezra 7:18; [אל] אחי ידניה וכנותה חילא יהודיא אחוכם חננ[יה] "[To] my brethren, Yedaniah and his colleagues, the Jewish garrison, your brother, Hananiah." *AP* 21:1-2, 11; אל אחי פל[טי בר יאו[ש] אחוך הושעיה בר נתן "To my brother, Pal[ti son of Ya'osh, your brother, Hoshaiah son of Nathan" *AP* 40:5; אל ברי שלמם [מ]ן אחוך אושע "To my son, Shalomam, from your kinsman, Osea" *Padua I* A 1; יא אחי ויא מרי "O my brother and my lord" (said by a wife to her husband) *1QapGen* 2:9. -- Cf. אחה (*'ăḥāh* < *'ăḥawat*), cst. אחת (*'ăḥāt*), w. suff. אחתי (*'ăḥātî*); pl. w. suff. אהותה (*'ăḥawā-teh*) (on -aw-, see אֲרָיֵה): **sister.** אח ואחה "brother or sister" *AP* 1:5; אחת מחת "sister of Mahath" *AP* 22:82; אל אחתי ת' מן אחכי מ "To my sister T., from your brother M." *Hermopolis* 2:1; I asked אחתך לאנתו "your sister for marriage" *BMAP* 7:3; שלם ה' ואחתהי "greetings to H. and his sister" *Hermopolis* 7:3-4; ס' ברת קניה ויתומה אחתה "S., daughter of Qenayah, and Yethomah, her sister" *AP* 1:1-2; אחותה "his sisters" *AP* 75:8;

אחתי היא "she is my sister" *1QapGen* 20:27; אל תצפי לה אחתי "do not be anxious about him, my sister" *4QTob^b (4Q197)* 4i3. [Hebr. אָח]. [1]

אַחֲוָיָה *: see חֲוָה Aphel infin.

אֲחִידָה * (*qatīl*, BL 54a, 188j), pl. אֲחִידָן : **riddle.** אַחֲוָיַת אֲחִידָן "explanation of riddles" Dan 5:12. [Hebr. חִידָה]. [1]

▲ אַחְמְתָא (< Persian *Hagmatāna*): **Ecbatana,** capital of Media, summer residence of Persian kings; today = Hamadān. A scroll was found בְּאַחְמְתָא בְּבִירְתָא דִּי בְּמָדַי מְדִינְתָּה "in Ecbatana, in the fortress, which is in the province of Media" Ezra 6:2. [1]

אַחַר *, pl. אַחֲרִין *: **latter part, later time** (*LFAA* 119i). -- עַל אחרין : **later, at last** (*LFAA* 121o; BL 256w, 372; cf. לקדמין, לקדמן, "formerly, heretofore" *AP* 32:8, 10). עַל אחרן יזכרני "later he will remember me" *Aḥ.* 53; [יזכר] . . . א׳ אחרן על זי עד "until afterwards E. . . . will remember" *Aḥ.* 64; עד . . . עַל אחרן צחא וחור שזבוני "Later Zeho and Hor . . . until they got me freed" *AP* 38:4-5; וְעַד אחרין עַל קֳדָמַי דָּנִיֵּאל "at last Daniel came in before me" (q. אָחֳרֵין, s.v. אָחֳרָן; read prob. עַל אַחֲרֵין) Dan 4:5. [1]
Adv. לאחרה, אחרה, אחר (*LFAA* 119i): (1) **afterwards, then** (cf. אֱדַיִן no. 2). הן פסמשך[ד] אחר . . . ישלח "If hereafter Psamshek sends . . ." *AD* 4:3; אחר כזי מצרין מרדת "Later, when Egypt revolted" *AD* 5:6; אחר עבדו קרבא[א] "then they joined battle" *Bisitun* 12; אחר וידרנג . . . אגרת שלח . . . לאמר אגורא זי ביב "Afterwards Widrang . . . sent a letter . . . saying, 'Let them destroy the temple that is in the fortress Yeb'; then Nephayan led forth the Egyptians" *AP* 30:6-8; למען לאחרה לתהנס ארצתי "lest you move my [Nerab's] sarcophagus later on" *Nerab* 7-8 (*KAI* 226). -- (2) **on that account, therefore.** I did not find the money and goods to pay you, אחר אנה יהבת לכי

29

לביתא זנה "therefore I give you this house" *AP* 13:5; that farm was not given to any other of my servants, אחר אנה בגה זי פמון זך יהבת לפטסורי "therefore I give (the domain) of that Pamun to Petosiri" *AD* 8:5. (3) **then** (inferential, at beginning of an apodosis; s.v. אֱדַיִן no. 3 and ן II 5). הן לא שלמת . . . אחר אנה ענני אחוב ואנתן לך כסף א[בג]דן "if I do not pay back . . ., then I, Anani, shall become liable to pay you a fine" *BMAP* 11:5-6 (also 11:8, 9-10); הן תנצר צלמא . . . זא אחרה ינצר זי לך "if you protect this image, then what is yours will be protected" *Nerab* 11-14 (*KAI* 225). [Hebr. the same].

Preposition. אַחֲרֵי, אחר : **after** (cf. בְּאתַר). אחר מותכי "after your death" *BMAP* 4:17-18; אחרי מותי "after my death" *BMAP* 4:21; אַחֲרֵי דְנָה "after this" (the present) Dan 2:29, 45; אַחֲרֵיהוֹן "after them" 7:24; אנת . . . ובניך אחריך 'you . . . and your children after you" *AP* 28:6-7; ובניך מן אחריך "and your children after you" *BMAP* 3:12; [מן אנ]ת מלך זי אחרי תהוה "Whoever yo]u are, O King, who will be after me" *Bisitun* 64; אחרי כן "afterwards" (adv.) *Aḥ.* 99. -- In a spatial sense: אחרי "after me" (i.e., accompanying me) *AD* 3:3; [א]חרין "(the king will send men) after us" *Aḥ.* 63; [י]אתה מן אחרוהי "(what) will come after it" *Aḥ.* 210. [Hebr. the same]. †

אַחֲרִי * (BL 197f), cst. אַחֲרִית; f. **end, latter part.** What will come בְּאַחֲרִית יוֹמַיָּא "at the end of days" Dan 2:28 (‖ אַחֲרֵי דְנָה "after the present time" 2:29, 45); may the guilty one die in misery ואחרתה תאבד "and may his posterity perish" *Nerab* 10 (*KAI* 226). [Hebr. אחרית]. [1]

אָחֳרִי (*'uḥrī* f. for m. *'uḥrān,* BL 200k), emph. אחריתא (*'uḥrītā'*); f. adj.: **other, another.** מַלְכוּ אָחֳרִי "another kingdom (will arise)" Dan 2:39a,b; 7:5-6; קֶרֶן אָחֳרִי "another horn (came up)" 7:8; עַל־קַרְנַיָּא . . . וְאָחֳרִי דִּי סִלְקַת "about (those) horns . . . and (about) the other (horn) that came up" (context requires the

emph.: that other horn) 7:20; ‏ואחריתא . . . חדה מן תרתי לחמא יהיבת‏
‏[י]היבת לתנינה די קאם‏ "(I watched until) one of the two loaves of
bread (= Hebr. ‏שתי הלחם‏) was given [to] the (High Priest) . . . and
the other was given to his deputy who was standing (nearby)"
2QNJ (2Q24) 4:15-16; ‏[מן] י [אוחרי בר מן]אהזינ‏ "he showed m[e]
another apart from [ ]" *2QNJ (2Q24)* 8:7. -- Cf. ‏איתי לי אנתה‏
‏אחרה‏ "I have another (perh. *'uḥrāh*) wife" *AP* 15:32; ‏לוח אחרה‏
‏אמן 9 ופלג‏ "another board of 9¹/₂ cubits" *AP* 79:3. †

‏אֳחֳרָן‏ (*'uḥrān*), in Dan 4:5 q. ‏אָחֳרָן‏ (for *ē*, see Brock. 1.
412), emph. ‏אחרנא‏ (*'uḥrānā'*); pl. ‏אחרנין‏ (*'uḥrānîn*); m. adj. (cf. f.
‏אָחֳרִי‏): **other, another.** ‏אֱלָה אָחֳרָן‏ "another god" Dan 3:29; 2:44;
7:24; ‏בנן אחרנן‏ "(I have) other children" *AP* 15:32; ‏אחרנן בעין מן‏
‏אתר אחרן‏ "they are seeking out other (slaves) from elsewhere"
AD 7:4; ‏מחר או יום אחרן‏ "tomorrow or some other (future) day"
AP 8:20; ‏ביומן אחרנן‏ "on other days" *AP* 71:4; ‏ליומן אחרנן שגיאן‏
"after many other days" *Aḥ*. 49-50; ‏[והא] אסף אוחרן‏ "and look,
another threshold" *5QNJ (5Q15)* 1 i 18; ‏תרעא אחרנא‏ "the other
gate" ibid. 1 ii 7; ‏אחרניא‏ "the others" *2QNJ (2Q24)* 8:4; ‏שליטין‏
‏בחלקי אחרנא אנה ענני‏ . . . "(my children shall) have authority over
my portion, the other (part), I, Anani . . ." *BMAP* 4:19; ‏פלג ביתא‏
‏[יהוה] לה . . . . ופלגא אחר[נא] אנת שליט בה‏ "half of the house shall be
hers . . . and the other half you shall have authority over" *AP*
9:11. -- Substantive: ‏לְאָחֳרָן הַב‏ "give (your rewards) to someone
else" Dan 5:17; ‏[הא ה]ות לאחרן‏ "it [came to be]long to someone
else" *Sefire III* 24; ‏לָא אִיתַי . . . לָהֵן אֱלָהִין אָחֳרָן‏ "there is no one
else but (the) gods . . ." Dan 2:11; ‏למנתנה לאחרנן‏ "(she will not
be able) to give it [the house] to others" *AP* 9:9; ‏ואחרן זי תמה הוה‏
"(they burned the furniture) and the other things that were there"
AP 30:11; ‏נכסן וכסף עבור ואחרן זי שלומם‏ "goods, and money,
grain, and other things belonging to Shelomam" *AP* 20:12; ‏עד‏
‏אחרן‏ "(I give you this house) until another (time)," i.e., for a
period (not ‏עד עלם‏ "forever") *BMAP* 10:10 (cf. 10:8); ‏עַד אָחֳרָן עַל‏

קֳדָמַי דָּנִיֵּאל "at last Daniel entered before me" Dan 4:5 (but read prob. עַל אַחֲרִין "at length," cf. k. and s.v. אַחַר).

אֲחַשְׁדַּרְפַּן *, emph. pl. אֲחַשְׁדַּרְפְּנַיָּא (Persian ḫšatra-pāvan "protector of the kingdom," Akk. aḫšad(a)rapanu; Gk. σατράπ-(π)ης, σαδράπας, (ἐ)ξατράπης): satrap, governor of a Persian satrapy, Dan 3:2-3, 27; 6:2-5, 7-8. [Hebr. אֲחַשְׁדַּרְפְּנִים]. †

אֵיך ('ayk), אִיכה ('aykāh), הֵיךְ * (s.v. הָא־כְדִי), adv.: how? אֵיךְ בִּיתָא עֲבִיד וְאֵיךְ נְפַקְתְּ "how the house was built and how you go out . . ." Padua I A 6; הוֹדַע אֵיךְ זִי עֲבִיד אַנְתְּ "make known how you act" Bisitun 66; לְמֶחֱזֵה אֵיךְ יִתְעֲבֵד "(the king appointed two other men) to see how it would be done" Aḥ. 37-38. -- Relative: in what way (cf. כְּדִי, לָקֳבֵל דִּי); אֵיךְ זִי תְקַד שְׁעוּתָא זָא בְּאֵשׁ כֵּן תְקַד אַרְפַּד "as this wax is burned by fire, so may Arpad be burned" Sefire I A 35; אֵיכָה זִי תְקַד . . . כֵּן יִקַּד מ[תעאל] "as (this wax) is burned, so may Ma[ti'el] be burned" ibid. 37; הָא־כְדִי . . . לָא מִתְעָרֵב עִם חַסְפָּא "as (= הֵיךְ דִּי) . . . (iron) does not mix with clay" Dan 2:43.

אִילָן ('īl-ān, BL 196b), emph. אִילָנָא; m. tree. Dan 4:7-8, 11, 17, 20, 23; קָאֵם אִילָנָא "the tree was standing" 4QFourKgdms (4Q552) 1ii2. [Hebr. אֵלָה, אֵלוֹן]. †

אֵימְתָן * ('aymatān, BL 197f), f. אֵימְתָנִי (s.v. אָחֳרִי); adj.: terrible, frightening. The beast of Dan 7:7. [cf. Hebr. אֵימָה "terror"]. [1]

אִיתַי (BL 254l, 256z), v.l. אִתַי; אִית, אִת (LFAA 119h); w. suff. אִיתָיךְ (Dan 2:26 k., אִיתָךְ q., BL 77o), אִיתוֹהִי, אִיתֵינָא (Dan 3:18 k., אִיתַנָא q., v.l. אִיתָנָא), אִיתֵיכוֹן; verbal particle: there is/are. (1) denoting presence in a place (BL 331t; cf. הֲוָה no. 1b); (a) w. noun subj., modified by a rel. cl.: אִיתַי גְּבַר . . . דִּי רוּחַ אֱלָהִין

קַדִּישִׁין בֵּהּ "there is a man in whom is the spirit of the holy gods" Dan 5:11; אִיתַי גֻּבְרִין יְהוּדָאיִן "there are Jewish men (whom you have appointed)" Dan 3:12; לָא אִיתַי אֱלָהּ אָחֳרָן "there is no other god (who can deliver)" 3:29: 2:10-11; חֲבָל לָא־אִיתַי בְּהוֹן "there is no damage on them," i.e., men in the furnace, 3:25; לָא אִיתַי דִּי־יְמַחֵא בִידֵהּ "there is no one who can stay his hand" 4:32; לָא אִיתַי זִי [מ]רִיר מִן ענוה "there is nothing more bitter than poverty" *Aḥ.* 105; אִיתַי אֱלָהּ בִּשְׁמַיָּא גָּלֵא רָזִין "there is a God in heaven who reveals mysteries" Dan 2:28; דִּי אִיתַי בִּי מִן־כָּל־חַיַּיָּא "(not by wisdom) that is in me more than all the living" 2:30; אף איתי תבא וללו ברה . . . "there is also Teba' . . . and Lilu, her son" *AP* 28:12-13. (b) Subj. is a cl. (introduced absolutely or by דִי), to which אִיתַי gives emphasis: הֵן אִיתַי דִּי . . . שִׂים טְעֵם "is it true that there is . . . a decree issued (by Cyrus)" Ezra 5:17; איתי זי בפק[דון] הפקדו "it is true that 'they are on deposit.' They were deposited" *AP* 20:7; איתי קצת מן גורנא . . . נדשו "it is true that they wrecked part of the stores. . ." *AP* 27:4-5; cf. הוה תרען . . . נדשו "it happened that they destroyed . . . gates" *AP* 30:9-10; הֵן אִיתַי אֱלָהַנָא יָכִל . . . לְשֵׁיזָבוּתַנָא "if it be so, our God . . . is able to deliver us (from the furnace)" Dan 3:17.

(2) Equals a more or less emphatic *copula* (BL 331u-w): (a) w. ptc. or adj. as predicate: הַאִיתֵיךָ כָּהֵל "are you really capable?" Dan 2:26; לָא אִיתֵיכוֹן פָּלְחִין "Is it true that you do not worship . . ." 3:14; הֵן אִיתֵיכוֹן עֲתִידִין "if you are really prepared to . . ." 3:15; לָא־אִיתַיְנָא פָּלְחִין "certainly (k.) we will not worship . . ." 3:18; לא איתיני ידע "I do not know" *Mur 72* 1:4. (b) w. prep. phrase as predicate: חֲלָק . . . לָא אִיתַי לָךְ "you shall have no possession (in the province)" Ezra 4:16; מְדָרְהוֹן עִם בִּשְׂרָא לָא אִיתוֹהִי "their dwelling is not with flesh [= humans]" Dan 2:11; בר . . . לא איתי לה "(if) she does not have . . . a child" *BMAP* 7:34-35; קנינה וכל זי איתי לה על אנפי ארעא "his possession and all that he has on the face of the earth" *AP* 15:19; איתי לי אנתה אחרה "I have another wife" *AP* 15:32; הן את ערב עליכי "if you have a

33

wager" *Hermopolis* 1:9; איתי לך עלי כסף "there is to your credit against me a sum . . ." *AP* 29:2-3; 35:3; את לי עליך כסף "I have against you (a claim for) money" *AP* 49:2; הב לי נפשא די איתי לי "give me the men [lit., the souls] that are mine" *1QapGen* 22:19; זילי עבידא לא איתי לך כעת אנת וגרדא "now as for you, you have no business with my domestic staff" (s.v. וֹ no. 12) *AD* 12:9. [Hebr. יֵשׁ, BL 254n]. †

אֲכַל *, 3 pl. אֲכַלוּ; impf. 3 sg. m. יֵאכַל, f. תֵּאכֻל ; impv. sg. f. אֲכֻלִי ; ptc. sg. f. אָכְלָה : **eat, devour.** אכלת ואשתית "I ate and I drank" *1QapGen* 21:20; כול דם לא תאכלון "you are not to eat any blood" *1QapGen* 11:17; יֵאכֻל . . . עִשְׂבָּא "he shall eat grass . . ." Dan 4:30; שַׂגִּיא קֻמִי אֲכֻלִי בְּשַׂר "Arise, devour much flesh!" 7:5; אָכְלָה וּמַדֲּקָה "(the beast) devoured and broke into pieces . . ." 7:7, 19; הן ישקר מתעא[אל] . . . יאכל ארבה . . . תאכל תולעה "if Mati'el should be unfaithful, . . . may the locust devour . . . may the worm eat . . ." *Sefire I* A 24-27; וישלחן אלהן מן כל מה אכל בארפד "may the gods send every sort of devourer against Arpad" *Sefire I* A 30. -- Transferred sense: תֵּאכֻל כָּל־אַרְעָא "it [the fourth kingdom] shall devour the earth" Dan 7:23; אֲכַלוּ קַרְצֵיהוֹן "they calumniated them" (lit., "ate their pieces," s.v. קְרַץ) 3:8; 6:25. [Hebr. אָכַל]. †

אַל , adv. of prohibition or negative wish (s.v. לָא no. 2), used w. juss. (BL 89d): **not, do not.** אַל־תְּהוֹבֵד "Do not destroy (the sages)" Dan 2:24; אַל־יְבַהֲלָךְ "let (the dream) not alarm you!" 4:16 (impf. * יְבַהֲלִנָּךְ "will alarm you"); אַל־יְבַהֲלוּךְ "let (your thoughts) not alarm you!" 5:10; יתיר פתף אל תנתנו להם "do not then assign them more provisions" *AD* 6:6; אל תפנו באשרה "do not (re)turn to his region" *Sefire III* 7; אל תצף לח' "do not be concerned about H." (*tiṣṣip*, < *yṣp*) *Hermopolis* 3:3; אל תצפי לה "do not be concerned (f.) about him" *Hermopolis* 1:4; 2:2; אל ילקחו "let them not get" *El. Ostr.* (*ASAE* 26 [1926] 25, line 5);

34

אל—אלה

אל ישלט . . . לטמיא אנתתי "may he not be able to defile my wife . .
." *1QapGen* 20:15. [Hebr. the same]. †

אֵל (*'il*; BL 83k) dem. pron. pl.: **these.** אֵל מָאנַיָא "these
vessels" Ezra 5:15 q. (k. אלה); כל מלכיא אל "all these kings" *Zkr*
A 9, 16 (*KAI* 202); חסניא אל "these fortifications" (ibid. B 8).

אלה (*'ilay*; BL 83j; Ezra 5:15 k.), אֵלֶּה (Jer 10:11 BL
83j), dem. pron. m. and f. (sg. דְּנָה ; cf. אִלֵּן): **these, those.** אֵלֶּה
מָאנַיָא "these vessels" Ezra 5:15; אֱלָהַיָּא . . . יֵאבַדוּ מֵאַרְעָא וּמִן־תְּחוֹת
שְׁמַיָּא אֵלֶּה "the gods . . . shall perish from the earth and from
under the heavens" (אֵלֶּה is perh. a gloss) Jer 10:11; גבריא אלה
"those men" *AP* 2:13; אלה נכסיא "these goods" *AP* 20:15; אלה
תחמי ביתא "these are the boundaries of the house" *BMAP* 3:7;
כמליא אלה "according to this account" (lit. "these words") *AD*
8:3. [Hebr. אֵלֶּה]. †

אֱלָה (*'ilāh*) abs. and cst., emph. אֱלָהָא, w. suff. אֱלָהָךְ, אֱלָהָנָא,
אֱלָהִי, (v.l. אֱלָהֲנָא, BL 73r, 76j, 79t, 122f), אֱלָהֲכֹם and אֱלָהֹם
אֱלָהֲכֹון, and אֱלָהֲהֹון ; pl. אֱלָהִין, cst. אֱלָהֵי, emph. אֱלָהַיָּא; w. suff.
אֱלָהָיִ,אֱלָהָיךְ k. אֱלָהָךְ q. BL 77o); w. prefix בֵּא׳, וֵא׳, לֵא׳, but cst.
sg. לֵאלָהּ : **god, God.** בִּשְׁמַיָּא אִיתַי אֱלָהּ "there is a God in heaven"
Dan 2:28; אֱלָהּ רַב הוֹדַע "a great God has made known (to the
king)" 2:45; לָהֵן אֱלָהִין דִּי "except the gods whose (dwelling is not
with flesh)" 2:11; . . . לָא עֲבַדוּ אֱלָהַיָּא דִּי "the gods who . . . did not
make" Jer 10:11; אֱלָהֵי דַהֲבָא "the gods of gold" Dan 5:4, 23 (אֱלָהֵי
דְּהַב * "gods of gold"); אלהי מצרין "gods of Egypt" *AP* 30:14. --
אֱלָהָא "God" Dan 2:20 +, Ezra 6:12; אֱלָהּ שְׁמַיָּא (cf. מָרֵא) "the
God of heaven" Ezra 5:11; 7:12 +, Dan 2:19, 37, 44; יהו אלה
שמיא "Yahu, the God of heaven" *AP* 30:27-28; אֱלָהָא עִלָּיָא "God
Most High" Dan 3:26, 32; אֱלָהָא חַיָּא "the living God" 6:21, 27;
אֱלָהָא רַבָּא "the great God" Ezra 5:8; יהו אלהא זי ביב "the God
Yahu who is in Yeb" *BMAP* 2:2; חנוב אלהא זי ביב "the god

35

Khnub who is in Yeb" *AP* 30:5; אֱלָהּ יִשְׂרָאֵל דִּי בִירוּשְׁלֶם מִשְׁכְּנֵהּ "the God of Israel, whose dwelling is in Jerusalem" Ezra 7:15; לְפָלְחָן בֵּית אֱלָהָךְ הַשְׁלֵם קֳדָם אֱלָהּ יְרוּשְׁלֶם "(the vessels given to you) for the service of the house of your God, you shall deliver before the God of Jerusalem" (Gk. ἐν Ιερ´; Syr.: who is in Jerusalem) Ezra 7:19. -- Gen. of quality (cf. s.v. דִּי I 2a): רוּחַ אֱלָהִין בָּךְ "the spirit of (the) gods (is) in you" Dan 5:14 (cf. רוּחַ יַתִּירָה 5:12); כְּחָכְמַת אֱלָהִין "like the wisdom of the gods" 5:11 (Hebr. חָכְמַת אֱלֹהִים 1 Kgs 3:28); רוּחַ־אֱלָהִין קַדִּישִׁין בֵּהּ "the spirit of the holy gods (is) in him" Dan 4:5, 15; 5:11; לְבַר־אֱלָהִין רֵוֵהּ דִּי רְבִיעָיָא דָמֵה "the appearance of the fourth one is like a son of the gods" 3:25 (in 3:28 he is called מַלְאֲכֵהּ "His angel"); אֱלָהֲכוֹן הוּא אֱלָהּ אֱלָהִין "your God is God of gods" 2:47 (Theod. θεὸς θεῶν; cf. s.v. מֶלֶךְ and BL 312i); עדי אלהן הם זי שמו אלהן "this is the treaty of gods, which gods have concluded" *Sefire I* B 6. Cf. אלהא ('*ilāhā*'), emph. אלהתא ('*ilāhatā*'): **goddess.** קדם אסי אלהתא "before Isis, the goddess" *AP* 72:16; ימאתי ... בסתי אלהתה "you swore ... by Sati, the goddess" *AP* 14:5. [Hebr. אֱלוֹהַ].

אֵלוּ and אֲרוּ (BL 266a,b); other forms: הלו, ארי, ארה, הֲלָא, אֲרוּ אֵלוּ (Ug. *hl*); an interjection that introduces a clause (sometimes abbreviated) about a new topic: **behold, look!** (s.v. הָא). וַאֲרוּ אַרְבַּע רוּחֵי שְׁמַיָּא מְגִיחָן "behold, the four winds of heaven were stirring up (the great sea)" Dan 7:2; וַאֲרוּ חֵיוָה אָחֳרִי "and look, another beast (like a bear was raised up)" 7:5, 6-7; וַאֲרוּ ... כְּבַר אֱנָשׁ אָתֵה הֲוָה "and behold, ... there came one like a son of man" 7:13. -- וַאֲלוּ ... סִלְקָת ... קֶרֶן וַאֲלוּ "and behold, there came up a horn ...; and behold, ..." 7:8; וַאֲלוּ אִילָן בְּגוֹא אַרְעָא "and behold, a tree in the middle of the earth" 4:7; 4:10; וַאֲלוּ צְלֵם חַד "(you saw) ... and look, a statue ..." 2:31. -- הלו בבית אוכן המו "behold, they (were) in Bīt-Amukkani" *Letter of Assur* 9 (*KAI* 233); הלו חלם 1 חזית "behold, I had a dream" *El. Ostr.* A 1-2 (*KAI* 270); הלו יהב להן פרס תנה "look, he gave them a stipend

there" *Hermopolis* 1:8-9; ארה לא אחי הו ח′ "look, Ḥ. is not my
brother" *Hermopolis* 1:8 (Milik reads לו "certainly" for לא "not");
ארה ספר לה שלחתי בשמה "behold, you did not send a letter in his
name" *Hermopolis* 1:5-6; ארי לך ולזרעך אנתננה "for I shall give it
(this land) to you and your descendants" *1QapGen* 21:14. †

אֵלֶן : s.v. אֵלָּין .

אֵלֶּך , dem. pron. m. pl. (f. pl. does not occur; sg. דֵּך):
those. גֻּבְרַיָּא אֵלֶּך "those men" Ezra 4:21; 6:8; Dan 3:12 + ; שָׂבֵי
יְהוּדָיֵא אֵלֶּך "those Jewish elders" Ezra 6:8: 5:9; כמריא זי חנוב אלך
"those priests of (the god) Khnub" *AP* 27:8; גבריא אלך תרין
"those two men" *Aḥ*. 56; יומיא אלך "those days" *AD* 6:6. --
Antepositive: אלך נכסיא "those goods" *AP* 20:8; אלך דיני[א]
"those judges" *AP* 16:4.

אֵלֶן and אֵלֵּין (graphic י), dem. pron. m. & f. pl. (sg. דְּנָה):
these (cf. אֵלֶּה * and אֵל). אֲחַשְׁדַּרְפְּנַיָּא אֵלֶּן "these satraps" Dan 6:7;
6:3 (אֵלֵּין); עדיא אלן "this treaty" (lit., "these pacts") *Sefire I* A 7;
חציא אלן "these arrows" *Sefire I* A 38; קדמת יומיא אלן "before
these days" *1QapGen* 21:23; לסוף חמש שניא אלן "at the end of
these five years" *1QapGen* 19:23. -- Antepositive: כָּל־אִלֵּין מַלְכְוָתָא
"all these kingdoms" Dan 2:44; 7:17. -- Substantive: כָּל־אִלֵּין "all
of these," i.e., kingdoms 2:40; כול אלן "all of these," i.e., kings
1QapGen 21:25. [Hebr. אֵלֶּה]. †

אֲלַף (*'alp*), cst. אֱלֶף (BL 46p), emph. אַלְפָּא ; pl. אַלְפִין q.
Dan 7:10 אלפים k., BL 201f): **thousand.** לְרַבְרְבָנוֹהִי אֲלַף וְלָקֳבֵל
אַלְפָּא "(the king made a feast) for a thousand of his nobles and in
the presence of the thousand (drank wine)" Dan 5:1; אֶלֶף אַלְפִין
"a thousand thousands (served him)" 7:10 (BL 251r, 312i); כסף
כנכרן אלף "the sum of a thousand talents" *AP* 31:27; יתיר מן זי כען
חד אלף "(may the God of heaven favor you before the king) a

thousand times more than now" *AP* 30:2-3 (BL 323p); עַל אַלְפֵי
מלכא "over the thousands (i.e., legions) of the king" *AP* 71:16.
[Hebr. אֶלֶף]. †

אַמָּה * (*qall*, BL 180o), pl. אַמִּין ; f. (but m. in *AP* 26:10,
12, 14): **cubit** (a measure). רוּמֵהּ אַמִּין שָׁתִּין פְּתָיֵהּ אַמִּין שֵׁת "its
height (i.e., of the statue) was sixty cubits, and its breadth six
cubits" Dan 3:1: Ezra 6:3 (cf. s.v. אֲרָךְ); לחד אמן חמשה פשכן תלתה
"(the planks are) each five cubits (and) three palms (long)" *AP*
26:14-15; 5 פתי אמן . . . 16 ארך אמין "in length (the house) is 16
cubits . . . in width 5 cubits" *BMAP* 12:15-16; שבע . . . אמן [פתיה]
"[its width] seven . . . cubits" *BMAP* 6:4. [Hebr. the same]. †

אֻמָּה (*qull*, BL 181w), pl. אֻמַּיָּא *, emph. אֻמַּיָּא and אֻמַיָא :
nation, people. כָּל־עַם אֻמָּה וְלִשָּׁן "any people, nation, or language. . ." Dan 3:29; שְׁאָר אֻמַיָּא דִּי הַגְלִי אָסְנַפַּר "the rest of the
peoples whom Osnappar deported" Ezra 4:10; עַמְמַיָּא אֻמַיָּא וְלִשָּׁנַיָא
"O peoples, nations, and languages . . ." Dan 3:4, 7, 31; 5:19;
6:26; 7:14 (in BHS אֻמַיָּא usually has *daghesh*, but sometimes it is
missing). [Hebr. the same]. †

אמן **Haph.** 3 sg. m. הֵימִן (BL 139i, 141e); pass. ptc.sg. m.
מְהֵימַן (BL 297c): **trust, believe.** דִּי הֵימִן בֵּאלָהֵהּ "because he (Daniel) trusted in his God" Dan 6:24; מְהֵימַן פִּשְׁרֵהּ "the interpretation
of it (the dream) is trustworthy" 2:45; דִּי־מְהֵימַן הוּא "because he
(Daniel) was faithful" 6:5; אן אשכחת אש מהימן אתה לכן מדעם "if I
find a trustworthy man, I shall make (Aph.) him bring you something" *Hermopolis* 4:9-10. Cf. חן גבר הימנותה "the beauty of a
man is his faithfulness," i.e., his fidelity accords him favor, *Aḥ.*
132. [Hebr. הֶאֱמִין]. †

אֲמַר , 3 sg. f. אֲמֶרֶת (BL 139g), 1 sg. אַמְרֵת (BL 138f), 1 pl.
אֲמַרְנָא ; impf. (BL 138a), 3 sg. m. יֵאמַר (< *yi'mar*), 2 sg. f. תאמרין

(< *ti'marīn*), 1 sg. אמר (< *'i'mar*, def.), 2 pl. m. תֵּאמְרוּן, 1 pl. נֵאמַר ; impv. (BL 132c) sg. m. אֱמַר, pl. m. אֱמַרוּ ; infin, מֵאמַר and מֵמַר and לֵאמַר (< *li'mar*) (cf. לְבְנֵא Ezra 5:3, 13); ptc. sg. m. אָמַר (BL 133g), pl. m. אָמְרִין : (1) **say, tell, ask, answer**, w. לְ or קֳדָם of the person; (a) w. an accus. of a thing: חֶלְמָא אֱמַרוּ לִי "tell me the dream" Dan 2:9; פִּשְׁרֵהּ נֵאמַר קֳדָם־מַלְכָּא "we shall tell the king its (the dream's) interpretation" 2:36; 5:17; 6:13-14; . . . מִלָּה כִדְבָה הִזְמִנְתּוּן לְמֵאמַר קָדָמַי "you have conspired to speak lying . . . words before me" 2:9; חֶלְמָא אֲמַר אֲנָה קֳדָמֵיהוֹן "I (the king) told them (the astrologers) the dream" (BL 294r) 4:4; אנה אמר לכם עטתא "I am telling you (my) counsel" *Aḥ.* 57; אנתי מה תאמרן "you (f.) what are you saying?" *El. Ostr.* 12 (*AH* I/1,13); יאמר מלין קדם ארשם "he will speak (lit., say words) before Arsames" *AP* 37:9; אמר ידניה . . . קדם וידרנג רב חילא "Jedaniah said . . .before Widrang, chief of the garrison" *AP* 25:2; ישימון טב בחנכה למאמר "(the gods) would put something good in his palate to speak" *Aḥ.* 115; לממר קדם ארשם על בית מדבחא "(Let this instruction be for you) to speak to Arsames about the altar-house" *AP* 32:2-3; לא [כות] הן יאמר "if he will speak [thus], no attention will be paid to him" *BMAP* 7:42. (b) w. dir. disc.: לא אכל אמר "I shall not be able to say, '(I have . . .')" *AP* 15:31; הן תאמר בנבשך "if you say to yourself , '(I am . . .')" *Sefire II* B 5; קְרִיבוּ וְאָמְרִין קֳדָם־מַלְכָּא עַל־אֱסָר "they came near and spoke before the king about the interdict" (BL 292l, 295u) Dan 6:13: 6:7; . . עֲנֵה מַלְכָּא וְאָמַר לְדָנִיֵּאל "the king said to Daniel, 'Are you . . .'" 2:26: 2:15; 3:24-25; 5:13; 6:21; אֲמַרְנָא "(then thus) we asked" (read rather אָמְרִין "they asked"; cf. v. 3) Ezra 5:4; ואמר לי מא "(Pharaoh summoned me) and asked me, 'What. . .'" *1QapGen* 20:26; [ה]וית אמר לי "have you been saying to me, '(She . . .')" *ibid.*; cf. Dan 7:16: 2:5, 8, 10 + (cf. עֲנָה); dir. disc. introduced by דִּי (BL 364c; cf. דִּי III 2): אָמְרִין דִּי לָא נְהַשְׁכַּח "(then these men) said, 'We shall not find . . .'" (BL 292l) Dan 6:6: 2:55; 5:7; 6:14. An obj. cl. (אמר די, "said that") does not occur; but after verbs of saying, dir.

disc. is introduced by some form of the verb אמר: פִּתְגָמָא הֲתִיבוּנָא
לְמֵמַר "they answered (lit., returned a word) us, saying . . ." Ezra
5:11; לאמר . . . אגרת שלח על נפין "he sent a letter to Nephayan . . .,
saying" *AP* 30:7; קדם מראי שלחת לאמר "to my lord I sent (a
letter), saying . . ." *AP* 16:8; רשין לאמר "we pleaded, saying" *AP*
20:6; זא אמר לי מראי מלכא לאמר "my lord, the king, said this to
me, saying" *Letter of Assur* 8 (*KAI* 233); זי מלתי לבתי לאמר "as
for what you (f.) mentioned about BTY, saying" (cf. זי III 3)
Hermopolis 1:6; שָׁאֵלְנָא . . . כְּנֵמָא אֲמַרְנָא "we asked (those elders
and) thus we spoke" Ezra 5:9; שלח עלי כן אמר "sent (word) to
me, saying thus" *AD* 4:1; עֲנָת מַלְכְּתָא וַאֲמֶרֶת "the queen spoke up
and said" Dan 5:10; עֲנוֹ אָמְרִין[א] וְאָמְרוּ לֵהּ "the sheep spoke up
and said to him" *Aḥ.* 121; עֲנֵה וְאָמַר לְאַרְיוֹךְ "he spoke up and said
to Arioch" (read perh. עֲנָה, cf. עֲנָה) Dan 2:15: 3:19 + ; כן אמיר לן
לאמר "so it was mentioned to us, saying" *Padua I* A 4; כן שמיע לן
לאמר "so it was heard by us, saying" *Padua I* B 6. (2) **order,
command:** אֲמַר לְהוֹבָדָה לְכֹל חַכִּימֵי בָבֶל "he ordered all the sages of
Babylon to be destroyed (lit., ordered to destroy)" Dan 2:12:
2:46; 3:13, 19-20; 4:23; 5:2; 6:24; אֲמַר ב׳ וְהַלְבִּישׁוּ לְדָנִיֵּאל "B.
commanded, and they clothed Daniel" 5:29: 6:17, 25; Ezra 6:9;
וְכֵן אָמַר גֹּדּוּ אִילָנָא "and he said thus, 'Cut down the tree'" Dan
4:11, 20; לְכוֹן אָמְרִין עַמְמַיָּא "You, O peoples, are ordered . . ." (BL
290c, 333d) 3:4; זי אמר אנה להם "(they do not obey me, in my
lord's business) about which I am telling them" *AD* 4:2; מן]
י]אמר להלדת ספריא [א]לן "whoever will give orders to efface these
inscriptions" *Sefire II* C 1-2; אמרת אזל <קטל> ח[י]ל[א זך מרדיא
"I ordered, 'Go, <kill> that rebel troop'" *Bisitun* 19. [Hebr. אָמַר].

אמר * (cf. Akk. *immeru* "sheep, ram"), pl. אִמְרִין : **lamb.**
For a sacrifice, Ezra 6:9, 17; 7:17; שבע שאן יהינקן אמר ו[אל יש]בע
"should seven ewes suckle a lamb, [may it not be sa]ted" *Sefire I*
A 23; ענו אמרי[א] ואמרו לה "the lambs answered and said to him"
Aḥ. 121. †

אֲנַב * or אֵב * (Akk. *inbu*; BL 50e, 221g), w. suff. אִנְבֵּהּ :
fruit. Fruit of a tree, Dan 4:9, 11, 18; cf. . . . . חשבן ענביא זי כתבת
אבהי "account of the produce that Abhi wrote" *AP* 81:1. †

אִנְדַּע : s.v. יְדַע

אֲנָה or אֲנָא, indep. pers. pron.: **I.** (1) Subj. of a nominal cl.:
אֲנָה נְבוּכַדְנֶצַּר "I see" Dan 3:25; יָדַע אֲנָה "I know" 2:8: 4:4;
מְשַׁבַּח . . . לְמֶלֶךְ שְׁמַיָּא "I, Nebuchadnezzar, praise . . . the king of
heaven" 4:34; מְשַׁבַּח אֲנָה . . . לָךְ "I praise . . . you" 2:23; . אנה עמך
ואנה מגן עליך . . "I am with you . . . and I (shall be) a shield over
you" *1QapGen* 22:30-31; אל תצפו לי לכן אנה יצף "do not be concerned (*tiṣṣipû*) about me; I am concerned (*yāṣip*) about you"
Hermopolis 3:12; כזי עבד אנה לחרוץ כות תעבד בנת עלי "as I am doing for Ḥaruṣ, so may Benit (the goddess) do for me" *Hermopolis*
1:7; לה שלחתן הן חי אנה והן מת אנה "you did not send (to find out)
whether I was alive or dead" *Hermopolis* 5:8-9; קא יהבנא [ ] (=
יהב אנא) "I am giving (back) the [dow]ry" *Mur* 19:8. Subj. of a
composite nominal cl. (BL 346e): אֲנָה דָנִיֵּאל . . . רַעְיוֹנַי יְבַהֲלֻנַּנִי "as
for me, Daniel, my thoughts alarm me" Dan 7:28; וַאֲנָה . . . רָזָא
דְנָה גְּלִי לִי "but as for me, . . . this mystery has been revealed to
me" (for the construction, see ¹לְהֵן no. 2) 2:30; ואנה נכתני חויה
"and as for me, a serpent bit me" *Hermopolis* 5:8.
        (2) Subj. of verbal cl. (BL 267a, c): אֲנָה יִדְעֵת "I know"
Dan 4:6: 4:16; דִּי־אֲנָה בֱנַיְתַהּ "(Is not this the great Babylon),
which I have built?" (BL 267a) 4:27. Before a name w. verb in 1
sg.: אֲנָה דָרְיָוֶשׁ שָׂמֵת טְעֵם "I, Darius, issued a decree" Ezra 6:12:
Dan 4:1, 15, 31; הן אנה ידניה רשיתכם "if I, Jedaniah, sue you" *AP*
25:12; חלמת אנה אברם חלם "I, Abram, had a dream" *1QapGen*
19:14. Before another subj.: שרית אנה ובני כולהון "I, and all my
sons, began (to cultivate the land)" *1QapGen* 12:13.
        (3) As an oblique case after 1 sg. suff. and before a name
(BL 69d, 267b): רוּחִי אֲנָה דָנִיֵּאל "as for me, Daniel, my spirit

(was disturbed)" Dan 7:15; מִנִּי אֲנָה אַרְתַּחְשַׁסְתְּא מַלְכָּא שִׂים טְעֵם "by me, Artaxerxes the king, a decree was issued" Ezra 7:21; לא הות ארק לדרגמן זילי הא אנה "it was no longer the land of Dargman, mine, that is (belonging to) me" *AP* 6:7; ביתי אנה דרגמן "my house, of me, Dargman" *AP* 6:8; בשמי אנה ידניה "in my name, me, Jedaniah" *AP* 25:12; מטא עלי בדינא אנה מלכיה "(the appeal) has been laid by the court upon me, on me, Malchiah" *AP* 7:7; מטאני בחלק אנה מחסיה "(this portion) has come to me as a share, to me, Mahseiah" *AP* 28:5. Before another obj.: אפקני אנה וברי "he made me go out, me and my son" *Hermopolis* 6:4. Indep. pers. pron.: **me.** לִי . . . יִבְעוֹן "(my counselors and my lords) sought me" Dan 4:33; קרא לי אלו "(the Pharaoh) called me to him" *1QapGen* 20:26. [Hebr. אֲנִי]. †

אִנּוּן m., אִנִּין f., indep. pers. pron. 3 pl. (cf. BL 124q, r, s): **they, them.** See הוּא.

אֱנָשׁ * s.v. אֱנַשׁ.

אֲנַחְנָה and אֲנַחְנָא , indep. pers. pron. (BL 70n): **we.** מְהוֹדְעִין אֲנַחְנָה לְמַלְכָּא "we make known to the king" Ezra 4:16; Dan 3:16; דִּי אֲנַחְנָא פָּלְחִין "(the God) whom we serve" 3:17; אֲנַחְנָא הִמּוֹ עַבְדוֹהִי "we are His servants" Ezra 5:11; אנחנה מחסיה ובני "we, Mahseiah and my children" *AP* 28:9; אנה בגזשת ואובל כל 2 אנחן זבן "I, Bagazusht, and Ubil, both of us, have sold" *BMAP* 3:10. [Hebr. אֲנַחְנוּ]. †

אנס , ptc. m. sg. אָנֵס : **crush.** כָּל־רָז לָא־אָנֵס לָךְ "no mystery is crushing for you," i.e., too difficult Dan 4:6; באדין אנסת רוחהא "then (my wife) crushed her spirit," i.e., suppressed her anger *1QapGen* 2:13. [Hebr. אָנַס *]. [1]

42

אֲנַף * (*'anp*), du. אַנְפִּין *, w. suff. אַנְפּוֹהִי (w. daghesh, BL 226x); m.: (1) **nose; du. nostrils, face, countenance.** מא רגג הוא כל לה אנפהא "how graceful is her (Sarai's) nose" *1QapGen* 20:3; גבר זי יבעה רוח אפוה "any man who rants [lit., "causes the breath of his nostrils to boil"] (and utters evil words against me)" *Sefire III* 1-2; נְפַל עַל־אַנְפּוֹהִי "fell upon his face" Dan 2:46; צְלֵם אַנְפּוֹהִי אֶשְׁתַּנִּי עַל שַׁדְרַךְ "the expression of his face was changed against Shadrach, . . ." 3:19; תחזין אנפי ואחזה אפיכי "you (f. sg.) will see my face, and I shall see your face" *El. Ostr.* 12-13 (*AH* I/1. 13); זי יחזני אפיכן בשלם "(the god Ptah), who may grant me to see your faces in peace" *Hermopolis* 5:2; כזי ח[ז]ית אנפי אסרחאדן מלך אתור טבן "when I s[a]w (that) the face of Esarhaddon, the king of Assyria, (was) favorable" *Aḥ.* 14; הן לו גלין אנפין על ארשם קדמן "if we had appeared [lit., showed our faces] before Arsames previously" *AP* 37:8; ירוקן באנפוהי "they will spit in his face" *Aḥ.* 133; ימחא על אפיה "one strikes her on the face" (*'appáyah*, cf. BL 49e) *Sefire I* A 42; כמה . . . שפיר לה צלם אנפיהא "how . . . beautiful the form of her face" *1QapGen* 20:2; באנפי יהוחנן זנה [ ] "[he said] this in the presence of Yohanan" *Mur 72* 1:6. (2) **surface.** כל זי איתי לה על אנפי ארעא "all that belongs to him on the face of the earth" *AP* 15:19; ינסחוהי וזרעה ושמה מן אנפי תימא "may (the gods) remove him, his descendants, and his name from the region of Tema" (*KAI* 228: A14-15); על אפי ארקה "(may calamity come up) on the face of its land" *Sefire I* A 28. [Hebr. אַף]. †

אֲנָשׁ (*'unāš*, BL 190u) abs. and cst. (in *1QapGen* always אנוש and always abs.); emph. אֲנָשָׁא and in Dan 4:13-14 k. אנושא (assimilated to *u*, *GBA* p. 21), in Dan 4:14 for Hebr. אֲנָשִׁים read אֲנָשָׁא (BL 201f); only sg. (BL 202m), m.: **man, human being.**
(1) Collective sense (sometimes expressed by בְּנֵי). (a) Indeterminate, abs. אֱנָשׁ (in *1QapGen* אנוש): "some men"; ואלהן ואנש לא ינ[פק] צלמשזב "let neither gods nor humans remove Zelemshezib (the priest, from this temple)" *Tema* 29-21 (*KAI* 228);

מְנִי עַמִּי אֲנוֹשׁ דִּי יַנְפְּק[וֹנַנִי] "(Pharaoh) appointed men who would escort me (out of Egypt)" *1QapGen* 20:32; וְבְ[נֵי] אֲנוֹשׁ אֲתוֹ "and some men came" *1QapGen* 19:15. (b) Determinate, emph. אֲנָשָׁא and cst w. determ. gen.: "the men"; אֱנָשׁ עֲבַר־נַהֲרָה "men of (the province) Beyond-the-River" Ezra 4:11; כֹּל אֲנָשׁ בֵּיתֵהּ "all the men of his house" *1QapGen* 20:16; וְאַשְׁכַּחַת כֹּל אַנְשֵׁי שְׁלָם "and I found all my men safe" ('ŭnāšī šĕlēm), i.e., my whole family *1QapGen* 21:19; כֹּל אֲנָשָׁא דִּי עִמֵּהּ "all the men who were with him" *1QapGen* 22:15; שַׁלִּיט עִלָּיָא בְּמַלְכוּת אֲנָשָׁא "the Most High rules the kingdom of men" Dan 4:14, 22, 29; 5:21; וּשְׁפַל אֲנָשִׁים יְקִים עֲלַיְהּ "and puts it over the lowliest of men" (read אֲנָשָׁא ; BL 320i) 4:14; לָךְ טָרְדִין מִן־אֲנָשָׁא "they will drive you out from among men" Dan 4:22, 29: 4:30; מִן־בְּנֵי אֲנָשָׁא טְרִיד "driven out from among mankind" 5:21; בְּכָל־דִּי דָארִין בְּנֵי־אֲנָשָׁא חֵיוַת בָּרָא וְעוֹף שְׁמַיָּא "wherever they dwell, the sons of men, beasts of the field, and birds of the heavens" 2:38.

(2) Individual sense (sometimes expressed by בַּר). (a) Indeterminate: abs. אֲנָשׁ (in *1QapGen* אנושׁ): "someone." אנשׁ זילי "some man of mine" *AP* 28:8; אישׁ לי ואנשׁ אחרן "anyone of mine or any other man" *BMAP* 8:5; כָּל־אֱנָשׁ דִּי "anyone" Dan 3:10; 5:7; 6:13a; Ezra 6:11: Dan 2:10; 6:8, 13b; אנשׁ לא שׁליט "no one has power" *BMAP* 8:8-9; בכל מה זי ימות בר אנשׁ שׁקרתם "in whatever way anyone shall die, you shall have been unfaithful (to all the gods)" *Sefire III* 16; כְּבַר אֱנָשׁ אָתֵה הֲוָה "there came one like a son of man" Dan 7:13 (cf. דָּמֵה לְבַר־אֱלָהִין "(someone) like a son of the gods" 3:25); דִּי לָא יִשְׁכַּח כֹּל בַּר אֱנוֹשׁ לְמִמְנֵיהּ "which no one can number" *1QapGen* 21:13. (b) Determinate: emph. אֲנָשָׁא : כן אנשׁא לא ידע אישׁ "so man knows not men" *Ah.* 116.

(3) As gen. of quality (see דִּי II 2a): "human." אֶצְבְּעָן דִּי יַד־אֱנָשׁ "fingers of a human hand (appeared)" Dan 5:5; לְבַב אֱנָשׁ יְהִיב לַהּ "a human mind was given to it (the beast)" 7:4; עַל רַגְלַיִן כֶּאֱנָשׁ "(to stand) on two feet like a man" (cf. BL 315c) 7:4; עַיְנִין כְּעַיְנֵי אֲנָשָׁא "(in the horn were) eyes like human eyes" (see above

אנתה

no. 2 b) 7:8; לְבָבֵהּ מִן־אֲנָשָׁא יְשַׁנּוֹן וּלְבַב חֵיוָה "let his mind be changed from a man('s mind), and let a beast's mind (be given to him)" 4:13 (brachylogy, see לְבַב ; one could have said: לִבְבֵהּ דִּי אֲנָשָׁא * "his human mind," cf. רַגְלוֹהִי דִּי פַרְזְלָא 2:34); לְהֵוֹן מִתְעָרְבִין בִּזְרַע אֲנָשָׁא "they will mingle with one another by human seed," i.e., in marriage, 2:43. [Hebr. אֱנוֹשׁ]. †

אַנְתָּה k. and אַנְתְּ k. Ezra 7:25; in q. always אַנְתְּ m., אנתי ('ántī) f.; indep. pers. pron. (BL 69e, 70k,l): **you.** (1) Subj. of nominal cl.: אֱלָהָךְ דִּי אַנְתָּה פָּלַח־לֵהּ "your God, whom you serve" Dan 6:17, 21; אַנְתְּה וְרַבְרְבָנָיךְ . . . שָׁתַיִן "you and your nobles . . . were drinking" 5:23; שליט אנת ידניה "you, Jedaniah, have authority" AP 28:6; אנתי שליטה בה "you (f.) have authority over it" AP 8:9; עמי את במתכדי "you (were) with me in the land of Akkad" Letter of Assur 2 (KAI 233); אנתה הוא ל]י א[ל] [ע]ל[מא] "You are to me the eternal God" 1QapGen 19:7-8. Subj. of composite nominal cl. (BL 346c): אַנְתָּה מַלְכָּא רַעְיוֹנָךְ . . . סְלִקוּ "You, O King, thoughts came to you" (read רַעְיוֹנָיךְ) Dan 2:29; 5:18; כעת אנת וגרדא זילי עבידא לא איתי לך "Now as for you, you have no business with my domestic staff" AD 12:9. Pred. of a nominal cl. (BL 330q): אִילָנָא . . . אַנְתָּה הוּא מַלְכָּא "(that) tree . . . is you, O king" Dan 4:17-19; אַנְתָּה־הוּא רֵאשָׁה . . . אַנְתָּה מַלְכָּא "You, O King, . . . the head (of gold) is you" 2:37-38; אַנְתָּה־הוּא דָנִיֵּאל דִּי־מִן־בְּנֵי גָלוּתָא "You are Daniel, one of the exiles (of Judah)" 5:13.
(2) Subj. of verbal cl.: אַנְתָּה מַלְכָּא שָׂמְתָּ טְעֵם "You, O King, issued a decree" Dan 3:10: 2:31; 5:22; הן אי[ן]י יקתלן את תאתה "if they kill me ('iyyātī), you must come" Sefire III 11; [א]ל מן את תעשקני את "you yourself shall not hinder me" Sefire III 20; תהנס צלמא זנה "whoever you are, who will carry off this statue, may the gods punish you" Nerab 5-7 (KAI 225). Before an impv.: אַנְתְּ עֶזְרָא . . . מֶּנִּי שָׁפְטִין "You, Ezra, . . . appoint judges" Ezra 7:25: Dan 4:15; אנת שם טעם "You, issue an order!" AD 3:7.

45

אנתה—אספרנא

(3) In an oblique case after 2 sg. suff. and before a name: מועה שמש לה ביתך אנת ענני "east of it is your house, Anani" *BMAP* 12:17; זך ביתא . . . זילכם הו אנת ידניה ומחסיה "that house . . . is yours, Jedaniah and Mahseiah" *AP* 25:8; לא אכהל אגרנך . . . אנת ובר לך "I shall not be able to stir up (a suit or process) against you . . . you and your son" *AP* 6:12-13. N.B. indep. pers. pron. "you": לָךְ . . . מְשַׁבַּח אֲנָה "You I praise" Dan 2:23; לָךְ טָרְדִין "(they will) drive you out" 4:22, 29. [Hebr. אַתָּה]. †

אַנְתָּה *: **wife,** see נְשִׁין.

אנתם, אַנְתּוּן indep. pers. pron. m. pl.: **you.** אַנְתּוּן זָבְנִין "you are buying (time)" Dan 2:8; אנתם כן לא עבדן "you are not doing so" *AD* 7:5; אנתם הבו [לה] "You, do give [him] . . . !" *AD* 6:2 (and often before an impv.). [Hebr. אַתֶּם]. [1]

אֱסוּר (BL 189s), pl. אֱסוּרִין : **bond, fetter.** לֶאֱסוּרִין "for bonds," i.e., imprisonment Ezra 7:26; וּבֶאֱסוּר דִּי־פַרְזֶל וּנְחָשׁ "(bound) with a band of iron and bronze" Dan 4:12, 20; see the list of accounts: נחשיא זי יהבו על תמריא "bronze bands that they put on the date palms" *AP* 81:111. [Hebr. אֱסוּר]. †

▲ אָסְנַפַּר , prob. a corruption of אס[רב]נפר, Ashurbanipal, **Osnapper,** king of Assyria (669-629 B.C.), Ezra 4:10. [1]

אָסְפַּרְנָא ('ospárnā'; < Persian *usprnā "completed"[?]). adv. **accurately, diligently, strictly.** אָסְפַּרְנָא עֲבַד "diligently produced (it)" Ezra 5:8; אָסְפַּרְנָא יִתְעֲבֵד "let it be done diligently" Ezra 6:12, 13; 7:21; אָסְפַּרְנָא דִּינָה לֶהֱוֵא מִתְעֲבֵד מִנֵּהּ "let judgment be executed strictly upon him" 7:26; אָסְפַּרְנָא נִפְקְתָא תֶּהֱוֵא מִתְיַהֲבָא "the cost is to be paid accurately" 6:8; אָסְפַּרְנָא תִקְנֵא . . . תּוֹרִין "(with this money) you shall buy diligently . . . bulls" 7:17; מנדת בגיא זי ורוהי אספרן . . . יהנפק "(to collect) the revenue of the estate

46

of Warohi accurately . . . (and) bring (it)" *AD* 10:4; אספרן לקבל
סתריא זי כספא "corresponding strictly to the silver stater" *Mysian
Lion-Weight* (*KAI* 263). †

אֱסָר (*'isār*) abs. (and cst.), emph. אֱסָרָא , m.: **prohibition, interdict.** לְתַקָּפָה אֱסָר "to enforce the interdict" Dan 6:8;
תְּקִים אֱסָרָא "(O King,) did you establish the interdict" 6:9: 6:12;
רְשַׁם כְּתָבָא וֶאֱסָרָא "(Darius) signed the document and the interdict"
6:10: 6:13-14. [Hebr. אִסָּר , w. suff. אֱסָרָהּ]. †

אָע , עק (* *'iḡ* > *'iq* > * *'a'* > *'ā'* ; BL 39d, 179f, *LFAA* 9k,
l), emph. אָעָא , m. **wood, beam, log.** יִתְנְסַח אָע מִן־בַּיְתֵהּ "a beam
shall be pulled from his house" Ezra 6:11; אָע מִתְּשָׂם בְּכֻתְלַיָּא
"logs are laid in the walls" 5:8; וְנִדְבָּךְ דִּי־אָע חֲדָה "and one course
of timber" 6:4; cf. 5:8; pl.: עקי ארז "planks of cedar" *AP* 26:17;
יהוספון על עקיא . . . בארכא לחד פשכן תלתה "they will add to the
planks . . . in length each three hand-breadths" *AP* 26:18; [למ]ה
ישפטון עקן עם אשה "Why should logs strive with fire?" *Aḥ.* 104;
איש מצלה עקן בחשוכא "a man splits logs in darkness" *Aḥ.* 125.
Gen. of material: אֱלָהֵי דַּהֲבָא . . . אָעָא "(they praised) the gods of
gold . . . wood . . ." Dan 5:4, 23; מאני עק וחוצן "(there are)
vessels of wood and ivory" *AP* 20:5-6. [Hebr. עֵץ]. †

אַף , adv.: **also;** adding simply something new: **and;** in
narrating and counting: **furthermore, moreover;** emphasizing:
even. וְאַף שְׁמָהָתְהֹם שְׁאֵלְנָא "we also asked their names" Ezra 5:10:
5:14; 6:5; וְאַף קֳדָמָיךְ . . . חֲבוּלָה לָא עַבְדֵת "and also before you, (O
King), I have done no wrong" Dan 6:23; . . . אף לא יכהל בר לי
יגרנכי "moreover, a son of mine . . . shall not be able to start a
suit against you" *BMAP* 4:13-14; אף לכל עבדיך אל[פנא] "and for
all your slaves, discipline" (*'ulpānā'*) *Aḥ.* 83; 1 ואף לכי תקבת
שפרת ואף משח בשם "and also for you (f.) 1 beautiful garment(?),
and also perfumed oil for . . ." *Hermopolis* 2:11-12; אף איתי תבא

שמה אמהם זי עלימיא "There is also Teba, by name, the mother of the lads" *AP* 28:12-13; multiple instances of אף "moreover," in *AP* 30:9-30; אף יהכון בדין "even (if) they go to court, (they will not win)" *AP* 10:19; טעמת אף זעררתא מררתא "I have tasted even the bitter sloe, (and nothing is more bitter than poverty)" *Aḥ.* 105; בעה . . . אף מן אתר אחרן גרד אמנן "from another place he also sought a staff of craftsmen" *AD* 7:2-3, 6; לא יכל למקרב בהא ואף לא ידעהא "he (the Pharaoh) was not able to approach her; nor did he have intercourse with her" *1QapGen* 20:17; אף אנה יהבת לה "moreover, I give (it) to her" *BMAP* 9:17-18. [Hebr. the same]. †

אֲפָרְסָי *, emph. pl. אֲפָרְסָיֵא (BL 196d), prob. read either פַּרְסָיֵא "Persians" or rather סִפָּרָיֵא "Sipparites," i.e., men of Sippar, a Babylonian town (*AH* I/2.17), as the context suggests: Ezra 4:9, "Rehum, the commander, and Shimshai. the scribe, and the rest of their associates, . . . and the rest of the peoples, whom . . . Osnappar deported and settled in the towns of Samaria and in (the province) Beyond-the-River." [1]

אֲפַרְסְכָי * (< Persian * *frasa-ka* "inquirer, spy" + Ar. *āy*), emph. pl. אֲפַרְסְכָיֵא prob. **investigator,** title of some Persian official: אֲפַרְסְכָיֵא דִּי בַּעֲבַר נַהֲרָה "investigators of (the province) Beyond-the-River" Ezra 5:6; 6:6. †

אֲפַרְסַתְכָי * (prob. < Persian * *fra-stā-ka* "prefect" [*GBA* p. 62] + Ar. *āy*): perh. **prefect,** title of some Persian official. דִּינָיֵא וַאֲפַרְסַתְכָיֵא "the judges (MT דִּינָיֵא) and the prefects" Ezra 4:9. [1]

אַפְּתֹם (v.l. אַפְּתֹּם and אַפְּתֹם) adv. **so, in this way.** וְאַפְּתֹם מַלְכִין תְּהַנְזִק "(if the city [Jerusalem] is rebuilt . . . , they will not pay tribute . . .) and in this way damage will affect kings" Ezra 4:13. From Akk. *appittum* (*appitumma, appittima*) "so, in this way" *CAD* I/2, s.v. *appitti.* Cf. the inscription of Darius I (*API*,

p. 7), Persian l. 6-7: *avākaram amiy* "so I am doing" (see R. G. Kent, *Old Persian*, p. 172) = Akk. l. 4: *appittum epšēka* "so I am doing." [1]

אֶצְבַּע * (BL 193o: w. prothetic א), pl. אֶצְבְּעָן , cst. אֶצְבְּעָת , emph. אֶצְבְּעָתָא ; f. **finger, toe.** אֶצְבְּעָן דִּי יַד־אֱנָשׁ "fingers of a man's hand (appeared)" Dan 5:5; אֶצְבְּעָת רַגְלַיָּא "the toes of the feet (of that statue)" 2:42: cf. 2:41; אצבעת ידיהא "the fingers of her hands" *1QapGen* 20:5. צבע (*qital*, *LFAA* 78k), m. **finger** (measure). על פתיא צבע חד "(they shall add) to the breadth one finger" *AP* 26:20; על פתיא ועביא צבען תרין "to the breadth and the thickness two fingers" *AP* 26:18; מסמרי נחש . . . לחד צבען עשרה "(as for the) bronze nails, . . . each ten finger(-breadths)" *AP* 26:15-16. [Hebr. אֶצְבַּע]. †

אַרְבַּע (BL 193m, 250i) m. (used w. f. noun), אַרְבְּעָה (used w. m. noun, BL 321g): **four.** Before a noun: אַרְבַּע חֵיוָן "four beasts" Dan 7:3; אַרְבְּעָה מַלְכִין "four kings" 7:17; אַרְבַּע רוּחֵי שְׁמַיָּא "the four winds of the heavens" 7:2; מן ארבע רוחיהון "(he fell on them) from four sides" (lit., "from their four winds") *1QapGen* 22:8. After a noun: גַּפִּין אַרְבַּע "four wings (of a bird)" Dan 7:6; גֻּבְרִין אַרְבְּעָה "four men" 3:25; אִמְּרִין אַרְבַּע מְאָה "four hundred lambs" Ezra 6:17; מסמרין ארבע מאה עשרין וחמש "425 nails" *AP* 26:16; //// שקלין "4, i.e., four shekels" *AP* 10:3-4; לשנין הו ארבעה "in the fourth year" *1QapGen* 12:13; בשנת ארבע עשרה "in the fourteenth year" (cf. עֲשַׂר) *1QapGen* 21:27. As a pred.: דִּי אִנּוּן אַרְבַּע "(these great beasts) which are four . . ." Dan 7:17. Pl. אַרְבְּעִין * "forty," emph. ארבעיא "the forty (in ?)" *AP* 81:60. Cf. רְבִיעִי . [Hebr. the same]. †

אַרְגְּוָן * (< Akk.), emph. אַרְגְּוָנָא : **purple.** אַרְגְּוָנָא יִלְבַּשׁ "he shall be robed in purple" Dan 5:7: 5:16, 29. As gen. of quality: לבוש שגי די בוץ וארגואן "many garments (collect. sg.) of fine linen and purple" *1QapGen* 21:31. [Hebr. אַרְגָּמָן]. †

אֲרוּ : see אֲלוּ .

אֲרַח * ('urḥ), emph. *ארחא ; pl. אָרְחָן , w. suff. אָרְחָתֵהּ
,אָ‏,; f.: (1) **way, route.** סלקו ארחא די מדברא "they came up
(by) the desert route" *1QapGen* 21:28; ארח מלכא "the highway
of the king" *AP* 25:6-7; שוק מלכא "the street of the king" *BMAP*
3:8. (2) Transferred meaning: **way of acting.** כָּל־מַעֲבָדוֹהִי קְשֹׁט
וְאָרְחָתֵהּ דִּין "all His works are right, and all His ways are just"
Dan 4:34; נפשי לא תדע ארחה "my soul knows not its way" *Aḥ.*
187; לֵאלָהָא דִּי־נִשְׁמְתָךְ בִּידֵהּ וְכָל־אָרְחָתָךְ לֵהּ לָא הַדַּרְתָּ "the God in
whose hand is your breath, and whose are all your ways, Him
you have not honored" Dan 5:23 (emphatic repetition of the obj.,
see הוּא no. 5; לְ no. I/3; or see דִּי no. II/1); מ]ן יום זי אזלת בארחא[
זך "from the day that you set out on that way" *Padua I* A 2.
[Hebr. אֹרַח]. †

אַרְיֵה ('aryēh < *'aryī), emph. אריא ('aryā'); emph. pl.
אַרְיָוָתָא (w. augm. -aw- see BL 233i); m. **lion.** קַדְמָיְתָא כְּאַרְיֵה "the
first (kingdom) was like a lion" Dan 7:4; גב אַרְיָוָתָא "the den of
lions" 6:8: 6:13 + ; אריה [לא אי]תי בימא "there is no lion in the
sea" *Aḥ.* 117; שבק חמר ולא יסבלנהי [ ] אריה "(for fear of) the
lion, the ass left (its burden) and would not carry it" *Aḥ.* 89-90;
אריה יהוה מסמה לאילא בסתר סוידא "the lion will scent out the hart in
the secrecy of (its) den (?)" *Aḥ.* 88; ענה חמרא ואמר לאריא "the ass
spoke up and said to the lion" *Aḥ.* 110. [Hebr. the same, BL 193
n. 2].

▲ אַרְיוֹךְ : **Arioch,** captain of the king's guard, Dan 2:14,
24-25. Cf. אריוך מלך כפתוך "Arioch, the king of Cappadocia"
1QapGen 21:23 (see *Letter of Mari* (II 63-64) *Ar-ri-wa-az / Ar-
ri-wu-uk,* son of the King of Zimrilim).

אֲרִיךְ (perh. < Persian *ārya-ka* "Arius, a man suited to Arius." BL 188i): **fitting.** לָא אֲרִיךְ לָנָא לְמֶחֱזֵא "it is not fitting for us to see (the king's ignominy)" Ezra 4:14. [1]

אֲרַךְ * (*'urk, LFAA* 76t), w. suff. ארכה (*'urkēh*), m.: **length** (spatial). הוה ארך אמן 8 ב 5 "(the) length (of which) was 8 cubits by 5" *AP* 15:8; ארכה . . . אמן 13 "its (the house's) length (was) 13 cubits" *AP* 8:4; על עקיא . . . בארכא לחד פשכן תלתה "(they will add) to the planks . . . in length to each three hand-breadths" *AP* 26:18; חזי כמן ארכהא "see how great (is) its length," i.e., of the promised land *1QapGen* 21:14; <אַמִּין אָרְכַּהּ תְּלָתִין> רוּמֵהּ אַמִּין שְׁתִּין אַמִּין פְּתָיֵהּ שְׁתִּין "its (the Temple's) height (shall be) <thirty cubits, its length> sixty <cubits>, its width sixty cubits" (or rather "twenty"; read עֶשְׂרִין) Ezra 6:3; ארוך בתי[א] "the length of the houses" *5QNJ (5Q15)* 1 ii 7; פותיה ואורכה משחה חדה "its width and its length (have) the same dimension" *5QNJ (5Q15)* 1 ii 3. [Hebr. אֹרֶךְ].

אַרְכֻּבָּה * (BL 44c, 193o), pl. w. suff. אַרְכֻבָתֵהּ (v.l. אַרְכֻּבָּתֵהּ , BL 241q), f.: **knee** (see בְּרַךְ). אַרְכֻבָּתֵהּ דָּא לְדָא נָקְשָׁן "his knees knocked, one against the other," because of fear" Dan 5:6; למאתה לה על ארבתה "to come to him (Noah) on his knees" *4QBirth-Noah*^a *(4Q534)* 1 i 6. [1]

אַרְכָה (*qatal*, BL 185s), f.: **lengthening, continuation.** תֶּהֱוֵה אַרְכָה לִשְׁלֵוְתָךְ "there may be a lengthening of your tranquillity" Dan 4:24; אַרְכָה בְחַיִּין יְהִיבַת עַד־זְמַן וְעִדָּן "a prolongation was given in life for a season and a time" 7:12. †

אַרְכְּוָי * (BL 196d), emph. pl. אַרְכְּוָיֵא q. (אַרְכְּוָיֵ k.), for the normal אַרְכָּיֵא * (sg. אַרְכִּי *). perh. read אַרְכָּיֵי (*AH* I/2.18), gentilic name: **Erechite**, an inhabitant of Uruk (today Warka), a town in Babylonia Ezra 4:9. [1]

ארע

אֲרַע and ארק (< *'arg̊*, see *AGI* p. 36), emph. אַרְעָא and אַרְקָא (Jer 10:11), f.: (1) **earth,** in a universal sense: כָּל־אַרְעָא "the whole earth" Dan 2:35, 39; 3:31; 6:26; סוֹף כָּל־אַרְעָא "the end (collect.) of the whole earth" 4:8, 17: 4:19; בְּגוֹא אַרְעָא "(a tree) in the midst of the earth" 4:7; דָּאֲרֵי אַרְעָא "the inhabitants of the earth" 4:32; שְׁמַיָּא וְאַרְעָא "heaven and earth." i.e., the universe Ezra 5:11; Dan 6:28; שְׁמַיָּא וְאַרְקָא . . . יֵאבַדוּ מֵאַרְעָא "(the gods who did not make) the heavens and the earth shall perish from the earth" Jer 10:11; שמיא וארקא "heaven and earth" *Adon Letter* 2 (*KAI* 266); דרכי ארקא בניח[א] "those who walk on the earth in tranquillity" *Ah.* 108; כל זי איתי לה על אנפי ארעא "all that he possesses on the face of the earth" *AP* 15:19; ארעא וכול די "the earth and all that (is) upon it" *1QapGen* 7:1; עליהא כול מלכי "all the kings of the earth" *1QapGen* 20:13, 15-16; מַלְכִין ארעא "(four) kings shall arise from the earth" 7:17; תֶּהֱוֵא יְקוּמוּן מִן־אַרְעָא "(a fourth kingdom) shall be on the earth בְּאַרְעָא . . . וְתֵאכַל כָּל־אַרְעָא . . . and it shall devour all the earth" 7:23; כל מה לחיה בארק ובשמין "every sort of evil (that exists) on earth and in heaven" *Sefire I* A 26; אלהי שמי[ן] ואלה[י] ארק "the gods of heave[n and the god]s of earth" *Zkr* B 25-26 (*KAI* 202).

(2) **land, region, territory:** על אפי ארקה "upon the face of its land (Arpad)" *Sefire I* A 28; יקח מן ארקי "(if) he should take some of my land" *Sefire I* B 27; למ[הך] לארע מצרין "to go to the land of Egypt" *1QapGen* 19:11; חזי כול ארעא דא "see all this land (that I am giving to you)" *1QapGen* 19:9-10; חלפנא ארענא "we passed through our land and ועלנא לארע לארע בני חם לארע מצרין entered the land of the sons of Ham, the land of Egypt" *1QapGen* 19:13; כול ארע צפונא "all the land of the north" *1QapGen* 16:10.

(3) **soil, ground, field** (see אֲתַר). נְטִילַת מִן־אַרְעָא "(the first beast) was lifted up from the ground" Dan 7:4; עלו באגורא זך "they entered that temple; they razed it to the נדשוהי עד ארעא ground" *AP* 30:9; תדבק לשטר ביתי מן ארעא ועד עלא "(this portico)

will adjoin the side of my house from the ground upwards" (or
"from below," *LFAA* 121o; see below no. 4, adv.) *AP* 5:5; עֲקַר
שָׁרְשׁוֹהִי בְּאַרְעָא שְׁבֻקוּ "leave the stump of its roots in the ground"
Dan 4:12, 20; חֲלָקֵהּ בַּעֲשַׂב אַרְעָא "(let) his lot (be) . . . in the grass
of the ground" 4:12; עבור ארקתא כלא "the crop of the field, all of
it" *AD* 12:6; שרית . . . למפלח בארעא "I began . . . to cultivate the
ground" *1QapGen* 12:13. -- Specifically, "empty ground" (not
built upon); cf. בַּיָּת "(urban) estate," on which a house can be
built: ותרבצה ארע הי ולא בניה "and the court is a plot, and it is not
built up" *BMAP* 3:4-5; עלדבר ארקא זך . . . ארעא זך "in regard to
that plot . . . , that plot" (surrounded by houses) *AP* 6:6, 16; בית
ביתא זנך ארק 1 "1 house (and) my plot" *AP* 8:3; ארק "that
house (and) a plot (I give to you)" *AP* 8:8; ארקא זך זיליכי בני והבי
"that plot is yours (f.); build (on it) or give (it)" *AP* 8:19; איתי
ארק בי 1 זילי "there is a plot of 1 house belonging to me" *AP* 9:3;
הן . . . ארקא זך תבנה "if . . . you build (on) that plot" *AP* 9:8; לא
יהבת לך ארקא זך למבנה "I did not give you that plot to build (on
it)" *AP* 9:14.

   (4) אֲרַע q. and אַרְעָא k. (BL 254o), adv. **below.** מַלְכוּ אָחֳרִי
אַרְעָא מִנָּךְ "another kingdom inferior to you" (see מִן no. 8) Dan
2:39; cf. above no. 1 and no. 3: *AP* 5:5. [Hebr. אֶרֶץ]. †

אַרְעִי * (BL 197f), cst. אַרְעִית , f.: **lower part, bottom.**
לָא־מְטוֹ לְאַרְעִית גֻּבָּא "they did not reach the bottom of the den"
Dan 6:25. [1]

אֲרַק * : see אֲרַע .

   ▲ אַרְתַּחְשַׁשְׂתָּא in Ezra 4:7 and in k. 4:8, 11-23; 6:14;
אַרְתַּחְשַׁסְתָּא in k. 7:12, 21; in pap. ארתחששש (< Persian *Artaḫšaṯ-
ra > Artaḫšača*; perh. by metathesis *-šača > -šasta* and *-šasta*, in
pap. *-šasša*): **Artaxerxes I,** king of the Persians (465-424 B.C.).
[Hebr. the same]. †

אֶשִׁין * (< Akk. only pl. *uššū*), emph. אֻשַּׁיָּא, w. suff. אֻשּׁוֹהִי; only pl.: **foundations** of a building (see *JNES* 17 [1958] 269-75). אֻשַּׁיָּא יַחִיטוּ "(the Jews) have repaired the foundations (of the walls)" (see יחט) Ezra 4:12; ... יְהַב אֻשַּׁיָּא דִּי־בֵית אֱלָהָא שֵׁשְׁבַּצַּר "Sheshbazzar . . . laid the foundations of God's house" 5:16; וְאֻשּׁוֹהִי מְסוֹבְלִין "and let its foundations be maintained" 6:3 (cf. 5:15; 7:6; and see סבל). †

אֶשָּׁה and אֶשָּׁא (< *'išāt: qitāl*, BL 56c, 189q), emph. אשתא (*'išātā*'); f.: **fire** (cf. נור). יְהִיבַת לִיקֵדַת אֶשָּׁא "(the beast) was given over to blazing fire" Dan 7:11; כלא באשה שרפו "all of it (the temple) they burned with fire" *AP* 30:12; || || באשתא שרפו *AP* 31:11; אשה יקדה הי "(a king's command) is a burning fire" *Aḥ.* 103; ישפטון עקן עם אשה "(Why) should logs strive with fire?" *Aḥ.* 104; בית רעה נשק באשה "the house of his friend caught fire" *Aḥ.* 222. [Hebr. אֵשׁ, אֶשֶּׁה *]. [1]

אָשֵׁף (< Akk. *[w]āšipu* ptc., BL30a, 190x), v.l. in Dan 2:10 אָשֵׁף and אַשָּׁף ; pl. אָשְׁפִין, emph. אָשְׁפַיָּא : **enchanter, exorcist.** Dan 2:10, 27; 4:4; 5:7, 11, 15; לא יכלו כול אסיא ואשפיא וכול חכימיא . . . לאסיותה "and none of the physicians, enchanters, or wise men were able . . . to cure him" *1QapGen* 20:20. [Hebr. אַשָּׁף]. †

אֲשַׁרְנָא (prob. < Persian; see *GBA* p. 63), m. **wooden structure** (see *JNES* 17 [1958] 269-275). וְאֲשַׁרְנָא דְנָה לְשַׁכְלָלָה "and to complete this wooden structure?" Ezra 5:3, 9 (cf. Ezra 5:8; Hag 1:8); עקי ארז ואר חדתן . . . אשרנא זנה בד לן[מע]ל "to [ma]ke this wooden structure . . . new planks of cedar and cypress" *AP* 26:9-10; סגן גריא . . . יד על יתיהב זנה אשרנא "this wooden material is to be delivered to . . . , the head of the carpenters" *AP* 26:21-22; אשרנא שירית עם "with the rest of the wooden furniture" *AP* 30:11; בנינא זי תבנה בה וכל אשרן זי יהכן על ביתא זך "the building

אשתדור—אתה

which you will build on it and all the lumber that may go into
that house" *BMAP* 3:22a, 23a.

אֶשְׁתַּדּוּר (either Hithpa. infin. שדר BL 193o, or < Persian
ā[ḫ]šti-drauga "breach of peace" *GBA* p. 63; cf. p. 49), m.: **in-
surrection, sedition.** אֶשְׁתַּדּוּר עָבְדִין "they were stirring up sedition (in it [Jerusalem]) from of old" Ezra 4:15; מְרַד וְאֶשְׁתַּדּוּר
מִתְעֲבֶד־בַּהּ "rebellion and sedition were stirred up in it" 4:19. †

אֶשְׁתִּי : see שתה.

אָת * (*qatalat*, *'awayat* BL 185s,t), pl. אָתִין, emph. אָתַיָּא,
w. suff. אָתוֹהִי ; m.: **sign, miracle.** עָבֵד אָתִין וְתִמְהִין "(God) works
signs and wonders" Dan 6:28; אָתַיָּא ... עֲבַד עִמִּי "the signs . . .
(that the Most High) has done for me" 3:32; אָתוֹהִי כְּמָה רַבְרְבִין
"His signs, how great!" 3:33. [Hebr. אוֹת]. †

אֲתָה and אֲתָא , 1 sg. אתית , 3 pl. אֲתוֹ (BL 154k); impf. 3
sg. m. יאתה (*yi'tēh*), 2 sg. m. תאתה, 1 sg. אתה (*'i'tēh*, def.
written), 3 pl. juss. יאתו ; impv. sg. m. אֱתָה (BL 153h), sg. f. אתי
(*Aḥ.* 118), pl. m. אֱתוֹ (BL 153i); infin. מאתה (*mi'tēh*), מֵתֵה (def.);
ptc. sg. m. אָתֵה , pl. m. אתין (*'ātáyin*, cf. BL 233g). **come** (see
opp. אֲזַל "go [away]).") אֲתָא יְהַב אֲשַּׁיָּא "(Sheshbazzar) came (and)
laid the foundations" Ezra 5:16; קִרְיְתָא ... עֲלַיְנָא אֲתוֹ לִירוּשְׁלֶם ...
בָּנַיִן "(the Jews) have come to us (and) to Jerusalem . . . and are
building (that) city" (transpose Atnaḥ; see ו no. 1; and BL 341u)
Ezra 4:12; זי מלך בבל אתו מטאו אפק [ ] "[the armies] of the king
of Babylon have come (and) have reached Aphek" *Adon Letter* 4
(*KAI* 266); לְמֵתֵא לַחֲנֻכַּת צַלְמָא "(the king ordered) . . . to come to
the dedication of the statue" Dan 3:2; למאתה לה על ארכובתה "to
come to him (Noah) on his knees" *4QBirthNoah^a (4Q534)* 1 i 6;
פֻּקוּ וֶאֱתוֹ "come out and come (here)" Dan 3:26; עַד דִּי־אֲתָה עַתִּיק
יוֹמַיָּא "until the Ancient of Days came" 7:22; אָתֵה הֲוָה וְעַד־עַתִּיק

55

אתה .

יוֹמַיָּא מְטָה "there came (one like a son of man), and he arrived at
the Ancient of Days" 7:13; .. [הן יאתה חד מלכן ויסבנ<י> יאתה ח]יל[ך]
והן . . . לתאתה בחילך "if one of (the) kings comes and surrounds
<me>, [your] ar[my] must come . . . and if . . . you (sg.) do not
come with your army" *Sefire I* B 28-31; אתי ואכסנכי משכי "(the
leopard said to the goat), 'Come, and I will cover you with my
hide" *Aḥ.* 118; בני אנוש אתו "some men came" *1QapGen* 19:15.
To a person (אל, על) : אֲתָה עֲלֵיהוֹן "(Tatenai) came to them" Ezra
5:3; הא אתין תמה עליכם "Look, they are coming there to you" *AP*
38:5; [ולא יא]ת[ו] עלי "and let them not come to me" *AD* 1:3; אתה
עלי חרקנוש ובעא מני די אתה ואצלה על מלכא "Hirqanos came to me
and begged that I might come and pray over the king" *1QapGen*
20:21; ויאתה אלי "and comes to me" *Sefire III* 20. To/into a
place (ל, בּ, עַל, or accus.): אתו לבירת יב "they came to the fortress
of Yeb" *AP* 30:8; אתה פסו . . . למנפי "Pasu . . . came to Memphis" *AP* 37:11; אתה לשלם "he came to Salem" *1QapGen* 22:13;
תבת ואתית לי לביתי "I returned and came home" *1QapGen* 21:19;
אנה לתנא אתית לו[ך] "I have come here to you" *1QapGen* 2:25; כזי
אתית עליך בביתך "I came to you in your house" *BMAP* 11:2-3; עם
יאתה עלי בבאל תאתה בזנה "when you come here" *AD* 12:7; מנדתא
"let him come to me in Babylon with the rent" *AD* 11:5;
כזי יאתה א' אנה [א]תית ביתך "I came (to) your house" *AP* 15:3; אשור
"when U. will come (to) Assyria" *Letter of Assur* 11 (*KAI*
233); כזי תאתון מצרין "when you (pl.) will come (to) Egypt"
Padua I A 5; אנה אתית על [בי]תך "I came to your house" *BMAP*
7:3; [כל מ]לה [זי] תאתה על בלך "every word that comes to your
mind" *Aḥ.* 96-97.
   Haph./Aph. (א > י , BL 169e; in *Hermopolis* def.), 3 sg.
m. הַיְתִי , 2 sg. f. התתי (*haytītī*), 1 sg. איתית (*'aytīt*), 3 pl. m. הַיְתִיו ;
impf. 3 sg. m. יהיתה (*yuhaytēh*), 1 sg. אתה (*'aytēh*), 2 pl. f. תהיתן
(*tuhaytān*), 3 pl. m. juss. יהיתו and יהתו and יתו , 3 pl. m. w. suff.
יתונה ; impv. sg. f. w. m. suff. אתיה (*'aytīyēh*); infin. הַיְתָיָה and
מתיה (*maytāyāh*, on *m-*, see *LFAA* 51g); ptc. sg. m. מהיתה

(*muhaytēh*), pl. m. מהיתין : "bring, lead, send." אֲבִי . . . הַיְתִי
זִי מִן־יְהוּד "(whom) . . . my father brought from Judah" Dan 5:13; זִי
כתן 1; *AD* 9:1 בגסרו היתי שושן "whom Bagasru brought (to) Susa"
הַיְתִיו ;3:3 *AD* "that man brought me . . . 1 tunic" . . . זך היתי עלי
לְדָנִיֵּאל וּרְמוֹ "they brought Daniel and threw (him)" Dan 6:17:
6:25; הַיְתִיו קֳדָמָיִךְ "they brought in before you (the vessels of the
temple)" 5:23: 5:3; אגרת ארשם זי היתיו על פסמשך "Arsames's
letter, which they brought to Psamshek" *AD* 12:4; כתנה זי התתי לי
סון "the tunic that you (f.) brought to me (at) Syene" *Hermopolis*
4:6; לא איתית המו מנפי "I did not bring them (the garments) to
Memphis" *Padua I* B 3; יהיתה עלי "let him bring (the rent of
those domains) to me" *AD* 10:3; והן תכלן תהיתן לן . . . יהתו לן ארון
תקם יתו ביד חרוץ "let them bring us a chest . . . and if you (f. pl.)
can send us (some) castor oil, let it come by Harus" *Hermopolis*
5:4-5; אנחן בען אלף בעו ויתונה לכן "we are looking for a boat that they
may bring it (a letter) to you" *Hermopolis* 6:9-10; אתה לכן מדעם
"I shall make something come to you" *Hermopolis* 4:10; הושרו
יהיתו עלי "dispatch (men) that they may bring (them [the sculp-
tures]) to me" *AD* 9:3; לְהַיְתָיָה לְמָאנֵי דַהֲבָא "(the king gave orders)
to bring the vessels of gold" Dan 5:2: 3:13; גנזא זי מני שים להיתיה
בבאל "the treasure which has been ordered by me to be brought
[lit., to bring] (to) Babylon" *AD* 10:5; לא שבקן [לן כמר]יא להיתיה
מנ[חה] "the [prie]sts will not allow [us] to bring a meal-offering"
AP 27:13-14; מנדעם מן תמה לא מהיתין עלי "they are not bringing
me anything from there" *AD* 10:2; מנדתא זי מהיתה נחתחור "the
rent that Nehtihur is bringing" *AD* 10:3-4; משח בשם למתיה לכן ולה
אשכחת אש למיתיה לכן "scented oil to send to you, but I did not
find anyone to bring (it) to you" *Hermopolis* 3:10-11.

Haph'al (BL 169f; prefix *hay*-; 3 sg. f. הֵיתָיַת (v.l. הֵיתַיַת ,
BL 169g), 3 pl. m. הֵיתָיוּ (v.l. הֵיתָיוּ, הַיְתָיוּ) : "be brought, led,
sent." הֵיתָיוּ קֳדָם מַלְכָּא "(these men) were brought before the king"
Dan 3:13; הֵיתָיִת אֶבֶן "a stone was brought" 6:18. Cf. *GBA* §167.
[Hebr. אָתָה]. †

אַתּוּן (< Akk. *atūnu*, BL 56c) abs./cst., emph. אַתּוּנָא , m.:
furnace. חֲזָה לְמֵזֵא לְאַתּוּנָא לְמֵזֵא עַל דִּי . . . "(the king gave orders)
to heat the furnace (seven times more) than it was wont to be
heated (lit., to heat it)" Dan 3:19; אַתּוּנָא אֱזֵה יַתִּירָא "the furnace
was very hot" 3:22; יָקֵדְתָּא אַתּוּן נוּרָא "a burning fiery furnace"
3:6, 11 + .

אֲתַר (*'atar*) abs./cst., w. suff. אַתְרֵהּ , m.: **place, site** (see
אֲרַע no. 3 and בַּיָת). יִתְבְּנֵא עַל־אַתְרֵהּ "(let the house of God) be
rebuilt on its site" Ezra 5:15; 6:7; למבניה באתרה כזי הוה לקדמן "to
rebuild it in its place, as it was before" *AP* 32:8; וִיהָךְ <כֹּלָּא>
לְהֵיכְלָא דִי בִירוּשְׁלֶם לְאַתְרֵהּ "let <all of it> go to the temple that is in
Jerusalem, (each) to its own place" Ezra 6:5; כָּל־אֲתַר לָא־הִשְׁתְּכַח
לְהוֹן "no trace of them was found" Dan 2:35; מן אשרה . . . יסחו
שמך ואשרך מן חין "from its place, may (the gods) exterminate
your name and your place among the living" *Nerab* 8-10 (*KAI*
225); הן יהוה באתר חד יתיר מן יום חד "if he is in one place more
than one day" *AD* 6:6; זי אתרה ביב בירתא "whose station is in the
fortress Yeb" *AP* 6:2-3; שלו על אשרכם . . . שבו לתחתכנ[ם] ואל תפנו
באשרה "'Stay quietly in your place' . . . 'Stay where you are and
do not turn to his place" *Sefire III* 5-7 (see F. Rosenthal, *JBL* 91
[1972] 552: "after him"); עם בנוה זי יסקן באשר[ה] "with his sons
who will come up after [him] (*or* in his place)" *Sefire I* A 5;
באתרא זנה משתרה אנה "in this place I ate breakfast" *Cilicia* 6 (*KAI*
261); לבית אל לאתרא די בנית תמן בה מדבחא "(I reached) Bethel, the
place where I had built the altar" *1QapGen* 21:1; תחומי אתרא דך
"boundaries of that place" *Bib* 38 (1957) 258 (line 3).
Adv. בכל אתר "everywhere," *Aḥ.* 97; מן אתר אחרן "from
elsewhere" *AD* 7:2, 6; אֲתַר דִּי "where" (without following בֵּהּ):
יִתְבְּנֵא אֲתַר דִּי־דָבְחִין דִּבְחִין "let the place be built where they offer
sacrifices" Ezra 6:3; תבעה אתר זי אנת תהשכח "you are to seek
(Aḥiqar in) a place where you will find (him)" *Aḥ.* 34; ביתאל אתר
די אנתה יתב "Bethel, the place where you are dwelling" *1QapGen*
21:9.

ב

Prep. בָּאתַר "after" (cf. אַחֲרֵי and אַחר (אַחר). בָּאתַר דְּנָה "after this (I saw a fourth beast)" Dan 7:6; בָּתְרָךְ תְּקוּם מַלְכוּ אָחֳרִי "after you another kingdom shall arise" 2:39; תרתין שנין בתר מבולא "two years after the flood" *1QapGen* 12:10; לבתר חמש שניא אלן "after these five years" *1QapGen* 19:23; בתר פתגמיא אלן "after these events" *1QapGen* 22:27; הוא רדף בתרהון "he went in pursuit of them" *1QapGen* 22:7; cf. הוא רדף להון *1QapGen* 22:9.

ב

בְּ , prefixed prep. (BL 257b-h); בַּ before shewa, בַּ and בֶּ before ḥateph, בִּי before בְ י, in בֵּאדַיִן and בֵּאלָהָהּ (Dan 6:24); w. suff. בִּי, בָךְ, בֵּהּ, בַהּ, בְּהוֹן . (1) **in, on, at** a place (or similarly; cf. בְּגוֹא, עַל). In Media Ezra 6:2; in the province Beyond-the-River 5:6; 6:6; in Babylon 5:17; in the province Babylon Dan 3:1; on the plain 3:1; in a house 4:1; in Jerusalem Ezra 4:22; 5:2+; in the temple Ezra 5:15; in the fortress 6:2; (God) in heaven Dan 2:28; in heaven and on earth 6:28; (kingdom) on earth 7:23; in your kingdom 5:11; (what is) in the darkness 2:22; (leave the stump) in the ground 4:12, 20; למפלח בארעא "(I began) to cultivate the earth" *1QapGen* 12:13; בטורא די בית אל "(I dwelt) on the mountain of Bethel" *1QapGen* 21:7; יְבַקַּר בְּסְפַר־דָּכְרָנַיָּא "let one search in the book of records" Ezra 4:15bis; בספרא זנה "(written) in this document" *BMAP* 9:12; בְּכָל־דִּי דָאֲרִין "wherever people dwell" Dan 2:38; [ב]כל אתר משריאתי "at every place of my encampments" *1QapGen* 21:1; באתר חד "in one place" *AD* 6:6; ביב "in Yeb" *BMAP* 4:2; בזנה "here" *AD* 3:2; 5:1; דבק לה בתחתיה "(the house of H.) adjoins it at the lower end" *AP* 25:5-6; לגמר יהב לקדמין בצפונא "to (the people of) Gomer he gave (an area) in the north" *1QapGen* 17:16; לְגַבְרִין . . בְחַיְלֵהּ. "(he ordered) men . . . in his army" Dan 3:20; אֲלֵךְ כְּפִת "these (men) were bound in their mantles" 3:21; . עֲקַר בְּסַרְבָּלֵיהוֹן

ב

בְּאֶסּוּר דִּי־פַרְזֶל . . . "(leave) the stump . . . (bound) with a band of iron" 4:12, 20; מָזוֹן לְכֹלָּא־בֵהּ "food for all in it (the tree)" 4:9, 18; כוין בה "windows are in it (the house)" *BMAP* 3:5; חָזֵה הֲוֵית בְּחֶזְוֵי "I saw in my visions" Dan 7:2, 7, 13; 4:10: 2:19; . . . אתחזי לי בחזוא "(God) appeared to me in a vision" *1QapGen* 21:8; בחלם חזה[ני] "he had seen [me] in a dream" *1QapGen* 20:22; בְּפֻם מַלְכָּא "(while words were still) in the king's mouth" Dan 4:28; תְּלָת עִלְעִין בְּפֻמַּהּ "three ribs in its mouth" 7:5; קַרְנַיָא עֲשַׂר דִּי בְרֵאשַׁהּ "ten horns that (were) on its head" 7:20; בְּקַרְנָא־דָא "on this horn (were eyes)" 7:8; לָא־הִשְׁתְּכַח בֵּהּ "(no damage) was found in him" 6:24; על ידה בימן "on his arm at the right" *AP* 28:4; *BMAP* 5:3; בְּדָת אֱלָהָךְ דִּי בִידָךְ "in the law of your God that is in your hand" Ezra 7:14; כְּחָכְמַת אֱלָהָךְ דִּי־בִידָךְ "like the wisdom of your God that is in your hand" 7:25; דִּי־נִשְׁמְתָךְ בִּידֵהּ "that your breath (is) in His hand" Dan 5:23; כסף שנא בראשה "the divorce money is on his head," i.e., he loses it *BMAP* 2:8; רוּחַ אֱלָהִין . . . בֵּהּ "the spirit of the (holy) gods (is) in him" Dan 5:11, 14: 6:4; הִשְׁתְּכַחַת בֵּהּ בְּדָנִיֵּאל "(the explanation of riddles) is found in this Daniel" (ב w. dem. element assimil. to proleptic pron. suff., *GBA* §89; cf. BL 270a, 314j) 5:12; מִלְּתָא בְּלִבִּי נִטְרֵת "I kept the matter in my mind" 7:28; הן תאמר בנבשך ותעשת בלבב[ך] "if you say in your soul and think in your min[d]" *Sefire II* B 5; חשבת בלבי "I thought to myself" *1QapGen* 2:1; [דחלת י]תירא בנפשה "[she feared v]ery much within her" *1QapGen* 19:23; יתבת באלוני ממרה די בחברון "I dwelt at the Oaks of Mamre, which are in Hebron" *1QapGen* 21:19; רצת בגלגל מראי "I ran alongside of the chariot-wheel of my lord" *Barrakib* 8-9 (*KAI* 216); דבק לה אגר באגר "(the house of Q.) adjoins it wall to wall" *BMAP* 9:9; למנפק בתרע זי "to go out through the gate of . . ." *BMAP* 9:14-15. Local בְּ is omitted: לְהֵיכְלָא דִּי בָבֶל "to the temple that is in Babylon" (could be "the temple of B." [*RSV*]) Ezra 5:14; בבל לם אגרת מן ארשם יהבת על "a letter from Arsames was delivered in Babylon to Psa[msh]ek" *AD* 12:1-2; כתוני זי שבקת . . . בית יהה "my tunic, which I left . . . in the temple of Yaho" *El. Ostr.* (*ASAE* 26

60

[1926] 27, lines 1-3); cf. בְּ 2 & לְ I 7.

(2) **into, to** a place (cf. לְ). יְהַב בִּידָךְ "(God) put (every-thing) into your hand" Dan 2:38: 7:25; Ezra 5:12; אָע מִתְּשָׂם בְּכָתְלַיָּא "timber is put into the walls (of the temple)" 5:8; אל תפנו אנה אתית עליך באשרה "do not (re)turn to his region" Sefire III 7; בביתך בסון "I came to you in your house in Syene" BMAP 11:2-3; לא תנפק בשוקא "you shall not go out (by it) into the street" AP 5:12; לא שנציו למנעל בבירתא "they did not succeed in entering into the fortress" AD 5:7; בתרבצא זיליהנעלו "bring (them) into my court" AD 7:7; כל זי הנעלת בביתה "all that she (a wife) brought into his (a husband's) house" BMAP 7:22; כזי תאתה בזנה "when you come into this (place)" AD 12:7; לא יכל למקרב בהא "he was not able to approach her" 1QapGen 20:17; נפל בעגיאין "(the king) fell into pits (of bitumen)" 1QapGen 21:33. In a hostile sense: מרדו בה "they rebelled against him (the king of Elam)" 1QapGen 21:27; אחזי ידך רבתא בה "show forth your great hand against him (the Pharaoh)" 1QapGen 20:14-15; אנתה שליט למעבד בכולהון דין "you have power to mete out justice on all of them" 1QapGen 20:13; שקרת בעדיא אלן "you will have been unfaithful to this treaty" Sefire I B 38; but שקרת לכל אלהי [ע]דיא "you will have been unfaithful to all the gods of the treaty" Sefire III 14. Cf. adv. accus.: [א]תית ביתך "I came to your house" AP 15:3 (see לְ I 7).

(3) **in** (of time). בִּשְׁנַת חֲדָה "in year one (of B.'s reign)" Dan 7:1; בְּיוֹמֵי אֲבוּךְ "in the days of your father" 5:11: 2:44; 6:11; זִמְנִין תְּלָתָה בְּיוֹמָא "three times a day" 6:14; בְּמַלְכוּת דָּרְיָוֶשׁ "in the reign of Darius" 6:29; בְּאַחֲרִית יוֹמַיָּא "in the latter days" 2:28; בִּשְׁפַּרְפָּרָא יְקוּם בְּנָגְהָא "at daybreak, (the king) got up at dawn" 6:20; אַרְכָה בְחַיִּין יְהִיבַת לְהוֹן "a prolongation of life was given to them (the beasts)" 7:12; בַּהּ זִמְנָא "at that time" 3:7, 8; 4:33; Ezra 5:3 (בְּ w. dem. element; see no. 1 above); בַּהּ שַׁעֲתָא "at that very moment" 3:6, 15; 4:30; 5:5; בַּהּ בְּלֵילְיָא "that very night" 5:30; בחיי ובמותי "then," see אֱדַיִן; בֵּאדַיִן בָּאתַר "after" (prep., see אַתַר);

"in my life or at my death" *BMAP* 10:13; בשנת תלת עשרה "in the thirteenth year" *1QapGen* 21:27; ב 5 לאפף "on the 5th of Epiphi" *BMAP* 13:8; בכפנא די "in the famine which" *1QapGen* 19:26; בְּעִדָּנָא דִּי־תִשְׁמְעוּן "at the time when you hear" Dan 3:5, 15; בעדן זי זא באישתא "at the time when this evil (was done to us)" *AP* 30:17; ביום זי יעב[ד] כן "on any day on which he will do so" *Sefire I* C 20-21; בכל מה די ימות בר אנש "in whatever way anyone shall die" *Sefire III* 16; ביום מפקך מן חרן "on the day you set out from Haran" *1QapGen* 22:30; בכל עדן "on every occasion" *BMAP* 13:1; [ו]לא ביומיך "[and] not in your time," i.e., prematurely *Aḥ.* 102; בזך עדנא "at that time" *Aḥ.* 70; בזא שנתא "in this year" *AP* 71:14; יוֹם בְּיוֹם דִּי־לָא שָׁלוּ "day by day without fail" Ezra 6:9; אשלמ[נה]י לך ירח בירח "I shall pay it to you month by month" *AP* 11:5.

(4) בְּ expressing instrument, cause, etc.: **by, from, through, with, because of.** חַתְמַהּ מַלְכָּא בְּעִזְקְתֵהּ "the king sealed it (the stone) with his signet-ring" Dan 6:18; וּשְׁאָרָא בְּרַגְלַיהּ רָפְסָה "and trod the rest with its feet" 7:7, 19; לָא בִידַיִן "not by (human) hands" 2:34, 45; בְּזָרַע אֲנָשָׁא "by human seed," i.e., in marriage 2:43; תְּקִילְתָּה בְמֹאזַנְיָא "you have been weighed by the balances" (read מֹאזַנְיָא) 5:27; וּמַצְלַח בְּיָדְהֹם "and it (the construction) prospers at their hands" Ezra 5:8; בְּצִדְקָה פְרֻק וַעֲוָיָתָךְ בְּמִחַן "break off (from your sins) by righteousness and your iniquities by showing mercy" Dan 4:24; בְּטַל שְׁמַיָּא "(let him be wet) with the dew of heaven" 4:12, 20; דִּי . . . בֱנַיְתַהּ . . . בִּתְקַף חִסְנִי "which I built . . . with my mighty power" 4:27; בִּגְזֵרַת עִירִין "(the sentence is) by decree of the Watchers" 4:14; לָא בְחָכְמָה . . . דְּנָה רָזָא גֱּלִי "not by any wisdom . . . has this mystery been revealed" 2:30; בִּנְבוּאַת חַגַּי "through the prophesying of Haggai" Ezra 6:14; ביד אנא "(you sent) by the hand of Ana" *AD* 13:2; מדעם זי יחיה בה איש "anything whereby a man may live" *AP* 49:3; תִּקְנֵא בְּכַסְפָּא דְנָה תּוֹרִין "with this money you will buy bulls" Ezra 7:17; לְמֶעְבַּד בִּשְׁאָר כַּסְפָּא . . . "to do with the rest of the money" 7:18; ביתי זי זבנת בכסף "my

house, which I bought with money" *BMAP* 9:3; . . . זי יהב לי
בדמוה[י] "which he gave me . . . for its price" *AP* 13:3; יהבתה לכי
ברחמן "I have given it to you in affection," i.e., gratis *BMAP* 4:4;
יהבת לך בתיא אלה ברחמה "I have given you these houses as a gift"
BMAP 6:14; טיב לבבן בדמיא זי יהבת לן "our mind is content with
the price that you have given us" *BMAP* 3:6-7; יאמיא אנה לך
בקדישא רבא "I swear to you by the Great Holy One" *1QapGen*
2:14; ימאת לי ביהו "you swore to me by Yaho" *AP* 6:11; ימאתי לי
עליהם בסתי אלההתה "you (f.) swore to me about them by the goddess Sati" *AP* 14:5; בצדקי הושבני מראי "because of my loyalty my
lord seated me [*hawšibnī*] (on the throne of my ancestor) *Barrakib* 4-5 (*KAI* 216); בזך שלח אנה עליכם "because of this, I am
sending (word) to you" *AP* 38:9. -- Conj. בְּדִי : **because.** נדחל בזי
בזי לא איתית זעירן אנחנה "we fear because we (are) few" *AP* 37:7;
המו מנפי "because I have not brought those (garments to) Memphis" *Padua I* B 3; בדי הוא רחים "because he (Enoch) is belov-
ed" *1QapGen* 2:20. -- Prep. בְּדִיל* (לְ בְּדִי)* (בְּדִי לְ *): **because of, on account of.** בדילהא . . . . שביקת אנה "I was saved because of her (Sarai)" *1QapGen* 20:10.

　　(5) Modal בְּ : **with.** בְּהִתְבְּהָלָה הַנְעֵל "(Arioch) brought in
(Daniel) in haste" Dan 2:25; 3:24; 6:20; אֲזַלוּ בִבְהִילוּ "they went
in haste" Ezra 4:23; בְּחֶדְוָה "(they celebrated the dedication of
the temple) with joy" 6:16; פָּלַח־לֵהּ בִּתְדִירָא "(may your God
whom you) adore continually" Dan 6:17, 21; קְרֵא בְחַיִל "shouted
aloud," lit., with might Dan 3:4; 4:11; 5:7; בְּקָל עֲצִיב זְעִק "he
cried out in an anguished tone" 6:21; בִּרְגַז וַחֲמָה אֲמַר "(the king)
in anger and rage commanded" 3:13; דִּי מַהְלְכִין בְּגֵוָה "those who
walk in pride" (read מְהַלְכִין) 4:34; לדרכי ארקא בניח[א] "to those
who walk on earth in tranquillity" *Aḥ.* 108; כולא בקושטא "(that
you make known to me) everything truthfully" *1QapGen* 2:5;
בקושט . . . ולא בכדבין "(that you are speaking to me) truthfully . . .
and without lies" 2:7; דבירת מני שרי באונס "Sarai was taken from
me by force" 20:11; די דברת אנתתי מני בתוקף "because my wife

has been taken away from me with force" 20:14; אתיבני לארעא דא
בשלם "He has brought me to this land in safety" 21:3-4; יחזני
אפיך בשלם "may (the god Ptaḥ) let me see your countenance in
peace" *Hermopolis* 1:2; כולא מנה ביצבא ינדע "let him learn
everything from him with certainty" *1QapGen* 2:20.

(6) **about, concerning** (see עַל no. 4): בְּדָת אֱלָהֵהּ "concerning the law of his God" Dan 6:6; בְּדָנִיֵּאל "(let nothing be
changed) about Daniel" 6:18; עַל־יְהוּד וְלִירוּשְׁלֶם בְּדָת אֱלָהָךְ "about
Judah and Jerusalem concerning the law of your God" Ezra 7:14;
בזנה . . . כלא ארשם לא ידע "about all this . . . Arsames knew nothing" *AP* 30:30; אגרת חדה בשלמך "(you did not send me) a letter
about your welfare" *AP* 41:5; בצבות מראי "(they do not obey
me) in my lord's business" *AD* 4:2.

(7) **as:** כסף שקלן 5 בדמי . . . "(you gave me) 5 silver
shekels as the price of . . ." *BMAP* 1:3; זי יהיב במכל "what (was)
delivered as food" *AP* 24:35; זי מטאך בחלק "which comes to you
as a share" *AP* 28:3; [ ] הקימני אל בצדיק עמך "set me up, O God,
as righteous with You" *Aḥ.* 173.

(8) **according to, by** (cf. כְּ no. 2 & לָקֳבֵל). הֲקִימוּ כָהֲנַיָּא
בִּפְלֻגָּתְהוֹן וְלֵוָיֵא בְּמַחְלְקָתְהוֹן "they set up the priests according to their
divisions and the Levites according to their courses" Ezra 6:18;
שקלן 4 באבני מלכא "4 shekels according to royal weight (lit.,
"stones of the king") i.e., Persian weight *BMAP* 3:6; במתקלת פרס
יתיהב [בא]בני "are to be supplied by Persian weight" *AP* 26:21; פתח
"(4 shekels) according to the weight of (the god) Ptaḥ" *AP*
11:2; במתקלת מלכא "(ten kerashin) by royal weight" *AP* 28:11.

(9) **Varia:** מְעָרַב בַּחֲסַף טִינָא "(iron) mixed with miry clay"
Dan 2:41, 43; הֵימִן בֵּאלָהֵהּ "he (Daniel) trusted in his God" 6:24;
יִשְׁתּוֹן בְּהוֹן מַלְכָּא וְר' "(that) the king and his nobles might drink
from them" 5:2, 3, 23; שַׁלִּיט . . . בְּמַלְכוּת אֲנָשָׁא "(that God) rules
over the kingdom of men" 4:14, 22, 29; 5:21; עָבֵד בְּחֵיל שְׁמַיָּא "He
does (according to His will) in the host of heaven" 4:32; מִשְׁתַּכַּל
חֲלָק בַּעֲבַר נַהֲרָא לָא אִיתַי "I considered the horns" 7:8; הֲוֵית בְּקַרְנַיָּא

לָךְ "you will have no share in (the province) Beyond-the-River" Ezra 4:16: Dan 4:12; בְּשֵׁם "in the name of"; cf. שֵׁם; קרית תמן בשם מרה עלמיא "there I called upon the name of the Lord of Ages" *1QapGen* 21:2; ימא לי מלכא במומה "the king swore to me with an oath" *1QapGen* 20:30; לָא אִיתַי דִּי־יְמַחֵא בִידַהּ "no one can stay His hand" Dan 4:32; הן ... לתאתה בחילך "if ... you do not come with your army" *Sefire I* B 31; תהך בחרב חילך "you will go with your mighty sword" *AP* 71:13; אזלת אנה אברם בנכסין שגיאין ... ואף בכסף ודהב "I, Abram, went forth (from Egypt) with many flocks and with silver and gold too" *1QapGen* 20:33;כל קטילו וחזין בהום "all (of them) were killed, and we saw (our desire) upon them" *AP* 30:17; כסף יון במנין סתתרי 6 "money of Yawan (Greece) in the amount (lit., number) 6 staters" *BMAP* 12:14; after vessels mentioned, בכל 5 "5 in all" *BMAP* 7:19; לבש 1 ... [א]מן 6 ב 4 "1 garment ... 6 cubits by 4" *BMAP* 7:8; בפתי אמן ... בעשתא 7 כ 1 "in the width of cubits ... it (the house) is by the one(-cubit-measure) 7 *k* 1" *BMAP* 4:7.

בְּאדָיִן : see אֱדַיִן .

בְּאִישׁ * (*ba'īš*), emph. f. בָּאִישְׁתָּא (*bīštā'*) (BL 22b, c, 60k, 67r; v.l. בישתא, באשתא), adj.: **bad, evil.** קִרְיְתָא מָרָדְתָּא וּבָאִישְׁתָּא "(Jerusalem), the rebellious and evil city" Ezra 4:12; איש מנדעם באיש לא יעבד לפירמא "let no one do any evil to Pirma" *AD* 5:8-9; כזי מלה באישה לא יהשכחון "when they find no fault" *AP* 38:6-7; זי בעו באיש לאגורא זך "who sought (to do) evil to that temple" *AP* 30:17; בעדן זי זא באישתא עביד "in the time when this evil (f.) was done (m. ptc.)" *AP* 30:17-18; מנדעם באיש לא עבדת "she has not done any evil" *Carpentras* 2 (*KAI* 269); רוח באישא "(God sent him) an evil spirit" *1QapGen* 20:16-17; תתגער מננה "let this evil spirit be expelled from us" *1Qap- רוחא דא באישתא Gen* 20:28. [1]

בְּאֵשׁ 3 sg. m.: **be evil, do evil, displease** (see BL 333e). שַׂגִּיא בְּאֵשׁ עֲלֹוהִי "much displeased was he (the king)" (cf. Theod.) Dan 6:15 (opp. טְאֵב "was glad" 6:24); באש עלי די פרש לוט "it grieved me that Lot had parted (from me)" *1QapGen* 21:7.
Haph.: יהבאשׁו ממתתה "may (the gods) make his death miserable" *Nerab* 9-10 (*KAI* 226). [Hebr. בָּאַשׁ]. [1]

בָּאתַר : see אֲתַר .

▲ בָּבֶל (Akk. *ba-bi-lu*, and in popular etymology *bāb-ili* "gate of god"; בבאל ; see *Bib* 37 [1956] 130). f.: **Babylon,** city. עַל כָּל־מְדִינַת בָּבֶל "over the whole province of Babylon" Dan 2:48, 49: Ezra 7:16 + ; מֶלֶךְ בָּבֶל "king of Babylon" Dan 7:1; Ezra 5:12; מַלְכָּא דִי בָבֶל "the king of Babylon" Ezra 5:13; הֲלָא דָא־הִיא בָּבֶל רַבְּתָא "Is not this the great Babylon?" Dan 4:27: Ezra 5:14; חַכִּימֵי בָבֶל "the wise men of Babylon" Dan 2:12, 18, 24, 48; 5:7; but חַכִּימֵי בָבֶל 2:14; אגרת מן ארשם . . . בבל "a letter from Arsames (was delivered in) Babylon " *AD* 12:1: 12:2; מנזי יהבו בבבאל "from those they delivered in Babylon" *AD* 12:5; להיתיה בבאל "to be brought to Babylon" *AD* 10:5. [Hebrew the same].

בַּבְלִי * (BL 196d), emph. בָּבְלָיָא *, emph. pl. בָּבְלָיֵא : **Babylonian.** Ezra 4:9; הדדנורי בבליא "Hadadnuri, the Babylonian" *AP* 6:19. [1]

בדר, **Pa.** impf. 3 pl. m. w. suff. יבדרונה (*yubaddirunnēh*); impv. m. pl. בַּדַּרוּ : **scatter.** בַּדַּרוּ "scatter (its fruit)" Dan 4:11; יבדרונה . . . ביתה קנינה "may (the goddesses) scatter his house, his possessions" *Lydia* B 7-8 (*KAI* 260). [Hebr. בְּדַר, פְּזַר]. [1]

בְּהִילוּ (BL 198g), f.: **haste.** אֲזַלוּ בִבְהִילוּ "they went in haste (to Jerusalem)" Ezra 4:23. [1]

בהל—בין

בהל **Hithpe.** infin. הִתְבְּהָלָה : **hasten.** אֲזַל . . . בְּהִתְבְּהָלָה "(the king) went hastily" Dan 6:20: 2:25; 3:24.

Pa. (BL 130i), impf. 3 pl. m. יְבַהֲלוּן *, w. suff. יְבַהֲלֻנֵּהּ יְבַהֲלֻנַּנִי, & יְבַהֲלוּנֵּהּ; juss. (BL 131k) 3 sg. m. w. suff. יְבַהֲלָךְ , 3 pl. m. יְבַהֲלוּ *, w. suff. יְבַהֲלוּךְ : **alarm, disturb.** חֶזְוֵי רֵאשִׁי יְבַהֲלֻנַּנִי "visions of my head alarmed me" (BL 283q) Dan 4:2; 7:15: 7:28; פִּשְׁרָא אַל־יְבַהֲלָךְ "let not the interpretation disturb you" 4:16; רַעְיֹנֹהִי יְבַהֲלֻנֵּהּ "his thoughts alarmed him" 4:16: 5:6; אַל־יְבַהֲלוּךְ רַעְיוֹנָךְ "let not your thoughts alarm you" 5:10.

Hithpa., ptc. sg. m. מִתְבָּהַל (BL 67t, 130f): **be alarmed.** מַלְכָּא . . . שַׂגִּיא מִתְבָּהַל "the king . . . was greatly alarmed" Dan 5:9; אנה למך אתבהלת "I, Lamech, became alarmed" *1QapGen* 2:3. [Hebr. the same]. †

▲ בּוֹזְנַי see שתר בוזני . שְׁתַר

בְּטֵל * (baṭil), 3 sg. f. בְּטֵלַת (BL 68x, 102r, 103w, x); ptc. act. sg. f. בָּטְלָה (BL 106i): **stop** (intrans.), **be interrupted.** בְּטֵלַת עֲבִידַת בֵּית־אֱלָהָא . . . וַהֲוָה בָּטְלָא "the work on the house of God stopped . . . and remained interrupted" (BL 293q) Ezra 4:24.

Pa. 3 pl. בַּטִּלוּ , infin. בַּטָּלָא : **stop** (trans.), **interrupt.** שִׂימוּ טְעֵם לְבַטָּלָא גֻּבְרַיָּא אִלֵּךְ "make a decree to stop those men!" (see לְ II 2) Ezra 4:21; וּבַטִּלוּ הִמּוֹ "(they went in haste) and stopped them" 4:23; לָא־בַטִּלוּ הִמּוֹ "they did not stop them" 5:5; תֶּהֱוֵא מִתְיַהֲבָא לְגֻבְרַיָּא אִלֵּךְ דִּי־לָא לְבַטָּלָא "let it be given to those men without delay" (see דִּי B I) 6:8. [Hebr. בָּטֵל]. †

בֵּין (bayn; BL 257i), בני (baynay, def.), בניהם (baynay-hom def.); w. m. suff. בֵּינֵיהוֹן k. (Dan 7:8), f. בֵּינֵיהֵן q. (BL 75h), prep.: **between, among.** תְּלָת עִלְעִין בְּפֻמַּהּ בֵּין שִׁנַּהּ "(a beast with) three ribs in its mouth, between its teeth" (read שִׁנַּהּ) Dan 7:5; סִלְקָת בֵּינֵיהוֹן "there came up among them (another horn)" 7:8; שוק מלכא ביניהם "the street of the king (is) between them" *BMAP*

67

3:8; בשוקא זי בינין "into the street that (is) between us (our hous-es)" *AP* 5:14; בשוקא זי בינין ובין בית פפטעיניית "(you shall not go out) into the street that is between us and the house of P." *AP* 5:12-13; אנה מהלך בין כרמיא "(while) I was walking among the vineyards" *Aḥ.* 40; ממנין הוו בין בגיא זילי "they were appointed among my domains" *AD* 5:5 + ; די היא בין נהרין "which is be-tween two rivers (naharayin)," i.e., in Mesopotamia *1QapGen* 21:24; לתשלח לשנך בניהם "you shall not interfere with them," lit., you shall not send your tongue between them *Sefire III* 17-18; בין יומן 20 הו עשרין "(I shall pay you) within 20 days, i.e., twenty" *BMAP* 11:7; נכסן זי יהוון בין ענני ותמר "property that may be between Anani and Tamar" *BMAP* 2:11; נכסן זי יהוון בין תמר ובין ענני "property that may be between Tamar and Anani" *BMAP* 2:12-13; אקרא לך על חרמביתאל אלהא בין 4 [נק]מן "(that) I should challenge you by the god Ḥ. before 4 avengers" (see *Bib* 38 [1957] 272-73) *AP* 7:7-8; קרית לך בין [נ]קמיא אלה "(if) I challenge you before these avengers" *AP* 7:10; ספר פלגנן נכתב בינין "we shall write a deed of partition between us" *AP* 28:14. [Hebr. the same]. †

בִּינָה (*qīl*, BL 180k), f.: **intelligence, understanding.** מַנְדְּעָא לְיָדְעֵי בִינָה "knowledge to those who have understanding" Dan 2:21. [Hebr. the same]. [1]

בִּירָה * (< Akk. *birtu*), emph. בִּירְתָא : **citadel, fortress, stronghold.** בְּאַחְמְתָא בְּבִירְתָא "in Ecbatana, in the citadel" (dl. בְּ [2] ?) Ezra 6:2; ביב בירתא "in Yeb, the fortress" *AP* 6:3; בבירת יב "in the fortress of Yeb" *AP* 6:3; בסון בירתא "in the fortress of Syene" *AP* 6:17. [Hebr. the same]. [1]

בית (denom. verb from בַּיִת), 3 sg. m. בָּת : **spend the night.** מַלְכָּא . . . בָּת טְוָת "the king spent the night fasting" Dan 6:19. N.B. The ordinary house was small and was especially

בית

used for spending the night; cf. the house of 11 x 7 cubits (*AP* 8:4), 11 x 7 (*BMAP* 4:7), 16 x 5 (*BMAP* 12:16). [1]

בַּיִת * (*qatl*, BL 182z, 247c): abs. בי (*bay, LFAA* 24k), cst. בֵּית, emph. בַּיְתָא & בַּיְתָה (Ezra 5:12; 6:15), w. suff. בַּיְתִי & בֵּיתִי (Dan 4:1, BL 231a), בבתה "in his house" *Hermopolis* 2:19, בַּיְתֵהּ; pl. בָּתִּין * & באתין *5QNJ (5Q15)* 1 ii 6 (BL 231b, prob. *bātīn*), w. suff. בָּתֵּיכוֹן, m.: **house.** אֲזַל לְבַיְתֵהּ "(Daniel) went to his house" Dan 2:17; 6:11; Ezra 6:11; בָּתֵּיכוֹן נְוָלִי יִתְּשָׂמוּן "your houses shall be laid in ruins" Dan 2:5: 3:29; יהבת לך בתיא אלה "I have given you these houses" *BMAP* 6:14; זבן לה בסודם בי "(Lot) bought himself a house in Sodom" *1QapGen* 21:6. -- **temple** (cf. הֵיכַל). בַּיְתָא; + ; עֲבִידַת בֵּית־אֱלָהָא "construction of God's house" Ezra 4:24 + ; בֵּית אֱלָהָא דִּי בִירוּשְׁלֶם "this temple" Ezra 5:9, 11, 12; 6:3, 15; דְּנָה "the house of God that is in Jerusalem" 5:2; דִּי־בֵית אֱלָהָא דִּי הֵיכְלָא בִירוּשְׁלֶם "the temple of the house of God that is in Jerusalem" (dl. "of the house of God" w. Theod., Vg.) Dan 5:3; על בית "about the altar-house" *AP* 32:3. -- **palace, royal house** (cf. הֵיכַל). הֲוֵית בְּבֵיתִי . . . בְּהֵיכְלִי "I was in my house . . . in my palace" Dan 4:1; לְבֵית מִשְׁתְּיָא עֲלַלת "(the queen) entered the banquet hall," lit., the house of drinking 5:10; בְנַיְתַהּ לְבֵית מַלְכוּ "(which) I built as a royal residence" 4:27; בי טב לישה לאבהי "my ancestors did not have a fine palace" (w. 3 sg. m. suff.) *Barrakib* 16 (*KAI* 216). -- **archives, treasury.** יִתְבַּקַּר בְּבֵית גִּנְזַיָּא דִּי־מַלְכָּא "let a search be made in the royal archives" Ezra 5:17; בְּבֵית סְפְרַיָּא דִּי גִנְזַיָּא מְהַחֲתִין תַּמָּה בְּבָבֶל "(a search was made) in the archives where the treasures were stored in Babylon" (explanation of 5:17) 6:1; אוצרא זי מלכא דבק לה "the treasury of the king (a building) joins it" *BMAP* 3:9; -- **administrative office.** מן אוצר מלכא . . . מן בית מלכא "from the storehouse of the king . . . from the house of the king" *BMAP* 11:4, 6; מִן־בֵּית מַלְכָּא תִּתְיְהֵב "(let the cost) be paid from the house of the king" Ezra 6:4; תִּנְתֵּן מִן־בֵּית גִּנְזֵי מַלְכָּא "you may provide (it) out of the king's treasury"

69

7:20 (LXX: "from the houses of the province Beyond-the-River"; see 7:21; BL 310b; see סְפַר). -- **family.** מלכא ובני ביתא "the king and the princes of the palace" *AP* 30:2-3; מן ארשם בר "From Arsames, prince of the palace" *AD* 5:1*; נשי ביתן "the women of our house," i.e., domestic servants *AD* 8:2; צלי עלי ועל ביתי "pray for me and for my household" *1QapGen* 20:28; אכלת ואשתית תמן אנה וכול אנש ביתי "I ate and drank there, I and all the men of my household" *1QapGen* 21:20-21; חד מן בני ביתי ירתנני "one of my houshold servants is to inherit me" *1QapGen* 22:33. -- **estate.** [פ]תף מן ביתא זילי "(travel) provisions from my estate" *AD* 6:2: 8:6; 30 א בית זרע ... בגה "his estate . . . a farm of 30 ardabs of seed" (cf. 1 Kgs 18:32) *AD* 8:4: 8:2. -- **receptacle.** בית זרע חנטין סאין תלת "a receptacle of three seahs of wheat seed" *Bib* 38 (1957) 259 (line 2); בית [ע]שרין ותר[ת]ין ערש[ין] "contains twenty-two beds," lit. a holder of *5QNJ (5Q15)* 1 ii 11; [בית דרג], "staircase," lit. a house of stairs *5QNJ (5Q15)* 1 ii 2. -- **plot of ground,** on which one can build. בניא זי אנת בנית בביתא זך "the building (*binnūyā'*, *LFAA* 83q) that you have constructed on that plot" *AP* 9:12; משחת ביתא זך "the dimension of that plot" *AP* 9:4, 6. Cf. ארקא זך "that land" *AP* 9:5, 14 (see אֲרַע no. 3); *AP* 8:3, 8; 9:3. [Hebr. the same].

בָּל (*qāl*, BL 179h): **mind.** עַל דָּנִיֵּאל שָׂם בָּל לְשֵׁיזָבוּתֵהּ "(the king) set (his) mind to deliver Daniel" Dan 6:15; cf. אתעשת על אגורא זך למבנה "take thought for that temple, to build it" *AP* 30:23; [כל מ]לה [זי] תאתה על בלך "[every w]ord [that] comes into your mind" *Aḥ.* 96-97. [1]

▲ בֵּלְאשַׁצַּר : see בֵּלְשַׁאצַּר .

בְּלָה * pass. ptc. sg. f. בליה (*baliyāh*; cf. BL 157j, *LFAA* 64f): **wear out.** כתן 1 בליה "1 worn out tunic" *BMAP* 7:12.

בלו—בנה

Pa. impf. 3 sg. m. יְבַלֵּא : "wear out." לְקַדִּישֵׁי עֶלְיוֹנִין יְבַלֵּא
"(a king) shall wear out the saints of the Most High" Dan 7:25.
[Hebr. בָּלָה]. [1]

בְּלוֹ (BL 196e; prob. < Akk. *biltu*, *AD* p. 97; read בְּלוֹ* ?,
ASA I, 149): **revenue, tribute.** מִנְדָּה־בְלוֹ וַהֲלָךְ לָא יִנְתְּנוּן "they will
not pay tribute, revenue, or toll" Ezra 4:13, 20; 7:24. †

▲ בֵּלְטְשַׁאצַּר Gk. Theod. Βαλτασάρ, Vg. Baltassar (prob.
Akk. *balāṭsu-uṣur* "protect his life!" or *balāṭ-šarri-uṣur* "protect the life of the king!"): **Belteshazzar,** name given to Daniel
Dan 2:26; 4:6, 15, 16; 5:12; שְׁמֵהּ ב' כְּשֻׁם אֱלָהִי "his name (was) B.
according to the name of my god" 4:5 (i.e., the god Bēl). [Hebr.
the same]. †

▲ בֵּלְשַׁאצַּר & בֵּלְאשַׁצַּר (v.l. בלשצר) Gk. Theod. Βαλτασάρ,
Vg. Baltassar: **Belshazzar,** King of Babylonia, son of King Nebuchadnezzar Dan 5:1, 2, 22, 29, 30; 7:1. Cf. Akk. *Bēl-šarra-
uṣur* "Bel, protect the king!," son of Nabonidus. The same name
בלסרצר & בלסראצר occurs in *Assur Tab.* Rs. 3 (*KAI* 234), Rs. 2
(*KAI* 235). †

בְּנָה *, 3 sg. m., w. 3 sg. m. suff. בְּנָהִי (BL 154n), 1 sg., w.
3 sg. f. suff. בֱּנֵיתַהּ (BL 155p, 267a), w. 3 sg. m. suff. בניתה; 3 pl.
בְּנוֹ (BL 154k); impf. 2 sg. m. תבנה (*tibnēh*), 3 pl. m. יִבְנוֹן (BL
153f); impv. sg. m. & f. בני (*běnī*); infin. לְבֵּנָא (old form wt. *m-*,
cf. לאמר), מִבְנֵא, emph. מִבְנָיָה (Ezra 5:9, v.l. מִבְנְיָא, *GBA* p. 51), w.
suff. מבניה (*mibniyēh*); ptc. act. sg. m. בָּנֵה *, pl. m. בָּנַיִן (BL
233g); ptc. pass. sg. m. בְּנֵה (BL 157e; *banēh* < *banī*), sg. f. בניה
(BL 157j, *LFAA* 64f; *baniyāh*). **Hithpe.** (pass.) 3 sg. f. אתבניאת
(*'itbaniyat*); impf. 3 sg. f. תִּתְבְּנֵא; ptc. sg. m. מִתְבְּנֵא : (1) **build,
construct,** (from context) **rebuild.** אֲנַחְנָא . . . בָּנַיִן בַּיְתָא דִּי־הֲוָא בְנֵה
מִקַּדְמַת דְּנָה "we . . . are rebuilding the house that was built long

71

ago" Ezra 5:11; רַב בְּנָהִי . . . מֶלֶךְ "(which) a great king . . . built"
Ezra 5:11; שָׁרִיו לְמִבְנֵא בֵּית אֱלָהָא "they began to rebuild God's
house" 5:2: 5:17; 6:8; בַּיְתָא דְנָה לִבְּנֵא "(who gave you a decree) to
rebuild this house?" 5:3: 5:13; בַּיְתָא דְנָה לְמִבְנְיֵה "to rebuild this
temple" 5:9; בֵּית־אֱלָהָא דַךְ יִבְנוֹן עַל־אַתְרֵה "let them rebuild this
house of God on its site" (see שְׁבַק no. 5) 6:7: 5:4, 15, 16; 6:3,
14bis; Dan 4:27; אבהין בנו אגורא זך ביב "our ancestors built that
temple in Yeb" AP 30:13; אגורא זך בנה השכח "(Cambyses) found
that temple built (already)" AP 30:14; אתעשת . . . למבנה בזי לא
שבקן לן למבניה "take thought . . . to rebuild (that temple), because
they will not allow us to rebuild it" AP 30:23; למבניה . . . . לקבל זי
בנה הוה קדמין "(let a letter be sent) to rebuild it . . . as it was built
before" AP 30:25; זי ביב . . . בנה הוה מן קדמן . . למבניה באתרה
"which was built formerly in Yeb . . . to rebuild it in its place"
AP 32:4-5, 8; שורא זך בנה במנציעת בירתא "that wall (was) built in
the middle of the fortress" AP 27:6; איתי באר חדה זי בניה בג]ו
בי]רתא "there is a well built within the fortress" AP 27:6-7; די
בנית תמן בה מדבחא ובניתה תניאני "where I built the altar, and I built
it again" 1QapGen 21:1; אתבנ]י]את חברון "(at that time) Hebron
was built" 1QapGen 19:9. -- W. accus. of material (BL 338m):
הוּא מִתְבְּנֵא אֶבֶן גְּלָל "it is being built with stone blocks" Ezra 5:8;
תרען זי אבן 5 בנין פסילה זי אבן "5 gateways of stone, built with
hewn blocks of stone" AP 30:9-10.
    (2) **construct, fortify.** בָּנַיִן . . . קִרְיְתָא לִירוּשְׁלֶם "they are
fortifying Jerusalem, (that) city . . ." Ezra 4:12; הֵן קִרְיְתָא דָךְ תִּתְבְּנֵא
וְשׁוּרַיָּא יִשְׁתַּכְלְלוּן "if that city is fortified and the walls are finished"
(read שׁוּרַיַּה "its walls") 4:13, 16; שִׂימוּ טְעֵם לְבַטָּלָה גֻּבְרַיָּא אִלֵּךְ וְקִרְיְתָא
דָךְ לָא תִתְבְּנֵא "issue a decree to stop those men, and let that city
not be fortified" (see ן no. 9) 4:21.
    (3) **build up.** תרבצה ארע הי ולא בניה "the court is below,
and it is not built up" (see אֲרַע) BMAP 3:4-5; אמרת לך ארקא זך בני
"I say to you, 'Build up this land!'" AP 9:5; הן . . . ארקא זך תבנה
"if . . . you build up this land" AP 9:8.

בנין—בעה

בִּנְיָן * (qutlān, BL 195z), emph. בִּנְיָנָא, m.: **building.**
נאבני דִּי־דְנָה בִנְיָנָא בָּנַיִן "who are building this building" Ezra 5:4;
זי תבנה הִיךְ להוא "the building that you will build" BMAP 3:22a;
בנינ[א]. "how the building will be" 4QTJacob (4Q537) 12:1.
[Hebr. בִּנְיָן, בִּנְיָה].[1]

בְּנִי *, בְּנֵי : see בַּר.

בְּנַס (v.l. בְּנֵס): **be angry.** מַלְכָּא בְּנַס וּקְצַף שַׂגִּיא "the king
was angry and very furious" Dan 2:12.[1]

בְּעָה & בְּעָא (BL 154k). 3 pl. בְּעוֹ, 1 pl. בְּעֵינָא , impf. 3 sg.
m. יִבְעֵה, 1 sg. אֶבְעֵא; infin. מִבְעֵא ; ptc. sg. m. בָּעֵא, pl. m. בָּעַיִן (BL
233g): (1) **seek.** בְּעוֹ דָנִיֵּאל ... לְהִתְקְטָלָה "they sought Daniel ...
that he might be put to death" (see לְ II 1 b) Dan 2:13; יבעה ראשי
להמתתי "(if any enemy) seeks my head to kill me" Sefire III 11;
בעי אנ[י]ש זי יזבן ביתא "seek out a man who will buy the house" AP
42:6; בעו ... מן אתר אחרן גרד "seek out from another place ... a
staff" AD 7:6-7; מן אתר אחרן לא תבעון "(if) you do not seek (them)
out from another place" AD 7:9; תבעה אתר זי אנת תהשכח "you are
to seek (Ahiqar in) a place where you will find (him)" Ah. 34; הֲווֹ
בָּעַיִן עִלָּה לְהַשְׁכָּחָה לְדָנִיֵּאל "they sought to find a ground for complaint against Daniel" Dan 6:5; אנחן בען אלף "we are looking for a
boat" Hermopolis 6:9. (2) **ask, ask for, beg** (cf. שְׁאֵל no. 2).
יַצִּיבָא אֶבְעֵא מִנֵּהּ ... וַאֲמַר־לִי "I asked for the truth (about this) from
him and he said to me" Dan 7:16; דִּי־בְעֵינָא מִנָּךְ "what we asked of
You (God)" 2:23; וְרַחֲמִין לְמִבְעֵא מִן־קֳדָם אֱלָהּ שְׁמַיָּא "to ask for mercy
of the God of Heaven" (cf. מִן II 2) 2:18; בְּעָה מִן־מַלְכָּא דִּי ... יִנְתֶּן־לַהּ
"he asked the king ... to give him (time)" 2:16; בעא מני די אתה
"he begged me to come" 1QapGen 20:21; בְּעָה מִן־מַלְכָּא וּמַנִּי "(Daniel) asked of the king, and he appointed (Shadrach)" (cf. אֲמַר no.
2; BL 352e) Dan 2:49; כָּל־דִּי־יִבְעֵה בָעוּ מִן־כָּל־אֱלָהּ "whoever makes
a petition to any god" 6:8: 6:13; בָּעֵא בָּעוּתֵהּ "(Daniel) makes his

73

petition (three times a day)" 6:14; בָּעֵא . . . קֳדָם אֱלָהֵהּ "making a petition . . . before his God" 6:12; צלית ובעית "(that night) I prayed and begged" *1QapGen* 20:12; זי יבעה רוח אפוה "(anyone) who rants," lit., "who seeks the breath of his nostrils" *Sefire III* 2. (3) **desire, wish, want.** יזכרני ועטתי יבעה "(the king) will remember me and desire my counsel" *Aḥ.* 53; יבעה . . . מלה זי צחא מנכם "(the) matter that Zaḥo . . . will desire of you (pl.)" *AP* 38:6; זי בעו באיש לאגורא זך "who wanted to do evil to that temple" *AP* 30:17; די יבעון למקטלני "who will wish to kill me" *1QapGen* 19:19; אתו ובעין למקץ . . . ל[א]רזא "(some men) came and wanted to cut down . . . the cedar" *1QapGen* 19:15.

  Pa. impf. 3 pl. יְבַעוֹן (BL158n), v.l. יְבָעוֹן (BL 58p, 130g): **seek out, hunt for.** לִי הַדָּבְרַי וְרַבְרְבָנַי יְבָעוֹן "my counselors and my nobles sought me out" Dan 4:33. [Hebr. ²בָּעָה]. †

  בָּעוּ (BL 197g), cst. בָּעוּת *, w. suff. בָּעוּתֵהּ : **petition, request.** כָּל־דִּי־יִבְעֵה בָעוּ מִן־כָּל־אֱלָהּ "whoever makes a petition to any god" Dan 6:8; בָּעֵא בָעוּתֵהּ "(Daniel) makes his petition (three times a day)" 6:14. †

  בְּעֵל (*ba'l*, BL 182x), cst. (& abs.): (1) **master, lord, owner** (cf. מָרֵא). בעל שמין "lord of heaven," Baal-shamayin *Zkr* A 3, 13 (*KAI* 202); בעלי ארפד "the lords of Arpad" *Sefire I* A 4; בעלי כסף ובעלי זהב "owners of silver and owners of gold" *Barrakib* 10-11 (*KAI* 216); יהודיא כל בעלי יב "the Jews, all (of them) masters (i.e., citizens) of Yeb" *AP* 30:22; בעל דגל וקריה "soldier or citizen," lit. "owner of a battle-standard and a town" *AP* 5:9; 13:10; בעל עטתא טבתא "master of good counsel" *Aḥ.* 42; חזי בעלי טבתך "look upon your well-wishers (and friends)," lit., "masters of your bounty" *AP* 30:23-24. (2) **husband, spouse.** הי אנתתי ואנה בעלה "she is my wife ('*intētī*), and I am her husband" (marriage contract formula) *AP* 15:4; שנאת לבעלי "I divorce

בקעה—בקר

(lit., I hate) my husband" *BMAP* 2:9; יזן בר אוריה בעלכי "Jezan son of Uriah, your husband" *AP* 8:6-7; בעל אחרן "(to live with) another husband" *BMAP* 7:33. (3) בְּעֵל טְעֵם (< Akk. *bēl ṭēmi*), does not occur as emph.: **prefect, commander,** title of an official who can send an authorized letter and can carry out its prescriptions. [עם]ט בעל ספרא ענני "Anani, the secretary, prefect" *AP* 26:23 (cf. the signature of the letter of Arsames, ארתוהי ידע טעמא זנה רשת ספרא "Artohi is aware of this prescription; Rasht is the scribe" *AD* 8:6); רְחוּם בְּעֵל־טְעֵם וְשִׁמְשַׁי סָפְרָא "Rehum, the commander, and Shimshai, the scribe" Ezra 4:8, 9, 17 (cf. 4:21). [Hebr. בַּעַל]. †

בִּקְעָה * (*qitl,* BL 184j), cst. בִּקְעַת , f.: **plain, valley.** אֲקִימֵהּ בְּבִקְעַת דּוּרָא "he set it (the statue) up on the plain of Dura" Dan 3:1; ויתב לה בבקעת ירדנא "and he settled in the valley of the Jordan" *1QapGen* 21:5; שרין בבקעת דן "encamped in the plain of Dan" *1QapGen* 22:8; והוא עמק מלכא בקעת בית כרמא "this is the Vale of the King, the Valley of Beth-haccherem" *1QapGen* 22:14. [Hebr. the same]. ¹

בקר , **Pa.** 3 pl. בַּקַּרוּ (BL 42v, 134t); impf. 3 sg. m. יְבַקַּר; infin. בַּקָּרָא (v.l. בַּקָּרָה): **search, investigate.** דִּי יְבַקַּר בִּסְפַר־דָּכְרָנַיָּא "that (someone) search in the book of records" Ezra 4:15; מִנִּי שִׂים טְעֵם וּבַקַּרוּ "I decreed, and they searched" (cf. אֲמַר no. 2) 4:19; 6:1; לְבַקָּרָא עַל־יְהוּד וְלִירוּשְׁלֶם בְּדָת אֱלָהָךְ "to investigate about Judah and Jerusalem according to the law of your God" 7:14; בקר ומני כול די איתי לך "examine and count all that you have" *1QapGen* 22:29. **Hithpa.,** impf. 3 sg. m. יִתְבַּקַּר : "be investigated": יִתְבַּקַּר הֵן אִיתַי דִּי־מִן־כּוֹרֶשׁ מַלְכָּא שִׂים טְעֵם . . . "let it be investigated . . . whether a decree was issued by Cyrus the King" Ezra 5:17. [Hebr. בָּקַר]. †

75

¹ בַּר (*bir* < **bin,* BL 179f) cst. (& abs.), emph. בְּרָא *, w. suff. בְּרֵהּ ; pl. בְּנִין * (< *banīn,* BL 247d), cst. pl. בְּנֵי, w. suff. בְּנַי *, בְּנֵיהוֹן *, בְּנַיָּה *, בְּנוֹהִי ; m. Cf. בְּרָה f. (< *bint, LFAA* 69i, > *birt,* perh. < *bir;* cf. *tintay > tirtay* "two," & *kussû > kursē* "seat, throne"), suff. ברתי , cst. pl. בְּנָת *, suff. בְּנָתֵהּ *. (1) **son, child.** מָלִין לְחַיֵּי מַלְכָּא וּבְנוֹהִי "they will be praying for the life of the king and his sons" Ezra 6:10: 7:23; Dan 6:25 אַנְתְּה בְּרֵהּ בַּלְשַׁאצַּר לָא הַשְׁפֵּלְתְּ "You, his son, Belshazzar, have not humbled" Dan 5:22; זְכַרְיָה בַר־עִדּוֹא "Zechariah, son (i.e., grandson, Zech 1:1) of Iddo" Ezra 5:1; 6:14: 5:2; מתעאל וברה ובר ברה "Mati'el and his son and his grandson" *Sefire II* C 14; בני בני ברגא[יה] "the grandsons of Bar-Ga'yah" *Sefire I* A 2; אנה ובר לי וברה לי "I and my son and my daughter" *AP* 6:12-13; קרית לבני ולבני בני . . . ולבנתהון "I invited my sons and the sons of my sons . . . and their daughters" *1QapGen* 12:16; אמות . . . די לא בנין וחד מן בני ביתי ירתנני "(when) I die . . . without children; even one of my house servants is to inherit me" *1QapGen* 22:33; ברא לם יהוה לי "surely he will be a son to me" *Aḥ.* 2; כזי ברי זי לא ברי בדא "when my son, who was not (really) my son, devised" *Aḥ.* 30; בר זכר ונקבה לאיתי לה "he does not have a child, male or female" *BMAP* 7:28-29; יהוישמע שמה ברי . . . יהוישמע ברתי "Yehoyishma by name, my child, . . . Yehoyishma, my daughter" *BMAP* 6:3, 8; מן ארשם בר ביתא "From Arsames, son of the house (palace)" *AD* 5:1*; לרחמן ישימנך . . . ובני ביתא "may (God) show mercy to you and the princes (lit., sons) of the palace" *AP* 30:2-3. (2) Meaning one or several individuals: גְּבַר מִן־בְּנֵי גָלוּתָא "a man from among the exiles," lit., "individuals of the exile" Dan 2:25; 5:13; 6:14; Ezra 6:16; בְּנֵי־יִשְׂרָאֵל "Israelites" Ezra 6:16; ארע בני חם "land of the sons of Ham" *1QapGen* 19:13; מן בנת [מצרין] "from the daughters of [Egypt]" *1QapGen* 20:34; [חד] בני שמין "[one of] the sons of heaven" (= angels) *1QapGen* 2:5; דָּמֵה לְבַר אֱלָהִין "one like a son of the gods" (= an angel) Dan 3:25 (cf. 3:28, מַלְאֲכֵהּ); כְּבַר אֱנָשׁ אָתֵה הֲוָה "there came one like a son of man" 7:13; בכל מה זי ימות

בר אנש "in whatever way anyone shall die" *Sefire III* 16; לא ישכח
כול בר אנוש לממניה "which no one can number" *1QapGen* 21:13;
ב]נ[י אנוש אתו "some individuals came" *1QapGen* 19:15; בְּנֵי
אֲנָשָׁא "people" Dan 2:38; 5:21; בְּנֵי תוֹרִין "young bulls" Ezra 6:9.
(3) **"Old"** (indicating age): כְּבַר שְׁנִין שִׁתִּין וְתַרְתֵּין "(the king),
being about sixty-two years old" Dan 6:1; ברת שנן 100 "(if you
[f.] die) at the age of 100 years" *BMAP* 4:17; בר שנן 100 "(if I
die) 100 years old" *BMAP* 4:18. [Hebr. בֵּן, בַּת]. †

^{2} בַּר * (*qall,* BL 180n), emph. בָּרָא (BL 221f): (1) **field,
meadow.** חֵיוַת בָּרָא "beasts of the field" Dan 2:38; 4:9 + ; דְּתְאָא
דִּי בָרָא "the grass of the meadow" 4:20; אל תה]חוי לערבי ימא
ולצידני ב]רא["[do not sh]ow the sea to an Arab or [the] fie[ld] to
a Sidonian" *Aḥ.* 208. (2) Adv. בָּרָא * (*bárrā, LFAA* 93b; cf .
BL 254o): **outside.** הו זי] תביר הנפקה ברא "[the one (vessel)
that] is broken sends it (its contents) outside" *Aḥ.* 109; למנסק עלא
ולמנחת ולמנפק ברא "to climb up above and to go down and to go
outside" *BMAP* 6:13-14. (3) Prep. בַּר מִן * & בָּרָא מִן *: **besides,
apart from.** בעל אחרן בר מ]ן[ענני "another husband besides
Anani" *BMAP* 7:33; בר מן בר זי אפולי "apart from a son of Apuli"
BMAP 3:21; ברא מן די אכלו כבר . . . וברא מן חולק תלתת גבריא "apart
from what they have eaten . . . and apart from the share of the
three men" *1QapGen* 22:23; לתקיף ברא מנך "against anyone
stronger than you" *1QapGen* 22:31. -- Conj. בַּר מִן דִּי * **except
if.** בר מן זי אנת תתרך לאמה "except if you drive out his mother"
BMAP 2:14. [Hebr. ^{2} בַּר].

^{1} ברך , ptc. pass. sg. m. בְּרִיךְ : **blest, blessed.** בְּרִיךְ אֱלָהֲהוֹן
"Blest be their God" Dan 3:28; בריך אל עליון "Blessed be God
Most High" *1QapGen* 22:16; בריכה תבא . . . קדם אוסרי בריכה הוי
"Blessed be Taba' . . . by Osiris. May she be blest!" *Carpentras*
1-3 (*KAI* 269); ברך אנת]ליהו אלהא["Blest are you [by Yaho the
God]" *Padua I* A 2; דכיר ובריך קדם בע>ל<שמין אלהא "Remembered

ברך—בשׂר

and blessed be N. by the god, Baal-shamayin" *Hatra* 1 (*KAI* 244).

Pa. 3 sg. m. בָּרֵךְ (* *barrik,* BL 130h), 1 sg. בָּרְכֵת ; ptc. pass. מְבָרַךְ (BL 112t): **bless, praise.** בָּרֵךְ לֶאֱלָהּ שְׁמַיָּא "(Daniel) blessed the God of Heaven" Dan 2:19; לְעִלָּיָא בָּרְכֵת "I blessed the Most High"(k.) 4:31; לֶהֱוֵה שְׁמֵהּ דִּי־אֱלָהָא מְבָרַךְ "let the name of God be blessed" 2:20; ברכת לאלהא "I blessed God" *1QapGen* 21:2-3; ברכתך ליהה "I bless you by Yaho" *RHR* 130 (1945) 20 line 3; ברכתכי לפתח זי יחזני אפיך בשלם "I bless you (f.) by Ptaḥ, who may let me see your countenance in peace" *Hermopolis* 1verso: 2; ברכנכן לפתח "we bless you (pl.) by Ptaḥ" *Hermopolis* 5verso:1-2; אמר בריך אברם לאל עליון "(Melchizedek) said, 'Blessed be Abram by God Most High" *1QapGen* 22:16. [Hebr. ² בֵּרֵךְ]. †

² ברך (denom. < בֶּרֶךְ "knee"), ptc. sg. m. בָּרֵךְ : **kneel, fall down.** הוּא בָּרֵךְ עַל־בִּרְכֹוהִי "he fell down upon his knees (and prayed)" (read rather הֲוָא, BL 293q) Dan 6:11. [Hebr. ¹ ברך]. ¹

בֶּרֶךְ * (*birk*); du. בִּרְכַּיִן *, w. suff. בִּרְכֹּוהִי (Dan 6:11 v.l.), pl. *birakīn*, w. suff. בִּרְכֹּוהִי ; f.: **knee** (cf. אַרְכֻבָּה). הוּא בָּרֵךְ עַל־בִּרְכֹוהִי "he fell down upon his knees" Dan 6:11. [Hebr. בֶּרֶךְ]. ¹

בָּרַם (< *bar-mā* "except for what," BL 264o), conj.: **but** (cf. ¹ לְהֵן). כֹּורֶשׁ שָׂם טְעֵם . . . לְבְנֵא . . . בָּרַם "but . . . Cyrus decreed . . . to rebuild" Ezra 5:13: Dan 2:28; 4:12, 20; 5:17. †

בְּשַׂר (*basar,* BL 184p), emph. בִּשְׂרָא (BL 218e), only sg. (BL 202m), m.: **flesh.** אֲכֻלִי בְּשַׂר שַׂגִּיא "devour much flesh!" Dan 7:5; דמה יאשד ובשרה יאכל "it (the lion) will shed its (the hart's) blood and devour its flesh" *Aḥ.* 89; [למ]ה ישפטון עקן עם אשה בשר עם סכין "why should wood strive with fire, flesh with a knife?" *Aḥ.* 104. -- Transferred sense: **living thing.** מִדָרְהֹון עִם־בִּשְׂרָא לָא אִיתֹוהִי "whose dwelling is not with living things (mortals)" Dan

78

2:11; מְנַהּ יִתְזִין כָּל־בִּשְׂרָא "all living things were fed from it (a tree)" 4:9. [Hebr. בָּשָׂר]. †

בַּת * (qall, BL 180n), pl. בַּתִּין ; liquid measure, **bath.** עַד־חֲמַר בַּתִּין מְאָה וְעַד־בַּתִּין מְשַׁח מְאָה "up to a hundred baths of wine and up to a hundred baths of oil" Ezra 7:22. [Hebr. the same]. †

בָּתַר : see אֲתַר .

ג

גַּב * (gabb), pl. גַּבִּין *, suff. גַּבַּיַהּ k. (גַּבֵּהּ q. = pl. + ah, BL 79s): **side, back.** עַל־גַּבַּיַהּ "(four wings) on its back" (Gk. Theod. Vg. "on it") Dan 7:6; [ב]נית גב בכל אל חסניא "I built those fortifications on every side (of the city)" Zkr B 8-9 (KAI 202). [1]

גֻּב * (gubb, BL 181v, 41r; > Akk. gubbu "cistern," Or 35 [1966] 8), cst. גֹּב, erroneously גוֹב (BL 222p); emph. גֻּבָּא : **cistern, pit, den.** לְגֹב אַרְיָוָתָא "(will be thrown) into the den of lions" Dan 6:8, 13, 17, 18, 20, 21, 24, 25. [Hebr. גֵּב * "cistern"].†

גְּבוּרָה * (qatūl, BL 189m), emph. גְּבוּרְתָא (v.l. גְּבוּרְתָּא, see BL 22b, c, 67r): **might, strength.** חָכְמְתָא וּגְבוּרְתָא דִּי לֵהּ־הִיא "to whom belong wisdom and might" Dan 2:20; חָכְמְתָא וּגְבוּרְתָא יְהַבְתְּ לִי "wisdom and might you gave to me (Daniel)" 2:23. [Hebr. the same]. †

גְּבַר (gabr, BL 41r, 182x) abs. (& cst.), emph. גַּבְרָא *; pl. גֻּבְרִין (Babyl. vocal. gabrīn), pl. גֻּבְרַיָּא : **man, someone, anyone.** אִיתַי גְּבַר בְּמַלְכוּתָךְ "there is a man in your kingdom" Dan 5:11; גְּבַר מִן־בְּנֵי גָלוּתָא "(I have found) a man among the exiles (of Judah) 2:25; איך זי יער גבר שעותא "just as a man of wax is blinded" Sefire I A 39; גבר עדן הא [אנה] "Look, [I] am an ally," lit. a man

79

with a treaty *Sefire I* B 24; גבר הוי "be a man!" *Padua* I A 7; גבריא די אזלו עמי "the (three) men who went with me" *1QapGen* 22:23-24; כל גבר זי יבעה "anyone who rants" *Sefire III* 1-2; גבר זי יחבל סותא זא "anyone who will destroy this stele" *Tema* A 12-13 (*KAI* 228); גבר זי תזבנון לה ביתא זך "anyone to whom you may sell that house" *AP* 25:11; גבר אחרן "someone else" *BMAP* 5:9; [אתו] לי תלתת גברין מן רברבי מצרי[ן] "three men from the nobles of Egypt [came] to me" *1QapGen* 19:24. **some, certain** (as substantivized adj. or pron., BL 318g): קְרִבוּ גֻּבְרִין כַּשְׂדָּאִין "some Chaldeans came forward" Dan 3:8; אִיתַי גֻּבְרִין יְהוּדָאִין "there are certain Jews" 3:12; גֻּבְרִין גִּבָּרֵי־חַיִל "certain mighty men" 3:20; לגברן חלכין תרין "(provisions) for two Cilicians" *AD* 6:4-5; לעלימוהי גב[ר]ן עשרה "(provisions) for some ten servants" *AD* 6:3; גברין בחרין לקרב "certain men chosen for war" *1QapGen* 22:6; גברא זי יהנצל ביתי "anyone who would snatch away my house" *BMAP* 4:20; מן גבר זי יקרב לה עלוה "(you will have more merit) than anyone who might offer Him a sacrifice" *AP* 30:28; מַן־אִנּוּן שְׁמָהָת גֻּבְרַיָּא דִּי . . . בָּנַיִן "what are the names of those who . . . are building" Ezra 5:4: 5:10; גֻּבְרַיָּא אִלֵּךְ "those individuals" Ezra 4:21; 6:8; Dan 3:12; 6:6 + . **each one.** וגבר חלקה נהחסן "we shall each take his share" *AP* 28:14; לגבר ל[ג]בר כסף [שׁ 2] "(names of those who donated), man by man the sum of [2 shekels]" *AP* 22:1. [Hebr. גֶּבֶר].

גְּבַר * (*gabbār*, BL 191c), cst. pl. גִּבָּרֵי as adj. **mighty, strong.** גִּבָּרֵי־חַיִל דִּי בְחַיְלֵהּ "mighty men of his army" Dan 3:20. [Hebr. גִּבּוֹר].[1]

גְּדָבַר * (< Pers.; prob. the same as גִּזְבַר), emph. pl. גְּדָבְרַיָּא: **treasurer,** title of some administrator. Dan 3:2, 3. †

גדד , impv. pl. גֹּדּוּ (*góddû*, BL 166c): **cut down.** גֹּדּוּ אִילָנָא, "cut down the tree" Dan 4:11, 20. [Hebr. the same]. †

גו—גזבר

גּוּ * (*gaww*, BL 220b), cst. גּוֹא (w. orthographic א), suff.
גַּוֵּהּ, גַּוַּהּ : **middle, midst.** בְּגוֹא : **in** (something): מְהַלְּכִין בְּגוֹא־נוּרָא
"walking in the midst of the fire" Dan 3:25; אִילָן בְּגוֹא אַרְעָא "a
tree in the middle of the earth" 4:7; אֶתְכְּרִיַּת רוּחִי . . . בְּגוֹא נִדְנֶה "my
spirit within its sheath (read נִדְנֵהּ) was anxious" 7:15; נשמתי לגו
נדנהא "my breath in the midst of its sheath" *1QapGen* 2:10; כְּדֵנָה
כְּתִיב בְּגַוֵּהּ "thus was it written in it" Ezra 5:7: 6:2; אֶשְׁתַּדּוּר עָבְדִין
בְּגַוַּהּ "(people) were making sedition in it (from of old)" 4:15;
רשה לא איתי לך עמי בגו דרתה די לי "you do not have a right against
me about my court" *Bib* 38 (1957) 264, lines 9-10. לְגוֹא : **into.**
יִתְרְמֵא לְגוֹא־אַתּוּן נוּרָא "he shall be cast into a furnace of (burning)
fire" Dan 3:6, 11, 15, 21, 23; לְ[גוֹ] נורא "[in]to the fire" 3:24 (as
read in *1QDanᵇ [1Q72]* 1:4); נָפְקִין . . . מִן־גּוֹא נוּרָא "(they) came
out of the fire" Dan 3:26. בגו (abs. as adv.), **there.** תב בגו עם
אנתתך "dwell there with your wife" *AP* 9:6; טיב לבבן בגו "our
heart is content therewith" *BMAP* 12:6; שהדיא בגו "the witnesses
thereto (are)" *AP* 5:15; בגו ליהו כ 12 ש 6 "therein (is paid) for
Yaho 12 k 6 sh" *AP* 22:123. †

גּוֹא : see גּוּ .

גּוּב : see גֹּב .

גֵּוָה (perh. < *ga'wā*, BL 60i, 183f): **pride.** מְהַלְּכִין בְּגֵוָה
יָכִל לְהַשְׁפָּלָה "those walking in pride he is able to abase" Dan 4:34.
[Hebr. the same]. ¹

גוח or גיח , **Aph.** ptc. pl. f. מְגִיחָן : **stir up.** רוּחֵי שְׁמַיָּא מְגִיחָן
לְיַמָּא "the winds of heaven were stirring up the sea" Dan 7:2.
[Hebr. the same]. ¹

גִּזְבַּר * (< Pers. *ganza-bara*; cf. γάζα ; see גְּנַז ; *AD* p. 77,
n. 2), emph. pl. גִּזַּבְרַיָּא (v.l. גִּזְבְרַיָּא cf. Hebr.): **treasurer.** לְכֹל
גִּזַּבְרַיָּא "(order) all the treasurers (in the province)" Ezra 7:21. ¹

81

גְּזַר *, ptc. sg. m. גָּזַר *, pl. m. גָּזְרִין, emph. גָּזְרַיָּא . **Hithpe./
Ithpe.** (pass.), 3 sg. m. הִתְגְּזַר *, 3 sg. f. הִתְגְּזֶרֶת (BL 108j, *GBA*
§104) & אִתְגְּזֶרֶת. (1) **cut, cut off.** מְטוּרָא אִתְגְּזֶרֶת אֶבֶן "a stone was
cut from the mountain" Dan 2:45: 2:34; מכדב גזיר קדלה "a liar
(has) his neck cut (?)" *Aḥ.* 134; יגזר עגלא זנה כן יגזר מתעאל] [
ויגזרן רבוה "[just as] this calf is cut in two (*yugzar*), so may Mati-
'el be cut in two and may his nobles be cut in two!" *Sefire I* A
40. (2) Transferred sense: **decide, conclude.** עדיא אלן זי גזר
[ברגא]יה "this treaty which Bar-Ga'[yah] has concluded" *Sefire I*
A 7; לָא . . . גָּזְרִין יָכְלִין "astrologers were not able" Dan 2:27: 4:4;
5:7, 11; חטאי שבק לה גזר והוא יהודי "as for my sin, a diviner
remitted it, and he was a Jew" *4QprNab (4Q242)* 1-3:4. [Hebr.
גָּזַר]. †

גְּזֵרָה * (*qatil*, BL 186y), cst. גְּזֵרַת : **decision, decree.** גְּזֵרַת
עֶלָּיָא הִיא "it is a decree of the Most High" Dan 4:21; בִּגְזֵרַת עִירִין
פִּתְגָמָא "the matter (was announced) by a decision of Watchers"
4:14 (see 4:10-11, 20-21). †

גיח : see גוח .

גִּיר * (*qīl*, BL 180j), emph. גִּירָא ; **plaster.** עַל־גִּירָא דִּי־כְתַל
הֵיכְלָא "(writing) on the plaster of the palace's wall" Dan 5:5.
[Hebr. גִּר]. [1]

גַּלְגַּל * (*qalqal*, BL 192h), pl. w. suff. גַּלְגִּלּוֹהִי : **wheel.**
גַּלְגִּלּוֹהִי נוּר דָּלִק "its (the throne-chariot's) wheels were burning
fire" Dan 7:9; רצת בגלגל מראי "I ran at the (chariot-)wheel of my
lord (the king of Assyria)" *Barrakib* 8-9 (*KAI* 216). [Hebr. the
same]. [1]

[1] גְּלָה *, infin. מִגְלָא ; ptc. act. sg. m. גָּלֵה & גָּלֵא . **Peʿīl**
perf. pass. 3 sg. m. גְּלִי & גֱּלִי (BL 41o, 156t): **reveal, manifest.**

גלה—גנז

גְּלֵה רָזִין דִּי יְכֵלְתָּ לְמִגְלֵא "a revealer of mysteries, because you have been able to reveal (this mystery)" Dan 2:47; גְּלָא רָזַיָּא הוֹדְעָךְ "the revealer of mysteries has made known to you (what is to be)" 2:29: 2:22, 28; רָזָה גֱלִי ... לְדָנִיֵּאל "(this) secret was revealed . . . to Daniel" 2:19: 2:30; [רז]יְךָ אל תגלי קדם [רח]מִיךָ "do not reveal your secrets before your [frie]nds" *Aḥ.* 141; הן לו גלין אנפין על "if we had appeared before Arsames earlier," lit., had manifested our faces *AP* 37:8. [Hebr. [1] גָּלָה]. †

[2] גְּלָה * (> Akk. *galū,* *Or* 35 [1966] 8): **emigrate, go into exile.** -- **Haph.** 3 sg. m. הַגְלִי : **deport, take into exile.** עַמָּה הַגְלִי לְבָבֶל "(the king) deported the people to Babylon" Ezra 5:12: 4:10. [Hebr. [2] גָּלָה]. †

גָּלוּ * (BL 197g), emph. גָּלוּתָא , f.: **exile.** בְּנֵי גָלוּתָא דִּי יְהוּד "exiles of Judah" Dan 2:25; 5:13; 6:14: Ezra 6:16. [Hebr. גָּלוּת]. †

גְּלָל (*galāl,* BL 187d; > Akk. *galālu* "hard rock, hewn stone," *Or* 35 [1966] 8): **hewn stone.** וְהוּא מִתְבְּנֵא אֶבֶן גְּלָל "and it is being built with hewn stones" Ezra 5:8; נִדְבָּכִין דִּי־אֶבֶן גְּלָל תְּלָתָא "three courses of hewn stones" 6:4 (cf. Palmyrene גללא "stone stele" *DISO* 50.35). †

גְּמִיר (*gamīr,* cf. BL 188h), adj.: **complete, perfect.** סָפַר דָּתָא דִּי־אֱלָהּ שְׁמַיָּא <שְׁלָם> גְּמִיר "(To Ezra), the scribe of the law of the God of heaven, (I bid) perfect <peace>!" (prob. hapl., see שְׁלָם) Ezra 7:12; דמין גמרין "complete price (of a house)" *Bib* 38 (1957) 264 line 6. [1]

גְּנַז * (< Pers. *ganza,* cf. גִּזְבָּר), cst. pl. גִּנְזֵי , emph. גִּנְזַיָּא : **treasure.** יאתה עם גנזא זי מני שים להיתיה בבאל "let him come with the treasure that has been ordered by me to be brought to Babylon" *AD* 10:5; יִתְבַּקַּר בְּבֵית גִּנְזַיָּא דִּי־מַלְכָּא "let a search be made in

83

the royal treasure-house" Ezra 5:17; בַּקָּרוּ בְּבֵית סִפְרַיָּא דִּי גִנְזַיָּא מְהַחֲתִין תַּמָּה "they searched in the records-house, where they store the treasures" 6:1 (explanation of 5:17); תִּנְתֵּן מִן־בֵּית גִּנְזֵי מַלְכָּא "(the needs) you may provide out of the king's treasures" (see Gk., BL 310b) 7:20; לְכֹל גִּזַּבְרַיָּא דִּי בַּעֲבַר נַהֲרָא "(I order) all the treasurers of (the province) Beyond-the-River" 7:21. In metonomy: "treasure house" or office of public administration (cf. בַּיִת): על גנזא . . . כלא יהיתה "all of it he is to bring . . . to the treasury," i.e., public storage *AP* 26:13; על המדכריא זי גנזא "to the accountants of the treasury," i.e., public administration *AP* 26:4; cf. אוצרא זי מלכא "royal treasury" in Elephantine next to the house of Ananiah *BMAP* 3:9. [Hebr. cst. pl. גִּנְזֵי cf. גַּנְזָךְ *]. †

גַּף * (BL 182c), pl. גַּפִּין , suff. גַּפַּיַּהּ k. (גַּפַּהּ q. = pl. + *ah*, BL 79s), f.: **wing.** וְלַהּ גַּפִּין אַרְבַּע "and it (the beast) had four wings" Dan 7:6; 7:4a, b. [Hebr. כָּנָף]. †

גְּרַם * or גֶּרֶם * (*garm*, BL 182x), pl. גַּרְמִין *, suff. גַּרְמֵיהוֹן, m. **bone.** כָּל־גַּרְמֵיהוֹן הַדִּקוּ "broke all their bones in pieces" Dan 6:25; גרמיך לא יחתון שאול "your bones shall not go down to Sheol" *AP* 71:15; ל[א] גרמין אנחנא ולא בשר "we are neither bones nor flesh" *4QEnGiants^c (4Q531)* 19:3. [Hebr. גֶּרֶם]. [1]

גְּשֵׁם * (*gišm*, BL 183g), suff. גֶּשְׁמֵהּ, גֶּשְׁמַהּ, גֶּשְׁמְהוֹן (BL 41s; v.l. גּוּשְׁמֵיהוֹן): **body.** לָא־שְׁלֵט נוּרָא בְּגֶשְׁמְהוֹן "the fire had no power over their bodies" (v.l. בְּגֶשְׁמֵיהוֹן; BL 306k) Dan 3:27; 3:28; 4:30; 5:21; קְטִילַת חֵיוְתָא וְהוּבַד גִּשְׁמַהּ "the beast was killed, and its body destroyed" 7:11. †

ד

In ancient Aramaic, the letter ד designated only
the sound *d*, but later it designated also the sound *d*
that arose from the primitive *ḏ*, written as ז .

דָּא : see דְּנָה .

דֹּב (*dubb*, BL 41r, 181v): **bear.** דָּמְיָה לְדֹב "(a second
beast) like a bear" Dan 7:5 [Hebr. the same]. [1]

דְּבַח * (*ḏabaḥ*), ptc. pl. m. דָּבְחִין : **sacrifice, immolate.**
יִתְבְּנֵא אֲתַר דִּי־דָבְחִין דִּבְחִין "let there be rebuilt a place where they
offer sacrifices," lit. "they sacrifice" Ezra 6:3; cf. בית מדבחא
"altar house," where sacrifice is offered *AP* 32:3. [Hebr. זָבַח]. [1]

דְּבַח * (*ḏibḥ*, BL 183j), pl. דִּבְחִין : **a sacrifice.** אֲתַר
דִּי־דָבְחִין דִּבְחִין "a place where they offer sacrifices" Ezra 6:3; זי
יקרב לה עלוה ודבחין דמי כסף כנכרן אלף "who offers Him a holocaust
and sacrifices worth the sum of a thousand talents" *AP* 31:27.
[Hebr. זָבַח]. [1]

דְּבַק *, ptc. pl. m. דָּבְקִין : **cling, hold together, arrive at.**
לָא לֶהֱוֺן דָּבְקִין דְּנָה עִם דְּנָה "(iron and clay) will not hold together,
this with that" Dan 2:43; אגרא זך . . . דבקה לביתא זילי לזויתה זי לעליה "that portico . . . adjoins my house at its upper corner" *AP*
5:4; לבבי לה דבק לה "my heart does not cling to it (a tunic)" *Her-
mopolis* 4:5; דבקת לטור תורא "I reached Mount Taurus" *1Qap-
Gen* 21:16. [Hebr. דָּבַק]. [1]

דִּבְרָה * (*qatal*, BL 185s), cst. דִּבְרַת : **reason, cause.**
Conj. עַל־דִּבְרַת דִּי "for that reason," "in order that . . .": עַל־דִּבְרַת
דִּי פִשְׁרָא . . . יְהוֹדְעוּן "in order that . . . they may make known the

interpretation" Dan 2:30; עַד־דְּבְרַת דִּי יִנְדְּעוּן "in order that ('addib-rat; BL 260z) they may know" 4:14; cf. the oath על דבר ארקא זך "in regard to that land" AP 6:6-7; על דברה "(you swore to me) in regard to it (the land)" AP 6:8; עדבר נונין "concerning fish" AP 45:3; אגרה על דבר כן "(he sent) a letter about it" AP 40:3. [Hebr. עַל־דִּבְרַת שֶׁ "so that" Qoh 7:14]. †

דְּהַב (dahab) abs. (& cst.), emph. דַּהֲבָא & דַּהֲבָה : **gold.** וְכֹל כְּסַף וּדְהַב דִּי תְהַשְׁכַּח "and all the silver and gold that you will find" Ezra 7:16: 7:15; בִּשְׁאָר כַּסְפָּא וְדַהֲבָה לְמֶעְבַּד "to do with the rest of the silver and gold" 7:18: Dan 2:35, 45; בעלי כסף ובעלי זהב "(mighty kings) owners of silver and of gold" Barrakib 10-11 (KAI 216); על זהב על זנה שלחן "as for gold, concerning this we have sent (a letter)" AP 30:28-29; אזלת . . . ואף בכסף ודהב "I went (forth) . . . with silver and gold too" 1QapGen 20:33. Gen. of material (see דִּי I 2): צְלֵם דִּי־דְהַב "a statue of gold" Dan 3:1; צְלֵם דַּהֲבָא "the statue of gold" 3:5, 7; מָאנֵי דַהֲבָא "the vessels of gold" 5:2, 3, 4, 23 = מָאנַיָּא . . . דִּי דַהֲבָא "(these) vessels of gold" Ezra 5:14; 6:5; מזרקיא זי זהבא "the basins of gold" AP 30:12; אַנְתְּה־הוּא רֵאשָׁה דִּי דַהֲבָא "you are the golden head of (that statue)" (BL 330q) Dan 2:38. As a predicate (see דִּי I 3): הוּא צַלְמָא רֵאשֵׁהּ דִּי־דְהַב טָב "as for that statue, its head (was) of fine gold" (BL 329j) 2:32. [Hebr. זָהָב].

דהוא k. (דְּהֵיא q.; vocalized as a gentilic noun, cf. אֲפַרְסָי, read דְּהוּא = דִּי הוּא : **that is.** שׁוּשַׁנְכָיֵא דֶהָיֵא עֵלְמָיֵא "men of Susa, that is (read דִּי הוּא) Elamites" Ezra 4:9; cf. יְ הִיא "that is" Ezra 6:15. [1]

דוק : see דקק .

דור *, impf. 3 sg. f. תְּדוּר, 3 pl. m. יְדֻרוּן k., 3 pl. f. יְדֻרָן q. (BL 144c); ptc. pl. m. דַּאֲרִין k. & דָּיְרִין q.; cst. דָּאֲרֵי k. & דָּיְרֵי q. (BL 51h, j): **inhabit, dwell** (cf. שְׁכַן). דָּאֲרֵי אַרְעָא "the inhabitants of the earth" Dan 4:32bis; דִּי־דָאֲרִין בְּכָל־אַרְעָא "that dwell on all the earth" 3:31; 6:26; יְהַב בִּידָךְ . . . בְּכָל־דִּי דָאֲרִין בְּנֵי־אֲנָשָׁא "into whose hand He has given, wherever they dwell, the sons of men" 2:38; תְּדוּר חֵיוַת בָּרָא "(the tree under which) the beasts of the field dwell" (‖ שכן) 4:18; יְדֻרוּן צִפֲּרֵי שְׁמַיָּא "the birds of the heavens dwell (in its branches)" 4:9. [Hebr. the same]. †

▲ דּוּרָא (v.l. דִּירָא): **Dura,** name of a Babylonian city (Akk. *dūru,* "fortified city"). עֲבַד צְלֵם . . . אֲקִימֵהּ בְּבִקְעַת דּוּרָא בִּמְדִינַת בָּבֶל "(the king) made a statue . . . and set it up on the plain of Dura, in the province of Babylon" (perh. Tulūl Dūra, SSE of Babylon) Dan 3:1. [1]

דּוּשׁ *, impf. 3 sg. f. w. suff. תְּדוּשִׁנַּהּ : **trample, grind** (cf. דקק, רְפַס, (חֲשַׁל) תְּדוּשִׁנַּהּ "(the beast) shall trample it (the whole earth)" Dan 7:23. [Hebr. the same]. [1]

דַּחֲוָה *, pl. דַּחֲוָן : uncertain meaning. "(the king spent the night fasting); וְדַחֲוָן לָא הַנְעֵל קֳדָמוֹהִי "and he had no diversions brought to him" (conjectures: "food" [Gk., Syr., Theod., Vg.], "tables" [Rashi], "sweet odors" [cf. Arab. *duḫān* "smoke"], "concubines" [read לְחֵנָן or רַחֲוָן * from רַחֲמָן*]) Dan 6:19. [1]

דְּחֵל * (*daḥil*), ptc. pl. m. דָּחֲלִין; ptc. pas. sg. m. דְּחִיל , sg. f. דְּחִילָה : **fear, be afraid.** וְדָחֲלִין מִן־קֳדָמוֹהִי "(all peoples were) fearing before him (the king)" Dan 5:19; לֶהֱוֹן זָאֲעִין וְדָחֲלִין אֱלָהֵהּ מִן־קֳדָם "they shall tremble and fear before his (Daniel's) God" 6:27; יזחל הא מן לד ספר[י]א "should that (man) be frightened from effacing the inscript[ion]s" *Sefîre II* C 6; אל תזחל כי אנה המל[כתך] "do not be afraid, for I have made you king" *Zkr* A 13 (*KAI* 202); דחלת לם אחיקר אמר "I, Aḥiqar, was really afraid" *Aḥ.* 45; נדחל בזי לי אל תדחל "he said to me (Aḥiqar), 'Fear not!'" *Aḥ.* 54; אל תדחל אנה עמך זעירן "we fear because we are few" *AP* 37:7;

"Do not be afraid; I am with you" *1QapGen* 22:30. -- דְּחִיל **fearsome, frightening** (BL 297c). רֵוֵהּ דְּחִיל "its (the statue's) appearance (was) frightening" Dan 2:31; אֲרוּ חֵיוָה רְבִיעָיָה דְּחִילָה "behold, the fourth beast (was) fearsome" 7:7; דְּחִילָה יַתִּירָה "(the beast was) very frightening" 7:19.

Pa., impf. 3 sg. m. w. suff. פְּשַׁר חֶלְמָא יְדַחֲלִנַּנִי "the interpretation of the dream terrified me" Dan 4:2. †

דִּי, זִי (*dī*), particle w. many & varied uses. (I) Dem. particle, substitute for the Gen. (cf. Hebr. זֶה , Arab. *ḏū,* BL 312a): almost = **that one.** (1) After determ. noun: דָּתָא דִּי מַלְכָּא = ὁ νόμος ὁ τοῦ βασιλέως "the law, that of the king," i.e., the law of the king" Ezra 7:26; גֻּבָּא דִּי אַרְיָוָתָא "the den of lions" Dan 6:17, 20; מַלְכָּא דִּי בָבֶל "the king of Babylon" Ezra 5:13; כל מלכיא זי סחרתי "all the kings of my vicinity" *Sefire III* 7-8; אגורא זי יהו "the temple of Yaho" *AP* 30:6. -- After indet. noun (BL 313c): אֶצְבְּעָן דִּי יַד "fingers of a hand" Dan 5:5; בְּקִרְיָה דִּי שָׁמְרָיִן "in a town of Samaria" (perh. collective: "towns" [Gk. ἐν πόλεσιν; BL 313g) Ezra 4:10; בר זי אפולי "a child of Apuli" *BMAP* 3:21. -- After a noun w. a proleptic suff. (BL 314j): שְׁמֵהּ דִּי אֱלָהָא "His name, that of God" = "the name of God" 2:20: 2:44; 3:26; Ezra 5:11; עבדיה זי מבטחיה אמן "the slaves of Mibṭaḥiah, our mother" *AP* 28:3; ביתה זי אפולי "the house of Apuli" *BMAP* 3:4; אבוהי זי אסרחאדן "the father of Esarhaddon" *Aḥ.* 47.

(2) דִּי before a gen. of quality or material. (a) Attributive gen. of quality is determ. when governed by a determ. noun, but indet. when governed by an indet. noun: שְׁבִיבָא דִּי נוּרָא "the flame of the fire" Dan 3:22; שְׁבִיבִין דִּי־נוּר "flames of fire" 7:9; נְהַר דִּי־נוּר "a stream of fire" 7:10; בְּחֶזְוָא דִּי־לֵילְיָא "in the vision of the night" 2:19; מָאנַיָּא דִי־בֵית־אֱלָהָא דִּי דַהֲבָא "the golden vessels of the house of God" Ezra 5:14: 6:5; צְלֵם דִּי־דְהַב "a statue of gold" Dan 3:1; רַגְלוֹהִי דִּי פַרְזְלָא "his feet of iron" 2:34; אֱסוּר דִּי־פַרְזֶל "a band of iron" 4:12, 20: 7:7; נִדְבָּךְ דִּי־אָע חֲדָה "one

course of wood" Ezra 6:4b: 6:4a; תרעון זי אבן 5 "5 gate-ways of stone" *AP* 30:9-10; עמודיא זי אבנא "the pillars of stone" *AP* 30:9; לבוש 1 זי קמר "1 garment of wool" *BMAP* 7:6; אוצרא זי מלכא "the treasury of the king" *BMAP* 3:9; מנן 2 זי מלך "2 royal minas" *CIS* II.6.5; אַנְתְּה־הוּא רֵאשָׁה דִּי דַהֲבָא "you are the golden head (of that statue)" (BL 330q) Dan 2:38; תְּקוּם מַלְכוּ תְלִיתָיָא אָחֳרִי דִּי נְחָשָׁא "another third kingdom of bronze shall arise" 2:39 (explains 2:38); מזרקיא זי זהבא וכסף "the basins of gold and silver (כסף error for כספא ; cf. *AP* 31:11: מזרקיא זי זהבא וזי כספא) *AP* 30:12; כל מלכיא זי סחרתי "all the kings of my vicinity" *Sefire III* 7-8. N.B. The same construction is found when a gen. of quality is introduced by a cst.: מַלְכוּת עָלַם "an everlasting kingdom" Dan 3:33; 7:27; חַי עָלְמָא "(He who) lives forever" 4:31; עַתִּיק יוֹמִין "(the) Ancient of Days" 7:9; עַתִּיק יוֹמַיָּא "the Ancient of Days" 7:13; צְלֵם דַּהֲבָא "the golden statue" 3:5, 7; יַד אֱנָשׁ "a man's hand" 5:5; חֶזְוֵי לֵילְיָא "the night visions" 7:7, 13; רוּחַ אֱלָהִין "a spirit of (holy) gods" 5:14; שׁוּק מלכא ביניהם "a street of the king is between them" *BMAP* 3:8; מנה מלך "a royal mina" *CIS* II.7.6; אֱסָר מַלְכָּא "the interdict of the king" Dan 6:12; מסמרי נחש ופרזל "nails of bronze and iron" *AP* 26:12; לְקַיָּמָה קְיָם מַלְכָּא "to establish a royal ordinance" (for the sense, see קְיָם) 6:8. (b) When the predicative gen. of quality is indet.: רֵאשֵׁהּ דִּי־דְהַב טָב . . . דְּרָעוֹהִי דִּי כְסַף מְעוֹהִי . . . דִּי נְחָשׁ "its (the statue's) head (was) of fine gold, . . . its arms of silver, its belly . . . of bronze" (BL 329j) 2:32; שָׁקוֹהִי רַגְלוֹהִי מִנְּהוֹן דִּי פַרְזֶל וּמִנְּהוֹן דִּי "its legs (were) of iron" 2:33; דִּי פַרְזֶל חֲסַף "its feet (were) partly of iron and partly of clay" 2:33 (cf. 2:41; 2:42).

(II) Rel. particle, which indicates that a descriptive cl. follows corresponding to what is called a rel. cl. (cf. Arab. *alladī*, BL 355e): Almost = **such a one as.** (1) A complete cl. follows: דִּי פֶחָה שָׂמֵהּ "whom he had set up as governor" Ezra 5:14: Dan 4:27; אֱלָהָךְ דִּי אַנְתְּה פָּלַח־לֵהּ "your God, whom you serve" 6:17, 21; וֵאלָהָא דִּי־נִשְׁמְתָךְ בִּידֵהּ וְכָל־אֹרְחָתָךְ לֵהּ "and the God in

whose hand is your breath, and whose are all your ways" (see
אָרַח) 5:23; מָאנַיָּא . . . "the vessels . . .
which Nebuchadnezzar had taken out . . . brought (to Babylon)"
Ezra 5:14: 4:10; . . . גֻּבְרִין "(there are) men . . .
whom you have appointed" Dan 3:12; דָּנִיֵּאל דִּי שְׁמֵהּ בֵּלְטְשַׁאצַּר
"Daniel, whose name (was) Belteshazzar" 2:26; 4:5, 16: 4:34a;
5:12, 23; אֱלָהִין דִּי מְדָרְהוֹן "(the) gods whose dwelling (is not with
flesh) 2:11; אַנְתָּה . . . דִּי אֱלָהּ . . . יְהַב־לָךְ "you . . . to whom God . .
. has given (the kingdom)" 2:37; גְּבַר . . . דִּי רוּחַ אֱלָהִין בֵּהּ "(there
is) a man . . . in whom the spirit of (the) gods is" 5:11; דִּי דָנִיֵּאל
חַד מִנְּהוֹן "(three prefects) of whom Daniel was one" 6:3; בְּבֵית
סִפְרַיָּא דִּי גִּנְזַיָּא מְהַחֲתִין תַּמָּה "in the house of the archives where they
stored documents" Ezra 6:1; ירחא זי לא אנתן לך בה "any month in
which I do not give you (interest)" AP 11:4 (see below, II 6).

(2) דִּי as obj. of a cl. (BL 356d, 357j): עדיא אלן זי גזר בר
גא[יה] "(it is) this treaty which Bar-Ga'[yah] has concluded" Sefire I A 7; עדי אלהן הם זי שמו אלהן "this is the treaty of gods,
which gods have set forth" Sefire I B 6; חֶלְמָא דִי־חֲזֵית "the dream,
which I saw" Dan 2:26b: 2:11a, 24; 4:6, 17a; . . . צַלְמָא דִּי הֲקֵם
"the statue which the king set up" 3:2; רְבוּתָא דִּי יְהַב לֵהּ מַלְכָּא "the
greatness which He gave him" 5:19; מָאנֵי . . . דִּי נְבוּ הַנְפֵּק "the
vessels of . . . which Nebuchadnezzar took out" Ezra 6:5; אִילָנָא
דִּי חֲזַיְתָ דִּי רְבָה "the tree which you saw (and) which became great"
Dan 4:17.

(3) דִּי as subj. of a cl. (BL 356d, e, i): מלכיא זי ימלכן "the
kings who will rule" Sefire I B 22; בר[י] זי ישב על כהסאי "[my]
son who sits upon my throne" Sefire III 17; אַבְנָא דִּי מְחָת לְצַלְמָא
"the stone that struck the statue" Dan 2:35: 6:14d; מַלְכָּא דִּי רְבַיְתָ
"you, O king, have grown" (BL 357k) 4:19; . . . אנה הו אחיקר זי
שזבך "I am Aḥiqar, who . . . saved you" Aḥ. 46; עמודיא . . . זי הוו
תמה "the pillars . . . which were there" AP 30:9; חַיְוָתָא . . . דִּי אִנִּין
אַרְבַּע "the beasts . . . which are four" Dan 7:17; תמת שמה זי אמתך
"Tamut, by name, who is your handmaiden" BMAP 2:3; לִירַח אֲדָר

90

דִּי־הִיא שְׁנַת־שֵׁת "until the month of Adar, which is the year six"
Ezra 6:15 (cf. בִּשְׁנַת־שְׁבַע "in the year seven" 7:7; שׁוּשַׁנְכָיֵא דְהוּא
עֵלְמָיֵא "the men of Susa, i.e., Elamites" 4:9). -- W. prep. pred.:
עדיא זי בספרא זנה "the treaty which is in this inscription" *Sefire I*
B 33; מלי ספרא זי בנצבא זנה "the words of the inscription which
is on this stele" *Sefire I* C 17; כהניא זי ביב "the priests who are in
Yeb (Elephantine)" *AP* 30:1; בשוקא זי בינין "into the street
which is between us (our houses)" *AP* 5:12-13; שהדיא זי על ספרא
זנה "the witnesses who(se names) are on this document" *AP*
11:16; גֻּבְרִין גִּבָּרֵי־חַיִל דִּי בְחַיְלֵהּ "mighty men who were in his
army" Dan 3:20; דָּת אֱלָהָךְ דִּי בִידָךְ "the law of your God, which is
in your hand," i.e., the book of the law Ezra 7:14: 7:25; הֵיכְלָא דִי
בִירוּשְׁלֶם "the temple that is in Jerusalem" Dan 5:2, 3; Ezra 5:14,
15; 6:5; cf. בֵּית־אֱלָהָא בִירוּשְׁלֶם "God's house in Jerusalem" (prep.
attribute; cf. BL 356f) Ezra 6:3: 5:17; הֵיכְלָא דִּי בָבֶל "the temple
which is (in) Babylon" (see לְ I 7) (*or* "the temple of Babylon"
[*RSV*]) Ezra 5:14b. -- דִּי לָא w. a noun = prep. **without** (see לָא
no. 4). -- דִּי לִי, דִּי לָךְ, etc. = poss. pron.: **my, mine; your, yours,**
etc. (see לְ no. 4; הוּא 2 b).

(4) דִּי substantivized rel. pron. = **he who, he whom;
that which.** הן השב זי לי "if he has restored what is mine" *Sefire
III* 20; ינצר זי לך "what is yours will be protected" *Nerab* 13-14
(*KAI* 225); דִּי הֲוָה צָבֵא הֲוָה מַחֵא "the one whom he would he kept
alive" Dan 5:19b: 5:19c, d; דִּי לָא יְדַע תְּהוֹדְעוּן "him who does not
know (the law) you (pl.) will teach" Ezra 7:25; דִּי־בָעֵינָא "(You
made known to me) what we asked for" Dan 2:23; וְדִי מַהְלְכִין
בְּגֵוָה "and those who walk (read Pa. ptc. מְהַלְכִין) in pride" 4:34; זי
יגרנכי "whoever shall sue you" *AP* 1:6; זי תעבדון לה "what you
do for him (will not be hidden)" *AP* 38:10-11; שא לך זי ת[נ]שא מנן
"take for yourself that which you will take from us" *Aḥ.* 121;
יאמר לזי לידע "he will say to someone who does not understand"
Sefire II C 7-8; עם זי רם מנך אל תעבר "with someone who is
taller than you do not argue(?)" *Aḥ.* 142; להן זי אל עמה "except

91

די

"I אנה אוספת לה על דילה שגי .107 *Aḥ* "him with whom God is
added much to that which he had" *1QapGen* 21:6; לָא אִיתַי
דִּי־יְמַחֵא בִידֵהּ "there is no one who can stay His hand" Dan 4:32;
לא איתי זי יקיר מן "there is nothing that is heavier than (debt)" *Aḥ.*
111. -- Used as a pred.: ביתא זילך ודי בניך ודי תנתן לה רחמת "the
house belongs to you and to your children and to whomever you
may give it as a gift" *BMAP* 12:30-31; לך יהוה וזי בניך . . . ולמן זי
צבית תנתן "(that slave) belongs to you and to your children . . .
and to whomever you wish to give (him)" *AP* 28:12; מַלְכוּתֵהּ דִּי־לָא
תִתְחַבַּל "His kingdom is one that shall not be destroyed" Dan 6:27
(cf. 7:14).

(5) דִּי in an indef. rel. cl. (BL 358n), מָה־דִּי, מַן־דִּי, כָּל־דִּי,
etc.: = **whoever, whatever.** כָּל־דִּי־יִבְעֵה בָעוּ "whoever makes a
petition" Dan 6:8; כל גבר זי יבעה רוח אפוה "anyone who rants," lit.
"causes the breath of his nostrils to boil" *Sefire III* 1-2; כָּל־אֱנָשׁ
דִּי־יִבְעֵה "anyone who petitions" Dan 6:13: 3:10; 5:7; Ezra 6:11;
כָּל־דִּי לָא לֶהֱוֵה עָבֵד דָּתָא "whoever does not obey the law" Ezra
7:26; כל זי רחם הא לי "anyone who is a friend of mine" *Sefire III*
8; גבר זי תזבנון לה ביתא זך "to whomever you sell that house" *AP*
25:11; מַן־דִּי לָא יִפֵּל "whoever does not fall down" Dan 3:6, 11;
לְמָן דִּי יִצְבֵּה יְהָקֵים עֲלַיהּ "(God gives it [kingdom of men]) to
whomever He will and sets over it (the lowliest of men)" 5:21;
למן זי רחמת תנתן או זי תזבן לה בכסף "to whomever you will you may
give it or to whom you sell (it for money)" *BMAP* 12:23-24;
ביתה וכל זי ב[ה] "his house and all that (is) in it" *Sefire I* C 22-23;
כָּל־דִּי יִשְׁאֲלָנְכוֹן "whatever is good" *Sefire III* 29; כל מה זי ט[ב]
"whatever he (Ezra) asks of you (pl.)" Ezra 7:21: 7:23; כל זי תצבה
שלח לי "for whatever you desire send (a letter) to me" *Hermopolis* 3:7; מן כול די איתי לך "from anything that is yours" *1QapGen*
22:22; מָה דִּי מה זי לקחת "whatever you have taken" *AD* 12:8;
לֶהֱוֵא "whatever will come to be" Dan 2:28, 29b, 45: Ezra 7:18;
טְעֵם לְמָא דִּי־תַעַבְדוּן "a decree about what you are to do" Ezra 6:8.

די

(6) דִי in an adverbial rel. cl. denoting time or place (even w. בָּהּ not following! See below III 7): כן [ביום זי יעב[ד "on any day on which he will do so" *Sefire I* C 20-21; בעדן זי זא באישתא עביד לן "at the time when this evil was done (m. ptc.) to us" *AP* 30:17-18; בזמן די תאמר לי "at a moment when you will say to me" *Mur 27* 1:5; בכל יום זי "on any day on which" *AP* 37:2; עד יום זי אשלמנהי לך "until the day on which I repay it to you" *AP* 11:10; בְּעִדָּנָא דִּי־תִשְׁמְעוּן "at the moment at which you hear" Dan 3:15; מן יום די נפקתה מן חרן "from the day on which you departed from Haran" *1QapGen* 22:28; [מ]ן יום זי אזלת "from the day that you went" *Padua I* A 2; בכל מה זי ימות בר אנש "in whatever way anyone shall die" *Sefire III* 16; תבעה אתר זי אנת תהשכח "you are to seek (Aḥiqar) in a place where (adv. accus.) you will find (him)" *Aḥ.* 34; יִתְבְּנֵא אֲתַר דִּי־דָבְחִין דִּבְחִין "let (the temple) be rebuilt in a place where they offer sacrifices" Ezra 6:3; לאתרא די בנית תמן בה מדבחא "to (Bethel), the place where I had built the altar" *1QapGen* 21:1; בְּכָל־דִּי דָאְרִין "wherever they dwell" (impers. BL 368c) Dan 2:38.

(III) דִּי as conj. (1) **that** (ὅτι, German "dass") after various verbs (but not אֲמַר), introducing a cl. as the obj. of a verb (BL 361d): שְׁמְעֵת . . . דִּי רוּחַ אֱלָהִין בָּךְ "I have heard . . . that the spirit of (the) gods is in you" Dan 5:14: 5:16; שמע מלך סודם די "the king of Sodom heard that Abram had brought back all the captives" *1QapGen* 22:12; חֲזַיְתָ דִּי . . . אִתְגְּזֶרֶת אֶבֶן "you saw that a stone was cut" Dan 2:45: 2:8; 3:27; . . . חזת די אשתני אנפי "(my wife) saw ... that my expression had changed" *1QapGen* 2:12; תִּנְדַּע דִּי שַׁלִּיט עִלָּיָא "you know that the Most High has power (over)" Dan 4:22, 29: 2:8-9; 4:6, 14, 23; 5:21; 6:11, 16; Ezra 4:15; תדען זי מדעם לה מפקן לן "you (pl.) will know that they are sending us nothing (לא = לה)" *Hermopolis* 5:2-3; ינדעוך מרי די אנתה מרה "that they may know that you are lord (of all the kings of the earth)" *1QapGen* 20:15 (w. prolep. obj.; cf. Dan 3:27; see חֲזָה no. 1); הַכְרִזוּ עֲלוֹהִי דִּי־לֶהֱוֵא שַׁלִּיט תַּלְתָּא "they

93

proclaimed about him (Daniel) that he would be the third ruler (in the kingdom)" Dan 5:29; ‏מְהוֹדְעִין אֲנַחְנָה לְמַלְכָּא דִּי. . . . לָא אִיתַי לָךְ‎ "we make known to the king that . . . you will have no (possession)" Ezra 4:16: 7:24; ‏חויה די שבי לוט‎ "he informed him that Lot had been taken captive" *1QapGen* 22:3; ‏חשבת בלבי די מן עירין הריאתא‎ "I thought to myself that the conception was from Watchers" *1QapGen* 2:1; ‏ימא לי . . . די לא ידעהא‎ "(the king) swore to me . . . that he had not known her" (euphemism) *1Qap-Gen* 20:30; ‏הן צבה אנת ברי זי תהוה [רם]‎ "if you, my son, wish that you become [exalted]" (instead of infin. ‏למהוא‎) *Aḥ.* 149. -- ‏דִּי‎ introducing a cl. that is subj. of a verb (BL 360b): ‏יְדִיעַ לֶהֱוֵא־לָךְ . . .‎ ‏דִּי לֵאלָהָיךְ לָא־אִיתַינָא פָלְחִין‎ "let it be known that we will not serve your gods" Dan 3:18: Ezra 4:12, 13; 5:8; ‏שִׂים טְעֵם . . . דִּי אִיתַי הֵן‎ ‏לְמִבְנֵא‎ "(let a search be made to see) whether a decree was issued to rebuild (the temple)" Ezra 5:17; ‏מִן־קְשֹׁט דִּי אֱלָהֲכוֹן הוּא אֱלָהּ אֱלָהִין‎ "it is true that your God is God of gods" Dan 2:47. -- ‏דִּי‎ introducing a cl. that is a complement to a noun (see ‏ו‎ II 3; ‏לְ‎ II 4): ‏דָּת לְמָדַי וּפָרַס דִּי־כָל־אֱסָר‎ "a law of the Medes and Persians that no interdict (can be changed)" Dan 6:16; ‏אַזְדָּא מִנִּי מִלְּתָא דִּי הֵן . . .‎ "the word from me is sure that, if . . . , (you will be killed)" 2:8-9; ‏הֵן אִיתַיכוֹן עֲתִידִין דִּי . . . תִּפְּלוּן‎ "if you are ready, that . . . you will fall down (and worship [BL 361e])" 3:15 (cf. Nabatean ‏לא‎ ‏לא רשי למכתב‎ ‏רשי אנוש . . . די יזבן‎ "no one has the right to sell"; "no one has the right to write" *DISO* 284:17, 19); ‏מהי דה זי ספר לה‎ ‏הושרתן לי‎ "what does this mean that you have not sent me a letter?" *Hermopolis* 5:7-8.

(2) ‏דִּי‎ introducing dir. disc. (BL 364c): ‏אָמְרִין דִּי לָא נְהַשְׁכַּח‎ "they said, 'We have not found'" Dan 6:6: 2:25; 5:7; 6:14; ‏אמרת‎ ‏שרי למלכא דאחי הוא‎ "Sarai said to the king, 'He is my brother'" *1QapGen* 20:9-10: 22:22; ‏בדיל [מה ה]וית אמר לי די אחתי היא‎ "why have you been saying to me, 'She is my sister?'" *1QapGen* 20:26-27: 19:20; ‏כן אמר זי שמע הוית זי אמר יהוחנן זנה‎ "he said thus, 'I have heard what this Yohanan has said'" *Mur 72* 1:5.

(3) דִי introducing a cl. that takes up a topic already mentioned and completes the sense of the main cl. (BL 364b): **that, as** (cf. below עַל זי). וְדִי חֲזַיְתָה רַגְלַיָּא . . . מַלְכוּ פְלִיגָה תֶּהֱוֵה "and as you saw the feet . . . , it will be a divided kingdom" Dan 2:41; וְדִי חֲזַיְתָ פַּרְזְלָא מְעָרַב . . . מִתְעָרְבִין לֶהֱוֹן "and as you saw the iron mixed . . . , (so) will they be mixed" 2:43; וְדִי חֲזָה מַלְכָּא עִיר . . . דְּנָה פִּשְׁרָא "and whereas the king saw a Watcher . . . ; this is the interpretation" 4:20-21; וְדִי אֲמַרוּ לְמִשְׁבַּק עִקַּר . . . מַלְכוּתָךְ לָךְ קַיָּמָה "and as they commanded to leave the stump . . . , your kingdom shall be stable for you" 4:23; אף זי הושרת עלי ביד אנא . . . כתן . . . זך היתי עלי "also what you sent to me by Ana . . . a tunic . . . that man has brought (it) to me" *AD* 13:2-3; מלתי לבתי לאמר לה שאל על חרוץ כעת "you spoke to Bitti saying, 'He did not ask about Haruṣ. Look, as I am doing for Haruṣ, so may Banit (the goddess) do for me" *Hermopolis* 1:6-7; על זי הלו כזי עבד אנה לחרוץ כות תעבד בנת עלי פסמשך] אמר "about what Psamshek said" *AD* 4:1*; על [ז]י יה[ו]ה כסנתו "as for what will be a loss" *AD* 7:1*.

(4) דִי introducing a causal cl. (BL 363u, 264r): **because, for.** דִּי חָכְמְתָא . . . דִּי לֵהּ־הִיא "because wisdom belongs to Him" Dan 2:20; דִּי חָכְמְתָא . . . יְהַבְתְּ לִי "for You have given me wisdom" 2:23; דִּי הֵימִן בֵּאלָהֵהּ "because he trusted in his God" 6:24; כָּל־קֳבֵל דִּי רוּחַ יַתִּירָא בֵּהּ "because an excellent spirit was in him" 6:4: 6:5; Ezra 4:14; קבלתך . . . די דברת אנתתי "I complain to you, (my Lord) . . . because my wife has been taken away (from me)" *1QapGen* 20:14; באש עלי די פרש לוט "it grieved me because Lot had parted (from me)" *1QapGen* 21:7; דִּי־מִלַּת מַלְכָּא הוֹדַעְתֶּנָא "for You have made known to us the king's affair" Dan 2:23; דִּי יְכֵלְתָּ לְמִגְלֵא רָזָא דְנָה "for you have been able to reveal this mystery" 2:47; כָּל־קֳבֵל דִּי כָּל־חַכִּימֵי . . . לָא־יָכְלִין "for none of the wise men of . . . was able" 4:15: 3:29; דִּי־הוּא אֱלָהָא חַיָּא "for He is the living God" 6:27; בריך אנתה אל עליון . . . די אנתה מרה "blessed (are) You, O God Most High, . . . for You are Lord" *1QapGen* 20:12-13.

(5) דְּ w. impf. after verbs of asking, commanding, etc.:
that (see וְ no. 10 & לְ II 2). בְּעָה מִן־מַלְכָּא דִּי זְמָן יִנְתֶּן־לֵהּ "he asked
the king that he would give him time" Dan 2:16; בעא מני די אתה
"he begged of me that I come" *1QapGen* 20:21; . . . שָׂמֶתָ טְעֵם דִּי
יִפֵּל "you decreed that (every one) . . . shall fall down" Dan 3:10;
מִנִּי שִׂים טְעֵם דִּי . . . הַדָּמִין יִתְעֲבֵד "it has been decreed by me that
(every blasphemer) shall be torn limb from limb" 3:29; שִׂים טְעֵם
דִּי . . . לֶהֱוֺן . . . דָּחֲלִין "it has been decreed (by me) that (people)
will fear (the God of Daniel)" 6:27; . . . דִּי . . . לְקַיָּמָה קְיָם מַלְכָּא
יִתְרְמֵא "the king should establish an ordinance that whoever . . .
will be cast (into the lions' den)" 6:8; זְקִיף . . . דִּי מִנִּי שִׂים טְעֵם
יִתְמְחֵא "it is decreed by me that (if anyone disobeys) . . . , he will
be impaled on a beam" Ezra 6:11; מִנִּי שִׂים טְעֵם . . . דִּי . . . לִמְהָךְ
עִמָּךְ יְהָךְ "it is decreed by me that (anyone who wishes) to לִירוּשְׁלֶם
go to Jerusalem with you may go" 7:13. -- דִּי omitted: שָׂמֶתָ טְעֵם
אָסְפַּרְנָא יִתְעֲבֵד "I decree, 'Let it be done with diligence'" Ezra
6:12; הושרו יהיתו עלי אפריע "send (word), 'Let them bring (them)
to me immediately'" *AD* 9:3; אקרא לך על חרמביתאל אלהא "I
should challenge you 'By Ḥerembethel, the god, . . .'" *AP* 7:7;
אנתם החווהי יהחסן "do notify him, 'Let him take possession of (the
estate)'" *AD* 8:5.

(6) דְּ w. the impf., expressing purpose: **that, in order
that** (cf. BL360c, 363v; see וְ no. 9; לְ II 1). דִּי יְבַקַּר בִּסְפַר־דָּכְרָנַיָּא
"in order that one search in the archives" Ezra 4:15; דִּי לֶהֱוֺן
מְהַקְרְבִין נִיחוֹחִין לֶאֱלָהּ "in order that they may offer pleasing sacrifices to God" 6:10; דִּי־פִשַׁר חֶלְמָא יְהוֹדְעֻנַּנִי "(let the sages be
brought in) that they might make known to me the interpretation
of the dream" Dan 4:3; דִּי לֶהֱוֺן בְּכָל־מַלְכוּתָא "in order that they
might be (satraps) in the whole kingdom" 6:2; דִּי לָא יְהֹבְדוּן "that
(Daniel and his companions) might not perish" 2:18; דִּי לָא־יִפְלְחוּן
"in order not to serve (other gods)" 3:28; דִּי לָא־תִשְׁנֵא צְבוּ בְּדָנִיֵּאל
"that nothing might be changed concerning Daniel" 6:18; דִּי־לֶהֱוֺן
. . . יָהֲבִין לְהוֹן טַעְמָא וּמַלְכָּא לָא־לֶהֱוֵא נָזִק "that (these satraps) might

דִּין

give an account, and the king might suffer no loss" 6:3. -- Mixed
construction (BL 301e; see וְ no. 9 & לְ II 1 c): דִּי־כְתָבָה דְנָה יִקְרוֹן
וּפִשְׁרֵהּ לְהוֹדָעֻתַנִי "(sages were brought in) that they might read this
writing and to make known to me its interpretation" (infin.
instead of יְהוֹדְעֻנַּנִי) 5:15; לְהוֹדָעוּתָךְ דִּי נִכְתֻּב שֻׁם־גֻּבְרַיָּא "for your in-
formation, that we might write down the names of the men" Ezra
5:10 (added explanation or hysteron proteron); דִּי־לָא לְבַטָּלָא "(be
paid fully to these men) without delay," lit., "in order not to interrupt" 6:8 (instead of תְּבַטְּלוּן; see בְּטֵל).

(7) Conj. דִּי in composite conjs. (cf. דִּי II 6): דִּי לְמָה = **lest
perhaps** (cf. מָה no. 4); cf. כְּדִי; מִן־דִּי; הֵיךְ־דִּי (cf. הֵא); עַד־דִּי (cf.
עַד no. 2); בְּדִי * (cf. בְּ no. 4); עַל־דִּבְרַת דִּי (cf. דִּבְרָה); לָקֳבֵל דִּי (cf.
קֳבֵל no. II).

דַּיָּן *, ptc. pl. m. דַּיָּנִין q. & דָּאנִין k. (BL 51h, j): **judge.**
דִּי־לֶהֱוֹן דָּאנִין לְכָל־עַמָּה "(appoint judges) who may judge all the
people" Ezra 7:25. [Hebr. the same]. [1]

דִּין (qīl, BL 180k) abs. (& cst.), emph. דִּינָא & דִּינָה; m.:
(1) **judgment, judicial suit, sentence.** דִּינָה לֶהֱוֵא מִתְעֲבֵד מִנֵּהּ "let
judgment be carried out on him (the guilty one)" Ezra 7:26; אנתה
שׁליט למעבד בכולהון דין "You have power to mete out judgment on
all of them" *1QapGen* 20:13; עבד לי דין מנה "mete out judgment
on him for me" *1QapGen* 20:14; לא אכהל אגרנכי דין ודבב "I shall
have no power to institute a suit or process against you (f.)" *AP*
14:7; מקריא על אלהן מטא עלי בדינא "the appeal to our god (i.e., an
oath) has been laid upon me by the court-sentence" *AP* 7:6-7; על
דינא זי עבדן בסון "according to the action (i.e. divorce) that we
took in Syene" *AP* 14:3.
(2) **juridical pact, agreement, contract.** יעבד [לה] דין ספרא זנה
"he shall fulfill [for her] the pact of this document" *BMAP* 7:32;
יעבד לה דין שנאה "he shall fulfill for her the pact of divorce"
BMAP 7:39. (3) **court, tribunal.** דִּינָא יְתִב "the court sat (in

97

judgment)" Dan 7:10; דִּינָא יִתֵּב "the court shall sit (in judgment)" 7:26; דִּינָא <יְתֵב וְשָׁלְטָנָא> יְהִיב "the court <sat (in judgment) and dominion> was given (to the saints)" 7:22 (prob. hapl., cf. 7:14, 27); אהך בדין "I shall go to court" AP 8:22. (4) **justice.** אָרְחָתֵהּ דִּין "His (God's) ways are justice," i.e., just Dan 4:34. (5) **custom, practice** (cf. Hebr. מִשְׁפָּט). לא יכהל ענניה ולא ויישמע אנתתה יעבד דין [חדה] ותרתין מן נשי כנותה לי[ה]"Ananiah shall not be able to do to Yehoyishma', his wife, (according to) the practice of [one] or two of the wives of his colleagues," i.e., render to her her conjugal rights (see *Bib* 38 [1957] 269-71) *BMAP* 7:37-38; [ל]א תכהל יהוישמע ולא תעבד דין חד ו[ת]רין לעניניה בעלה "Yehoyishma' shall not be able to do to Ananiah, her husband, (according to) the practice of one or [t]wo . . ." *BMAP* 7:39-40. [Hebr. the same]. †

דַּיָּן * (*qattāl*, BL 191c), pl. דַּיָּנִין, emph. דַּיָּנַיָּא *: **judge.** מִנִּי . . . דַּיָּנִין "appoint . . . judges" Ezra 7:25; וּשְׁאָר כְּנָוָתְהוֹן דִּינָיֵא "and the rest of their colleagues, judges . . . " 4:9 (cf. דִּינָיֵא q., but read דַּיָּנַיָּא); קדם דמידת וכנותה דיניא "before Damidath and his colleagues, the judges" AP 6:5-6; הן אזד יתעבד מן דיניא "if inquiry be made of the judges" AP 27:8-9; זי יהבו לן דיני מלכא "(the share) which the king's judges granted to us" AP 1:3; דיני מדינתא "the judges of the province" AP 16:7; שאילת [קד]ם תר[וח ו]דינא "I was questioned [be]fore Tar[uḥ and] the judge, and I said before [the] judge" AP 16:3. [Hebr. the same]. †

דִּינָיֵא, gentilic term (Gk. Διναιοί), but read דַּיָּנַיָּא "the judges" (cf. דַּיָּן & the context s.v. אֲפָרְסָי) Ezra 4:9.

דֵּךְ m., דָּךְ f. (cf. דִּכֵּן & pl. אִלֵּךְ) dem. adj. & pron.: **that, that one.** בֵּית־אֱלָהָא דֵךְ "that house of God (in Jerusalem)" Ezra 5:17; 6:7, 8, 12; שֵׁשְׁבַּצַּר דֵּךְ "that Sheshbazzar" 5:16; קִרְיְתָא דָךְ "that city" 4:13, 15, 16, 19, 21; עֲבִידְתָּא דָךְ "that work" 5:8; ספרא

זך אנה יהבתה לכי "that deed I have given to you (f.)" *AP* 8:25; ידניה זך "that Yedaniah" *BMAP* 8:7, 8. Prepositive (BL 269b, c): זך ספרא זי יהנפקון עליכי כדב יהוה "that deed, which they produce against you, will be forged" *AP* 8:16; זך פתפא הב לה "give him that ration" *AD* 9:1-2; בזך עדנא "at that time" *Aḥ.* 70. -- Pron.: זך אבד "that one perished" *AD* 8:2; זך היתי עלי "that man brought (them) to me" *AD* 13:3; בזך שלח אנה עליכם "for this reason I am sending to you" *AP* 38:9.

דְּכֵן dem. adj. sg. m. & f. (= דָּךְ & דִּךְ): **that.** צַלְמָא דְכֵן "that statue (m.)" Dan 2:31; קַרְנָא דְכֵן "that horn" 7:20, 21.

דְּכַר * (*dakar*), pl. דִּכְרִין : **male.** בר דכר ונקבה "a child male or female" *AP* 15:17, 20; בר זכר ונקבה "a child male or female" *BMAP* 7:28-29. **ram.** דִּכְרִין "rams" (for sacrifice) Ezra 6:9, 17; 7:17. Cf. שאת = שאה *, pl. שאן : **ewe,** *Sefire I* A 21, 23. [Hebr. זָכָר]. †

דִּכְרוֹן * (*dakar-ān?*, BL 53t, 195y), emph. דִּכְרוֹנָה : **memorial, reminder, record.** וְכֵן־כָּתִיב בְּגַוַּהּ דִּכְרוֹנָה "and thus was written in it: A record" Ezra 6:2; מה כתבת א[נ]ה מתע[אל לזכרן לברי "what I, [Mati']el, have written (is) a reminder for my son" *Sefire I* C 1-3; זכרן זי בגוהי ודליה אמרו לי "A record of what Bagohi and Daliah said to me" *AP* 32:1-2; זכרן לם יהוי לך במצרין לממר "let it be a reminder to you in Egypt to say . . ." *AP* 32:2; זכרן על מנחם "a reminder about Menahem" *AP* 63:10. [Hebr. זִכָּרוֹן]. [1]

דָּכְרָן * (*dukrān*), emph. pl. דָּכְרָנַיָּא : **memorandum, record.** יְבַקַּר בִּסְפַר־דָּכְרָנַיָּא "let one search in the book of the records" Ezra 4:15 bis. [Hebr. זִכָּרוֹן]. †

דְּלַק *, ptc. sg. m. דָּלֵק : **burn** (cf. יְקַד). גַּלְגִּלּוֹהִי נוּר דָּלִק "its wheels were burning fire" Dan 7:9; [נוּר ד]לִק אִשָּׁן בֵּינָת[הוֹן]. "the ground between them burned with fire" *4QEn^d (4Q205)* 1 xi 6 [Hebr. דָּלַק]. [1]

דְּמָה * ptc. sg. m. דָּמֵה, f. דָּמְיָה : **be like, be similar.** . . . חֵיוָה רְוַה . . . דָּמֵה לְבַר־אֱלָהִין . . . דָּמְיָה לְדֹב "a beast . . . like a bear" Dan 7:5; "his appearance . . . is like a son of (the) gods" 3:25 (brachylogy, cf. לְבַב). Cf. the noun, בַּיִת לִדְמוּת בֵּיתָך "a house in the likeness of your house" *BMAP* 3:21. [Hebr. דָּמָה]. †

דְּנָה, דְּנָא, זנה (dinā), דֵּן m., דָּא & זא (da') f. (cf. pl. אִלֵּן, אֵל q., אִלֵּה *), dem adj. & pron.: **this** (cf. דָּךְ, דֵּךְ, that). רָזָא דְנָה "this mystery" Dan 2:18, 30, 47: 5:7 + ; בֵּית־אֱלָהָא דְנָה "this house of God" Ezra 5:13; 6:16; 7:24; בְּקַרְנָא דָא "in this horn" Dan 7:8; מִן יוֹמָא זנה ועד עלם "from this day and forever" *BMAP* 2:4; שנתא זא "this year" *AP* 21:3; בארעא דא כולא "in all this land" *1Qap-Gen* 19:10; רוחא דא באישתא "this evil spirit" *1QapGen* 20:28; בתר יומא דן "after this day" (see BL 66j) *1QapGen* 21:5. -- Prepositive (BL 269c). דְּנָה בִנְיָנָא "this building" Ezra 5:4; זנה ספרא "this document" *BMAP* 10:16; זא באישתא "this evil" *AP* 30:17; עד זנה יומא "until this day" *AP* 30:20; בזא שנתא "in this year" *AP* 71:14. -- Pron.: דְּנָה חֶלְמָא "this (was/is) the dream" Dan 2:36; 4:15; כָּל־דְּנָה יְדַעְתְּ "you knew all this" 5:22: 7:16; דְּנָה פִּשְׁרָא "this is the interpretation" 4:21: 5:25, 26; Ezra 4:11; דָּא־הִיא בָבֶל "Is (not) this (great) Babylon?" Dan 4:27; דְּנָה הוּא "(your dream) is this" 2:28; דְּנָה עִם־דְּנָה "together," lit., "this with that" 2:43; דָּא לְדָא "this against that" 5:6; דָּא מִן־דָּא "(different,) this one from that one" 7:3; זנה שמהת חילא "these (!) are the names of the army (soldiers)" *AP* 22:1: 34:2; זנה תחומי ביתא "these are the boundaries of the house" *BMAP* 4:8 (but אלה תחומי ביתא *BMAP* 3:7); לא מהידה זי ירתנך דן "this one shall not inherit you" *1QapGen* 22:34; ספר לה הושרתן לי "what is this (mā hī dāh) that you did not send

(*hawširten* f.) me a letter" *Hermopolis* 5:7-8. -- W. preps.:
אַחֲרֵי־דְנָה "hereafter" Dan 2:29, 45; בָּאתַר דְּנָה "after this" 7:6, 7;
בזנה "here," lit. "in this" *AD* 3:2 + ; לָקֳבֵל דְּנָה "because of this"
Ezra 4:16; עַל־דְּנָה "for this (reason)" 4:14, 15; 6:11; עַל־דְּנָה
"about this" Dan 3:16; מִקַּדְמַת דְּנָה "ago," lit., "before this" Ezra
5:11. See כִּדְנָה "so, thus"; [ה]עלי לי ולתרשה בזא בי לתמשל "you
shall not dominate me in this (respect) or assert your authority
over me about [it]" *Sefire III* 9.

▲ דָּנִיֵּאל name: **Daniel** ("God has judged," cf. Hebr. אֲבִידָן
שְׁפַטְיָה, אֱלִישָׁפָט,); passim in Dan.

דקק, 3 pl. דָּקוּ (as if < דוק *, but read as a v.l. דַּקּוּ , BL
166d): **be broken in pieces.** דָּקוּ . . . וַהֲווֹ כְעוּר "they were broken
in pieces . . . and became like chaff" Dan 2:35. [Hebr. the
same]. [1]

Haph./Aph. 3 sg. m. הַדֵּק * (for *hadiqq*), f. הַדֵּקֶת & הַדֵּקַת
(BL 167i), 3 pl. הַדִּקוּ; impf. 3 sg. m. יְהַדֵּק & יַדֵּק *, f. תַּדֵּק, w.
suff. תַּדְּקִנַּהּ (v.l. דְּ, BL 167i); ptc. sg. m. מְהַדֵּק, f. מַדֱּקָה & מַדְּקָה:
crush, break in pieces (cf. רעע חֲשַׁל,). וְכָל־גַּרְמֵיהוֹן הַדִּקוּ "and (the
lions) broke all their bones in pieces" Dan 6:25; אָכְלָה מַדֱּקָה "(the
beast) devoured (and) broke in pieces" 7:19: 7:7; וּתְדוּשִׁנַּהּ וְתַדְּקִנַּהּ
"and trample it down and break it to pieces" 7:23; הַדֵּקֶת הִמּוֹן "it
broke them (the feet of the statue) in pieces" 2:34; הַדֵּקֶת פַּרְזְלָא "it
crushed the iron" 2:45; כָּל־קֳבֵל דִּי פַרְזְלָא מְהַדֵּק וְחָשֵׁל כֹּלָּא [ ] כָּל־אִלֵּין
תַּדִּק וְתֵרֹעַ "just as iron crushes and shatters everything, [ ] it (the
fourth kingdom) will crush and smash all these (others)" 2:40
(about [ ], see פַּרְזֶל;) תַּדִּק וְתָסֵיף כָּל־אִלֵּין מַלְכְוָתָא "it (the fifth
kingdom) shall break in pieces all these kingdoms and bring
(them) to an end" 2:44. [Hebr. the same]. †

דָּר (*qāl*, BL 179h): **generation** (only sg., BL 202m).
עִם־דָּר וְדָר "(His dominion is) from generation to generation" Dan
3:33; 4:31. [Hebr. דּוֹר]. †

דריוש—דתא

▲ דָּרְיָוֶשׁ (< Pers. *Dārayawauš, Dārayawahūš*): **Darius.**
(1) דָּרְיָוֶשׁ מֶלֶךְ־פָּרַס "Darius, king of Persia" Ezra 4:24: 5:5-7;
6:1, 12-15, Darius I, son of Hystaspes (522-485 B.C.). (2) דָּרְיָוֶשׁ
מָדָיָא "Darius the Mede" Dan 6:1; דָּרְיָוֶשׁ מַלְכָּא "Darius, the king"
6:7, 10, 26: 6:2, 29. -- דריוהוש "Darius" *BMAP* 7:1; 8:1; *AP*
20:1 + ; דריהוש *BMAP* 6:1; דריוש *AP* 1:1. †

דְּרָע * (*dirā'*). pl. w. suff. דְּרָעוֹהִי, f.: **arm** (specifically
"upper arm," from elbow to shoulder; cf. אֶדְרָע & יַד). וּדְרָעוֹהִי דִּי
כְסַף "and its (the statue's) arms (were) of silver" Dan 2:32;
דרעיהא מא שפירן "her arms, how beautiful!" *1QapGen* 20:4.
[Hebr. זְרוֹעַ]. [1]

דָּת (> Pers.) abs. & cst., emph. דָּתָא, w. suff. דָּתְכוֹן, cst.
pl. דָּתֵי (see below), f.: **law, decree.** דָּת מָדַי וּפָרַס "the law of the
Medes and Persians" Dan 6:9, 13: 6:16; דָּתָא נָפְקַת "the decree
went forth" Dan 2:13: 2:15; חֲדָה־הִיא דָתְכוֹן "there is but one
decree for you" 2:9 (the sentence already announced); סָפַר דָּתָא
דִּי־אֱלָהּ שְׁמַיָּא "scribe of the law of the God of Heaven" Ezra 7:12,
21 (see סָפַר); דָּתָא דִּי־אֱלָהָךְ וְדָתָא דִּי מַלְכָּא "the law of your (Ezra's)
God and the law of the king" 7:26; בְּדָת אֱלָהָךְ דִּי בְידָךְ "according
to the law of your God, which is in your hand," i.e., how the
written law should be observed 7:14 (cf. 7:25; 6:18); כָּל־יָדְעֵי דָּתֵי
אֱלָהָךְ וְדִי לָא יָדַע "all those who know the law (read w. Gk. דָּת) of
your God and those who do not know " 7:25; הִשְׁתְּכַחְנָה עֲלוֹהִי בְּדָת
אֱלָהֵהּ "(unless) we find it (an accusation) against him in connec-
tion with the law of his God" Dan 6:6; יִסְבַּר לְהַשְׁנָיָה זִמְנִין וְדָת "he
will plot to change (the) times and (the) law" 7:25. [Hebr. the
same]. †

דֶּתֶא * (*dat'*, BL 183f), emph. דִּתְאָא (only sg., BL 202m):
grass (cf. עֵשֶׂב). דִּתְאָא דִּי בָרָא "the grass of the field" Dan 4:12,
20. [Hebr. דֶּשֶׁא]. †

102

דְּתָבַר * (< Pers. *dāta-bara* "legal expert"), emph. pl.
דְּתָבְרַיָּא "the justices" Dan 3:2, 3. †

ה

הַ, הָ, prefixed interrog. particle (BL 253g): **?** (cf. הֵן no.
2). הַאִיתָיךְ כָּהֵל "are you able?" (BL 253j) Dan 2:26; . . . אֱלָהָךְ
הַיְכִל לְשֵׁיזָבוּתָךְ "has your God been able to deliver you?" 6:21 (BL
253i); פָּלְחִין . . . לֵאלָהַי לָא אִיתֵיכוֹן הַצְדָּא "is it true that . . . you do
not serve my gods?" 3:14 (cf. BL 253i & s.v. צְדָא); פלסר [יש]אל
הצדא הני מליא אלה . . . שאל המו הצד[א מלי]א אלה אלה "Pilsar [will as]k,
'Are these words true?' . . . Ask them, 'Are these [wor]ds true?'"
Assur Ostr. 12-13 (*KAI* 233); הלבתי מלא את . . . למה לבתי מלא [את]
"Are you full of anger (at me)? . . . Why are [you] full of anger
(at me)?" (לבתי מלא = Akk. *malû libbāti*) *Assur Ostr.* 19-20 (*KAI*
233); הֲלָא גֻבְרִין תְּלָתָא רְמֵינָא "Did we not throw three men (bound
into the fire)?" Dan 3:24: 6:13; but: הֲלָא דָא־הִיא בָּבֶל "Is not this
the (great) Babylon?" 4:27 (cf. אֲלוּ ; Hebr. הֲלֹא 2 Kgs 15:36 = הִנֵּה
2 Chr 27:7).

הָא, interjection (BL 266c): **behold, lo, look** (see אֲלוּ &
הֲלָא). הָא־אֲנָה חָזֵה גֻבְרִין אַרְבְּעָה "lo, I see four men" Dan 3:25; והא
זנה חלקא "and look, this is the share (that comes to you)" *AP*
28:3; והא אלה תחומי ביתא זך "and note, these are the boundaries of
that house" *BMAP* 3:7; לא הות ארק לדרגמן זילי הא אנה "it was not
the land of Dargman; (it is) mine; look, (belonging to) me" *AP*
6:7; הא כן אנשא לא ידע איש "Lo, similarly man does not know
humanity" *Aḥ.* 116; הא באדין השבת בלבי "so then I thought to
myself" *1QapGen* 2:1; הא אנתתך דברה "Here is your wife; take
her away" *1QapGen* 20:27. [Hebr. הֵא]. [1]

הֵיךְ דִּי for הֵאכְדִי q. , . . . **look, as** הָא כְדִי k. : הָא־כְדִי * **as**
(BL 264w): הָא־כְדִי פַרְזְלָא לָא מִתְעָרַב עִם־חַסְפָּא "just as iron is not
mixed with clay" Dan 2:43 (see אֵיךְ). [Hebr. אֵיךְ]. [1]

הַדָּבַר (< Pers. *hada-bāra "companion"), cst. pl. הַדָּבְרֵי,
emph. הַדָּבְרַיָּא, w. suff. הַדָּבְרוֹהִי, הַדָּבְרֵי : **companion, counselor.**
הַדָּבְרֵי מַלְכָּא "the king's counselors" Dan 3:27; אֲמַר לְהַדָּבְרוֹהִי "(the
king) said to his companions" 3:24; הַדָּבְרֵי וְרַבְרְבָנַי יְבַעוֹן "my
counselors and my nobles sought me" 4:33: 6:8. †

הַדָּם (< Pers. *handāma), pl. הַדָּמִין : **limb, member.**
הַדָּמִין יִתְעֲבֵד "he will be made limbs," i.e., "he will be torn limb
from limb" (BL 338l) Dan 3:29: 2:5 (cf. μέλη ποιεῖν τινα,
2 Macc 1:16). †

¹ הֲדַר * (hadar), emph. הַדְרָה (v.l. הַדְרָא), w. suff. הַדְרִי :
glory, splendor. הַדְרָה יְהַב לְ . . . אֲבוּךְ "(God) gave glory to . . .
your father" Dan 5:18; וְלִיקָר הַדְרִי "and for the honor of my
glory" 4:27; וְלִיקָר מַלְכוּתִי הַדְרִי וְזִוִי יְתוּב עֲלַי "and for the honor of
my kingdom, my glory and my splendor returned to me" 4:33
(instead of הַדְרִי, prob. read w. Theod., Vg,. Rashi הַדְרֵת "I came
back"); יקיר הדרה לדרכי ארקא בניח[א] "and precious is his (a
king's) glory (= sovereignty) to those who walk on the earth in
tranquillity" Aḥ. 108. [Hebr. הָדָר]. †

² הֲדַר *, 1 sg. הַדְרֵת *: **come/go back.** See Dan 4:33 (s.v.
¹הֲדַר).

³ הֲדַר * **Pa.** (denom. verb, BL 273g), 2 sg. m. הַדַּרְתְּ, 1
sg. הַדְּרֵת (v.l. הִדְּרֵת); ptc. act. sg. m. מְהַדַּר : **glorify.** וְלֵאלָהָא . . . לֵהּ
לָא הַדַּרְתְּ "(you praised the gods of silver) but the God . . . you did
not glorify" Dan 5:23 (cf. אֲרַח): 4:31, 34. [Hebr. הָדָר]. †

הוּא הָא (hū'), הו (hū) m., הָא הִיא (hī'), הי (hī) f.; m. pl.
הִמּוֹ, הִמּוֹן, אִנּוּן ; f. pl. הִנִּי (KAI 233:12), אִנִּין ; indep. pers. pron.:
he, she, they. (1) As a subj. or anaphoric emphasis for a subj.:
(a) in a verbal cl.: הוּא יְשֵׁזְבִנָּךְ "(your God), may He deliver you!"

Dan 6:17; וְהִיא תְקוּם לְעָלְמַיָּא "and it (God's kingdom) shall stand forever" 2:44: 7:24; אסחור הו ירתנה "as for Asḥor, he will inherit her" *AP* 15:21; וְהו החסן ולא התיב לה "(goods were deposited), but he retained (them) and did not return (them) to him" *AP* 20:7; בני המו ישלמון לך "my children are to pay you" *AP* 10:15; ויזחל הא מן לד ספר[י]א "should he be frightened from effacing the inscriptions" *Sefire II* C 6; המו עמה הוו "they were with him" *AD* 5:7-8; עבידתך הו יעבד [לי] "he (your son) will do your service [for me (the king)]" *Aḥ.* 21; והיא הואת אנתתך "when she was (really) your wife" *1QapGen* 20:27; והוא הוא כהן לאל עליון "and he was a priest of God Most High" *1QapGen* 22:15. (b) in a nominal cl.: הוּא אֱלָהָא חַיָּא "He is the living God" Dan 6:27: 2:21, 22, 47; 7:7; Ezra 5:8; הוא בָּרֵךְ עַל בִּרְכוֹהִי "he (Daniel) got down upon his knees" Dan 6:11 (but read w. v.l. of v. 1 הֲוָא בָרֵךְ); הי אנתתי ואנה בעלה "she is my wife, and I am her husband" (marriage formula) *AP* 15:4; בניך מן מבטחיה . . . המו שליטן בה "your children by Mibtaḥiah . . . have authority over it" *AP* 9:7, 9-10, 12-13; אנון שליטין בחולקהון "they have authority over their portion" *1QapGen* 22:24; פהא בית שתוא להם "and that was a winter-house for them" *Barrakib* 18-19 (*KAI* 216).

(2) Pron. הוא, etc. = copula (BL 268d). (a) before a pred.: אֲנַתְּה־הוּא דָנִיֵּאל "Are you Daniel?" (BL 318e) Dan 5:13; אֲנַחְנָא הִמוֹ עַבְדוֹהִי "we are His servants" Ezra 5:11; די המון "(78 denarii) which are (19 tetradrachms)" *Bib* 38 (1957) 259, line 7(?); חנום הו עלין "(that the god) Khnum is against us" *AP* 38:7; הֲלָא דָא־הִיא בָבֶל "Is not this Babylon . . . ?" Dan 4:27; דִּי אִנִּין אַרְבַּע "(those beasts) which are four" 7:17; מָא־אִנּוּן שְׁמָהָת גֻּבְרַיָּא "What are the names of the men?" Ezra 5:4; מַן־הוּא אֱלָהּ דִּי "Who is the god who . . ." Dan 3:15; מן הו זי יקום קדמוהי "Who is he that can stand before him (a king)?" *Aḥ.* 107; מהידה זי ספר לה הושרתן "What is this that you did not send a letter?" *Hermopolis* 5:7; הצדא הני מליא אלה "Are these words true?" *Assur Letter* 12 (*KAI* 233).

הוא

תמת הי שליטה בכל . . . עֵנָני הו "I am Aḥiqar" *Ah.* 46; אנה הו אחיקר
שליט [ ] בכל "Tamut is with power over all . . . Anani is with
power [ ] over all" *BMAP* 2:11-12. (b) after a pred.: צנפר הי
מלה "a word is (like) a bird" *Ah.* 98; אַנְתָּה־הוּא רֵאשָׁה דִּי דַהֲבָא "the
head of gold is you" (BL 330q) Dan 2:38; חֲדָה־הִיא דָתְכוֹן "your
sentence is one," i.e., unchanged 2:9 (see the sentence in 2:5);
אִילָנָא . . . אַנְתָּה־הוּא "your dream . . . is this" 2:28; דְּנָה הוּא . . . חֶלְמָךְ
"(that) tree . . . is you" 4:17-19 (BL 330q); אגרא זך זילך הי "that
portico is yours" *AP* 5:4 (see לְ I 4); דִּי . . . גְּבוּרְתָא דִּי לַהּ־הִיא "to
Whom belongs might" Dan 2:20; ימאת לה כזי זילי הי "I swore to
him that it was mine" *AP* 8:24-25; עדי אלהן הם "this is the treaty
of gods" *Sefire I* B 6; כל זי רחם הא לי "anyone who is a friend of
mine" *Sefire III* 8; כָּל־קֳבֵל דִּי־מְהֵימַן הוּא "because he (Daniel) was
faithful" Dan 6:5 (BL 328d); גְּזֵרַת עִלָּיָא הִיא "it is a decree of the
Most High" 4:21; הן לא יעבד כות שנאה [הי] "if he (the husband)
does not act thus, divorced [is she]" *BMAP* 7:38-39; הן לא תעב[ד]ה
לה שנאהי "if she does not act (thus) toward him, she is divorced"
(*šanī'ā' hī*) *BMAP* 7:40; ועטה טבה הי "and it is a good counsel"
Ah. 57; והן קריה הא נכה תכוה בחרב והן חד אחי הא או חד עבדי "and if it
is a city, you must strike it with a sword; if it is one of my brothers or one of my slaves, . . ." *Sefire III* 12-13; אחתי היא "she is
my sister" *1QapGen* 20:27; כדב הו זנה ספרא . . . הו יצב "(whoever
produces a document), it is false; this document (that I . . . have
written) is valid" *BMAP* 10:16-17 (cf. כדב יהוה "it will be false"
AP 8:17).

(3) Explanatory הוא : עֵלְמָיֵא דְּהַוֵא (= דִּי־הוּא) שׁוּשַׁנְכָיֵא "men
of Susa, that is, Elamites" Ezra 4:9 (see דהוא); לִירַח אֲדָר דִּי־הִיא
שְׁנַת־שֵׁת "to the month of Adar, that is, (in) the sixth year (of the
reign of Darius)" 6:15 (cf. 7:8 Hebr.); יומן 20 הו עשרן "(within)
20, that is, twenty days" *BMAP* 11:7; שלם היא ירושלם "Salem,
that is, Jerusalem" *1QapGen* 22:13.

(4) Dem. הוא : מן עדנא הו "from that time" *El. Ostr.* A 2-
3 (*KAI* 270); יומא הו "on that day" *AP* 22:120; פלגא הו "that

106

half" *AP* 9:12; מַלְכַיָא אִנּוּן "those kings" Dan 2:44; הוּא צַלְמָא "that statue" 2:32 (BL 268e).

(5) Pl. pron. as obj.: יְהַב הִמּוֹ בְיַד "(God) gave them into the hand of (Nebuchadnezzar)" Ezra 5:12: 4:23; 5:5, 14bis, 15; 7:17; דִי . . . הוֹתֵב הִמּוֹ "whom . . . he settled (in Samaria)" 4:10; נפלג המו עלין "we shall divide them (the slaves) between us" *AP* 28:13-14; קרא המו שאל המו "call them (and) ask them" *Assur Letter* 12 (*KAI* 233); נְשָׂא הִמּוֹן רוּחָא "the wind lifted them up" Dan 2:35: 2:34; 3:22; רְמוֹ אִנּוּן "they threw them (into the den of lions)" 6:25; לא איתית המו מנפי "I did not bring them (the clothes) to Memphis" *Padua I* B 3; אשכח אנון . . . תבר אנון "(Abram) found them . . . he routed them" *1QapGen* 22:7, 9. -- Cf. מַנִּיתָ יָתְהוֹן "you appointed them" Dan 3:12; הוא רדף להון "he pursued them" *1QapGen* 22:9; לֵהּ לָא הַדַּרְתָּ "you have not honored Him" Dan 5:23; לה שבק אנה לה "I am not leaving him (alone)" *Hermopolis* 3:4. N.B. הוּא & הִיא do not occur in the accus.; but see הִי מלבש אנה "I have put it (the tunic) on" *Hermopolis* 4:6-7. [Hebr. sg. the same; pl. הֵם, הֵמָּה].

הֲוָה & הֲוָא , 3 sg. f. הֲוָת & הֲוָת (BL 154k, l), 2 sg. m. הֲוַיְתָ, 1 sg. הֲוֵית, הוית, & הות (*Hermopolis*), 3 pl. הֲווֹ, 1 pl. הוין ; impf. 3 sg. m. לֶהֱוֵה & לֶהֱוֵא (BL 152d), & יהוה (*yahwēh*), in the Old Ar. juss. יהוי ; 3 sg. f. תֶּהֱוֵה & תֶּהֱוֵא, in the Old Ar. juss. תהוי ; 1 sg. אהוה ; 3 pl. m. לֶהֱוֹן & יהוון ; 3 pl. f. לֶהֱוְיָן (BL 153g, *lehĕwyān* for *yahwiyān*); impv. sg. m. & f. הוי , pl. הֲווֹ & הֱווֹ (BL 153i); infin. מהוא (*mihwē'*); ptc. sg. m. הוה (*hāwēh*). (1) **become, happen.** לעקרה תהוי מלכתה כמלכת חל "(and for his son and) his offspring may his kingdom become like a kingdom of sand" *Sefire I* A 25; דִי לֶהֱוֵא "what will happen" Dan 2:28, 29, 45; כזי יוזא הוה במצרין "when the rebellion occurred in Egypt" *AD* 8:4; שלחי כל טעם זי הוה בביתי "write about whatever happens in my house" *Hermopolis* 1:12; וַהֲווֹ כְּעוּר "and (the metals) became like chaff" Dan 2:35a; אַבְנָא . . . הֲוַת לְטוּר "the stone . . .

הוה

became a mountain" 2:35b (BL 341x); תהוי ארפד תל "let Arpad become a mound" *Sefire I* A 32; הוה מלך באתור "(Esarhaddon) became king in Assyria" *Aḥ.* 5; הֵן תֶּהֱוֵא אַרְכָה לִשְׁלֵוְתָךְ "if perhaps it may become a lengthening of your tranquillity" Dan 4:24 (BL 366h); שלם יהוי לך "may peace come to you" *Aḥ.* 110; פתפא זי כזי חבזו הוה לי "the allowance which became mine" *AP* 43:8; אלהן בית [אבי הא ה]ות לאחרן "when (the) gods struck [my father's] house, [it came to belong] to another" *Sefire III* 24; דִּי־לְמָה לֶהֱוֵא קְצַף עַל־מַלְכוּת מַלְכָּא "lest His wrath come upon the realm of the king" Ezra 7:23 (cf. כֹּלָּא מְטָא עַל־נְבוּכַדְנֶצַּר, "all this happened to Nebuchadnezzar" Dan 4:25); אף הוה תרען . . . נדשו "it also happened: they destroyed . . . (five) gates" *AP* 30:9-10.

(2) **be.** עמודיא . . . זי הוו תמה "the pillars . . . which were there" *AP* 30:9; כזי [ע]דן יהוה נפלג המו "when it is time, we shall divide them" *AP* 28:13; ספינתא . . . עדן הוה אופשרה למע[בד] "as for the boat . . . , it is (ptc.) time to make its repairs" *AP* 26:3. (a) w. a prep.: [מן אנ]ת זי אחרי תהוה "[Whoever y]ou are, O King, who will be after me" *Bisitun* 64; כזי הוה לקדמן "(to re-build the temple) as it was before" *AP* 32:8; נכסין זי יהוון בין ענני ותמת "the goods that there may be between Anani and Tamut" (a married couple) *BMAP* 2:11; מַלְכוּ רְבִיעָיָא תֶּהֱוֵא בְאַרְעָא "there will be a fourth kingdom on the earth" Dan 7:23; הן יהוה באתר חד "if he (a traveler) will be in one place" *AD* 6:6; הלו כספה זי הוה בידה יהב[ ] "Look, the money that was in his hand he gave [to ?]" *Hermopolis* 6:6-7; הוא כפנא בארעא דא כולא "there was a famine in all this land" *1QapGen* 19:10; מַתְּנָתָךְ לָךְ לֶהֱוְיָן "let your gifts be for yourself," i.e., keep them, Dan 5:17; [ח]שבונוהי להוון לעלמין "his intuitions will remain forever" *4QBirthNoah^a* (4Q534) 1 i 11; צדקה יהוה לך יהוה "(the slave) will belong to you" *AP* 28:12; לך קדם יהו "it will be a merit for you before Yaho" *AP* 30:27; מַלְכִין תַּקִּיפִין הֲווֹ עַל־יְרוּשְׁלֶם "mighty kings have been over Jerusalem" Ezra 4:20; עֵין אֱלָהֲהֹם הֲוָת עַל־שָׂבֵי יְהוּדָיֵא "the eye of their God was upon the elders of the Jews" 5:5 (cf. חֲזָה עַל; על עטתה ומלוהי);

108

חיל [אתו]ר כלא הוו "by his counsel and words all the army (soldiers) were (guided)" *Ah.* 60-61; עִם־חֵיוַת בָּרָא לֶהֱוֵה מְדֹרָךְ "with the
beasts of the field shall your dwelling be" Dan 4:22; המו עמה הוו
"they were with him" *AD* 5:7-8; כול שביא די הואת עמה "all the
captives (collect. sg.) that were with him" *1QapGen* 22:25. (b)
w. a pred. noun: זי פרתרך תנה הוה "who was governor here" *AP*
27:4; והיא הואת אנתתך "and she was your wife" *1QapGen* 20:27;
הוא הוא כהן "he was a priest" *1QapGen* 22:15; לא אהוה לך אנתת "I
will not be to you a wife" *BMAP* 7:25; זכרן לם יהוי לך "let (this)
be for you a reminder" *AP* 32:2; ברא לם יהוה לי "surely, he shall
be to me a son" *Ah.* 2; הוה כסף חלרן 8 לירח חד "(interest) being at
the rate of 8 hallurin per month" *AP* 10:5-6; תהוה מרבית כספך חלרן
1 לירח [8] "the interest on your money shall be [8] hallurin per
month" *AP* 11:3-4; תונה הוה . . . אמן "a chamber being . . .
cubits" *BMAP* 4:6; קרבני למהוא "bring me forward to be (your
servant)" *4QLevi^b (4Q213a)* 1:18; גבר הוי "be a man!" *Padua I*
A 7. (c) w. a pred. adj.: שְׁלֵה הֲוֵית "I was at ease" Dan 4:1; מַלְכוּ
. . . תֶּהֱוֵא תַקִּיפָה "(the fourth) kingdom shall be strong (as iron)"
2:40: 2:42; לֶהֱוֵא שַׁלִּיט "(Daniel) should be powerful (in the kingdom)" 5:29; רַחִיקִין הֲווֹ מִן־תַּמָּה "stay far away from there," lit. "be
remote" Ezra 6:6: 4:22; ברה שליט יהוה למנשא "his son shall be
empowered to take" *AD* 2:4; דכין הוו "be clean" *AP* 21:6; חדה
ושריר הוי בכל עדן "be happy and prosperous at every time!" *AP*
30:3; זך ספרא . . . כדב יהוה "that document . . . will be false," i.e.,
a forgery *AP* 8:16-17 (cf. כדב הו *BMAP* 10:16).
    (3) Periphrastic usage, w. ptc.: (a) to indicate continuous
or repeated action (BL 292i, j; 293p, q): In the past: חָזֵה הֲוֵית "I
was gazing" Dan 4:7, 10 + ; אָתֵה הֲוָה וַעַד . . . מְטָה "(. . . a son of
man) was coming . . . and arrived at (the Ancient of Days)" 7:13
(BL 298b); הֲווֹ בָעַיִן "they were seeking" Dan 6:5: 6:4, 27; 7:8;
דִּי־הֲוָה צָבֵא הֲוָא קָטֵל "whomever he would he used to slay" 5:19 (8
instances); הוּא בָרֵךְ (read הֲוָא) "he used to kneel" 6:11a: 6:11b;
ירח בירח הוו שלחן עלי "month by month they were sending to me"

AP 17:3; כסף ומרבי זי אהוה משלם לך "money and interest that I shall be paying to you" *AP* 11:7; שקקן לבשן הוין וצימין "we were wearing sack-cloth and were fasting (ṣāyĕmîn)" *AP* 30:15; לקדמין "(as) formerly was done" *AP* 32:10-11; בגה זי הוה "his domain, of which (my father) was in possession" *AD* 8:2; הוא יתב בחברון "(Abram) was living in Hebron" *1QapGen* 22:2-3; [גבר]יא זי קדמן עמי הוו "the [men] who formerly were with me" *Bisitun* 74; [ ] זי הוה י[א]תה עליך הוית אשלח שלמך "who used to come to you; I used to send greetings to you" *AP* 41:3. In the future & as an impv.: לֶהֱוֵא מִתְיְהֵב לְהֹם יוֹם בְּיוֹם . . . דִּי־לֶהֱוֹן "let (that) be given to them day by day . . . that they may be (offering sacrifices)" Ezra 6:9-10: 6:8; Dan 6:3; מֶנִּי . . . דַּיָּנִין דִּי־לֶהֱוֹן דָּאֲנִין "appoint . . . judges who may judge" Ezra 7:25; . לָא לֶהֱוֵא עָבֵד דָּתָא "(whoever) will not obey the law . . . , let judgment be executed upon him" 7:26; דלמא תהוה אמר "lest you will say" *1QapGen* 22:22; הוי לקח שערן מן תשי "take barley from Tishi" *Hermopolis* 3:9; הוי חזית על ינקיא אלכי "be vigilant (f. ptc. cst.) of those little children" *Hermopolis* 7:2-3. (b) to indicate quality or status: דִּי־הֲוָת שָׁנְיָה מִן־כָּלְּהֵון "(the fourth beast), which was different from all of them" Dan 7:19; בְּטֵלַת . . . וַהֲוָת בָּטְלָא "(work on the temple) was interrupted . . . , and it remained interrupted" Ezra 4:24; אנה נכתני חויה והות מית "as for me, a serpent bit me, and I was (almost) dead (māyit)" *Hermopolis* 5:8. -- w. pass. ptc. (BL 296a-c): מַלְכוּ פְּלִיגָה תֶּהֱוֵה "it will be a divided kingdom" Dan 2:41: 2:42; יְדִיעַ לֶהֱוֵא־לָךְ "be it known to you" 3:18: Ezra 4:12, 13; 5:8; כן יד[י]ע יהוה לך "so shall it be known to you" *AD* 4:3; לֶהֱוֵא שְׁמֵהּ . . . מְבָרַךְ "Blessed be His name" Dan 2:20; בַּיְתָא דִּי־הֲוָא בְנֵה "the house that was built (many years ago)" Ezra 5:11; זי בנה הוה קדמין, "which was built before" *AP* 30:25: 32:4-5; ממנין הוו בין בגיא זילי "they had been appointed (mŭmannayîn; see BL 160v) in my domains" *AD* 5:5 (cf. גושכיא זי ממנין במדינת "the police who are set up in the province of . . ." *AP* 27:9). [Hebr. הָיָה].

110

הִיא : see הוּא .

הֵיכַל (< Akk. *ekallu*) cst. (& abs.), emph. הֵיכְלָא , w. suff.
הֵיכְלָהּ, הֵיכְלִי : **big house, temple, palace.** אֲזַל מַלְכָּא לְהֵיכְלֵהּ "the
king went to his palace" Dan 6:19; בְּהֵיכְלִי . . . הֲוֵית בְּבֵיתִי "I was
in my house . . . in my palace" 4:1; מְלַח הֵיכְלָא מְלַחְנָא "we ate the
salt of the palace," i.e., were obligated to the king, Ezra 4:14;
למפלח בבב היכלא "(I am unable) to serve in the gate of the palace," i.e., be in the king's service, *Aḥ.* 17; זי הקימת בתרע היכלא
"(your son), whom you set up in the gate of the palace" *Aḥ.* 44;
עַל־הֵיכַל מַלְכוּתָא דִּי בָבֶל "on the royal palace of Babylon" Dan 4:26;
כְּתַל הֵיכְלָא דִּי מַלְכָּא "(interior) wall of the royal palace" 5:5; הֵיכְלָא
דִּי בִירוּשְׁלֶם "the temple that is in Jerusalem" Ezra 5:14, 15;
6:5bis; Dan 5:2 (on Dan 5:3, see בַּיִת); הֵיכְלָא דִּי בָבֶל "the temple
that is in Babylon" (*or* "the temple of Babylon" [*RSV*]) Ezra
5:14b; יתבנא היכל מלכות רבא "a royal temple of the Great One will
be built" *4QEnᵍ (4Q212)* 1 iv 18. [Hebr. הֵיכָל]. †

הֵימַן : see אמן Haph.

הֵיתִי : see אָתָה Haph.

הֲךְ * (BL 143a, 144b, 146p), impf. 3 sg. m. יְהָךְ , 3 pl. m.
יהכון ; infin. מְהָךְ (perf., impv., ptc. from אֲזַל): **go, reach** (w. לְ of
place). לִמְהָךְ לִירוּשְׁלֶם עִמָּךְ יְהָךְ "(whoever wishes) to go to Jerusalem may go with you" Ezra 7:13; וִיהָךְ <כֹּלָא> לְהֵיכְלָא "let <all of
it (the vessels)> go to the temple (in Jerusalem [what is in < > is
prob. hapl.]) 6:5; עַד־טַעְמָא לְדָרְיָוֶשׁ יְהָךְ "until the report should
reach Darius" (not עַל "to" Darius; cf. "the decree went forth"
Dan 2:13; BL 280k, n. 1; *GBA* §178) 5:5; חוכמתה לכול עממיא תהך
"his wisdom will reach all people" *4QBirthNoahᵃ (4Q534)* 1 i 8;
תהך לבית אבוה "(the divorced woman) shall go to the house of her
father" *BMAP* 7:28; תהך לה אן זי צבית "she shall go wherever she

will" *AP* 15:28-29; רשיא בנפשכי למהך "you yourself have the right to go (and marry any man)" *Mur 19* 6; אף יהכון בדין ולא יצדקון "even (if) they go to court, they shall not win the case" *AP*10:19: 8:22; *BMAP* 10:15; תהך בחרב חילך "you will go with the sword of your army" *AP* 71:13; הן . . . יהכן חלב "if . . . they go to Aleppo" *Sefire III* 4-5; עד אהך אנה "until I go" *Sefire III* 6; תהך [ו]לא ביומיך "(beware lest) you go (die) before your time" *Ah.* 102; אנה כדי אמות ערטלי אהך די לא בנין "when I die, I shall depart bereft (and) without children" *1QapGen* 22:33; [ה]ן לבית עלמא תהך "[i]f you go to the house of eternity (before me)" *Mur 20* 7; [ה]ן אנה אהך לבית[א] דך "[i]f I go to that hou[se] (before you)" *Mur 21* 14.

הלך , **Pa.** ptc. sg. m. מְהַלֵּךְ : **walk, walk about.** מְהַלֵּךְ הֲוָה "(the king) was walking" Dan 4:26; אנה מהלך בין כרמיא "I was walking among the vineyards" *Ah.* 40; קום הלך ואזל וחזי כמן "rise, walk about, go, and see how great (is this land)" *1QapGen* 21:13-14.

Haph. ptc. pl. m. מַהְלְכִין (read Pa. מְהַלְכִין * BL 216s, 274n): חָזֵה גֻּבְרִין . . . מהלכין "(I) see men . . . walking (in the midst of the fire)" Dan 3:25; דִּי מהלכין בְּגֵוָה (those who walk with pride" 4:34. [Hebr. הָלַךְ]. †

הֲלָךְ (< Akk. *ilku*): **tribute, tax** (cf. מִנְדָּה, בְּלוֹ). הֲלָךְ לָא יִנְתְּנוּן "they will not pay tribute (to the king)" Ezra 4:13; וַהֲלָךְ מְתְיְהֵב לְהוֹן "and a tax was paid to them" 4:20; הֲלָךְ לָא שַׁלִּיט לְמִרְמֵא עֲלֵיהֹם "it shall not be lawful to impose a tax on them"(see לָא no. 3) 7:24; הלכא . . . יחשל על ביתא זילי "the tax . . . let him pay to my estate" *AD* 8:5-6. †

הִמּוֹ (in Ezra, BL 52p) & הִמּוֹן (in Daniel, BL 71p), indep. pers. pron.: **they, them**; see הוּא.

112

* הַמְיָנַךְ (< Pers. *hamyānaka*, *GBA* §189), emph. הַמְיָנְכָא * (k. המונכא, q. הַמְנִיכָא, v.l. הַמְיָנְכָא, etc. cf. *BH*): **chain, necklace.** אַרְגְּוָנָא יִלְבַּשׁ והמונכא דִי־דַהֲבָא עַל־צַוְּארֵהּ "he shall be robed in purple, with a chain of gold about his neck" (BL 331s) Dan 5:7: 5:16, 29. †

הֵן, conj. (1) introducing a conditional cl. (BL 365a): **if**, -- w. impf.: הֵן קִרְיְתָא דָךְ תִּתְבְּנֵא "if that city is rebuilt" Ezra 4:13: 4:16; Dan 2:6; 5:16; הֵן לָא תְהוֹדְעוּנַּנִי "if you do not make known to me" 2:5: 2:9; הן יאתה חד מלכן "if one of (the) kings comes" *Sefire I* B 28; הן כן תעבד "if you do so" *AP* 31:26; . . . הן תאמר פלאכהל לאשלח י[ד בך] "if you say . . . , then (*pa*- marking the apodosis) I shall not be able to raise a ha[nd against you]" *Sefire II* B 5-6. -- w. perf. (for the fut. [BL 365c]): הן לא שלמת לך כל כספך "if I do not pay you all your money" *AP* 11:7-8; . הן יהב לכי שלחי לי והלה יהב לכי . . "if he gives you (f.) . . . , send word to me; and if he does not (= *wahēn lāh*) give you" *Hermopolis* 2:9-10; אן אשכחת אש מהימן "if I find a trustworthy man" *Hermopolis* 4:9; הן כן עבדו . . . וצדקה יהוה לך קדם יהו "if they do so . . . , it shall be a merit for you before Yaho" *AP* 30:27; הן לו גלין אנפין על ארשם קדמן "if we had appeared before Arsames previously," lit. "had revealed our faces" (contrary-to-fact [see below on *Aḥ.* 35-36, 81]) *AP* 37:8. -- in a nominal cl.: הֵן עַל־מַלְכָּא טָב "if it seems good to the king" Ezra 5:17; הן על מראן טב "if it seems good to our lord" *AP* 30:23; הן צבה אנת ברי "if you, my son, wish (ptc. = verbal adj.)" *Aḥ.* 149; הן לו [אח]יק[ר] זך שבא ספר חכים . . . למה הו יחבל מתא "even if this Aḥiqar, the old man, be a wise scribe . . . , why should he corrupt the land?" *Aḥ.* 35-36. -- w. an ellipse: הֵן תִּתְרְמוֹן . . . וְהֵן לָא תִסְגְּדוּן . . תִּסְגְּדוּן לְצַלְמָא דִי־עַבְדֵת "if . . . you worship the statue that I have made; and if you do not worship . . . , you will be cast" Dan 3:15 (BL 366f); הֵן אִיתַי . . . וְהֵן לָא יְדִיעַ לֶהֱוֵא־לָךְ "if it be so (that you will cast us into the furnace) . . . ; but if not, be it known to you" Dan 3:17-18 (BL 365b); ערקי

113

אלפא מחר בשבה . . . הן לא נפשׁכ[י] אלקח "meet (f. impv.) the boat tomorrow, on the Sabbath . . . ; if not, I shall take your life" *El. Ostr.* 2-4 (*AH* I/1 p. 12 §5); הן להן שׁקרתם "if (you do) not (do so), you shall be unfaithful (to all the gods)"*Sefire III* 4; הן לו לא תכהל תהנצלנ[הי] "if you could not keep [him] (from evil)" *Aḥ.* 81. -- Postpositive הֵן : כְּעַן הֵן תּוּכֵל "Now if you can" Dan 5:16; אנחן הן קמן "if we rise" *BMAP* 5:13; [קדמ]ת מלך הן פקיד לך "[in the presence] of a king, if (something) is commanded you" *Aḥ.* 103.

(2) introducing an indir. question (BL 366h, i): **whether** (w. the idea of expectation or attempt): יתבקר . . . הֵן אִיתַי דִּי "let a search be made . . . (to see) whether it is (true [see אִיתַי 1 b]) that" Ezra 5:17; לה שלחתן הן חי אנה והן מת אנה "you (f. pl.) did not send, (asking) whether I were alive or whether I were dead" *Hermopolis* 5:8-9; הֵן תֶּהֱוֵא אַרְכָה לִשְׁלֵוְתָךְ "whether there may be a lengthening of your tranquillity" (BL 366h) Dan 4:24; קרא . . . אסי "he summoned . . . physicians of Egypt (to see) whether they could cure him" *1QapGen* 20:19.

(3) in a disjunction: **whether . . . or.** הֵן לְמוֹת הֵן לִשְׁרֹשׁו הֵן-לַעֲנָשׁ נִכְסִין "whether for death or for banishment or for confiscation of goods" Ezra 7:26.

(4) as enclitic: **perhaps.** למה הן יאבד "lest perhaps (the pot-herb) perish" *El. Ostr.* 3 (*AH* I/1 p. 12 §5); כזי הן הנדיז "when perhaps it is supervised(?)" *AP* 27:7. [Hebr. אִם, הֵן]. †

הַצְדָּא : see הֵ & צְדָא .

הַרְהֹר * (qalqāl, BL 192i; < root hrr), pl. הַרְהֹרִין : **imagination, fancy.** וְהַרְהֹרִין . . . יְבַהֲלֻנַּנִי "and the fancies (of my head) . . . alarmed me" Dan 4:2. [1]

ו

ו

וֵ, וִ, וְ, וִי, וּ, וַאֲלָהָא Ezra 6:12 (BL 36a-c, 262b, 263c-j),
prefixed conj. (*wa-*), coordinate (& subordinate). (1) **and.** Poly-
syndetic joins (BL 323b): מַתְּנָן וּנְבִזְבָּה וִיקָר "gifts and a reward
and glory" Dan 2:6: 2:10; 5:11, 14; Ezra 6:9; joining the last
word (BL 323c); חֲנַנְיָה מִישָׁאֵל וַעֲזַרְיָה "Hananiah, Mishael, and
Azariah" Dan 2:17; עַמְמַיָּא אֻמַּיָּא וְלִשָּׁנַיָּא "peoples, nations, and
languages" 3:4: 2:35, 45; 3:5, 7; 4:4; 6:25; Ezra 4:13, 20; 6:9, 17;
גשורן כון ודשש "beams, windows, and portals" *BMAP* 12:13;
דברה אזל ועדי "take her, go, and depart" *1QapGen* 20:27. --
joining two words (BL 324e, f): מַלְכָּא וְרַבְרְבָנוֹהִי שֵׁגְלָתֵהּ וּלְחֵנָתֵהּ
"the king and his nobles, his wives and his concubines" Dan 5:2,
3: 5:23; 6:8; כסף ודהב נחש ופרזל עבד ואמה "silver and gold, bronze
and iron, male and female slave" *AP* 10:9-10. -- joining words
freely (BL 324d): לֵאלָהֵי דַּהֲבָא וְכַסְפָּא נְחָשָׁא פַרְזְלָא אָעָא וְאַבְנָא "(they
praised) the gods of gold and silver, bronze, iron, wood, and
stone" Dan 5:4: 2:37; 3:2, 3, 21, 27; Ezra 7:17, 24. -- joining
words expressing from which and to which: מִן־אֱדַיִן וְעַד־כְּעַן "from
then and until now" Ezra 5:16; מן יומא זנה ועד עלם "from this day
for ever" *BMAP* 2:4 (cf. מן יומא זנה עד עלם *BMAP* 7:4); מן ארעא
ועד עלא "from bottom to top" *AP* 5:5; בחייך ועד מותך "during
your life until your death" *BMAP* 5:12. -- ו is omitted often (BL
286h, 351b): לָא חַכִּימִין אָשְׁפִין חַרְטֻמִּין גָּזְרִין יָכְלִין "no sages, sorcer-
ers, magicians, soothsayers were able" Dan 2:27: 5:11; שקלן 7
חלרן 7 פלג "7 shekels, 7 (and) a half hallurs" *BMAP* 2:6-7; עֲבַד
צְלֵם . . . אֲקִימֵהּ "(the king) made a statue . . . set it up" Dan 3:1;
אָכְלָה מַדֲּקָה "(the beast) devoured, broke in pieces" 7:19 (cf. אָכְלָה
וּמַדֲּקָה 7:7); קוּמִי אֲכֻלִי "Arise, devour!" (BL 299a) 7:5; . . . שְׁאֵלְנָא
כְּנֵמָא אֲמַרְנָא לְהֹם "we asked . . . thus we said to them" Ezra 5:9;
שלח עלי כן אמר "he has sent (word) to me; he said thus" *AD* 8:1;
דֵּךְ אֲתָא יְהַב אֻשַּׁיָּא "that one came; he laid the foundations" Ezra
5:16; בָּנַיִן . . . אֲתוֹ לִירוּשְׁלֶם "they have come to Jerusalem; . . .
they are building" 4:12 (see BL 341u); שָׂא אֵזֶל־אֲחֵת הִמּוֹ "take (the

sacred vessels), go, deposit them" (read as v.l. אֶחָת) Ezra 5:15;
נָפְלִין ... סָגְדִין לְצֶלֶם "fell down ... worshiped the statue" Dan 3:7;
חֲזַיִן לְגֻבְרַיָּא ... מִתְכַּנְּשִׁין "(the satraps) gathered together ... saw
the men" 3:27; ברך יאתה יקם דם ברי "your son must come (and)
avenge the blood of my son" *Sefire III* 11-12 (cf. את תאתה ותקם
דמי "you must come and avenge my blood" *Sefire III* 11); קרא
המו שאל המו "call them (and) ask them" *Assur Letter* 12 (*KAI*
233); זי לקחת כלא התב הב "anything you have taken, restore (and)
give" *AD* 12:7; עלו באגורא זך נדשוהי "they entered that temple
(and) destroyed it" *AP* 30:9; שלחן הודען "we sent (and) made
known" *AP* 30:29 (cf. שְׁלַחְנָא וְהוֹדַעְנָא Ezra 4:14); אזלת השכחת
לאחיק[ר] "I went (and) I found Aḥiqar" *Aḥ.* 76; שלחת קרית לממרה
"I sent (and) invited Mamre" *1QapGen* 21:21.

(2) **finally, to sum up,** completing an enumeration: וְכֹל
שִׁלְטֹנֵי מְדִינָתָא "(the satraps, pre-fects, officials), finally all the
governors of the provinces" Dan 3:2, 3; וְכֹל זְנֵי זְמָרָא "(horn, pipe,
lyre), to sum up, every kind of musical instrument" 3:10, 15;
וְפָלְחֵי בֵית-אֱלָהָא "(priests, levites, singers), finally all the servants
of the house of God" Ezra 7:24; וכול חכימיא "(none of the physicians, magicians), nor even any of the wise men (were able)"
1QapGen 20:20.

(3) **also, moreover** (cf. אַף): וּבְעוֹ דָנִיֵּאל "they also sought
Daniel" Dan 2:13; וַהֲקִימוּ כָהֲנַיָּא "moreover, they set up the
priests" Ezra 6:18; וּמָאנַיָּא ... הַשְׁלֵם "also deliver ... the vessels"
7:19; וּמַלְכִין תַּקִּיפִין הֲווֹ עַל יְרוּשְׁלֶם "also mighty kings were over
Jerusalem" 4:20; וְעַל-קַרְנַיָּא עֲשַׂר "also about the ten horns" Dan
7:20; וּלְגֻבְרִין ... אֲמַר לְכַפָּתָה "he also ordered men ... to bind"
3:20; וּמִנִּי שִׂים טְעֵם "moreover, I make a decree" Ezra 6:8, 11.

(4) **then, thereupon** (cf. אֱדַיִן no. 2; BL 351a): וַעֲבַדוּ
בְנֵי-יִשְׂרָאֵל כָהֲנַיָּא "then the Israelites, the priests, (the Levites,)
made" Ezra 6:16; וְדָנִיֵּאל עַל וּבְעָה "thereupon Daniel went in and
begged" Dan 2:16: 2:40, 49; 3:2, 4; 6:18, 25; 7:26; ואשא ידי אל
בעלש[מי]ן ויענני בעלשמי[ן] "then I lifted up my hands to Baal-

shamen, and Baal-shamen answered me" *Zkr* A 11 (*KAI* 202); [ויאמר ל]י בעלשמין] "thereupon Baal-shamen said to me" *Zkr* A 15 (*KAI* 202) cf. Degen, *AGI* 114-15. -- Often omitted: קְרֵא מַלְכָּא בְחַיִל "(then) the king cried aloud" Dan 5:7; עַלַּלת . . . מַלְכְּתָא "(then) the queen . . . entered" 5:10; always before עָנֵה מַלְכָּא וְאָמַר "(then) the king spoke up, saying" 2:5 + .

(5) **indeed, namely** (BL 324g): וּגְזֵרַת עִלָּיָא הִיא "indeed, it is a decision of the Most High" Dan 4:21; לָךְ טָרְדִין "namely, they shall drive you out" (BL 264r) 4:22; . . . וּמָה חַשְׁחָן וּבְנֵי תוֹרִין מְתִיהֵב "and let whatever is needed, namely, young bulls . . . , be given (to them)" (BL 324g) Ezra 6:9; וְאֻשּׁוֹהִי מְסוֹבְלִין "namely, its foundations (should) be maintained" Ezra 6:3; . . . שַׁכְלִלוּ וְשֵׁיצִיא בַּיְתָא דְנָה "they finished . . . indeed, they completed this house" (read rather וְשֵׁיצִיו) 6:14-15; . . . שְׁבֻקוּ לַעֲבִידַת בֵּית-אֱלָהָא דֵךְ וּלְשָׂבֵי יְהוּדָיֵא בֵּית-אֱלָהָא דֵךְ יִבְנוֹן "let the work on that house of God alone . . . indeed, let the elders of the Jews rebuild that house of God" 6:7 (יִבְנוֹן instead of לְמִבְנֵה; see לְ II 1 c); וּמִנִּכְסֵי מַלְכָּא "namely, from the treasures of the king" 6:8; מֶנִּי שָׁפְטִין וְדַיָּנִין "appoint judges (Hebr.), that is, judges (Ar.)" 7:25; בְּאַרְעָא שְׁבֻקוּ וּבֶאֱסוּר "leave (the stump) in the earth, namely, with a band" (BL 324g) Dan 4:12, 20; . . . לָא סָגְדִין וּצְלֵם "(they do not serve your gods); indeed, they do not worship . . . the statue" 3:12: 3:14, 18; עַד-עַתִּיק יוֹמַיָּא מְטָה וּקְדָמוֹהִי הַקְרְבוּהִי "he came to the Ancient of Days; indeed, they presented him before Him" 7:13: 4:14; ומן עלא כוין פתיחן תמה בתחתיה "at the lower end, that is, above, open windows are there" *AP* 25:6; ארע הי ולא בניה "it is a plot of ground, that is, not built (upon)" *BMAP* 3:5 (see בְּנָה no. 3).

(6) **but, however** (BL 264p): וְהֵן חֶלְמָא . . . תְּהַחֲוֹן "(if you do not tell me the dream . . .), but if you do show the dream" Dan 2:5-6; וּמַן-דִּי-לָא יִפֵּל "but whoever does not fall down (and worship)" 3:6; וְהֵן לָא "but if not, (be it known to you)" 3:18; וּפִשְׁרֵהּ לָא-מְהוֹדְעִין לִי "but they did not make known to me its interpretation" 4:4; וְאַנְתָּה כָּהֵל "but you are able" 4:15; וּכְדִי רַם לִבְבֵהּ "but

ו

when his heart was lifted up" 5:20; וְלָא שְׁלִם "but not yet finished" Ezra 5:16; וְדָנִיֵּאל בִּתְרַע מַלְכָּא "but Daniel was at the king's
court" Dan 2:49.

(7) **or** (= אוֹ *): וְלֶאֱסוּרִין "or for imprisonment," lit., "for
bonds" (BL 263n, 324j) Ezra 7:26; לכם . . . לבר וברה לכם אח ואחה
או גבר זי "(we shall not be able to sue) any son or daughter of
yours, a brother or sister . . . of yours, or any man to whom" *AP*
25:10-11; בשמי . . . ובשם בני "in my name . . . or in the name of
my sons" *AP* 25:12; ינתן לכם או לבניכם ולמן זי "he shall pay you or
your sons or whomever" *AP* 20:14; עִיר וְקַדִּישׁ נָחִת "a Watcher or
a Holy One coming down" (BL 324h) Dan 4:10, 20; . . . מִן עִירִין
ומן קדישין "from Watchers . . . or from Holy Ones" *1QapGen* 2:1
(cf. Dan 4:14).

(8) introducing a consequence or conclusion: **and so, so
that:** וְשָׂבֵי יְהוּדָיֵא בָּנַיִן "and so the elders of the Jews (were) rebuilding" Ezra 6:14; וְלָא־בַטִּלוּ הִמּוֹ "so that they did not interrupt
them" 5:5; וַאֲמַר לְהוֹבָדָה "and so (the king) gave orders to destroy" Dan 2:12; וְכָל־אֲתַר לָא־הִשְׁתְּכַח לְהוֹן "so that not a trace of
them was found" (BL 353e; cf. 350) Dan 2:35; ותהוה מרבית כספך
1 לירח [8] חלרן "and so the interest on your money shall be [8]
hallurs per month" *AP* 11:3-4; ואחזי ידך רבתא בה "(mete out
justice to him) so that I may see your great hand against him"
1QapGen 20:14-15; וְאִנְדַּע דִּי . . . תְּהַחֲוַנַּנִי "(tell me the dream) so
that I may know that . . . you are making known to me (its meaning)" Dan 2:9; שלח לי לבשה זי עליך ויחטנה "send me the garment
that you are wearing, so that they can sew it" *El. Ostr.* 4-5 (*RHR*
103 [1945] 20); הוי יהבת עבר לוחפרע ויהוי זבן גשרן "give grain to
WḤPRʿ so that he may buy beams" *Hermopolis* 2:14; וְרוּמֵהּ יִמְטֵא
לִשְׁמַיָּא "(the tree grew) so that its top reached to heaven" Dan
4:8, 17 (cf. 4:19: 'your greatness has grown וּמְטָת so that it
reaches to heaven"); ואל יפק חצר וליתחזה ירק "may the grass not
come forth so that no green may be seen" *Sefire I* A 28 (see *AGI*
p. 128).

118

ו

(9) introducing a purpose cl.: **in order that, so that.** שלח
לי ואקבל עליהן תנה "send me word so that I may complain here
against them" *Hermopolis* 2:10; שלחי לתבי ותושר לכי עמר "write
to Tabi so that she may send you wool" *Hermopolis* 2:6-7; וְיִשְׁתּוֹן
בְּהוֹן "(the king bade them bring the vessels) in order that they
might drink from them" Dan 5:2; וְיַצִּיבָא אֶבְעֵא־מִנֵּהּ "(I approached
one of those standing by) in order that I might learn the truth
from him" 7:16; וְקִרְיְתָא דָךְ לָא תִתְבְּנֵא "(decree that these men
stop), in order that that city not be rebuilt" Ezra 4:21; ויעבד
פתכרן "(give him the same provision), so that he may make
sculptures" *AD* 9:2; שבק חמר ולא יסבלנהי "the ass relinquished (its
burden) in order not to carry it" *Aḥ.* 90; [אמרי] עלי די אחי הוא ואחי
"[say] about me, 'He is my brother,' in order that I may live"
1QapGen 19:20; אסמוך ידי עלוהי ויחה "(that) I should lay my
hands upon him in order that he might live" *1QapGen* 20:22;
אנחן בען אלף ויתונה לכן "we are looking for a boat so that they may
bring it to you" *Hermopolis* 6:9-10. -- Mixed pleonastic construction (see לְ II 1 c; BL301e): וּפִשְׁרָא לְהַחֲוָיָה "(Daniel begged
for time) in order to make known the meaning" (infin. instead of
יְהַחֲוֵה) Dan 2:16; וְרַחֲמִין לְמִבְעֵא "(Daniel told his companions) to
beg for mercy (of the God of heaven)" (infin. instead of יִבְעוֹן)
2:18.

(10) introducing an obj. or subj. cl.: **that, and** (cf. דִּי III 5
& לְ II 2). אמר למלכא וישלח אנתתה מנה "tell the king that he should
send his (Abram's) wife away from him" *1QapGen* 20:23; לְמָא
דִי־תַעַבְדוּן . . . וּמִנִּכְסֵי מַלְכָּא . . . נִפְקְתָא תֶּהֱוֵה מִתְיַהֲבָא "(I decree) for
what you shall do . . . that from the royal revenues . . . the cost
shall be paid" Ezra 6:8; דָּתָא נֶפְקַת וְחַכִּימַיָּא מִתְקַטְּלִין "the sentence
went forth that the wise men were to be slain" (BL 293o) Dan
2:13; אחוב ואנתן לך כסף א[בג]דן "I shall become liable to pay you
a fine" *BMAP* 11:6; לא יכהל עניה ולא יעבד "Ananiah will not be
able not to do" *BMAP* 7:37-38 (cf. [ד]ין לאכהל לאשלח "I shall not
be able to raise a han[d]" *Sefire II* B 6; לא יכלון ינפקון "they will

119

ו

not be able to produce (a document)" *BMAP* 10:15). -- With an
ellipse: וְהַלְבִּישׁוּ . . . אֲמַר "(Belshazzar) commanded . . . and they
clothed (Daniel)" Dan 5:29: 6:17, 25; Ezra 6:1; (cf. wt. ellipse:
וְהֻסַּק דָּנִיֵּאל . . . לְהַנְסָקָה אֲמַר לְדָנִיֵּאל "[the king] bade [them] take up
Daniel . . . so Daniel was taken up" 6:24); שָׂם טְעֵם וּבַקַּרוּ "(the
king) decreed, and they searched" Ezra 6:1; בְּעָא מִן מַלְכָּא וּמַנִּי
"(Daniel) requested of the king that he appoint" Dan 2:49; שְׁפַר
מִלְכִּי יִשְׁפַּר עֲלָיךְ קֳדָם דָּרְיָוֶשׁ וַהֲקִים "it pleased Darius to set up" 6:2;
וַחֲטָאָךְ . . . פְרֻק "let my counsel be acceptable to you . . . break off
your sins" (read חֲטָאַיךְ) 4:24.

(11) introducing a modal cl. (cf. ל II 5): לתשלח לשנך בניהם
ותאמר "you shall not interfere with them, saying," lit., "shall not
send your tongue between them" *Sefire III* 17-18 (*AGI* p. 128).

(12) introducing a circumstantial cl. (cf. BL 352a): וספרא
זנה בידכי "(another document shall not be admitted) as long as
this deed is in your (f.) hand" *AP* 8:18; ואנה ימין סב לא כהל הוית
בידי "(she supported me) when I was old in days and unable (to
work) with my hands" *BMAP* 9:17; וְרַעְיֹנֹהִי יְבַהֲלֻנֵּהּ "(Daniel was
dismayed) as his thoughts alarmed him" Dan 4:16; וּמַנְדְּעִי עֲלַי יְתוּב
"(I lifted up my eyes to heaven) as my reasoning returned (to
me)" 4:31; חָזֵה הֲוֵית וְקַרְנָא דִכֵּן עָבְדָה קְרָב "I was gazing, as that
horn made war" 7:21; ועמי תמלל "(she suppressed her emotion)
as she spoke to me" *1QapGen* 2:13; וְזִמְנָא מְטָה וּמַלְכוּתָא הֶחֱסִנוּ
קַדִּישִׁין "and the time came, when saints received the kingdom"
Dan 7:22; וְהֻסַּק דָּנִיֵּאל מִן־גֻּבָּא וְכָל־חֲבָל לָא־הִשְׁתְּכַח בֵּהּ "when Daniel
was taken up from the den, no damage was found on him" (cf.
BL 353e) 6:24; וַאֲמַר־לִי וּפְשַׁר מִלַּיָּא יְהוֹדְעִנַּנִי "so he told me, making
known to me the meaning of the things" 7:16; ואנה נכתני חויה והות
מית "(you did not write to me) even though a serpent had bitten
me and I was almost dead" (*māyit*) *Hermopolis* 5:8; והיא הואת
אנתתך "(you said, 'She is my sister'), when she was (really) your
wife" *1QapGen* 20:27; ודמעי נחתן "(in sorrow I spoke), as my
tears ran down (my cheeks)" *1QapGen* 20:12.

(13) introducing an apodosis (cf. אֱדַיִן no. 3 & אַחַר no. 3): כזי צידא עבד אנה תנה ובאתרא זנה משתרה אנה "whenever I go hunting there, in this place I take my lunch" *Cilician Inscr.* 4-6 (*KAI* 261); הן כן עבדו . . . וצדקה יהוה לך "if they do so (at your bidding) . . . , it will be a merit for you" *AP* 30:27; אהאבד ספר[י]א . . . ויזחל הא מן לד ספר[י]א "(whoever will say), 'I shall destroy the inscriptions . . . should that one be frightened from effacing the inscriptions" *Sefire II* C 4-6; הן תאמר . . . פלאכהל לאשלח י[ד] "if you say . . . , then I shall not be able to raise a hand" *Sefire II* B 5-6.

(14) ו after the subj. of a composite nominal cl.: וְקַרְנָא דִּכֵּן וְעַיְנִין לַהּ "as for that horn, it had eyes" Dan 7:20; כעת אנת וגרדא זילי עבידא לא איתי לך "now, as for you, you have no business with my domestic staff" *AD* 12:9; וכל מלכיא זי סחרתי או כל זי רחם הא לי . . . ואשלח מלאכי א[ל/ל]וה . . . פתחה לי ארחא "as for all the kings of my vicinity or anyone who is a friend of mine, when I send my messenger to him . . . , the road shall be open to me" (see *AGI* 134s) ו[מ]לכן [זי סחר]תי ויקרק קרקי אל חדהם . . . הן השב זי לי "as for kings [of my vicin]ity, if a fugitive of mine flees to one of them . . . if he has restored mine, I will restore [his]" *Sefire III* 19-20.

ז

The letter ז in Old Aramaic designated two primitive sounds: (1) *z*; (2) *ḏ*, later pronounced *d* and written with the letter ד : *ḏī* = זִי & *ḏī* = דִּי .

זְבַן * ptc. pl. m. זָבְנִין : **buy.** ביתא זי זבנת מן אוביל "the house that I bought from Ubil" *BMAP* 4:3; ביתי זי זבנת בכסף "my house that I bought with money" *BMAP* 9:3; זבן לה בסודם בי "(Lot) bought himself a house in Sodom" *1QapGen* 21:6. In transferred sense: עִדָּנָא אַנְתּוּן זָבְנִין "you are buying time," i.e., to forestall the sentence, Dan 2:8; זבניא "buyers" (of a plot of land), *Bib* 38 (1957) 259, line 9.

Pa. perf. 3 sg. m. זֶבֶן *: **sell.** גבר זי תזבנון לה ביתא זך "a man to whom you will sell that house" *AP* 25:11; או' מזבנה "U. the seller" *Bib* 38 (1957) 259 line 11. [1]

זָהִיר * (*zahīr*, BL 188h). pl. m. זְהִירִין, adj.: **cautious, attentive.** זְהִירִין הֱווֹ שָׁלוּ לְמֶעְבַּד "be cautious to cause negligence" Ezra 4:22. Cf. זהר Ithpe. impv.: דכין הוו ואזדהרו "be (ritually) clean and take heed!" *AP* 21:6; אזדהרי בה "be attentive to her" *Hermopolis* 2:17; 4:8. [Hebr. נִזְהָר]. [1]

זוד *: see זיד.

זון *, **Hithpe.** impf. 3 sg. m. יִתְּזִין (daghesh forte because of t-z, BL 46m, 145n, 220x, y; cf. שִׂים Hithpe.); v.l. יִתְּזִין : **nourish oneself, take food.** וּמִנֵּהּ יִתְּזִין כָּל־בִּשְׂרָא "and all flesh was fed from it (the tree)" Dan 4:9; מתזנה ומכסיא "(you [my wife] will) be fed and clothed (in my house)" *Mur 20* 10. Cf. מָזוֹן "food" Dan 4:9, 18. [Hebr. the same]. [1]

זוע *, ptc. pl. m. זָאֲעִין k., זָיְעִין q. (v.l. זַיְעִין ; BL 51h, j): **tremble, quake.** לֶהֱוֺן זָאֲעִין וְדָחֲלִין מִן־קֳדָם "(people) must tremble and fear before (God)" Dan 6:27: 5:19. [Hebr the same]. †

זיד , **Haph.** infin. הֲזָדָה : **act proudly.** רוּחֵהּ תִּקְפַת לַהֲזָדָה "his spirit was hardened to deal proudly" (see לְ II 5) Dan 5:20. [Hebr. זִיד *]. [1]

זִיו * (< Akk. *zīmu* usually in the pl.), sg. w. suff. זִוִי (v.l. זִיוִי, זְוִי), זִיוַהּ ; pl. w. suff. זִיוָיְ k. (זִיוָךְ q. = pl., BL 78o), זִיוֹהִי m.: (1) sg. **splendor.** צַלְמָא דְּכֵן רַב וְזִיוֵהּ יַתִּיר "that statue (was) mighty, and its splendor exceeding" Dan 2:31; in a transferred sense: וְזִיוִי יְתוּב עֲלַי "and my splendor returned to me" 4:33 (cf. [1] הֲדַר). (2) pl. (BL 202n, 305e) **face, countenance, color** (used always of the face changed by terror): וְזִיוַי יִשְׁתַּנּוֹן עֲלַי "(I was alarmed), and my color changed" Dan 7:28; וְזִיוָיךְ אַל־יִשְׁתַּנּוֹ "let not your countenance change" 5:10; וְזִיוֹהִי שָׁנַיִן עֲלוֹהִי "(the king was alarmed), and his countenance changed on him" 5:9; מַלְכָּא זִיוֹהִי שְׁנוֹהִי "the king, his countenance changed" 5:6 (for the dative suff., see *Bib* 45 [1964] 227); cf. וּצְלֵם אַנְפּוֹהִי "and the expression of his face" Dan 3:19; צלם אנפיהא "the form of her face" *1QapGen* 20:2. †

זָכוּ (< Akk. *zakūtu*, as a legal term, *GBA* §188), f.: (legal) **innocence.** קֳדָמוֹהִי זָכוּ הִשְׁתְּכַחַת לִי "innocence was found in me before Him" (BL 338l) Dan 6:23; cf. מן קטל זכי "from an undeserved death" *Ah.* 46. N.B. the Ar. root differs: דך (*dk*), Hebr. זַ "clean": דכין הוו "be (ritually) clean!" *AP* 21:6 (see F. Rosenthal, *JBL* 91 [1972] 552). [1]

▲ זְכַרְיָה : a Hebr. name, **Zechariah**, a prophet Ezra 5:1; 6:14. †

זמן (denom. verb, BL 276x), perf. 2 pl. m., assimil. (BL 32a), either partially (*hizd-*) or totally (*hizz-*), **Hithpe.** (BL 109m) הִזְדְּמִנְתּוּן q., הִזַּמִנְתּוּן k.; or **Hithpa.** (BL 111k) הִזְדְּמִנְתּוּן (so many MSS. & Edd.), הִזַּמִנְתּוּן k.: **agree together, conspire.** מִלָּה כִדְבָה . . . הִזְמִנְתּוּן לְמֵאמַר קֳדָמַי "you have conspired to speak before me . . . a deceptive word" Dan 2:9 (v.l. **Haph.** הַזְמִנְתּוּן "you have agreed together to say"); כול אלן אזדמנו כחדא לקרב "all these (kings) united together for battle" *1QapGen* 21:25. [1]

זְמַן & vocalized questionably זְמָן (*zaman, GBA* §52), emph. זִמְנָא ; pl. (BL 218e) זִמְנִין , emph. זִמְנַיָּא , m.: **time,**

moment, season (cf. עִדָּן). דִּי זְמָן יִנְתֶּן־לֵהּ . . . בְּעָא "he begged . . . that one give him time (to interpret)" Dan 2:16; עַד־זְמַן וְעִדָּן "(the beasts' lives were prolonged) for a season and a time" 7:12; וְזִמְנָא מְטָה "and the time arrived (when the saints attained the kingdom)" 7:22; בֵּהּ־זִמְנָא "at that moment" (dem. suff. assimil. to proleptic pron. suff., *GBA* §89) Dan 3:7, 8; 4:33; Ezra 5:3; זִמְנִין תְּלָתָה בְּיוֹמָא "(he used to pray) three times in the day" Dan 6:11, 14; יִסְבַּר לְהַשְׁנָיָה זִמְנִין וְדָת "he intends to change times and (the) law" 7:25; וְהוּא מְהַשְׁנֵא עִדָּנַיָּא וְזִמְנַיָּא "and He changes the times and seasons" 2:21, cf. עַד דִּי עִדָּנָא יִשְׁתַּנֵּא "till the time changes" 2:9; בזמן די תאמר לי "at the moment when you tell me" *Mur 27* 5. [Hebr. זְמָן]. †

זְמָר * (*zamār*, BL 187d), emph. זְמָרָא : **music, musical instrument.** קָל . . . כֹּל זְנֵי זְמָרָא "the sound of . . . every kind of musical instrument" Dan 3:5, 7, 10, 15. [Hebr. זִמְרָה]. †

זַמָּר * (*qattāl,* BL 191c) emph. pl. זַמָּרַיָּא, m.: **singer, cantor.** זַמָּרַיָּא "singers (in the temple)" Ezra 7:24. [1]

זַן * (< Old Pers. *zana*), cst. pl. זְנֵי : **kind, sort.** כֹּל זְנֵי זְמָרָא "every kind of music" Dan 3:5, 7, 10, 15; זן זן ירח בירח "(they were sending me) each item month by month," lit., "kind (for) kind" *AP* 17:3. [Hebr. the same]. †

זְעֵיר * (*qutayl,* BL 190v), f. sg. זְעֵירָה, adj.: **small.** קֶרֶן אָחֳרִי זְעֵירָה "another horn, a small one" Dan 7:8; איש זעיר "a little man" *Aḥ.* 114, 145; זעירן אנחנה "we are few" *AP* 37:7; ובזעריהם [אל תבחת] "(in a multitude of children, do not exult), and in the fewness of them [do not be ashamed]" *Aḥ.* 106; שומן זוערן על "tiny marks on his thighs" *4QBirthNoah (4Q534)* 1 i 3. [Hebr. the same]. [1]

124

זְעֵק : **cry out.** לְדָנִיֵּאל בְּקָל עֲצִיב זְעִק "(the king) cried out in a tone of anguish to Daniel" Dan 6:21. [Hebr. זָעַק]. [1]

זְקַף *, pass. ptc. sg. m. זְקִיף : **lift up.** זָקִיף יִתְמְחֵא עֲלֹהִי "(the guilty one), lifted up, shall be impaled on it (a beam pulled from his house)" Ezra 6:11 (cf. Akk. *ana iṣē izzagapu-šunuti* "they lifted them up on beams" CAD s.v. *zaqāpu* d; BL 339n). [Hebr. זָקַף]. [1]

▲ זְרֻבָּבֶל : **Zerubbabel,** Ezra 5:2.

זְרַע (*zar'*, BL 183e), cst. (& abs.): **seed; offspring** (cf. עֵקָר). בית זרע א׳ 30 "an estate (holding) 30 ardabs of seed" *AD* 8:2. 4; מִתְעָרְבִין לֶהֱוֹן בִּזְרַע אֲנָשָׁא "(so) they will mix with one another by the seed of man," i.e., in marriage Dan 2:43; אנה ובני "I and my children and my offspring" *AP* 13:8; מנך זרעא וזרע זילי "this seed (child) is from you" *1QapGen* 2:15; די אנה יהב לך ולזרעך "(this land) which I am giving to you and your descendants" *1QapGen* 21:10; ינסחוהי וזרעה "may they extirpate him and his offspring" *Tema* A 14 (*KAI* 228). [Hebr. זֶרַע]. [1]

ח

אַף קֳדָמָיךְ . . . חֲבוּלָה (*qatūl,* BL 189m): **evil, crime.** חֲבוּלָה לָא עַבְדֵת "also before you . . . I have done no evil" Dan 6:23; חבל רב חנבלו בא[רעא] "great evil they inflicted on [the land]" *4QEn-Giantsᵈ (4Q532)* 2:9. [1]

חַבֵּל *, **Pa.** 3 pl. w. suff. חַבְּלוּנִי ; impv. pl. w. suff. חַבְּלוּהִי (BL 53q); infin. חַבָּלָה ; act. ptc. sg. m. מְחַבֵּל *; pass. ptc. sg. m. מְחַבַּל *. **Hithpa.** impf. 3 sg. f. תִּתְחַבַּל : **hurt, destroy.** וְלָא חַבְּלוּנִי "and they (the lions) have not hurt me" Dan 6:23; גדו

אִֽילָנָא וְחַבְּלֽוּהִי "cut down the tree and destroy it" 4:20; לְחַבָּלָה
בֵּית־אֱלָהָא דֵּךְ "(who will put forth a hand) to destroy that house of
God" Ezra 6:12 (cf. לְ II 1a); איש מנדעם באגורא זך לא חבל "no one
did any harm to that temple" AP 30:14; למה הו יחבל מתא עלין
"why should he destroy the land against us?" Aḥ. 36; [ברא זי
רבי]ת חבלך . . . "[the son whom] you [have raised] . . . has hurt
you" Aḥ. 44; [שׁ]לם ומחבל לא איתי "(we have) [p]eace, and there
is no one to hurt (us)" Padua I A 7; [לא] אשתכח לן ומנדעם מחבל
"and [no]thing destructive was found in us" AP 27:2; . . . מַלְכוּ דִּי
לָא תִתְחַבַּל "a kingdom that . . . will not be destroyed" Dan 2:44;
6:27; 7:14. [Hebr. חָבֵל]. †

חֲבַל * (ḥabāl, BL 187d), emph. חֲבָלָא, m. **damage, harm.**
חֲבָל לָא־אִיתַי בְּהוֹן "there is no damage on them (the men in the
furnace)" Dan 3:25; וְכָל־חֲבָל לָא הִשְׁתְּכַח בֵּהּ "and no damage was
found on him (Daniel)" 6:24 (cf. וְ no. 10); לְמָה יִשְׂגֵּא חֲבָלָא "why
should damage increase (to hurt the king)?" Ezra 4:22. †

חֲבַר * (ḥabir, BL 185v), pl. w. suff. חַבְרוֹהִי (BL 218b):
companion, ally. וּבְעוֹ דָּנִיֵּאל וְחַבְרוֹהִי "and they sought Daniel and
his companions" Dan 2:13, 17, 18; למלך סודם ולכול חברוהי "(the
kings prevailed) over the king of Sodom and all his allies" 1Qap-
Gen 21:26. [Hebr. חָבֵר]. †

חַבְרָה * (qatil, BL 186y), pl. w. suff. חַבְרָתַהּ (v.l. חַבְרָתָהּ,
BL 81z): **female companion.** וְחֶזְוַהּ רַב מִן־חַבְרָתַהּ "and its (the
horn's) appearance was greater than its (ten) companions" Dan
7:20. [Hebr. *חֲבֵרָה]. [1]

▲ חַגַּי (v.l. חַגִּי): **Haggai,** a prophet, Ezra 5:1; 6:14. †

חַד m. (< qatal, 'aḥad BL 185q, 249e), f. חֲדָה, adj. (1)
one, the same. כס כסף חד "a silver cup, one" AP 61:4; הן יהוה

126

חד

באתר חד יתיר מן יום חד "if he (a traveler) is in one place more than one day" *AD* 6:6; חֲדָה־הִיא דָתְכוֹן "(there is but) one sentence for you" Dan 2:9; פותיה ואורכה משחה חדה "its width and its length (are of) the same measurement" *5QNJ (5Q15)* 1 ii 3; לִשְׂטַר־חַד "(the beast) was raised up on one side" Dan 7:5 (see קוּם הֳקֵמַת Hoph.); נִדְבָּךְ דִּי־אָע חֲדַת "one course of timber" Ezra 6:4; ולא תעבד דין חד ו[ת]רין "and she shall not go to court (with) one or two (colleagues)" *BMAP* 7:40. In the counting of years, etc. (BL 252y): **first.** בִּשְׁנַת חֲדָה לְכוֹרֶשׁ "in the first year of Cyrus" Ezra 5:13; 6:3: Dan 7:1; ביום חד לשתא חמישיתא "on the first day of the fifth year" *1QapGen* 12:15.

(2) indef.: **one, a(n).** צְלֵם חַד שַׂגִּיא "a great statue" Dan 2:31; כְּתַבוּ אִגְּרָה חֲדָה "they wrote a letter (against Jerusalem)" Ezra 4:8: 6:2; Dan 6:18; אֶשְׁתּוֹמַם כְּשָׁעָה חֲדָה "(Daniel) was dismayed for a moment" Dan 4:16; באגרה חדה שלחן "(an explanation) we have sent in a letter" *AP* 30:29; רכב ב[ס]וסה חד קלי[ל] "riding on a swift horse of his (*sûseh*)" *Ah.* 38; ארז חד ותמרא חדא "a cedar-tree and a date-palm" *1QapGen* 19:14-15. -- Used as a pron.: דָּנִיֵאל חַד־מִנְּהוֹן "Daniel (was) one of them" Dan 6:3: 7:16; אל תשתק חדה מן מלי ספרא זן[ה] "let not one of the words of thi[s] inscription be silent," i.e., as a witness of the treaty, *Sefire I* B 8; חד מלכן או חד שנאי "(if) one of the kings or one of my enemies (should speak against me)" *Sefire I* B 26; אל חד מלכי ארפד "(whoever will come) to one of the kings of Arpad" *Sefire III* 1; ויקרק קרקי אל חדהם "if a fugitive of mine flees to one of them" *Sefire III* 19; הן חד אחי הא או חד עבדי "if it is one of my brothers or one of my slaves" *Sefire III* 13; ויקם חד [דמי] "someone will avenge [my blood]" *Sefire III* 22; חד מן בני ביתי ירתנני "one of my household servants is to inherit me" *1QapGen* 22:33; . . . והן מן חד אחי או מן חד שנאי ויבעה "and if one (*man had*) of my brothers . . . or one of my enemies seeks (to kill me, you must come)" *Sefire III* 9-11.

127

(3) in a distrib. sense: **each, each one.** הוה כסף חלרן 8
ליךח חד "being (at the) rate of 8 hallurs each month" *AP* 10:5-6;
מסמרי נחש . . . לחד פשכן תלתה "bronze nails . . . each 3 hand-
breadths (long)" *AP* 26:15; לחד ליומא קמח חפן חדה "for each,
daily, one measure of meal" *AD* 6:4; לגבר לגבר ליומא קמח חפן חדה
"for each (and) every man, daily, one measure of meal" *AD* 6:4-
5.

(4) used as an adv.: כַּחֲדָא **together** (cf. כְּ no. 4). אכלו
כחדא עמי "they ate together with me" *1QapGen* 21:21-22; הוא
יתב בסודם כחדא עמהון "he was dwelling in Sodom together with
them" *1QapGen* 22:1; אנחנה אשתוין כחדא ופלגן "we have agreed
together and have divided (the slaves)" *AP* 28:2-3; כול אלן אזדמנו
כחדא.לקרב "all these (kings) united together for battle" *1QapGen*
21:25; . . . דָּקוּ כַחֲדָא פַּרְזְלָא "(then) the iron . . . (all) together were
broken in pieces" Dan 2:35; אתכנשנא כחדא ואזלנא "we gathered
together and went" *1QapGen* 12:16. -- לחדא **very.** . . . אזלת
בנכסין שגיאין לחדא "I (Abram) went forth . . . with very many
flocks" *1QapGen* 20:33; עתרך ונכסיך ישגון לחדא "your wealth
and your flocks will increase very much" *1QapGen* 22:31-32. --
ירבה מרביתא כרשא חד כחד "it will yield interest like the capital,
both alike," lit., "one like one" *AP* 10:6-7; כל 2 כפם חד "(husband
and wife) both of them in full accord," lit., "like one mouth"
BMAP 12:11; פם חד תלתהון ממללין "the three of them spoke as
one man," lit., "(with) one mouth" *1QapGen* 20:8. -- to express
manifold meaning (BL 254p, 323p): לְמֵזֵא לְאַתּוּנָא חַד־שִׁבְעָה עַל דִּי
"(he ordered them) to heat the furnace seven times more than
what (was usual)" Dan 3:19; יתיר מן זי כען חד אלף "a thousand
times more than now" *AP* 30:3. [Hebr. אֶחָד]. †

חֲדֵה * (*ḥadēh* < **ḥadī*), w. suff. חדיה (*ḥadiyah*), m.:
breast, chest. כמא יאא לה חדיה "how lovely is her (Sarai's)
breast" *1QapGen* 20:4; חֲדוֹהִי וּדְרָעוֹהִי דִּי כְסַף "its (the statue's)
chest and its arms were of silver" Dan 2:32 (prob. read w. Ginsberg [*TS* 28 (1967) 577] חַדְיֵהּ *). [Hebr. חָזֶה]. ‖

חדוה—חדוה

חֶדְוָה (*qitl*, BL 184k): **joy.** חֲנֻכַּת בֵּית־אֱלָהָא דְנָה בְּחֶדְוָה
"(they celebrated) the dedication of this house of God with joy"
Ezra 6:16. Cf. חדה ושריר הוי בכל עדן "be joyous and prosperous at
all times!" *AP* 30:3. [Hebr. the same]. [1]

חֲדַת (*ḥadat*, BL 185q), f. חדתה (*AP* 36:3): **new.** וְנִדְבָּךְ
דִּי־אָע חֲדַת "and (one) course of new timber" Ezra 6:4 (read חַד);
ספר חדת ועתיק בשמי "(bring out) a document, old or new, in my
name" *AP* 8:16; עקי ארז חדתן "new beams of cedar" *AP* 26:14.
[Hebr. חָדָשׁ]. [1]

חוה, **Pa.** 3 sg. m. חַוִּי *, w. suff. חויּנא (*ḥawwīnā'*) & חויה
(*ḥawwiyēh*); impf. 3 sg. m. יְחַוֵּה * w. suff. יְחַוִּנַּנִי & יְחַוִּנַּה, 2 sg. f.
w. suff. תחוינני (*tĕḥawwinnánî*), 1 sg. אֲחַוֵּא, 1 pl. נְחַוֵּא & נחוי,
juss. 3 sg. m. w. suff. יחוני (*yĕḥawwinî*); ptc. sg. m. מְחַוֵּה, pl. m.
מחוין : **announce, make known, show** (w. accus. or suff. of a
thing, w. לְ or suff. of a person). פִּשְׁרָא לְמַלְכָּא אֲחַוֵּא "I shall show
the king the meaning" Dan 2:24; וּפִשְׁרֵהּ יְחַוִּנַּנִי "and makes known
to me the interpretation of it" 5:7; לָא אִיתַי דִּי יְחַוִּנַּהּ קֳדָם מַלְכָּא
"there is no one who will show it to the king" 2:11; פִּשְׁרָא נְחַוֵּא
"we shall show (you) the interpretation" 2:4; לה מחוין כולא "they
make everything known to him (Enoch)" *1QapGen* 2:21; לך אנה
מחוה "to you I make known" *1QapGen* 5:9; כולא בקושטא תחוינני
"(that) you (f.) truthfully make everything known to me" *1Qap-
Gen* 2:5; וחויה די שבי לוט "and he informed him (Abram) that Lot
had been taken captive" *1QapGen* 22:3; נחוי זי ביד פסמסנית "we
report that by Psamsineth" *AP* 26:7; זי יחוני אפיכי בש[לם] "that
you show me your countenance in pe[ace]" *Hermopolis* 6:1-2;
חוינא בוידרנג זך "he let us see (our desire) on that Widrang" *AP*
31:15 (cf. ‖ 30:16 under Haph.).
        Haph. 3 sg. m. הַחֲוִי *, w. suff. החוין (*haḥwînā*); 1 pl.
החוין (*haḥwînā*); impf. 3 sg. m. יְהַחֲוֵה ; 2 pl. m. תְּהַחֲוֹן (for תְּהַחֲוֻן *
BL 158n), w. suff. תְּהַחֲוֻנַּנִי; 1 pl. נְהַחֲוֵה ; impv. m. pl. w. suff.

129

הַחֲוֹנִי (for הַחֲוֹנִי * BL 159p) & הַחֲוִוהִי (haḥwûhî); infin. הַחֲוָיָה, Aph. infin. cst. אַחֲוָיַת : **announce, make known, show**. ... בְּעָא וּפִשְׁרָא לְהַחֲוָיָה לְמַלְכָּא "(Daniel) begged (for time) . . . and to show the king the interpretation" Dan 2:16 (see וְ no. 9): 2:27; חֶלְמָא וּפִשְׁרֵהּ הַחֲוֹנִי "show me the dream and its meaning" 2:6b; 2:9. -- w. the accus. of thing only: הֵן חֶלְמָא וּפִשְׁרֵהּ תְּהַחֲוֹן "if you show the dream and its meaning" 2:6a; 2:7, 10; 3:32; 5:15; החוין ספינתא "(the boatman) showed us the boat" *AP* 26:7; ואנחנה החוין לשמשלך "and we have reported to Shemsillek" *AP* 26:8; החווהי יהחסן "inform him (that) he should take possession (of the estate)" *AD* 8:5; אַחֲוָיַת אֲחִידָן . . . הִשְׁתְּכַחַת בֵּהּ "the explanation of riddles . . . was found in him (Daniel)" Dan 5:12; זי החוין בוידרנג זך "who let us see (our desire) on that Widrang" *AP* 30:16 (cf. חזין בהום "we saw them [punished]" *AP* 30:17; 31:16). [Hebr. חִוָּה]. †

חוט or חיט : **sew, repair** (cf. יחט). שלח לי לבשא זי עליך ויחטנה "send me the garment that you are wearing and they will repair it" *El. Ostr.* 4-5 (*RHR* 130 [1945] 20); וְאָשַּׁיָּא יַחִיטוּ (v.l. יַחִיטוּ; read יַחְטוּ Pa.) "they have repaired the foundations" Ezra 4:12.

חִוָּר (quttāl, BL 52n), adj.: **white.** לְבוּשֵׁהּ כִּתְלַג חִוָּר "his robe (was) white as snow" Dan 7:9; צִיפִין באבן חור [ר] "paved with white stone" *5QNJ (5Q15)* 1 i 6. [Hebr. חָוַר *].

חֲזָה *, w. suff. חזהא (ḥăzā-hā'), 3 sg. f. חזת (ḥăzat), 2 sg. m. חֲזַיְתָ & חֲזַיְתָה, 1 sg. חֲזֵית & חזית, 2 pl. m. חֲזַיתוּן, 1 pl. חזין ; impf. 3 sg. m. w. suff. יחזנה (yaḥzinnah), 2 sg. f. תחזין (taḥzîn), 1 sg. אחזה ('aḥzēh); impv. sg. m. חזי (ḥăzî), pl. m. חזו ; infin. מֶחֱזָא ; act. ptc. sg. m. חָזֵה, cst. sg. f. חזית, pl. m. חָזַיִן (BL 233g); pass. ptc. sg. m. חֲזֵה & חזה (ḥăzēh). **Ithpe.** 3 sg. m. אתחזי ('itḥăzî); impf. 3 sg. m. יתחזה (yitḥăzēh); ptc. מתחזה (mitḥăzēh): (1) **see, perceive** (w. accus.): וּמַלְכָּא חָזֵה פַּס יְדָה

130

"and the king saw the palm of a hand" Dan 5:5; חֶלְמָא דִי־חֲזֵית
"the dream that I saw" 2:26: 4:2, 6, 15; 7:1; אִילָנָא דִּי חֲזַיְתָ "the
tree that you saw" 4:17; [בר אנוש] די לא יחזנה כול "(she feared)
lest someone would see her" *1QapGen* 19:23; וחזהא ואתמה "and
seeing her, he marvelled at (her beauty)" *1QapGen* 20:9; תחזין
אנפי ואחזה אפיכי "you will see my face, and I shall see yours (f.)"
El. Ostr. 12-13 (*AH* I/1, 13). W. pred. accus. (BL 338k): חֲזַיְתָ
פַּרְזְלָא מְעָרַב "(as) you saw the iron (was) mixed (with clay)" Dan
2:41b, 43: 2:41a; 3:25; 4:20; כזי ח[ז]ית אנפי אסרחאדן מלך אתור טבן
"when I s[a]w that the face of Esarhaddon, king of Assyria, (was)
favorable" *Aḥ.* 14. W. conj.: חֲזַיְתָ דִּי . . . אִתְגְּזֶרֶת אֶבֶן : דִּי "(as) you
saw that . . . a stone was cut" Dan 2:45; הֲזַיְתוּן דִּי אַזְדָּא מִנִּי מִלְּתָא
"you saw that the word from me is true" 2:8; כדי חזת . . . די אשתני
אנפי "when (Bitenosh) saw . . . that my expression had changed"
1QapGen 2:12. W. a prolep. subj.: . . . חָזַיִן לְגֻבְרַיָּא אֵלֵּךְ דִּי
לָא־שְׁלֵט נוּרָא "(the satraps) gathered together (and) . . . saw that
the fire had no power (over their bodies)" Dan 3:27 (cf. the prolep. subj. in *1QapGen* 20:15; see יְדַע no. 1). In isolation: דִּי
לָא־חָזַיִן "(gods of silver) that do not see" Dan 5:23. After the
verb חָזֵה הֲוֵית "I was looking," a new detail is introduced: (a) עַד
דִּי "when suddenly" Dan 2:34; 7:4, 9, 11. (b) וַאֲרוּ / וַאֲלוּ "and
lo" 2:31; 4:7, 10; 7:2, 6-7, 13; cf. חזית בחלמי [וה]א ארז חד "I saw
in my dream, [and l]o there was a cedar-tree" *1QapGen* 19:14.
(c) חָזֵה הֲוֵית וְקַרְנָא דִכֵּן עָבְדָה קְרָב "I was looking, and that horn was
making war" Dan 7:21. -- Pass. usage: אל יפק חצר וליתחזה ירק
"may grass not come out so that no green may be seen" *Sefire I*
A 28; כמותא זי [ל]א מתחזה "like death, (the cause of) which is not
perceived," prob. the plague, *Aḥ.* 106; אתחזי לי אלהא בחזוא "God
appeared to me in a vision," lit., "was seen" *1QapGen* 21:8; איש
מצלח עקן בחשוכא ולא חזה "a man cuts beams in darkness and is not
seen" (pass. ptc.) *Aḥ.* 125. -- Pregnant usage: וחזין בהום "and we
saw (our desire) on them," i.e., that they were punished *AP*
30:17; 31:16; ואחזי ידך רבתא בה "and may I see Your powerful
hand against him" *1QapGen* 20:14-15 (cf. ואחי "that I may live"

חזו

1QapGen 19:20).

(2) **look at, look upon, inspect.** עֲרְוַת מַלְכָּא לָא אֲרִיךְ לָנָא לְמֶחֱזֵא "it is not fitting for us to look on the king's dishonor" Ezra 4:14; חזי אגרת ארשם "look at the letter of Arsames" *AD* 12:4; פגרה זי אחיקר זנה למחזה "(the king will send others) to inspect the corpse of this Aḥiqar" *Aḥ.* 63; חזי למדנחא . . . וחזי כול ארעא דא "look at the east . . . and look at all this land" *1QapGen* 21:9-10; וחזי כמן ארכהא "and look at how great is its length" *1QapGen* 21:14; למחזה איך יתעבד "(the king appointed men) to inspect how it (the command) would be done" *Aḥ.* 37-38.

(3) **look after, attend to.** חזי על עלימיא וביתי "look after the servants and my house" *AP* 41:6; חזו עליהם מה צבו "attend to them for what they want" (*sĕbiw*) *AP* 38:5-6; הוי חזית על ינקיא אלכי "look after those children" (f. cst. ptc.?) *Hermopolis* 7:2-3; חזי בעלי טבתך "attend to (us) your well-wishers" *AP* 30:23-24; חזו כתוני זי שבקת . . . בית יהה "look (pl.) for my tunic which I have left . . . in the temple of Yaho" *El. Ostr.* 1-3 (*ASAE* 26 [1926] 27).

(4) **Peil** pass. ptc. sg. m. חֲזֵה : **be seen, be fitting** (i.e., necessary and sufficient, BL 297c). חַד־שִׁבְעָה עַל דִּי חֲזֵה לְמֵזְיֵהּ "(the king bade the furnace to be heated) seven times more than it was wont to be heated" Dan 3:19; כדי חזה להון "as was fitting for them" (= ὡς καθήκει αὐτοῖς) *Test. Twelve Patr.* (ed. R. H. Charles, p. 250, lines 11-12).

(5) **Pa.** infin. חזיה (*ḥazzāyāh*), ptc. sg. m. מחזה (*mĕḥaz-zēh*): **contemplate, gaze.** פקחו עיניכם לחזיה עדי בר גאיה "open your eyes, (O gods), to gaze on the treaty of Bir Ga'yah" *Sefire I* A 13; בעיני מחזה אנה בני רבע "(and what) did I contemplate with my eyes? Children of four (generations)" *Nerab* 5 (*KAI* 226).

חֱזוּ * (*ḥizw*, BL 232p, s), emph. חֶזְוָא, w. suff. חֶזְוֵהּ, cst. pl. חֶזְוֵי, m.: (1) **vision.** בְּחֶזְוָא דִי־לֵילְיָא "in a vision of the night" Dan 2:19; 7:2, 7, 13; חֶזְוֵי רֵאשִׁי "the visions of my head" 4:2, 7,

חזות—חי

10; 7:15: 2:28; 7:1; חֶזְוֵי חֶלְמִי "visions of my dream" 4:6 (but read חֶלְמִי אֲחַוֵּא "I shall make known my dream" BL 232r); אתחזי לי אלהא בחזוא די ליליא "God appeared to me in a vision of the night" *1QapGen* 21:8. (2) **aspect, appearance** (cf. צְלֵם). וְחֶזְוַהּ רַב מִן־חַבְרָתַהּ "and the appearance of it (the last horn seemed) greater than its companion" Dan 7:20 (brachylogy; cf. לְבַב). Cf. מחזה ידיהא "the appearance of her hands" *1QapGen* 20:5. [Hebr. חִזָּיוֹן]. †

חֲזוֹת * (*qatal-at,* BL 185s), w. suff. חֲזוֹתֵהּ (v.l. חֲזוּתֵהּ), f.: **visibility.** חֲזוֹתֵהּ לְסוֹף כָּל־אַרְעָא "the visibility of it (reached) to the end of the whole earth," i.e., it could be seen even at the end of the earth, Dan 4:8, 17. [Hebr. חָזוּת]. †

חטא , **Pa.** infin. חַטָּאָה * > חַטָּיָה k. > חַטָּאָה q. (cf. BL 51k, l): **atone, expiate.** לְחַטָּאָה עַל־כָּל־יִשְׂרָאֵל "(they offered sacrifices) to atone for all Israel" Ezra 6:17. [prob. from Hebr. חִטֵּא]. [1]

חֲטָא * (*qatāl,* BL 187d), w. suff. חטיך k.; חֲטָאָךְ q. can mean "your sin" or "your sins" (cf. BL 74w, z, 77o), read prob. pl. חטאיך w. Gk., Theod., Syr., Vg.: **sin.** חֲטָאָךְ בְּצִדְקָה פְרֻק "do away with your sins by (practising) righteousness" Dan 4:24; והעדית חטאיך קדמוהי "and I took away your sins before him (Senacherib)," i.e., I obtained from him forgiveness for you, *Aḥ.* 50; וחטאי שבק לה גזר "and a diviner remitted my sin for Him" *4Qpr-Nab (4Q242)* 1-3:4; יסרון חטאה וחוביא "they will investigate his sin and the faults" *4QBirthNoahᵃ (4Q534)* 1 ii + 2:16. [Hebr. חֵטְא, חֲטָאָה]. [1]

[1] חַי (*ḥayy,* BL 181q, r) cst. (& abs.), emph. חַיָּא ; pl. חַיִּין *, emph. חַיַּיָּא ; adj.: **alive, living.** לְחַי עָלְמָא שַׁבְּחֵת "I (Nebuchadnezzar) praised Him who lives forever" Dan 4:31 (see דִּי I 2); אֱלָהָא חַיָּא "the living God" 6:21, 27; כָּל־חַיַּיָּא "all the living" 2:30:

133

4:14; [ ]06 אחדו [חין[ו] "[and] they took alive [ ]06 (men)"
Bisitun 11; יסחו שמך ואשרך מן חין "may they extirpate your name
and your status from among the living" *Nerab* 9-10 (*KAI* 225);
הן חי אנה והן מת אנה "whether I was alive or was dead" *Hermopolis* 5:9. [Hebr. the same]. †

[2] חַי * (*ḥayy, LFAA* 70q), only in pl. (BL 305e) חַיִּין, cst.
חַיֵּי : **life.** אַרְכָה בְחַיִּין יְהִיבַת "a prolongation in life was granted (to
the first beasts)" Dan 7:12; לְהֱוֹן . . . מְצַלִּין לְחַיֵּי מַלְכָּא "they will be
praying for the life of the king" Ezra 6:10; חין אריכן ינתן לך "may
(God) grant you long life" *AP* 30:3; שלם וחין שלחת לך "I send you
(greetings of) safety and life" *Hermopolis* 3:5; בחייך ועד מותך
"(we will serve you) in your life-time and until your death"
BMAP 5:12; חי ליהה "by the life of Yaho" *El. Ostr.* 3, 7 (*AH* I/1.
12). [Hebr. חַיִּים]. †

[3] חַי * (*ḥayy;* double 'ayin verb, see BL 170k; cf. חָיָה)
perf. 3 sg. m. חַי (*ḥayy*); impf. 3 sg. m. יחה (*yaḥḥēh < yaḥḥī <
yaḥiyy*), 1 sg. אחי (*'aḥḥī/'aḥḥēh < 'aḥiyy*): **live, be cured.**
אסמוך ידי עלוהי ויחה "(that) I might lay my hands upon him that he
might be cured" *1QapGen* 20:22; וחי וקם "he was cured and got
up" *1QapGen* 20:29; די אחי הוא ואחי "(say about me,) 'He is my
brother'; then I shall live" *1QapGen* 19:20.
    Haph./Aph., perf. 3 sg. m. החי * (*haḥḥī < haḥiyy*), 1 sg.
w. suff. החיתך (*haḥḥītāk < haḥiyyytāk*); impf. 3 sg. m. w. suff.
יהחיני (*yĕḥaḥḥiy-annî < yuḥaḥiyy-annî,* cf. *LFAA* 68h); ptc. sg.
m. מַחֵא (*maḥḥē' < maḥḥī < maḥiyy*): **keep alive.** [תקר[בני
עלוהי ויהחיני "[br]ing me to him, and he will let me live" *Aḥ.* 54;
על זי החיתך ולא קטלתך "because I had kept you alive and had not
killed you" *Aḥ.* 51; וְדִי־הֲוָה צָבֵא הֲוָה מַחֵא "and whom he would he
kept alive" Dan 5:19. [Hebr. the same]. †

חיה—חיל

חֲיָה * (BL 170k), impf. 3 sg. m. יִחְיֵה (yaḥyēh); impv. sg.
m. חֱיִי (BL 153h): **live.** מַלְכָּא לְעָלְמִין חֱיִי "O king, live for ever!"
Dan 2:4; 3:9; 5:10; 6:7, 22; כל מדעם זי יחיה בה איש "anything
whereby a man may live" AP 49:3. Cf. ³ חַי . [Hebr. חָיָה]. †

חֵיוָה (< ḥayiw-at, BL 186y), cst. חֵיוַת , emph. חֵיוְתָא; pl.
חֵיוָן, emph. חֵיוָתָא, f.: **beast, wild animal.** חֵיוָה רְבִיעָיָה "a fourth
beast" Dan 7:7a: 4:13; 7:5; חֵיוְתָא רְבִיעָיְתָא "the fourth beast"
7:19, 23: 7:6, 11; אַרְבַּע חֵיוָן רַבְרְבָן "four great beasts" 7:3; אִלֵּין
חֵיוָתָא רַבְרְבָתָא אִנִּין אַרְבַּע "these great beasts are four" 7:17: 7:7b,
12; לִבְבֵהּ עִם־חֵיוְתָא שַׁוִּי "his mind was made like (that) of a beast"
5:21 (brachylogy; see לְבַב); collect. sg.: תְּנֻד חֵיוְתָא "let the wild
animals flee" 4:11: 4:12; חֵיוַת בָּרָא "beasts of the field" 2:38; 4:9,
18, 20, 22, 29. [Hebr. חָיָה]. †

חיט : see חוט .

חַיִל (qatl, BL 182z; erroneously חָיִל , BL 23d), cst. חֵיל
(BL 230z), w. suff. חַיְלֵהּ , m.: (1) **strength, might.** קְרָא בְחָיִל
"cried out mightily," i.e., aloud, Dan 3:4; 4:11; 5:7; וּבַטִּלוּ הִמּוֹ
בְּאֶדְרָע וְחָיִל "and by force and might they made them stop" Ezra
4:23. -- as gen. of quality: גֻּבְרִין גִּבָּרֵי־חַיִל "men of great strength"
Dan 3:20 (cf. גְּבַר); תהך בחרב חילך "you will go with the sword of
your might (?)" AP 71:13. (2) **army;** collect. sg.: **troops.** דִּי
בְחַיְלֵהּ "which were in his army" Dan 3:20; וּכְמִצְבְּיֵהּ עָבֵד בְּחֵיל שְׁמַיָּא
"and according to His will He acts among the host of heaven"
4:32; רב חילא זי סון "head of the army of Syene" BMAP 8:2;
ח]ילא זילי קטלו למרדיא אלך] "[my] tr[oops killed those rebels]"
Bisitun 5; דבר מצריא עם חילא אחרנן "led out the Egyptians with
other troops" AP 30:8; זנה שמהת חילא יהודיא "this (is a list of) the
names of the Jewish troops" AP 22:1. [Hebr. the same]. †

135

חַכִּים * (*qattīl*, BL 192e), pl. חַכִּימִין, cst. חַכִּימֵי, emph. חַכִּימַיָּא, adj.: **wise.** ספר חכים . . . [מ]לי אחיקר "the [w]ords of Aḥiqar . . . the wise scribe" *Aḥ.* 1. -- as a noun: **sage.** חַכִּימֵי מַלְכָּא "the sages of the king" Dan 5:8; חַכִּימֵי בָבֶל "the wise men of Babylon" 2:12, 14 + . [Hebr. חָכָם].

חָכְמָה (*qutl-at*, BL 184n), cst. חָכְמַת, emph. חָכְמְתָא, f.: **wisdom.** דִּי לַהּ־הִיא . . . חָכְמְתָא "to Whom belongs wisdom" Dan 2:20; יָהֵב חָכְמְתָא לְחַכִּימִין "giving wisdom to sages" 2:21: 2:23; חָכְמָה כְּחָכְמַת־אֱלָהִין "(in Daniel there is) wisdom like the wisdom of the gods" 5:11; חָכְמָה יַתִּירָה "excellent wisdom" 5:14; לָא בְחָכְמָה דִּי־אִיתַי בִּי "not by wisdom that I have," i.e., more than others, 2:30. -- In a transferred sense: כְּחָכְמַת אֱלָהָךְ דִּי־בִידָךְ "(appoint officials) according to the wisdom of your God which is in your hand," i.e., according to your written law, Ezra 7:25. [Hebr. the same]. †

חֵלֶם (*ḥilm*, BL 183g, 224h, i), emph. חֶלְמָא, w. suff. חֶלְמָךְ, חֶלְמִי ; pl. חֶלְמִין (BL 225r), m.: **dream** (cf. חֵזוּ). חֵלֶם חֲזֵית "I had a dream," lit., "I saw" Dan 4:2: 4:6, 15; 7:1 + ; חֶלְמָא וּפִשְׁרֵהּ "the dream and the interpretation of it" 2:5 + ; חֶלְמָךְ וְחֶזְוֵי רֵאשָׁךְ עַל־מִשְׁכְּבָךְ "your dream and the visions of your head as you lay in bed" 2:28; חֶזְוֵי חֶלְמִי "visions of my dream," but read חֶלְמִי אַחֲוֵא "I shall make my dream known" (or something similar, cf. BL 232r) 4:6; יַצִּיב חֶלְמָא "the dream is certain (and its meaning sure)" 2:45; חֶלְמָא לְשָׂנְאָיךְ "let (the contents of) the dream (be) for those who hate you" 4:16; חלמת . . . חלם בליליה . . . וחזית בחלמי "I had a dream . . . in a dream of the night. . . I saw in my dream and lo, there was a cedar-tree" *1QapGen* 19:14. [Hebr. חֲלוֹם].

חֲלַף *, impf. 3 sg. m. יַחֲלֵף * (see *LFAA* 52a), 3 pl. m. יַחְלְפוּן : **pass through/over, come after.** חלפנא ארענא "we

חלק—חמא

passed through our land (and entered Egypt)" *1QapGen* 19:13;
וְשִׁבְעָה עִדָּנִין יַחְלְפוּן עֲלוֹהִי "and let seven times (years) pass over
him" Dan 4:13, 20, 22, 29; והו יחלף לי ספר "let him (my son)
come after me as scribe" *Aḥ.* 18.

Haph./Aph.: substitute, replace. אחלף לכי שטרא "I
shall replace (this) document for you" *Mur 19* 10-11; החלפי לי
שערן "replace (the) barley for me" *El. Ostr.* 5 (*AH* I/1.13). Cf.
the prep. חֲלָף *: פקיד עבד חלפוהי "has been made an an officer
instead of him" *AD* 2:3. [Hebr. חָלַף]. †

חֲלָק (ḥalāq, BL 187d), w. suff. חֲלָקֵהּ, m.: **part, portion.** זנה חלק ביתא זי . . . יהבתה לכי "this is the part of the house
which . . . I have given to you (f.)" *BMAP* 4:11-12; עליה לה חלקא
דבק לה . . . זי לי "above it the portion, which belongs to me, . . .
adjoins it" *BMAP* 4:9; שליטן בחלקי אחרנא "(my children shall
have) authority over my other portion" *BMAP* 4:19; זנה חלקא זי
מטאך בחלק "this is the part (of the inheritance) that comes to you
as a share" *AP* 28:3; וגבר חלקא נהחסן "and we shall each take
possession of his share" *AP* 28:14; לָקֳבֵל דְּנָה חֲלָק בַּעֲבַר נַהֲרָא לָא אִיתַי
לָךְ "because of this you will have no part in (the province) Beyond-the-River" Ezra 4:16; עִם חֵיוְתָא חֲלָקֵהּ בַּעֲשַׂב אַרְעָא "and let his
portion be with the beasts in the grass of the earth" Dan 4:12;
עִם־חֵיוַת בָּרָא חֲלָקֵהּ "let his portion be with the beasts of the field"
4:20 (cf. עִם־חֵיוַת בָּרָא לֶהֱוֵה מְדֹרָךְ "your dwelling shall be with the
beasts of the field" 4:22). -- Cf. חולק (Jewish Ar. ḥullāq). ברא מן
חולק תלתת גבריא די אזלו עמי "except for the portion of the three
men who went with me" *1QapGen* 22:23-24; אנון שליטין בחולקהון
"they have authority over their portion" *1QapGen* 22:24. [Hebr.
חֵלֶק]. †

חֵמָא (qil-at, BL 179g), חֲמָה, f.: **anger, fury.** בִּרְגַז וַחֲמָה
אֲמַר "(the king) in rage and fury bade" Dan 3:13; הִתְמְלִי חֱמָא "he
was filled with anger" 3:19. [Hebr. חֵמָה]. †

137

חֲמַר (*ḥamr*, BL 183e), emph. חַמְרָא, m.: **wine.** For cultic use: מְלַח חֲמַר וּמְשַׁח "salt, wine, and oil" Ezra 6:9: 7;22; חַמְרָא שָׁתֵה "(Belshazzar was) drinking wine" Dan 5:1: 5:2, 4, 23; בְּטַעַם חַמְרָא "in the tasting of the wine" 5:2; זי ישתה חמרא "the one who drinks wine" *Ah*. 93; חמר לא שתין "we do not drink wine" *AP* 30:21; חמר מצרין מאנן 5 "wine of Egypt: 5 vessels" *AP* 72:4; נצבת כרם . . . עבד לי חמר שגיא "I planted a vineyard . . . it made much wine for me" *1QapGen* 12:13. [Hebr. חֶמֶר]. †

חִנְטָה * (*qitl-at*, BL 183g), pl. חִנְטִין f.: **wheat** (used in pl. or collect. sg., BL 305h). For cultic use: חִנְטִין מְלַח חֲמַר וּמְשַׁח "wheat, salt, wine, and oil" Ezra 6:9; את לי עליך כסף וחטן ושערן "I have against you (a claim for) money and wheat and barley" *AP* 49:2; חִנְטִין כֹּרִין מְאָה "a hundred cors of wheat" Ezra 7:22; נצבתא זי זבדיה חנטן ס 1 "the plantation of Zebadiah (produced) 1 seah of wheat" *AP* 81:2; שטר 1 בחנטן א 24 "1 bond for 24 ardabs of wheat" *AP* 81:25; ביד [יו]נתן חנטא [זי] "in the hand of [Jo]nathan, the wheat [of . . .]" *AP* 81:28; זף דגנא וחנטתא זי תאכל "borrow grain and wheat that you may eat" *Ah*. 129. [Hebr. חֶטָה, חִטִּים]. †

חֲנֻכָּה * (*qutul-at*, BL 187b), cst. חֲנֻכַּת f.: **dedication, inauguration.** לְמֵתֵא לַחֲנֻכַּת צַלְמָא "to come to the dedication of the statue" Dan 3:2, 3; עֲבַדוּ . . . חֲנֻכַּת בֵּית-אֱלָהָא דְנָה בְּחֶדְוָה "they celebrated . . . the dedication of this house of God with joy" Ezra 6:16: 6:17. [Hebr. the same]. †

חנן, infin. מְחַן (< *miḥḥan*, BL 166f): **show mercy.** בְּמִחַן עֲנָיִן "by showing mercy to the miserable" Dan 4:24. **Hithpa.,** ptc. sg. m. מִתְחַנַּן (v.l. מִתְחַנֵּן, BL 166h): **ask for mercy.** בָּעֵא וּמִתְחַנַּן קֳדָם אֱלָהֵהּ "(Daniel) begging and asking for mercy from his God" Dan 6:12; צלית ובעית ואתחננת "I prayed, I begged, and I asked for mercy" *1QapGen* 20:12. [Hebr. the same]. †

▲ חֲנַנְיָה : **Hananiah,** companion of Daniel, Dan 2:17.[1]

138

חַסִּיר (*qaṭṭīl*, BL 192e), adj.: **lacking, deficient.** וְהִשְׁתְּכַחַתְּ חַסִּיר "and you have been found deficient" Dan 5:27. Cf. ptc.: איתי באר חדה . . . ומין לא חסרה "there is a well . . . and not lacking water" *AP* 27:6-7; זי לי חסרן "whatever is lacking to me" *AP* 38:9. [Hebr. חָסֵר]. [1]

חסן , **Haph./Aph.** 3 sg. m. הַחְסָן *, 3 pl. m. הֶחֱסָנוּ (for הַחְסָנוּ *, BL 128f); impf. 3 sg. m. יְהַחְסָן *, 3 pl. m. יַחְסְנוּן ; impv. sg. f. w. suff. החסני ; ptc. sg. m. מהחסן. (1) **obtain, acquire, possess.** מַלְכוּתָא הֶחֱסָנוּ קַדִּישִׁין "(the time came when) saints obtained the kingdom" Dan 7:22 (see וְ no. 12); וגבר חלקה נהחסן "and we shall each take possession of his share" *AP* 28:14; ינתנו לי אהחסן "(that) they give to me (so that) I may acquire (the domain)" *AD* 8:3; אנתם החווהי יהחסן "make known to him (so that) he may take possession (of the domain)" *AD* 8:5. (2) **hold, have, retain, possess.** וְיַחְסְנוּן מַלְכוּתָא עַד־עָלְמָא "(the saints) shall hold the kingdom for ever" Dan 7:18; אנתי החסני "(I give you this document); you (f.) are to retain it" *AP* 8:25-26; איתי זי בפק[דון] הפקדו והו החסן ולא התיב "(those goods) were on deposit; they were deposited, but he kept possession and did not return (them)" *AP* 20:7; בגה זי הוה מהחסן פמון "his domain, which Pamun retained" *AD* 8:2; זי ביב הו מהחסן "(the house) that he possessed in Yeb" *BMAP* 12:4-5; ספינתא זי מהחסנן א[נח]נה "the boat that w[e] have" *AP* 26:3; מלכיה . . . ארמי מהחסן ביב "Malchiah . . . an Aramean, holding property in *Yeb*" *AP* 7:2. [Hebr. the same]. †

חֲסַן * (*ḥisn*, BL 183j), emph. חִסְנָא, w. suff. חִסְנִי : **force, power.** חִסְנָא וְתָקְפָּא "(God gave the king) power and might" Dan 2:37; בִּתְקָף חִסְנִי "(which I built) with my mighty power" 4:27; [על[ת [בביתי] כחסן "you [entered my house] by force" *AP* 7:4-5: 7:8; מה זי לקחת כחסן מן גרדא "(restore) whatever you have taken forcibly from (my) staff" *AD* 12:9-10. Cf. adj.

139

מ[ה] חסין הו מן חמר : *חַסִּין "what is stronger than wine?" *Ah.* 79; adv.: חסין תשתאלון "you (pl.) will be interrogated strictly" *AD* 7:9. †

חֲסַף (*hasp*, BL 182x) abs. & cst., emph. חַסְפָּא : **clay, earthenware.** דְקוּ כַחְדָה פַּרְזְלָא חַסְפָּא "(then) the iron, the clay (of the statue) all together were broken in pieces" Dan 2:35: 2:45; פַּרְזְלָא מְעָרַב בַּחֲסַף טִינָא "the iron mixed with miry clay" 2:41, 43bis (see דִי I 2). -- as gen. of material: עַל־רַגְלוֹהִי דִי . . . חַסְפָּא "on its feet of . . . clay" 2:34 (*רַגְלַיִן דִּי חֲסַף* "two feet of clay"); as a pred.: וּמִנְּהוֹן דִּי חֲסַף . . . רַגְלוֹהִי "its feet were . . . and partly of clay" 2:33; אֶצְבְּעָת רַגְלוֹהִי . . . וּמִנְּהֵין חֲסַף "the toes of its feet were . . . and partly of clay" 2:42; אֶצְבְּעָתָא . . . חֲסַף דִּי־פֶחָר "the toes were . . . of potter's clay" 2:41a. †

חצף, **Haph./Aph.**, ptc. sg. f. (prob. pass., BL 129r, s) מַחְצְפָה, מְהַחְצְפָה (v.l. BL 45i, 130u): **urgent, severe.** עַל־מָה דָתָא מְהַחְצְפָה "why is the sentence so severe?" Dan 2:15; מִלַּת מַלְכָּא מַחְצְפָה "the king's order was severe" 3:22. †

חֲרֵב *, **Haph.** הַחֲרֵב *. **Hoph.** 3 sg. m. הָחֳרַב *, f. הָחָרְבַת (*hŏhorbát*, BL 129j): **lay waste, devastate.** קִרְיְתָא דָךְ הָחָרְבַת "that city was devastated" Ezra 4:15. [Hebr. חרב]. [1]

חַרְטֹם (BL 221d), pl. חַרְטֻמִּין, emph. חַרְטֻמַיָּא (v.l. חַרְטֻמַיָּא): **magician, soothsayer.** Dan 2:10, 27; 4:4; רַב חַרְטֻמַיָּא "chief of the magicians" 4:6: 5:11. Cf. Akk. *hartibi* "interpreter of dreams" (< Egyp. *hr.tp*). [Hebr. the same]. †

חרך, **Hithpa.** 3 sg. m. הִתְחָרַךְ (BL 130h): וּשְׂעַר רֵאשְׁהוֹן לָא הִתְחָרַךְ "and the hair of their heads was not singed" Dan 3:27. [1]

חרץ—חשחו

חֲרַץ * (ḥaraṣ, BL 185p), w. suff. חַרְצֵהּ : **hips** (cf. יַרְכָה).
קִטְרֵי חַרְצֵהּ מִשְׁתָּרַיִן "the joints of his hips gave way" Dan 5:6.
[Hebr. חֶלֶץ]. [1]

חֲשַׁב *, pass. ptc. pl. m. חֲשִׁיבִין : **think, consider.** חשבת
בלבי די "I thought to myself that" *1QapGen* 2:1; וְכָל־דָּאֲרֵי אַרְעָא
כְּלָה חֲשִׁיבִין "and all the inhabitants of the earth are considered as
nothing" Dan 4:32 (see לָא no. 5; כְּ no. 5; BL 297c); cf. חשבן
עלביא זי כתבת "account of the produce which A. wrote" *AP* 81:1.
[Hebr. חָשַׁב]. [1]

חֲשׁוֹךְ * (ḥašāk, BL 188g), emph. חֲשׁוֹכָא : **darkness.** יָדַע
מָה בַחֲשׁוֹכָא "(God) knows what is in the darkness" Dan 2:22; איש
מצלח עקן נחשוכא ולא חזה "a man cuts beams in the dark and is not
seen" (pass. ptc.) *Aḥ.* 125; ק מנה [א]ואעברת על[א] מן חשוכא רח[י] "and
I passed ov[er] the (region of) darkness, fa[r] from it" *4QEn[e]*
(4Q206) 1 xxvi 20-21. [Hebr. חֹשֶׁךְ]. [1]

חֲשַׁח *, pl. m. חַשְׁחִין, pl. f. חַשְׁחָן, < Akk. ḥašāḫu "have
need." w. accus.; חֲשַׁח perh. stative = Akk. ḥašiḫ (CAD 6.134-
35) w. Ar. construction (*JNES* 17 [1968] 9): **have need** (w. accus.). לָהֲתָבוּתָךְ . . . אֲנַחְנָא לָא־חַשְׁחִין "we have no need . . . to answer you" Dan 3:16; וּמָה־חַשְׁחָן "and whatever need they have"
Ezra 6:9 (prob. read חַשְׁחִין ; differently BL 185s, *GBA* §44). †

חַשְׁחוּ * (BL 198g), cst. חַשְׁחוּת, f.: **things needed.** שְׁאָר
תִּנְתֵּן . . . חַשְׁחוּת בֵּית־אֱלָהָךְ "the rest of the things needed for the
house of your God . . . you may provide (out of the royal treasur-
y)" Ezra 7:20. From Akk. ḥišiḫtu (ḥašaḫtu*) "necessities": *ana
. . . ḥišiḫti ekallim* "(I am not oblivious) of the things needed for
the palace" (CAD 6.204). [1]

חֲשַׁל *, ptc. sg. m. חָשֵׁל : **shatter, crush.** פַּרְזְלָא מְהַדֵּק וְחָשֵׁל כֹּלָּא "the iron breaks to pieces and shatters everything" Dan 2:40. Cf. Akk. *ḥašālu* "shatter, crush." [1]

חֲתַם *, 3 sg. m. w. suff. חַתְמַהּ (v.l. חַתְמֵהּ, BL 129l): **seal, sign.** וְחַתְמַהּ מַלְכָּא בְּעִזְקְתֵהּ "and the king sealed it (the stone of the den) with his signet" Dan 6:18. [Hebr. חָתַם]. [1]

ט

The letter ט designated in Old Aramaic only its primitive sound *ṭ*, but later it designated also the sound *ṭ* that arose from primitive *ṣ̌*; cf. צ .

טְאֵב (BL 141g; cf. בְּאֵשׁ); = טִיב *, 3 sg. f. טִיבַת *; cf. יְטַב *: **be good, be content;** used impersonally: **it is good, it pleases** (w. עַל, "someone"): טְאֵב עֲלוֹהִי "it pleased him (the king)" Dan 6:24; טיב לבבן בדמיא "our heart is pleased at the price: *BMAP* 3:6-7; עטתא זנה טיבת על כנותה "this counsel seemed good to his companions" *Aḥ.* 66-67; לי טיב אף אמך "it is good for me, also (for) your mother" *Padua I* A 2. [Hebr. טוב]. [1]

טָב (*qāl*, BL 179h), sg. f. טָבָה *, emph. pl. f. טָבָתָא *, adj.: **good.** דְּהַב טָב "good gold," i.e. pure, Dan 2:32 (cf. כסף צריף "purified silver" *AP* 28:10-11; הֵן עַל־מַלְכָּא טָב יִתְבַּקַּר "if it seems good to the king, let a search be made" Ezra 5:17 (BL 328h); שמני שם טב "(the god) put on me a good name" *Nerab* 3 (*KAI* 226); כזי [יח]זה גבר טב לגבר ל[חה] "when a good man [se]es an e[vil] man" *Aḥ.* 163; [מא]ן טב כס[ה] "a good pot hid[es]" *Aḥ.* 109; עטה טבה הי "it is good advice" *Aḥ.* 57; בעל עטתא טבתא "giver of good advice" *Aḥ.* 42; ח[ז]ית אנפי אסרחאדן מלך אתור טבן "I saw (that) the countenance of Esarhaddon, king of Assyria, (was) favorable" *Aḥ.* 14; הן על מראן טב אתעשת "if it seems good to our lord (you), take thought" *AP* 30:23; הן עליך כות טב "if it seems good to you in this way" *AD* 5:8; על כול נכסיא וטבתא די יהב לי "for all the flocks and the good things that He had given to me" *1QapGen* 21:3. [Hebr. טוב]. †

טַבָּח * (*qattāl,* BL 191c), emph. pl. טַבָּחַיָא : **slaughterer, executioner, militia-man.** רַב־טַבָּחַיָא "chief of the militia-men" Dan 2:14. [Hebr. the same]. [1]

טוּר (*qūl,* BL 180l), emph. טוּרָא, m.: **mountain.** מְטוּרָא הֲוָת אֶתְגְּזֶרֶת אֶבֶן "a stone was cut from the mountain" Dan 2:45; לְטוּר רַב "(the stone) became a great mountain" 2:35; לֹא דבקתה לטורא קדישא "I had not reached the holy mountain" *1QapGen* 19:8; טור תורא דן "this Mount Taurus" *1QapGen* 17:10; חד מן טורי הוררט "one of the mountains of Ararat" *1QapGen* 10:12; יתקטל בי[נ] טוריא [אל]ה תרין "let him be killed betw[een th]ese two mountains" *Aḥ.* 62; בימיא ובטוריא "over the seas and over the mountains" *1QapGen (1Q20)* 7:1. [Hebr. צוּר]. †

טְוָת (*qatal-at,* root *ṭwy,* BL 185s, 237h; "fasting"), adv. (*GBA* §88; differently BL 337f): **fasting.** וּבָת טְוָת "and (the king) spent the night fasting" Dan 6:19. [1]

טִין * (*qīl,* BL 180j), emph. טִינָא : **clay.** פַּרְזְלָא מְעָרַב בַּחֲסַף טִינָא "iron mixed with miry clay" Dan 2:41, 43; קנינה טין ומין "his possession: clay and water and whatever else" *Lydia* B 8 (*KAI* 260). [cf. Hebr. טִיט]. †

טַל (*qall,* BL 180n) cst. (& abs.): **dew.** בְּטַל שְׁמַיָא יִצְטַבַּע "let him be wet with the dew of the heavens" Dan 4:12, 20: 4:22, 30; 5:21. [Hebr. the same]. †

* טְלַל, **Aph.** impf. 3 sg. f. תַּטְלֵל , denom. verb from טְלָל "shade, protection," BL 274m; conjugated as a strong verb, and not as ʿAyin ʿAyin, BL 167j): **have shade, protection.** תְּחֹתוֹהִי תַּטְלֵל חֵיוַת בָּרָא "the beasts of the field found shade under it" Dan 4:9 (cf. תְּחֹתוֹהִי תְּדוּר "[the beasts] lie down under it" 4:18). -- Cf. * מַטְלַל (BL 167j) "covering": מטלל אגורא זך כלא עקהן זי ארז "the roof of that temple, all of it, (was) beams of cedar" AP 31:10. [Hebr. צלל]. [1]

* טְעַם, 1 sg. טעמת ; impf. 3 sg. m. w. suff. יטעמנהי : **taste** (food or drink). טעמת אף זעררתא מררתא "I have tasted even the bitter sloe" Aḥ. 105; חמרא הו זי יטעמנהי "(he who treads out) the wine is the one who should taste it" Aḥ. 209. -- **Pa.** impf. 3 pl. m. יְטַעֲמוּן, w. suff. יְטַעֲמוּנֵּהּ : **make eat.** עִשְׂבָּא . . . לָךְ יְטַעֲמוּן "they will make you eat . . . grass" Dan 4:22, 29: 5:21. [Hebr. טָעַם]. †

טְעֵם (qatl, BL 183e, 223f, g), cst. טְעֵם & טְעֵם (BL 228f), emph. טַעְמָא . (1) **taste.** אֲמַר בִּטְעֵם חַמְרָא "(Belshazzar) ordered, in the tasting of the wine, that" Dan 5:2. (2) **prudence.** הֲתִיב עֵטָא וּטְעֵם לְאַרְיוֹךְ "(Daniel) replied to Arioch with prudent advice" 2:14 (cf. 2:24). (3) **attention.** לָא־שָׂמוּ עֲלָיךְ מַלְכָּא טְעֵם "(these men) have paid no attention to you, O King" 3:12: 6:14. (4) **account.** דִּי־לְהֵוֹן . . . יָהֲבִין לְהוֹן טַעְמָא "to whom (the satraps) should give an account (of their administration)" 6:3 (cf. Akk. turru ṭēmu "render an account, report"). (5) **business, happening.** שלחי כל טעם זי הוה בביתי "send (me word about) everything that goes on in my house" Hermopolis 1:12 (cf. מִנְדַע & צְבוּ). (6) **decree, command.** מִנִּי שִׂים טְעֵם "I make a decree," lit. "a decree has been set forth by me" Dan 3:29; Ezra 4:19+; עַד־טַעְמָא לְדָרְיָוֶשׁ יְהָךְ "until the decree of Darius should come" Ezra 5:5 (see הָךְ); וְשַׁכְלִלוּ מִן־טַעַם אֱלָהּ יִשְׂרָאֵל וּמִטְּעֵם כּוֹרֶשׁ "and they finished (building the temple) by command of the God of Israel and by the decree of Cyrus" 6:14; כָּל־דִּי מִן־טַעַם אֱלָהּ שְׁמַיָּא יִתְעֲבֵד "what-

טפר–יבל

ever is commanded by the God of Heaven, let it be done," lit., "is from the command of God" 7:23; בְּעֵל־טְעֵם "commander" 4:8, 9, 17 (see בְּעֵל). [Hebr. טַעַם].

טְפַר* (ṭipr, BL 183g), pl. טִפְרִין *, w. suff. טִפְרֹוהִי, טִפְרַיַּה k. (טִפְרַהּ q. BL 75c): **nail** (of finger/toe), **claw.** וְטִפְרֹוהִי כְצִפְּרִין "and his nails (became) like (claws of) birds" Dan 4:30 (brachylogy, s.v. לְבַב); טִפְרַיַּה דִּי־נְחָשׁ "(the beast had) claws of bronze" 7:19. [Hebr. צִפֹּרֶן]. †

טְרַד *, act. ptc. m. pl. טָרְדִין ; perf. pass. 3 sg. m. טְרִיד : **drive out.** לָךְ טָרְדִין מִן־אֲנָשָׁא "they shall drive you out from among humans" Dan 4:22: 4:29; מִן־אֲנָשָׁא טְרִיד "driven out from among humans" 4:30: 5:21. †

טַרְפְּלָי * (BL 196d), gentilic adj. (*GBA* §42, 58), emph. pl. טַרְפְּלָיֵא (BL 204l): **Tripolite** (someone coming from the Phoenician town of Tripolis [?]; but see *HALOT*, 1886). Ezra 4:9 (check the context; s.v. אֲפָרְסָי). [1]

י

יְבַל *, 3 sg. m. w. suff. יבלך , 1 sg. w. suff. יבלתך ; impf. 3 sg. m. יבל (yibbil), 1 pl. נבל; impv. sg. m. w. suff. בלני (bilnî); infin. מובל (môbal) : **carry, bring, lead.** יבלתך לביתא זילי "I led you to my house" *Aḥ.* 48; שעריא זי חנם זי יבלך המו "the barley that Khnum brought to you" *El. Ostr.* 2-4 (*ASAE* 26 [1926] 25; cf. *Bib* 45 [1964] 227); יבל סון "let him carry (this letter to) Syene" *Hermopolis* 1:14; אנחנה נבל עבורא [זנה] "we shall bring [this] grain" *AP* 2:9; בלני לביתך "bring me to your house" *Aḥ.* 52; על ידן למובל לגבריא אלה "(the grain delivered) to us to carry to those men," lit., "(delivered) to our hand(s)" *AP* 2:13.

145

יד—יבשה

Haph. 3 sg. m. הֵיבֵל ; infin. הֵיבָלָה : **bring, lead.** וְהֵיבֵל
הִמּוֹ לְהֵיכְלָא דִּי בָבֶל "and he (Nebuchadnezzar) brought them (the
Jerusalem vessels) into the temple of Babylon" Ezra 5:14; 6:5;
לְהֵיבָלָה כְּסַף וּדְהַב דִּי־מַלְכָּא "to bring the king's silver and gold (to
the God of Israel)" 7:15.
Hoph. 1 sg. הובלת (*hûbĕlēt*). [למד]נח תמה הובלת ומן "and
from there I was carried [to the Ea]st" *4QEn^e (4Q206)* 1 xxvi 18-
19 (*BE*, 232). On מְסוֹבְלִין (Ezra 6:3), see BL 92k (Saphel) & s.v.
סְבַל. [Hebr. יבל]. †

יַבֶּשָׁה * (*qattal-at,* BL 191a), emph. יַבֶּשְׁתָּא ; f. **dry land,**
earth. לָא־אִיתַי אֱנָשׁ עַל־יַבֶּשְׁתָּא "there is not anyone on earth (who
can do that)" Dan 2:10. [Hebr. יַבָּשָׁה]. [1]

יְגַר (*yagr,* BL 182x), (abs. &) cst.: **heap of stones.** יְגַר
שָׂהֲדוּתָא "the heap of testimony" confirming the pact between
Arameans and Hebrews (= Hebr. גַּל עֵד) Gen 31:47. [1]

יַד (*qal,* BL 178c), cst. (& abs.), emph. יְדָא & יְדָה, w.
suff. יְדִי, יְדָךְ, יְדָה, יֶדְהֹם (BL 81y); du. יְדַיִן, w. suff. יְדָי . (1)
hand, arm (below the elbow; opp. דְּרָע "upper arm" & כַּף *
"palm [of hand]"; cf. רְגַל & *AP* 28:5-6). נְפַקוּ אֶצְבְּעָן דִּי יַד־אֱנָשׁ
"fingers of a man came forth" Dan 5:5; פַּס יְדָה 5:5 = פַּסָּא דִּי־יְדָא
5:24 "(the) part of a hand"; לבשך שבק בידה "(if the wicked seize
the skirts of) your garment, leave (it) in his hand" *Aḥ.* 171; סמכת
ידי על [ראי]שה "I laid my hands upon his [he]ad" *1QapGen* 20:29;
דרעיהא מא שפירן וידיהא כמא כלילן וחמיד כול מחזה ידיהא כמא יאין כפיהא
"her arms, how beautiful! And her hands, how perfect! And
(how) attractive all the appearance of her hands! How lovely
(are) her palms!" *1QapGen* 20:4-5; ואצבעת כפי וידי "and the
fingers of my hands and my hands" *4QLevi^b (4Q213a)* 1:9; יוד 1
שנית על ידה בימין "a yodh is marked on his hand at the right (of a
mark)" *AP* 28:4; *BMAP* 5:3. In a transferred sense: וְלָא אִיתַי

146

דִּי־יְמַחֵא בִידֵהּ "and no one can stop His hand," i.e., hinder God, Dan 4:32; דִּי יִשְׁלַח יְדֵהּ לְהַשְׁנָיָה "who will send forth his hand to change (this decree)" Ezra 6:12; וישלח ידה ויקח מן ארקי "and (if anyone) should raise his hand and take some of my land" *Sefire I* B 27. (2) **side.** ואתית ליד ימא "and I (Abram) moved alongside the Sea" *1QapGen* 21:15; ואזלת ליד טור תורא "and I went along-side Mount Taurus" *1QapGen* 21:16; וסחרת ליד פורת "and I traveled along the Euphrates" *1QapGen* 21:17; ואחלפת ליד פרדס קשט[א] "and I passed along the Paradise of Righteousness" *4QEn^e (4Q206)* 1 xxvi 21; ותרעא ליד כותלא גויה "and the gate at the side of the inner wall" *5QNJ (5Q15)* 1 i 18; ודרגא די סלק לידה "and the staircase that mounts at its side" *5QNJ (5Q15)* 1 ii 5. (3) **work.** הִתְגְּזֶרֶת אֶבֶן דִּי־לָא בִידָיִן "a stone was cut without (the work of) hands" Dan 2:34, 45; וּמַצְלַח בְּיֶדְהֹם "(the construction) prospers at their hands," i.e., by their work, Ezra 5:8; זי הושרת עלי ביד אנא "which you sent to me through Ana," i.e., by the hand/work of, *AD* 13:2; [ואמר] בעל שמין אלי [ב]יד חזין וביד עדדן "Baal-shamen [said] to me through seers and through sooth-sayers" *Zkr* A 12 (*KAI* 202). (4) **possession.** כְּדָת אֱלָהָךְ דִּי בִידָךְ "according to the law of your God that is in your hand," i.e., that you hold in writing, Ezra 7:14: 7:25; ספרא זנה בידך "this docu-ment is in your hand," i.e., in your possession, *AP* 10:12; אתנא זי ביד פ[מסי] "the she-ass that is in the possession of Pa[msi]" *AP* 44:4-5; כספה זי הוה בידה יהב "he gave [me] the money that was in his hand" *Hermopolis* 6:6-7; כל זי הנעלת בידה תהנפק "all that I have put into her hand she shall give up," if she is divorced, *AP* 15:24-25; הנחת לי כתון 1 בידך "bring down to me 1 tunic in your possession" *AP* 42:13; יהבת על ידן שע[רן] "you have delivered to us bar[ley]" *AP* 2:3; אשרנא זנה יתיהב על יד . . . סגן נגריא "let this material (for the repair of the boat) be delivered to the hand . . . of the head of the carpenters" *AP* 26:21-22; זי הוה בידכי יהבתהי לי "what was in your possession, you have given to me" *AP* 43:7. (5) **power, ability.** דִּי־נִשְׁמְתָךְ בִּידֵהּ "(God) in whose power is your breath" Dan 5:23; חד עמיא זי בידי "one of the peoples who are

under my control" *Sefire III* 10; . . . לא בידי אנ[ש]א מ[נש]א רגלהם
לא בידיך מ[נש]א רגלך "it is not in the power of me[n] to l[if]t up
their foot . . . it is not in your power to l[if]t up your foot" *Aḥ.*
122-23; כדי מטאה ידי "as my ability arrives," i.e., to the extent
that I can, *Hermopolis* 3:4; זבני עמר כזי תמטה ידכי "buy wool
whenever your ability arrives," i.e., whenever you can, *Hermopolis* 6:5-6; לקבל זי זי ידכם "according to your ability" *AP* 38:9; ואחזי
ידך רבתא בה "and may I see Your great power against him"
1QapGen 20:14-15; יְהַב בִּידָךְ "(God) has given into your power
(all dwellers of the earth)" Dan 2:38; Ezra 5:12; יִתְיַהֲבוּן בִּידֵהּ
"(the saints) will be given into his power," i.e., for persecution,
Dan 7:25; סגר שנאיך בידך "(God) has delivered your enemies into
your hand" *1QapGen* 22:17; ולחילא זי לידך "and as for the troop
that is in your control" *AD* 4:2; דִּי יְשֵׁיזְבִנְכוֹן מִן-יְדָי "who will
deliver you from my power" Dan 3:15; 3:17; דִּי שֵׁיזִיב לְדָנִיֵּאל מִן-יַד
אַרְיָוָתָא "who has delivered Daniel from the power of the lions"
6:28; את תאתה ותקם דמי מן יד שנאי "you must come and avenge
my blood from the hand of my enemies" *Sefire III* 11 (cf. ברך
יאתה יקם דם ברי מן שנאוה "your son must come and avenge the
blood of my son from his enemies" *Sefire III* 11-12); [את ל[תקח
מליא מן ידה "[you] must [not] accept such words from him" *Sefire
III* 2. [Hebr. the same]. †

ידה, **Haph./Aph.** 1 sg. אוֹדִית (*'ôdît*); ptc. sg. m. מְהוֹדֵא
& מוֹדֵא (BL 140d, 169i): **praise, give thanks.** לָךְ . . . מְהוֹדֵא
וּמְשַׁבַּח אֲנָה "to You, (O God) . . . I give thanks and praise" Dan
2:23; מוֹדֵא קֳדָם אֱלָהֵהּ "(Daniel three times a day) was giving
thanks before his God" 6:11; אודית תמן קודם אלהא "I gave thanks
there before God" *1QapGen* 21:3. -- **Ithpa.** 3 sg. m. איתודי
(*'itwaddî*): **confess, declare.** איתודי . . . מניה עמי . . . כסף "he
declared . . . was charged against me . . . a sum (of 20 zuz)" *Mur
18* 2-4 (*maniyēh* is pass. ptc. w. suff.). [Hebr. the same]. †

148

יְדַע , 3 sg. m. w. suff. ידעהא (yěda‘hā’), 2 sg. m. יְדַעְתָּ, 1 sg. יִדְעֵת ; impf. 2 sg. m. תִּנְדַּע (< תִּדַּע *), 1 sg. אֶנְדַּע, 2 pl. m. תדעון (tidda‘ûn), 3 pl. m. יִנְדְּעוּן, 3 pl. m. juss. w. suff. ינדעוך (yin-da‘ûk); impv. sg. m. דַּע ; infin. מִנְדַּע (minda‘); act. ptc. sg. m. יָדַע, pl. m. יָדְעִין ; cst. יָדְעֵי ; pass. ptc. sg. m. יְדִיעַ : **know, understand, recognize.** In a cl. w. obj.: חֶלְמָא אֱמַרוּ לִי וְאֶנְדַּע דִּי פִּשְׁרֵהּ תְּהַחֲוֻנַּנִי "tell me the dream, and I shall know that you can make known its meaning" Dan 2:9; דִּי . . . דִּי יִנְדְּעוּן "that (the living) may know . . . that (God rules)" 4:14; עַד דִּי תִנְדַּע דִּי שַׁלִּיט "until you understand that (God) rules" 4:22, 29: 5:21; מִן־דִּי תִּנְדַּע דִּי שַׁלִּטִן שְׁמַיָּא "from the time you will know that Heaven rules" 4:23; תְּהַשְׁכַּח . . . וְתִנְדַּע דִּי קִרְיְתָא דָךְ "you will find . . . and you will recognize that that city . . ." Ezra 4:15; מִן־יַצִּיב יָדַע אֲנָה דִּי עִדָּנָא אַנְתּוּן זָבְנִין "I certainly know that you are gaining time" Dan 2:8; אֲנָה יִדְעֵת דִּי רוּחַ אֱלָהִין קַדִּישִׁין "I recognize that the spirit of holy gods (is in you)" 4:6: 6:11; יְדִיעַ לֶהֱוֵה־לָךְ מַלְכָּא דִּי "be it known to you, O King, that (we shall not serve your gods)" 3:18: Ezra 4:12, 13; 5:8; ידִ[י]ע יהוה לך הן פסמש[ך] אחר קלבת מנך ישלח עלי "be it known to you (that) if later Psamshek sends me a complaint about you" *AD* 4:3; תדען זי מדעם לה מפקן לן "you must understand that they have produced nothing for us" *Hermopolis* 5:2-3; דַּע מַלְכָּא דִּי־דָת לְמָדַי וּפָרַס "know, O King, that (it is) a law of the Medes and Persians" Dan 6:16 (cf. 6:13). -- W. accus.: וְרַעְיוֹנֵי לִבְבָךְ תִּנְדַּע "(the mystery has been revealed) that you may understand the thoughts of your mind" Dan 2:30; כָּל־קֳבֵל דִּי כָּל־דְּנָה יְדַעְתָּ "(you did not humiliate yourself) although you knew all this" 5:22; בזנה זי עביד לן כלא ארשם לא ידע "Arsames did not know about all that was done to us" *AP* 30:30; למנדע מנה כולא "to learn everything from him" *1QapGen* 2:22; אף לא ידעהא "nor did he know her," i.e., have intercourse with her, *1QapGen* 20:17; נפשי לא תדע ארחה "my soul does not know its path" *Aḥ.* 187. -- W. prolep. subj. (cf. Dan 3:27 s.v. חֲזָה): ינדעוך מרי די אנתה מרה לכול מלכי ארעא "(that) they may know you, my Lord, that you

are the Lord of all the kings of the earth" *1QapGen* 20:15. In
isolation: וְלָא יָדְעִין "(gods of silver that) do not know" Dan 5:23.
  Ptc.: יָדַע מָה בַחֲשׁוֹכָא "(God) knows what is in the dark"
Dan 2:22; יָדְעֵי בִינָה "(those who) have understanding" 2:21 (cf.
Hebr. בִינָה יוֹדְעֵי 1 Chr 12:33); כָּל־יָדְעֵי דָתֵי אֱלָהָךְ וְדִי לָא יָדַע "all
those who know the law of your God and those who do not know
(it)" Ezra 7:25 (read w. Gk. דָּת); ארתוהי ידע טעמא זנה "Artohi is
cognizant of this command" (signature of letter) *AD* 8:6 + ; שגיאן
[כ]וכב]י שמיא זי] שמהתהם לא ידע איש הא כן אנשא לא ידע איש "many
are the [s]tar[s of heaven] whose names one does not know: so
one knows not mankind" *Aḥ.* 116; פרעה ידע כי עבד[ך] "Pharaoh
knows that [your] slave [   ]" *Adon Letter* 6 (*KAI* 266).
  Haph. (BL 140d), 3 sg. m. הוֹדַע, w. suff. הוֹדְעָךְ ; 2 sg. m.
w. suff. הוֹדַעְתַּנִי, הוֹדַעְתָּנָא (BL 53r), הודען (*hôda'nā*); impf. 3 sg.
m. יְהוֹדַע, w. suff. יְהוֹדְעִנַּנִי ; 1 sg w. suff. אֲהוֹדְעִנַּה ; 3 pl. m.
יְהוֹדְעוּן, w. suff. יְהוֹדְעִנַּנִי ; 2 pl. m. תְּהוֹדְעוּן, w. suff. תְּהוֹדְעוּנַּנִי &
תְּהוֹדְעִנַּנִי ; impv. sg. m. הודע (*hôda'*); infin. הוֹדָעָה, w. suff.
הוֹדָעֻתַנִי & הוֹדָעֻתָךְ, הוֹדִעֻתִי ; ptc. pl. m. מְהוֹדְעִין : **explain, make
known, teach** (cf. חוה Pa. Haph.), w. accus. of a thing, w. לְ or
suff. of a person: הוֹדַע לְמַלְכָּא מָה דִי לֶהֱוֵא "(God) made known to
the king what will be (hereafter)" Dan 2:45: 2:15, 25 + ; פִּשְׁרֵה
לָא־מְהוֹדְעִין לִי "the meaning of it they did not make known to me"
4:4; פִּשְׁרָא אֲהוֹדְעִנַּה "I shall explain to him the interpretation"
5:17: 2:5, 9, 23, + ; שְׁלַחְנָא וְהוֹדַעְנָא לְמַלְכָּא "we sent (word) and
made known to the king" Ezra 4:14; על זהב על זנה שלחן הודען "as
for gold, we have sent (word) and explained about this" *AP*
30:28-29; דִּי לָא יָדַע תְּהוֹדְעוּן "(and him) who does not know (the
law) you (pl.) shall teach" Ezra 7:25; הודע איך זי עביד אנת "make
known how you are acting" *Bisitun* 66. [Hebr. יָדַע].

יְהַב, 3 sg. m. w. f. suff. יהבה (*yĕhabah*), 3 sg. f. יהבת
(*yahbat*); 2 sg. m. יְהַבְתְּ (v.l. יְהַבְתָּ, BL 101e), w. m. suff. יהבתה,
w. f. suff. יהבתה ; 1 sg. יהבת, w. m. suff. יהבתה ; 3 pl. m. יהבו, 1

יהב

pl. יהבן, w. f. suff. יהבנה ; impf. 2 sg. m. תהב (< *tihhab*); impv. sg. m. הַב, w. m. suff. הבה; sg. f. הבי, w. m. suff. הבהי (*habīhī*), pl. m. הבו ; ptc. sg. m. יָהֵב, pl. m. יָהֲבִין . **Peil** perf. 3 sg. m. יְהִיב, 3 sg. f. יְהִיבַת & יְהִיבַת , 3 pl. m. יְהִיבוּ . **Hithpe.** impf. 3 sg. m. יִתְיְהִב, 3 sg. f. תִּתְיְהִב (v.l. תִּתְיְהַב), 3 pl. m. יִתְיַהֲבוּן ptc. sg. m. מִתְיְהֵב, sg. f. מִתְיַהֲבָא, pl. m. מִתְיַהֲבִין (cf. נְתַן). (1) **give.** יְהַב חָכְמְתָא לְחַכִּימִין "(God) gives wisdom to sages" Dan 2:21: 2:23, 37; 5:18, 19; יְהַב־לֵהּ . . . רַבְרְבָן מַתְּנָן "(the king) gave him . . . great gifts" 2:48: 5:17; וִיהִיבַת לְמָדַי "and (your kingdom) was given to the Medes" 5:28; דִּינָא <יְתִב וְשָׁלְטָנָא> יְהִיב לְקַדִּישֵׁי "judgment <was given and sovereignty> was bestowed on the saints of . . ." (prob. haplography) 7:22; לֵהּ יְהִיב שָׁלְטָן "dominion was given to him" 7:14: 7:6; וְאַרְכָה בְחַיִּין יְהִיבַת לְהוֹן "and a prolongation in life was given to them (the beasts)" 7:12; רְבוּתָא . . . יְהִיבַת לְעַם קַדִּישֵׁי "greatness . . . was given to the people of the saints of . . ." 7:27 (the context demands תִּתְיְהִב "will be given"); לְבַב אֱנָשׁ יְהִיב לַהּ "the mind of a man was given to it (the beast)" 7:4; לְבַב חֵיוָה יִתְיְהִב לֵהּ "let the mind of a beast be given to him (the king)" 4:13; מָה חַשְׁחָן . . . לֶהֱוֵא מִתְיְהֵב לְהֹם "whatever is needed . . . let (that) be given to them" Ezra 6:9 (read prob. חַשְׁחָן); יהב המו לי מראי מלכא "my lord, the king, gave them to me" *Assur Letter* 7 (*KAI* 233); זי הוה בידכי יהבתהי לי "what was in your possession you have given to me" *AP* 43:7; לא אנחן יהבנה לכי "we did not give it to you" *AP* 1:5; הן יהב לכי עמרה "if he has given you the wool" *Hermopolis* 2:9; הן לתהב לחמי "if you do not give (me) my food" *Sefire I* B 38. -- Contract perf. (in deeds): אנה יהבת לכי "I have given you the house that Meshullam . . . gave me for its price and wrote for me a document about it" *AP* 13:2-3; ויהבתה למפטחיה ברתי חלף נכסיא זי יהבת לי "and I have given it to my daughter, Miphṭaḥiah, in place of the property which she gave me" *AP* 13:4; יהבת לך בתיא אלה ברחמה "I have given you these houses as a gift" *BMAP* 6:14. Perf. in writs of divorce: s.v. שׂנא (cf. perf. in letters: s.v. אגרה ; perf. in a decree: s.v. שׂים no. 4).

151

יהב

(2) **hand over, deliver, yield.** יְהַב בִּידָךְ "(God) has handed over into your hand (all men, etc.)" Dan 2:38: Ezra 5:12;
וְיִתְיַהֲבוּן בִּידֵהּ "and (the saints) will be handed over to him (King
Antiochus)," i.e., in persecution, Dan 7:25; יְהַבוּ גֶשְׁמְהוֹן "(the
pious ones) yielded their bodies," i.e., to death or torture, 3:28;
גִּשְׁמַהּ וְהִיבַת לִיקֵדַת אֶשָּׁא "its (the beast's) body . . . , and it was
handed over to burning by fire" 7:11; מָאנַיָּא . . . יְהִיבוּ לְשֵׁשְׁבַּצַּר
"the vessels . . . were delivered to Sheshbazzar," i.e., to take to
Jerusalem, Ezra 5:14; וּמָאנַיָּא דִּי־מִתְיַהֲבִין לָךְ "and the vessels that
have been handed over to you" 7:19; אף נשתונא כתיב יהיב לן "a
written document also was delivered to us" *AP* 17:3; בבל לם אגרת
מן ארשם יהבת על פס[מש]ך "a letter from Arsames was delivered in
Babylon to Psa[msh]ek" *AD* 12:1-2; אשרנא זנה יתיהב על יד שמו . . .
סגן נגריא "let this material be delivered to Shemaw . . . the head
of the carpenters" *AP* 26:21-22; כל 2 זבן ויהבן לך ביתן "both of us
have sold and handed over to you our house" *BMAP* 12:3.

(3) Varied examples: מִדָּה . . . מִתְיְהֵב לְהוֹן "tribute . . . was
delivered to them (kings of Jerusalem)" Ezra 4:20: 6:4, 8; הוא
יהבין מדתהון למלך עילם "they kept paying their tribute to the king
of Elam" *1QapGen* 21:26-27; יהבת לן דמי ביתא כסף כרש חד "you
paid to us the price of our house, the sum of one karsh" *BMAP*
12:5; דִּי־לְהֵוֹן . . . יְהַבִין לְהוֹן טַעְמָא "to whom . . . they should give
account" Dan 6:3; התב הבלהם "return, give (back) to them" *AD*
12:10; אַרְכָה בְחַיִּין יְהִיבַת לְהוֹן "a prolongation in life was given to
them" Dan 7:12; יהב להן פרס תנה ויתלקח קדמתהן בסון "he has given
them a salary here (Memphis), and it will be taken to them in
Syene" *Hermopolis* 1:8-9; לעלים אחרן זילי לא יהיב אחר אנה בגה . .
יהבת לפטסורי "to no other servant of mine was it (the farm)
given; later I gave the estate . . . to Petosiri" *AD* 8:5; שאלת מנך . .
אחתך לאנתו ויהבתה לי "I asked of you . . . your sister, and you
gave her to me for marriage" *BMAP* 7:3; יהבת לי תרע ביתא זילך
למבנה אגר "you have given me the gateway of your house to build
a portico" *AP* 5:3-4; אֲתָה יְהַב אֲשַׁיָּא דִּי־בֵית אֱלָהָא "he came (and)

152

laid the foundations of God's house" Ezra 5:16; נחשיא זי יהבו על תמריא "bronze-bands, which they put on the palm trees" *AP* 81:111. †

▲ יְהוּד (BL 189n *yahūd*): **Judah, Judea.** גְּבַר מִן־בְּנֵי גָלוּתָא דִּי יְהוּד "a man among the exiles of Judah" Dan 2:25: 5:13; 6:14; יְהוּדָיֵא דִּי בִיהוּד וּבִירוּשְׁלֶם: the Jews who are in Judah and in Jerusalem" Ezra 5:1: 7:14; אֲזַלְנָא לִיהוּד מְדִינְתָּא "we went to the (Persian) province of Judah" 5:8; אל מראן בגוהי פחת יהוד "To our lord, Bagohi, governor of Judea" *AP* 30:1; חרי יהוד "the nobles of Judea" *AP* 31:18. [Hebr. יְהוּדָה]. †

▲ יְהוּדִי * (BL 196d), emph. יְהוּדָיֵא *; pl. יְהוּדָיִן q. (יְהוּדָאִין k., BL 52k, l), emph. יְהוּדָיֵא : **Jew, Jewish.** אִיתַי גֻּבְרִין יְהוּדָיִן "there are Jewish men" Dan 3:12; שָׂבֵי יְהוּדָיֵא "the elders of the Jews" Ezra 5:5; 6:8, 14: 4:12, 23; 6:7; Dan 3:8; יְהוּדָיֵא דִּי בִיהוּד "Jews who were in Judah" (not in exile) Ezra 5:1; קוניה . . . יהודי לדגל אתרופרן "Qoniah . . . , a Jew of the detachment of Athruparan" *AP* 6:8-9; חֵ[י]לָא י[הודיא] "the Jewish gar[rison]" *AP* 21:2; יהודין זי יב בירתא "Jews of the fortress Yeb" *AP* 20:2; חרי יהודיא "the nobles of the Jews" *AP* 30:19. Cf. the personal name יהודה "Judas" *AP* 81:78. [Hebr. יְהוּדִי]. †

יוֹם (*yawm, qatl,* BL 182a), emph. יוֹמָא; pl. יוֹמִין, cst. יוֹמֵי & (f.) יוֹמָת, emph. יוֹמַיָּא, w. suff. יוֹמֵיהוֹן , m.: (1) **day.** עַד־יוֹמִין תְּלָתִין "within thirty days" Dan 6:8, 13; יתיר מן יום חד "more than one day" *AD* 6:6; ביום חד בכף חדה "(she shall take away everything) on one day, at one time" *AP* 15:28; זילכי הו מן יומא זנה עד עלם "yours (f.) it is from this day forever" *BMAP* 4:4-5; עד זנה יומא אנחנה שקקן לבשן וצימין "up to this day we are wearing sackcloth and fasting" *AP* 30:20; מחר או יום אחרן "tomorrow or another (later) day" *BMAP* 2:7; יומא דן "on this day" *1QapGen* 22:21; יומא הו "on that day" *AP* 22:120; [ ] וביום חרן לכל

"and on a day of wrath for all [   ]" *Sefire II* B12; וקדם יום ולילה "(the treaty is concluded) in the presence of Day and Night" *Sefire I* A 12. -- **day of the calendar.** עַד יוֹם תְּלָתָה לִירַח אֲדָר "(they finished the temple) on the third day of the month of Adar" Ezra 6:15; עד יום 15 מן יום עד יום 21 לנ[יסן] "from the 15th day to the 21st day of [Nisan] (are seven days of Unleavened Bread)" *AP* 21:5-6 (cf. line 8); עד יום שבה "up to the day of the Sabbath" *El. Ostr.* A 1 (*RSO* 32 [1957] 404); ביום 6 לפאפי "on the 6th day of Paophi (the letter arrived)" *AP* 37:15; ב 25 לכיחך זי הו לנדר "on the 25th of Khoiak, which was the day of a vow" *AP* 72:18; מן זכי ועד יום שנת 17 דריהוש "from that (time) until (this) day in the 17th year of Darius, (the king, sacrifices have not been offered)" *AP* 30:21; ביום חד לשתא חמישיתא "on the first day of the fifth year" *1QapGen* 12:15. -- In a distributive sense: וְזִמְנִין תְּלָתָה בְּיוֹמָא "and three times a day (Daniel got down on his knees)" Dan 6:11, 14; יוֹם בְּיוֹם דִּי־לָא שָׁלוּ "day by day without fail" Ezra 6:9; יום ליום . . . לחד ליומא . . . לגבר ליומא . . . לגבר לגבר "(give him provisions) day by day . . . (meal) for each one daily . . . every man daily (one measure of meal)" *AD* 6:3-5. -- W. a modifying rel. cl. (cf. דִּי II 6): כן יעב[ד]זי ביום "on any day on which he will d[o] so" *Sefire I* C 20-21; עד יום זי אשלמנהי לך "until I restore it to you" *AP* 11:10; [   ] בכל יום זי "as long as [   ]" *AP* 37:2; עשר שנין שלמא מן יום די נפקתה מן חרן "ten years have elapsed since the day you departed from Haran" *1QapGen* 22:28; כול די נפקו עמך ביום מפקך "all that went forth with you on the day of your departure" *1QapGen* 22:30.

(2) **time** (pl.): בְּיוֹמֵי אֲבוּךְ "in the time of your father" Dan 5:11; 2:44; בְּאַחֲרִית יוֹמַיָּא "in the latter time (of the kingdom)" 2:28; לִקְצָת יוֹמַיָּא "with the passing of (that) time," i.e., seven years, 4:31; עד זי לעד[ן א[חרן ולימן אחרנן שגיאן קרבתך "until a later date and much time thereafter I brought you" *Aḥ.* 49-50; מִן־יוֹמָת עָלְמָא "from of old" Ezra 4:15, 19; מן יומי מלך מצרין "(already) in the time of the kings of Egypt" (read מלכי, as in 31:12) *AP*

30:13; סבלתני ואנה ימין סב "she sustained me when I was old in time" (שֵׂב = סב) *BMAP* 9:17; עַתִּיק יוֹמִין "(one who was) ancient of days" (BL 310a) Dan 7:9; עַתִּיק יוֹמַיָּא "the Ancient of Days" 7:13, 22 (see דִּי I 2a). -- **time of life:** יומיך יארכון "may your days last long" *Bisitun* 72; בצדקתי קדמות . . . האָרך יומי "because of my righteousness toward him, (my god) made the time of my life long" *Nerab* 2-3 (*KAI* 226); ותהך [ב]לא ביומיך "and (that) you go away not in your time," i.e., you die prematurely, *Aḥ.* 102; מן בתיהם ומן יומיהם "(may the gods remove the infidels) from their homes and from their days" *Sefire II* C 16-17; קושטא כול יומי "all my days have I practised uprightness" *1QapGen* 6:2. [Hebr. the same]. †

▲ יוֹצָדָק : **Jozadak,** son of Seraiah (1 Chr 5:40-41), High Priest until 586 B.C. and father of Jeshua, who returned from the exile. Ezra 5:2. [Hebr. יְהוֹצָדָק]. [1]

יזב : see שֵׁיזֵב.

יחט, יַחִיטוּ (v.l. יְחִיטוּ , BL 148e), vowels indicate the **Pa.**, perf. 3 pl. * יַחִטוּ (*yaḥḥiṭū, GBA* §178), of the root יחט (related to חוט , as יטב is to טיב); cf. חוט : **sew, repair.** לירוּשְׁלֶם . . . קִרְיְתָא . . . בְּנַיִן וְשׁוּרַיָ אֶשְׁכְלִלוּ וְאֻשַׁיָּא יַחִיטוּ "(the Jews are accused of) rebuilding Jerusalem, the city . . . , they are finishing the walls and repairing the foundations" Ezra 4:12 (see D. Bodi, *Transeuphratène* 34 [2007] 51-63; cf. 4:13, 16, 21). †

יטב (cf. perf. טְאֵב), impf. 3 sg. m. יֵיטַב (BL 141f): **be good, be content, please.** מָה דִּי עֲלָיִךְ . . . יֵיטַב . . . לְמֶעְבַּד "whatever pleases you . . . to do (with the rest . . . , you may do)" Ezra 7:18. **Haph.: make good, satisfy.** הוטבת לבבי על ארקא זך "you have satisfied my mind about that land" *AP* 6:11-12; אחזת בית אבי והיטבתה מן בית חד מלכן רברבן "I took over my father's house

155

and made it finer than the house of any one of mighty kings"
Barrakib 11-13 (*KAI* 216). [Hebr. the same]. [1]

יְכֵל (BL 140a), 2 sg. m. יְכֵלְתָּ, 3 pl. יכלו (*yĕkílû*); impf.
(BL 142j) 3 sg. m. יִכַּל & יוּכַל k. (BL 142k, *GBA* §171), 2 sg.
m. תִּכַּל q. & תוּכַל k., 2 sg. f. תכלן (*tikkĕlīn*), 3 pl. m. יכלון
(*yikkĕlûn*), 1 pl. נכל (*nikkul*); ptc. sg. m. יָכֵל, sg. f. יָכְלָה, pl. m.
יָכְלִין : **be able, be capable, prevail, have right** (cf. כהל, שְׁלֵט
שַׁלִּיט,). וְיָכְלָה לְהוֹן "(the horn made war on the saints) and prevailed over them" Dan 7:21. -- W. לְ & infin.: יְכֵלְתָּ לְמִגְלֵא רָזָא דְנָה
"you were able to reveal this mystery" 2:47; הַיְכִל לְשֵׁיזָבוּתָךְ "has
(God) been able to rescue you (from the lions)?" 6:21; לא יכלו כול
אסיא . . . לאסיותה "none of the physicians . . . were able . . . to
cure him" *1QapGen* 20:20; לא יכל למקרב בהא "(the pharaoh) was
not able to approach her" *1QapGen* 20:17; . . . לצליא לא יכול אברם
על מלכא "Abram will not be able (*yikkûl*) . . . to pray for the
king" *1QapGen* 20:22-23; יָכֵל לְהַשְׁפָּלָה "He is able to humiliate
(the proud)" Dan 4:34: 2:10, 27; 3:17, 29; 4:15; 5:16; 6:5. -- W.
a finite verb: כדי תכלן תעבדן לה עבד אנה לה "just as you are able to
do for him, I (shall be) doing for him" *Hermopolis* 1:4-5; לא נכל
נגרנך דין "we will have no right to start a case against you"
BMAP 3:12; לא יכלון ינפכון עליכי ספר "they shall not be able to
produce a document against you" *BMAP* 10:15; לא אכל אמר "I
will have no right to say" ('*i'mar*) *AP* 15:31. [Hebr. יָכֹל]. †

יָם * (*qall*, BL 180n), emph. יַמָּא, m.: **sea.** מְגִיחָן לְיַמָּא
רַבָּא "(four winds of heaven) stirring up the great sea" Dan 7:2:
7:3; לשן ים סוף די נפק מן ים שמוקא "tongue of the Reed Sea that
goes forth from the Red Sea," i.e., Gulf of Suez, *1QapGen* 21:18;
ומן ימא רבא עד חורן "and (I looked at the land) from the Great Sea
to Hauran (south of Damascus)" *1QapGen* 21:11; מן ל[יד] ימא
רבא דן די מלחא "(I journeyed) from the [coast] of this Great Sea of
Salt" *1QapGen* 21:16; התסוג בדשין ימא "will you hold back the
sea with portals" *11QtgJob (11Q10)* 30:6. [Hebr. יָם]. †

יסף, **Haph./Aph.** 1 sg. הוספת (*hôsĕpēt*) & אוספת; impf. 3 pl. m. יהוספון (*yĕhôsĕpûn*), 2 pl. m. תהוספון : **add, annex.** ולא זילי ביתא על תהוספון "and (if) you do not annex (them) to my estate" *AD* 7:9; . . . עקיא על יהוספון על טף באdרבא לחד פשכן תלתה "they shall add to the logs . . . to each board in length three handbreadths" *AP* 26:18; והוספ[ת לה] אית כל מחנת "and [I] added [to it] all the circuit of [ ]" *Zkr* B 4-5 (*KAI* 202); אוספת לה על שגי דילה "I added much to what he had" *1QapGen* 21:6. -- **Hoph.,** 3 sg. f. הוספת (BL 141h): רבו יתירה הוספת לי "exceeding majesty was added to me" Dan 4:33. [Hebr. the same]. [1]

יעט * (BL 140b), ptc. sg. m. יעט, pl. m. w. suff. יעטוהי & יעטוהי : **advise, give counsel.** מלכא ויעטוהי "the king and his counselors" Ezra 7:15: 7:14; [ס]פרא חכימא יעט אתור כלה "(Aḥi-qar), the wise [s]cribe, counselor of all Assyria" *Aḥ.* 12. -- **Ith-pa.,** 3 pl. אתיעטו (BL 130g): **be agreed in advice.** אתיעטו כל . . . לקימה קים מלכא . "all (the officials of the kingdom) are agreed that the king should issue an ordinance" Dan 6:8 (cf. די I 2 a). †

יצא : see שיציא .

יצב, **Pa.** (denom. verb < יציב, BL 273g), infin. יצבא : **know for sure.** צבית ליצבא על חיותא "I wanted to know for sure about the (fourth) beast" Dan 7:19 (v.l. ליציבא ; cf. ויציבא אבעא־מנה על־כל־דנה "(that) I might ask him the truth about all this" 7:16). [1]

יציב (*qattīl*, BL 192e), emph. יציבא, f. abs. יציבא, adj.: **sure, certain, true** (cf. תקיף). יציב חלמא ומהימן פשרה "certain is the dream, and the meaning of it is trustworthy" Dan 2:45; יציבא מלתא "the matter is sure," i.e., immutable 6:13; זי יהנפק כדב הו זנה ספרא . . . הו יצב "whoever produces (a document), it is a fake; this document (that I wrote) is true" *BMAP* 10:16-17; ויציבא

אֶבְעֵא־מִנֵּהּ עַל־כָּל־דְּנָה‎ "(that) I might ask him the truth about all this" Dan 7:16. -- Used as an adv.: מִן־יַצִּיב יָדַע אֲנָה‎ "I know for sure" Dan 2:8 (BL 255s); וכולא מנה ביצבא ינדע‎ "and learn everything from him with certainty" *1QapGen* 2:20 (cf.: למנדע‎ מנה כולא בקושטא‎ "to learn everything from him in truth" 2:22); יַצִּיבָא מַלְכָּא‎ "(they replied,) 'Certainly, O King!'" Dan 3:24 (emph. state, BL 254p, 337d; or old accus., *GBA* §88.4). [Hebr. יצב‎ verb]. †

יְקַד‎ *, ptc. sg. f. יקדה‎ (*yāqĕdāh*), emph. יָקְדְתָּא‎ (BL 241t): **burn.** אַתּוּן נוּרָא יָקִדְתָּה‎ "a burning fiery furnace" Dan 3:6, 11 + ; אשה יקדה‎ "a burning fire" *Ah.* 103; איך זי תקד שעותא זא באש‎ כן תקד ארפד‎ "just as this wax is burned by fire, so may Arpad be burned" *Sefire I* A 35. [Hebr. יָקַד‎].

יְקֵדָה‎ * (*qatil*, BL 186y), cst. יְקֵדַת‎, f.: **a burning.** וִיהִיבַת‎ לִיקֵדַת אֶשָּׁא‎ "and (the beast's body) was given over to a burning with fire" Dan 7:11. [Hebr. יָקַד‎].

יַקִּיר‎ (*qattīl*, BL 192e), emph. יַקִּירָא‎, f. יַקִּירָה‎, adj.: **grave, noble, precious.** מִלְּתָא . . . יַקִּירָה‎ "the matter . . . is difficult" Dan 2:11; ז[]פתא יקירתא ומן גבר לחה אל תזף‎ "the loan is heavy, and from a wicked man borrow not" *Ah.* 130; לא איתי זי‎ יקיר מן‎ [ ] "there is nothing heavier than [ ]" *Ah.* 111; אָסְנַפַּר‎ רַבָּה וְיַקִּירָא‎ "the great and noble Osnappar" Ezra 4:10; הא זנה יקיר‎ [קדם] שמש‎ "lo, this is precious [before] Shamash" *Ah.* 93; ויקיר‎ הדרה לדרכי ארקא בניח[א]‎ "and precious is his (a king's) sovereignty to those who walk on the earth in tranquillity" *Ah.* 108; אף‎ לאלהן יקירה הי‎ "even to gods (wisdom) is precious" *Ah.* 95; סב‎ לוחיא יקריא‎ "take up (these) precious tablets" *Sem* 5 (1955) 38, line 3. [Hebr. יָקָר‎]. †

יָת, אית (prob. *'iyyāt*), w. suff. יָתְהוֹן : sign of the accus.
דִּי־מַנִּית יָתְהוֹן "(Jews) whom you appointed" Dan 3:12; אהבד אית
כתך ואית מלכה "I shall destroy KTK and its king" *Sefire II* C 5-6;
והוספ[ת לה] אית כל [ת]י אין[הן "if they kill me" *Sefire III* 11; יקתלן
[ ] מחנת "and [I] added [to it] all the circuit of [ ]" *Zkr* B 4-5
(*KAI* 202); תשלחון לי ית אלעזר "you will send to me Eleazar" *IEJ*
11 (1961) 44. line 4; שלח יתהן "send them" ibid., 48, line 4;
[משח] . . . ית ד[שין ל]ה "[he measured] . . . it[s] por[tals]" *5QNJ*
(5Q15) 1 i 17. [Hebr. אֵת, אוֹת]. [1]

יְתֵב (*t* < *ṯ*), יתב (*yĕtib*), 1 sg. יתבת ; impf. 3 sg. m. יִתֵּב ;
impv. sg. m. תב (*tib*), pl. m. שבו ; ptc. sg. m. יתב (*yātib* or *yātēb*),
pl. m. יָתְבִין : (1) **settle, sit.** וְעַתִּיק יוֹמִין יְתִב "and an ancient of
days took his seat" Dan 7:9; דִּינָא יְתִב "the court sat in judgment"
7:10; דִּינָא יִתִּב "the court shall sit in judgment" 7:26: 7:22 (conjecture, see דִּין no. 3); ראש מלוכתא כזי ארתחשסש מלכא יתב בכרסאה
"the beginning of the reign, when King Artaxerxes sat on his
throne" *AP* 6:1-2; מלכא נפעורת יתב [בא]פף] "the King Nepherites
sat (enthroned) [in the month E]piphi"*BMAP* 13:3; [י]ברן ירב והן
זי ישב על כהסאי "and if [my] son, who sits on my throne, quar-
rels" *Sefire III* 17. (2) **dwell, live, remain.** ותב . . . ארקא זך בני
בגו עם אנתתך "build on that land . . . and dwell there with your
wife" *AP* 9:5-6; בהברון . . . אזלת ויתבת "I went and I lived . . . in
Hebron" *1QapGen* 21:19; זבן לה בסודם בי ויתב בה ואנה הוית יתב
בטורא די בית אל "(Lot) bought himself a house in Sodom and
dwelt in it; and I was living (then) on the mountain of Bethel"
1QapGen 21:6-7; שבו לתחתכ[ם] "remain where [yo]u are" *Sefire*
III 7; דִּי יָתְבִין בְּשָׁמְרָיִן "who live in Samaria" Ezra 4:17.
Haph. 3 sg. m. הוֹתֵב, w. suff. הושבני (*hôšibnî*): **seat,**
settle. הושבני . . . על כרסא אבי "(God) seated me . . . on my
father's throne" *Barrakib* 5-7 (*KAI* 216); הוֹתֵב הִמּוֹ בְּקִרְיָה דִּי שָׁמְרָיִן
"(the king of Assyria) settled them in the cities (v.l. בְּקִרְיָה pl.) of
Samaria" Ezra 4:10. [Hebr. יָשַׁב]. †

יַתִּיר (qattīl, BL 192e), f. יַתִּירָה & יַתִּירָא , adj.: **exceed-ing, superlative.** וְזִיוֵהּ יַתִּיר "and its splendor was exceeding" Dan 2:31; וְחָכְמָה יַתִּירָה הִשְׁתְּכַחַת בָּךְ "and superlative wisdom has been found in you" 5:14: 5:12; 6:4; רְבוּ יַתִּירָה הוּסְפַת לִי "exceed-ing majesty was added to me" 4:33. -- Used as adv.: יַתִּירָה, יַתִּירָה יַתִּיר *; (either f., BL 254p, or old accus., GBA §88.4): **very, ex-ceedingly.** אַתּוּנָא אֵזֵה יַתִּירָא "the furnace was fired excessively" Dan 3:22 (seven times as hot, 3:19); תַּקִּיפָא יַתִּירָא "(the fourth beast was) exceedingly strong" 7:7; דְּחִילָה יַתִּירָה "exceedingly frightful" 7:19; הן יהוה באתר חד יתיר מן יום חד "if he is more than one day in any one place" AD 6:6; יתיר מן זי כען חד אלף . . . ישימנך "may (the God of Heaven) give you favor . . . a thousand times more than (you have) now" AP 30:2-3; אל ת[ב]ט יתרא "do not chatter excessively" Aḥ. 96. †

כ

כְּ, (ka-) before a shewa כְּ, before a Ḥateph כַּ & כֶּ (BL 265x-a'), prep. particle prefixed to a noun (BL 258k). (1) **as, like.** וּמַלְכוּ . . . תַּקִּיפָה כְּפַרְזְלָא "and a kingdom . . . strong as iron" Dan 2:40; קַדְמָיְתָא כְּאַרְיֵה "the first (beast was) like a lion" 7:4 (cf. לְבוּשֵׁהּ כִּתְלַג חִוָּר וּשְׂעַר רֵאשֵׁהּ כַּעֲמַר נְקֵא דָּמְיָה לְדֹב "like a bear" 7:5); "his raiment was white as snow, and the hair of his head like pure wool" 7:9: 5:11; 7:6, 8; הֲווֹ כְּעוּר "(the metals) became like chaff" 2:35; כְּבַר אֱנָשׁ אָתֵה הֲוָה "(one) like a son of man came" 7:13 (BL 315d); פתפא הב לה . . . כאחרנן "give to him . . . the (same) provision as (to) the others" AD 9:1-2; הן כן הו כמליא אלה "if it is as (described in) these words" AD 8:3; הן מטת מרביתא לרשא ירבה מרביתא כרשא חד כחד "if the interest is added to the capital, it will pay interest like the capital, one like the other" AP 10:6-7; תהוי מלכתה כמלכת חל "may his kingdom become like a kingdom of sand" Sefire I A 25; ואשגה זרעך כעפר ארעא "and I shall make your descendants as numerous as the dust of the earth" 1QapGen

21:13; שַׂעְרֵהּ כְּנִשְׁרִין רְבָה וְטִפְרוֹהִי כְצִפְּרִין "his hair grew as long as
eagles' (feathers), and his nails (were) like (claws of) birds" Dan
4:30 (brachylogy, cf. לְבַב); עַל־רַגְלַיִן כֶּאֱנָשׁ "(the beast was made
to stand) on two feet like a man" 7:4 (cf. BL 315c); cf. כִּדְנָה .

(2) **according to** (cf. לָקֳבֵל & בְּ no. 8). כְּדָת־מָדַי וּפָרַס
"according to the law of the Medes and the Persians" Dan 6:9,
13: Ezra 6:18; 7:25; וּכְמִצְבְּיֵהּ עָבֵד בְּחֵיל שְׁמַיָּא "and (God) does according to His will in the host of heaven" Dan 4:32: Ezra 6:9;
7:18; כְּשֻׁם אֱלָהִי "(Daniel, who was named Belteshazzar) according to the name of my god" Dan 4:5; כתב . . . ספרא זנה כפם קוניה
"(Pelatiah) wrote . . . this document according to the dictation of
Koniah" *AP* 5:15.

(3) **when,** used before an infin. (cf. כְּדִי no. 3): כְּמִקְרְבֵהּ
לְגֻבָּא "when (the king) came near the den" Dan 6:21.

(4) כְּ as an adv.: כַּחֲדָה "together" Dan 2:35 (cf. חַד no.
4); כְּעַן "now" 3:15 (see כְּעַן); אֶשְׁתּוֹמַם כְּשָׁעָה חֲדָה "(Daniel) was
alarmed for a moment" 4:16; כחסן בביתך [לֹא] עלת "I did [not]
enter your house by force" *AP* 7:8; כל 2 כפם חד "both of them in
full accord," lit. "with one voice" *BMAP* 12:11 (cf. פם חד *1Qap-*
Gen 20:8); כלמדנח צפון חברון "(Mamre is) to the northeast of
Hebron" *1QapGen* 21:20; כלצפון מדנחה[ו]ן "to the northeast of
them (the mountains)" *4QEnᶜ (4Q204)* 1 xii 30: *4QEnᵉ (4Q206)*
1 xxvi 17; cf. כל־קֳבֵל , i.e., כְּלָקֳבֵל * (= לָקֳבֵל); כלקבל זי מן עלא
כת[יב] "according to what is writ[ten] above" *Mur 72* 6; כְּמָה
"how" (cf. מָה no. 2): אָתוֹהִי כְּמָה רַבְרְבִין "how great are His
signs!" Dan 3:33a: 3:33b; דרעיהא מא שפירן וידיהא כמא כלילן "Her
arms, how beautiful! And her hands, how perfect!" *1QapGen*
20:4-5.

(5) emphatic כְּ : קַבֵּל מַלְכוּתָא כְּבַר שְׁנִין שִׁתִּין וְתַרְתֵּין "(Darius)
received the kingdom, being about sixty-two years old" Dan 6:1;
שמעת כעמלא זי מלך כרחמן "a king (is) truly merciful" *Ah.* 107;
עמלת "I have heard of the great trouble that you took" *AP* 40:2;

כעשק עביד לי "truly a wrong was done to me" *AP* 16:5, 8; כעשק אל יתעבד לי "indeed, let no wrong be done to me" *AP* 16:9; וְכָל־דָּאֲרֵי אַרְעָא כְּלָה חֲשִׁיבִין "and all the inhabitants of the earth are considered as nothing" Dan 4:32. [Hebr. the same]. †

כְּדַב * (d < ḏ; *kadab*), f. כִּדְבָה , adj. (BL 319e: perh. a noun): **lying, deceitful, false.** מִלָּה כִדְבָה . . . לְמֵאמַר "to utter . . . a deceitful word" Dan 2:9; זך ספרא זי יהנפקון עליכי כדב יהוה לא אנה כתבתה "that document that they will produce against you will be false; I shall not have written it" *AP* 8:16-17; זי יהנפק כדב הו זנה ספרא זי אנה ענני כתבת לכי הו יצב "whoever produces (another document), it is deceitful; this document that I, Anani, have written for you, is valid" *BMAP* 10:16-17; כרסאא לכדבא . . . [ית]נשגון כדבתה "a throne (is set up) for the liar, (but later) his lies will be [ex]posed" *Aḥ*. 133; מן כדבן שגיאן אזהר "guard yourself from many lies" *Bisitun* 65; בקושט עמי תמללין ולא בכדבין "(that) you are speaking to me truthfully and without lies" *1QapGen* 2:7: 2:6. -- Cf. כדבה f. "untruth": [יה]נשגון כדבתה "they will [un]cover his falsehood" *Aḥ*. 133; חן גבר הימנותה [כי] שנאתה כדבת שפותה "the charm of a man is his fidelity, [for] his hatefulness is the untruth of his lips" *Aḥ*. 132. [Hebr. כָּזָב]. [1]

כְּדִי (כְּ + דִי): (1) **as.** נסבלנך כזי יסבל בר לאבוהי "we shall care for you as a son cares for his father" *BMAP* 5:13-14 (cf. 5:12: למבניה באתרה כזי "like a son who . . . "); כבר זי יסבל לאבוהי הוה לקדמן "to rebuild it (the temple) in its place as it was before" *AP* 32:8; יעבד כזי שים טעם "let him do (it) as the order was issued" *AP* 26:22; וביתי כזי תעבד לביתך "and (look after) my house as you do for your own house" *AP* 41:6; כדי תכלן תעבדן לה עבד אנה לה "as you (pl.) were able to do for him, I am doing for him" *Hermopolis* 1:4-5; הלו כזי עבד אנה לחרוץ כות תעבד בנת עלי "lo, as I am doing for Ḥaruṣ, so may (the goddess) Banit do for me" *Hermopolis* 1:7 (reading הלו w. Milik instead of the editors'

ועבדו על ביתא זילי כן כזי פקידיא [קד]מיא הוו עבדן ;(מלו) "and do for
my house just as the [for]mer officers used to do" *AD* 7:7-8; כן
[כזי עבדת לבנוה[י "thus as you did for hi[s] sons" *AP* 71:19. (2)
according to what (cf. פ no. 2): לה שבק אנה לה 1 כדי מטאה ידי "I
shall not leave him alone according to what I can do," lit., "what
my hand succeeds" *Hermopolis* 3:4; זבני עמר כזי תמטה ידכי "buy
wool according to what you can" *Hermopolis* 6:5-6. Cf. הָא־כְדִי .
(3) **when, as soon as** (cf. פ no. 3); of the past: כְּדִי יְדַע דִּי־רְשִׁים
כְּתָבָא "(Daniel), when he knew that the document had been
signed" Dan 6:11: 6:15; כְּדִי שָׁמְעִין כָּל־עַמְמַיָּא קָל קַרְנָא "as soon as
all the peoples heard the blast of the horn" 3:7 (BL 293n); כְּדִי רִם
לְבְבֵהּ "when his mind was elated" 5:20 (BL 361h); כזי חבזו אלהן
בית [אבי הא ה]ות לאחרן "when the gods struck [my father's] house,
it [came to belong] to another" *Sefire III* 24; כזי אנה הוית אתה [ע]ל
"when I was coming [t]o [my lord]" *AD* 3:2; כזי יוזא הוה במצרין
אבד "when the revolt occurred in Egypt, he perished" *AD* 8:4;
בליליא כדי דבירת מני שרי "on the night when Sarai was taken from
me" *1QapGen* 20:11. -- of the future: כזי תאתה בזנה "when you
come here, (restore what has been taken)" *AD* 12:7; כזי יאתה
אפקנרביל אשור . . . יהתב המו לאפק[נרביל] "when Upaqana-Arbayl
comes to Assyria, let him restore them to Upaqana-Arbayl" *Assur Letter* 11 (*KAI* 233); כדי אמות ערטלי אהך די לא בנין "when I
die, I shall depart bereft (and) without children" *1QapGen* 22:33.
-- w. a correlative particle in the apodosis: קדמן כזי מצריא מרדו
אדין <פ>סמשך . . . נטר "previously, when the Egyptians rebelled,
then Psamshek . . . took care of (my property)" *AD* 7:1-2, cf.
קדמת זנה בעדן זי זא באישתא עביד לן "before this, at the time when
this evil was done to us" *AP* 30:17-18; . . . אחר כזי מצרין מרדת
אדין פרימא זך וכנותה לא שנציו "later, when Egypt rebelled . . . , then
that Piryama and his colleagues did not succeed" *AD* 5:6-7; כדי
חזת בתאנוש . . . באדין אנסת רוחהא "when Bitenosh saw . . . , then
she suppressed her emotion" *1QapGen* 2:12-13; כזי צידא עבד אנה
תנה ובאתרא זנה משתרה אנה "when I go hunting here, I take my
lunch in this place" *Cilicia* 4-6 (*KAI* 261). (4) **that, so that.**

164

טרו כן כזי מ[נ]דעם כסנתו לא יהוה מן ביתא זילי "take good care so that
my house suffers no loss" *AD* 7:6: 7:2; כן כזי [מס]פת קבילה תובא
לא ישלח "so that Mispat does not send a complaint again" *AD*
12:11; כדי הוית מתגר על דילהא "(Sarai said, 'He is my brother'),
so that I might be benefited on her account" *1QapGen* 20:10; מנך
יתשם טעם כזי איש מנדעם באיש לא יעבד לפירמא "may an order be
issued by you so that no one will do any harm to Pirma'" *AD* 5:8-
9; אגרת . . . תשתלח . . . כזי הנדרז יעבדון לחתובסתי "let a letter be
sent . . . so that they provide an order for Ḥatubasti" *AD* 10:2-3;
למומא ביהו . . . כזי לא הות ארק לדרגמן "(you had) to swear by Yaho .
. . that it was not the land of Dargman" *AP* 6:6-7; כן שמיע לי כזי
פקידיא . . . מתנצחן "thus it has been heard by me that the officers .
. . are active (in the disturbances)" *AD* 7:3-4; אל ת[ב]ט . . . [כל]
מ[ל]ה [זי] תאתה על בלך כזי בכל אתר [עיני]הם ואדניהם "do not u[tt]er . .
. [every w]ord [that] comes into your mind, for in every place are
their [eyes] and their ears" *Aḥ.* 96-97. Cf. בזי, s.v. בְּ no. 4.

כְּדְנָה ("like this"): **so, thus, in this way** (cf. כֵּן). לָא אִיתַי
אֱלָה אָחֳרָן דִּי־יִכֻּל לְהַצָּלָה כִּדְנָה "there is no other god who can deliver
in this way" Dan 3:29; כִּדְנָה תֵּאמְרוּן לְהוֹם "thus you shall say to
them" Jer 10:11; יוד 1 שניח על ידה . . . ארמית כזנה למבטחיה "a yodh
is inscribed on his hand . . . in Aramaic thus 'Belonging to Mibṭaḥiah'" *AP* 28:4-5; לכן לא כזנה הו[ה] "but it was not so" *AP*
37:8; [למא צלם] אנפיך כדנא עליך שנא "[Why is the expression of]
your face so changed?" *1QapGen* 2:16-17; כָּל־מֶלֶךְ . . . מִלָּה כִדְנָה
כִּדְנָה כְּתִיב בְּגַוֵּהּ "no king has asked such a thing" Dan 2:10; לָא שְׁאֵל
"in it was written thus" Ezra 5:7 (cf. 6:2, כֵּן כְּתִיב); וכזי כזנה עביד
"(no one harmed that temple), but when it was done in this way"
AP 30:14-15; רוחך כדן עליבא "(why) is your spirit so depressed?"
1QapGen 2:17. †

כָּה (BL 252b), adv.: (1) **so.** כה אמרן "thus we have
spoken" *Sefire I* C 1. -- (2) **here.** עַד־כָּה סוֹפָא דִי־מִלְּתָא "up to here

is the end of the affair" Dan 7:28 (cf. מִלָּה no. 1). Cf. די לתנא
[ל]ך אתית "that I have come here to [you]" *1QapGen* 2:25.
[Hebr. כֹּה]. ¹

כהל , impf. 3 sg. m. *יִכְהַל ; ptc. sg. m. כָּהֵל, pl. m. כָּהֲלִין :
can, be able, have right (cf. יְכִל). -- W. ל & infin.: לָא־כָהֲלִין
כָּתָבָא לְמִקְרֵא "(the king's sages were) not able to read the writing"
Dan 5:8; 5:15; לָא־יָכְלִין פִּשְׁרָא לְהוֹדָעֻתַנִי וְאַנְתָּה כָּהֵל "(the sages)
cannot make known to me the interpretation of it, but you can"
4:15 (read w. MSS. פִּשְׁרָה): 2:26; לא אכהל . . . למרשה עליך "I will
not be able . . . to start a court-case against you" *AP* 28:7-8; לא
אכהל למפלח בבב היכלא "I cannot serve in the gate of the palace"
Aḥ. 17. -- W. a finite verb: לא יכהל זכור יאמר "Zakkur shall have
no right to say" *BMAP* 7:40-41; לא יכהלון יהנפקון עליכי ספר חדת
ועתיק "they will not be able to produce against you a document,
new or old" *AP* 8:15-16; פלאכהל לאשלח י[ד בך] "then I shall not
be able to raise a han[d against you]" *Sefire II* B 6; ליכהל ברי
[ל]י[שלח יד בבר]ך "my son will [not] be able to raise a hand
against [your] son" *Sefire I* B 25; לא יכהל ענניה ולא יעבד דין
"Ananiah shall not be able to go to court" *BMAP* 7:37-38 (cf. דִּין
no. 5); לא כהל הוית בידי "I was not able (to work) with my hands"
BMAP 9:17. †

כָּהֵן * (kāhin), emph. כָּהֲנָא ; emph. pl. כָּהֲנַיָּא, w. suff.
כָּהֲנוֹהִי : **priest.** עֶזְרָא כָּהֲנָא "Ezra the priest" Ezra 7:12, 21; יחנן
כהנא "Johanan the priest" *AP* 81:8; כָּהֲנַיָּא דִי־בִירוּשְׁלֶם "the priests
who are in Jerusalem" Ezra 6:9: 6:16, 18; 7:16, 24; כהניא זי ביב
"the priests who are in Yeb" *AP* 30:1; כהניא זי יהו אלהא "the
priests of the god Yaho" *AP* 38:1; מִן־עַמָּה יִשְׂרָאֵל וְכָהֲנוֹהִי "(any) of
the people of Israel and its priests" Ezra 7:13; אגרה שלחן . . . על
ירושלם יהוחנן כהנא רבא וכנותה כהניא זי בירושלם "we sent a letter . . . to
Johanan, the High Priest, and his colleagues, the priests, who are
in Jerusalem" *AP* 30:18; הוא הוא כהן לאל עליון "he was a priest of
God Most High" *1QapGen* 22:15. [Hebr. כֹּהֵן]. †

כַּוָּה * (*qall-at*, BL 180o), emph. כַּוְתָא *, pl. כַּוִּין, f.:
window. כַּוִּין פְּתִיחָן לֵהּ בְּעִלִּיתֵהּ "windows in his upper chamber
open (toward Jerusalem)" Dan 6:11; בתחתיה ומן עלא כוין פתיחן
"at its lower end and above there are open windows" *AP* 25:6;
כוין בה "windows (are) in it (the house)" *BMAP* 3:5; 3 כון בה "3
windows (are) in it" *BMAP* 9:13; כותא י [ ] . . . עשרה כוין [חדה]
"[ele]ven windows . . . [ ]of the window" *5QNJ (5Q15)* 1 ii
11-12. [1]

▲ כּוֹרֶשׁ : **Cyrus,** king of the Persians. וּבְמַלְכוּת כּוֹרֶשׁ פָּרְסָיָא
"and in the reign of Cyrus the Persian" Dan 6:29: Ezra 5:13, 14,
17; 6:3, 14. [Hebr. the same]. [1]

כַּכַּר * (*karkar*, BL 192h), pl. כַּכְּרִין (v.l. כִּכְּרִין), m.:
talent (in monetary sense; = 60 minas). עַד־כְּסַף כַּכְּרִין מְאָה "up to
a hundred talents of silver" Ezra 7:22; דמי כסף כנכרן אלף "the
value of a thousand silver talents" *AP* 31:27 (cf. BL 50d; *LFAA*
17i); כנכר חד מנן עשרה כלא "one talent, ten minas in all" *AP*
26:17; ככרן 3 "3 talents" *AP* 83:29. [Hebr. כִּכָּר]. [1]

כֹּל (*kull*), cst. כֹּל & כָּל־, emph. כֹּלָּא (*kóllā',* on the
accent, see BL 88h); w. suff. כָּלְּהוֹן, 3 pl. f. כָּלְּהֵין (Dan 7:19 q.,
kolléhên): **totality, all.** (1) **as cst.:** (a) before a determ. sg.:
whole, entire, any. וּמְלָת כָּל־אַרְעָא "and it filled the whole earth"
Dan 2:35; לכל חפצי "for any of my business" *Sefire III* 8; כל עלי
ארם "all Upper Aram" *Sefire I* A 6; כל כספך "your entire
money" *AP* 11:7-8; וּמִנֵּהּ יִתְּזִין כָּל־בִּשְׂרָא "and all living beings are
fed from it" Dan 4:9; כָּל־דְּנָה "all of this" 5:22; 7:16. -- (b) before
a determ. pl.: **all.** כֹּל עַמְמַיָּא "all peoples" Dan 7:14; כָּל חַכִּימֵי
מַלְכָּא "all the king's sages" 5:8; כָּל־מַעֲבָדוֹהִי "all His deeds" 4:34:
5:23; 6:25; כל מלכיא זי ימלכן בארפד "all the kings who will rule in
Arpad" *Sefire I* B 22; כל מלכי ארפד "all the kings of Arpad"
Sefire II C 15; אף לכל עבדיך אל[פנא] "and for all your slaves,

disci[pline]" *Ah.* 83; כָּל־אִלֵּין תַּדִּק וְתֵרֹעַ "it shall break and crush all these (kingdoms)" Dan 2:40 (see בְּבַרְזֶל); וְהַשְׁלְטָךְ בְּכָלְּהוֹן "(God) has made you rule over all of them" 2:38; דִּי־הֲוָת שָׁנְיָה מִן־כָּלְהֵין "(the fourth beast) which was different from all of them" 7:19 (q.); ולנשי כלנא "(I invited my sons) and the wives of all of us" *1QapGen* 12:16; ועליא שפרהא לעלא מן כולהן "and in her beauty she ranks high above all of them," i.e., other women, *1QapGen* 20:7; כל 2 כפם חד "both of them in full agreement," lit., "as with one mouth" *BMAP* 12:11. -- w. a negative: **no one, none.** לא יכלו כל אסיא "none of the physicians (of Egypt) were able" *1Qap-Gen* 20:20. -- (c) before indet. sg. (rarely pl.): **every, any.** כֹּל כְּסַף וּדְהַב דִּי תְהַשְׁכַח "any silver or gold that you shall find" Ezra 7:16; כָּל־מֶלֶךְ וְעַם דִּי יִשְׁלַח יְדֵהּ "(may God overthrow) any king or people that will stretch forth a hand to . . ." 6:12; כָּל־אֱנָשׁ דִּי יִשְׁמַע קָל "every man who hears the sound" Dan 3:10; 5:7; 6:13; Ezra 6:11; בכל גב [ ] חסניא אל "these fortifications on every side" *Zkr* B 8 (*KAI* 202); כל גבר זי יבעה רוח אפוה "anyone who rants," lit., "causes the breath of his nostrils to boil" *Sefire III* 1-2; עם כל עלל בית מלך "with all who enter the royal palace" *Sefire I* A 6; עם עקר כל מה מלך זי "with the offspring of any king who" *Sefire I* B 2; [ז]י כל לח[י]ה לתתעבד] "[th]at [no] ev[il may be done]" *Sefire I* C 6-7; כל מה לחיה בארק ובשמין "every sort of evil (existing) on earth and in heaven" *Sefire I* A 26; בכל עדן "at all times" *AP* 30:2, 3; כל מדעם זי יחיה בה איש "everything by which a man may live" *AP* 49:3; כל ירחן "in every month" *AP* 45:8; כל נכסן וקנין "all properties and acquisitions" *AP* 14:4. -- w. a negative (usually postpositive): **no, none.** וְכָל־חֲבָל לָא־הִשְׁתְּכַח בֵּהּ "no sort of harm was found on him" Dan 6:24; וְכָל־רָז לָא־אָנֵס לָךְ "and no mystery is difficult for you" 4:6; 2:35; 6:5bis; כול דם לא תאכלון "you are to eat no blood" *1QapGen* 11:17; כל בתולן . . . לא ישפרן מנהא "there are no virgins . . . more beautiful than she (Sarai)" *1QapGen* 20:6; כָּל־מֶלֶךְ . . . מִלָּה כִדְנָה לָא שְׁאֵל לְכָל־חַרְטֹם "no king . . . has asked any magician such a thing" Dan 2:10; לָא נְהַשְׁכַּח לְדָנִיֵּאל כָּל־עִלָּא . . . "we shall not find any basis of complaint against

כל

Daniel" 6:6: 3:28. -- (d) כל w. suff. in apposition to a determ. noun (cf. no. 3b): יעט אתור כלה "(Aḥiqar) counselor of all Assyria" *Aḥ.* 12; עם ארם כלה "with all Aram" *Sefire I* A 5; שרית אנה ובני כולהון למפלח בארעא "I, with all my sons, began to cultivate the earth" *1QapGen* 12:13; ועל כול ארעא כולהא "and for the entire earth" *1QapGen* 10:13; כול בני שם כולהון "all the sons of Shem, altogether" *1QapGen* 12:10; כל זי איתי לה על אנפי ארעא כלה "all that he has on the face of the earth, all of it" *AP* 15:19-20.

(2) **as abs.**: (a) **all, each** (as indef. pron.): כָּל־דִּי־יִבְעֵה "whoever makes a petition" Dan 6:8; כָּל־דִּי־לָא לֶהֱוֵא עָבֵד דָּתָא "whoever will not obey the law" Ezra 7:26; כָּל־דִּי יִשְׁאֲלֶנְכוֹן עֶזְרָא "whatever Ezra requires of you" 7:21: 7:23; כל זי איתי לה "all that he possesses" *AP* 15:19; כול די שבוא וכול די בזו "all that they had captured and all that they had plundered" *1QapGen* 22:10-11; וּבְכָל־דִּי דָאֲרִין בְּנֵי־אֲנָשָׁא "and wherever the sons of men dwell" Dan 2:38; בכל מה זי ימות בר אנש שקרתם "in whatever way anyone shall die, you will have been unfaithful" *Sefire III* 16. -- (b) כל following an enumeration: **in all**. אנת ואנתתך וברך כל 3 "you and your wife and your son, 3 in all" *AP* 6:4-5; חלכין תרין אמן חד כל "two Cilicians, one craftsman, in all three servants of mine" *AD* 6:4; כל גבר 1 נשן 1 "altogether, 1 man 1 woman" *BMAP* 3:3; אנה בגזשת ואובל כל 2 אנבחי זבן "I, Bagazusht, and Ubil, both of us, have sold" *BMAP* 3:10; כל תרין נופתיא זי כרכיא "(P. and X.), in all, two boatmen of the fortifications" *AP* 26:8; כל גברן 5 "in all, 5 men" *AP* 33:5; כל לבשן זי עמר וכתן 8 "all the garments of wool and linen 8" *BMAP* 7:13; after the enumerated vessels: בכל 5 "in all, 5" *BMAP* 7:19. -- (c) כל as an appositive instead of כלא (only in *AP* 30 & 39:1; cf. no. 3b): **all**. אלהיא כל "may the gods all wish you well," lit. "seek your welfare" *AP* 39:1; אגורי אלהי מצרין כל מגרו "the temples of the gods of Egypt, all (of them), they overthrew" *AP* 30:14.

(3) **as emph.**: (a) **all, everything** (see *Bib* 38 [1957] 178-83). מָזוֹן לְכֹלָּא־בֵהּ "in it was food for all" Dan 4:9, 18; ... פַּרְזְלָא

כֹּלָּא מְטָא עַל . . . "the iron . . . shatters everything" 2:40; . . . חָשֵׁל כֹּלָּא
אנתה מרה ושליט . . . the king" 4:25; מַלְכָּא "all (of this) came upon . . . the king" 4:25;
על כולא "You are Lord and Sovereign over all" *1QapGen* 20:13;
כלא זי עביד לן ארשם לא ידע "Arsames knew nothing about all that
was done to us" *AP* 31:29; זי לקחת כלא התב הב למספת "what you
have received, restore and give all of it to Maspath" *AD* 12:7;
נשמן על דליה כלא מליא באגרת חדה שלחן "we sent all (these) matters
in a letter in our name to Delaiah" *AP* 30:29. -- (b) כלא as an
appositive to a determ. noun: לְדָרְיָוֶשׁ מַלְכָּא שְׁלָמָא כֹלָּא "To Darius,
the king, all peace!" Ezra 5:7 (BL 318e); שלם מראי אלהיא כלא
[ישאלו] "may all the gods [desire] the peace of my lord" *BMAP*
13:1; הות אתור כלא ירעך "(by his advice and words) all Assyria
was guided(?)" *Aḥ.* 43; יהודיא כלא זי תנה "all the Jews who are
here" *AP* 31:26; נשי ביתן כלא א[בדו] "all the women of our house
per[ished]" *AD* 8:2; כנכר חד מנן עשרה כלא "(all the materials are
worth) one talent, ten minas, in all" *AP* 26:17; וכ]ל זי[בעה באיש
לאגורא זך כלא קטילו "and al[l who] sought (to do) evil to that
temple, all of them were killed" *AP* 31:15-16 (cf. 30:16 ‖ כל);
יהודיא כלא בעלי יב "the Jews, all (of them), citizens of Yeb" *AP*
31:22 (cf. 30:22 ‖ כל); יהודיא כלא די תנה "the Jews, all (of them),
who are here" *AP* 31:26 (cf. 30:26-27 ‖ כל).

שכלל : see כלל .

כְּמָה : see מָה .

כֵּן , adv. **so, thus** (cf. כְּדְנָה). -- (1) before dir. disc.: כֵּן
כֵּן אָמְרִין "he said thus to him" Dan 2:24, 25; 7:23: 4:11; אֲמַר לֵהּ
"they said thus: 6:7; 7:5; Ezra 5:3; שלח עלי כן אמר "he sent
(word) to me, saying thus" *AD* 4:1; עבדיך . . . כן אמרן "your
servants . . . say thus" *AP* 33:1-7; כֵּן כְּתִיב "so it is written" Ezra
6:2; כן ידיע יהוי לך "let it thus be known to you" *AD* 7:8. --
before an obj. cl.: כן שמיע לי כזי "thus I hear that," lit. "it is heard

כנה

by me" *AD* 7:3. -- (2) in a comparison: איך זי תקד שעותא זא באש כן תקד ארפד "just as this wax is burned by fire, so may Arpad be burned" *Sefire I* A 35; לקבל זי אנה עבדת לך כן אפו עבד לי "according as I did for you, so do also for me" *Ah.* 52; [זי] שמהתהם לא ידע איש הא כן אנשא לא ידע איש "(many are the stars) [whose] names a man does not know; so man does not know mankind" *Ah.* 116; ואנתם כן לא עבדן "(others are adding to their lord's domain), but you are not doing so" *AD* 7:5; כן כזי פקידיא [קד]מיא הוו עבדן כן ידיע לך "just as the [ear]lier officials were doing, so let it be known to you" *AD* 7:7-8. -- (3) before a purpose or result cl.: כן עבד כזי לאלהיא וארשם תחד[י] "so act as to please the gods and Arsames" *AD* 13:2; התב הב להם כן כזי [מס]פת קבילה תובא לא ישלח "restore and give (it) to them so that [Mas]path does not again send a complaint" *AD* 12:10-11; אנתם קמו קבלהם כן כזי מלה באישה לא יהשכחון לכם יהו[דעון] "help them so that, when they find no fault in you, [they] will acknow[ledge] to you," lit., "rise up before them" *AP* 38:6-7; הן כן עבדו עד זי אגורא זך יתבנה "if they do so, that that temple is rebuilt, (it will be a merit for you)" *AP* 30:27. -- (4) in adverbial expressions: ומן כן רשינכם "and so we sue you" *AP* 20:7; על כן "therefore" *Ah.* 117; ושלח אגרה על דבר כן "and he sent a letter about this matter" *AP* 40:3; סלקת למחרתי כן לרמת חצור "the next day I climbed up to Ramat-Hazor" *1QapGen* 21:10. [Hebr. the same]. †

כְּנָה * (< Akk. *kinātu*); w. suff. כנתה (*kĕnātēh*), כנתהם; pl. (w. augm. -*aw*-), w. suff. כְּנָוָתֵהּ , כְּנָוָתְהוֹן, m.: **colleague, associate.** שְׁמְשַׁי סָפְרָא וּשְׁאָר כְּנָוָתְהוֹן דִּינָיָא "Shimshai, the scribe, and the rest of their colleagues, the judges" Ezra 4:9: 4:17, 23; תַּתְּנַי וּשְׁתַר בּוֹזְנַי וּכְנָוָתְהוֹן ... "Tattenai ... and Shethar-bozenai and their associates" 5:3: 5:6; 6:6, 13; דמידת וכנותה דיניא "Damidat and his colleagues, the judges" *AP* 6:6; על יהוחנן כהנא רבא וכנותה כהניא זי בירושלם "to Johanan, the High Priest, and his associates, the priests, who are in Jerusalem" *AP* 30:18; חרוץ וכנותה ספרי מדינ[תא]

171

"Ḥaruṣ and his colleagues, notaries of [the] province" *AP* 17:6;
אזדכרא כנתהם "the herald, their associate" *AP* 17:7. -- (2)
companion, comrade (cf. חֲבַר): אחי ידניה וכנותה חילא יהודיא [אל]
"[to] my brethren, Yedaniah and his comrades, the Jewish garrison" *AP* 21:11; רביא אמר לכנותה גבריא אלך תרין "the officer said
to his companions, those two men (who were with him)" *Aḥ.* 56;
[פ]סם[שכחסי] זכי וכנותה עבדי עחחפי "that [P]sam[shek-ḥasi] and his
companions, the slaves of 'Aḥ-ḥapi" *AD* 3:6-7; [לא ידע] איש מה
בלבב כנתה "a man does not know what is in the mind of his comrade" *Aḥ.* 163 (cf. אנשא לא ידע איש "man does not know mankind" *Aḥ.* 116); חמר . . . ינשא בות מן כנתה "an ass . . . shall bear
shame before his companion" *Aḥ.* 90. [Hebr. קְנוֹתָו Ezra 4:7]. †

כְּנֵמָא , adv. (BL 253d): **so, thus.** Before indir. disc.:
כְּנֵמָא אֲמַרְנָא לְהֹם "thus we spoke to them" Ezra 5:9: 5:11; כְּנֵמָא
אֲמַרְנָא "so we said" (but read אָמְרִין "they said," cf. v. 3) 5:4;
כְּתַבוּ אִגְּרָה . . . כְּנֵמָא "they wrote a letter . . . (saying) thus" 4:8 (but
the letter begins only in v. 11b). -- In a comparison: לָקֳבֵל דִּי־שְׁלַח
דָּרְיָוֶשׁ מַלְכָּא כְּנֵמָא . . . עֲבַדוּ "according to what Darius, the king, had
ordered, so . . . they did" 6:13. †

כְּנַשׁ *, infin. מִכְנַשׁ : **assemble.** שְׁלַח לְמִכְנַשׁ לַאֲחַשְׁדַּרְפְּנַיָּא
"(the king) sent to assemble the satraps" Dan 3:2. -- **Hithpa./
Ithpa.,** ptc. pl. m. חָזַיִן . . . וּמִתְכַּנְּשִׁין "and (the satraps et al.)
gathered together (and) saw" Dan 3:27: 3:3; יתכנשון אלהי מצרין
"the gods of Egypt will be assembled" *AP* 71:8; [מרדיא] אתכנשו
"[the rebels] gathered together" *Bisitun* 15; ואתכנשנא כחדא ואזלנא
"we gathered together and went" *1QapGen* 12:16. [Hebr. כָּנַס]. †

▲ כַּשְׂדָּי *: see כַּשְׂדָּי.

כְּסַף (*kasp*), emph. כַּסְפָּא, m.: **silver.** כַּסְפָּא . . . דְּקוּ כַחֲדָה
וְדַהֲבָא "the silver and the gold (of the statue), all together, were

172

broken up" Dan 2:35: 2:45; כֹּל כְּסַף וּדְהַב דִּי תְהַשְׁכַּח "all the silver and gold that you will find" Ezra 7:16: 7:15; בִּשְׁאָר כַּסְפָּא וְדַהֲבָא "(do) with the rest of the silver and gold (whatever you wish)" 7:18; כסף צריף "refined silver" *BMAP* 5:15. -- as a gen. of material: מָאנֵי דַהֲבָא וְכַסְפָּא "vessels of gold and silver" Dan 5:2: 5:4, 23; מָאנַיָּא . . . דִּי דַהֲבָא וְכַסְפָּא "the vessels . . . of gold and silver" Ezra 5:14: 6:5; דְּרָעוֹהִי דִּי כְסַף "its (the statue's) arms (were) of silver" Dan 2:32 (cf. דִּי I 2b). -- **money** (silver as used in commerce). תִּקְנֵה בְּכַסְפָּא דְנָה "with this money you will acquire" Ezra 7:17; וזי תנתן לה בכסף או רחמת "or to whomever you give (it) for money or gratis" *BMAP* 12:26; למזלכי מנדת כסף "to sell you (a slave) for a payment of money" *BMAP* 5:7; כסף שנאה בראשה "the divorce money is on her head" *BMAP* 7:25. -- **sum of money** (abs.), with a following number of units as an appositive: תתב על מוזנא ותתקל ל[אס]חור כסף שקלן 7 "she shall return to the scales and weigh out to [As]hor the sum of 7 shekels" *AP* 15:23-24; והן כספא זנה חד כרש חד שקלן ארב[עה לא ש]למת "and if I do [not p]ay (you) this sum of one karash, fou[r] shekels" *AP* 29:6; אביגרנא זי כסף כרשן עשרה "the penalty of a sum of ten karashes (by the scales of the king)" *AP* 20:14; ננתן לך אביגרנא כסף צריף כרשן עשרה במתקלת מלכא "we shall pay you a penalty of refined money, ten karashes, by royal weight" *AP* 28:10-11; לבשיה דמי כסף כ[רש]ן שבעה "her garments valued at the sum of seven ka[rash]es" *BMAP* 7:23; יהבת לן דמוהי כסף כרש חד שקלן 3 כסף יון במנין סתתרי 6 שקל 1 "you gave us its price, the sum of one karash, 3 shekels in Greek money, in the number of 6 staters (and) 1 shekel" *BMAP* 12:13-14; עַד־כְסַף כַּכְּרִין מְאָה "up to a sum of a hundred talents" Ezra 7:22. [Hebr. כֶּסֶף]. †

כְּעַן (< כְּעֶת כְּעֶנֶת (v.l. כְּעֶן), *'itt* <* *'idt*; cf. עִדָּן & BL 255u; ענתא "time" *1QapGen* 2:10), adv. "at this time" (see כְּ no. 4). -- (1) **now.** וּכְעַן הוֹדַעְתַּנִי דִּי־בְעֵנָא מִנָּךְ "and now You have made known to me what we asked of You" Dan 2:23; וּמִן־אֱדַיִן וְעַד־כְּעַן

מִתְבְּנֵא "and from then until now it (the temple) is being built"
Ezra 5:16; חנום הו עלין מן זי חנניה במצרין עד כען "Khnum is against
us from the time that Hananiah (was) in Egypt until now" *AP*
38:7; עד כען לא דבקתה לטורא "up till now I had not reached the
mountain" *1QapGen* 19:8; וכעת השבו אלהן שיבת בי[ת אבי] "but
now the gods have brought about the return of [my father's]
hou[se]" *Sefire III* 24; ברה . . . . כען פקיד עבד חלפוהי "his son . . .
has been made an officer now instead of him" *AD* 2:2-3; יתיר מן
זי כען חד אלף "(God grant you favor before the king) a thousand
time more than now" *AP* 30:2-3. (2) **and so, therefore.** כְּעַן דָּנִיֵּאל
יִתְקְרֵי "and so let Daniel be called upon" Dan 5:12; כְּעַן מַלְכָּא
תְּקִים אֱסָרָא "therefore, O King, establish the prohibition" 6:9:
4:24; Ezra 4:13, 14, 21; כְּעַן הֵן אִיתֵיכוֹן עֲתִידִין "and so, if you are
ready" Dan 3:15: 5:16; וּכְעַן הֵן עַל־מַלְכָּא טָב יִתְבַּקַּר "therefore, if it
seems good to the king, let a search be made" Ezra 5:17: Dan
5:15; וכען צלי עלי "and so, pray for me" *1QapGen* 20:28. -- (3)
and now (וכען) etc., introducing in a letter, after the name of the
addressee, the body of the message): מן ארשם על ארתהנת שלם
ושררת שגיא הושרת ל[ך] וכעת "From Arsames to Artahunt, I send
yo[u] (a greeting of) abundant peace and prosperity: And now"
AD 5:1; אל מראן בגוהי פחת יהוד עבדיך ידניה וכנותה . . . שלם . . . כען
"To our lord, Bagohi, governor of Judah, your servants Jedaniah
and his colleagues . . . (send you a greeting of) peace . . . : Now"
AP 30:1-4; מן ארשם על ארמפי וכעת "From Arsames to Armapi:
And now" *AD* 4:1; מן ארשם על נחתחור וכעת . . . וכען . . . כען אף
"From Arsames to Nehtihur: And now . . . , and now . . . ; more-
over now" *AD* 7:1, 3, 5; in the body of a letter: וכעת (seven
times) *Hermopolis* 1:5-11; וּכְעֶנֶת . . . עַל־אַרְתַּחְשַׁשְׁתָּא מַלְכָּא עַבְדָּיך
"To Artaxerxes, the king, your servants . . . : And now" Ezra
4:11 (dl. וּכְעֶנֶת in 4:10b); the king's reply: שְׁלָם וּכְעֶנֶת . . . עַל־רְחוּם
"To Rehum . . . peace! And now" 4:17b; כְּעַן תַּתְּנַי . . . שְׁתַר בּוֹזְנַי וּכְנָוָתְהוֹן "Now Tattenai . . . Shethar-bozenai and their associates"
6:6; גְּמִיר <שְׁלָם> דִּי־אֱלָהּ שְׁמַיָּא . . . כָּהֲנָא לְעֶזְרָא מַלְכַּיָּא מֶלֶךְ אַרְתַּחְשַׁשְׁתְּא
וּכְעֶנֶת "Artaxerxes, king of kings, to Ezra, priest . . . of the heav-

enly God, Perfect <Peace!> And now" 7:12. [Hebr. עַתָּה]. †

כְּפַת *, **Peil** perf. pass. 3 sg. m. כְּפִית *, 3 pl. m. כְּפִתוּ. **Pa.** infin. כַּפָּתָה; pass. ptc. sg. m. מְכַפַּת *, pl. m. מְכַפְּתִין : **bind, tie up.** גֻּבְרַיָּא אִלֵּךְ כְּפִתוּ "those men were tied up" Dan 3:21; אֲמַר לְכַפָּתָה לְשַׁדְרַךְ "(the king) bade (them) to bind Shadrach" 3:20; נְפַלוּ לְגוֹא־אַתּוּן . . . מְכַפְּתִין "they fell bound into the furnace" 3:23; 3:24. †

כֹּר *, pl. כֹּרִין : **cor** (a measure of capacity). עַד־חִנְטִין כֹּרִין מְאָה "up to a hundred cors of wheat" Ezra 7:22. [Hebr. the same]. [1]

כַּרְבְּלָה * (Akk. *karballatu*), pl. w. suff. כַּרְבְּלָתְהוֹן : **tiara, hat.** וְכַרְבְּלָתְהוֹן וּלְבֻשֵׁיהוֹן וּרְמִיו "(these men, bound in) their tiaras and their clothes were thrown (into the furnace)" Dan 3:21; וכרבלה 1 "and 1 hat" *AP* 55:11; [כ]רבלן 2 "2 hats" *AP* 57:2. [1]

כְּרָה *, **Itpe.** 3 sg. m. אִתְכְּרִי *, 3 sg. f. אֶתְכְּרִיַּת (BL 159r): **be anxious.** אֶתְכְּרִיַּת רוּחִי "my spirit was anxious" Dan 7:15. [1]

כָּרוֹז *, emph. כָּרוֹזָא : **herald.** כָּרוֹזָא קָרֵא בְחָיִל "the herald proclaimed aloud" Dan 3:4. [1]

כְּרַז * (denom. verb < כָּרוֹז , BL 274m), **Haph.** 3 pl. הַכְרִזוּ: **proclaim.** הַכְרִזוּ עֲלוֹהִי דִּי־לֶהֱוֵא שַׁלִּיט "they proclaimed about him that he would rule" Dan 5:29. [1]

כָּרְסֵא *, < Akk. *kussīum, kussû* (> *kursī > kursē'*); dissim. *ss > rs* (cf. BL 50f; *AHW* 512a); cst. כָּרְסֵא , emph. כָּרְסְיָא* (on the yodh, see BL 233 n. 1) & כָּרְסְאָא * (*Aḥ.* 133), w. suff. כָּרְסְיֵה & כרסאה (*korsě'ēh*), כרסאי (*korsě'î*), pl. כָּרְסָוָן (w. augm. -*aw*-): **seat, throne.** מִן־כָּרְסֵא מַלְכוּתֵה "(the king was deposed)" from his kingly throne" Dan 5:20; כָּרְסָוָן רְמִיו "seats were placed (for judgment)" 7:9; כָּרְסְיֵהּ שְׁבִיבִין דִּי־נוּר "his throne was flames of fire" 7:9; עַל כרסא אבי ... הושבני "have seated me ... on the throne of my father" *Barrakib* 5-7 (*KAI* 216); מלכא יתב בכרסאה "(when Artaxerxes), the king, (was) sitting on his throne" *AP* 6:2; בר[י] זי ישב על כהסאי "[my] son who sits on my throne" *Sefire III* 17 (correct to כרסאי). †

▲ כַּשְׂדָּי * (BL 196d), emph. כַּשְׂדָּיָא k. & כַּשְׂדָּאָה q. (BL 51k), כַּסְדָּיָא k. & כַּסְדָּאָה q. (BL 27h); pl. כַּשְׂדָּיִין * & כָּשְׂדָּאִין, emph. כַּשְׂדָּיֵא k. & כַּשְׂדָּאֵי q. (BL 204l). -- (1) **Chaldean.** בֵּלְאשַׁצַּר מַלְכָּא כַשְׂדָּיָא "Belshazzar, the Chaldean king" Dan 5:30 (for k., read כַּשְׂדָּיָא q.); גֻּבְרִין כַּשְׂדָּאִין "Chaldean men" 3:8 (BL 318g); נְבוּכַדְנֶצַּר מֶלֶךְ־בָּבֶל כַּסְדָּיָא "Nebuchadnezzar, king of Babylon, the Chaldean" Ezra 5:12 (for k., read כַּסְדָּיָא q.). -- (2) **soothsayer.** אֲמַר לְכַשְׂדָּיֵא "he said to the soothsayers" Dan 2:5: 2:10bis; 4:4; 5:7, 11. [Hebr. כַּשְׂדִּי]. †

כְּתַב, כְּתַב, 1 sg. כתבת (*kitbēt*), 3 pl. כְּתַבוּ; impf. 2 sg. m. תכתב (*tiktub*), 1 pl. נִכְתֻּב; ptc. act. sg. f. כָּתְבָה, pl. f. כָּתְבָן; pass. ptc. sg. m. כתב, כְּתִיב (*kĕtîb*), pl. m. כתיבן (*kĕtîbīn*): **write** (cf. רְשַׁם, שְׁלַח). אֶצְבְּעָן ... כָּתְבָן עַל־גִּירָא "fingers ... writing on the plaster (of the wall)" Dan 5:5; פַּס יְדָה דִּי כָתְבָה "part of the hand as it wrote" 5:5; מַלְכָּא כְתַב לְכָל־עַמְמַיָּא "the king wrote to all the peoples" 6:26; כְּתַבוּ אִגְּרָה ... לְאַרְתַּחְשַׁשְׂתְּא "they wrote a letter ... to Artaxerxes" Ezra 4:8; בֵּאדַיִן חֶלְמָא כְתַב "then he wrote the dream" Dan 7:1; דִּי נִכְתֻּב שֻׁם־גֻּבְרַיָּא דִּי בְרָאשֵׁיהֹם "that we might write down the names of the men who are at their head" Ezra 5:10 (cf. דִּי III 6); כֵּן כְּתִיב בְּגַוֵּהּ "on it was written thus" 6:2: 5:7; ותכתב לי נבו על כל כסף "and you shall write for me a receipt for all the money" *AP* 11:6-7; זי ... זנה ביתא זי תחומוהי כתיבן בספרא זנה ... לא כתב על ספר אנתתכי "this is the house, of which the boundaries are written in this document ... which is not written in the docu-

ment of your marriage" *BMAP* 10:7; כה אמרן [וכה כ]תבן מה כתבת
א[נה מתע]אל "thus we have spoken [and thus] we have [writ]ten;
what I, [Matiʻ]el, wrote" *Sefire I* C 1-2. [Hebr. כְּתַב]. †

כְּתַב (BL 189r; v.l. כְּתָב) abs. & cst., emph. & כְּתָבָה
כְּתָבָא , m.: **book, document, writing.** דִּי-יִקְרֵא כְּתָבָה דְנָה "who
will read this writing" Dan 5:7: 5:8 + ; תְּקִים אֱסָרָא וְתִרְשֻׁם כְּתָבָא
"establish the interdict and sign the document" 6:9: 6:10, 11;
כִּכְתָב סְפַר מֹשֶׁה "according to the writing in the book of Moses"
Ezra 6:18; וּמְלַח דִּי-לָא כְתָב "and salt without limit," lit., "without
a writing" Ezra 7:22. [Hebr. the same].

כְּתַל (*kutl,* BL 184m, 224k; v.l. כֹּתַל ; < Akk. *kutlu*),
emph. pl. כַּתְלַיָּא : **wall.** עַל-גִּירָא דִּי-כְתַל הֵיכְלָא "on the plaster of
the wall of the palace" Dan 5:5; אָע מִתְּשָׂם בְּכֻתְלַיָּא "timber is laid
in the walls (of the temple)" Ezra 5:8; תרעה ליד כתלא גויא "its
gate was by the inner wall" *4QNJ^a (4Q554)* 2 iii 16. [Hebr.
כֹּתֶל]. †

ל

ל (*la-*), prefixed prep. (BL 258m-r); לְ before a shewa, לַ
לַ & לֵ &; before Hateph, לַ before יְ , לֵ before אֱלָה , but before
cst. sg. לֵאלָהּ ; w. sg. suff. לִי, לָךְ, לֵהּ, לַהּ; pl. לַנָא, לְכֹם & לְכוֹן,
לְהוֹן & לְהֹן & לְהֹם:
I. לְ **before a noun or pron.** -- (1) לְ for dative, after
verb of giving, saying, etc.: זְמָן יִנְתֶּן-לֵהּ "(that the king) might
give him time" Dan 2:16; מְהַקְרְבִין נִיחוֹחִין לֶאֱלָהּ שְׁמַיָּא "offering
fragrant sacrifices to the God of Heaven" Ezra 6:10; דִּי יִפֶּל-לָךְ
לְמִנְתַּן "you will have occasion to give," lit., "it will fall to you to
give" 7:20; כֵּן אֲמַר-לֵהּ "thus he said to him" Dan 2:24; כְּתָבָא
אֶקְרֵא לְמַלְכָּא "I shall read the writing for the king" 5:17; כְּתַב
כְּתַבוּ אִגְּרָה לְכָל-עַמְמַיָּא "(the king) wrote to all the peoples" 6:26; . . .

177

לְאַרְתַּחְשַׁשְׂתְּא מַלְכָּא . "they wrote a letter . . . to Artaxerxes, the king" Ezra 4:8; שלחי לי "send (word) to me" Hermopolis 2:8; in the address of a letter: אַרְתַּחְשַׁסְתְּא מֶלֶךְ . . . לְעֶזְרָא כָהֲנָא "Artaxerxes, king of . . . to Ezra, the priest" Ezra 7:12: 5:7; מַן־שָׂם לְכֹם טְעֵם "who gave you the decree?" Ezra 5:3, 9: 7:21; יְדִיעַ לֶהֱוֵא־לָךְ "let it be known to you" Dan 3:18; כן ידיע יהוי לך "let it thus be known to you" AD 7:8; רָזָא גֲלִי . . . לְדָנִיֵּאל "the mystery was revealed . . . to Daniel" Dan 2:19; לא ישתמע לה "heed shall not be paid to her" AP 18:3; וכען תנה כן שמיע לי "and now here, so I hear," lit., "it is heard by me" AD 7:3; כן שמיע לן "so we have heard" Padua I B 6; דָּמְיָה לְדֹב . . . חֵיוָה אָחֳרִי "another beast . . . (was) like a bear" Dan 7:5: 3:25.

(2) לְ of the accus. (BL 335a, 336b): אֶבֶן . . . מְחָת לְצַלְמָא "a stone . . . shattered the statue" Dan 2:34; רוּחֵי שְׁמַיָּא מְגִיחָן לְיַמָּא רַבָּא "winds of the heavens were stirring up the great sea" 7:2; כתשת לאנתתי "you struck my wife" AP 7:5; אנה יהבת לכי לביתא "I give you the house" AP 13:2; יתיבו נה לשרי לאברם בעלה "let them return Sarai to Abram, her husband" 1QapGen 20:25; דִּי סְלִקוּ . . . עֲלַיְנָא אֲתוֹ לִירוּשְׁלֶם . . . בָּנַיִן "(the Jews), who came up . . . to us, have gone (and) are rebuilding Jerusalem" Ezra 4:12 (BL 341u); שְׁבֻקוּ לַעֲבִידַת בֵּית־אֱלָהָא דֵךְ פַּחַת יְהוּדָיֵא וּלְשָׂבֵי יְהוּדָיֵא בֵּית־אֱלָהָא דֵךְ יִבְנוֹן "let the work on that house of God alone; let the prefect of the Jews and the elders of the Jews rebuild that house of God" Ezra 6:7 (prob. dl. "the prefect of the Jews and" and read לְמִבְנֵה for יִבְנוֹן; cf. לְ II 1c). -- W. suff.: לא שבקן לן למבניה "they do not allow us to build it" AP 30:23; יָבַעוֹן . . . לִי "(my counselors) were seeking for me" Dan 4:33; קרא לי אלו "(the Pharaoh) summoned me" 1QapGen 20:26; לָךְ . . . מְהוֹדֵא וּמְשַׁבַּח אֲנָה "to You . . . I give thanks and praise" Dan 2:23: 4:22, 29; לֵאלָהֵי כַסְפָּא . . . שַׁבַּחְתָּ וְלֵאלָהָא דִּי־נִשְׁמְתָךְ בִּידֵהּ . . . לֵהּ לָא הַדַּרְתָּ "you praised the gods of silver . . . but the God, in whose hand is your breath, . . . you have not honored" 5:23 (obj. is emphasized by לֵהּ; cf. הוּא no. 5, or דִּי II 1); לה שבק אנה לה 1 "I am not leaving him alone"

ל

Hermopolis 3:4; והוא רדף להון "and he (Abram) pursued them"
1QapGen 22:9. -- Cf. לְ before a pred. nominative: הֲוָת . . . אַבְנָא
לְטוּר רַב "the stone . . . became a great mountain" Dan 2:35: 4:27
(BL 341x).

(3) לְ of the gen. (BL 315f, g): מֶלֶךְ לְיִשְׂרָאֵל "a king of
Israel" Ezra 5:11; עַד יוֹם תְּלָתָה לִירַח אֲדָר "on the third day of the
month of Adar" 6:15; עַד שְׁנַת תַּרְתֵּין לְמַלְכוּת דָּרְיָוֶשׁ "until the
second year of the reign of Darius" 4:24: 5:13; 6:3; Dan 7:1;
ענניה . . . לחן ליהו אלהא "Ananiah . . . agent of the god Yaho"
BMAP 3:3: 4:2; ארדיכל לסון בירתא "architect of the fortress,
Syene" *AP* 14:2; מחסיה, , , ארמי זי סון לדגל וריזת "Mahseiah . . . ,
an Aramean of Syene, of the detachment of Warizath" *AP* 5:2-3;
תחומוהי עליה לה זי בית דרגמן "its boundaries: at the upper end of it,
the house of Dargman" *AP* 8:5 (cf. מִן no. 8); לבש 1 זי קמר [ח]דת
לאמן 7 "1 garment of wool, [n]ew, (length) of 7 cubits" *BMAP*
7:6; אנתה מרה לכול מלכי ארעא "You are lord of all the kings of the
earth" *1QapGen* 20:15-16; והוא הוא כהן לאל עליון "and he
(Melchizedek) was a priest of God Most High" *1QapGen* 22:15.

(4) Poss. לְ: דִּי־דָת לְמָדַי וּפָרַס "that it is a law of the Medes
and the Persians" Dan 6:16: 7:4, 6, 7, 20; כַּוִּין פְּתִיחָן לֵהּ בְּעִלִּיתֵהּ נֶגֶד
יְרוּשְׁלֶם "he (Daniel) had windows in his upper room open toward
Jerusalem" 6:11; מַתְּנָתָךְ לָךְ לֶהֶוְיָן "let your gifts be for yourself"
5:17; חֲלָק . . . לָא אִיתַי לָךְ "you will have . . . no share" Ezra 4:16;
שלם לן תנה [אבי] כזי חבזו אלהן בית "here we have peace" *AP* 37:2;
הא ה[י]ות לאחרן "when gods struck [my father's] house, [it came to
be]long to somebody else" *Sefire III* 24; לא איתי לי בר וברה "I
have no son or daughter" *AP* 8:10; כָּל־אֲתַר לָא־הִשְׁתְּכַח לְהוֹן "no
trace of them was found" Dan 2:35. -- דִּי לִי & לִי, etc. = poss.
pron.: **my, mine,** etc., w. דִי, it can express possession attribu-
tively or predicatively. (a) as attributive: בר לי "a son of mine"
AP 6:12; בר לה "a son of his" *AP* 5:9; או בר זילה "or a son of
his" *AP* 8:26; איש לכם . . . איש זי לכם "any one of yours . . . any
one of yours" *AP* 20:12-14; עלים זילי "a servant of mine" *AD*

179

סריסא [זנ]ה עלימא זילי 8:1;‎ "[th]is eunuch, a slave of mine" *Ah.*
63;‎ אנתי ובר וברה לכי ואיש זילכי "you (f.) or a son or daughter of
yours or any one belonging to you" *AP* 8:12;‎ בית 1 ארק זילי "a
house (and) a land of mine" *AP* 8:3;‎ זי תהשכח לי ביב "whatever
you find of mine in Yeb" *BMAP* 11:11 (cf. שכח);‎ לא הות ארק
לדרגמן זילי הא אנה "it was not the land of Dargman, (but) mine,
that is (belonging to) me" *AP* 6:7. -- (b) as predicative (cf. הוא 2
b):‎ לך יהוה וזי בניך אחריך "(that slave) will belong to you and to
your sons after you" *AP* 28:12;‎ ארקא זך זיליכי "that land is yours"
AP 8:19;‎ אגרא זך זילך הי "that portico is yours" *AP* 5:4;‎ ימאת לה
כזי זילי הי "I swore to him that it was mine" *AP* 8:24-25;‎ די חכמתא
וגבורתא די לה־היא "to Whom belong wisdom and might" Dan
2:20.

     (5) ל of interest or disinterest:‎ וּמָזוֹן לְכֹלָּא־בֵהּ "and on it
food for all" Dan 4:9;‎ לַעֲלָוָן לֶאֱלָהּ שְׁמַיָּא "for holocausts for the
God of Heaven" Ezra 6:9:‎ 7:15, 16;‎ יִתְעֲבֵד . . . לְבֵית אֱלָהּ שְׁמַיָּא "let
it be done . . . for the house of the God of Heaven" 7:23;‎ וּמְצַלַּיִן
לְחַיֵּי מַלְכָּא וּבְנוֹהִי "that they may pray for the life of the king and of
his sons" 6:10;‎ מַלְכוּתָךְ לָךְ קַיָּמָה מִן־דִּי תִנְדַּע דִּי שַׁלִּטִן שְׁמַיָּא "your
kingdom shall be stable for you from the time that you know that
Heaven reigns" Dan 4:23;‎ להן בני זי ילדתי לי "but my children
whom you bore to me" *BMAP* 4:20;‎ למלקח לך כל ערבן "(you have
the right) to take any security for yourself" *AP* 10:9;‎ וצדקה יהוה
לך קדם יהו "and it shall be a merit for you before Yaho" *AP*
30:27;‎ כזי תעבד לביתך "as you would do for your own house" *AP*
41:6;‎ למה לי "for what good will it be for me?" *Ah.* 119;‎ לוט קנה
לה נכסין שגיאין ונסב לה אנתה "Lot acquired many flocks and took
for himself a wife" *1QapGen* 20:34;‎ ל designates a creditor, and
עַל a debtor:‎ לא אשתאר לן עליך מן דמיא "there is not outstanding to
us against you any part of the price" *BMAP* 12:6; --‎ חֶלְמָא לְשָׂנְאָיךְ
וּפִשְׁרֵהּ לְעָרָיךְ "(My lord), may the dream be for those who hate
you and its interpretation for your enemies" Dan 4:16;‎ וכעשק
זי בעו באיש עביד לי "and a wrong was done to me" *AP* 16:5;‎

ל

לאגורא זך "(all) who sought (to do) evil to that temple" *AP* 30:17;
זי לי חסרן "what is lacking to me (makes no difference to you)"
AP 38:9.

(6) ל as ethical dative (giving emphasis): תהך לה אן זי צבית
"(a divorced wife) shall go away wherever she wishes" *AP*
15:28-29; אזלת לי לביתי "I (Aḥiqar) went away to my house" *Aḥ.*
22; פמך אשתמר לך "keep guard over your mouth" *Aḥ.* 97; עדי לך
מן כול מדינת מצרין "depart (at once) from all the provinces of
Egypt" *1QapGen* 20:27-28; דכר לך על עדינתי "recall my pleasure" *1QapGen* 2:9; אזל ויתב לה בבקעת ירדנא "(Lot) went and
settled in the valley of the Jordan" *1QapGen* 21:5; תבת ואתית לי
לביתי בשלם "I returned and came home safely" *1QapGen* 21:19.

(7) ל of direction: **to, into,** following a verb of motion (cf.
עַל "to" a person): דָּנִיֵּאל לְבַיְתֵהּ אֲזַל "Daniel went to his house"
Dan 2:17: 6:19, 20; Ezra 4:23; 5:8; עַל לְבַיְתֵהּ "he entered his
house" Dan 6:11: 5:10; לִמְהָךְ לִירוּשְׁלֵם עִמָּךְ יְהָךְ "(whoever offers)
to go to Jerusalem may go with you" Ezra 7:13; <כֹּלָּא> וִיהָךְ
לְהֵיכְלָא . . . לְאַתְרֵהּ "and let <all of it> go back to the temple . . . to
its place" 6:5 (see הָךְ); אתו לבירת יב "they came to the fortress of
Yeb" *AP* 30:8; קְרֵב נְבוּכַדְנֶצַּר לִתְרַע אַתּוּן "Nebuchadnezzar drew
near to the gateway of the furnace" Dan 3:26: 6:21; רוּמֵהּ יִמְטֵא
לִשְׁמַיָּא "its top reached to the heavens" 4:8, 17: 4:19; 6:25; וְגֻבְרַיָּא
אִלֵּךְ . . . נְפַלוּ לְגוֹא־אַתּוּן "and those men . . . fell into the furnace"
3:23: 3:21, 24; אֲמַר לְכַפָּתָה לְשַׁדְרַךְ . . . לְמִרְמֵא לְאַתּוּן "he bade
(them) to tie up Shadrach . . . to throw (him) into the furnace"
3:20: 6:25; הוּבַד גִּשְׁמַהּ וִיהִיבַת לִיקֵדַת אֶשָּׁא "its (the beast's) body
was destroyed, and it was given over to a burning of fire" 7:11;
עַיְנַי הַגְלִי לְבָבֶל . . . עַמָּה הַגְלִי לִשְׁמַיָּא נִטְלֵת "I raised my eyes to heaven" 4:31; הַיְבֵל
"the people he carried away to Babylonia" Ezra 5:12: 6:5a;
הִמּוֹ לְהֵיכְלָא דִּי בָבֶל "he brought them (the vessels) into the temple
of Babylon" 5:14: 6:5b; דבקת לטור תורא "I reached Mount Taurus" *1QapGen* 21:16; [אל]תהרכב חטך לצדיק "[do not] shoot your
arrow at a righteous person" *Aḥ.* 126-28; מַלְכָּא . . . נְפַל . . . וּלְדָנִיֵּאל

181

ל

סְגִד "the king . . .fell down . . . and did homage to Daniel" Dan
2:46; ותרעא עלה פתיח לשוק מלכא "the upper gate opens onto the
street of the king" *BMAP* 12:21; ומן תחתיא לעליא פתי אמן 5 "and
from below to above in width it is 5 cubits" *BMAP* 12:8. --
Accus. instead of לְ : זי אזלן עמה מצרין "who are going with him
to Egypt" *AD* 6:4; עד ימטא מצרין "until he reaches Egypt" *AD*
6:5; מטא צחא מנפי "Seḥo arrived at Memphis" *AP* 83:2; חת מנפי
"go down to Memphis" *AP* 42:7; גרמיך לא יחתון שאול "your
bones shall not go down to Sheol" *AP* 71:15; תנעל ביתא זנה "you
shall enter this house" *BMAP* 12:22; כזי תאתון מצרין "when you
will come to Egypt" *Padua I* A 5; אתו מטאו אפק "they have
come (and) have reached Aphek" *Adon Letter* 4 (*KAI* 266); כזי
יאתה . . . אשור "when he will come to Asshur" *Assur* 11 (*KAI*
233); ויהכן חלב בגסרו זי "and they go to Aleppo" *Sefire III* 5; זי
כתנה היתי שושן "whom Bagasru has brought to Susa" *AD* 9:1; זי
התתי לי סון "the tunic that you (f.) brought to me in Syene" *Hermopolis* 4:6; סון יבל "let (the letter) be brought to Syene" *Hermopolis* 1:14 + ; לא איתית המו מנפי "I did not bring them (the
clothes) to Memphis" *Padua I* B 3; עם גנזא זי מני שים להיתיה בבאל
"with the treasure that has been ordered by me to be brought to
Babylon" *AD* 10:5; יאתה עלי בבאל "let him come to me in Babylon" *AD* 11:5 (cf. בְּ 1.2).
    (8) לְ of place: **in** (cf. בְּ). הֲוֹו בָעַיִן עִלָּה לְהַשְׁכָּחָה לְדָנִיֵּאל "they
were seeking to find in Daniel a ground for complaint" Dan 6:5
(BL 338l): 6:6, 23 (cf. "wisdom . . . was found [בֵּהּ] in him"
5:11: 5:12, 14; 6:24); כזי מלה באישה לא יהשכחון לכם "when they
find no fault in you" *AP* 38:6-7; לרחמן ישימנך קדם דריוהוש מלכא
"may (God) set you in favor before Darius, the king" *AP* 30:2;
לתחתיה לה "in the lower part of it" *AP* 6:10 (= 25:6 = תחתיה
בתחתיה adv. accus. 8:6); נשמתי לגו נדנהא "my breath in the midst
of its sheath" *1QapGen* 2:10; כלצפון מדנחהון "to the northeast of
them (the mountains)" *4QEnᶜ (4Q204)* 1 xii 30; *4QEnᵉ (4Q206)*
1 xxvi 17; באלוני ממרה די בחברון כלמדנח צפון חברון "at the Oaks of

182

Mamre, which are in Hebron, to the northeast of Hebron" *1Qap-Gen* 21:19-20.

(9) לְ of time: **in, after.** מַלְכָּא לְעָלְמִין חֱיִי "O King, live forever!" Dan 2:4: 2:44; לִקְצָת יַרְחִין תְּרֵי־עֲשַׂר "at the end of twelve months" 4:26: 4:31; כזי הוה זי לקדמין . . . לקבל זי לקדמין "as it was before . . . as (was done) formerly" *AP* 32:8-10; לממטה מרד[י]א[אתכנשו "at his arrival, the rebe[l]s rallied" *Bisitun* 20; אחר לי[ו]מן אחרנן תלתה "then after three more days" *Aḥ.* 39; לשנין ארבע עבד לי חמר שגיא "after four years it produced for me much wine" *1QapGen* 12:13-14; לעד[ן]א[חרן וליומן אחרנן שגיאן "at a later tim[e] and after many other days" *Aḥ.* 49-50; לבתר חמש שניא אלן "at the end of those five years" *1QapGen* 19:23.

(10) לְ of purpose: **for.** לְמֵתֵא לַחֲנֻכַּת צַלְמָא "to come for the dedication of the statue" Dan 3:2: 3:3; Ezra 6:17; . . . מָאנַיָּא דִי לְפָלְחָן בֵּית אֱלָהָךְ . "the vessels which . . . are for the service of the house of your God" 7:19; וְאִמְּרִין לַעֲלָוָן לֶאֱלָהּ שְׁמַיָּא "and sheep for burnt offerings to the God of Heaven" 6:9; הֵן לְמוֹת הֵן לִשְׁרֹשׁוּ "whether for death or for banishment" 7:26a,b: 7:26c,d; לְבֵית מַלְכוּ . . . וְלִיקָר הַדְרִי "for a royal residence . . . and for the glory of my honor" Dan 4:27: Ezra 4:22; ברתך למלקחה לאנתו "your daughter, to take her for marriage" *AP* 48:3; למה הו יחבל מתא עלין "for what reason should he corrupt the land against us?" *Aḥ.* 36.

(11) Varied uses of לְ : **about, according to, by, through.** עֻזִּין . . . תְּרֵי־עֲשַׂר לְמִנְיָן שִׁבְטֵי יִשְׂרָאֵל "twelve he-goats . . . , according to the number of the tribes of Israel" Ezra 6:17 (cf. עמיר לקבל רכשה "fodder according to (the number of) his horses" *AD* 6:4); נתן לך בית לדמות ביתך "we shall give you a house according to the likeness of your house" *BMAP* 3:21; שְׁלִיחַ לְבַקָּרָה עַל־יְהוּד וְלִירוּשְׁלֶם "(you were) sent to inquire about Judah and about Jerusalem" Ezra 7:14 (BL 324k); לְמָא דִי־תַעַבְדוּן "(I decree) about what you are to do (for these elders)" 6:8; כְּדְנָה תֵּאמְרוּן לְהֹם "thus shall you say about them" Jer 10:11; ברכתך לפתח "I bless you by (the god) Ptaḥ" *Hermopolis* 3:1-2; בריך אברם לאל עליון "Blest be Abram by

God Most High" *1QapGen* 22:16. -- Distributive or Proportional
לְ : "יום ליום "(let provision be made) day by day" *AD* 6:3; לגבר
לגבר ליומא "for each and every man daily" *AD* 6:4-5; 2 כסף חלרן
לתקל 1 לירח 1 הוה כסף חלרן 8 לירח חד "at the rate of 2 hallurs per
shekel per month, being at the rate of 8 hallurs for each month"
AP 10:5-6; 8 כסף חלרן 2 לכסף ש 1 לירחא . . . ותהוה מרבית כספך חלרן
1 לירח "at the rate of 2 hallurs for the sum of 1 shekel per month
. . . and the interest on your money shall be 8 hallurs each month"
AP 11:2-4; ואשלמ[נה]י לך ירח בירח "and I shall pay [it] to you
month by month" *AP* 11:5; יהוה רבה עלי ירח לירח "(if I do not pay
the interest, your money) will grow against me month by month"
AP 11:9.

　　II. לְ before an infin. -- (1) לְ of purpose: **to, in order
that** (cf. דִּי III 6; וְ no. 9). -- (a) subj. of the infin. is the same as
the subj. of the governing finite verb: נְפַק לְקַטָּלָה לְחַכִּימֵי בָבֶל "he
went to slay the wise men of Babylon" Dan 2:14: 2:9; 6:15; Ezra
5:10; 6:12; שְׁלִיחַ לְבַקָּרָה עַל־יְהוּד וְלִירוּשְׁלֶם "(you were) sent to
inquire about Judah and about Jerusalem" Ezra 7:14: 7:15; זי
יקום עליכי לתרכתכי מן בתיא "whoever rises up against you to drive
you out of the houses" *BMAP* 6:16; יבעה ראשי להמתתי "(whoever) seeks my head to kill me" *Sefire III* 11. -- (b) subj. of the
infin. different from the governing finite verb: מַלְכָּא שְׁלַח לְמִכְנַשׁ . . .
לְמֵתֵא . "the king sent to assemble (the satraps, etc.) in order that
they might come" Dan 3:2: 2:24; וּבְעוֹ דָּנִיֵּאל וְחַבְרוֹהִי לְהִתְקְטָלָה;
"and they sought Daniel and his companions that they might be
killed" 2:13; . . . לְמִבְנֵא בֵּית אֱלָהָא דָךְ תַּעַבְדוּן "(what) you are to do .
. . that (they might) build that house of God" Ezra 6:8; אנה [א]תית
ביתך למנתן לי [ל]ברתך מפטיה לאנתו "I came to your house that you
might give me your daughter, Miphtayah, in marriage" *AP* 15:3;
יהבת לי תרע ביתא זילך למבנה אגר 1 תמה "you gave me the gateway
of your house that I might built 1 portico there," i.e., you gave
me the right to build *AP* 5:3-4; אתעשת על אגורא זך למבנה "think
about that temple that they might build it" *AP* 30:23; מני עמה גברן

ל

2 אחרנן למחזה איך [יתעבד] "(the king) appointed with him 2 other
men to see how [it would be done]" *Ah.* 37; לא יהבת לך ארקא זך
למבנה "I did not give you that land that you might build" *AP*
9:14. -- (c) Mixed construction (cf. דִּי III 6; וְ II 2; BL 301e):
בְּעָה . . . דִּי זְמָן יִנְתֶּן־לֵהּ וּפִשְׁרָא לְהַחֲוָיָה "(Daniel) begged (the king) . . .
that he would give him time, and (that) he would make known
the meaning" Dan 2:16 (instead of וִיהַחֲוֵה); רַחֲמִין לְמִבְעֵא מִן־קֳדָם
אֱלָהּ שְׁמַיָּא "that they might beg mercy from the God of Heaven"
2:18 (instead of יִבְעוֹן); . . . דִּי־כְתָבָה דְנָה יִקְרוֹן וּפִשְׁרֵהּ לְהוֹדָעֻתַנִי
"(the sages) were brought in . . . that they might read this writing
and make known to me its meaning" 5:15 (instead of וִיהוֹדְעֻנַּי);
תֶּהֱוֵא מִתְיַהֲבָה לְגֻבְרַיָּא אִלֵּךְ דִּי־לָא לְבַטָּלָא "let (the cost of building) be
given to those men without delay," lit., "in order not to delay (it)"
Ezra 6:8 (instead of תְבַטְּלוּן or the impers. וִיבַטְּלוּן); לממר קדם
ארשם על בית מדבחא . . . למבניה . . . ולבונתא יקרבון "to speak to Arsames about the altar-house . . . to rebuild it . . . that they may offer
incense (on it)" *AP* 32:2-3, 8-9 (instead of לְהַקְרָבָה); לְהוֹדָעוּתָךְ דִּי
נִכְתֵּב שֶׁם־גֻּבְרַיָּא "(we asked them their names) to inform you, that
we were writing down the names of the men (at the head of
them)" Ezra 5:10; למבניה ביב בירתא . . . ועלותא יקרבון "to rebuild it
(the temple) in the fortress of Yeb . . . , and they shall offer
burnt-offerings (in it)" *AP* 30:25.

(2) לְ w. an infin. after a verb of commanding, etc. (cf. דִּי
III 5; וְ no. 10). לְגֻבְרִין . . . אֲמַר לְכַפָּתָה לְשַׁדְרַךְ "(the king) bade the
men . . . to tie up Shadrach" Dan 3:20; וַאֲמַר לְהוֹבָדָה לְכֹל חַכִּימֵי בָבֶל
"(the king) ordered (them) to destroy all the sages of Babylon"
2:12: 2:46; 3:13, 19; 5:2; 6:24; וְדִי אֲמַרוּ לְמִשְׁבַּק עִקַּר שָׁרְשׁוֹהִי "and
as it was commanded to leave the stump of its roots," lit., "they
(impers.) commanded" 4:23; מַלְכָּא שְׁלַח לְמִכְנַשׁ "the king sent
word to assemble (the satraps)" 3:2; מִנִּי שִׂים טְעֵם לְהַנְעָלָה "I made
a decree to bring in (all the sages of Babylon)" 4:3: 5:7; Ezra
4:21; עם גנזא זי מני שים להיתיה בבאל "with the treasure that has
been ordered by me to be brought to Babylon" *AD* 10:5; לְקַיָּמָה

185

קְיָם מַלְכָּא וּלְתַקָּפָה אֱסָר "to establish an ordinance and to enforce an interdict" Dan 6:8 (cf. לְ I 2 N.B.).

(3) לְ w. an infn. after other verbs. -- (a) as the obj. of the verb: הֲווֹ בָעַיִן עִלָּה לְהַשְׁכָּחָה "they were seeking to find a ground for complaint" Dan 6:5; פִּתְגָם לַהֲתָבוּתָךְ . . . לָא חַשְׁחִין אֲנַחְנָא "we have no need . . . to give you an answer" 3:16; יְכֵלְתָּ לְמִגְלֵא "you were able to reveal this mystery" 2:47: 5:8; רָזָא דְנָה צְבִית לְיַצָּבָא עַל־חֵיוְתָא "I wanted to ascertain the truth about the beast" 7:19; לִמְהָךְ . . . כָּל־מִתְנַדַּב "everyone who offers . . . to go" Ezra 7:13; וְשָׁרִיו לְמִבְנֵא בֵּית אֱלָהָא "and they began to build the house of God" 5:2; שְׁחִיתָה הִזְמִנְתּוּן לְמֵאמַר "you have plotted to speak lying words" Dan 2:9; יִסְבַּר לְהַשְׁנָיָה זִמְנִין וְדָת "he will think to change times and law" 7:25; עֲשִׁית לַהֲקָמוּתֵהּ עַל־כָּל־מַלְכוּתָא "(the king) intended to set him over the whole kingdom" 6:4; לא שבקן לן למבניה "they do not allow us to build it" AP 30:23; לא . . . אכלאנך למבנה עלוי "I . . . shall not hinder you from building upon it" AP 5:6; לא שנציו למנעל בבירתא "they did not succeed in entering the fortress" AD 5:7. -- (b) as the subj. of the verb: דִּי יִפֵּל לָךְ לְמִנְתַּן "which you will have occasion to supply," lit., "it will fall to you" Ezra 7:20; מָה דִּי עֲלָיךְ . . . יֵיטַב . . . לְמֶעְבַּד "whatever seems good to you . . . to do" 7:18; שְׁפַר קֳדָמַי לְהַחֲוָיָה "it pleased me to manifest" Dan 3:32; לָא אֲרִיךְ לַנָא לְמֶחֱזֵא "it is not fitting for us to behold (the king's disgrace)" Ezra 4:14; לְמֵזֵא . . . חַד־שִׁבְעָה עַל דִּי חֲזֵה לְמֵזְיֵהּ "to heat (the furnace) seven times more than it was usual to heat it" Dan 3:19; שפיר מלך למחזה "it is splendid to see a king" Ah. 108.

(4) לְ w. an infin. as a complement to a noun (cf. דִּי III 1; וְ no. 10): וּזְהִירִין הֱווֹ שָׁלוּ לְמֶעְבַּד עַל־דְּנָה "and be careful not to neglect this matter," lit., "of negligence to act" Ezra 4:22; אנת שליט למפתח תרעא זך "you have the authority to open that gate" AP 5:14; וַהֲלָךְ לָא שַׁלִּיט לְמִרְמֵא עֲלֵיהֹם "and it shall not be lawful to impose a toll on them" Ezra 7:24; איתי באר . . . ומין לא חסרה להשקיא חילא "there is a well . . ., and it never lacks water for the

troops to drink" *AP* 27:6-7; לא השכחת כסף ונכסן לשלמה לכי "I did not find money and property to pay you" *AP* 13:5; בבא זילך למנפק "your gate to go out" *BMAP* 10:4; ישימון טב בחנכה למאמר "(the gods) will put something good in his palate to utter" *Aḥ*. 115; כפן למנשא משח "bowls to carry oil" *BMAP* 7:19.

(5) לְ w. an infin. as gerund: פִּתְגָמָא הֲתִיבוּנָא לְמֵמַר "they replied to us, saying" Ezra 5:11; זי מלתי לבתי לאמר "as for what you uttered about BTY, saying" *Hermopolis* 1:6; וְרוּחֵהּ תִּקְפַּת לַהֲזָדָה "and his spirit hardened, acting proudly" Dan 5:20; שָׁלְטָנֵהּ יְהַעְדּוֹן לְהַשְׁמָדָה וּלְהוֹבָדָה "they will take away his dominion, (utterly) consuming and destroying" 7:26. -- לְ w. an infin. as gerundive (BL 302g): כָּל־אֱסָר . . . דִּי־מַלְכָּא יְהָקֵים לָא לְהַשְׁנָיָה "no interdict . . . that the king establishes is to be changed" Dan 6:16; תְּקֵים אֱסָרָא . . . דִּי לָא לְהַשְׁנָיָה "establish the interdict . . . that is not to be changed" 6:9 (cf. Hebr. : כִּי כְתָב אֲשֶׁר־נִכְתָּב . . . אֵין לְהָשִׁיב "for an edict which is written . . . is not to be revoked" Esth 8:8); כוכה דנה . . . . לא למפתח "this tomb . . . is not to be opened" *AH* I/1. 2b 1-4 (p. 52).

לָא, לָה & לְ (lā-) negative particle, sometimes prefixed. -- (1) negating a cl.: **not.** דִּי־שְׁמַיָּא וְאַרְקָא לָא עֲבַדוּ "who did not make the heavens and the earth" Jer 10:11; לָא יָכְלִין פִּשְׁרָא לְהוֹדָעֻתַנִי "(the sages) are unable to make known to me the interpretation (of the dream)" Dan 4:15; לה אשכחת אש "I have not found anyone" *Hermopolis* 3:11; ליקתל וליאסר "he will not kill and will not imprison (him)" *Sefire III* 18; הֵן לָא תִסְגְּדוּן "if you will not worship" Dan 3:15; וְלָא מְטוֹ לְאַרְעִית גֻּבָּא "and they did not reach the bottom of the den" 6:25 (BL 287i, 353d); זי לא עד נפלג עלין "whom we do not yet divide between us" *AP* 28:13; הן מיתת ולעד "if I die and have not yet paid back" *BMAP* 11:8; שב אנה שלמת לא אכהל למפלח בבב היכלא "I am old. I cannot serve in the gate of the palace" *Aḥ*. 17; אנה ימין סב לא כהל הוית בידי "I am old in days; I cannot (work) with my hands" *BMAP* 9:17; אָחֳרָן לָא אִיתַי דִּי יְחַוִּנַּהּ

לֹא

"there is no other who will show it (to the king)" Dan 2:11; כָּל־מֶלֶךְ . . . מִלָּה כִדְנָה לָא שְׁאֵל "no king . . . has asked such a thing (of any sage)" 2:10; ה[ן] ימות עבניה ובר זכר ונקבה לאיתי לה "[if] Ananiah dies and has no child, male or female" *BMAP* 7:28-29. -- w. ellipsis of the verb: וְהֵן לָא "but if not" Dan 3:18. -- negating two verbs: דִּי־לָא יִפֵּל וְיִסְגֻּד "whoever does not fall down and worship" 3:6, 11. -- double negation: לא יכהל ענניה ולא יעבד דין "Ananiah will not be able to recuse a court-case" *BMAP* 7:37-38; [ל]יכהל ברי [ל]ישלח יד בבר[ך] "my son will not be able to raise a hand against [your] son" *Sefire I* B 25. -- in a prohibitive sense (BL 300e): הן יאמר [כות] לא ישתמע לה "if he speaks [thus], let no attention be paid to him" *BMAP* 7:42. -- (2) **not** (in negative purpose cl.): וִיהַבוּ גֶשְׁמֵיהוֹן דִּי לָא־יִפְלְחוּן "and they yielded up their bodies in order not to serve (any other god)" Dan 3:28; 2:18; 6:18; יָהֲבִין לְהוֹן טַעְמָא . . . וּמַלְכָּא לָא־לֶהֱוֵא נָזִק "to whom (the satraps) . . . would give an account and the king would suffer no damage" 6:3; שִׂימוּ טְעֵם לְבַטָּלָא גֻּבְרַיָּא אִלֵּךְ וְקִרְיְתָא דָךְ לָא תִתְבְּנֵא "issue a decree to impede those men so that that city may not be rebuilt" Ezra 4:21; דִּי־לָא לְבַטָּלָא "in order not to impede (them)" 6:8 (cf. לְ II 1c; וְ I 5). -- (3) לָא = **(there/it) is not** (cf. Hebr. אֵין). עֲרְוַת מַלְכָּא לָא אֲרִיךְ לַנָא לְמֶחֱזֵא "it is not fitting for us to behold the king's disgrace" Ezra 4:14; ואנש לא שליט למשנתה "and there is no one with authority to mark him (a slave)" *BMAP* 8:8-9; וְהַלָךְ לָא שַׁלִּיט לְמִרְמֵא עֲלֵיהֹם "and there is no one with authority to impose a toll on them" Ezra 7:24; לטב הא מך "he is not better than you" (read מנך ?) *Sefire III* 22; ברי זי לא ברי "my son, who is not my son" *Ah.* 30; לא בידיך מ[נש]א רגלך "it is not in your power to l[if]t your foot" *Ah.* 123; ולא דין "and there shall be no suit" *BMAP* 4:15. -- לָא לְ w. an infin., see לְ II 5. -- (4) לָא negating a word: לָא חַכִּימִין אָשְׁפִין "no wise men, soothsayers (can manifest this mystery): Dan 2:27; לא אנה כתבתה "not I have written it (the deed produced)" *AP* 8:17; [ה]לא כזנה הו[ן] "not so did it hap[pen]" *AP* 37:8; כָּל־דָּאֲרֵי אַרְעָא כְּלָה חֲשִׁיבִין "all who dwell on the earth are accounted as nothing" Dan 4:32 (cf. כְּ

188

no. 4). -- לָא before prep. בְּ : **not by, without.** לָא בְחָכְמָה דִּי־אִיתַי בִּי
"not by any wisdom that I have" Dan 2:30; ותהך [ו]לָא ביומיך "and
you shall go (i.e., die) [and] not in your time" *Aḥ.* 102; ימותון שאני
ולא בחרבי "my enemies shall die, but not by my sword" *Aḥ.* 174;
בקושט עמי תמללין ולא בכדבין "(that) you are speaking to me truthfully and without lies" *1QapGen* 2:7. -- דִּי־לָא (בְּ) as a prep.:
without (BL 261l, 359u). הִתְגְּזֶרֶת אֶבֶן דִּי־לָא בִידַיִן "a stone was cut
out without (human) hands" Dan 2:34, 45; יוֹם בְּיוֹם דִּי־לָא שָׁלוּ
"day by day, without fail" Ezra 6:9; וּמְלַח דִּי־לָא כְתָב "and salt
without limit," lit., "without a writing" 7:22; ערטלי אהך די לא בנין
"I shall depart (from this life) bereft (and) without children"
1QapGen 22:33. -- הֲלָא : see הֵ . [Hebr. לֹא].

לֵב * (libb), w. suff. לְבִּי : **heart, mind.** וּמִלְּתָא בְּלִבִּי נִטְרֵת
"and I kept the matter in my mind" Dan 7:28; חשבת בלבי "I
thought to myself" *1QapGen (1Q20)* 2:1. [Hebr. the same]. [1]

לְבַב (libab) cst. (& abs.), w. suff. לִבְבָךְ (BL 218c),
לְבְבֵהּ, m.: **heart, mind.** וְרַעְיוֹנֵי לִבְבָךְ תִּנְדַּע "(that) you may
understand the thoughts of your mind" Dan 2:30; רִם לִבְבֵהּ "his
mind was puffed up" 5:20: 5:22; לְבַב חֵיוָה יִתְיְהִב לֵהּ "let the mind
of a beast be given to him" 4:13: 7:4; לִבְבֵהּ מִן־אֲנָשָׁא יְשַׁנּוֹן "let his
mind be changed from a man's," i.e., "let them change his mind
from (that of) a man" 4:13 (מִן in brachylogy); לִבְבֵהּ עִם־חֵיוָתָא שָׁוִי
"his mind was made like that of a beast," lit., "was equated with
the beast" (עִם in brachylogy) 5:21 (cf. brachylogy after מִן s.v.
נְשַׁר 2:3, & חֲבָרָה 7:20, after לְ s.v. רְעוּ , after כְּ s.v. טְפַר & מַלְכוּ
4:20); אל תהשגא לבבא "do not lead (your) mind astray" *Aḥ.* 137;
[לא ידע] איש מה בלבב כנתה "a man [does not know] what is in the
mind of his companion" *Aḥ.* 163; מלת מלך בחמר לבבא "a word of
a king is with wrath of mind" *Aḥ.* 104; והן אשבקן על לבבך [לא
תחיה] "(if I strike you, you will not die), and if I leave (you) to
your own heart, [you will not live]" *Aḥ.* 82; בשגיא בנן לבבך אל

יחדה "in an abundance of children let your mind not rejoice" *Ah.*
106; ולבבי זי יהבת לך בחכמה עיני זי נטלת עליך "my eyes that I have
lifted up to You and my heart that I have given to You in wisdom" *Ah.* 169; לבבי לה דבק לה "my mind has not clung to it (the
gift)" *Hermopolis* 4:5; לא אכל אנצל לפלטי מן תחת לבבך "I shall not
be able to take away Palti from your heart," i.e., your possession
BMAP 2:13-14; מאן טב כס[ה] מלה בלבבה "a good vessel hid[es] a
thing in its heart" *Ah.* 109. [Hebr. לֵבָב]. †

לְבוּשׁ * (BL 189o), w. suff. לְבוּשֵׁהּ, pl. w. suff. לְבֻשֵׁיהוֹן
m.: **(outer) garment, cloak.** לְבוּשֵׁהּ כִּתְלַג חִוָּר "his robe was white
as snow" Dan 7:9; גֻּבְרַיָּא אִלֵּךְ . . . וּלְבֻשֵׁיהוֹן וּרְמִיו לְגוֹא אַתּוּן "those
men . . . and their garments, and they were thrown into the fur-
nace" 3:21; אי[תי] נכסיא לבשי קמר וכתן "there are goods: garments
of wool and linen" *AP* 20:5; לבוש ועבור "clothing and produce"
(in a collective sense) *BMAP* 11:11; הן יאחדן רשיעא בכנפי לבשך
שבק בידה "if the wicked seizes the skirts of your cloak, leave (it)
in his hand" *Ah.* 171; שלח לי לבשא זי עליך "send me the garment
that you are wearing" *El. Ostr.* 4-6 (*RHR* 130 [1945] 20); לבוש
שגי די בוץ וארגואן "(the king gave Sarai) many garments of fine
linen and purple" *1QapGen* 20:31; לבש 1 זי עמר . . . הוה ארך אמן 8
ב 5 "1 garment of wool . . . (of which) the length was 8 cubits by
5" *AP* 15:7-8 (cf. גמירה 1 זי קמר חדת לאמן 6 ב 4 "1 full-cloth garment of new wool, in cubits 6 by 4" *BMAP* 7:7). Such a garment
stands in contrast to כֻּתּוּן * **(inner) garment, tunic.** זי . . . כתון
קמר "a tunic . . . of wool" *AP* 42:9; על כתון ולבש כתונך ולבשך
עבידן "(you wrote in your letter) about a tunic and a cloak: your
tunic and your cloak have been made" *Padua I* B 2; כעת זבנת לי
אנה [כ]תן 1 זי כתן "now I have bought for myself 1 [tu]nic of
linen" *Padua I* B 4; בזע כתונה "he rent his tunic" *Ah.* 41. [Hebr.
the same]. †

לבש—להן

לבש *, impf. 3 sg. m. יִלְבַּשׁ, 2 sg. m. תִּלְבַּשׁ : **put on, don, be clothed.** אַרְגְּוָנָא יִלְבַּשׁ . . . כָּל־אֱנָשׁ דִּי יִקְרֵא כְּתָבָה "anyone who will read the writing . . . shall be clothed in purple" Dan 5:7 (BL 331s): 5:16; אנחנה . . . שקקן לבשן הוין וצימין "we have put on sack-cloth and are fasting" AP 30:15, -- **Haph.**, 3 pl. m. הַלְבִּשׁוּ (BHS הַלְבִּישׁוּ): **clothe, put on.** הַלְבִּשׁוּ לְדָנִיֵּאל אַרְגְּוָנָא "they clothed Daniel with purple" Dan 5:29; כתנה זי התתי לי סון הי מלבש אנה "the tunic that you brought to me in Syene, I have put it on" Hermopolis 4:6-7. [Hebr. לָבֵשׁ]. †

לָה : see לָא .

הֲוָה see : לֶהֱוֵה, לֶהֱוֹן, לֶהֱוֹן, לֶהֱוֵה .

¹ לָהֵן conj. (< לָא הֵן , BL 264q): -- (1) conditional conj.: **unless, except** (BL 266l; often with the predicate not repeated). -- W. neg. cl. preceding: לָהֵן הַשְׁכַּחְנָא עֲלוֹהִי בְּדָת אֱלָהֵהּ "unless we find (it) against him regarding the law of his God" Dan 6:6; לָהֵן אֱלָהִין דִּי מְדָרְהוֹן עִם־בִּשְׂרָא לָא אִיתוֹהִי "unless it is gods who do not dwell with flesh" 2:11; לָהֵן לֵאלָהֲהוֹן "(they do not worship any god) except their own God" 3:28; שליט בארקא זך להן אנתי ובניכי "(no one has) authority over that land except you and your children" AP 8:11; לא [ישא]ל שלם טביא להן למונק דמה "(the leopard) does not greet the goat except to suck its blood" Aḥ. 119-120; ספר חדת ועתיק להן ספרא זנה "(they cannot produce any) document, new or old, except this document" BMAP 9:22. -- W. positive cl. preceding: כָּל־דִּי יִבְעֵה בָעוּ מִן־כָּל . . . לָהֵן מִנָּךְ מַלְכָּא "whoever petitions anyone . . . except you, O King" Dan 6:8, 13; מן הו זי יקום קדמוהי להן זי אל עמה "who is the one who can stand before him except the one with whom God is?" Aḥ. 107; לא אכל אמר איתי לי אנתה אחרה להן מפטיה "I shall have no right to say, 'I have another wife besides Miphṭaḥiah'" AP 15:31-32; והן להן שקרת "and if (you do) not (do) so, you will have been unfaithful (to all the gods)" Sefire III 14.

191

(2) adversative conj.: **but.** -- W. a preceding neg. cl.: לָא
יְהוֹדְעוּן . . . רָזָא דְנָה גֱּלִי לִי לָהֵן עַל־דִּבְרַת דִּי . . . בְּחָכְמָה "not because of
(my) wisdom . . . was this mystery revealed to me, but in order
that . . . they might make (it) known (to the king)" Dan 2:30; לא
שליט אנת לזבנה . . . להן בניך . . . שליטן בה "you shall have no
authority to sell it (the house), but your children . . . (shall have)
authority over it" AP 9:6-7; מקלו ל[א יתעבד תמה להן לבונה מנחה
"(animals as) burnt-sacrifice shall not be offered there, but rather
incense (and) meal-offering" AP 33:10-11; להן ברי יהוה "(no one
shall enslave him) but he shall be my son" BMAP 8:9; לא ירתנך דן
להן די יפוק "this one shall not inherit you, but the one who shall
go forth (from your loins)" 1QapGen 22:34. W. a preceding
positive cl.: לָהֵן מִן־דִּי הַרְגִּזוּ אֲבָהֳתַנָא לֶאֱלָהּ שְׁמַיָּא "(the temple stood
for a long time), but because our ancestors angered the God of
Heaven, (He destroyed it)" Ezra 5:12; תב בגו . . . להן ביתא זנך לא
שליט אנת לזבנה "dwell in it (the land) . . ., but you shall have no
authority to sell that house" AP 9:6; וביתא אפם זילכי להן הן מיתתי
ברת שנן 100 "and the house in addition is yours, but if you die at
the age of 100 years" BMAP 4:16-17.

לָהֵן ² adv. (BL 256x): **therefore, on that account.** לָהֵן
חֶלְמָא וּפִשְׁרֵהּ הַחֲוֹנִי "therefore show me the dream and its meaning"
Dan 2:6; 2:9; 4:24; [הקי]ם . . . [בבית צ]לם . . . להן אלהי תימא צ[דק]ו
לצלמשזב "[erec]ted (a stele) [in the temple of Š]LM . . . ; therefore the gods of Tema showed themselve loyal to ŠLMŠZB" Tema A 9-11 (KAI 228). [Hebr. the same]. †

לְוִי * (BL 196d), emph. pl. לֵוָיֵא (in MSS. לְוָאֵי q. BL
51k): **Levite.** חֲנֻכַּת בֵּית־אֱלָהָא . . . וְלֵוָיֵא כָּהֲנַיָּא בְנֵי־יִשְׂרָאֵל עֲבַדוּ "the
Israelites, the priests and the Levites... celebrated the dedication
of the house of God" Ezra 6:16: 6:18; 7:13, 24. [Hebr. לֵוִים
לֵוִי,]. †

לָוָת prep. (BL 259s): **at** (chez). יְהוּדָיֵא דִּי סְלִקוּ מִן־לְוָתָךְ עֲלֶינָא "the Jews who went up from you (de chez toi) to us" Ezra 4:12; פרש לוט מן לואתי "Lot parted from me" *1QapGen* 21:5: 21:7; "send men לות (to) Jonatham" (*IEJ* 11 [1961] 48, line 2); they will send palm branches לותך "to you" and send others מלותך "from you" (ibid., line 3). [1]

לְחֶם (*laḥm*; v.l. לְחַם), m.: **bread, food, feast.** מַלְכָּא עֲבַד לְחֶם רַב "the king made a great feast" Dan 5:1; ישתבע כעס מן לחם "let him that is afflicted be sated with food" *Aḥ.* 189; זי לחם אבי "who ate the bread of my father" *Aḥ.* 33; [י]כלאו מנה לחם ומין "let them deprive him (a captive) of food and water" *El. Ostr.* A 3 (*HSSD* 54). [Hebr. לֶחֶם]. [1]

לְחֵנָה * (< Akk. *laḥḥinatu* CAD 4. 62), pl. w. suff. לְחֵנָתֵהּ, לְחֵנָתָךְ: **concubine.** וְרַבְרְבָנוֹהִי שֵׁגְלָתֵהּ וּלְחֵנָתֵהּ "his nobles, his wives, and his concubines" Dan 5:2, 3, 23. †

לֵילָה * (*laylēh* < *laylī*), emph. לֵילְיָא (< *layliyā'*), m.: **night.** בֵּהּ בְּלֵילְיָא קְטִיל בֵּלְאשַׁצַּר "that very night Belshazzar was killed" Dan 5:30 (for the dem. suff. see בְּ no. 1); קדם יום ולילה "(the treaty was concluded) in the presence of Day and Night" *Sefire I* A 12; חלמת אנה . . . חלם בלילה מעלי "I had a dream in the night of my entering (Egypt)" *1QapGen* 19:14; בליליא כדי דבירת מני שרי "on the night when Sarai was taken from me" *1QapGen* 20:11. -- As a gen. of quality (cf. דִּי I 2): בְּחֶזְוָא דִי־לֵילְיָא רָזָא גְלִי "the mystery was revealed in visions of the night" Dan 2:19: 7:7, 13; חָזֵה הֲוֵית בְּחֶזְוֵי עִם־לֵילְיָא "I beheld in my vision during the night" 7:2. [Hebr. לַיְל]. †

מָה : see מָא, לְמָה .

לְשָׁן (lišān, BL 56c, 189p), emph. pl. לְשָׁנַיָּא, m.: **tongue, speech, language; bay** (of a sea). ינסח לשנ[ה] "(God) will tear out his tongue" *Ah.* 156; רכיך לשן מלך ועלעי תנין יתבר "smooth is the speech of a king, but it will break the ribs of a dragon" *Ah.* 105-6; לתשלח לשן בביתי "you shall not interfere in my house," lit., "send a tongue into it" *Sefire III* 21; כָּל־עַם אֻמָּה וְלִשָּׁן דִּי־יֵאמַר "every people, nation, or language that speaks" Dan 3:29: in pl. 3:4, 7 + ; עד די דבקת ללשן ים סוף די נפק מן ימא שמוקא "until I reached the bay of the Reed Sea, which goes forth from the Red (simmôqā') Sea" *1QapGen* 21:18; בחבל תחרז לשנה "will you tie its tongue with a cord?" *11QtgJob (11Q10)* 35:4. [Hebr. לָשׁוֹן]. †

מ

מָא : see מָה .

מְאָה (mi'ā, qil-at, BL 179g), du. מָאתַיִן (= Hebr. מָאתַיִם *, BL 250q); f. noun. -- (1) **hundred.** הַקְרִבוּ . . . תּוֹרִין מְאָה דִּכְרִין מָאתַיִן אִמְּרִין אַרְבַּע מְאָה "they offered . . . a hundred bulls, two hundred rams, four hundred lambs" Ezra 6:17; עַד־חֲמַר בַּתִּין מְאָה וְעַד־בַּתִּין מְשַׁח מְאָה "(let there be given) up to a hundred baths of wine and up to a hundred baths of oil" Ezra 7:22 (invert order: מְשַׁח בַּתִּין); כרשן מאה "a hundred karashes" *AP* 26:17; מסמרי נחש ופרזל מאתין "two hundred bronze and iron nails" *AP* 26:12-13. -- If other numbers follow, at least the last has "and": . . . הֲקִים לַאֲחַשְׁדַּרְפְּנַיָּא מְאָה וְעֶשְׂרִין "(the king) set up . . . one hundred and twenty satraps" Dan 6:2; כרשן מאה ותמנין "one hundred and eighty karashes" *AP* 26:14; מסמרי נחש מאה וחמשן לחד פשכן תלתה "one hundred and fifty nails of bronze for every three hand-breadths; two hundred and seventy-five . . . " *AP* 26:15; מאתין שבען וחמשה כל מסמרין ארבע מאה עשרין וחמשה "total nails: four hundred and twenty-five" *AP* 26:16; גברין בחרין לקרב תלת מאא ותמניאת עשר

"(the) best men for war, three hundred and eighteen" *1QapGen* 22:6 (cf. עֲשַׂר); [ו]שת ועשרי[ן] פותי אמין מא[ה "in width a hundred and twenty-six cubits" *5QNJ (5Q15)* 1 i 4; תלת מאה [א[מין] ו]חמשין ושבע לכל [רו[ח "[three hundred and] fifty-seven [c]ubits in every [di]rection" *5QNJ (5Q15)* 1 i 1. -- (2) מאה, cst. מאת, emph. מאתא, w. suff. מאתה, pl. w. suff. מאותהם (*mi'awāthom*, w. augm. -*aw*-): **century** (subdivision of the *degel*, a military detachment). כל מאת שנדן "all (the men) of the century Siniddin" *AP* 22:19; [גבר]ן זי מאתה זי ביתאלתקם 11 "11 [me]n of the century of Betheltaqem" *AP* 2:6; מאתא ורבני "the century and the officers" *AP* 3:11; [ר]בי מאותהם "the [of]ficers of their centuries" *AP* 80:3. [Hebr. מֵאָה]. †

מאזן *: see מוֹזֵן .

מֵאמַר (*mi'mar*, BL 194s), infin. used as a noun: **saying, command.** מֵאמַר קַדִּישִׁין שְׁאֵלְתָא "the decision (is by) the word of the holy ones" Dan 4:14; כְּמֵאמַר כָּהֲנַיָא . . . לֶהֱוֵא מִתְיְהֵב לְהֹם "according to the word of the priests . . . let it be given to them" Ezra 6:9. [Hebr. מַאֲמָר]. †

מָאן * (< *ma'nī, maqtal*, root 'ny, BL 194r); emph. pl. *ma'niyayyā* by haplography > מָאנַיָא , whence the abs. מָאנִין *, cst. מָאנֵי, sg. מָאן * BL 55a); m.: **vessel, furniture.** לְהַיְתָיָה לְמָאנֵי דַהֲבָא וְכַסְפָּא "to bring the gold and silver vessels" Dan 5:2; 5:3; מָאנֵי בֵית-אֱלָהָא דִּי דַהֲבָא "the gold vessels of the house of God" Ezra 6:5; 5:14, 15; 7:19; וּלְמָאנַיָא דִי-בַיְתֵהּ הַיְתִיו . . . חַמְרָא שָׁתַיִן בְּהוֹן "they brought the vessels of His house . . . (and) were drinking wine from them" Dan 5:23; מאני נחש ופרזל מאני עק "vessels of bronze and iron, furniture of wood" *AP* 20:5; מאן נחש ופרזל "vessels of bronze and iron" *BMAP* 11:11 (collect. sg.); מאני נחש מחזי 1 ... תמסא 1 ... כס 1 "vessels of bronze: 1 mirror . . . 1 dish . . . 1 cup" *BMAP* 7:14; מאן טב כס[ה] מלה בלבבה ו[הו זי "

195

תביר הנפקה ברא "a good vessel hid[es] a thing in its heart; but
[that which is] broken spills it out" *Ah.* 109; חמר מצרין מאנן 5 "wine from Egypt, 5 vessels" *AP* 72:4. [Hebr. cf. אֳנִי "ship," BL 55a]. †

מְגִלָּה (BL 194u), f.: **scroll.** הִשְׁתְּכַח . . . מְגִלָּה "a scroll . . . was found" Ezra 6:2; בין ספריא אשתכח<ת>מגלה "among the books was found a scroll" *4QProtoEsth^a (4Q550)* 1:4-5. [1]

מגר **Pa.** impf. 3 sg. m. יְמַגַּר : **destroy, overthrow** (cf. חַבֵּל). אֱלָהָא . . . יְמַגַּר כָּל־מֶלֶךְ וְעַם "may God . . . overthrow any king or people" Ezra 6:12; אגורי אלהי מצרין כל מגרו ואיש מנדעם באגורא זך לא חבל "(the soldiers of Cambyses) destroyed all the temples of the gods of Egypt, but no one did any harm to that temple (of Yaho)" *AP* 30:14. [Hebr. the same]. [1]

מַדְבַּח * (*maqtil,* BL 194t), emph. מַדְבְּחָא : **altar.** וּתְקָרֵב הִמּוֹ עַל־מַדְבְּחָה "and you will offer them on the altar" Ezra 7:17; עלותא יקרבון על מדבחא זי יהו "they are to offer holocausts on the altar of Yaho" *AP* 30:25-26; על בית מדבחא זי אלה שמיא "about the altar-house of the God of Heaven" *AP* 32:3-4; כול בשרהון על מדבחא אקטרת "I burned all their flesh on the altar" *1QapGen* 10:15; די בנית תמן מדבח "there I built an altar" *1QapGen* 21:20; בנית תמן בה מדבחא ובניתה תניאני "where I (had) built the altar, and I built it again" *1QapGen* 21:1. [Hebr. מִזְבֵּחַ]. [1]

מִנְדָּה : see מְדָה .

מָדָר *, מְדֹר *, מְדוֹר * (*maqtal,* root דּוּר, BL 194r, 42x), w. suff. מְדָרְהוֹן (v.l. מְדוֹרְהוֹן), מְדָרָךְ, מְדוֹרָךְ: **dwelling.** עִם־חֵיוַת בָּרָא לֶהֱוֵה מְדֹרָךְ "your dwelling shall be with the beasts of the field" Dan 4:22, 29: 5:21; אֱלָהִין דִּי מְדָרְהוֹן עִם־בִּשְׂרָא לָא אִיתוֹהִי "gods whose dwelling is not with (mortal) flesh" 2:11 (vocal. perh. distinctive, see BL 288f). [Hebr. דּוֹר]. †

▲ מָדַי (< Akk. *Madai* < Persian *Māda*): **Media, Medes.** דִּי בְּמָדַי מְדִינְתָּה "(Ecbatana), which is in the province of Media" Ezra 6:2; דָּת לְמָדַי וּפָרַס "law of the Medes and Persians" Dan 6:16: 5:28; 6:9, 13; [י]במד שמה בכנדור מדי לממטה "upon arrival in Media, in Kundur in Med[ia]" *Bisitun* 25; פרס זי חילא [ר]ושא [י]ומד "and the res[t of the army of] Persia and Med[ia]" *Bisitun* 40. [Hebr. the same]. †

▲ מָדַי * (BL 196d), emph. מָדָיָא k. & מָדָאָה q. (BL 51k), emph. pl. * מָדָיֵא (BL 208e): **Mede.** דָּרְיָוֶשׁ מָדָיָא "Darius, the Mede" Dan 6:1. [Hebr. מָדַי]. [1]

מְדִינָה * (*maqtil*, root דִּין, BL 194u), cst. מְדִינַת, emph. מְדִינְתָּא & מְדִינְתָּה (BL 43g); pl. מְדִינָן, emph. מְדִינָתָא, f.: **province, administrative region, city.** מְדִינַת בָּבֶל "the province of Babylonia" Ezra 7:16; Dan 2:48, 49; 3:1, 12, 30; [מן] מדינת נא "[from] the region of No (= Thebes, Egypt)" *AP* 24:36; עדי לך מן כול מדינת מצרין "depart from all the provinces of Egypt!" *1Qap-Gen* 20:27-28; ואזלין למדינת דרמשק "and making their way to the city of Damascus" *1QapGen* 22:4-5; דִּי בְּמָדַי מְדִינְתָּא "which is in the province of Media" Ezra 6:2; אֲזַלְנָא לִיהוּד מְדִינְתָּא "we went to the province of Judah" 5:8; מַלְכִין וּמְדִנָן וְאֶשְׁתַּדּוּר עָבְדִין בְּגַוַּהּ "(damaging) kings and provinces, and stirring up sedition in it" 4:15 (perh. read וּמַרְדִין "rebellions" [see *AH* I/1.18]); וְכֹל שִׁלְטֹנֵי מְדִינָתָא "and all the prefects of the provinces" Dan 3:2, 3; דִּינֵי [פ]תף מן ביתא זילי זי "the judges of the province" *AP* 16:7; מדנתא במדינתכם "[pro]visions from my estate that is in your provinces" *AD* 6:2; מן פקיד על פקיד . . . מן מדינה עד מדינה "from prefect to prefect . . . from province to province (until he reaches Egypt)" *AD* 6:5. [Hebr. the same]. †

מְדוֹר : see מְדוֹר, מְדָר .

מָה עֲבַדְתְּ -- .(מֵן .cf) **what?** :.interrog. pron (1) -- מָא, מָה
"what did You do?" Dan 4:32; מָה דִּי לֶהֱוֵא אַחֲרֵי דְנָה "(thoughts
about) what would be hereafter" 2:29; מה טב שג[יא] כבי[ך לזי נ]גע
[באנ]ביך "what is the good of the abun[dance] of [your] thorns
[to him who tou]ches [your fr]uit?" *Ah.* 165; למה לי נסיכי "for
what (good is this) to me, my lord?" *Ah.* 119; למה הו יחבל מתא
עלין "why should he damage the land against us?" *Ah.* 36; עַל־מָה
דָתָא "why is the decree (so severe)?" Dan 2:15; מהידה זי ספר לה
הושרתן לי "What is this (= מָה הִי דָא) that you did not send a letter
to me?" *Hermopolis* 5:7-8. -- (2) adv. (BL 348e) מָה & כְּמָה
(cf. כְּ no. 4): **how!** אָתוֹהִי כְּמָה רַבְרְבִין "how great are His signs"
Dan 3:33a: 3:33b; כמה נצ[י]ח ושפיר לה צלם אנפיהא "how splen-
[did] and beautiful the form of her face!" *1QapGen* 20:2; דרעיהא
מא שפירן וידיהא כמא כלילן "her arms, how beautiful! And her
hands, how perfect!" *1QapGen* 20:4-5; כמא יאין כפיהא ומא אריכן
וקטינן כול אצבעת ידיהא "how lovely (are) her palms, and how long
and dainty all the fingers of her hands!" *1QapGen* 20:5. -- Cf.
כְּמָן *: **how great!** (about -*n*, see BL 82h, j; *LFAA* 118b). אזל וחזי
כמן ארכהא וכמן פתיהא "go and see how great is its (the land's)
length and how great its width" *1QapGen* 21:13-14; וחזי כמן כפלין
שגיו מן כול "and see how greatly they have doubled and multiplied beyond all" *1QapGen* 22:29-30. -- (3) indef. rel. pron. מָה
מָה דִּי לֶהֱוֵא & דִּי (BL 357m-o): **that which, what, whatever.** מָה דִּי לֶהֱוֵא
בְּאַחֲרִית יוֹמַיָּא "what will be at the end of days" Dan 2:28: 2:29,
45; Ezra 7:18; לְמָא דִי־תַעַבְדוּן עִם־שָׂבֵי יְהוּדָיֵא "about what you are to
do for the Jewish elders" 6:8; מה זי תעבדון לחור ל[תריה]ם עבדו
"whatever you do for Hor, do for [both of] them" *AP* 38:8; חזו
עליהם מה צבו "look after them, as to that which they need" *AP*
38:6; מה זי לקחת זיני תשלם "you are to pay the penalty (for) whatever you have taken" *AD* 12:8; יָדַע מָה בַחֲשׁוֹכָא "(God) knows
what is in the darkness" Dan 2:22: Ezra 6:9; מה טב בעיני "whatever is good in my sight" *Sefire III* 3; כל מה לחיה בארק ובשמין
"whatever evil there is on earth and in heaven" *Sefire I* A 26;

מוזן—מות

ישלחן אלהן מן כל מה אכל בארפד ובעמה "may gods send every sort of devourer against Arpad and its people" *Sefire I* A 30; בכל מה זי ימות בר אנש שקרתם "in whatever way anyone shall die, you shall have been unfaithful (to the gods of the treaty)" *Sefire III* 16. -- (4) neg. conj. of purpose לְמָה & דִּי לְמָה w. impf. (BL 363w; cf. Hebr. פֶּן): **so that not, lest (perhaps).** לְמֶעְבַּד עַל־דְּנָה לְמָה יִשְׂגֵּא חֲבָלָא "to do in this matter lest the damage grow (worse)" Ezra 4:22; דִּי־לְמָה לֶהֱוֵא קְצַף עַל מַלְכוּת מַלְכָּא "so that (His) wrath not come upon the realm of the king" 7:23; למה כזי תאתה בזנה מה זי לקחת זיני תשלם "lest, when you come hither, you are to pay the penalty (for) whatever you have taken" *AD* 12:7-8; [אל תדרג] ק[שתך . . . לצדיק למה אלהא . . . יהתיבנהי עליך "[do not bend] your [b]ow . . . against a righteous person lest God . . . turn it back on you" *Aḥ.* 126; למה הן יאבד "so that (the herb) may not perish" *El. Ost.* (*AH* I/1. 12); דלמה תהוה אמר "lest you say" *1QapGen* 22:22. [Hebr. מָה, מַה].

מוֹזֵן * (*maqtal*, root *wzn*, BL 2341, *LFAA* 85z, a), emph. מוזנא (*môzĕnā'* *AP* 15:24); du. מוֹזְנַיִן *, emph. מֹאזְנַיָּא (Dan 5:27 v.l.; א perh. < Hebr. אָזְנַיִם "two ears"); secondary form מוזנה * (*môzĕnēh*), emph. מוזניא * (*môzanyā'*) & מֹאזַנְיָא (Dan 5:27); pl. מֹוזְנָן(*Tg. Onq. Lev.* 19:36; w. augm. -*aw*-): **balance, scales.** תְּקִילְתָּה בְמֹאזַנְיָא "you have been weighed in the scales" Dan 5:27; תתב על מוזנא ותתקל . . . כסף שקלן 7 "she will come back to the scales and weigh out . . . the sum of 7 shekels" *AP* 15:23-24. ¹

מוֹת (*mawt*): **death.** הֵן לְמוֹת הֵן לִשְׁרֹשׁוּ "(execution) whether by death or by exile" Ezra 7:26; אנה יהבת לכי בחיי ובמותי בית 1 "I have given to you for my lifetime and after my death 1 house" *AP* 8:3; 8:8; שבקתכי במותי "I have released you (effective) at my death" *BMAP* 5:4; בחייך ועד מותך נסבל לזכור "in your lifetime and up until your death we shall support Zakkur" *BMAP* 5:12; עלעי

199

מזון—מחלקה

תנין יתבר כמותא זי [ל]א מתחזה א[ל] "(the speech of a king) breaks the ribs of a dragon, like the death that is not seen (i.e., the plague)" *Ah.* 106. [Hebr. מָוֶת]. [1]

מָזוֹן * (*maqtal*, root זון "be nourished," BL 194r): **food, nourishment.** וּמָזוֹן לְכֹלָּא־בֵהּ "and food for all was on it (the tree)" Dan 4:9: 4:18; cf. זון "provision," i.e., supply of food kept in a house: וכל זון זי תשכח לי "and any provisions that you may find of mine" *AP* 10:10: 10:17. [Hebr. the same]. †

מַחָא : see חֲיָה, Aph. ptc.

מְחָא * (ל"ה > ל"א), 3 sg. f. מְחָת (v.l. מְחַת, BL 154l), 3 pl. m. מחאו (*mĕḥá'û*) & מחו (*mĕḥô*); impf. 3 sg. m. ימחא (*yimḥē'*), 1 sg. w. suff. אמחאנך ('*imḥa'innāk*); ptc. pl. m. מחין (*māḥáyin*). **Hithpe.** impf. 3 sg. m. יתמחא; ptc. מתמחין (*mitmĕḥáyin*): **strike. Pa.** impf. 3 sg. m. יְמַחֵא : **strike.** . . . אֶבֶן מְחָת לְצַלְמָא עַל־רַגְלוֹהִי "a stone . . . struck the statue on its feet" Dan 2:34: 2:35; מחאו עליך מצר "(these kings) set up a siege-wall against you" *Zkr* A 15 (*KAI* 202); הן אמחאנך ברי לא תמות "if I strike you, my son, you will not die" *Ah.* 82; וימחא על אפיה "and one strikes (her) on her face" *Sefire I* A 42; סלקו . . . והוא מחין ובזין מן פורת נהרא ומחו "they came up . . . and kept striking and plundering from the Euphrates River (onward). They struck (the Rephaim)" *1QapGen* 21:28; זְקִיף יִתְמְחֵא עֲלֹהִי "he shall be lifted up and impaled on it" Ezra 6:11; ומתמחין מן אחיהון "and they are being struck by their brothers" *1QapGen* 0:15; לָא אִיתַי דִּי־יְמַחֵא בִידֵהּ "there is no one who hinders His hand," lit., "who strikes on His hand" Dan 4:32. [Concerning מחא and Hebr. מחץ, see Degen, *AGI* §21 n.] †

מַחְלְקָה * (*maqtul-at*, BL 194v), pl. w. suff. מַחְלְקָתְהוֹן; f.: **class, division** (cf. פְּלֻגָּה). וַהֲקִימוּ . . . לְוָיֵא בְּמַחְלְקָתְהוֹן עַל־עֲבִידַת אֱלָהָא "and they set up . . . the Levites in their classes for the service of

200

מחן—מטא

God" Ezra 6:18. [Hebr. מַחֲלֹקֶת]. [1]

מְחַן : see חנן Pe. infin.

מְטָא & מְטָה (ṯ > ṭ; ל"ה > ל"א), 3 sg. m. w. suff. מטאך (mĕṭa'āk), מטאני; 3 sg. f. מטאת (miṭ'at) & מְטָת (v.l. מְטַת), w. suff. מטתכי (miṭṭĕkî); 3 pl. מְטוֹ; impf. ימטא (yimṭa') & יְמְטָא, w. suff. תמטנך (timṭinnāk); infin. ממטה (mimṭēh); ptc. sg. f. מטאה (māṭĕ'āh): **arrive, reach, come to, happen** (w. לְ, עַל, עַד, accus.). . . . רְמוֹ אָנוּן וְלָא מְטוֹ לְאַרְעִית גֻּבָּא "they threw them . . . and they did not reach the bottom of the den" Dan 6:25; רב חילא מטא למטה "the officer of the army came to Abydos" AP 38:3; לאבוט מדי "upon arrival in Media" Bisitun 25; כְּבַר אֱנָשׁ אָתֵה הֲוָה וְעַד־עַתִּיק יוֹמַיָּא מְטָה "there came one like a son of man, and he reached the Ancient of Days" Dan 7:13 (BL 298b); עד ימטא מצרין "until he reaches Egypt" AD 6:5; מטא צחא מנפי "Ṣeḥa' arrived at Memphis" AP 83:2; הן מטאך סרחלצה שלח לי "if SRḤLṢH comes to you, send me" Hermopolis 3:6; ביום 6 לפאפי מטו אגרתא "on day 6 of Paophi the letters arrived" AP 37:15; כזי תמטנך אג[רתי] "when [my] letter reaches you" BMAP 13:2; וכזי אגרתא זא [ת]מטא עליך "and when this letter [rea]ches you" AP 42:6-7; [מ]טאת ספינתא "(a sheep) arrived to be shorn" Sachau p. 233 n. 76 A 1.3; רְבָה אִילָנָא מטית למגז "the boat [ca]me here to us" BMAP 13:7; תנה עלין . . . וְרוּמֵהּ יְמְטֵא לִשְׁמַיָּא "the tree grew . . . and its top reached to the heavens" Dan 4:8, 17. -- In a transferred sense: רְבוּתָךְ רְבַת וּמְטָת לִשְׁמַיָּא "your majesty has grown and has reached the heavens" Dan 4:19; זִמְנָא מְטָה וּמַלְכוּתָא הֶחֱסִנוּ קַדִּישִׁין "and the time arrived, and holy ones took possession of the kingdom" 7:22; הן מטא תנין שנה "if a second year arrives" AP 10:7; הן מטת מרביתא לרשא "if the interest is added to the capital," lit., "comes to the capital" AP 10:6; גְּזֵרַת עֶלָּיָא הִיא דִּי מְטָת עַל־מָרְאִי מַלְכָּא "it is a decree of the Most High that has come upon my lord, the king" Dan 4:21; כֹּלָּא . . . עַל מְטָא מַלְכָּא "all (this evil) has happened to . . . the king"

201

4:25 (cf. דִּי־לְמָה לֶהֱוֵא קְצַף עַל־מַלְכוּת מַלְכָּא "lest (His) wrath be upon the realm of the king" Ezra 7:23); מקריא על אלהן מטא עלי בדינא "an appeal to our god has been imposed on me in the court," lit., "has arrived at me" *AP* 7:6-7; מומאה מטאה עליכי "an oath was imposed on you" *AP* 14:4-5 (cf. טעונך לי מומאה "they imposed on you an oath to me" *AP* 6:6); הא זנה חלקא זי מטאך . . . זי מטאני "look, this is the share that comes to you . . . that comes to me" *AP* 28:3-5; חלף פלג מנתא זי מטתכי "instead of half of the share that accrued to you" *AP* 1:3-4; לה שבק אנה לה 1 כדי מטאה ידי "I am not leaving him alone, to the extent that it is possible for me," lit., "that it arrives at my hands" *Hermopolis* 3:4 (cf. Hebr. מָצְאָה יָדִי לְ "my hand succeeds in . . ." Isa 10:10, 14); זבני עמר כזי תמטה ידכי "buy wool, whenever you can," lit., "your hand arrives (at it)" *Hermopolis* 6:5-6. [Hebr. מָצָא]. †

▲ מִישָׁאֵל : **Mishael**, companion of Daniel. לַחֲנַנְיָה מִישָׁאֵל וַעֲזַרְיָה . . . מִלְּתָא הוֹדַע "to Hananiah, Mishael, and Azariah . . . he made the matter known" Dan 2:17.

▲ מֵישַׁךְ : **Meshach**, companion of Daniel. וּמַנִּי . . . לְשַׁדְרַךְ מֵישַׁךְ וַעֲבֵד נְגוֹ "and he appointed . . . Shadrach, Meshach, and Abednego" Dan 2:49; 3:12, 14 + .

מְלָא * (ל״ה > ל״א), 3 sg. f. מְלָת (v.l. מְלָאת ,מְלַת ,מְלָאת, BL 154m). **Hithpe.** (pass.) 3 sg. m. הִתְמְלִי : **fill.** מְלָת . . . וְאַבְנָא "and the stone . . . filled all the earth" Dan 2:35; הִתְמְלִי כָּל־אַרְעָא "(Nebuchadnezzar) was filled with rage" 3:19; עד תתמלא חֱמָא בכספך "until you are filled with your money," i.e., have received full payment *AP* 10:11. [Hebr. מָלֵא]. †

מַלְאַךְ * (*maqtal*, BL 194q), w. suff. מַלְאֲכֵהּ : **messenger, angel.** אֱלָהִי שְׁלַח מַלְאֲכֵהּ "my God sent his angel" Dan 6:23: 3:28; אשלח מלאכי א[ל]וה לשלם . . . או ישלח מלאכה אלי "(when) I send my messenger to h[i]m for peace . . . or he sends his messenger to me" *Sefire III* 8. -- Cf. מלאכתי אשלח לך "I send you my message" *Assur Letter* 19 (*KAI* 233). [Hebr. מַלְאָךְ]. †

מִלָּה (qill-at, BL 181u, 199h), cst. מִלַּת, emph. מִלְּתָא; pl. מִלִּין (BL 238r), cst. מִלֵּי, emph. מִלַּיָּא, f.: -- (1) **word.** מִלִּין לְצַד עִלָּיָא יְמַלִּל "he shall utter words against the Most High" Dan 7:25; ימלל מלן לחית לעלי "(whoever) utters evil words against me" *Sefire III* 2; מִלָּה כִדְבָה וּשְׁחִיתָה . . . לְמֵאמַר קָדָמַי "to speak lying and corrupt words before me" Dan 2:9; עוֹד מִלְּתָא בְּפֻם מַלְכָּא "(while) the word was still in the king's mouth" 4:28; מִן־קָל מִלַּיָּא רַבְרְבָתָא דִּי קַרְנָא מְמַלְלָה "because of the sound of the great words that the horn was uttering" 7:11; מִלְּתָא סָפַת עַל "the (prophetic) word was fulfilled upon (Nebuchadnezzar)" 4:30; כדי שמע מלכא מלי חרקנוש ומלי תרין חברוהי "when the king heard the words of Hirqanos and the words of his two companions" *1QapGen* 20:8; איש זעיר וירבה מלוהי מסרסרן לעלא מנה "(when) a little man multiplies his words, they fly away above him" *Aḥ.* 114; ישמע מלה ולא יהחוה "(a wise man) will hear a word and not reveal it" *Aḥ.* 93; לָקֳבֵל מִלֵּי מַלְכָּא וְרַבְרְבָנוֹהִי "because of the words of the king and his nobles" Dan 5:10 (cf. v. 7); בכת שרי על מלי בלייא דן "Sarai wept because of my words that night" *1QapGen* 19:21. -- **decree.** דִּי אֲזְדָּא מִנִּי מִלְּתָא "(you perceive) that the decree from me is certain" (‖ דָּת v. 9) Dan 2:8: 2:5; וּמְלַת מַלְכָּא שַׁנִּיו "and transgressed the decree of the king" 3:28: 3:22; 6:13. -- **description, account.** חֶלְמָא כְתַב רֵאשׁ מִלִּין אֲמַר . . . עַד־כָּה סוֹפָא דִּי־מִלְּתָא "(Daniel) wrote down the dream beginning of the words (and) told (an account of the matter) . . . up to here, the end of the description" Dan 7:1-28 (glosses, BL 353f); הן כן הו כמליא אלה זי פטסרי שלח ע[לי] "if it is as (described in) this account that Petosiri has sent to [me]" *AD* 8:3; כלא מליא חדה באגרה שלחן בשמן "the whole account we have sent in a letter in our name," lit., "all the words" *AP* 30:29; ומלוהי כתיב בספרא זנה "(the boundaries and dimensions of the house), and the description of it is recorded in this document" *BMAP* 9:16.

(2) **matter, affair, business** (cf. פִּתְגָּם, צְבוּ). דִּי מִלַּת מַלְכָּא
יוּכַל לְהַחֲוָיָה "(there is no one) who can explain the king's matter"
Dan 2:10: 2:11, 23; מִלְּתָא הוֹדַע אַרְיוֹךְ לְדָנִיֵּאל "Arioch explained
the matter to Daniel" 2:15: 2:17; מַלְכָּא כְּדִי מִלְּתָא שְׁמַע שַׂגִּיא בְּאֵשׁ
"the king, when he heard the affair, was much distressed" 6:15;
אֲמַר־לִי וּפְשַׁר מִלַּיָּא יְהוֹדְעִנַּנִי "he spoke to me and made known the
meaning of the business" 7:16; מִלְּתָא בְּלִבִּי נִטְרֵת "I kept the affair
in my mind" 7:28; לָא־כָהֲלִין פְּשַׁר־מִלְּתָא לְהַחֲוָיָה "(the wise men)
could not explain the meaning of the matter," i.e., the writing on
the wall 5:15: 5:26; מלה זי צחא יבעה מנכם "(in the) business that
Ṣeḥaʾ asks of you, (assist him)" AP 38:6; כזי מלה באישה לא יהשכחון
לכם "when they find no fault in you," lit., "no evil matter" AP
38:6-7; [ואנחנה] נעבד מלה "and [we] shall do business" AP 37:16;
מאן טב כס[ה] מלה בלבבה "a good vessel hid[es] a matter within
itself" Aḥ. 109. [Hebr. the same]. †

מְלַח (milḥ, BL 183g), abs. & cst.: **salt.** חִנְטִין מְלַח חֲמַר
וּמְשַׁח "wheat, salt, wine, and oil (for the temple)" Ezra 6:9: 7:22;
מְלַח הֵיכְלָא מְלַחְנָא "(since) we eat the salt of the palace," lit., "we
taste" (see next entry) 4:14; נשאית חלא וטענת מלח "I have lifted
sand and have carried salt" Aḥ. 111; ימא רבא דן די מלחא "this
great Salt Sea" 1QapGen 21:16. [Hebr. מֶלַח]. †

מלח (denom. verb, 1 pl. מְלַחְנָא : **taste, season with salt.**
מְלַח הֵיכְלָא מְלַחְנָא "(since) we eat the salt of the palace," lit., "we
taste" (= our salary is paid by the king; but W. Rudolph would
read מְלָחֲנָא "the salt of the palace is our salt") Ezra 4:14; cf.
וכולהון מליחין במלח = καὶ πάντα ἡλισμένα ἐν ἅλατι (Test. Levi
9:14[?]) "and all of them were salted with salt." [1]

מֶלֶךְ (malk [w. Hebr. vocal.]) abs. & cst., emph. & מַלְכָּה
מַלְכָּא ; pl. מַלְכִין (כ wt. daghesh, BL 226x: < malakīn); (מַלְכִים
Ezra 4:13: error, BL 10v, 201f), emph. מַלְכַיָּא : **king.** לְבֵלְאשַׁצַּר

מלך—מלכה

מֶלֶךְ־בָּבֶל "of Belshazzar, king of Babylon" Dan 7:1: Ezra 5:12, but מַלְכָּא דִי בָבֶל 5:13; מַלְכָּא כַשְׂדָּיָא . . . קְטִיל "the Chaldean king was killed" Dan 5:30; לְמַלְכוּת דָּרְיָוֶשׁ מֶלֶךְ־פָּרָס "of the reign of Darius, king of Persia" Ezra 4:24; וּמֶלֶךְ לְיִשְׂרָאֵל רַב בְּנָהִי "and a great king of Israel built it (the temple)" 5:11; מַלְכָּא דָּרְיָוֶשׁ רְשַׁם "King Darius signed the document" Dan 6:10: 4:15; and אַנְתָּה מַלְכָּא מֶלֶךְ ; + 7 ,5:6 דָּרְיָוֶשׁ מַלְכָּא "Darius the king" 6:26; Ezra מַלְכַיָּא "You, O King, king of kings" (cf. דִי I 2) Dan 2:37; אַרְתַּחְשַׁסְתְּא מֶלֶךְ מַלְכַיָּא "Artaxerxes, king of kings" (Persian title, BL 312i) Ezra 7:12; אֲנָה . . . מְשַׁבַּח . . . לְמֶלֶךְ שְׁמַיָּא "I praise . . . the King of Heaven" Dan 4:34; אֱלָהֲכוֹן הוּא . . . וּמָרֵא מַלְכִין "your God is . . . and lord of kings" 2:47; מרא מלכן פרעה "Pharaoh, the lord of kings" Saqqara Letter 1, 6 (KAI 266). -- As gen. of quality (cf. דִי I 2): royal. רַב־טַבָּחַיָּא דִי מַלְכָּא "the officer of the royal guards" Dan 2:14; לְאַרְיוֹךְ שַׁלִּיטָא דִי־מַלְכָּא "to Arioch, the king's captain" 2:15; דָּנִיֵּאל בִּתְרַע מַלְכָּא "Daniel (was) at the royal court" 2:49; עַל גִּירָא דִי־כְתַל הֵיכְלָא דִי מַלְכָּא "on the plaster of the wall of the royal palace" 5:5; נִפְקְתָא מִן־בֵּית מַלְכָּא תִּתְיְהִב "let the cost be paid from the royal revenue" Ezra 6:4: 6:8; 7:20; [כ]זי יתנתן לי פתפא מן בית מלכא "[wh]en the ration is given to me from the royal house" BMAP 11:5-6; מן אוצר מלכא "from the royal treasury" BMAP 11:4; ושוק מלכא ביניהם "and the Street of the King is between them" BMAP 3:8; וארח מלכא בניהם "and the Royal Highway is between them" AP 25:6-7. [Hebr. מֶלֶךְ].

מְלַךְ (milk), w. suff. מִלְכִּי : advice (cf. עֵטָא). לָהֵן מַלְכָּא מִלְכִּי יִשְׁפַּר עֲלָיִךְ "therefore, O King, let my advice be pleasing to you" Dan 4:24; לא בהיל על כול מלך "he was not troubled by any advice" 4QEnGiants^c (4Q531) 14:2. [1]

מַלְכָּה (qatl-at, BL 182d), emph. מַלְכְּתָא : queen. מַלְכְּתָא . . . לְבֵית מִשְׁתְּיָא עַלְלַת עֲנָת מַלְכְּתָא וַאֲמֶרֶת "the queen . . . entered the banquet-hall; the queen spoke up, saying" Dan 5:10; שלם בית

205

בתאל ובית מלכת שמין "Greetings (to) the temple of Bethel and (to) the temple of the queen of heaven" *Hermopolis* 4:1. [Hebr. the same]. †

מַלְכוּ (BL 197g; כ wt. a daghesh), cst. מַלְכוּת, emph. מַלְכוּתָא, w. suff. מַלְכוּתֵהּ ,מַלְכוּתָךְ ,מַלְכוּתִי ; pl. (BL & מַלְכוּתָה 245c, d) מַלְכְוָן *, cst. מַלְכְוָת, emph. מַלְכְוָתָא : -- (1) **kingdom, royal majesty.** מַלְכוּתָה וְשָׁלְטָנָא וּרְבוּתָא דִּי מַלְכְוָת תְּחוֹת כָּל־שְׁמַיָּא יְהִיב לְעַם "regal status and dominion and the majesty of kingdoms under all the heavens is given to the people of (the saints of the Most High)" Dan 7:27 (BL 310c): 2:37, 44; 4:33; 5:18, 28; 7:14; שַׁלִּיט עִלָּיָא בְּמַלְכוּת אֲנָשָׁא "the Most High has power over the kingdom of man" 4:14, 22, 29; 5:21; דָּרְיָוֶשׁ . . . קַבֵּל מַלְכוּתָא "Darius . . . received royal majesty" 6:1: 7:18; וְיַחְסְנוּן מַלְכוּתָא עַד־עָלְמָא "and (the holy ones) shall possess the kingdom for ever and ever" 7:18: 7:22; מַלְכוּתָה עֲדָת מִנָּךְ "kingly power has departed from you" 4:28 (cf. שָׁלְטָנֵהּ יְהַעְדּוֹן "they will take away his dominion" 7:26); מַלְכוּתָךְ לָךְ קַיָּמָה מִן־דִּי תִנְדַּע "your kingdom shall be sure for you from the time that you recognize" 4:23; פְּרִיסַת מַלְכוּתָךְ וִיהִיבַת לְמָדַי וּפָרָס "your kingdom is divided and given to the Medes and Persians" 5:28; מַלְכוּתֵהּ מַלְכוּת עָלַם "His kingdom is an everlasting kingdom" 3:33: 4:31; 6:27; תהוי מלכתה כמלכת חל "may his kingdom become like a kingdom of sand, a kingdom of sand" (dittography) *Sefire I* A 25. -- (2) **royal dignity, kingdom** (concretely, as in a series of kings): וּבָתְרָךְ תְּקוּם מַלְכוּ אָחֳרִי אֲרַעא מִנָּךְ "and after you shall arise another kingdom inferior to you" Dan 2:39a (brachylogy); מַלְכוּ תְלִיתָיָא . . . דִּי "a third kingdom . . . shall rule over all the earth" תִּשְׁלַט בְּכָל־אַרְעָא 2:39b; מַלְכוּ פְלִיגָה תֶּהֱוֵה "(the fourth) will be a divided kingdom," i.e., w. several kings 2:41 (cf. vv. 42-43); אַרְבְּעָה מַלְכִין יְקוּמוּן "(the four beasts are) four kings (who) shall arise" 7:17; חֵיוְתָא רְבִיעָיְתָא מַלְכוּ רְבִיעָיָא תֶּהֱוֵה בְאַרְעָא "the fourth beast represents the fourth kingdom (that) will be on the earth" 7:23; מִנַּהּ מַלְכוּתָה

מלל—ממר

עֲשָׂרָה מַלְכִין יְקֻמוּן "from this kingdom shall arise ten kings," i.e.,
one after the other 7:24. -- (3) **people and land**, where kingly
power dominates. כָּל־חַכִּימֵי מַלְכוּתִי לָא יָכְלִין "all the wise men of
my kingdom are unable (to interpret the dream)" 4:15: 6:8; אִיתַי
גְּבַר בְּמַלְכוּתָךְ "there is a man in your kingdom" 5:11: 5:7, 16, 29;
6:2, 4; Ezra 7:13. -- (4) **time of reign.** עַד שְׁנַת תַּרְתֵּין לְמַלְכוּת
דָּרְיָוֶשׁ מֶלֶךְ־פָּרָס "until the second year of the reign of Darius, king
of Persia" Ezra 4:24: 6:15, 29bis; ראש מלוכתא כזי ארתחששש מלכא
יתב בכרסאה "the beginning of the reign when Artaxerxes, the
king, sat on his throne" *AP* 6:1-2 (read מלכותא); מְנָה־אֱלָהָא מַלְכוּתָךְ
וְהַשְׁלְמַהּ "God has numbered (the days of) your reign and brought
it to an end" Dan 5:26. -- (5) Gen. of quality: = **royal.**
עַל־הֵיכַל מַלְכוּתָא דִּי בָבֶל מְהַלֵּךְ הֲוָה "(the king) was walking on the
(roof of) royal palace of Babylon" Dan 4:26; בָּבֶל רַבְּתָא דִּי־אֲנָה
בֱנַיְתַהּ לְבֵית מַלְכוּ "great Babylon which I built for a royal residence" 4:27: 5:20; בְּכָל־שָׁלְטָן מַלְכוּתִי "in all my royal dominion"
6:27.

מלל (denom. verb < מִלָּה, BL 273g), **Pa.** 3 sg. m. מַלִּל ;
impf. 3 sg. m. יְמַלִּל ; ptc. sg. m. מְמַלִּל , sg. f. מְמַלְלָה : **speak,
utter.** מִלִּין לְצַד עִלָּיָא יְמַלִּל "he shall utter words against the Most
High" Dan 7:25; וּפֻם מְמַלִּל רַבְרְבָן "and a mouth speaking great
things" 7:8, 20: 7:11; ימלל מלן לחית לעלי "(whoever) will speak
evil words against me" *Sefire III* 2; דָּנִיֵּאל עִם־מַלְכָּא מַלִּל "Daniel
spoke with the king" Dan 6:22; בקושט עמי תמללין "(that) you are
speaking to me truthfully" *1QapGen* 2:7; עמי מללת ובּ[כת] ואמרת
"she spoke to me and we[pt] and said" *1QapGen* 2:8-9; מלל על
פטנפחתף "he spoke about Peṭenefḥotef" *AP* 69:A2; פם חד תלתהון
ממללין "the three of them were speaking with one voice" *1Qap-
Gen* 20:8. [Hebr. מִלֵּל]. †

מֵמַר : see אֲמַר infin.

207

מן

מַן , (1) Interrog. pron.: **who?** (cf. מָה). מַן־שָׂם לְכֹם טְעֵם
בַּיתָא דְנָה לִבְּנֵא "Who gave you a decree to build this house?" Ezra
5:3, 9; מַן־הוּא אֱלָהּ דִּי יְשֵׁזְבִנְכוֹן מִן־יְדָי "who is the god who will save
you from my hands?" Dan 3:15; מַן־אִנּוּן שְׁמָהָת גֻּבְרַיָּא "what are
the names of the men?" (construction acc. to sense) Ezra 5:4 (cf.
Hebr. מִי שְׁמֶךָ Judg 13:17); מן הו זי יקום קדמהי "who is he that can
stand before him?" *Aḥ.* 107; ועם מן אצדק "and with whom shall I
be justified" *Aḥ.* 139; לא איתיני ידע למן הוה אמר "I do not know to
whom (I) was saying" *Mur 72* 1:4.

(2) Indef. rel. pron. מַן־דִּי & מַן : **whoever, the one who,
etc.** מַן־דִּי לָא יִפֵּל וְיִסְגֻּד "whoever does not fall down and adore"
Dan 3:6, 11; וּלְמַן־דִּי יִצְבֵּא יִתְּנִנַּהּ "and (the Most High) gives it (the
kingdom) to whom He pleases" 4:14, 22, 29; וּלְמַן־דִּי יִצְבֵּא יְהָקֵים
עֲלַיהּ "and He sets over it (the kingdom) whom He pleases" 5:21;
[י']קתל מן יקתל "let him kill whomever he would kill" *Sefire II* B
9; או מן ישלח "or whoever will send" *Zkr* B 21 (*KAI* 202); ולמן
די צבית למנתן "and he to whom you will want to give (it)" *BMAP*
3:12; לבר לך וברה ולמן זי צבית למנתן "to your son or daughter or to
whomever you want to give (it)" *BMAP* 3:14; ינתן לכם או לבניכם
ולמן זי ירשון אביגרנא "he shall pay the fine to you or to your sons
or to whomever they sue" *AP* 20:14; מן את תהנס צלמא זנה "whoever you (are that) will remove this statue" *Nerab* 5-7 (*KAI* 225);
מן זי את תתב יתבון "whoever you (are that) will damage (?) the
(boundary)" *Cilicia* 2 (*KAI* 259); הן מן חד אחי . . . או מן חד שנאי
. . . ויבעה להמתתי "if anyone of my brothers . . . or anyone of my
enemies seeks . . . to kill me" *Sefire III* 9-11. †

מִן , prep., w. suff. (BL 259t-w) sg. מִנִּי, מִנָּךְ, מִנַּהּ, מִנֵּהּ ;
pl. m. מִנְּהוֹן, f. מִנְּהֵין (Dan 2:33 q.): -- (1) מִן meaning separa-
tion, etc.: **from, out of.** עִיר וְקַדִּישׁ מִן־שְׁמַיָּא נָחִת "a Watcher, a holy one, came down from heaven" Dan 4:10; 4:28; הָנְחַת מִן־כָּרְסָא
מַלְכוּתֵהּ "he was deposed from his kingly throne" 5:20; . . . נָפְקִין
מִן־גּוֹא נוּרָא "came out . . . from the midst of the fire" 3:26; מִן יוֹם

208

מן

דִּי נִפְקְתָה מִן חָרָן "since the day that you departed from Haran" *1QapGen* 22:28; לְמָאנֵי דַהֲבָא דִּי . . . הַנְפֵּק . . . אֲבוּהִי מִן־הֵיכְלָא "the vessels of gold . . . that his father . . . had brought from the temple" Dan 5:2: 5:3; לְהַנְסָקָה מִן־גֻּבָּא "to bring (Daniel) up from the den" Dan 6:24; דִּי הַיְתִי מַלְכָּא אֲבִי מִן־יְהוּד "(exiles) whom my father, the king, brought from Judah" 5:13; וּמִן־אֲנָשָׁא טְרִיד "and (Nebuchadnezzar) was driven out from among men" 4:30: 4:22, 29; 5:21; נְטִילַת מִן־אַרְעָא "(the beast) was lifted up from the ground" 7:4; יִתְנְסַח אָע מִן־בַּיְתֵהּ "a log shall be pulled out of his house" Ezra 6:11: Dan 2:45; וּמַן־הוּא אֱלָהּ דִּי יְשֵׁיזְבִנְכוֹן מִן־יְדָי "and who is the god that will save you from my hand" (read prob. יְדִי) Dan 3:15: 3:17; 6:21, 28; נכסן לקח מנה "he has taken property from it" *AD* 12:9; אגורא זי יהו אלהא . . . יהעדו מן תמה "the temple of the god Yaho . . . let them remove from there" *AP* 30: 6; לא יתכסון מן ענני "it will not be hidden from 'Anani" *AP* 38:11; הצפנתך מנה "I hid you from him" *Ah.* 49; אל ישלט . . . לטמיא אנתתי מני "may he not be able . . . to defile my wife" *1QapGen* 20:15. -- Distance: רַחִיקִין הֲווֹ מִן־תַּמָּה "keep far from there" Ezra 6:6; לשטר ביתי מן ארעא ועד עלא "the side of my house from the ground upwards" *AP* 5:5; מן תחתיא לעליא "from the lower part to the upper" *BMAP* 9:6. -- Change, succession: לְבָבֵהּ מִן־אֲנָשָׁא יְשַׁנּוֹן "let his mind be changed from a man's" Dan 4:13 (cf. לְבַב); שָׁנְיָן דָּא מִן־דָּא "(beasts) differing, one from the other" 7:3: 7:7, 19, 23, 24; מן פקיד על פקיד . . . מן מדינה עד מדינה "from prefect to prefect . . . from province to province" *AD* 6:5. -- Compos. prep.: יֵאבַדוּ מֵאַרְעָא וּמִן־תְּחוֹת שְׁמַיָּא "(the gods) shall perish from the earth and from under the heavens" Jer 10:11: Dan 4:11; לא אכל אנצל לפלטי מן תחת לבבך "I shall not be able to take Palti away from under your care," lit., "your heart" *BMAP* 2:13-14; מִן־קֳדָם, see קֳדָם.

(2) מִן in comparison: **than, more than** (cf. עַל no. 9). לָא בְחָכְמָה דִּי־אִיתַי בִּי מִן־כָּל־חַיַּיָא "not by a wisdom that I have more than all living beings" Dan 2:30: חֶזְוַהּ רַב מִן־חַבְרָתַהּ "its appearance was greater than its fellows" 7:20 (brachylogy); הרמו שר מן

209

שׁר חזרך "they erected a wall higher than the wall of Ḥazrak" *Zkr* A 10 (*KAI* 202); צדקה יהוה לך קדם יהו אלה שמיא מן גבר זי יקרב לה עלוה "you will have merit before Yaho, the god of heaven, (great-er) than one who offers him a burnt sacrifice" *AP* 30:27-28; יתיר מן יום חד "more than one day" *AD* 6:6; עזיז ארב פם מן ארב מלחם "mightier is the ambush of the mouth than the ambush of war" *Aḥ.* 99; זעיר כצפה מן ברק "swifter is his (a king's) wrath than lightning" *Aḥ.* 101; עם זי רם מנך אל תעבר בנ[צוי "enter not into a quar[rel?] with one that is taller than you" *Aḥ.* 142; זי יעז מנך "who will be stronger than you" *Sefire II* B 20; כל בתולן . . . לא, ישפרן מנהא "there are no virgins . . . more beautiful than she" *1QapGen* 20:6.

(3) Partitive מִן (BL 316h): **of, from, from among.** -- (a) הַשְׁכַּחַת גְּבַר מִן־בְּנֵי גָלוּתָא "I have found a man from among the exiles (of Judah)" Dan 2:25: 5:13; 6:14; Ezra 7:13; דִּי דָנִיֵּאל חַד־מִנְּהוֹן "of whom Daniel (was) one" Dan 6:3: 7:8, 16 (cf. חד מלכן "one of the kings" *Sefire I* B 26); יהבת לכי קצת מן ביתי "I have given to you part of my house" *BMAP* 9:2-3; . אשלמ[נה]י לך מן פרסי . . "I shall pay [it] to you . . . from my salary" *AP* 11:5-6. -- (b) מִן = **part** (of a thing), **some** (in a quasi-nominal sense; see Brock. II, 360, 397): רַגְלוֹהִי מִנְּהֵן דִּי פַרְזֶל וּמִנְּהוֹן דִּי חֲסַף "its feet partly of iron, partly of clay" Dan 2:33: 2:41, 42; מִן־קְצָת מַלְכוּתָא תֶּהֱוֵה תַקִּיפָה וּמִנַּהּ תֶּהֱוֵה תְבִירָה "the kingdom shall be partly strong and partly fragile" 2:42 (see קְצָת); מִן־נִצְבְּתָא דִּי פַרְזְלָא לֶהֱוֵא־בַהּ "some of the firmness of iron shall be in it" 2:41; זי יכלא מנהם ינתן לה כספא "whoever will impede anyone of them shall pay him the money" *AP* 5:10; יקח מן ארקי "(if) he takes away some of my land" *Sefire I* B 27; ישלחן אלהן מן כל מה אכל "may the gods send every sort of devourer (against Arpad)" *Sefire I* A 30; לא אשתאר לן עליך מן דמיא "there is not outstanding to us against you any part of the price" *BMAP* 12:6; הן מן גרדא או מן נכסיא אחרנן זילי מנדעם כסנתו יהוה "if my staff or other property suffers any damage" *AD* 7:8.

(4) Temporal מִן : **from, since.** מְבָרַךְ מִן־עָלְמָא וְעַד־עָלְמָא
"blessed for ever and ever" Dan 2:20; מִן־אֱדַיִן וְעַד־כְּעַן "from then
until now" Ezra 5:16; מן יומא זנה עד עלם "from this day for ever"
BMAP 7:4; מן ירח תמוז "since the month of Tammuz" *AP* 30:19;
דִּי־הֲוָא עָבֵד מִן־קַדְמַת דְּנָה "what he (Daniel) had been doing previously," lit., "from before this" Dan 6:11: Ezra 5:11; מִן־יוֹמָת
עָלְמָא עַל־מַלְכִין מִתְנַשְּׂאָה "(this city, Jerusalem,) from of old has
risen up against kings" 4:19: 4:15; מן יומי מלך מצרין אבהין בנו
אגורא זך "since the days of the king(s) of Egypt, our ancestors
built that temple" *AP* 30:13 (see 31:13: בנה הוה מן קדמן קדם כנבוזי
מלכי מצרין); "(the temple) was built previously, before Cambyses" *AP* 32:4-5 (cf. בנה הוה קדמין "was built before" 30:25); מן
יום די נפקתה מן חרן "since the day that you departed from Haran"
1QapGen 22:28; ה[וי]ת אנתתי מן קדמת דנא "y[ou] were my wife
previously," lit., "before this" *Mur 19* 16-17.

(5) מִן of origin: **from, out of.** נִפְקְתָא מִן־בֵּית מַלְכָּא תִּתְיְהִב
"let the cost be paid out of the king's treasury" Ezra 6:4: 7:20;
[כ]זי יתנתן לי פתפא מן בית מלכא "[wh]en the ration is supplied to
me from the king's house" *BMAP* 11:5-6; אַרְבַּע חֵיוָן רַבְרְבָן סָלְקָן
מִן־יַמָּא, "four great beasts coming up from the sea" Dan 7:3, i.e.,
אַרְבְּעָה מַלְכִין יְקוּמוּן מִן־אַרְעָא "four kings shall arise from the earth"
7:17; מִנַּהּ מַלְכוּתָה עַשְׂרָה מַלְכִין יְקֻמוּן "from this kingdom ten kings
shall arise" 7:24 (suff. = dem. pron.; cf. בְּ no. 1); בְּעָה מִן־מַלְכָּא
"(Daniel) besought the king," lit., "begged from" 2:16: 2:33, 49;
6:8, 13; 7:16; שאלת מנך לנשן "I asked of you the woman" *BMAP*
7:3 (but: שְׁאֵל לְ Dan 2:10; Ezra 5:9); ביתא זי זבנת מן אוביל "the
house that I bought from 'Ubil" *BMAP* 4:3; אבוכם לקח מן שלומם
"your father received (these goods) from Shelomem" *AP* 20:6;
בר דכר ונקבה לא איתי לה מן אסחור בעלה "there is no child, male or
female, belonging to her from Ashor, her husband" *AP* 15:20-21.
-- In an attributive phrase (BL 316h): הֲווֹ כְּעוּר מִן־אִדְּרֵי־קַיִט "they
became like chaff of the summer threshing-floors" Dan 2:35;
בניך מן מבטחיה ברתי "your children from Mibṭaḥiah, my daugh-

מן

ter" *AP* 9:7; שהד מן חברן [ ] מן ירושלם [ ] "[name] from Jerusalem; [name] a witness from Hebron" *Judean Desert Papyrus* verso 19-20 (Milik, *Bib* 38 [1957] 259).

(6) מן of authorship: **by.** מנּי שׂים טְעֵם "I make a decree," lit., "a decree is issued by me" Dan 3:29; 4:3; Ezra 4:19 + ; מנך יאתה עם גנזא זי יתשׂם טעם "let a decree be issued by you" *AD* 5:8; מני שׂים להיתיה בבאל "let him come with the treasure that has been ordered by me to be brought to Babylon," lit., "to bring" *AD* 10:5; מִלְּתָא מִנּי אַזְדָּא "the matter is guaranteed by me" Dan 2:5, 8; הן אזד יתעבד מן דיניא "if an investigation be made by the judges" *AP* 27:8-9; לעלים אחרן זילי מני לא יהיב "(the farm) was not given by me to any other servant of mine" *AD* 8:5; בגא לם זי מן מראי יהיב לי "the estate, indeed, which was given to me by my lord" *AD* 10:1; אגרת מן מראי תשתלח על נחתיחור "let a letter be sent to Neḥitiḥur" *AD* 10:2 (cf. address of a letter: מן ארשם על וחפרעמחי "from Arsames to Waḥprimaḥi" *AP* 26:1.

(7) Causal מן : **because of, from.** חְזֵה הֲוֵית . . . מִן־קָל מִלַּיָּא רַבְרְבָתָא "I looked . . . because of the sound of the great words" Dan 7:11; מְטַל שְׁמַיָּא לָךְ מְצַבְּעִין "(you shall be) made wet from the dew of the heavens" 4:22: 4:30; 5:21 (cf. בְּטַל "by dew" 4:12, 20); מִן־רְבוּתָא . . . כָּל עַמְמַיָּא . . . הֲוֹו . . . דָּחֲלִין מִן־קֳדָמוֹהִי "because of the greatness (of the king) . . . all peoples . . . were in fear before him" 5:19; וּמִנַּהּ יִתְּזִין כָּל־בִּשְׂרָא "and all flesh was fed from it (the tree)" 4:9; ישׂתבע כעס מן לחם "let the one who is annoyed be sated with food" *Aḥ.* 189; פרש לוט מן לואתי מן עובד רעותנא "Lot separated from me because of the conduct of our shepherds" *1QapGen* 21:5; שַׁכְלִלוּ מִן־טַעַם אֱלָהּ יִשְׂרָאֵל וּמִטְּעֵם כּוֹרֶשׁ "they finished (the building) because of the command of the God of Israel and because of the decree of Cyrus" Ezra 6:14 (Gk.: ἀπὸ γνώμης, Vg. *iubente*); כָּל־דִּי מִן־טַעַם אֱלָהּ שְׁמַיָּא יִתְעֲבֵד אַדְרַזְדָּא "let all that is from the command of the God of Heaven be done diligently" Ezra 7:23; אנה מן רעותי . . . זבנת לך . . . לבתה דילי "I of my own accord . . . have sold to you . . . my house" *?Hev B* 3 (Milik, *Bib* 38 [1957] 264). Cf. מִן־דִּי.

212

(8) מִן of specification: **in respect of, with regard to.**
הֲווֹ בָעַיִן עִלָּה לְהַשְׁכָּחָה לְדָנִיֵּאל מִצַּד מַלְכוּתָא "they were seeking to find a ground for complaint against Daniel with regard to the kingdom" Dan 6:5 (cf. לָהֵן הַשְׁכַּחְנָה עֲלוֹהִי בְּדָת אֱלָהֵהּ "unless we find [it] against him in regard to the law of his God" 6:6); דִּינָה לֶהֱוֵא מִתְעֲבֵד מִנֵּהּ "let judgment be carried out with regard to him" Ezra 7:26; עבד לי דין מנה "mete out justice with regard to him for me" 1QapGen 20:14 (cf. אנתה שליט למעבד בכולהון דין "you have power to mete out justice on all of them" 20:13); הן . . . קבלת מנך ישלח עלי "if . . . he sends me a complaint with regard to you" AD 4:3; ומתמחין מן אחיהון, "being smitten by their brothers" 1QapGen 0:15; מן נפשה כתב "(she) wrote with regard to herself" Mur 21 23 (stereotyped masc. sg. witness's signature). -- מִן used as = adv. accus.: תחתיא מנה אגר דרגא "below it (is) the wall of the stairwell" BMAP 9:10 (cf. in the same sense לְ: עליה לה "at the upper end of it" AP 8:5 (see לְ I 3; or w. gen.: ממרא . . . כלמדנח צפון חברון "Mamre . . . to the northeast of Hebron" 1QapGen 21:19-20); בָּתְרָךְ תְּקוּם מַלְכוּ אָחֳרִי אֲרְעָה מִנָּךְ "another kingdom will arise after you inferior to you" Dan 2:39 (k. אֲרַעא, q. אֲרַע BL 319h); וְעֲלָא מִנְּהוֹן סָרְכִין תְּלָתָא "and over them three superiors," lit., "above with regard to them" 6:3; עליא שפרהא לעלא מן כולהן "in her beauty she ranks high above all of them" 1QapGen 20:7; ברא מן חולק תלתת גבריא די אזלו עמי "except for the portion of the three men who went with me" 1QapGen 22:23-24.

(9) מִן in a compos. adv. (BL 255s): מִן־יַצִּיב יָדַע אֲנָה "I know for sure" Dan 2:8 (cf. כולא מנה ביצבא ינדע "he will learn everything from him with certainty" 1QapGen 2 :20); מִן־קְשֹׁט דִּי אֱלָהֲכוֹן הוּא אֱלָהּ אֱלָהִין "truly (I know) that your God is God of gods" Dan 2:47 (cf. למנדע מנה כולא בקושטא "to learn all from him in truth" 1QapGen 2:22); בתחתיה ומן עלא כוין פתיחן "at the lower end and above (there are) open windows" AP 25:6; זי מנעל כתיב "which is written above (in the document)" AP 35:8; כתיבן בספרא "(the boundaries) are written (this) document from מן תחת ומ]נעל]

below and a[bove]" *BMAP* 6:9; ולא התיב לה ומן כן רשינכם "and he did not return (them) to him; therefore we are suing you" *AP* 20:7 (cf. על כן "therefore" *Aḥ.* 117).

מְנָא , מנה (*manē'/h* < Akk. *manû*), pl. מנין, מנן: m.: **mina** (unit of money = 50 shekels, 5 karashes, 1/60 of a talent). מְנֵא מְנֵא תְּקֵל וּפַרְסִין "counted: a mina, a shekel, and halves (of a shekel)" Dan 5:25 (cf. מְנָה ; read perh. sg. פְּרַס); מְנֵא מְנָה־אֱלָהָא מַלְכוּתָךְ "a mina: God has numbered (the days of) your reign" 5:26; כנכר חד מנן עשרה כלא "one talent, ten minas in all" *AP* 26:17; מנה מלך "a royal mina" *CIS* II/1.7 #6; חמשת עשר מנין "fifteen minas" *CIS* II/1.2 #1b; מנן 2 זי מלך "2 royal minas" *CIS* II/1.6 #5. [Hebr. מָנֶה, מָנִים]. †

מִנְדָּה & מִדָּה (< Akk. *mandattu, maddattu*): **tax, tribute, impost** (cf. בְּלוֹ.& הֲלָךְ). בְּכָל עֲבַר נַהֲרָא וּמִדָּה בְלוֹ וַהֲלָךְ מִתְיְהֵב לְהוֹן "(they ruled) over the whole (province of) Beyond-the-River and tribute, custom, and toll were paid to them" Ezra 4:20; . . . מִנְדָּה מִנְכְסֵי מַלְכָּא דִי מִדַּת לָא יִנְתְּנוּן "they will not pay . . . the tax" 4:13; עֲבַר נַהֲרָה "(the cost is to be paid) from the royal revenue, which is the tribute of (the province) Beyond-the-River" 6:8; מִנְדָּה בְלוֹ וַהֲלָךְ לָא שַׁלִּיט לְמִרְמֵא עֲלֵיהֹם "no one (shall have) authority to impose tribute, custom, and toll on them (the temple ministers)" 7:24; מנדת חילא "the army's tax" *AP* p. 318, line 6; זי עד מנדת בגיא אלך יהנפק ויהיתה עלי עם מנדתא זי מהיתה נחתחור "that he collect the tax on those estates and bring (it) to me along with the tax that Neḥtiḥur is bringing" *AD* 10:3-4; שויו עליהון מדא "they imposed tribute on them" *1QapGen* 21:26; תרתי עשרה שנין הווא יהבין מדתהון למלך עילם "for twelve years they kept paying their tribute to the king of Elam" *1QapGen* 21:26-27. [Hebr. מִדָּה]. †

מִן־דִּי conj.: -- (1) **since, from the time that.** מִן־דִּי פַּרְשֶׁגֶן נִשְׁתְּוָנָא . . . קֱרִי "once the copy of the decree . . . was read," lit.,

מנדע

"from the time that" Ezra 4:23; מן זי נפקת מן סון שאל לה הושר לי
ספר "since I departed from Syene, Saul has not sent me a writing" *Hermopolis* 5:3-4; חנום הו עלין מן זי חנניה במצרין עד כען
"(that) Khnum is against us (ever) since Hananiah was in Egypt
until now" *AP* 38:7; הא עשר שנין שלמא מן יום די נפקתה מן חרן "Lo,
ten years have elapsed since the day when you departed from Haran" *1QapGen* 22:27-28; וחדא מן די תבת מן מצרין "and one (year)
since you returned from Egypt" *1QapGen* 22:28-29. -- (2) **be-
cause.** מֶן־דִּי הַרְגִּזוּ אֲבָהֳתָנָא לֶאֱלָהּ שְׁמַיָּא "because our fathers had
enraged the God of Heaven, (He handed them over)" Ezra 5:12;
כָּל־קֳבֵל דְּנָה מִן־דִּי מִלַּת מַלְכָּא מַחְצְפָה "consequently, because the order
of the king was severe" Dan 3:22; מַלְכוּתָךְ לָךְ קַיָּמָה מִן־דִּי תִנְדַּע דִּי
שַׁלִּיט שְׁמַיָּא "your kingdom shall be secure for you because you
understand that Heaven rules" 4:23 (or possibly "from the time
that").

מַנְדַּע (< מַדַּע, *maqtal,* BL 194r, < root *yd'*), abs. & cst.,
emph. מַנְדְּעָא, w. suff. מַנְדְּעִי, m.: **knowledge, intelligence;
thing, matter** (cf. טְעֵם no. 5). יָהֵב חָכְמְתָא לְחַכִּימִין וּמַנְדְּעָא לְיָדְעֵי בִינָה
"He gives wisdom to the wise and knowledge to those who have
understanding," lit., "to those knowing intelligence" Dan 2:21:
5:12; מַנְדְּעִי עֲלַי יְתוּב "my understanding returned to me" 4:31, 33;
אסרחאדן מלכא רחמן הו כמנדע "King Esarhaddon is (as) merciful as
anything," i.e., "very merciful" *Aḥ.* 53. -- Cf. * מִנְדַּעַם & * מִדַּעַם
(< *manda'-ma, LFAA* 37d): **anything, whatever.** ואיש מנדעם
באגורא זך לא חבל "and no one did any damage to that temple" *AP*
30:14; כל מדעם זי יחיה בה איש "everything by which a man may
live" *AP* 49:3; כל מנדעם זי חמיר א[יתי בה] "(do not eat) anything
[in] which th[ere is] leaven" *AP* 21:7; י[ש]ל[ח] ע[ל]יכם מדעם מכל
"he will [se]nd [y]ou some food" *AP* 49:4; הן מן גרדא או מן נכסיא
אחרנן זילי מנדעם כסנתו יהוה "if my staff or other property suffers
any damage" *AD* 7:8; ומנדע[ם] אחרן זי לקחת כלא התבהב "and
restore all (of) anything else that you have taken" *AD* 12:6-7;

מנה

מנדעם באיש לא עבדת "she did nothing wrong" *Carpentras* 2 (*KAI* 269); חזי קדמתך מנדעם קשה "look at something difficult before you" *Aḥ.* 101; ומזרקיא . . . ומנדעמתא זי הוה באגורא זך "and the vessels . . . and everything else that was in that temple (they took)" *AP* 30:12; קנינה טין ומין ומנדעמתה יבדרונה "his property, land and water, and whatever else they will destroy for him" *Sardes (Lydia)* B 8 (*KAI* 260). [Hebr. מַדָּע]. †

מְנָה , impv. sg. m. מני (*mĕnî*); infin. w. suff. ממניה ; pass. ptc. sg. m. מְנֵא, w. suff. מניה (*manĕyēh*). **Hithpe.** impf. 3 sg. m. יתמנה (*yitmĕnēh*): **count, number.** מְנָה־אֱלָהָא מַלְכוּתָךְ "God has numbered (the days of) your reign" Dan 5:26; מְנֵא מְנֵא תְּקֵל וּפַרְסִין "counted: a mina, a shekel, and halves (of a shekel)" 5:25 (but BL 157i; Gk., Theod., Vg. omit first מְנֵא ; perh. from 5:26); אנתם כן מנו ארב[עת עשר] יומן "accordingly, you (must) count four[teen] days" *AP* 21:4-5; מני כול די איתי לך "count all that you have" *1QapGen* 22:29; די לא ישכח כול בר אנוש לממניה "which no one can number" *1QapGen* 21:13; זרעך לא יתמנה "your descendants will be without number" *1QapGen* 21:13; מניה עמי . . . כסף זוזין עס[רי]ן "numbered with (i.e., borrowed from) me . . . the sum of tw[en]ty denarii" (pass. ptc. w. dative suff; see *Bib* 45 [1964] 227) *Mur* 18 3-4.
    Pa. 3 sg. m. מַנִּי , 2 sg, m. מַנִּיתָ ; impv. sg. m. מֶנִּי (BL 159p); pass. ptc. pl. m. ממנין : **appoint, designate.** מֶנִי שָׁפְטִין וְדַיָּנִין דִּי־לֶהֱוֹן דָּאנִין לְכָל־עַמָּה "designate magistrates and judges who will judge all the people" Ezra 7:25; מַנִּי עַל עֲבִידְתָּא "(the king) appointed (them) over the affairs (of the province)" Dan 2:49: 3:12; דִּי מַנִּי מַלְכָּא לְהוֹבָדָה לְחַכִּימֵי בָבֶל "whom the king had appointed to destroy the sages of Babylon" 2:24; [מלך א[תור מני עמה גברן "[the king of As]syria appointed with him 2 other men to see how it was to be done" *Aḥ.* 37; ומני עמי אנוש די "(the king) appointed men to escort me (out of Egypt)" *1QapGen* 20:32; זי ממנין במדינת תשטרס "who are designated over the province of Tishteres(?)" *AP* 27:9. [Hebr. מָנָה]. †

216

מנחה—מעה

מְנְחָה (< Hebr.), emph. pl. מנחתא (*minḥātā'*), w. suff.
מִנְחָתְהוֹן : **offering** (especially cereal), (non-bloody) **sacrifice.**
תִּקְנֵא . . . אִמְּרִין וּמִנְחָתְהוֹן וְנִסְכֵּיהוֹן "you shall buy . . . lambs and their
cereal offerings and drink offerings" Ezra 7:17; וּלְדָנִיֵּאל סְגִד וּמִנְחָה
וְנִיחֹחִין אֲמַר לְנַסָּכָה לֵהּ "and (the king) did homage to Daniel and
ordered (them) to offer an offering and fragrances to him" Dan
2:46; מנחה ולבו[נ]ה ועלוה לא עבדו באגורא זך "they do not offer in
that temple (of Yeb) a meal offering, ince[n]se, or holocaust" *AP*
30:21-22; ומ>נ<חתא ולבונתא ועלותא יקרבון על מדבחא זי יהו אלהא
"and they shall offer the cereal offerings, incense, and holocausts
on the altar of Yaho the God" *AP* 30:25-26; ואקרבת עלוהי עלוון
ומנחה לאל עליון "and I offered on it holocausts and a meal offering
to God Most High" *1QapGen* 21:2. †

מִנְיָן (*qutlān*, BL 195z) cst. (& abs.): **number.** . . . הַקְרִבוּ
צְפִירֵי עִזִּין . . . תְּרֵי־עֲשַׂר לְמִנְיָן שִׁבְטֵי יִשְׂרָאֵל . "they offered . . . twelve .
. . he-goats according to the number of the tribes of Israel" Ezra
6:17; 1 כסף יון במנין סתתרי 6 שקל "(in) the money of Greece, by
number, 6 staters (and) 1 shekel" *BMAP* 12:14; לך [כל אבורא זי]
במנין בבית מלכא "(if we do not give you) [all the grain that] is
yours in (full) measure at the royal office," lit., "in number at the
house of the king" *AP* 2:13-14. ׀

מַעֲבָד * (*maqtāl*, BL 195w), pl. w. suff. מַעֲבָדוֹהִי : **work,**
deed. כָּל־מַעֲבָדוֹהִי קְשֹׁט "all His deeds are right" Dan 4:34; מרא כול
מעבדיא "Lord of all the works" *4QTKohath (4Q542)* 1 i.2. [Hebr.
מַעֲבָד]. ׀

מֵעָה * (*mě'ēh* < *mi'ī*), pl. w. suff. מְעוֹהִי ; only pl.: **belly.**
הוּא צַלְמָא . . . דִּי . . . מְעוֹהִי . . . נְחָשׁ "that statue . . . the belly of
which . . . (was) bronze" Dan 2:32. [Hebr. מֵעִים]. ׀

מְעַל * (*maqtāl,* root עלל, BL 57i, 195w), cst. pl. מֵעֲלֵי (*ma''ālay;* v.l. מֶעֲלֵי): **entering, entry.** עַד מֶעָלֵי שִׁמְשָׁא "until the setting of the sun," lit., "the entry (into night)" Dan 6:15; בלילה מעלי לארע מצרין "in the night of my entering into the land of Egypt" *1QapGen* 19:14. Cf. . [ו]מן [מן] מערב שמשא עד יום 21 לניס[ן] "from sunset until 21 Nisan" *AP* 21:8. [1]

מַצְלַח : **success,** see צלח.

מָרֵא (*māri',* BL 190y, 233d, f) & מרה , abs. & cst.; w. suff. מָרְאִי k., מָרִי q. (BL 60k; cf. שַׂגִּיא): **lord.** -- For God or a king: אֱלָהֲכוֹן הוּא אֱלָהּ אֱלָהִין וּמָרֵא מַלְכִין "your God is God of gods and Lord of kings" Dan 2:47; מרא מלכן פרעה "Pharaoh, the lord of kings" *Adon Letter* 1, 6 (*KAI* 266); עַל מָרֵא־שְׁמַיָּא "against the Lord of Heaven" Dan 5:23; הוין . . . מצלין ליהו מרא שמיא "we were . . . praying to Yaho, the Lord of Heaven" *AP* 30:15; דִּי מְטָת עַל־מָרְאִי מַלְכָּא "which has come upon my lord, the king" Dan 4:21: 4:16; אמר לי מראי מלכא "my lord, the king, said to me" *Assur Letter* 8 (*KAI* 233); ותאמר להם קתלו מראכם "and you shall (not) say to them, 'Kill your lord'" *Sefire III* 21-22; ואמר אברם מרי אלהא "and Abram said, 'My Lord God'" *1QapGen* 22:32; וקרית תמן בשם מרה עלמיא "and there I called upon the name of the Lord of Ages" *1QapGen* 21:2; אנתה מרה ושליט על כולא "you are Lord and Sovereign over all" *1QapGen* 20:13. -- For a superior: כזי מראן ארשם אזל על מלכא "when our lord, Arsames, went to the king" *AP* 27:2-3; in a letter: אל מראן בגוהי פחת יהוד "To our lord, Bigwahi, governor of Judah" *AP* 30:1; על מראי פסמי עבדך מכבנת . . . "To my lord, PSMY, your servant MKBNT . . . to my father, PSMY, from MKBNT, son of PSMY" אל אבי פסמי מן מכבנת בר פסמי . . *Hermopolis* 3:1-14; ש[לם] . . . שלם מראי מנחם . . . אל מראתי שלוה "To my lady (see *LFAA* 110r), Selawa, gree[t-ings]! . . . Greeting to my lord, Menahem! Greeting to my lady, שלם מראתי אביהי Abihi!" *AP* 39:1-2; a wife to her husband: יא אחי ויא מרי "O my

brother and my lord!" *1QapGen* 2:9. -- For an owner: נכסיא זי
לקחו אתבו אם על מריהם "the property, which they had taken, they
have restored, indeed, to their owners" *AP* 34:6. †

מְרַד (*mard*), m.: **revolt.** וּמְרַד וְאֶשְׁתַּדּוּר מִתְעֲבֵד־בַּהּ "and
revolt and sedition have been wrought in it (Jerusalem)" Ezra
4:19 (recall the conjecture in 4:15 [see מְדִינָה]). Cf. כזי מצרין מרדת
"when Egypt rebelled" *AD* 5:6; כזי מצריא מרדו "when the Egyptians rebelled" *AD* 7:1; בשנת תלת עשרה מרדו בה "in the thirteenth
year (the kings) rebelled against him (the king of Elam)" *1Qap-
Gen* 21:27. [Hebr. מָרַד]. [1]

מָרָד * (*marrād,* BL 191c), f. מָרָדָא, emph. מָרָדְתָּא, adj.:
rebellious. אֲתוֹ לִירוּשְׁלֶם קִרְיְתָא מָרָדְתָּא "(the Jews) have gone to
Jerusalem, the rebellious city" Ezra 4:12; קִרְיְתָא דָךְ קִרְיָה מָרָדָא
[בתלתי "(you will find that) that city is a rebellious city" 4:15;
מרדיא] אתכנשו "[for a third time the rebels] rallied" *Bisitun* 15. [1]

מְרַט *, **Peil** perf. pass. 3 pl. m. מְרִיטוּ : **pluck off.** חָזֵה
הֲוֵית עַד דִּי מְרִיטוּ גַפֵּיהּ "as I looked, its wings were plucked off"
Dan 7:4; עמרא ... מתמרט בכבא "the wool (of the lamb) ... was
plucked off by thorns" *APO* 76 i A 4. [Hebr. מָרַט]. [1]

מְשַׁח (*mišḥ*): **oil, ointment.** מְלַח חֲמַר וּמְשַׁח "(whatever is
needed in the temple) salt, wine, and oil" Ezra 6:9: 7:22; משח
לא משחן "we have not anointed ourselves with oil" *AP* 31:20;
זבנת משח זית ... ואף משח בשם "I bought olive oil ... and also perfumed oil" *Hermopolis* 2:11-12; כפן למנשא משח "bowls for
carrying ointment" *BMAP* 7:19. [Hebr. מִשְׁחָה]. †

מִשְׁכַּב * (*miqtal,* BL 194q), w. suff. מִשְׁכְּבֵהּ, מִשְׁכְּבָךְ
מִשְׁכְּבִי, : **bed, couch.** וִידַחֲלִנַּנִי ... עַל־מִשְׁכְּבִי "and it frightened me
... (as I lay) on my bed" Dan 4:2: 4:7, 10; 2:28, 29; 7:1. [Hebr.
מִשְׁכָּב]. †

מִשְׁכַּן * (*miqtal*, BL 194q), w. suff. מִשְׁכְּנֵהּ : **dwelling.** דִּי
בִּירוּשְׁלֶם מִשְׁכְּנֵהּ "(the God of Israel) whose dwelling is in Jerusalem" Ezra 7:15; cf. יהו אלהא שכן יב "Yaho the god dwelling (in)
Yeb" *BMAP* 12:2. [Hebr. מִשְׁכָּן]. [1]

מַשְׁרוֹקִי * (*maqtāl* + *i*, BL 195w, 197f), emph. מַשְׁרוֹקִיתָא,
f.: **pipe** (musical instrument). תִּשְׁמְעוּן קָל קַרְנָא מַשְׁרוֹקִיתָא "(when)
you hear the sound of the horn, the pipe" Dan 3:5, 15: 3:7, 10
(collect. sg.). [Hebr. שָׁרַק "hiss, whistle"]. †

מִשְׁתֵּא *, משתה (*mištēh* < **mištī*), emph. מִשְׁתְּיָא (Babyl.
vocal. *mištiyā'*, BL 38a): **drink, drinking, banquet.** . . . מַלְכְּתָא
לְבֵית מִשְׁתְּיָא עַלַּת "the queen . . . entered the banquet hall (of the
palace)" Dan 5:10; [ ] במאכל שגי ובמשתה [שגי] "with much eat-
ing and with [much] drinking" *1QapGen* 19:27; אנפק . . . מלכיצדק
מאכל ומשתה לאברם "Melchizedeq . . . brought out food and drink
for Abram (and his companions)" *1QapGen* 22:14-15. [Hebr.
מִשְׁתֶּה]. [1]

מֵתָא : see אֲתָה infin.

מַתְּנָה * (*maqtal-at*, BL 194r), pl. מַתְּנָן, w. suff. מַתְּנָתָךְ,
f.: **gift.** מַתְּנָן . . . תְּקַבְּלוּן מִן־קֳדָמַי "you will receive from me . . .
gifts" Dan 2:6: 2:48; מַתְּנָתָךְ לָךְ לֶהֶוְיָן "let your gifts be for yourself," i.e., keep them 5:17. [Hebr. מַתָּנָה]. †

נ

נבא (א"ל < ה"ל). **Hithpa.** 3 sg. m. הִתְנַבִּי (MSS. q. הִתְנַבִּיא,
BL 168a): **prophesy.** הִתְנַבִּי . . . עַל־יְהוּדָיֵא "(Haggai and Zechariah) prophesied to the Jews (in Judah)" Ezra 5:1 (BL 334i). [Hebr.
the same]. [1]

נְבוּאָה * (*qatūl-at*, BL 189m), cst. נְבוּאַת : **prophesying.** מַצְלְחִין בִּנְבוּאַת חַגַּי "(the Jewish elders) were prospering through the prophesying of Haggai (and Zechariah)" Ezra 6:14. [Hebr. the same]. [1]

▲ נְבוּכַדְנֶצַּר & נְבַכַדְנֶצַּר (Akk. *Nabū-kudurri-uṣur*, "Nabu, protect the boundary!"): **Nebuchadnezzar**, king of Babylonia. לְמַלְכָּא נְבוּכַדְנֶצַּר "to the king Nebuchadnezzar" Dan 2:28: 2:46; Ezra 5:12, 14; + ; ל[בב] מלך [נ]בוכדרצר "[Ne]buchadrezzar, king of [Baby]lonia" *Contract*, verso 5-6 (*KAI* 227).

נְבִזְבָּה (< Akk. or Persian?), v.l. נְבִזְבָּה ; pl. w. suff. נְבִזְבְּיָתָךְ (*něbozběyātāk*), v.l. נְבֵז, נְבֵז (BL 244l): **reward.** מַתְּנָן וּנְבִזְבָּה "(you shall receive) gifts and a reward" Dan 2:6; נְבָזְבְּיָתָךְ לְאָחֳרָן הַב "give your rewards to someone else" 5:17. †

נְבִיא * (*qatīl*, BL 188h), emph. נְבִיאָה k., נְבִיָּא q. (BL 210o); emph. pl. נְבִיאַיָּא k. (נְבִיַּיָּא q., BL 212z): **prophet.** חַגַּי נְבִיאָה "Haggai, the prophet" Ezra 5:1a: 5:1b, 2; 6:14; [ש]קרא נביאי די קמו "the false prophets who have arisen (in Israel)" *4QFal-Proph (4Q339)* 1:1. [Hebr. נָבִיא]. †

נֶבְרְשָׁה * (perh. < Persian., *GBA* §190), emph. נֶבְרַשְׁתָּא : **lamp, lampstand.** לָקֳבֵל נֶבְרַשְׁתָּא "opposite the lampstand" Dan 5:5. [1]

נְגַד *, ptc. sg. m. נָגֵד : **go forth, issue, make one's way.** נְהַר דִּי־נוּר נָגֵד וְנָפֵק מִן־קֳדָמוֹהִי "a stream of fire made its way and came out from before Him" Dan 7:10; נגדת ל] [והוית אזל לדרומא "I set out for [   ] and I kept going southward" *1QapGen* 19:8-9; נגדת למ[הך] לארע מצרין "I set out to [go] to the land of Egypt" *1QapGen* 19:10-11; די שבי לוט . . . ודי נגדו מלכיא "that Lot had been taken captive . . . and that the kings had set out (by the route

of the Great Valley)" *1QapGen* 22:3-4; נגדו עמה והוא רדף בתרהון
"(Arnem, Eshcol, and Mamre) set out with him, and he went in
pursuit of them" *1QapGen* 22:7. [1]

נֶגֶד , prep. **toward, facing.** וְכַוִּין פְּתִיחָן . . . נֶגֶד יְרוּשְׁלֶם
"and (with) windows opened . . . facing Jerusalem" Dan 6:11
(perh. a Hebr. gloss, *GBA* §84). [Hebr. the same]. [1]

נָגַהּ * (*nugh,* BL 184n), emph. נָגְהָא (v.l. נַגְהָא, BL 32i):
light, dawn. מַלְכָּא בִּשְׁפַּרְפָּרָא יְקוּם בְּנָגְהָא "at break of day the king
rose at dawn" Dan 6:20. [Hebr. נֹגַהּ]. [1]

נדב **Hithpa.** 3 pl. m. הִתְנַדַּבוּ ; infin. הִתְנַדָּבָה *, cst.
הִתְנַדָּבוּת (BL 246n); ptc. sg. m. מִתְנַדַּב, pl. m. מִתְנַדְּבִין : **offer freely; be ready, wish** w. לְ & infin.; infin. as noun: **spontaneous
gift** (BL 302i). כְּסַף וּדְהַב דִּי . . . הִתְנַדַּבוּ לֶאֱלָהּ יִשְׂרָאֵל "silver and gold
which (the king and his counselors) offered freely to the God of
Israel" Ezra 7:15; הִתְנַדָּבוּת עַמָּה וְכָהֲנַיָּא <דִּי> מִתְנַדְּבִין לְבֵית אֱלָהֲהֹם "the
spontaneous gift of the people and the priests <which> they offer
freely to the house of their God" 7:16 (BL 339n); . . . כָּל־מִתְנַדַּב
לִמְהָךְ לִירוּשְׁלֶם עִמָּךְ יְהָךְ "anyone who freely offers . . . to go to
Jerusalem, may go with you" 7:13. [Hebr. the same]. †

נִדְבָּךְ (< Akk. *nadbāku*), pl. נִדְבָּכִין , m.: **row, course.**
נִדְבָּכִין דִּי־אֶבֶן גְּלָל תְּלָתָא וְנִדְבָּךְ דִּי־אָע חֲדַת "(with) three courses of
stone blocks and one (read חַד) course of wood" Ezra 6:4; cf.
מִתְבְּנֵא אֶבֶן גְּלָל וְאָע מִתְּשָׂם בְּכֻתְלַיָּא "(God's house) constructed with
stone block(s) and timber laid in the walls" 5:8. [1]

נדד , 3 sg. f. נַדַּת (BL 166d): **flee.** שְׁנָתֵהּ נַדַּת עֲלוֹהִי "his
sleep fled from him" Dan 6:19; cf. נוד [Hebr. the same]. [1]

נְדֵן * (< Persian *nidāni*), נִדְנֶה , read נִדְנַה * : **vagina, sheath** (cf. Hebr. וַיָּשֶׁב חַרְבּוֹ אֶל־נְדָנָה "and he put his sword back into its scabbard" 1 Chr 21:27). -- In a transferred sense: אֶתְכְּרִיַּת רוּחִי . . . בְּגוֹא נִדְנֶה "my spirit was disturbed in its sheath" Dan 7:15; נשמתי לגו נדנהא "(recall) my breath in the midst of its sheath" *1QapGen* 2:10. [Hebr. נָדָן]. [1]

נְהוֹר * (*nahār*, BL 188g), emph. נְהוֹרָא q., נְהִירָא k. (BL 188h), m.: **light.** יָדַע מָה בַחֲשׁוֹכָא וּנְהִירָא עִמֵּהּ שְׁרֵא "(God) knows what is in the darkness, and the light abides with Him" Dan 2:22. [Hebr. נְהָרָה]. [1]

נַהִירוּ (*qattīl+ū*, BL 198g; v.l. נְהִירוּ): **intelligence.** נַהִירוּ וְשָׂכְלְתָנוּ וְחָכְמָה . . . הִשְׁתְּכַחַת בֵּהּ "intelligence and understanding and wisdom . . . were found in him (Daniel)" Dan 5:11: 5:14. †

נְהַר (*nahar*, BL 185p), emph. נַהֲרָא & נַהֲרָה : **river, stream.** נְהַר דִּי־נוּר נָגֵד וְנָפֵק "a stream of fire made its way and came out" Dan 7:10; וּשְׁאָר עֲבַר־נַהֲרָא "and (in) the rest of (the province) Beyond-the-River" (to the west of the Euphrates River) Ezra 4:10, 17: 4:11, 16, +; עד די דבקת לפורת נהרא "until I reached the Euphrates River" *1QapGen* 21:17: 21:28; תדעל מלך גוים די היא בין נהרין "Tidal, the king of Goiim, which is Mesopotamia," lit., "between two rivers" *1QapGen* 21:23-24; מן נהר מצרין עד לבנן "from the River of Egypt to Lebanon" *1QapGen* 21:11. [Hebr. נָהָר].

נוד *, impf. 3 sg. f. תְּנֻד (read תְּנֹד from נדד ?): **flee.** תְּנֻד חֵיוְתָא מִן־תַּחְתּוֹהִי "let the beasts (collect. sg.) flee from under it" Dan 4:11 (BL 334i). [Hebr. the same, but "wander about"]. [1]

223

נְוָלִי, נְוָלוּ (< Akk.?, BL 197f): **heap of splinters, ruins.**
וּבָתֵּיכוֹן נְוָלִי יִתְּשָׂמוּן "and your houses will be made ruins" Dan 2:5
(BL 338k, l); וּבַיְתֵהּ נְוָלִי יִשְׁתַּוֵּה "and his house shall be laid in
ruins" 3:29; וּבַיְתֵהּ נְוָלוּ יִתְעֲבֵד "and his house shall be made ruins"
Ezra 6:11. †

נוּר (qūl, BL 180l), emph. נוּרָא m. & f. (BL 200j): **fire**
(cf. אֶשָּׁא). הֲלָא גֻבְרִין תְּלָתָא רְמֵינָא לְגוֹא־נוּרָא "Did we not cast three
men into the fire?" Dan 3:24; נָפְקִין . . . מִן־גּוֹא נוּרָא "came out
from the fire" 3:26b; לָא־שְׁלֵט נוּרָא בְּגֶשְׁמְהוֹן "the fire (m.) had no
power over their bodies" (collect. sg.) 3:27a. -- As gen. of quality (cf. דִּי I 2): קַטִּל הִמּוֹן שְׁבִיבָא דִּי נוּרָא "the flame of fire killed
them" Dan 3:22; לְגוֹא־אַתּוּן נוּרָא יָקִידְתָּא "into the burning fiery
furnace" 3:6, 11 + ; כָּרְסְיֵהּ שְׁבִיבִין דִּי־נוּר גַּלְגִּלּוֹהִי נוּר דָּלִק "his throne
was fiery flames, and its wheels burning fire (m.)" 7:9; נְהַר דִּי־נוּר
נָגֵד וְנָפֵק "a stream of fire made its way and came out" 7:10; רֵיחַ
נוּר לָא עֲדָת בְּהוֹן "no odor of fire had come upon them" 3:27.

נְזַק *, ptc. sg. m. נָזִק : **lose, suffer loss.** וּמַלְכָּא לָא־לֶהֱוֵא
נָזִק "so that the king might suffer no loss" Dan 6:3. **Haph.**
impf. 3 sg. f. תְּהַנְזִק ; infin. הַנְזָקָה *, cst. הַנְזָקַת (BL 246n); ptc.
sg. f. cst. מְהַנְזְקַת : **damage, cause loss, injure.** מַלְכִין תְּהַנְזִק "it
(rebuilt Jerusalem) will cause loss for kings" Ezra 4:13; וּמְהַנְזְקַת
מַלְכִין "and it will damage kings" 4:15; לְמָה יִשְׂגֵּא חֲבָלָא לְהַנְזָקַת
מַלְכִין "why should damage increase to cause loss for kings" 4:22
(cf. cst. infin. אַחֲוָיַת Dan 5:12). [Hebr. נֶזֶק]. †

נְחָשׁ (nuḥāš, BL 190t), emph. נְחָשָׁא : **copper, bronze**
(copper & tin alloy). דָּקוּ כַחֲדָה . . . נְחָשָׁא כַּסְפָּא "the bronze, the
silver . . . altogether were smashed" Dan 2:35: 2:45; נחשיא זי
יהבו על תמריא "the bronze bands that they put on the date-palms"
AP 81:111. -- As a gen. of quality (cf. דִּי I 2): שַׁבַּחוּ לֵאלָהֵי דַהֲבָא
וְכַסְפָּא נְחָשָׁא "they praised the gods of gold and silver, bronze. . ."

Dan 5:4: 5:23; וּבֶאֱסוּר דִּי־פַרְזֶל וּנְחָשׁ "(leave the stump in the earth) and (bound) with a band of iron and bronze" 4:12, 20; מֶחֱזִי זִי נחש 1 "1 mirror of bronze" *AP* 15:11; מאני נחש . . . אין[תי] "there [are] . . .vessels of bronze" *AP* 20:5. Used as pred.: צִירֵיהֶם זִי דשׁשׁיא אלך נחש "the hinges of those doors were of bronze" *AP* 30:10-11; יַרְכָתֵהּ דִּי נְחָשׁ "its thighs (were) of bronze" Dan 2:32: 7:19; .אָחֳרִי דִּי נְחָשָׁא . . תְּקוּם מַלְכוּ "there will arise . . . another kingdom of bronze" 2:39 (cf. דִּי I 2). [Hebr. נְחֹשֶׁת]. †

נְחַת *, 2 sg. m. נחת (*něhatt[ā]*); impf. 3 pl. m. יחתון (*yěhhutûn*); impv. sg. m. חת (*hut*); infin. מנחת (*minhat*); ptc. sg. m. נָחֵת , pl. f. נחתן (*nāhětān*): **go down, descend.** עִיר וְקַדִּישׁ מִן־שְׁמַיָּא נָחִת "(I saw) a Watcher, a holy one, descending from heaven" Dan 4:10: 4:20; חת מנפי "go down (to) Memphis!" *AP* 42:7; הן נחת אנת למנפי "if you go down (prob. ptc.) to Memphis" *AP* 42:11; [הן א[שׁ נחת יתו ל]] "[if any]one goes down, let them bring to [ ]"*Hermopolis* 8:5-6; גרמיך לא יחתון שאול "your bones shall not descend to Sheol" *AP* 71:15; [למ]נסק [למ]נחת בדרגא "(you shall be able) [to] go up and [to] go down by the stairway" *BMAP* 6:10: 9:15; ודמעי נחתן "as my tears ran down (my cheeks)" *1QapGen* 20:12.

Haph./Aph. 1 sg. w. suff. *ah-hi-te-e* (= *'ahhitēh* "I put him," *Warka* 3); impf. 2 sg. m. תַחֵת (*tahhēt,* BL 135a); impv. sg. m. הנחת (*hanhit*) & אֲחֵת (read v.l. אַחֵת , BL 137p; *'ahhit*); infin. w. suff. מנחתותהם (*manhātûtěhom*); ptc. pl. m. מְהַחֲתִין : **put, deposit, bring.** שֵׂא אֵזֶל־אֲחֵת הִמּוֹ בְּהֵיכְלָא "take (the vessels), go, and put them in the Temple" Ezra 5:15; וִיהָךְ <כֹּלָּא> לְהֵיכְלָא . . וְתַחֵת בְּבֵית אֱלָהָא . "let <all of it> go to the Temple . . . and you shall put (it) in God's house" 6:5 (instead of וְתַחֵת read perh. יְהֵחַת "let it be put"); בְּבֵית סִפְרַיָּא דִּי גִנְזַיָּא מְהַחֲתִין תַּמָּה "(they searched) in the house of the archives, where they deposited the treasures" 6:1 (explanation of 5:17); חת לעבק . . . הנחת לי כתון 1 "come down at once, (and) bring down to me 1 tunic in בידך

כִּי לָא בִּידֵי אנ[ש]א מ[נש]א רגלהם ומנחתותהם מן
בלע[די אלהן] "for it is not in the ability of m[en] to lift up their
foot and to put them down with[out the gods]" *Ah.* 122. --
Hoph. (BL 135b) 3 sg. m. הָנְחַת ; impf. 3 sg. m. יְהַנְחַת * or יֻנַּח *.
הָנְחַת מִן־כָּרְסֵא מַלְכוּתֵהּ "(the king) was deposed from his kingly
throne" Dan 5:20 (cf. above Ezra 6:5). [Hebr. נָחַת]. †

עֵינַי **lift up.** : נְטִילַת 3 sg. f. נְטָלַת . **Peil** perf. נְטַלַת . 1 sg. *, נְטַל
לִשְׁמַיָּא נִטְלֵת "I lifted my eyes to heaven" Dan 4:31; עֵינַי זִי נטלת
עֲלָיךְ "my eyes which I lifted up to you" *Ah.* 169; וּנְטִילַת מִן־אַרְעָא
"and (the beast) was lifted up from the ground (and made to
stand on two feet like a man)" Dan 7:4. †

נְטַר *, 1 sg. נִטְרֵת ; impv. pl. m. טָרוּ *; infin. מִנְטַר * :
keep, take care of, watch. מִלְּתָא בְּלִבִּי נִטְרֵת "I kept the matter in
my mind" Dan 7:28; הן יפקד לך מראך מין למנטר "if your lord
entrusts to you water to guard" *Ah.* 192; חסין נטר "he took strict
care of (our domestic staff)" *AD* 7:2; חסין טרו "take strict care!"
AD 7:6; מן כל מנטרה טר פמך "beyond all watchfulness guard your
mouth" *Ah.* 98. [Hebr. נָטַר]. [1]

נִיחוֹחַ * (*qatlāl*, BL 193l; < Hebr.; cf. נוח "rest"), pl.
דִּי־לֶהֱוֹן מְהַקְרְבִין נִיחוֹחִין לֶאֱלָהּ : **pleasing offering.** נִיחֹחִין & נִיחוֹחִין
שְׁמַיָּא "that they may offer pleasing offerings to the God of Heav-
en" Ezra 6:10; וּלְדָנִיֵּאל סְגִד וּמִנְחָה וְנִיחֹחִין אֲמַר לְנַסָּכָה לֵהּ "and
(Nebuchadnezzar) did homage to Daniel and ordered that a meal-
offering and pleasing offerings be submitted to him" Dan 2:46.
[Hebr. the same]. †

נְכַס * (< Akk. *nikasu*), pl. נִכְסִין , cst. נִכְסֵי , m. (only pl.):
flocks; goods, possessions, property. הֵן־לַעֲנָשׁ נִכְסִין וְלֶאֱסוּרִין
"whether for confiscation of (his) property or for imprisonment"

Ezra 7:26; וּמִנִּכְסֵי מַלְכָּא דִּי מִדַּת עֲבַר נַהֲרָא "and (the cost is to be paid) from the property of the king, which is the tribute of (the province) Beyond-the-River" 6:8; על נכסיא אלכי "(you swore) concerning those goods of yours" *AP* 14:6; לבשיה . . . וש[א]רת נכסיא זי כתיב "her clothes . . . and the r[e]st of the possessions which are written (above)" *BMAP* 7:23; והוא רעה נכסוהי "and (Lot) kept pasturing his flocks (in the valley of the Jordan)" *1QapGen* 21:6; אודית תמן . . . על כול נכסיא וטבתא די יהב לי "I gave thanks there (to God) . . for all the flocks and the good things that He had given me" *1QapGen* 21:3; כסף ונכסן יהבו לה "they gave him money and possessions" *AP* 27:4; ולא השכחת כסף ונכסן לשלמה לכי "and I did not find money and possessions to pay you" *AP* 13:5; [בא]חדה ביתה ונכסוהי וקנינה "(Y. shall control) his [pr]operty(?). his house, his goods, and his possessions" *BMAP* 7:29-30; גרדא ונכסיא זילנא [זי] במצרין חסין נטר "(P.) took strict care of our staff and property [which were] in Egypt" *AD* 7:1-2. [Hebr. נְכָסִים]. †

נְמַר (*namir*, BL 185u): **leopard, panther.** אָחֳרִי כִּנְמַר "another (beast) like a leopard" Dan 7:6; נמרא פגע לעזנא "the leopard met the she-goat" *Aḥ.* 118; . . . פם נמרה [יאכל] "may the mouth of a panther . . . [devour]" *Sefire I* A 30-31. [Hebr. נָמֵר]. [1]

נְסַח *, impf. ינסח (*yinsaḥ*), 3 pl. m. juss. יסחו (*yissěḥû*), w. suff. ינסחוהי (*yinsěḥûhî*). **Hithpe.,** impf. 3 sg. m. יִתְנְסַח : **tear out, pluck out.** אל . . . וינסח לשנ[ה] "God . . . and will tear out [his] tongue" *Aḥ.* 156; יסחו שמך ואשרך מן חין "may (the gods) tear your name and your status out from among the living" *Nerab* 9-10 (*KAI* 225); אלהי תימא ינסחוהי וזרעה ושמה מן אנפי תימא "may the gods of Tema pluck him and his offspring and his name from the face of Tema" *Tema A* 13-15 (*KAI* 228); יִתְנְסַח אָע מִן־בַּיְתֵהּ "let a log be torn out from his house, (and let him be impaled on it)" Ezra 6:11. [Hebr. נָסַח]. [1]

נסך—נפק

נְסַךְ *, impf. 3 sg. m. יסך (yissak): **pour out, shower, offer.** יסך על ארפד [אבני ב]רד "may he (Hadad) shower upon Arpad [h]ail-[stones]" *Sefire I* A 26-27; ותסך להם לחם "and (if) you offer them food" *Sefire III* 7. -- **Pa.** infin, נַסָּכָה (BL 111n): **pour out, offer.** וּמִנְחָה וְנִיחֹחִין אֲמַר לְנַסָּכָה לֵהּ "he ordered that a meal-offering and pleasing sacrifices be offered to him (Daniel)" Dan 2:46. [Hebr. נָסַךְ & Piel]. [1]

נְסַךְ * or נְסֵךְ * (nisk), pl. w. suff. נִסְכֵּיהוֹן (BL 226z): **libation, drink offering.** תִּקְנֵא . . . אִמְּרִין וּמִנְחָתְהוֹן וְנִסְכֵּיהוֹן "you shall buy . . . lambs, and their meal-offerings and their drink offerings" Ezra 7:17. [Hebr. נֶסֶךְ]. [1]

נְפַל , 3 pl. m. נְפַלוּ , 3 pl. f. נְפַלָה q. (BL 101k, 134r); impf. 3 sg. m. יִפֵּל & ־יִפֵּל , 2 pl. m. תִּפְּלוּן ; ptc. pl. m. נָפְלִין : -- (1) **fall, be thrown down.** קָל מִן־שְׁמַיָּא נְפַל "a voice sounded from heaven," lit., "fell from" Dan 4:28; נְפַלוּ לְגוֹא־אַתּוּן . . . גֻּבְרַיָּא אִלֵּךְ "those men . . . fell into the furnace" 3:23; וּנְפַלוּ מִן־קֳדָמַיהּ תְּלָת "and three (of the horns [f.]) were thrown down before it" (the little horn; see vs. 8; q. נְפַלָה) 7:20. -- (2) **prostrate oneself.** נְפַל עַל־אַנְפּוֹהִי וּלְדָנִיֵּאל סְגִד "(the king) prostrated himself and did homage to Daniel," lit. "fell on his face" 2:46; יִפֵּל וְיִסְגֻּד לְצֶלֶם דַּהֲבָא "let him prostrate himself and adore the golden statue" 3:10: 3:5, 6, 11, 15; נָפְלִין כָּל־עַמְמַיָּא . . . סָגְדִין לְצֶלֶם דַּהֲבָא "all the peoples prostrated themselves . . . (and) adored the golden statue" 3:7. -- (3) **happen, have occasion.** דִּי יִפֵּל־לָךְ לְמִנְתַּן "which you (Ezra) will have occasion to provide" Ezra 7:20. [Hebr. נָפַל]. †

נְפַק , 3 sg. f. נֶפְקַת (v.l. נפקת, נְפַקַת), 2 sg. m. נפקתה (něpaqtāh), 1 sg. נפקת (nipqēt), נפקו (něpáqû, Dan 5:5 k.). 3 pl. f. נָפְקָה q.; impf. 3 sg. m. יפק & יפוק (yippuq), 3 sg. f. תנפק (tinpuq); impv. pl. m. פֻּקוּ ; infin. מנפק (minpaq), w. suff. מפקך (mippěqak); ptc. sg. m. נָפֵק , sg. f. נפקה (nāpěqāh), pl. m. נָפְקִין:

228

נפק

go out, come out, depart. מִן־גּוֹא נוּרָא . . . נָפְקִין בֵּאדַיִן נְפַקוּ וֶאֱתוֹ
"come out and come (here). Then they came out from the fire"
Dan 3:26; נְפַק לְקַטָּלָה לְחַכִּימֵי בָבֶל "(Arioch) went out to slay the
sages of Babylon" 2:14; נְהַר דִּי־נוּר נָגֵד וְנָפֵק "a stream of fire
made its way and came out" 7:10; שליטא אנת למנפק בתרע זי תחית
"you (shall) be able to go out by the gate of the lower part"
BMAP 9:14-15; בבא זילך למנפק "(to the west) is your gate to go
out" *BMAP* 10:4; ולמנפק ברא "and to go outside" *BMAP* 6:14;
תרעא זך לא זילך הו ילא תנפק בשוקא זי ביניך "that gateway is not
yours, and you shall not go out (by it) into the street that is between us" *AP* 5:12-13; כזי ארשם נפק ואזל על מלכא "when Arsames
departed and went to the king" *AP* 30:4-5; מן יום [ז]י נפקתה מן
מצרין "from the time [t]hat you departed from Egypt" *Padua I* A
3; מן זי נפקת מן סון "since I departed from Syene" *Hermopolis*
5:3; הן . . . ברתי תשנאנך ותנפק מנך "if . . . my daughter divorces
you and departs from you" *AP* 9:8-9; מן יום די נפקתה מן חרן "since
the day you departed from Haran" *1QapGen* 22:28; כול די נפקו
עמך ביום מפקך מן חרן "all that went forth with you on the day that
you departed from Haran" *1QapGen* 22:30; ינפק עלי "let him
come out to me" *El. Ostr.* Convex 2 (*HSSD* 55). -- Specifically:
נְפַקוּ (נְפָקָה) אֶצְבְּעָן דִּי יַד־אֱנָשׁ וְכָתְבָן "the fingers of a man's hand
came forth (appeared) and were writing" Dan 5:5; דָּתָא נֶפְקַת "the
decree went forth" Dan 2:13; אל יפק חצר וליתחזה ירק "may grass
not come forth so that no green may be seen" *Sefire I* A 28; הן
נפקה טבה מן פם א[נשא] טב "if good comes forth from a hu[man]
mouth, it is good" *Aḥ.* 123; לא ירתנך דן להן די יפוק "this one shall
not inherit you, but the one who will go forth [from your loins]"
1QapGen 22:34; דבקת ללשן ים סוף די נפק מן ימא שמוקא "I reached
the tongue (Gulf of Suez) of the Reed Sea, which goes forth from
the Red Sea" *1QapGen* 21:18.

Haph./Aph. 3 sg. m. הַנְפֵּק & אנפק (*'anpēq*), 2 sg. m.
הנפקת (*hanpēqt*), 3 pl. m. הַנְפִּקוּ ; impf. 3 sg. m. יְהַנְפֵּק , 3 pl. m.
יהנפקון (*yĕhanpĕqûn*): **make go out, bring out, remove, take**

away. מָאנַיָּא . . . דִּי נְבוּכַדְנֶצַּר הַנְפֵּק מִן־הֵיכְלָא "the vessels . . . that Nebuchadnezzar took away from the temple" Ezra 5:14a: 6:5; Dan 5:2, 3; הַנְפֵּק הִמּוֹ כּוֹרֶשׁ מַלְכָּא מִן־הֵיכְלָא דִּי בָבֶל "Cyrus the king took them (the vessels) from the temple of Babylon" Ezra 5:14b; נכסן כחסן הנפקת מן ביתי "removed property from my house by force" *AP* 7:5; כלביא הנפקו כבלא מן רגלוהי "the dogs tore the anklet from his legs" *AP* 30:16; לא יכהלון יהנפקון עליכי ספר חדת ועתיק "they will not be able to bring out a document, new or old, against you" *AP* 8:15-16; ו]הו זי[תביר הנפקה ברא "but [the vessel that] is broken lets it (the contents) go out" *Aḥ.* 109; מדעם לה מפקן לן מן סון "they are allowing nothing to come to us from Syene" *Hermopolis* 5:2-3; מנדת בגיא אלך יהנפק "let him collect the rent on those domains," lit., "let him bring out" *AD* 10:3; מלכיצדק . . . אנפק מאכל ומשתה לאברם "Melchizedek . . . brought out food and drink for Abram" *1QapGen* 22:14-15; מני עמי אנוש די ינפק]וני מן מצרין["(Pharaoh) appointed men to escort [me out of Egypt]," lit., "to make [me] go out" *1QapGen* 20:32. †

נִפְקָה * (*qatal-at*, BL 185s), emph. נִפְקְתָא (BL 238p): **cost, expenses.** נִפְקְתָא מִן־בֵּית מַלְכָּא תִּתְיְהֵב "let the cost be paid from the royal house" Ezra 6:4: 6:8; נפקתה בירח פאפי "expenses in the month of Paophi" *AP* 72:1; נ]פקת נפשה["personal expenses," lit., "of the soul," i.e., private expenses, *AP* 73:7; נפקת מדינתא "town expenses" *AP* 73:14. †

נִצְבָּה * (*qitl-at*, BL 184j), emph. נִצְבְּתָא . -- (1) **planting, farm.**]דן[ומנך נצבת פריא "and from you is the planting of [this] fruit" (collect. sg. פֵּר *) 1QapGen* 2:15; נצבתא זי זבדיה חנטן ס 1 ′ "the farm of Zebadiah: 1 seah of wheat" *AP* 81:2; cf. שרית אנה . . . למפלח בארעא ונצבת כרם רב "I began to cultivate the earth and planted a large vineyard" *1QapGen* 12:13. -- (2) Metaphorical sense: **quality, nature** (what is planted [נְצִיב] in a thing [= ἔμφυτος]) מִן־נִצְבְּתָא דִּי פַרְזְלָא לֶהֱוֵא־בַהּ "some of the quality of iron shall be in it (the fourth kingdom)" Dan 2:41b. [1]

230

נצח , **Hithpa./'Ithpa.** ptc. sg. m. מִתְנַצַּח (BL 133g): **excel, distinguish oneself.** הֲוָא מִתְנַצַּח עַל־סָרְכַיָּא "(Daniel) distinguished himself among the magistrates" Dan 6:4; [אלה] שגיא עמ[י'] אתנצחו "[these men who were] with [me] excelled (in war)" *Bisitun* 75; פקידיא . . . בשוזיא מתנצחן "(that) the officers have been distinguishing themselves in the disturbances" *AD* 7:3-4; על זנה אנתם [א]תנצחו "for this reason, distinguish yourselves, you (too)!" *AD* 7:5.[1]

נצל , **Haph./'Aph.** 3 sg. m. אנצל (*'anṣil/'anṣēl*) & אצל (*'aṣṣil*), 2 sg. m. w. suff. אצלתה (*'aṣṣiltēh*), 1 sg. w. suff. הנצלתה (*hanṣiltēh*); impf. 2 sg. m. תהנצל (*tĕhanṣēl*), 1 sg. אהנצל (*'ăhanṣil*) & אנצל (*'anṣil*); infin. הַצָּלָה , w. suff. , הצלתי הַצָּלוּתַהּ ; ptc. sg. m. מֵצַל . -- (1) **rescue, free, save.** מְשֵׁיזִב וּמַצִּל "(Daniel's God) delivers and rescues" Dan 6:28; לָא אִיתַי אֱלָהּ אָחֳרָן דִּי־יִכֻּל לְהַצָּלָה כִּדְנָה "there is no other god who can save like this" 3:29; שָׂם בָּל...לְהַצָּלוּתַהּ "(the king) set his mind...to rescue him (Daniel)" 6:15; למשלח חיל להצלתי "to send an army to rescue me" *Adon Letter* 7 (*KAI* 266); הן לו לא תכהל תהנצלנ[הי מן באישתא] "if you were not able to keep [him from wickedness]" *Aḥ.* 81; אצל מנהון כול די שבוא "(Abram) rescued from them all (the men) that they had captured" *1QapGen* 22:10; הב לי נפשא די איתי לי די שביא עמך די אצלתה מן מלך עילם "give me the men that are mine, who are captives with you, whom you have rescued from the king of Elam" *1QapGen* 22:19. -- (2) **take away, remove.** כען צבית אהנצל הם "now I want to take them away" *AP* 18:2-3; הן אמר אהנצל מנך "if I say, 'I shall take (it) away from you" *BMAP* 10:10; לא אכל אנצל לפלטי מן תחת לבבך "I will not be able to remove (the slave) Palti from your care," lit., "from under your heart" *BMAP* 2:13-14; והן הנצלתה מנך אנתן לענני כסף "and I do remove him, I will pay Anani silver" *BMAP* 2:14a; הן . . . ברתי תשנאנך ותנפק מנך . . . הן תהנצל מנך "if . . . my daughter divorces you and goes away from you . . . (or) if you remove (her) from you . . ." *AP* 9:8-10. [Hebr. the same]. †

231

נקא—נשין

נְקֵא (*nĕqē' < *naqī*): adj. **pure, innocent.** וּשְׂעַר רֵאשֵׁהּ כַּעֲמַר נְקֵא "and the hair of his head like pure wool" Dan 7:9; לא חטא לי ונקא "I have no sin and am innocent" *11QtgJob (11Q10)* 22:3. [Hebr. נָקִי]. [1]

נְקַשׁ *, ptc. pl. f. נָקְשָׁן : **dash against, knock at.** אַרְכֻבָּתֵהּ דָּא לְדָא נָקְשָׁן "his knees knocked one against the other," lit., "this one to that one" Dan 5:6. [1]

נְשָׂא (ל"א > ל"ה), 1 sg. נשאית (*niś'ît*); impf. 2 sg. m. תנשא (*tinśā'*) & תשא (*tiśśā'*), 1 sg. אשא ; impv. sg. m. שָׂא ; infin. מנשא (*minśā'*): **lift up, take, bear** (cf. סְבַל, נְטַל). נְשָׂא הִמּוֹן רוּחָא "the wind bore them (the smashed metals) away" Dan 2:35; נשאית חלא "I have lifted sand (to carry it)" *Aḥ.* 111; ואשא ידי אל בעלש[מי]ן "I lifted up my hand to Ba'al shamayn" *Zkr* A 11 (*KAI* 202); שָׂא אֵזֶל־אַחֵת הִמּוֹ "take (the vessels), go and deposit them (in the Temple)" Ezra 5:15 (read אַחֵת); אמרו לה שא לך זי ת[נ]שא מנן "(the lambs) said to him, 'Take for yourself whatever you want to take from us" *Aḥ.* 121; ברה שליט יהוה דשנא למנשא זכי "his son shall have authority to take that grant" *AD* 2:4; הן יסק על לבבך ותשא על שפתיך להמתחתי "if (the idea) should come to your mind and you should express with your lips (the intention) to kill me" *Sefire III* 14-15; כפן למנשא משח "bowls for carrying ointment" *BMAP* 7:19. **Hithpa.** ptc. sg. m. מִתְנַשָּׂא *, sg. f. מִתְנַשְּׂאָה : **exalt oneself.** עַל־מַלְכִין מִתְנַשְּׂאָה "(Jerusalem) has exalted itself against kings" Ezra 4:19. [Hebr. נָשָׂא]. †

נְשִׁין * (*nišîn*, BL 179f), only pl. (BL 305e), w. suff. נְשֵׁיהוֹן : -- (1) **wives.** גֻּבְרַיָּא אִלֵּךְ . . . בְּנֵיהוֹן וּנְשֵׁיהוֹן "those men . . . their children and their wives" Dan 6:25; אנחנה עם נשין ובנין שקקן לבשן הוין "we with our wives and our children have been wearing sack-cloth" *AP* 30:15; נשיא זילן כארמלה עבידין "our wives have been made widow-like" *AP* 30:20. -- sg. אִנְתָּה * = **wife.** הי אנתתי

נשמה—נתין

ואנה בעלה "she is my wife, and I am her husband" *AP* 15:4. --
(2) **women, females.** [בדה]א כלא ביתן נשי "the women of our
house perished altogether" *AD* 8:2; על כול נשין שופר שפרה "she
(Sarai) greatly surpasses in beauty all women," lit., "above all
women is she beautiful (in) beauty" *1QapGen* 20:6-7. -- (3)
woman (pl. w. sg. sense; see *LFAA* 92j). ונשן אובל . . . אמר בגזשת
כל גבר 1 נשן 1 . . . ברת שתבר "said Bagazusht . . . and the woman
Ubil, daughter of Shatibar, in all 1 man, 1 woman" *BMAP* 3:1-3;
ונשין תפמת אנתתה . . . אמר ענני "said Anani . . . and the woman,
Tapmut, his wife" *BMAP* 12:1-2. [Hebr. נָשִׁים]. [1]

נִשְׁמָה * (qatal-at, BL 185s, 238p), w. suff. נִשְׁמְתָךְ :
breath, life. לֵאלָהָא דִּי־נִשְׁמְתָךְ בִּידֵהּ . . . לָא הַדַּרְתָּ "you did not
honor the God in whose hand your life was" Dan 5:23 (cf. לְ I
2); דכרלך . . . נשמתי לגו נדנהא "recall . . . my breath in the midst of
its sheath" *1QapGen* 2:9-10. [Hebr. נְשָׁמָה]. [1]

נְשַׁר (našr), pl. נִשְׁרִין : **eagle.** עַד דִּי שַׂעְרֵהּ כְּנִשְׁרִין רְבָה
"until his hair grew like (the feathers of) eagles" Dan 4:30 (brachylogy); וְגַפִּין דִּי־נְשַׁר לַהּ "and (the first beast) had the wings of
an eagle" 7:4. [Hebr. נֶשֶׁר]. †

נִשְׁתְּוָן * (< Persian *ništāvan* "written precept"), emph.
נִשְׁתְּוָנָא **written document, letter, rescript.** נִשְׁתְּוָנָא דִּי שְׁלַחְתּוּן
עֲלֶינָא "the letter that you sent to us" Ezra 4:18 (‖ אִגַּרְתָּא "letter"
4:11); נִשְׁתְּוָנָא דִּי אַרְתַּחְשַׁשְׂתָּא מַלְכָּא קֱרִי "the rescript of Artaxerxes
the king has been read" 4:23 (‖ פִּתְגָמָא "reply" 4:17); וֶאֱדַיִן יְתִיבוּן
נִשְׁתְּוָנָא עַל־דְּנָה "and then they return the answering letter about it"
5:5; אף נשתונא כתיב יהיב לן "a written document also was given to
us: *AP* 17:3. [Hebr. נִשְׁתְּוָן]. †

נְתִין * (*natīn* "given," BL 188h), emph. pl. נְתִינַיָּא :
temple servant. תָּרָעַיָּא נְתִינַיָּא וּפָלְחֵי בֵית אֱלָהָא "the gatekeepers,

233

נתן

the temple servants, and (other) servants of God's house" Ezra
7:24. [Hebr. the same]. [1]

גְּתַן * 2 sg. m. נתנת (*nětant[ā]*); impf. 3 sg. m. יִנְתֵּן (v.l.
יִנְתֵּן), w. suff. יִתְּנַּהּ, 2 sg. f. תנתנן (*tintěnīn*), 3 pl. m. יִנְתְּנוּן, juss.
ינתנו (*yintěnû*); infin. מִנְתַּן. **Hithpe.** impf. 3 sg. m. יתנתן
(*yitnětēn*); cf. יְהַב : -- (1) **give, grant, hand over.** דִּי זְמָן יִנְתֶּן־לֵהּ
"(he asked the king) that he would give him time" Dan 2:16;
וּלְמַן־דִּי יִצְבֵּא יִתְּנַנַּהּ "and (God) gives it to whomever he desires"
4:14, 22, 29; ינתנו לי אהחסן "let them hand (it) over to me (that) I
may take possession (of it)" *AD* 8:3; וחיין אריכן ינתן לך "and may
(God) grant you long life" *AP* 30:3; ולמן זי צבית תנתן "and to
whomever you want you may give (him [the slave])" *AP* 28:7;
למן זי רחמתי תנתנן "to whom you (f.) wish you may give it" *AP*
8:9-10; זי. . . אמתך לאנתו . . . למנתן לי לתמת "to give me Tamut . . . ,
who is your handmaiden, in marriage" *BMAP* 2:3. -- (2) **pay,
provide.** מִנְדָּה־בְלוֹ וַהֲלָךְ לָא יִנְתְּנוּן "(if Jerusalem is rebuilt), they
will not pay tribute, tax, or toll" Ezra 4:13; דִּי יִפֶּל־לָךְ לְמִנְתַּן תִּנְתֵּן
מִן־בֵּית גִּנְזֵי מַלְכָּא "which you will have to provide, you may provide from the king's treasury" 7:20; [כ]זי יתנתן לי פתפא מן בית
מלכא "[w]hen the ration is paid to me from the king's house"
BMAP 11:5-6; מן פרסי זי ינ[ת]נון לי מן אוצרא "from my salary,
which they pa[y] me from the treasury" *AP* 11:6. -- (3) **sell,
lend.** זי תנתן לה בכסף או רחמת "which you sell for money or (give)
as a gift" *BMAP* 12:26 (cf. זי תזבן לה בכסף "which you sell (Pa.)
for money" 12:23-24); נתנת לי כסף [שקלן 4] . . . וירבה עלי כסף חלרן
2 לכסף ש 1: you have lent me the sum of [4 shekels] . . . and the
interest shall grow against me at the rate of 2 hallurs for the sum
of 1 sh(ekel per month [5%])" *AP* 11:1-3 (cf. לְ I 11); יזפת מנך
ויהבת לי כנתן . . . אשלם ואנתן לך כנתניא אלך "I borrowed from you
and you lent me spelt . . . I shall pay back and give you that spelt
(pl.)" *BMAP* 11:3-4; כל זי הנעלת בביתה ינתן לה "all that she
brought into his house he shall give (back) to her" *BMAP* 7:22.
[Hebr. נָתַן]. †

234

נתר Aph. m. pl. impv. אַתַּרוּ (BL 113f, 133j) **cut out, excise.** (Cut down the tree; cut off its branches and) אַתַּרוּ עָפְיֵהּ "cut off its leaves" Dan 4:11. [1]

ס

שַׂבְּכָא see , סַבְּכָא .

סְבַל *: **carry.** שבק חמר ולא יסבלנהי "the ass abandoned (his load) and would not carry it" *Ah.* 90; [לחם ומין] יסתבלון קדם מראי "[bread and water] will be carried to my lord" *Ah.* 72-73. -- **Pa.** סַבֵּל *: **sustain, take care of.** ברתי . . . סבלתני ואנה ימין סב "my daughter . . . sustained me, when I was elderly" *BMAP* 9:17; יבלתך לביתא זילי תמה הוית מסבל לך "I brought you to my house; there I was taking care of you" *Ah.* 48; ותפמת ואחתסן מסבלן לה "and T. and A. were taking care of him" *Hermopolis* 1:5. -- **Poel** (BL 91d, 92k), ptc. pl. m. (act. or pass.?) מְסוֹבְלִין (hardly Saph'el of יבל < Akk. *šūbulu* "send" something to someone, cf. CAD 1. 24-27), אֲתַר דִּי־דָבְחִין דִּבְחִין וְאֱשׁוֹהִי מְסוֹבְלִין "the place where they offer sacrifices and present burnt offerings" Ezra 6:3 (cf. 5:13; 6:7; *AP* 32:8; an order to lay foundations would be tautological). [Hebr. סָבַל]. [1]

סְבַר *, impf. 3 sg. m. יִסְבַּר . **think, intend.** יִסְבַּר לְהַשְׁנָיָה זִמְנִין "(this king) shall intend to change times (of the calendar)" Dan 7:25; [הוית סב[ר די אלהין ה[מון] "I thought that they were gods" *4QPrNab (4Q242)* 1-3:8. [1]

סְגֵד , impf. 3 sg. m. יִסְגֻּד , 3 pl. m. יִסְגְּדוּן , 2 pl. m. תִּסְגְּדוּן , 1 pl. נִסְגֻּד ; ptc. pl. m. סָגְדִין : **bend over** (in reverence), **kneel; prostrate oneself, worship, do homage** (cf. Hebr. הִשְׁתַּחֲוָה לְ). נְפַל עַל־אַנְפּוֹהִי וּלְדָנִיֵּאל סְגִד "(the king) prostrated himself and did homage to Daniel," lit., "fell on his face" Dan 2:46; יִפֵּל וְיִסְגֻּד

לְצֶלֶם דַּהֲבָא "let (everyone) fall down and worship the golden statue" 3:10: 3:5, 6, 11, 15; נָפְלִין כָּל־עַמְמַיָּא . . . סָגְדִין לְצֶלֶם דַּהֲבָא "all
the peoples fell down . . . (and) worshiped the golden statue" 3:7;
לֵאלָהָיךְ לָא פָלְחִין וּלְצֶלֶם . . . לָא סָגְדִין "they do not serve your gods
and the statue . . . they do not worship" 3:12: 3:14, 18, 28; גהנת
וסגד[ת] לם אחיקר קדם אסרח[אדן] "I, Aḥiqar, bowed down and did
homage to Esarh[addon]" *Aḥ.* 13. -- Cf. מַסְגֵּד * **place of worship, temple:** ימא למשלם . . . במסגדא ובענתיהו "he swore to Meshullam by the temple and by ʻAnatyahu" *AP* 44:2-3. [Hebr. סגד
ל , < Ar.]. †

סְגַן * or סָגֵן * (*LFAA* 103b; *BMAP* pp. 36, 243; < Akk.
sagānu [see *Or* 37 (1968) 265]), pl. סְגְנִין, emph. סִגְנַיָּא : (1)
governor, prefect of a province (= פֶּחָה, see *BMAP* p. 36). לְמִכְנַשׁ
לַאֲחַשְׁדַּרְפְּנַיָּא סִגְנַיָּא וּפַחֲוָתָא "to assemble the satraps, governors, and
prefects" Dan 3:2: 3:3, 27; אֲתִיעַטוּ כֹּל סָרְכֵי מַלְכוּתָא סִגְנַיָּא
וַאֲחַשְׁדַּרְפְּנַיָּא הַדָּבְרַיָּא וּפַחֲוָתָא "all the ministers of the kingdom, the
governors, the satraps, the counselors, and the prefects are a-
greed" 6:8. -- (2) **presider, head** (in a generic sense; see *BMAP*
pp. 36, 243). רַב־סְגְנִין עַל כָּל־חַכִּימֵי בָבֶל "(the king made Daniel)
chief presider over all the sages of Babylon" Dan 2:48; זי יקבל
עליך לסגן ומרא ודין "whoever brings a complaint against you to a
presider or lord or judge (about this house)" *BMAP* 12:28; אשרנא
זנה יתיהב על יד . . . סגן נגריא "this material is to be delivered to . . .
the head of the carpenters" *AP* 26:21-22. [Hebr. סְגַן * or סָגֵן *;
LFAA 104b]. †

סְגַר *, וּסֲגַר * (BL 36b, 40m): **close, shut.** אֱלָהִי שְׁלַח מַלְאֲכֵהּ
וּסֲגַר פֻּם אַרְיָוָתָא "my God sent His angel and shut the lions'
mouths" Dan 6:23. [Hebr. סָגַר]. [1]

סוּמְפֹּנְיָה (< Gk. συμφωνία), סִיפֹנְיָה k., סוּפֹנְיָה q. Dan 3:10:
bagpipe (?); double-barrelled flute (?). וְסִיפֹנְיָה וְכֹל . . . קָל קַרְנָא

236

זְנֵי זְמָרָא "the sound of the horn . . . and the bagpipe, and every sort of music" Dan 3:10 (see *JBL* 24 [1905] 172; *BA* 4 [1941] 40-42; *DSD* 7 [2000] 99): 3:5, 15. †

סוף *, 3 sg. f. סָפַת : **come to an end, be finished** (cf. שְׁלֵם). מִלְתָא סָפַת עַל־נְבוּכַדְנֶצַּר "the verdict was fulfilled on Nebuchadnezzar," lit., "came to an end" Dan 4:30; [וכ]ל חשבוניהון [ן]עלוהי יסופו "[and a]ll their forebodings were fulfilled on him" *4QBirthNoah^a (4Q534)* 1 i 9. -- **Aph.** impf. 3 sg. f. תָּסֵיף (BL 148c, d): **bring to an end, destroy.** תַּדִּק וְתָסֵיף כָּל־אִלֵּין מַלְכְוָתָא "it shall smash all those kingdoms and bring (them all) to an end" Dan 2:44.

סוֹף (*sawp*, BL 182a) cst. (& abs.), emph. סוֹפָא : **end.** וַחֲזוֹתֵהּ לְסוֹף כָּל־אַרְעָא "it (the tree) was visible to the end of the whole earth," lit., "sight of it to the end . . . " Dan 4:8; וְשָׁלְטָנָךְ לְסוֹף אַרְעָא "and your dominion (reaches) to the end of the earth" 4:19; רֵאשׁ מִלִּין "beginning of the story" 7:1, סוֹפָא דִי מִלְתָא "the end of the story" 7:28 (two added glosses, BL 353f); לסוף תרתין שנין "at the end of two years" *1QapGen* 20:18. -- עַד־סוֹפָא = **for ever, in perpetuity** : קָיָם לְעָלְמִין . . . וְשָׁלְטָנֵהּ עַד־סוֹפָא "(God) enduring for ever . . . and His dominion (lasts) in perpetuity" Dan 6:27; שָׁלְטָנֵהּ יְהַעְדּוֹן לְהַשְׁמָדָה וּלְהוֹבָדָה עַד־סוֹפָא "they shall take away his dominion to consume and destroy (it) for ever" 7:26. [Hebr. the same]. †

סְלַק *, סלק (*sĕliq*), 3 sg. f. סִלְקַת, סְלָקַת Dan 7:8 (v.l. סְלָקָת, סָלְקַת, סָלְקַת, read סְלָקַת, BL137e), 3 pl. m. סְלִקוּ ; impf. 3 sg. m. יִסַּק (*yissaq*), 3 pl. m. יִסְּקוּן (*yissĕqūn*); impv. סְלַק (*sĕlaq*); infin. מִסְלַק (*mislaq*, > מִסַּק > מִנְסַק [*minsaq*]); ptc. pl. f. סָלְקָן : **go up, come up, ascend.** אַרְבַּע חֵיוָן רַבְרְבָן סָלְקָן מִן־יַמָּא "four great beasts came up from the sea" Dan 7:3; יְהוּדָיֵא דִּי סְלִקוּ מִן־לְוָתָךְ עֲלֶינָא אֲתוֹ "the Jews who came up from you to us have come (to Jeru-

salem)" Ezra 4:12; עם בנוה זי יסקן באשר[ה] "with his sons who
will come after [him]," lit., "in [his] place" *Sefire I* A 5; שליטא
ולמנחת "you (f.) shall have power over half אנתי בפלג דרגא למסלק
of the stairway to go up and to go down" *BMAP* 9:15; ש]ל[י]טה
אנת] למ[נסק [ולמ[נחת בדרגא "you (f.) will be able to go up [and to]
go down by the stairway" *BMAP* 6:10: 6:13; סלק לך לרמת חצור
"go up to Ramath-Hazor!" *1QapGen* 21:8; סלק לעורעה ואתה לשלם
"(the king of Sodom) went up to meet him (Abram) and came to
Salem" *1QapGen* 22:13. -- Specifically: וַאֲלוּ קֶרֶן אָחֳרִי זְעֵירָה סִלְקָת
"and lo, another horn, a little one, came up among them" בֵּינֵיהֵין
Dan 7:8 (read rather סִלְקַת); . . . סְלִקוּ מָה דִּי לֶהֱוֵא אַחֲרֵי דְנָה
רַעְיוֹנָךְ "your thoughts . . . arose (in your mind about) what would be
after this" Dan 2:29; הן יסק על לבבך . . . להמתתי "if (the idea)
should come to your mind . . . to kill me" *Sefire III* 14-15. --
Haph. 3 pl. m. הַסִּקוּ; infin. הַנְסָקָה. **Hoph.** הֻסַּק: **lift up, take
up.** גֻּבְרַיָּא אִלֵּךְ דִּי הַסִּקוּ לְשַׁדְרַךְ "those men who lifted up Shadrach
(to throw him into the furnace)" Dan 3:22; לְדָנִיֵּאל אֲמַר לְהַנְסָקָה
מִן־גֻּבָּא וְהֻסַּק "(the king) ordered (them) to take Daniel up from the
den; so he was taken up" 6:24. †

סעד, **Pa.** 3 sg. m. w. suff. סעדני (*sā'ădánî*); ptc. pl. m.
מְסָעֲדִין (*musa''idīn*): **help, assist.** וְעִמְּהוֹן נְבִיַּאיָּא דִי־אֱלָהָא מְסָעֲדִין
לְהוֹן "and with them (were) God's prophets assisting them" Ezra
5:2; אהורמזד סעדני "Ahuramazda helped me (in battle)" *Bisitun*
32. [Hebr. סָעַד]. [1]

סְפַר (*sipr*, BL 224i) cst. (& abs.), pl. סְפָרִין, emph.
סִפְרַיָּא, m.: **book, document, deed, letter, inscription** (cf.
כְּתָב). הֲקִימוּ כָהֲנַיָּא . . . כִּכְתָב סְפַר מֹשֶׁה "they set up the priests . . .
according to the writ of the book of Moses" Ezra 6:18; דִּינָה יְתִב
וְסִפְרִין פְּתִיחוּ "the court took its seat, and books were opened" Dan
7:10; דִּי יְבַקַּר בִּסְפַר־דָּכְרָנַיָּא דִי אֲבָהָתָךְ "so that one might search in
the book of records of your ancestors" Ezra 4:15a: 4:15b (BL

310b); בְבָבֶל . . . וּבַקַּרוּ בְּבֵית סִפְרַיָּא "and they searched (for the document) in the archives . . . in Babylon," lit., "in the house of books" Ezra 6:1; וספר אנתו "and a marriage document" AP 14:4; ספר פלגנן "a document of our division" AP 28:14: 28:17; יהבן לך ספרא עתיקא זי כתב לן בגזשת ספר זבנתא "we have given to you the old document that Bagazusht had written for us as the deed of sale" BMAP 12:31; ספר חדת ועתיק בשמי "a document, new or old, with my name" AP 8:16; זך ספרא . . . כדב יהוה "that document . . . will be false" AP 8:16-17; זנה ספרא זי אנה ענני כתבת לכי הו יצב "this document that I, Anani, have written for you is valid" BMAP 10:16-17; ספר לה הושרתן לי "you did not send me a letter" Hermopolis 5:7-8; מן ליצר מלי ספרא זי בנצבא זנה "whoever will not observe the words of the inscription that is on this stele" Sefire I C 16-17; [ומן י]אמר להלדת ספריא [א]לן מן בתי אלהיא "[and whoever will] give orders to efface [th]ese inscriptions from the bethels" Sefire II C 1-3; כתב ספריא ש.[ ] "X wrote the deeds" (i.e., a double document) XHev/Se 50 frgs. d + e 29. [Hebr. סֵפֶר]. †

סָפַר (< Akk. šāpiru) cst (& abs.), emph. סָפְרָא : -- (1) **secretary, clerk.** רשת ספרא "Rasht is the clerk" AD 8:6; 9:3; 10:5; ענני ספרא בעל [טע]ם "Anani, the secretary, (was) the author of (the) order" AP 26:23; [אל מראן ארש]ם עבדיך אחמנש וכנותה . . . וספרי מדינתא "[To our lord, Arsa]mes, (from) your servants, Aḥmenesh and his colleagues . . . and the secretaries of the province" AP 17:1; וקדם ספרי אוצרא "and in the presence of the clerks of the treasury" AP 2:12; ספרא, "scribe" KAI 227, B6 and 236, B6. -- (2) **scribe.** עֶזְרָא כָהֲנָא סָפַר דָּתָא דִּי־אֱלָה שְׁמַיָּא "Ezra, the priest, the scribe of the law of the God of Heaven" Ezra 7:12, 21 (cf. Hebr. 7:6, 10, 11; disputed meaning, see ASA, 4ff.); [לאחיקר ס]פרא חכימא יעט אתור כלה "[for Aḥiqar], the wise scribe, counselor of all Assyria" Aḥ. 11-12; [אלה מ]לי אחיקר . . . ספר חכים "[these are the wor]ds of Aḥiqar . . . , a wise and expert ומהיר

scribe" *Aḥ.* 1; ספרא חכימא [אנת הו] "[Are you] the wise scribe?"
Aḥ. 42; רְחוּם בְּעֵל־טְעֵם וְשִׁמְשַׁי סָפְרָא "Rehum, the commander, and
Shimshai, the scribe" Ezra 4:8: 4:9, 17, 23. [Hebr. סֹפֵר]. †

סַרְבָּל * (< Persian *salavāra;* cf. modern Persian *šalvār;*
Arab. *sirwāl* & *širwāl*), pl. w. suff. סַרְבָּלֵיהוֹן ([שרבל[י]הון *1Q-
Danb [1Q72]* 1:10 [DJD 1. 151]): **mantle** (meaning uncertain).
גֻּבְרַיָּא אִלֵּךְ כְּפִתוּ בְּסַרְבָּלֵיהוֹן . . . וּרְמִיו לְגוֹא־אַתּוּן "those men were
bound in their mantles . . . and thrown into the furnace" Dan
3:21: 3:27. †

סָרֵךְ * (< Persian *sāraka,* "head"; see *GBA* §189), pl.
סָרְכִין , cst. סָרְכֵי , emph. סָרְכַיָּא : **official, supervisor.** סָרְכִין תְּלָתָא
דִּי דָנִיֵּאל חַד־מִנְּהוֹן "three supervisors, of whom Daniel was one"
Dan 6:3: 6:4, 5, 7, 8. †

סתר [1], **Pa.,** pass. ptc. sg. m. מסתר (*mĕsattar*), pl. f.
emph. מְסַתְּרָתָא : **hide.** הוּא גָּלֵא עֲמִיקָתָא וּמְסַתְּרָתָא "He reveals deep
and hidden things" Dan 2:22. [Hebr. the same]. [1]

סְתַר [2] *, שׂתר, w. suff. סַתְרֵהּ : **destroy, break.** וּבַיְתָא דְנָה
סַתְרֵהּ "and he (Nebuchadnezzar) destroyed this house (temple)"
Ezra 5:12; [מע]כאיש גנב זי שתר בי וישת "like a thief who breaks
into a house and is hea[rd]" *Aḥ.* 125. [Hebr. שׂתר]. [1]

ע

The letter ע designated in Old Aramaic the sound ʿ
(and perh. ġ); later it designated also the sound derived
from primitive ġ̆ (< ḍ*), written of old with the letter ק.

עבד

עֲבַד , 2 sg. m. עֲבַדְתָּ , 1 sg. עַבְדֵת , 3 pl. m. עֲבַדוּ ; impf. 2 pl. m. תַּעַבְדוּן (v.l. תֶּעְבְּדוּן); infin. מֶעְבַּד ; ptc. sg. m. עָבֵד , sg. f. עָבְדָה , pl. m. עָבְדִין . **Hithpe.** impf. 3 sg. m. יִתְעֲבֵד & יִתְעַבֵד, 2 pl. m. תִּתְעַבְדוּן ; ptc. sg. m. מִתְעֲבֵד & ־מִתְעֲבָד , sg. f. מִתְעַבְדָא : (1) **do, make, produce.** מַלְכָּא עֲבַד צְלֵם "the king made a statue" Dan 3:1; צַלְמָא דִי־עַבְדֵת "the statue that I made" 3:15; אֱלָהַיָּא דִּי־שְׁמַיָּא וְאַרְקָא לָא עֲבַדוּ "the gods who did not make the heavens and the earth" Jer 10:11; ספרא זמה זי אנה עבדת לכי "this document, which I have made for you" *BMAP* 9:22; יעבד פתכר . . . לקבל זי קדמי קדמן עבד "(that) he may make a sculpture . . . such as the one he made for me previously" *AD* 9:2; כרם רב . . . עבד לי חמר "a great vineyard . . . produced wine for me" *1QapGen* 12:13; מַלְכָּא עֲבַד לְחֶם רַב לְרַבְרְבָנוֹהִי "the king made a great dinner for his nobles" Dan 5:1; עדיא וטבתא ז[י] עבדו אלהן "the treaty and the amity that (the) gods have produced" *Sefire II* B 2. -- (2) **make, cause, produce** (often instead of a simple verb). אֶשְׁתַּדּוּר עָבְדִין "causing sedition" Ezra 4:15; עֲבַדוּ בְנֵי יִשְׂרָאֵל . . . לַחֲנֻכַּת בֵּית־אֱלָהָא דְנָה "the people of Israel . . . made the dedication of this house of God," i.e., "dedicated" 6:16; קַרְנָא דִכֵּן עָבְדָה קְרָב עִם־קַדִּישִׁין "that horn was making war with holy ones" Dan 7:21; אזלו לערק[ה] זי דדרש "they went to an encoun[ter] with Dadarsh to make war" *Bisitun* 15; למעבד קרב ועבדו קרב עם ברע מלך סודם "and they made war on Bera, the king of Sodom" *1QapGen* 21:24; אָסְפַּרְנָא יִתְעֲבֵד "let it be done with all diligence," i.e., "let it be given" Ezra 7:21; חלפיך עבידתך הו ועבד כל עבידה "and do every work!" *Aḥ.* 127; יעבד [לי] "instead of you, he shall do your service [for me]" *Aḥ.* 21; דִּינָה לֶהֱוֵא מִתְעֲבֵד מִנֵּהּ "let judgment of him be made," i.e., "let him be judged" Ezra 7:26; עבד לי דין מנה "mete out justice to him for me," i.e., "do for me" *1QapGen* 20:14; הן אזד יתעבד מן דיניא ומראן אודיס "if inquiry be made of the judges" *AP* 27:8-9; יעב]ד על זנה["let our lord mak[e] an investigation [about this]" *AP* 33:12; על דינה זי עבדן בסון "according to the legal action that we made in Syene" *AP* 14:3; מומאה דכא זי עבדתי לי על נכסיא אלכי

241

"that oath that you made to me about those goods of yours" *AP* 14:6; זנה זי בפרתו עבדת "this is what I did in Parthia" *Bisitun* 29; עֲבֵד אָתִין וְתִמְהִין "(God) produces signs and wonders" Dan 6:28: 4:32; זְהִירִין הֱוֹו שָׁלוּ לְמֶעְבַּד עַל־דְּנָה "take care not to produce negligence in this matter" Ezra 4:22; לְמֶעְבַּד . . . . תַּעַבְדוּן . . . בִּשְׁאָר כַּסְפָּא "(whatever seems good to you) to do . . . with the rest of the silver . . . you may do" 7:18; למעבד בה כול די תצבה "to do with it whatever you wish" *XḤev/Se papDeed of Sale G (XḤev/Se 23)* 1:3. -- (3) **do, commit.** קָדָמָיךְ מַלְכָּא חֲבוּלָה לָא עַבְדֵת "against you, O King, I have done no wrong" Dan 6:23; [והן ת]עבד מרמת עלי "[and if you] commit treachery against me" *Sefire III* 22; אָתַיָּא וְתִמְהַיָּא דִּי עֲבַד עִמִּי עֱלָהָא "the signs and wonders that God has done for me" Dan 3:32; ודי עבד עמי טב "and because He has done good to me" *1QapGen* 21:3; לְמָא דִי־תַעַבְדוּן עִם־שָׂבֵי יְהוּדָיֵא "regarding what you must do for the elders of the Jews" Ezra 6:8; בעדן זי זא באישתא עביד לן "at the time when this evil was done to us" *AP* 30:17-18; וכעשק עביד לי "and a wrong was done to me" *AP* 16:5; איש מנדעם באיש לא יעבד לפירמא זך "(that) no one do any evil to that Pirma" *AD* 5:8-9; מה טב בעיני אעבד להם "whatever is good in my sight, I will do for them" *Sefire III* 3; מה זי תעבדון לחור ל[תריה]ם עבדו "what you do for Ḥor, do for [both of th]em" *AP* 38:8; יִתְעֲבֵד אָדְרַזְדָּא לְבֵית אֱלָהּ שְׁמַיָּא "let it be done diligently for the house of the God of Heaven" Ezra 7:23. -- (4) **make** someone something (w. two accus. or two nom.) למשנתה ולמעבדה עבד "to mark him and to make him a slave" *BMAP* 8:7; [פס]משך . . זי "[Psa]mshek . . . who now has been made an officer in his (father's) place" *AD* 2:2-3; בַּיְתֵהּ נְוָלוּ יִתְעֲבֵד "his house shall be made a dunghill" Ezra 6:11; הַדָּמִין תִּתְעַבְדוּן "you shall be made limbs," i.e., torn limb from limb Dan 2:5; 3:29. -- (5) **do, act** (absolutely). לְקֵבֵל דִּי־שְׁלַח . . . מַלְכָּא כְּנֵמָא . . . עֲבַדוּ "according to the word that the king sent, . . .so they did" Ezra 6:13; אנת לקבל זי אנה עבדת לך כן אפו עבד לי "as I have done for you, so do also for me" *Aḥ.* 51-52; עבד לקבל זי אנת עשת "do according to what you intend" *Aḥ.* 68; כזי עבד אנה לחרוץ כות תעבד

בנת לי "as I am acting toward Ḥaruṣ, so may (the goddess) Banit act toward me" *Hermopolis* 1:7; כן [ביום זי יעב[ד "on the day on which he will d[o] so" *Sefire I* C 20-21; הן כן עבדו עד זי אגורא זך יתבנה "if they have done so that that temple is built" *AP* 30:27; הן תעבד כות שנאה "when it was so done" *AP* 30:15; כזי כזנה עביד הי "if she does thus, she is divorced," lit., "is hated" *BMAP* 7:33-34. -- עבד generically resuming sense of a preceding verb: מְצַלֵּא . . . כָּל־קֳבֵל דִּי־הֲוָא עָבֵד מִן־קַדְמַת דְּנָה "(Daniel) was praying, . . . as he had done before" Dan 6:11; חזי על עלימיא וביתי כזי תעבד לביתך "look after the servants and my house, as you would do for your own house" *AP* 41:6; יקרבון על מדבחא זך לקבל זי לקדמין הוה מתעבד "let them offer on that altar as it was done formerly" *AP* 32:9-11; נסבל לזכור ברך כבר זי יסבל לאבוהי כזי הוין עבדן לך בחייך "we shall provide for Sakkur, your son, as the son who provides for his father, just as we were doing for you in your lifetime" *BMAP* 5:12-13; ועבדו על ביתא זילי כן כזי פקידיא [קד]מיא הוו עבדן "and make (the servants) over to my house, just as the [for]mer prefects used to do" *AD* 7:7-8. -- (6) Specifically: כָּל־דִּי־לָא לֶהֱוֵא עָבֵד דָּתָא "whoever will not observe the law" Ezra 7:26: 6:12; עלוה לא עבדו באגורא זך "they have not been offering a holocaust in that temple" *AP* 30:21-22; קן תור ענז מקלו [ל]א יתעבד תמה "sheep, oxen, (and) goats will [n]ot be sacrificed there as a burnt-offering" *AP* 33:10; כלא לקחו ולנפשהום עבדו "they took all of it away and made (it) their own" *AP* 30:12-13; נכסן . . . הנפקת מן ביתי "goods . . . removed from my house, and appropriated" ולקחת לנפש[ך] עבדת "you removed goods . . . from my house and took (them and) made (them) your own" *AP* 7:5-6; ועבד על ביתא זילי "(he sought out a staff of craftsmen) and appropriated (it) to my estate" *AD* 7:3; תרתין (שנין) עבדתה תנה ושבע במצרין "you passed two (years) here and seven in Egypt" *1QapGen* 22:28. [Hebr. עָבַד]. †

עֲבֵד (*'abd*) cst. (& abs.); pl. עבדין (*'abdîn* [ד wt. da-ghesh]), w. suff. עַבְדָיִךְ k. & עַבְדָךְ q. (BL 74z, 77o), עֲבְדוֹהִי (BL

עבידה–עבד נגו

226x), עבדיה (ʿabdáyah, BL 49e); m. **slave, servant.** אֲמַר חֶלְמָא לְעַבְדָּיךְ "tell the dream to your servants!" i.e., to us Dan 2:4: 2:7; Ezra 4:11; אֲנַחְנָא הִמּוֹ עַבְדוֹהִי דִי־אֱלָהּ שְׁמַיָּא "we are the servants of the God of Heaven" Ezra 5:11: Dan 3:26, 28; עֲבֵד אֱלָהָא חַיָּא "(O Daniel,) servant of the living God" Dan 6:21; למעבדה עבד "to make him a slave" *BMAP* 8:7; פלגן עלין עבדיה זי מבטחיה אמן "we have divided between us the slaves of Mibṭaḥiah, our mother" *AP* 28:3; אל מרא מלכן פרעה עבדך אדן "To the lord of kings, Pharaoh, your servant Adon" *Adon Letter* 1 (*KAI* 266); על מראי פסמי עבדך מכבנת "To my lord, Pasmi, your servant, Makkibanit" *Hermopolis* 3:1; תדברנה לעבד עלם "you will take him as a slave forever" *11QtgJob (11Q10)* 35:7. [Hebr. עֶבֶד]. †

עֲבִידָה * (qatil-at, BL 188j), cst. עֲבִידַת, emph. עֲבִידְתָּא, f.: **work, labor, service, business.** בְּטֵלַת עֲבִידַת בֵּית־אֱלָהָא "work on the house of God stopped," i.e., construction Ezra 4:24; עֲבִידְתָּא דָךְ אָסְפַּרְנָא מִתְעַבְדָא "that work is done diligently" 5:8; שְׁבֻקוּ לַעֲבִידַת בֵּית־אֱלָהָא דָךְ "leave that work on the house of God alone" 6:7; עבד כל עבידה אדין תאכל ותשבע "do every work; then you shall eat and be satisfied" *Aḥ.* 127; עבידתא זילי יעבדו כזי קדמן "let them perform my service, as previously" *AD* 5:9; בניך . . . המו שליטן בה "your children . . . have authority over it in exchange for the work that you have done" *AP* 9:9-10; הֲקִימוּ כָהֲנַיָּא . . . עַל עֲבִידַת <בֵּית> אֱלָהָא "they set up priests . . . for the service of <the house of> God," Ezra 6:18 (add בֵּית w. Gk., Syr.); וּמַנִּי עַל עֲבִידְתָּא דִּי מְדִינַת בָּבֶל "and he appointed for the (governing) service of the province of Babylon" Dan 2:49: 3:12; כעת אנת [לי] יעבד "he shall do your service [for me]" *Aḥ.* 21; וגרדא זילי עבידא לא איתי לך "now (as for) you, you have no business with my staff" *AD* 12:9. [Hebr. עֲבֹדָה]. †

▲ עֲבֵד נְגוֹ : **Abednego,** companion of Daniel. וּמַנִּי עַל עֲבִידַת דִּי מְדִינַת בָּבֶל לְשַׁדְרַךְ מֵישַׁךְ וַעֲבֵד נְגוֹ "and for the service of the pro-

244

עבר נהרה—עד

vince of Babylon, he appointed Shadrach, Meshach, and Abed-nego" Dan 2:49: 3:12 +; עֲבֵד נְגוֹא 3:29.

▲ עֲבַר נַהֲרָה & עֲבַר נַהֲרָא (< Akk. *Eber nāri*): **Beyond-the-River**, i.e., west of the Euphrates. וּשְׁאָר עֲבַר נַהֲרָה "and the rest of (the province) Beyond-the-River" Ezra 4:10: 4:11, 16 + . Cf. תדעל מלך גוים די היא בין נהרין "Tidal, the king of Goiim, which is between two rivers," i.e., in Mesopotamia *1QapGen* 21:24-25. [Hebr. עֵבֶר הַנָּהָר].

עַד . -- (1) prep. of place and time: **up to, to, into.** וְעַד־עַתִּיק יוֹמַיָּא מְטָה "and he came up to the Ancient of Days" Dan 7:13; עַד־כָּה סוֹפָא דִי־מִלְּתָא "up to here the end of the story" 7:28; בפתי אמן מן מועה עד מערב "in the width of cubits, from east to west" *BMAP* 4:7; לשטר ביתי מן ארעא ועד עלא "at the side of my house from the ground upwards" *AP* 5:5; נדשוהי עד ארעא "they destroyed it (the temple) to the ground," i.e., thoroughly *AP* 30:9; ודבק עד סודם "and he came to Sodom," lit., "he arrived at" *1Qap-Gen* 21:6; לקבל אדונא זי מן מדינה עד מדינה "according to (his) journey which (is) from province to province" *AD* 6:5; עַד־כְּסַף כַּכְּרִין מְאָה "up to a hundred talents of silver" Ezra 7:22: 7:22 (three times); וכל . . . תהנפק מן חם עד חוט "she shall take away . . . everything, from straw to thread" *BMAP* 2:10 + ; אן מן חוט עד ערקא דמסאן אן אסב מן כול די איתי לך "that I will not take so much as a thread or a sandal-strap from anything that is yours" *1QapGen* 22:21-22. -- עַד שְׁנַת תַּרְתֵּין לְמַלְכוּת דָּרְיָוֶשׁ "until the second year of the reign of Darius" Ezra 4:24: 6:15; וּמִן־אֱדַיִן וְעַד־כְּעַן מִתְבְּנֵא "and from then until now it (the temple) is being built" 5:16; וּלְהוֹבָדָה עַד־סוֹפָא "and to destroy (it) to the end," i.e., thoroughly Dan 7:26: 6:27; עד ירח תחות "up to the month of Thoth" *AP* 11:8; אשלמן לכי עד 30 לפרמתי "I shall pay you in full by the 30th of Pharmuthi" *AP* 35:5-6; עַד־עָלְמָא "for ever" Dan 2:20: 7:18; מן יומא זנה . . . עד עלם "from this day . . . for ever" *BMAP* 10:8; על

245

ספר אנתותכי עד אחרן "on the document of your marriage until another (time)," i.e., in the interim *BMAP* 10:9-10. -- עַד **for, during, within** (a space of time; BL 260y): כָּל־דִּי־יִבְעֵה בָעוּ מִן־כָּל־אֱלָהּ וֶאֱנָשׁ עַד־יוֹמִין תְּלָתִין "whoever makes a petition from any god or human being during thirty days" Dan 6:8, 13; עַד־עִדָּן וְעִדָּנִין וּפְלַג "for a time, (two) times, and a half time" 7:25 (cf. עִדָּן (עִדָּן); וְאַרְכָה בְחַיִּין יְהִיבַת לְהוֹן עַד־זְמַן וְעִדָּן "and a prolongation in life was given to them (the beasts) for a season and a time" 7:12. -- עַד־דִּבְרַת דִּי "to the end that" Dan 4:14 (where עַל is assimilated to עַד); וְעַל אַחֲרֵין [cf. אַחֲרֵין]). ועד אחרין "and at last" 4:5 (read perh. וְעַל אַחֲרֵין [cf. אַחֲרֵין]).

(2) עַד & עַד דִּי , conj.: **until.** עַד־מִנִּי טַעְמָא יִתְּשָׂם "until the decree is issued by me" Ezra 4:21; עַד־טַעְמָא לְדָרְיָוֶשׁ יְהָךְ וֶאֱדַיִן יְתִיבוּן נִשְׁתְּוָנָא "until the report should go to Darius, and then they return an answering letter" Ezra 5:5 (cf. הָךְ); עד אהך אנה "until I come" *Sefire III* 6; עד ימטא מצרין "until he arrives in Egypt" *AD* 6:5; וְעִם־חֵיוַת בָּרָא חֲלָקֵהּ עַד דִּי־שִׁבְעָה עִדָּנִין יַחְלְפוּן עֲלוֹהִי "and with the beasts of the field let his lot be until seven times will have passed over him" Dan 4:20 (BL 280k, n. 2); עַד דִּי־תִנְדַּע "until you realize" 4:22, 29: 2:9; עַד דִּי־יָדַע "until he knew" 5:21: 4:30; 7:22; עד זי שזבוני "until they rescued me" *AP* 38:5; עד זי . . . קרבתך קדם סנחאריב מלכא "until . . . I brought you before Sennacherib, the king" *Ah.* 49-50. -- עַד דִּי : **when.** לָא־מְטוֹ לְאַרְעִית גֻּבָּא עַד דִּי־שְׁלִטוּ בְהוֹן אַרְיָוָתָא "they did not reach the bottom of the den, when the lions overpowered them" Dan 6:25; חָזֵה הֲוֵית עַד דִּי "you were looking when a stone was cut loose" 2:34: 7:4, 9 (see חֲזָה no. 1). -- עד זי, זי עד, עַד (cf. דִּי III 1, 5, 6 & כְּדִי no. 4): **that, so that.** הן כן עבדו עד זי אגורא זך יתבנה "if they do so that that temple be rebuilt" *AP* 30:27; זי עד מנדת בגיא אלך יהנפק ויהיתה עלי "(instruct my officer) that he collect the rent on those domains and bring (it) to me" *AD* 10:3; עד מנדת [בגיא זילי יהי]תה עלי "that [he br]ing the rent of [my domains] to me" *AD* 11:3; עד כולא בקושטא תחוינני "that you truthfully make known to me everything" *1QapGen* 2:5. [Hebr. עַד]. †

עֲדָה*, 3 sg. f. עֲדָת (BL 154l); impf. 3 sf. m. יְעָדֵּה, 3 sg. f. תֵּעְדֵּא ; impv. sg. m. עֲדִי (*'ădî): **go away, depart, perish.** אזל וְעֵדִי לָךְ מִן כֹּל מְדִינַת מִצְרֵין "go, depart from all the provinces of Egypt" *1QapGen* 20:27-28; מַלְכוּתָךְ עֲדָת מִנָּךְ "your kingship has departed from you" Dan 4:28; שָׁלְטָן עָלַם דִּי־לָא יֶעְדֵּה "an everlasting kingdom that shall not perish" 7:14; כְּדָת־מָדַי וּפָרַס דִּי־לָא תֵעְדֵּא "according to the law of the Medes and the Persians, which does not perish" 6:9, 13; וְרֵיחַ־נוּר לָא עֲדָת בְּהוֹן "and no odor of fire had come on them" 3:27 (v.l. [ ] עד]ה בהון[, as read in *1QDanᵇ [1Q72]* 2:1; or should one read: לָא עַד בְּהוֹן "was no longer on them"?). -- **Haph.,** 1 sg. העדת & העדית , 3 pl. m. הֶעְדִּיו (*BHS* Dan 7:12) & הֶעְדִּיו (*BHS* Dan 5:20, BL 128f); impf. 3 pl. m. יְהַעְדּוֹן (BL 158n); juss. 2 sg. תהעדי , 3 pl. m. יהעדו ; infin. העדיה , w. suff. אעדיותכי ; ptc. sg. m. מְהַעְדֵּה : **take away, remove, destroy.** וְהוּא . . . מְהַעְדֵּה מַלְכִין "and He . . . removes kings" Dan 2:21; וִיקָרָה הֶעְדִּיו מִנֵּהּ "and his glory was taken away from him," lit., "they took away" 5:20; 7:12, 26; אל תהעדי מנך "remove not wisdom from yourself " *Aḥ.* 146; הן העדת המו חכמתא "remove not wisdom from yourself " *Aḥ.* 146; מנה "if I remove them (the goods) from her" *AP* 15:35-36; להעדיה ביתא זנה מן קדמיכי "to take this house away from you" *BMAP* 10:13; והעדית חטאיך קדמוהי "and I removed your offenses before him (the king)" *Aḥ.* 50; אגורא זי . . . ביב בירתא יהעדו מן תמה "let them remove from there the temple which . . . is in the fortress Yeb" *AP* 30:6; לאעדיותכי [יב]על]ון[מני "they [will] seek to take you away from me" *1QapGen* 19:21. [Hebr. עָדָה]. †

עִדָּן (< *'id-ān*, root *w'd*, BL 56c, 196z), emph. עִדָּנָא, pl. עִדָּנִין , emph. עִדָּנַיָּא , m.: **time, moment; space** (of time), **delay** (cf. זְמָן). בכל עדן "at all times" *AP* 30:2, 3 + ; בזך עדנא אשתמיע "at that time it was heard" *Aḥ.* 70; [מ]ן זך ע[דנ]א ועד ז[נה] "[fr]om that t[im]e until t[his]" *AP* 31:20; לעד[ן א]חרן וליומן אחרנן "after [s]ome ti[me] and many days later" *Aḥ.* 49-50; כזי שגיאן [ע]דן יהוה נפלג המו עלין "when it is time, we shall divide them (the

slaves) between us" *AP* 28:13-14; [עדן הוה . . . למע[בד "it is time
. . . to do (the repairs)" *AP* 26:3, 9; בְּעִדָּנָא דִּי־תִשְׁמְעוּן קָל קַרְנָא "at
the moment that you hear the sound of the horn" Dan 3:5, 15 (cf.
בַּהּ זִמְנָא כְּדִי שָׁמְעִין דִּי II 6 = "at the time [the people] heard" 3:7);
קדמת זנה בעדן זי זא באישתא עביד לן "before this, at the time when
this evil (f.) was done (m.) to us" *AP* 30:17-18; וְאַרְכָה בְחַיִּין יְהִיבַת
לְהוֹן עַד־זְמַן וְעִדָּן "and a prolongation in life was granted to them
(the beasts) for a season and a time" Dan 7:12; עִדָּנָא אַנְתּוּן זָבְנִין
"you are buying time," i.e., seeking a delay 2:8; עַד דִּי עִדָּנָא יִשְׁתַּנֵּא
"until the time changes" 2:9; וְהוּא מְהַשְׁנֵא עִדָּנַיָּא וְזִמְנַיָּא "and He
changes times and seasons" 2:21; שִׁבְעָה עִדָּנִין יַחְלְפוּן עֲלוֹהִי "let
seven times (i.e., years) pass over him" 4:13, 20: 4:22, 29;
עַד־עִדָּן וְעִדָּנִין וּפְלַג עִדָּן "for a time, two times, and a half-time" 7:25
(BL 306l), i.e., for 3½ years (cf. 8:14; 9:27). [Hebr. עֵת, מוֹעֵד]. †

עוֹד , עַד , adv.: **still, yet.** עוֹד מִלְּתָא בְּפֻם מַלְכָּא "(while) the
word was still in the king's mouth" Dan 4:28. --. לָא עוֹד : (1)
not yet. לא עד נפלג עלין "we do not yet divide between us" *AP*
28:13; הן מיתת ולעד שלמת "if I die and have not yet paid back (the
money)" *BMAP* 11:8; לעד אשכח אש למושרתהם לכן "I have not yet
found anyone to send them to you" *Hermopolis* 2:12-13 (Aph.
infin., see *LFAA* 51g); ולא יתכלא עוד "and it will not yet be
finished" *2QNJ (2Q24)* 8:6; cf. וְלָא מְטוֹ לְאַרְעִית גֻּבָּא "and they did
not yet reach the bottom of the den" Dan 6:25. -- (2) **no longer.**
כל שקר לא עוד ישתכח "no longer will any deceit be found" *Sem* 5
(1955) 38 (line 2); עוד טעם לא עד יהוי להן תנה "they shall have no
further authority here" *AP* 34:7; וְרֵיחַ־נּוּר לָא עֲדָת בְּהוֹן "and no
odor of fire had come on them" Dan 3:27 (or should one read: לָא
עֹד בְּהוֹן "was no longer on them"?), see עֲדָה ; cf. שב אנה לא אכהל
למפלח בבב היכלא "I am an old man; I shall no (longer) be able to
serve in the court of the palace" *Aḥ.* 17. [Hebr. the same]. [1]

248

עֲוָיָה * (*qatāl-at*, BL 187f), pl. w. suff. עֲוָיָתָךְ : **iniquity.**
חֲטָיָךְ . . . פְּרֻק וַעֲוָיָתָךְ "break off . . . your sins and your iniquities"
Dan 4:24. [Hebr. עָוֹן]. [1]

עוֹף ('*awp*, BL 182a), sg. often collect.: **birds** (cf. צִפַּר
"bird"). עוֹף שְׁמַיָּא "birds of the heavens" Dan 2:38. -- Gen. of
quality: כְּנְמַר וְלַהּ גַּפִּין אַרְבַּע דִּי־עוֹף "like a leopard, and it had four
wings of a bird" 7:6; לבעירא ולחיותא לעופא "to the cattle and to the
animals, to the birds" *1QapGen (1Q20)* 6:26. [Hebr. the same]. †

עוּר (*qūl*, BL 180l), only sg.: **chaff, straw.** וַהֲווֹ כְּעוּר
מִן־אִדְּרֵי־קַיְט "and they (the metals) became like the chaff of the
summer threshing-floors" Dan 2:35 (cf. BL 316h). [1]

עֵז *, ענז (Akk. *enzu, ezzu*), pl. עִזִּין , f.: **she-goat.** קן תור
ענז מקלו [ל]א יתעבד תמה "sheep, oxen, goats are not offered there
as a burnt-sacrifice" *AP* 33:10; ענה נמרא ואמר לענזא אתי ואכסנכי
משכי "the leopard spoke up, saying to the goat, 'Come, and I
shall cover you with my hide" *Aḥ.* 118; וּצְפִירֵי עִזִּין לְחַטָּיָא "and
he-goats for sins" Ezra 6:17. [Hebr. the same]. [1]

עִזְקָה * (< Akk. *izqātu*), cst. עִזְקַת (in v.l.), w. suff. עִזְקְתֵהּ ;
cst. pl. עִזְקָת : **signet ring.** חַתְמַהּ מַלְכָּא בְּעִזְקְתֵהּ וּבְעִזְקָת רַבְרְבָנוֹהִי "the
king sealed it with his signet ring and with the signets of his
nobles" Dan 6:18; [צב]ית עזקתה זי שנחאריב "(Aḥiqar was) the
[be]arer of the signet ring of Sennacherib" *Aḥ.* 3. [1]

▲ עֶזְרָא : **Ezra,** the priest. לְעֶזְרָא כָהֲנָא "to Ezra, the priest"
Ezra 7:12, 21: 7:25. [Hebr. the same]. †

▲ עֲזַרְיָה : **Azariah,** companion of Daniel. לַחֲנַנְיָה מִישָׁאֵל
וַעֲזַרְיָה חַבְרוֹהִי "(Daniel made the matter known) to Hananiah,
Mishael, and Azariah, his companions" Dan 2:17. [1]

עֵטָה (*qil-at,* BL 179g, root *y't*), f.: **counsel, advice.** אנה אמר לכם עטתא [זילי] ועטה טבה הי "I give you [my] advice, and it is good advice" *Aḥ.* 57; עטתי יבעה "he will desire my counsel" *Aḥ.* 53; בעל עטתא טבתא "giver of good advice," lit., "master of" *Aḥ.* 42; על עטתה ומלוהי חיל [אתו]ר כלא הוו "on his counsel and his words all the army of [Assy]ria depended" *Aḥ.* 60-61; דָּנִיֵּאל הֲתִיב עֵטָה וּטְעֵם לְאַרְיוֹךְ "Daniel replied to Arioch with prudent advice" Dan 2:14. [Hebr. עֵצָה]. [1]

עַיִן (*'ayn,* BL 182z), cst. עֵין ; pl. (also for du., BL 306m) עַיְנִין ; du. עַיְנִין, cst. עַיְנֵי, w. suff. עַיְנַי (BL 203d, e), f.: **eye.** עַיְנַי לִשְׁמַיָּא נִטְלֵת "I lifted my eyes to heaven" Dan 4:31; עַיְנִין כְּעַיְנֵי אֲנָשָׁא "(in the little horn there were) eyes like the eyes of a human being" Dan 7:8: 7:20 (read perh. עַיְנִין, BL 306m); עֵין אֱלָהֲהֹם הֲוָת עַל־שָׂבֵי יְהוּדָיֵא "the eye of their God was on the Jewish elders" Ezra 5:5 (cf. חֲזָה); מה טב בעיני אעבד להם "whatever is good in my sight, I will do for them" *Sefire III* 3; זי יעבד לעינוהי "what he will do in his presence," lit., "for his eyes" *AP* 41:7; עיני זי נטלת עליך ולבבי זי יהבת לך בחכמה מאסת "my eyes, which I have lifted up to you, and my mind, which I have given to you in wisdom, you have despised" *Aḥ.* 169-70. [Hebr. the same]. †

עִיר , pl. עִירִין , m.: **Watcher,** a sort of guardian angel. עִיר וְקַדִּישׁ מִן־שְׁמַיָּא נָחִת "a Watcher, a Holy One, came down from heaven" Dan 4:10: 4:20 (cf. BL 324h); בִּגְזֵרַת עִירִין פִּתְגָמָא וּמֵאמַר קַדִּישִׁין שְׁאֵלְתָא "the sentence is by the decree of the Watchers, and the question by the word of the Holy Ones" 4:14; די מן עירין הריאתא ומן קדישין זרעא "that the conception was from Watchers or the seed from Holy Ones" *1QapGen* 2:1; ולא מן כול עירין ולא מן כול בני ש[מין] "and (the conception is) not from any of the Watchers or from any of the sons of hea[ven]" *1QapGen* 2:16. [Hebr. עוּר , ptc. עֵר "watching"]. †

עַל verb-form: see עלל .

עַל prep., w. suff. (BL 260b, c) sg. עֲלֵי‎, עֲלָיִךְ k. & עֲלָךְ‎
q., עֲלֹוהִי & עֲלֹהִי‎ , עֲלָיַהּ k. & עֲלַהּ (BL 49e, 79s); pl. , & עֲלֵיהֹון‎
עֲלֵיהֹם‎ , עֲלֵינָא : (1) **above.** -- (a) **above, in, on, upon** a place (=
בְּ): חֶלְמָךְ וְחֶזְוֵי רֵאשָׁךְ עַל־מִשְׁכְּבָךְ דְּנָה הוּא "your dream and the visions
of your head upon your bed are these" Dan 2:28 (cf. BL 316j):
2:29; 4:2, 7, 10; 7:1; לָא־אִיתַי אֱנָשׁ עַל־יַבֶּשְׁתָּא "there is not a man
on the dry land" 2:10; וכל זי איתי לה על אנפי ארעא "and all that he
has on the face of the earth" AP 15:19; שלו על אשרכם "stay
quietly in your place" Sefire III 5; ק תוי על אפי ארקה ס[י "may
TWY [come] up on the face of its land" Sefire I A 27-28;
עַל־הֵיכַל מַלְכוּתָא . . . מְהַלֵּךְ הֲוָה "(the king) was walking . . . on the
(roof of the) royal palace" Dan 4:26; אֶבֶן חֲדָה . . . שֻׂמַת עַל־פֻּם גֻּבָּא
"a stone . . . was laid upon the mouth of the den" 6:18; תְּקֻרַב הִמֹּו‎
עַל־מִדְבְּחָה "you shall offer them on the altar" Ezra 7:17; וּבֵית‎
אֱלָהָא יִתְבְּנֵא עַל־אַתְרֵהּ "and let God's house be rebuilt on its (former) site" 5:15: 6:7; עַל־גִּירָא דִּי־כְתַל הֵיכְלָא . . . וְכָתְבָן "and
(fingers) were writing on the plaster of the wall of the palace"
Dan 5:5; על ספר אנתותכי "on the document of your (f) marriage"
BMAP 10:9-10 (cf. בספרא 10:15); נכסיא זי על ספר אנתותכי "the
goods that are (mentioned) in the document of your marriage"
AP 35:4-5; אמתה זי שניתה על ידה בימן "his handmaiden on whose
hand is a mark, on the right" BMAP 5:3; זְקִיף יִתְמְחֵא עֲלֹהִי "he
shall be impaled upon it" Ezra 6:11; לָא הִשְׁתְּכַחַת עֲלֹוהִי "no (fault)
was found in him" Dan 6:5; נחשיא זי יהבו על תמריא "bronze bands
which they put on the date-palms" AP 81:111. -- **in** time: על
אחרן "later, at last" (cf. אַחַר). -- (b) **above, in, on**, of bodily
members: לַהּ גַּפִּין אַרְבַּע דִּי־עֹוף עַל־גַּבַּיַהּ "it (the beast) had four
wings of a bird on its back" Dan 7:6 (עַל־גַּבַּהּ k., עַל־גַּבֵּיהּ q.); זי
יהבת על יד[ן] "which you delivered to u[s]," lit., "into our hand"
AP 3:14; וְהַמְונְכָא דִי־דַהֲבָא עַל־צַוְּארֵהּ "and a chain of gold on his
neck" Dan 5:7, 29 (BL 331s): 5:16; לבשא זי עליך "the garment
that is on you" El. Ostr. 4-5 (RHR 130 [1945] 20); נְפַל עַל־אַנְפֹּוהִי‎
"(the king) fell upon his face" Dan 2:46; הוּא בָרֵךְ עַל־בִּרְכֹוהִי‎

עַל

"(Daniel) knelt upon his knees" 6:11; וְעַל־רַגְלַיִן כְּאֱנָשׁ הֳקִימַת "(the beast) was made to stand on two feet like a man" 7:4; וּמְחָת לְצַלְמָא עַל־רַגְלוֹהִי "and (the stone) struck the statue on its feet" 2:34; יִמְחָא עַל אפיה "one strikes (her) on her face" *Sefire I* A 42. -- cf. דִּי הִתְרְחִצוּ עֲלוֹהִי "who trusted in Him" Dan 3:28; אל תתכלי על משלמת "do not trust in Mishlemet" *El. Ostr.* 4 (*AH* I/1 12). -- (c) **over,** of authority: מַלְכִין תַּקִּיפִין הֲוֹו עַל־יְרוּשְׁלֶם "mighty kings have been over Jerusalem" Ezra 4:20; מַנִּי עַל עֲבִידְתָּא דִּי מְדִינַת בָּבֶל "(the king) appointed over the affairs of the province of Babylon" Dan 2:49: 3:12; עַל־עֲבִידַת <בֵּית> <בֵּית> אֱלָהָא . . . הֲקִימוּ "they set up . . . over the service of <the house of> God" Ezra 6:18 (add w. Gk., Syr. בֵּית, hapl.); הֲקֵים עַל־מַלְכוּתָא "(Darius) set up over the kingdom" Dan 6:2: 6:4; הַשְׁלְטֵהּ עַל כָּל־מְדִינַת בָּבֶל "(the king) made him (Daniel) ruler over all the province of Babylon" 2:48: 4:14; 5:21; עַל־מַלְכוּתִי הָתְקְנַת "I was set up over my kingdom" Dan 4:33 (read rather הָתְקְנֵת); וגבר אחרן לא שליט עליכי ועל יהישמע "and no other man shall have authority over you or over Yeho-yishma" *BMAP* 5:9-10 (cf. לא שליט בכי 5:6). -- (d) **upon, against,** used of a calamity: כֹּלָּא מְטָא עַל־נְבוּכַדְנֶצַּר מַלְכָּא "all of that came upon King Nebuchadnezzar" Dan 4:25; גְּזֵרַת עִלָּיָא . . . מְטָת עַל־מָרְאִי "a decree of the Most High . . .has come upon my lord" 4:21; יסך על ארפד [אבני ב]רד "may he (the god Hadad) shower upon Arpad [ha]il-[stones]" *Sefire I* A 26-27; מקריא על אלהן מטא עלי בדינא "the appeal to our god has been laid upon me by the court" *AP* 7:6-7; דִּי־לְמָה לֶהֱוֵא קְצַף עַל־מַלְכוּת מַלְכָּא "lest (His) wrath be against the realm of the king" Ezra 7:23; הֲלָךְ לָא שַׁלִּיט לְמִרְמֵא עֲלֵיהֹם "it shall not be lawful to impose a toll on them" 7:24; שִׁבְעָה עִדָּנִין יַחְלְפוּן עֲלוֹהִי "let seven times (calamitous years) pass over him" Dan 4:13, 20: 4:23, 29; 2 איתי לכי עלי כסף ש "you have a claim on me for the sum of 2 sh(ekels)" *AP* 35:3; עמרה זי על מכי שלחי לי "send me the wool that (is owed) to Makki" *Hermopolis* 2:9.

252

עַל

(2) **to, toward, on,** of direction. -- (a) **to** a person, after a verb of motion (cf. לְ = "to" a place): עַל עַל־אַרְיוֹךְ "(Daniel) went in to Arioch" Dan 2:24 (BL 351d); מַנְדְּעִי עֲלַי יְתוּב "my reason returned to me" 4:31: 4:33; הַרְגִּשׁוּ עַל־מַלְכָּא "(all the ministers) put pressure on the king" 6:7, 16; קִרְבֵת עַל־חַד מִן־קָאֲמַיָּא "I drew near to one of those standing (there)" 7:16; אֲזַלוּ . . . לִירוּשְׁלֶם עַל־יְהוּדָיֵא "they went . . . to the Jews at Jerusalem" Ezra 4:23; אֲתָה ארשם אזל על מלכא "Arsames went to the king" AP 27:2-3; עֲלֵיהוֹן תִּתְּנַי אנה אתית עליך "Tattenai came to them" Ezra 5:3; בביתך בסון "I came to you in your house in Syene" BMAP 11:2-3; כזי אגרתא זא [ת]מטא עליך "when this letter [r]eaches you" AP 42:6-7; [מ]טאת ספינתא תנה עלין "the boat has [rea]ched us here" BMAP 13:7; כסף . . . על עלי "I have received . . . the money," lit., "it has entered to me" AP 15:15; ינתן לכי ועל בניכי אביגדן "he shall pay a fine to you and to your children" BMAP 10:13-14; פתכרן אחרנן . . . יהיתו עלי "let them bring to me . . . other sculptures" AD 9:3; נכסיא זי לקחו אתבו אם על מריהם "the property that they have taken they have returned, indeed, to the owners of it" AP 34:6; פתפא זנה הבו להם מן פקיד על פקיד "give them this provision (each of you) from officer to officer" AD 6:5; מקריא על אלהן מטא עלי בדינא . . . אקרא לך על חרמביתאל "appeal to our god has been laid on me by the court . . . that I should challenge you by Ḥerembethel (the god)" AP 7:6-7; חזי אגרת ארשם זי היתיו על פסמשך "look at the letter of Arsames that they have brought to Psamshek" AD 12:4; אִגְּרָא דִּי שְׁלַחוּ עֲלוֹהִי "a letter that they sent to him" Ezra 4:11: 4:17, 18; 5:6, 7, 17. -- שְׁלַח w. an ellipsis of the obj., **wrote, sent word:** פסמשך זילי שלח עלי פקידא "Psamshek, my officer, wrote to me" AD 4:1; ישתלח על ארתון[ת] "let word be sent to Artawont" AD 3:5; שלחי על תבי ותושר לכי עמר "write to Tabbi, and have her send wool to you" Hermopolis 2:6-7. -- In the address of a letter: עַל־אַרְתַּחְשַׁשְׂתְּא מַלְכָּא עֲבָדָיְךָ "To Artaxerxes, the King, your servants" Ezra 4:11; על מראי פסמי עבדך מכבנת "To my lord, Pasmi, your servant, Makkibanit" Hermopolis 3:1;

253

עַל

מן ארשם על ארמפי "From Arsames, to Armapi" *AD* 4:1 (cf. אֵל מראן בגוהי פחת יהוד עבדיך ידניה וכנותה "To our lord, Bagohi, governor of Judah, your servants, Jedaniah and his colleagues" *AP* 30:1; אל אחתי רעיה מן אחכי מכבנת "To my sister, Ra'yah, from your brother, Makkibanit" *Hermopolis* 1:1.). -- (b) **to, for, on, upon,** w. obj. of attention, etc.: דִּי עֲלָךְ טְעֵם וְעַל־אֱסָרָא . . . לָא־שָׂם עֲלָיךְ רְשַׁמְתָּ "(Daniel) has paid no heed to you . . . or to the interdict that you have signed" Dan 6:14: 3:12; עַל־דָּנִיֵּאל שָׂם בָּל לְשֵׁיזָבוּתֵהּ "about Daniel, (the king) set his mind to deliver him" 6:15; אתעשת על אגורא זך למבנה "give thought to that temple to rebuild (it)" *AP* 30:23; חזו עליהם מה צבו "look after them as to what they have desired" *AP* 38:5-6; הוי חזית על תשי ועל ברה "be sollicitous for Tishi and for his son" *Hermopolis* 1:11-12; הוי חזית על ינקיא אלכי "be sollicitous for those small children" *Hermopolis* 7:2-3; עיני זי נטלת עליך "my eyes, which I have lifted up to you" *Aḥ.* 169; הן עיני אלהן על א[נשא] "if the eyes of (the) gods are on man[kind]" *Aḥ.* 124; עֵין אֱלָהֲהֹם הֲוָת עַל־שָׂבֵי יְהוּדָיֵא "the eye of their God was upon the elders of the Jews" Ezra 5:5; על עטתה ומלוהי חיל [אתו]ר כלא "on his advice and his words all the army of [Assyr]ia (depended)" *Aḥ.* 60-61; מלל על פטנפתחתף "he spoke about P." *AP* 69:2; הִתְנַבִּי . . . עַל־יְהוּדָיֵא . . . בְּשֻׁם אֱלָהּ יִשְׂרָאֵל עֲלֵיהוֹן "he prophesied . . . to the Jews . . . in the name of the God of Israel for them" Ezra 5:1 (cf. 5:5, BL 316j); הן יסק על לבבך ותשא על שפתיך להמתתי "if it should come into your mind and you express (it) with your lips to kill me" *Sefire III* 14-15. -- (c) **to,** expressing addition: ויהוספון על עקיא . . . ועל פתיא ועביא צבען תרין "and (the carpenters) shall add to the planks . . . and to the breadth and thickness two fingers (measurement)" *AP* 26:18; ולא תהוספון על ביתא זילי "and (if) you do not add (them) to my estate" *AD* 7:9; ועבד על ביתא זילי "and he made (them) over to my estate" *AD* 7:3.

(3) **against.** וּצְלֵם אַנְפּוֹהִי אֶשְׁתַּנִּי עַל שַׁדְרַךְ "and the expression of his face was changed against Shadrach" Dan 3:19; דִּי יֵאמַר שָׁלֻה עַל אֱלָהֲהוֹן "who utters nonsense against their God" 3:29;

254

עַל

עַל מָרֵא שְׁמַיָּא הִתְרוֹמַמְתָּ "you have exalted yourself against the God of Heaven" 5:23: Ezra 4:19; כְּתַבוּ אִגְּרָה חֲדָה עַל־יְרוּשְׁלֶם לְאַרְתַּחְשַׁשְׁתְּא "they wrote a letter to Artaxerxes against Jerusalem" 4:8; חנום הו "(the god) Khnum is against us" *AP* 38:7; [והן ת]עבד מרמת עלין "[if you com]mit treachery against me" *Sefire III* 22; זי קבלת עלי "about which you lodged a complaint against me" *BMAP* 1:3-4; זי ינפק עליך ספר חדת ועתיק בשם ביתא זנה "whoever will produce a document, new or old, with mention of this house" *BMAP* 12:29.

(4) **concerning, about.** שְׁמְעֵת עֲלָיִךְ "I have heard about you" Dan 5:14, 16; הַכְרִזוּ עֲלוֹהִי "they proclaimed concerning him (Daniel)" 5:29; עַל־אֱסָר מַלְכָּא . . . קְרִבוּ וְאָמְרִין "they drew near and spoke . . . about the king's interdict" 6:13; שְׁלִיחַ לְבַקָּרָה עַל־יְהוּד וְלִירוּשְׁלֶם "(you) have been sent to make an investigation about Judah and Jerusalem" Ezra 7:14; וּרְעוּת מַלְכָּא עַל־דְּנָה יִשְׁלַח עֲלֶינָא "and let the king send us his decision concerning this" 5:17: Dan 7:16; עַל־רָזָה דְּנָה . . . וְרַחֲמִין לְמִבְעֵא "to seek (God's) mercy . . . concerning this mystery" 2:18; וּזְהִירִין הֱווֹ שָׁלוּ לְמֶעְבַּד עַל־דְּנָה "and take care not to be negligent about this matter," lit., "to commit negligence" Ezra 4:22; על זהב על זנה שלחן הודען "as for (the) gold, we have sent (word and) given instructions concerning this (matter)" *AP* 30:28-29; אף איתי ספר . . . זי . . . כתב לי על ארקא זך "there is also a document . . . which . . . he wrote for me about this land" *AP* 8:23-24; לה שאל על חרוץ "he did not ask about Ḥaruṣ" *Hermopolis* 1:6; תשתאל על זנה "you will be interrogated about this (matter)" *AD* 12:8; זי ימאתי לי עליהם "concerning which you (f.) have sworn to me" *AP* 14:8; טעונך לי מומאה למומא ביהו על דבר ארקא זך "they imposed on you an oath to me, to swear by Yaho about the matter of this land" *AP* 6:6-7; ושלח אגרה על דבר כן "and he sent a letter about it" *AP* 40:3; [אנה רשיתך] עדבר נונין "[I sued you] about the matter of fish" *AP* 45:3 (על דבר = עדבר). -- Conj. : על זי פסמש[ך] אמר לא משתמ[ע/ע]ן לי "about what Psamshek said, '(the troop) does not obe[y] me'" *AD* 4:1a. *עַל דִּי (cf. דִּי III 3):

-- Adv. עֲלָא* : = "in this matter": הן רשינך דינא עלא "if we move the court against you in this matter" *AP* 28:9 (cf. *DISO* 211₁).

(5) **because of, on account of.** עַל־דְּנָה קִרְיְתָא דָךְ הָחָרְבַת "because of this that city was laid waste" Ezra 4:15: 6:11; עַל־מָה דָתָא מְהַחְצְפָה מִן־קֳדָם מַלְכָּא "on account of what is the decree from the king (so) severe?" Dan 2:15; זי השכחו גניב ... אסרני על דבר אבן ביד רכליא "he locked me up because of the stone . . . , which they found stolen in the hands of dealers" *AP* 38:3-4; אל יח[ון]הי על א[מ]ריך "let not (the king) display it (his wrath) because of your w[o]rds" *Aḥ.* 102; לבי . . . משתני על עולימא דנא "my mind wavered because of this child" *1QapGen* 2:2; בכת שרי על מלי "Sarai wept on account of my words" *1QapGen* 19:21; על כן יקראון "therefore they call" *Aḥ.* 117. -- Conj.: לָהֵן עַל־דִּבְרַת דִּי פִשְׁרָא לְמַלְכָּא יְהוֹדְעוּן "but in order that the interpretation may be made known to the king," lit., "they may make known" Dan 2:30; על זי החיתך "that I had kept you alive" *Aḥ.* 51.

(6) **for.** הַקְרִבוּ . . . תּוֹרִין מְאָה . . . עַל־כָּל־יִשְׂרָאֵל "they offered . . . one hundred bulls . . . for all Israel" Ezra 6:17; פלגן עלין עבדיה "we divided the slaves for ourselves" *AP* 28:3; ונצלה עליך בכל עדן "and we shall pray for you at all times" *AP* 30:26; מְצַלַּיִן לְחַיֵּי מַלְכָּא "they were praying for the life of the king" Ezra 6:10; אודית תמן קודם אלהא על כול נכסיא "I gave thanks there to God for all the flocks (He had given me)" *1QapGen* 21:3.

(7) **according to the opinion/judgment of** (cf. בְּעֵינֵי). מִלְכִּי יִשְׁפַּר עֲלָיךְ "may my advice be good in your opinion," i.e., please you Dan 4:24; מָה דִי עֲלָיךְ . . . יֵיטַב "whatever in your judgment . . . will be good" Ezra 7:18; הֵן עַל־מַלְכָּא טָב "if it seems good in the king's judgment" 5:17 (BL 328h); הן על מראן טב "if it seems good in the opinion of our lord" *AP* 30:23; הן עליך כות "if it so seems good in your opinion" *AD* 5:8; ועטתא זנה טיבת על כנותה "and this advice was good in the judgment of his colleagues" *Aḥ.* 67. -- Cf. הן איתי כסף הבי על פמי "if there is money, give (it) according to my instruction," lit., "to my mouth" *Padua II* A 4.

(8) **in, on, at,** expressing affect or emotion: זִיוֹהִי שְׁנֵין
עֲלוֹהִי "his color changed on him" Dan 5:9; 7:28; לבי עלי משתני
"my mind in me wavered" *1QapGen* 2:2; די אשתני אנפי עלי "that
my expression had changed in me" *1QapGen* 2:12; [למא צלם]
שנא אנפיך כדנא עליך "[Why is the expression of] your face so
changed in you?" *1QapGen* 2:16-17; שְׁנַתֵּהּ נַדַּת עֲלוֹהִי "his sleep
fled from him," lit., "his sleep in him" Dan 6:19; . . . אֱדַיִן מַלְכָּא
שַׂגִּיא בְּאֵשׁ עֲלוֹהִי "then the king . . . was much distressed at him"
6:15; . . . טָאֵב עֲלוֹהִי בֵּאדַיִן מַלְכָּא "then the king . . . was glad about
him" 6:24; באש עלי די די פרש לוט "there was grief in me that Lot
had parted" *1QapGen* 21:7.

(9) **above, over, more than.** הֲוָא מִתְנַצַּח עַל־סָרְכַיָּא "(Daniel) became distinguished above (all) the officials" Dan 6:4; אֲמַר
לְמֵזֵא לְאַתּוּנָא חַד־שִׁבְעָה עַל דִּי חֲזֵה לְמֵזְיֵהּ "(the king) ordered (them) to
heat the furnace seven times more than it was usual to heat it"
3:19; על כול נשין שופר שפרה "above all women she is beautiful
indeed" *1QapGen* 20:6-7.

עַל * (*'il;* root *'lī,* * *'lū,* but see BL 196d), noun: **upper
part, top;** adv. * עַל, עֵלָּא (*-ā* accus., BL 254o, *LFAA* 119i,
GBA §88): **above, over, upwards, to the top.** תדבק לשטר ביתי מן
ארעא ועד עלא "(the portico) will adjoin the side of my house from
the bottom to the top" *AP* 5:5; אנת שליט למבנה עלויה עד עלא "you
have the right to build above it upwards" *AP* 5:11; וירבה מלוהי
מסרסרן לעלא מנה "and he multiplies his words that fly upwards
away from him" *Aḥ.* 114; ועליא שפרהא לעלא מן כולהן "(in) her
beauty (Sarai) ranks high above all of them (other women)"
1QapGen 20:7 (cf. מן no. 8); וְעֵלָּא מִנְּהוֹן סָרְכִין תְּלָתָא "and over
them three officials" Dan 6:3; אחלפ[ת] [על]א מן י[מא] שמוקא "[I]
was conveyed high above the Red Sea" *4QEn^e (4Q206)* 1 xxvi
19-20; למנסק עלא ולמנחת "to go up above and to go down"
BMAP 6:13; יהבת לך כספא זילך זי מנעל כתיב "I have given you
your money, which is mentioned above" *BMAP* 11:8 (cf. מן no.

257

9); בתחתיה ומן עלא כוין פתיחן תמה "at the lower end (of the house) and above, open windows are there" *AP* 25:6; זבניא די מן עלא "the buyers who are (mentioned) above" *XHev/Se . . .* frg. d:12 (DJD 27. 127). -- Cf. עֲלָא * s.v. עַל no. 4. [1]

עֲלָה & עֲלָא (BL 181u), f.: **fault.** הֲווֹ בָעַיִן עִלָּה לְהַשְׁכָּחָה לְדָנִיֵּאל . . . . וְכָל־עִלָּה . . . . לָא־יָכְלִים לְהַשְׁכָּחָה "they were seeking to find a fault in Daniel . . . but they could not find . . . any fault" Dan 6:5: 6:6. †

עלה * & עלא (*'ălā'*) & עלוה (*'alwāh*? root: *'ly, 'lw*), pl. עֲלָוָן, emph. עלותא (*'alăwātā'*): **holocaust, burnt offering.** אָמְרִין לַעֲלָוָן לֶאֱלָהּ שְׁמַיָּא "lambs for burnt offerings to the God of Heaven" Ezra 6:9 (BL 315e); מנחה לבונה ועלוה "meal offering, incense, and holocaust" *AP* 31:21; 30:21; גבר זי יקרב לה עלוה ודבחן "a man who offers Him a holocaust and sacrifices" *AP* 31:27; 30:28; מחתא ולבונתא ועלותא יקרבון "they shall offer the meal offerings, incense, and holocausts" *AP* 30:25 (read rather מנחה ומנחתא); אקרבת עלוהי עלואן ומנחה "I offered on it holocausts and a meal offering" *1QapGen* 21:2; ואסקת עלוה[י] עלא ומנחא לאל עליון "I offered on i[t] a holocaust and a meal offering to God Most High" *1QapGen* 21:20. [Hebr. עוֹלָה]. [1]

עֲלָי * (*'ilāy;* root: *'ly,* *'lw,* but see BL 196d), emph. עִלָּיָא k. & עִלָּאָה q. (BL 51k); f. עֶלְיָה *, emph. עֶלָיְתָא, adj.: **high, lofty, superior.** עַבְדוֹהִי דִּי־אֱלָהָא עִלָּיָא "servants of God Most High" Dan 3:26: 3:32; 5:18, 21; וּלְעִלָּיָא בָּרְכֵת "and I (Nebuchadnezzar) blessed the Most High" 4:31: 7:25 + ; ועליא שפרהא לעלא מן כולהן "and (in) her beauty she ranks high above all of them (women)" *1QapGen* 20:7. -- As a noun: **upper part.** -- (1) עלי : ארם כלה . . . . כל עלי ארם ותחתה "(with) all Aram . . . all Upper-Aram and Lower(-Aram)" *Sefire I* A 5-6. -- (2) עליה : וישמו תחתיתה [לע]ליתה "may (the gods) make its lower part its

258

[up]per part" *Sefire I* C 23-24; בגיא זילי זי בעליתא ותחתיתא "my domains, which are in Upper (Egypt) and Lower"*AD* 5:5-6. -- Specifically: עליה : **upper part, north** (opp. תחתיה , "south," see *BMAP* pp. 77-78). מן מועה שמש למערב . . . ומן עליה לתחתיא "(the dimensions of the house) from east to west . . . and from north to south" *BMAP* 12:15-16; תחמי ביתא זך . . . לעליה לה בית שתבר "the boundaries of that house: . . . to the north of it, the house of Shatibar" *BMAP* 3:7-8; עליה לה חלקא זי לי "north of it, the portion that is mine" *BMAP* 4:9; דבקה לביתא זילי לזויתה זי לעליה "it adjoins my house at the corner that is to the north" *AP* 5:4. [Hebr. עֲלִי].

עֲלִי * (BL 197f), cst. עֲלִית *, w. suff. עֲלִיתֵהּ ; f.: **upper chamber.** כַּוִּין פְּתִיחָן לַהּ בְּעִלִּיתֵהּ נֶגֶד יְרוּשְׁלֶם "windows in his upper chamber opened towards Jerusalem" Dan 6:11. [Hebr. עֲלִיָּה].

עֶלְיוֹן (*'ilyān*, w. Hebr. vocal.), pl. עֶלְיוֹנִין : **Most High.** וִיקַבְּלוּן מַלְכוּתָא קַדִּישֵׁי עֶלְיוֹנִין "but the saints of the Most High shall receive the kingdom" Dan 7:18 (attract. of the pl., BL 202o, 305g): 7:22, 25, 27; אל עליון "God Most High" *1QapGen* 20:12, 16. Cf. קדם אל ועלין "(the treaty was concluded) in the presence of 'El and 'Elyan" *Sefire I* A 11. †

עלל (paradigm: *GBA*, pp. 73-74), 3 sg. m. עַל , 3 sg. f. עֲלַת q. & עַלְלַת k. (Dan 5:10, BL 54y, 144d, e), 1 sg. עלת , 3 pl עָלּוּ , 1 pl. עלנא ; impf. 3 sg. m. יעל (*yi''ul*), 2 sg. m. תנעל (*tin'ul*, cf. BL 57f, 50d), 3 pl. f. יעלן (*yi''ulān*); infin. מנעל (*min'al*), w. suff. מעלי (*mi''ălî*); ptc. pl. m. עָלְלִין k. & עָלִין q. (*'āllin*): **come/go in(to), enter.** עַל וּבְעָה מִן־מַלְכָּא "(Daniel) went in and begged the king" Dan 2:16: 4:4; 5:8; עם כל עלל בית מלך "with all who enter the royal palace" *Sefire I* A 6. -- W. prep. לְ of place: עַל לְבַיְתֵהּ "(Daniel) entered his house" 6:11; . . . מַלְכְּתָא לְבֵית מִשְׁתְּיָא עַלְלַת "the queen . . . went into the banquet hall" 5:10;

עלל

כזי כנבוזי על למצרין עלו לסון "they went into Syene" *AP* 16:6; עלנא לארע בני חם "when Cambyses came into Egypt" *AP* 30:13; לארע מצרין "we entered the land of the sons of Ham, the land of Egypt" *1QapGen* 19:13; בלילה מעלי לארע מצרין "in the night of my entering into the land of Egypt" *1QapGen* 19:14; כלאן די יעלן לגנון "brides who enter a bridal chamber" *1QapGen* 20:6. -- W. prep. בְּ of place: כחסן בביתך [לא] עלת "I did [not] enter your house by force" *AP* 7:8; עלו באגורא זך "they entered that temple" *AP* 30:9; בתיא זי עלו בהן ביב "the houses that they entered in Yeb" *AP* 34:6; לא שנציו למנעל בבירתא "they did not succeed in entering the fortress" *AD* 5:7. -- W. accus. of place: מן תמה תנפק ותנעל ביתא זנה "from there you shall go out and go into this house" *BMAP* 12:22. -- W. preps. עַל, קֳדָם : דָּנִיֵאל עַל עַל־אַרְיוֹךְ "Daniel went in to Arioch" Dan 2:24 (BL 351d); עלת על בתאנוש "I went to Bitenosh" *1QapGen* 2:3; על עליך "it (the sum of money) entered into you," i.e., you received it *AP* 15:5; עַל קֳדָמַי "(Daniel) entered my presence," lit., "before me" Dan 4:5.

Haph. 3 sg. m. הַנְעֵל (< *ha''il*, BL 167i), 3 sg. f. הנעלת (*han'ălat*); impv. sg. m. w. suff. הַעֵלְנִי (BL 57f, 166i), pl. m. הנעלו (*han'ălû*); infin. הֶעָלָה & הַנְעָלָה : **bring in, introduce.** הַעֵלְנִי קֳדָם מַלְכָּא "bring me in before the king" Dan 2:24; . . . אַרְיוֹךְ הַנְעֵל לְדָנִיֵּאל "Arioch . . . brought Daniel in" 2:25: 6:19; לְהַנְעָלָה קֳדָמַי לְכָל חַכִּימֵי בָבֶל "(I ordered them) to bring into my presence all the sages of Babylon" 4:3; קָרֵא מַלְכָּא . . . לְהֶעָלָה לְאָשְׁפַיָּא "the king called for (them) to introduce the enchanters" 5:7; בעו והנעלו "seek out and bring (them) into my court" *AD* 7:7; זילי בתרבצא "seek out and bring (them) into my court" *AD* 7:7; הנעלת לי יהוישמע אחתך לביתי תכונה "your sister, Yehoyishma, brought to me, to my house, a dowry" *BMAP* 7:5; הנעלת לי תמת בידה "Tamut has brought in to me in her hand" *BMAP* 2:4.

Hoph. (BL 57h, 167k) 3 sg. m. הֻעַל (*hu''al*), 3 pl. m. הֻעַלוּ (*BHS* Dan 5:15: wrongly הֶעַלוּ ; see *GBA* §164): **be brought in, be introduced.** הֻעַלוּ קֳדָמַי חַכִּימַיָּא "the sages were brought in before me" Dan 5:15: 5:13. -- **Hithaphal**: impf. 3

260

עלם

sg. m. יִתְאֵעַל (yit'a''al, GBA §99): כל די יתאעל "whoever will be introduced" Sem 5 (1955) 38 (line 4). †

עָלַם (qātal, BL 190x) abs. & cst., emph. עָלְמָא ; pl. עָלְמִין , emph. עָלְמַיָּא **remote time,** past or future. -- (1) indet.: אנתי . . . עד עלם . . . שליטה בה מן יומא זנה "you (f.) shall have authority over it from this day . . . for ever" BMAP 10:8 (opp.: עד אחרן "until another (time) BMAP 10:10). In a marriage contract: הי אנתתי ואנה בעלה מן יומא זנה ועד עלם "she is my wife, and I am her husband from this day forward" AP 15:4; BMAP 2:3-4; 7:4; 14:4; ורחקן מנה מן יומא זנה ועד עלמן "we have withdrawn from it from this day for ever" BMAP 3:11; מַלְכָּא לְעָלְמִין חֱיִי "O King, live forever!" Dan 2:4; 3:9; 5:10; 6:7, 22; הוּא אֱלָהָא חַיָּא וְקַיָּם לְעָלְמִין "He is a living God, enduring forever!" 6:27 (|| עַד סוֹפָא); מַלְכוּ דִּי לְעָלְמִין לָא תִתְחַבַּל "a kingdom that will never be destroyed" 2:44. -- (2) determ.: especially **eternity;** all remote ages, past or future. מְבָרַךְ מִן־עָלְמָא וְעַד־עָלְמָא "(God's name be) blessed for ever and ever!" Dan 2:20; וְיַחְסְנוּן מַלְכוּתָא עַד־עָלְמָא וְעַד עָלַם עָלְמַיָּא "(the saints) shall possess the kingdom for ever, for ever and ever" 7:18 (BL 312i); וְהִיא תְּקוּם לְעָלְמַיָּא "and it (the kingdom) shall stand forever" 2:44; לך ולזרעך אחריך אנתננה עד כול עלמיא "to you and to your descendants after you I shall give it (this land) for all ages" 1QapGen 21:14. -- (3) as gen. of quality (cf. דִּי I 2): = **very old, eternal, everlasting.** מִן־יוֹמָת עָלְמָא "(Jerusalem was rebellious) from very old days" Ezra 4:15, 19; מַלְכוּתֵהּ מַלְכוּת עָלַם "His kingdom will be an everlasting kingdom" Dan 3:33; 7:27: 4:31b; 7:14; וּלְחַי עָלְמָא שַׁבְּחֵת וְהַדְּרֵת "and I praised and honored Him who lives as eternal" 4:31; קודם מרה עלמא "before the eternal Lord" 1QapGen 0:18; קרית תמן בשם מרה עלמיא "there I called upon the name of the eternal Lord" 1QapGen 21:2; [ה]ן [i]f you go off to the house of eternity [before me]" Mur 20 1:7. [Hebr. עוֹלָם]. †

261

עלמי—עם

▲ עֵלְמָי * (BL 196d, 204l), emph, pl. עֵלְמָיֵא : **Elamite,**
inhabitant of the land of Elam, the capital of which was Susa.
שׁוּשַׁנְכָיֵא דָּהֲוֵא עֵלְמָיֵא "Susanites, i.e., Elamites" Ezra 4:9 (read
rather דִּי הוּא). †

עֲלַע * (dila', BL 26c, 186z), pl. עֲלְעִין , f.: **rib.** תְּלָת עֲלְעִין
בְּפֻמַּהּ "(the beast) had three ribs in its mouth" Dan 7:5; רכיך לשן
מ[לך] ועלעי תנין יתבר "smooth is the speech of a k[ing], but it
breaks the ribs of a dragon" Aḥ. 105-6. [Hebr. צֵלָע]. †

עַם ('amm, BL 180n), abs. & cst., emph. עַמָּא & עַמָּה ;
emph. pl. עַמְמַיָּא ('amamayyā', BL 68w, 221h), m.: **people.**
וּמַלְכוּתֵהּ לְעַם אָחֳרָן לָא תִשְׁתְּבִק "and its kingship shall not be left to
another people" Dan 2:44; כָּל־מֶלֶךְ וְעַם דִּי יִשְׁלַח יְדֵהּ לְהַשְׁנָיָה "every
king or people that will extend its hand to alter (this)" Ezra 6:12:
Dan 3:29; דִּי לֶהֱוֺן דָּאֲנִין לְכָל־עַמָּה "who will judge all the people"
Ezra 7:25; מִן־עַמָּה יִשְׂרָאֵל "from among the people (of) Israel"
7:13: 5:12; 7:16; יְהִיבַת לְעַם קַדִּישֵׁי עֶלְיוֺנִין "it shall be given to the
people of the saints of the Most High" Dan 7:27; כָּל עַמְמַיָּא אֻמַּיָּא
וְלִשָּׁנַיָּא "all the peoples, nations, and languages" 3:7, 31; 5:19;
6:26; 7:14: 3:4; in sg., 3:29; חד עמא זי בידי "one of the people
who are under me" Sefire III 5; מן חד עמיא זי בידי "from one of
the peoples who are under me" Sefire III 10; ולישמע עמה "and
(if) his people will not obey" Sefire II B 3. [Hebr. the same]. †

עם prep. (BL 260e), w. suff. עַמִּי, עִמָּךְ, עִמַּהּ, עִמְּהוֺן : **with.**
-- (1) to act together **with** someone: עִמָּךְ יְהָךְ "let him go with
you" Ezra 7:13; זי אזלן עמה מצרין "who are going with him to
Egypt" AD 6:4; תב בג בגו עם אנתתך "dwell on it with your wife" AP
9:6; זנה דושכרתא זי . . . [עבד]ו . . . המונית עם וידרנג "this is the
crime that . . . they [comit]ted . . . in concert with Widrang" AP
27:3-4; אבד עם נשי [ביתה] "he perished with the women of [his
house]" AD 8:4; כול די נפקו עמך "all that went forth with you"

262

עם

1QapGen 22:30; אכלו כחדא עמי ואשתיו עמי "they ate together with me and drank with me" *1QapGen* 21:21-22; די הוא יתב בסודם כחדא עמהון "who was dwelling in Sodom together with them" *1QapGen* 22:1. -- (2) to be **with** someone: עִם־חֵיוַת בָּרָא לֶהֱוֵה מְדֹרָךְ "with the beasts of the field shall your dwelling be" Dan 4:22: 4:29; עִם־חֵיוְתָא חֲלָקֵהּ "(let) his lot (be) with the beasts" 4:12: 4:20; דִּי מְדָרְהוֹן עִם־בִּשְׂרָא לָא אִיתוֹהִי "(the gods) whose dwelling is not with flesh" 2:11; וּנְהִירָא עִמֵּהּ שְׁרָא "the light resides with Him" 2:22; גבריא אלך תרין זי עמה "those two men who were with him" *Ah.* 56; אחד המו עמה הוו "he seized them, (and) they were with him" *AD* 5:7-8; [ואז[ל [לוט] בר אחי עמי "and [Lot], my brother's son, [we]nt with me" *1QapGen* 20:33-34; וכול נכסוהי עמה "and all his flocks (were) with him" *1Qap-Gen* 21:5-6; ולשמו עמי מאן כסף ונחש "they have not deposited with me a vessel of silver or bronze," i.e., in my grave, *Nerab* 6-7 (*KAI* 226); חכמא שגיא עמהא "(there is) much wisdom in her," lit., "with her" *1QapGen* 20:7. -- (3) to be **with** someone, **assist, help:** וְעִמְּהוֹן נְבִיַּאיָא דִּי־אֱלָהָא מְסָעֲדִין לְהוֹן "and with them (were) God's prophets, assisting them" Ezra 5:2; אנה עמך ואהוה לך סעד ותקף "I am with you, and I shall be to you support and strength" *1QapGen* 22:30-31; [אלה גבר]יא זי קדמן עמי הוו "[these are the me]m who were with me previously" *Bisitun* 74; להן זי אל עמה "except one with whom God is" *Ah.* 107; cf. [הן לא י]עמד איש עם אלהן "[if] one [s]tands [not] with (the) gods" *Ah.* 160. -- (4) to act **with** someone, **for, toward, against:** דָּנִיֵּאל עִם־מַלְכָּא מַלִּל "Daniel spoke with the king" Dan 6:22; עמי תמלל ולי תאמר "she spoke with me and said to me" *1QapGen* 2:13; קַרְנָא דִכֵּן עָבְדָה קְרָב עִם־קַדִּישִׁין "that horn was making war against (the) saints" Dan 7:21; אָתַיָּא וְתִמְהַיָּא דִּי עֲבַד עִמִּי אֱלָהָא "the signs and wonders that God has wrought toward me" 3:32; [ ] וצדק אנה עם "and I am faithful toward [ ]" *Barrakib* 5 (*KAI* 217); [למ]ה ישפטון עקן "[wh]y should wooden logs strive against fire?" *Ah.* 104; עם אשה אשתדרו עם וידרנג . . . עד שזבוני "they insisted with Widrang . . . until they set me free" *AP* 38:4-5; לְמָא דִי־תַעַבְדוּן עִם שָׁבֵי יְהוּדָיֵא אִלֵּךְ

לְמִבְנֵא בֵּית אֱלָהָא דֵךְ וּמִנְּכְסֵי מַלְכָּא "about what you are to do for these elders of the Jews for the rebuilding of that house of God, and from the royal property . . . " Ezra 6:8; ורשה לא איתי לך עמי בגו ליד דרתה די לי "and you (will) have no right against me within the courtyard that is mine" XHev/SeDeedSaleC (XHev/Se8a) 1:9-10. -- In an attributive sense (see BL 314a): עדי בר גאיה מלך כתך עם מתעאל "the treaty of Bar-Ga'yah, king of KTK, with Mati'el" Sefire I A 1; זי לא כתב על ספר אנתתכי עם ענני "which is not written in the document of your marriage with Anani" BMAP 10:7-8; אנת כל[ך] כבן עם זי נגע בך "you are al[l] thorns for the one who touches you" Aḥ. 166. -- (5) **with** a thing: לָא־לֶהֱוֹן דָּבְקִין דְּנָה עִם־דְּנָה פַּרְזְלָא לָא מִתְעָרַב עִם־חַסְפָּא . . . "they will not cling one to the other, (as) iron does not mix with clay" Dan 2:43; עם כול שפרא דן חכמא שגיא עמהא "with all this beauty there is much wisdom in her (Sarai)" 1QapGen 20:7; עם לבשי שמוני "(only) with my (burial-) clothes they laid me (to rest)" Nerab 7 (KAI 226); לִקְבֵהּ עִם־חֵיוְתָא שַׁוִּי "his mind was equated with (that of a) beast" Dan 5:21; עִם־עֲנָנֵי שְׁמַיָּא כְּבַר אֱנָשׁ אָתֵה הֲוָה "with the clouds of the heavens there came one like a son of man" 7:13 (LXX: ἐπὶ τῶν νεφελῶν); אתו לבירת יב עם תליהם "they came to the fortress of Yeb with their weapons" AP 30:8; מנדת בגיא אלך . . . יהיתה עלי עם מנדתא "let him bring the rent of those domains to me (along) with the rent . . . " AD 10:3; יאתה עם גנזא "let him come with the treasure" AD 10:5; ותנפק מנה עם שארת תכונתה ונכסיה "and (the divorced wife) shall forth from him with the rest of her dowry and her goods" BMAP 7:26-27. -- In a temporal sense: וְשָׁלְטָנֵהּ עִם־דָּר וְדָר "and His dominion (will last) with generation and generation" Dan 3:33; בְּחֶזְוֵי עִם־לֵילְיָא "in my vision of the night," lit., "with the night" 7:2 (BL 316k; cf. בחזוא די ליליא 1QapGen 21:8). -- (6) עם "with" often = **and:** כֹּל כְּסַף וּדְהַב דִּי תְהַשְׁכַּח . . . עִם הִתְנַדָּבוּת עַמָּה "all the silver and gold that you will find . . . and the free-will offerings of the people" Ezra 7:16; מצריא עם חילא אחרנן אתו לבירת יב "the Egyptians and the other soldiers came to the fortress of Yeb" AP 30:8; כלא זי עם שירית אשרנא ואחרנן זי תמה "all of it and the rest

of the furniture and other things that were there (they burned)"
AP 30:11; אנחנה עם נשין ובנין שקקן לבשן הוין "we and our wives
and our children have donned sack-cloth" *AP* 30:15; ארמפי עם
חילא זי לידה לא משתמען לי "Armapi and the troop that is under him
do not obey me" *AD* 4:1; יעבד פתכר סוסה עם רכבה "let him make
a sculpture of a horse and its rider" *AD* 9:2; לָא יְהֹבְדוּן דָּנִיֵּאל
וְחַבְרוֹהִי עִם־שְׁאָר חַכִּימֵי בָבֶל "(so that) they do not slay Daniel and
his companions and the rest of the sages of Babylon" Dan 2:18.
[Hebr. the same]. †

עַמִּיק * (*qattīl*, BL 192e; v.l. עֲמִיק, cf. BL 188j), emph.
pl. f. עַמִּיקָתָא (v.l. עֲמִיקָתָא), adj.: **deep, profound.** הוּא גָּלֵא
עַמִּיקָתָא "He reveals profound things" Dan 2:22 (BL 319c). [Hebr.
עָמֹק]. I

עֲמַר (*'amr*, BL 182x; < *ḏamr*), m.: **wool.** שְׂעַר רֵאשֵׁהּ
כַּעֲמַר נְקֵא "the hair of his head was like pure wool" Dan 7:9; לבש
1 זי עמר "1 garment of wool" *BMAP* 2:4; לבש 1 זי קמר "1 garment of wool" *BMAP* 7:6; כל לבשן זי קמר וכתן 12 "all the garments of wool and linen were 12" *BMAP* 7:13. [Hebr. צֶמֶר]. I

עַן, see כְּעַן .

עֲנָה *, 3 sg. f. עֲנָת (BL 63w, 154l; v.l. עֲנַת), 1 sg. עניה
(*'ănêt*), 3 pl. עֲנוֹ ; ptc. sg. m. עָנֵה, pl. m. עָנַיִן (BL 233g): **answer, speak (up), entreat.** This verb occurs in narrative style in
Daniel and Aḥiqar introducing אֲמַר, often with some solemnity,
and preceding dir. disc.; the two verbs have the same subj. and
often the same personal obj.; the subj. (if mentioned) follows
עֲנָה, and sometimes the obj. too: עֲנָה מַלְכָּא לְדָנִיֵּאל וְאָמַר "the king
spoke up and said to Daniel" Dan 2:47; עֲנָה דָנִיֵּאל קֳדָם־מַלְכָּא וְאָמַר
"Daniel spoke up in the presence of the king and said" 2:27:
2:10; עֲנֵה וְאָמַר לְאַרְיוֹךְ "he spoke up and said to Arioch" 2:15 + ;

265

Ah. 45, 110, 118, 121; עֲנָה דָנִיֵּאל וְאָמַר קֳדָם מַלְכָּא "Daniel spoke up and said in the presence of the king" Dan 5:17: 6:14. -- Tenses: (a) perf. + perf.: עֲנָת מַלְכְּתָא וַאֲמֶרֶת "the queen spoke up and said" Dan 5:10; ענית ואמרת "I spoke up and said" *Ah.* 45; [א]ענו אמרי "the lam[bs] spoke up and said to him" *Ah.* 121; ענה ואמרו לה חמרא ואמר לאריא "the ass answered and said to the lion" *Ah.* 110; ענה נמרא ואמר לענזא "the leopard spoke up and said to the goat" *Ah.* 118. -- (b) perf. + ptc.: עֲנוֹ וְאָמְרִין "they spoke, saying" Dan 3:9; 6:14: 2:7, 10; 3:16. -- (c) ptc. + ptc. (perh. read perf. + ptc., BL 164, n, 1; 295u): עֲנָה מַלְכָּא וְאָמַר "the king answered and said" Dan 2:5, 8 + ; עֲנַיִן וְאָמְרִין "they answered and said" 3:24 (read עֲנוֹ ?). -- Meaning: After introductory עֲנָה, the verb אֲמַר means either "say" or, according to the context (s.v. אֲמַר): (i) **ask:** עֲנָה וְאָמַר . . . עַל מָה "he spoke up and asked . . . , 'Why . . .?'" Dan 2:15: 2:26; 3:24a; 5:13; 6:21 (cf. קְרִיבוּ וְאָמְרִין . . . הֲלָא "they drew near and asked, 'Did not . . .'" 6:13): Ezra 5:4. (ii) **command, order:** עֲנָה וְאָמַר לְמֵזֵא לְאַתּוּנָא "(the king) spoke up and ordered (them) to heat the furnace" Dan 3:19. (iii) **tell, recount:** עֲנָה דָנִיֵּאל וְאָמַר "Daniel spoke up and recounted" 7:2 (Gk. & Theod. omit). (iv) **reply:** עֲנָה מַלְכָּא וְאָמַר "the king spoke up and replied" Dan 2:5, 8: 2:10, 27; 3:16, 24b, 25; 4:16b; 5:17; 6:13, 14; *Ah.* 45, 110 (cf. אֲבָעֵא־מִנֵּהּ . . . וַאֲמַר־לִי "I sought from him . . . , and he replied" Dan 7:16: 3:16; Ezra 5:11). (v) Does עֲנָה have the Hebr. sense of "answer"? It often cannot have that meaning, e.g., in a soliloquy: עֲנָה מַלְכָּא וְאָמַר "the king spoke up and said" Dan 4:27: 2:20; 3:28; at the beginning of a dialogue: Dan 2:47; 3:9, 14, 26; 4:16a; 5:7, 10; 6:17; *Ah.* 118; כזי ח[ז]ית אנפי אסרהאדן טבן עניה ואמרת . . . "when I saw that the face of Esarhaddon . . . was favorable, I spoke up and said" *Ah.* 14. N.B. In Dan 2:5, עֲנָה picks up from the Hebr. וַיְדַבְּרוּ "they said" (2:4); עֲנוֹ תִנְיָנוּת וְאָמְרִין "they answered a second time, saying" 2:7; ואשא ידי אל בעלש[מי]ן ויענני בעלשמנין [וימלל] בעלשמין אלי [ב]יד חזין וביד עדדן [ויאמר אלי] בעלשמין "I raised my hands to Belshamayin, and B. answered me; B. spoke to me through seers and through soothsayers; B.

עֲנַה—עֲקַר

[said to me]" *Zkr* A 11-12 (*KAI* 202). †

עֲנֵה * (*'ănēh* < **'anī*), pl. m. עֲנַיִן *, in pause עֲנַיִן (v.l. עֲנַיִן, BL 233h), adj.: **poor.** בְּמִחַן עֲנַיִן "by showing mercy to the poor" Dan 4:24; [ ] אנה שיזבת לענא מן "I saved a poor person from" *11QtgJob (11Q10)* 14:6. [Hebr. עָנִי]. [1]

עֲנַן * (*'ănān*), cst. pl. עֲנָנֵי : **cloud.** וַאֲרוּ עִם־עֲנָנֵי שְׁמַיָּא כְּבַר אֱנָשׁ אָתֵה הֲוָה "and lo, with the clouds of heaven there came one like a son of man" Dan 7:13. {Hebr. עָנָן]. [1]

עֲנַף * (*'ănap*), pl. w. suff. עַנְפּוֹהִי (פ wt. daghesh in pl.; cf. du. אַנְפּוֹהִי): **branch.** בְּעַנְפּוֹהִי יְדֻרוּן צִפֲּרֵי שְׁמַיָּא "in its branches dwell the birds of the heavens" Dan 4:9: 4:11bis, 18. [Hebr. עָנָף]. [1]

עֲנַשׁ (*'ănāš*) cst. (& abs.): **penalty.** עֲנַשׁ נִכְסִין "a property penalty," i.e., confiscation of property, Ezra 7:26. [Hebr. עֹנֶשׁ]. [1]

עֲנֵת : see כְּעַן .

עֳפִי * (*'upy*), w. suff. עָפְיֵהּ ; only collect. sg. (BL 202m), m.: **leaf, foliage.** עָפְיֵהּ שַׁפִּיר "its leaves were beautiful" Dan 4:9, 18; אַתַּרוּ עָפְיֵהּ "cut off its foliage" 4:11. [Hebr. the same]. †

עֲצִיב (*'ăṣīb;* v.l. עַצִּיב), adj.: **sorrowful, anguished.** בְּקָל עֲצִיב זְעִק "(the king) cried out in an anguished voice" Dan 6:21. [Hebr. עָצוּב]. [1]

עקר , **'Ithpe.** 3 pl. m. אֶתְעֲקַרוּ k., 3 pl. f. אֶתְעֲקַרָה q. (BL 101k, 134r), v.l. **'Ithpa.** אֶתְעֲקַרוּ : **be plucked, be overturned.** וּתְלָת מִן־קַרְנַיָּא קַדְמָיָתָא אֶתְעֲקַרוּ מִן־קֳדָמַיהּ "and three of the first horns were plucked up by their roots" Dan 7:8 (cf. ‖ נְפַלוּ מִן־קֳדָם "they

267

fell down," i.e., were overtuned, 7:20); cf. אתו ובעין למקץ ולמעקר
ל[א]רזא "(some men) came, seeking to cut down and pluck out
the [ce]dar" *1QapGen* 19:15. [Hebr. the same]. [1]

עֲקַר * (or עִקַּר *, BL 192f; v.l. עֵקַר), cst. עִקַּר : (1)
sprout, stump, which comes forth from a root (Theod. φυή, Vg.
germen, cf. Hebr. עֵקֶר ; acc. others: the **main stem** of the root).
בְּרַם עִקַּר שָׁרְשׁוֹהִי בְּאַרְעָא שְׁבֻקוּ "but leave the stump of its roots in
the ground" Dan 4:12, 20: 4:23. -- (2) **offspring** (cf. זֶרַע). עדי
בני בני בר גא[י]ה ועקר[]ה עם עקר מתעאל "the treaty of the grandsons
of Bar Ga'[yah and] his [offspring] with the offspring of Mati'el"
Sefire I A 2-3; הן ישקר מתע[א]ל <לבר גאיה> [ול]ברה ולעקרה "if
Mati'[el] should be unfaithful <to Bar Ga'yah> [and to] his son
and to his offspring" *Sefire I* A 24-25. [Hebr. עֵקֶר]. †

עַר * (*'arr,* < **darr*), pl. w. suff. עָרָיִךְ k. (עָרָךְ q., BL
77o): **adversary.** חֶלְמָא לְשָׂנְאַיִךְ וּפִשְׁרֵהּ לְעָרָיִךְ "may the dream be
for your enemies and its interpretation for your adversaries" Dan
4:16. [Hebr. צַר]. [1]

ערב , **Pa.,** pass. ptc. מְעָרַב : **mix.** פַּרְזְלָא מְעָרַב בַּחֲסַף
"(you saw) the iron mixed with clay" Dan 2:41: 2:43a. **Hithpa.,**
ptc. sg. m. מִתְעָרַב, pl. m. מִתְעָרְבִין : **be mixed.** הֵא־כְדִי פַרְזְלָא לָא
מִתְעָרַב עִם־חַסְפָּא "just as iron is not mixed with clay" Dan 2:43c;
מִתְעָרְבִין לֶהֱוֹן בִּזְרַע אֲנָשָׁא "they will be mixed with one another in
marriage," lit., "in the seed of human beings" 2:43b. [Hebr.
ערב[1]]. †

עֲרָד * (*'arād*), emph. pl. עֲרָדַיָּא : **wild ass, onager.**
עִם־עֲרָדַיָּא מְדוֹרֵהּ "with the wild asses was his dwelling" Dan 5:21.
[Hebr. עָרוֹד]. [1]

עֶרְוָה * (qatl-at, BL 183f), cst. עֶרְוַת, f.: **nudity,
ignominy.** עֶרְוַת מַלְכָּא לָא אֲרִיךְ לַנָא לְמֶחֱזֵא "it is not fitting for us to
behold the ignominy of the king" Ezra 4:14. [Hebr. עֶרְוָה]. [1]

עֲשַׂב * ('iśb, BL 40n, 183f, 225p), emph. עִשְׂבָּא , only
collect. sg. (BL 202m): **grass, herb.** עִשְׂבָּא כְתוֹרִין יֵאכֻל "he ate
grass like oxen" Dan 4:30: 4:22, 29; 5:21. [Hebr. עֵשֶׂב]. †

עֲשַׂר m. ('aśr: qatl, BL 182x), עַשְׂרָה f. ('aśarāh, LFAA
77a): **ten.** -- (1) w. nouns: -- (a) **m.** noun: עַשְׂרָה מַלְכִין יְקֻמוּן
"ten kings shall arise" Dan 7:24; מִנַן עשׂרה . . . כרשׁן עשׂרה "ten
minas . . . ten kerashin" AP 26:17; טף אמן עשׂרה "(each) plank,
ten cubits" AP 26:10; צבען עשׂרה "(a measurement of) ten
fingers" AP 26:16. -- (b) **f.** noun: וְקַרְנַיִן עֲשַׂר לַהּ "and it had ten
horns" Dan 7:7; עַל־קַרְנַיָּא עֲשַׂר דִּי בְרֵאשַׁהּ "about the ten horns that
were on its head" 7:20: 7:24; הא עשׂר שׁנין שׁלמא "lo, ten years
have elapsed" 1QapGen 22:27. -- (2) In numbers **11-19:** עֲשַׂר m.
('aśar), עשׂרה f. ('aśrēh). In the numbers 1-2, the gender
always agrees with the gender of the noun; in the number 3-9, it
always differs from it; the 10 can agree or differ. -- (a) The
number 10, when it stands behind units, agrees with the gender
of the noun: (i) w. **m.** noun: חד* עשׂר "eleven"; יְרַחִין תְּרֵי־עֲשַׂר
"twelve months" Dan 4:26; וּצְפִירֵי עִזִּין לְחַטָּיָא עַל־כָּל־יִשְׂרָאֵל תְּרֵי־עֲשַׂר
"and as sin offerings for all Israel twelve he-goats" Ezra 6:17;
וארבעת עשׂר "[thir]teen ro[ds]" 5QNJ (5Q15) 1 i 6; קנ]ין תל[תת עשׂר
באתין כה]נין "and fourteen prie[sts]" 2QNJ (2Q24) 4:13; . . . עשׂר
חמשׁת [עשׂר] "[fifteen] houses . . ." 5QNJ (5Q15) 1 ii 6;
קנין תמנית עשׂר "fifteen minas" CIS II/1.2, no. 1b; עשׂר מנין
גברין . . . תלת מאא ותמניאת עשׂר "eighteen rods" CIS II/1.189 (I:4);
"three hundred and eighteen . . . men" 1QapGen 22:6. -- (ii) w.
f. noun: שׁנת חדה ע[שׂרה] "(in) year ele[ven]" Mur 20 recto 1;
אמין] [חדה] עשׂרה כוין "[e]leven windows" 5QNJ (5Q15) 1 ii 11;
תרתי עשׂרה תר[תי "[tw]elve [cubits]" 5QNJ (5Q15) 1 ii 11;

שנין "for twelve years" *1QapGen* 21:26; בשנת תלת עשרה "in year thirteen" *1QapGen* 21:27; בשנת ארבע עשרה "in the fourteenth year" *1QapGen* 21:27; אמין ארבע עשרה "fourteen cubits" *5QNJ (5Q15)* 1 ii 3; [ה]אמין תשע ע[שר] "nine[teen] cubits" *5QNJ (5Q15)* 1 ii 10. -- (b) The number 10, when it stands before units, differs from the gender of the noun, and the units are added w. ן, as in 21-99 (cf. עֲשָׂרִין): בגו סגנן אמין עשרה ותרין "among them ribs(?) (of) twelve cubits" *AP* 26:10-11; שף עשרה וחמשה "fifteen yards(?)" *AP* 26:11; אמי[ן] ע[שר ופלג "[t]en and a half cubit[s]" *5QNJ (5Q15)* 1 i 11. [Hebr. עָשָׂר etc.]. †

עֶשְׂרִין (invariable, as in other multiples of "ten"): **twenty.** אֲחַשְׁדַּרְפְּנַיָּא מְאָה עֶשְׂרִין "the one hundred (and) twenty satraps" Dan 6:2; read perh. עֶשְׂרִין in Ezra 6:3 (cf. אֲרָךְ); עשרן בין יומן 20 הו 20 "within 20 days, that is twenty" *BMAP* 11:7; [א]מין עשרין [וחדה] "twenty-one cubits" *5QNJ (5Q15)* 1 i 1-2; [ע]שרין ות[ר]תין ערש[י]ן "[tw]enty-t[w]o bed[s]" *5QNJ (5Q15)* 1 ii 11; כל מסמרין ארבע מאה עשרן וחמשה "all (the) nails: four hundred (and) twenty-five" *AP* 26:16; אמין מא[ה ועשרי]ן [ו]שת "a hund[red and twen]ty-six cubits" *5QNJ (5Q15)* 1 i 4. Cf. [אמין תלתין וחמש] "[thirty-five cubits]" *5QNJ (5Q15)* 1 i 13; בכסף זוזין עשר[ין] ותמניה "in silver: twen[ty-]eight denarii" *XHev/SeDeedSale (XHev/Se 9)* recto/upper 5-6 (DJD 27.40). [Hebr. עֶשְׂרִים]. [1]

עֲשֵׁת *, 1 sg. עשתת (*'aštēt*); impf. 2 sg. m. תעשת ; act. ptc. sg. m. עָשֵׁת *, pass. ptc. sg. m. עֲשִׁית (w. act. meaning, BL 90k, or as adj., BL 297e; or should one read עָשֵׁת ?). **Ithpe.** impv. sg. m. אתעשת (*'it'ašit*): **think, intend, decide, plan.** מַלְכָּא עֲשִׁית לַהֲקִימוּתֵהּ עַל־כָּל־מַלְכוּתָא "the king decided to set him over the whole kingdom" Dan 6:4; עבד לקבל זי אנת עשת "do as you are planning" *Ah.* 68; " עשתת לכי בחיי ויהבת לכי קצת מן ביתי "I have thought about you during my life, and I have given to you part of my house" *BMAP* 9:2-3; אנה עשתת לכי . . . שבקתכי "I

have thought about you . . . I have released you" *BMAP* 5:3-4; זי
[באישתא] אנה רבית עשת על[י "(my [nephew]), whom I raised,
planned [evils] against [me]" *Aḥ.* 25; הן . . . תעשת בלבב[ך גבר עדן
אנה "if . . . you think in your mind, '[I am an ally . . .]'" *Sefire II*
B 5; אתעשת על אגורא זך למבנה "think about that temple to rebuild
(it)" *AP* 30:23 (cf. עַל דָּנִיֵּאל שָׂם בָּל לְשֵׁיזָבוּתֵהּ "(the king) set his
mind on Daniel, to deliver him" Dan 6:15); אתעשת לי ינתנו לי
אהחסן "think of me; let them give (it) to me (that) I may take
possession (of it)" *AD* 8:3. [Hebr. ² עשת Hithpael]. ¹

עֵת *: see כְּעַן .

עֲתִיד * (*'atīd*), pl. עֲתִידִין , adj.: **ready.** הֵן אִיתֵיכוֹן עֲתִידִין דִּי
תִּפְּלוּן וְתִסְגְּדוּן לְצַלְמָא . . . "if you are ready that . . . you will fall
down and adore the statue" Dan 3:15 (see דִּי III 1). [Hebr.
עָתִיד]. ¹

עַתִּיק (*qattīl*, BL 192e), adj.: **old, ancient.** וְעַתִּיק יוֹמִין יְתִב
"and one that was ancient of days took his seat" Dan 7:9 (BL
310a; cf. דִּי I 2); עַתִּיק יוֹמַיָּא "the Ancient of Days" 7:13, 22; cf.
סבלתני ואנה ימין סב "she supported me, since I (was) old in days"
BMAP 9:17; ספר חדת ועתיק "a document new or old" *AP* 8:16;
13:11-12 (another scribe in a similar context wrote rather עטיק
BMAP 9:22; 10:15: 12:31); יהבת לכי ספרא עתיקא זי [כתב] לי משלם זך
"I give to you the old document, which that Meshallem [wrote]
for me" *AP* 13:6-7. [Hebr. עָתִיק & עַתִּיק]. †

פ

פֶּחָה (*peḥḥāh* for *paḥā*; < Akk. *pī/āḫātu* "administrative
region" & "governor," abbreviation of *bēl pī/āḫāti*), cst. פַּחַת
(*paḥḥát* for *paḥāt*); pl. (w. augm. -*aw*-) פַּחֲוָן *, emph. פַּחֲוָתָא (BL

271

פחר—פלג

238t): **governor, magistrate** (major or minor). סְגְנַיָּא וּפַחֲוָתָא "the prefects and governors" Dan 3:2, 3, 27: 6:8; תַּתְּנַי פַּחַת עֲבַר־נַהֲרָה "Tattenai, governor of (the province) Beyond-the-River" Ezra 5:3, 6; 6:6, 13; אל מראן בגוהי פחת יהוד "to our lord, Bagohi, governor of Judah" *AP* 30:1; סנאבלט פחת שמרין "Sanballaṭ, governor of Samaria" *AP* 30:29; וִיהִיבוּ לְשֵׁשְׁבַּצַּר שְׁמֵהּ דִּי פֶחָה שָׂמֵהּ "and they were delivered to one named Sheshbazzar, whom he had made magistrate" Ezra 5:14; קבלן לפחותא על פרסכן תנה ב[מ]גדל["we complained to the magistrates about your wages (not paid) here in [Mig]dol" *Padua I* A 4; פַּחַת יְהוּדָיֵא "governor of the Jews" Ezra 6:7 (prob. dl. acc. context; cf. ן no. 5). [Hebr. the same]. †

פֶחָר (*pehhār*, BL 191c; < Akk. *paḫāru*): **potter.** רַגְלַיָּא מִנְּהֵן חֲסַף דִּי־פֶחָר . . . "the feet . . . (were) partly of potter's clay" Dan 2:41. [1]

פטיש, pl. w. suff. פַּטִּישֵׁיהוֹן (or פְּטִישֵׁיהוֹן) k., פַּטְּשֵׁיהוֹן q. = *paṭĕšēhōn* (daghesh forte to avoid *ṯš*, BL 46m; in Babyl. vocal. *ṯš* is avoided by metathesis *pišṭēhôn*, BL 220x, y): **tunic, mantle** (meaning uncertain). כְּפִתוּ בְּסַרְבָּלֵיהוֹן פַּטְּשֵׁיהוֹן "they were bound in their mantles, their tunics" Dan 3:21. [1]

פְּלַג *, pass. ptc. sg. f. פְּלִיגָה : **divide, apportion, cut in half** (cf. פְּרַס). מַלְכוּ פְלִיגָה תֶּהֱוֵה "(the fourth kingdom) shall be a divided kingdom" Dan 2:41 (cf. 2:42-43); פלגן עלין עבדיה "we have divided between us the slaves (of Mibtahiah)" *AP* 28:3; לא עד נפלג עלין כזי [ע]דן יהוה המו נפלג המו עלין "(other slaves) we do not yet divide between us; when it is [ti]me, we shall divide them between us" *AP* 28:13-14; [עם קדישין] עדבה פליג "[with the Holy Ones] is his lot apportioned" *1QapGen* 2:20-21; ספר פלגן עבד "a document of the apportioning of a slave" *AP* 28:17. [Hebr. פלג Piel & Niphal). [1]

272

פלג—פלח

פְּלַג (*palg* or *pilg*, *LFAA* 74j), m.: **half.** עַד־עִדָּן וְעִדָּנִין וּפְלַג
עִדָּן "for a time, two times, and a half-time" (= 3¹∕₂ years) Dan
7:25; חלף פלג מנתא . . . . יהבן לכי פלג מנ[ת]א "we have given to you
half of (our) sh[are] . . . in exchange for half of (your) share" *AP*
1:2-3; פלג ביתא [יהוה] לה למלקח ופלגא אחר[נא] אנת שליט בה "half of
the house [shall be] hers to take, and as for [the] oth[er] half, you
have authority over it" *AP* 9:11; ותוב פלגא הו בניך . . . המו שליטן בה
"and again, as for that half, your children . . . shall have authority over it" *AP* 9:12-13; [הא] פלגה זילי הו צדיק "[lo,] the half that is
mine is (so) legally" *AP* 44:6. Following a number: אמן 9 ופלג
"9 and a half cubits" *AP* 79:3; אמן 8 ופלג "8 and a half cubits"
BMAP 9:6; מחזי 1 שויה כסף חלרן 7 פלג "1 mirror worth 7 hallurs
(and) a half" *BMAP* 2:5; כסף שקלן 7 חלרן 7 פלג "7 silver shekels,
7 hallurs (and) a half" *BMAP* 2:6-7.

פְּלֻגָּה (BL 187b), pl. w. suff. פְּלֻגָּתְהוֹן , f.: **class, course**
(cf. מַחְלְקָה). הֲקִימוּ כָהֲנַיָּא בִּפְלֻגָּתְהוֹן "they set up the priests in their
courses" Ezra 6:18. [Hebr. the same].[1]

פְּלַח *, impf. 3 pl. m. יִפְלְחוּן ; infin. מפלח (*miplaḥ*); ptc.
sg. m. פָּלַח , pl. m. פָּלְחִין , cst. פָּלְחֵי : **cultivate, serve, minister,
worship.** שרית אנה . . . למפלח בארעא "I began . . . to cultivate the
earth" *1QapGen* 12:13; יפלחנך זי יסבל בר וברה לאבוהי בחייך "we
shall serve you during your life-time as a son or daughter provides for his (or her) father" *BMAP* 5:11-12 (read נפלחנך and כזי,
as in line 12); שב אנה לא אכהל למפלח בבב היכלא "I am an old man;
I cannot serve in the court of the palace" *Aḥ.* 17; . . . כָּל־כָּהֲנַיָּא
וּפָלְחֵי בֵּית אֱלָהָא דְנָה "all the priests . . . and those ministering in
this house of God" Ezra 7:24; לֵהּ יְהִיב שָׁלְטָן . . . וְכָל עַמְמַיָּא . . . לֵהּ
יִפְלְחוּן "to him was given sovereignty . . . that all peoples . . .
should serve him" Dan 7:14 (BL 281m); וְכֹל שָׁלְטָנַיָּא לֵהּ יִפְלְחוּן
וְיִשְׁתַּמְּעוּן "and all the dominions shall serve and obey it" 7:27;
אֱלָהָךְ דִּי אַנְתָּא פָּלַח־לֵהּ "your God whom you are worshiping" 6:17,

273

21: 3:17, 28; לָא סָגְדִין . . . לֵאלָהָךְ לָא פָלְחִין וּלְצֶלֶם "they do not
worship your god and . . . do not adore the statue" 3:12: 3:14,
18; הוי פלחה "be a (god)-worshiper!" *Carpentras* 4 (*KAI* 269).
[Hebr. פָלַח "plough"]. †

פָּלְחָן (*pulḥān*): **service, ministry.** לְפָלְחָן בֵּית אֱלָהָךְ "for
the service of the house of your God" Ezra 7:19 (cf. עֲבִידַת אֱלָהָא
6:18 s.v. פְּלַח); פלחן צמחין "service of sprouts" (Gen 1:2 Neofiti). †

פֻּם (*pum*, BL 178b; v.l. פֹּם) abs. & cst., w. suff. פֻּמֵּהּ ;
m.: **mouth.** עוֹד מִלְּתָא בְּפֻם מַלְכָּא "(while) the word was still in
the king's mouth" Dan 4:28; עַיְנִין לַהּ וְפֻם מְמַלִּל רַבְרְבָן "it had eyes
and a mouth uttering great things" 7:20: 7:8; וּתְלָת עִלְעִין בְּפֻמַּהּ
"and three ribs in its (the beast's) mouth" 7:5: 6:23;]יֵאכֻל פ[ם
חוה ופם עקרב . . . ופם נמרה וסס "[may the mou]th of a snake [de-
vour] and the mouth of a scorpion . . . and the mouth of a panther
and a moth" *Sefire I* A 30-31; עַל־פֻּם גֻּבָּא "on the mouth of the
(lions') den" Dan 6:18; טר פמך "guard your mouth" *Aḥ.* 98; הן
נפקה טבה מן פם א[נשא טב] והן לחיה תנפק [מן] פמהם "if good comes
forth from the mouth of m[en, it is a benefit], and if evil comes
forth [from] their mouth(s, the gods will curse them)" *Aḥ.* 123-
24; עזיז ארב פם מן ארב מלחם "more mighty is the ambush of the
mouth than the ambush of war" *Aḥ.* 99; ביום מתת פמי לאתאחז מן
מלן "on the day that I died, my mouth was not closed off from
words" *Nerab* 4 (*KAI* 226); כל 2 כפם חד "both of them (spoke)
with one voice" *BMAP* 12:11; פם חד תלתהון ממללין "the three of
them were speaking as one man," lit. "with one mouth" *1Qap-
Gen* 20:8; כתב פלטיה . . . ספרא זנה בפם קוניה "Pelatiah . . . wrote
this document at the dictation of Qoniah," lit., "in the mouth of
Q." *AP* 5:15; הן איתי כסף הבי על פמי "if there is money (there),
give (it out), as I have said," lit., "according to my mouth" *Padua
II* A 4. [Hebr. פֶּה]. †

274

פס—פרזל

פַּס (pass, BL 180n), emph. פַּסָּא , m.: **part, portion.**
מַלְכָּא חֲזָה יְדָה פַּס דִּי כָתְבָה "the king saw part of a hand that was
writing" Dan 5:5; שְׁלִיחַ פַּסָּא דִּי־יְדָא וּכְתָבָא דְּנָה רְשִׁים "the part of the
hand was sent (by God), and this message was inscribed" 5:24;
יהבתה לך פס שרת "I have given it (the house) to you as a remainder (?) portion" BMAP 10:7: 10:9; 12:9, 18 (cf. Nab. פס ראש
"part of the capital"; see RB 61 [1954] 164 C₂). [Mish. Hebr.
פְּסִיסָה "partition"]. †

פְּסַנְתֵּרִין & פְּסַנְטֵרִין (Dan 3:7) (< Gk. ψαλτήριον, BL
11z): **trigon** (triangular stringed instrument). קָל . . . פְּסַנְתֵּרִין
"the sound of . . . (the) trigon" Dan 3:5, 7, 10, 15 (collect.). †

פַּרְזֶל (BL 42w), emph. פַּרְזְלָא , m.: **iron.** דָּקוּ כַחֲדָה פַּרְזְלָא
חַסְפָּא "there were broken together the iron, the clay, . . . " Dan
2:35: 2:45; למלקח לך . . . נחש ופרזל "to take for yourself . . .
(whatever) bronze and iron . . . (you may find of mine)" AP 10:9-
10. -- In a symbolic sense: מַלְכוּ רְבִיעָיָה תֶּהֱוֵא תַקִּיפָה כְּפַרְזְלָא "a
fourth kingdom shall be as strong as iron" Dan 2:40a; פַּרְזְלָא
מְהַדֵּק וְחָשֵׁל כֹּלָּא וּכְפַרְזְלָא דִּי־מְרָעַע כָּל־אִלֵּין תַּדִּק "(because) iron breaks
to pieces and shatters everything; and like iron that crushes, (it
will crush) all these things" 2:40bc; הֵא־כְדִי פַרְזְלָא לָא מִתְעָרַב "just as iron is not mixed with clay" 2:43c; מִן־נִצְבְּתָא דִּי עַם־חַסְפָּא
פַּרְזְלָא לֶהֱוֵא־בַהּ "some of the firmness of iron shall be in it" 2:41b.
-- As a gen. of material: (1) attributive: עַל־רַגְלוֹהִי דִּי פַרְזְלָא "on
its feet of iron" Dan 2:34; לֵאלָהֵי דַהֲבָא וְכַסְפָּא נְחָשָׁא פַרְזְלָא "(they
worship) gods of gold and silver, bronze, iron . . . " 5:4, 23; שִׁנַּיִן
בְּאֵסוּר דִּי־פַרְזֶל וּנְחָשׁ דִּי־פַרְזֶל לַהּ רַבְרְבָן "it had great iron teeth" 7:7;
"in a band of iron and bronze" 4:12, 20; מאני נחש ופרזל "vessels
of bronze and iron" AP 20:5; מאן נחש ופרזל "vessels of bronze
and iron" BMAP 11:11; מסמרי נחש ופרזל מאתין "two hundred
nails of bronze and iron" AP 26:12-13. -- As a gen. of material:
(2) predicative: שָׁקוֹהִי דִּי פַרְזֶל רַגְלוֹהִי מִנְּהוֹן דִּי פַרְזֶל "its legs were of

iron; its feet were partly of iron . . ." Dan 2:33: 2:41a, 42; שְׁנַּהּ
דִּי־פַרְזֶל "its teeth were of iron" 7:19; חֲזַיְתָה פַּרְזְלָא מְעָרַב בַּחֲסַף "you
saw the iron mixed with clay" 2:41c, 43a. [Hebr. בַּרְזֶל]. †

פְּרַס *, **Peil** perf. 3 sg. f. פְּרִיסַת : **divide.** פְּרִיסַת מַלְכוּתָךְ
"your kingdom has been divided (and given to the Medes and
Persians) Dan 5:28. [Hebr. פָּרַס ; cf. Akk. *parāsu* "divide,
separate from"]. [1]

פְּרַס (= Akk. *parsu*), pl. פַּרְסִין (= du., as in Dan 7:25; cf.
BL 306l): **half** (acc. context, it means ½ shekel or ½ mina or ½
dimension, etc. [see *ZAW* 63 (1951) 111; *DISO* 236: 26-30]).
מְנֵא מְנֵא תְּקֵל וּפַרְסִין "counted: mina, shekel, and (two) half (shekels)" Dan 5:25 (see Theod. [Μανη θεκελ φαρες]; Vg. [*mane
thecel fares*] cf. v. 28); פְּרַס פְּרִיסַת מַלְכוּתָךְ וִיהִיבַת לְמָדַי וּפָרָס "a half:
your kingdom has been divided and given to the Medes and the
Persians" 5:28. †

▲ פָּרַס, in pause פָּרָס (BL 23d, 65h): **Persia.** דָּת לְמָדַי וּפָרַס
"it is a law of Media and Persia" Dan 6:16: 6:9, 13 (commonly
tr. "of the Medes and the Persians"); מַלְכוּתָךְ יְהִיבַת לְמָדַי וּפָרָס
"your kingdom has been given to the Medes and the Persians"
5:28; דָּרְיָוֶשׁ מֶלֶךְ־פָּרָס "Darius, King of Persia" Ezra 4:24: 6:14;
ושא[ר חילא זי] פרס ומד[י] "and the res[t of the army of] Persia and
Media" *Bisitun* 40; פרסי יתב בפרס "a Persian dwelling in Persia"
Bisitun 36; זנה זי אנה בפרס [עבדת] "this is what [I did] in Persia"
Bisitun 50; במתקלת פרס "by the weight-standard of Persia" *AP*
26:21. [Hebr. the same]. †

▲ פָּרְסָי * (BL 196d), emph. sg. פָּרְסָיָא k. & פַּרְסָאָה q. (BL
51k); emph. pl. פָּרְסָיָא * (cf. אֲפָרְסָיֵא Ezra 4:9): **Persian.** כּוֹרֶשׁ
פָּרְסָיָא "Cyrus the Persian" Dan 6:29; וידזת . . . שמה פרסי "a Persian named Vahyazdat" *Bisitun* 36. [Heb. פַּרְסִי & פָּרְסִי]. [1]

פְּרַק *, impv. sg. m. פְּרֻק : **break off.** חֲטָיָךְ בְּצִדְקָה פְרֻק "break off your sins by practising righteousness" Dan 4:24. [Hebr. פָּרַק]. [1]

פְּרַשׁ *: **separate oneself, part.** פרש לוט מן לואתי "Lot parted from me" 1QapGen 21:5; 21:7. -- **Pa.,** pass. ptc. sg. m. מְפָרַשׁ : **separate, divide.** נִשְׁתְּוָנָא . . . מְפָרַשׁ קֱרִי קָדָמַי "the letter . . . has been plainly read before me," lit., "discretely," i.e., in separate details, Ezra 4:18 (cf. *ASA*, 4- 6); מפרש זן זן יִרח [ ] בירח הוו שלחן עלי "plainly divided, each item they were sending me, month by month" *AP* 17:3. [Hebr. פָּרַשׁ]. [1]

פַּרְשֶׁגֶן (< Persian *pati-čagna*): **copy.** דְּנָה פַּרְשֶׁגֶן אִגַּרְתָּא "this is a copy of the letter" Ezra 4:11; 5:6; פַּרְשֶׁגֶן נִשְׁתְּוָנָא "a copy of the letter" 4:23; פרשגן לוחא תני[נ]א "copy of the second tablet" *4QEnGiants^a* (4Q203) 8:3. [Hebr. פַּתְשֶׁגֶן]. †

פְּשַׁר *, infin. מִפְשַׁר : **interpret, explain.** תוּכַל פִּשְׁרִין לְמִפְשַׁר "are you able to interpret (the) meanings?" Dan 5:16 (BL 336c). -- **Pa.,** ptc. sg. m. מְפַשַּׁר : **interpret, explain.** שָׂכְלְתָנוּ מְפַשַּׁר חֶלְמִין "(had) understanding interpreting dreams" 5:12 (read rather Peal infin. מִפְשַׁר ?). [Hebr. פָּתַר]. †

פְּשַׁר (*pišr,* BL 183j), emph. פִּשְׁרָא (for פְּשָׁרָא Dan 4:15a, 16) & פִּשְׁרָה (Dan 2:7; 5:12; but read prob. פִּשְׁרֵהּ, BL 229i), w. suff. פִּשְׁרֵהּ ; pl. פִּשְׁרִין ; m.: **interpretation, mean-ing.** פְּשַׁר חֶלְמָא יְהוֹדְעַנַּנִי "(that) they might make known to me the interpretation of the dream" Dan 4:3: w. the same verb, 2:25, 26, 30; 4:4; 5:8 + חֶלְמִי . . . וּפִשְׁרֵהּ אֱמַר "my dream . . . and tell (me) its interpretation!" 4:6; 2:36; 4:15; פִּשְׁרָא נְחַוֵּא "we shall show the interpretation" 2:4; 2:24; 5:7; פִּשְׁרֵהּ תְּהַחֲוִנַּנִי "you will show to me the interpretation of it" 2:9; 2:7, 16; 5:12; וְיַצִּיב חֶלְמָא וּמְהֵימַן פִּשְׁרֵהּ "and the dream is certain, and the interpretation of it is trustworthy" 2:45; דִּי־יִקְרֵה כְתָבָה דְנָה וּפִשְׁרֵהּ יְחַוִּנַּנִי "whoever reads this inscription and shows me the interpretation of it" 5:7; וְלָא־כָהֲלִין פְּשַׁר־מִלְּתָא לְהַחֲוָיָה "and they were unable to give an interpretation of the word(s written on the wall)" 5:15; פְּשַׁר מִלַּיָּא "the interpretation of the things (seen)" 7:16; תּוּכַל פִּשְׁרִין לְמִפְשַׁר "are you able to interpret (the) meanings?" Dan 5:16. [Hebr. פְּשַׁר & פִּתָּרוֹן].

פִּתְגָּם (ג wt. daghesh; < Persian *pati-gāma*), emph. פִּתְגָמָא; m.: (1) **word, reply, decree, report**. . . . לָא־חַשְׁחִין אֲנַחְנָה פִּתְגָם לַהֲתָבוּתָךְ "we have no need . . . to give you a reply" Dan 3:16 (cf. Hebr. הֵשִׁיב דָּבָר); כְּנֵמָא פִּתְגָמָא הֲתִיבוּנָא "so they returned a reply to us" Ezra 5:11; פִּתְגָמָא שְׁלַחוּ עֲלוֹהִי "they sent him the report" 5:7; פִּתְגָמָא שְׁלַח מַלְכָּא "the king sent word" 4:17; בִּגְזֵרַת עִירִין פִּתְגָמָא וּמֵאמַר קַדִּישִׁין שְׁאֵלְתָּא "the decree is by a decision of Watchers, and the sentence by the word of holy ones" Dan 4:14; בפתגם א[לה]א "by the decree of G[o]d" *4QPrNab (4Q242)* 1-3:2; דִּי יְהַשְׁנֵא פִּתְגָמָא דְנָה "(anyone) who alters this decree" Ezra 6:11 (cf. גסת פתגם יתעבד לך "an evil report will be made about you" *AD* 4:3-4: 7:9) -- (2) **thing, event** (cf. מִלָּה). בתר פתגמיא אלן "after these events" *1QapGen* 22:27. [Hebr. the same]. †

פְּתַח *, **Peil** perf. 3 pl. m. פְּתִיחוּ ; ptc. sg. m. פְּתִיחַ *, pl. f. פְּתִיחָן : **open.** כַּוִּין פְּתִיחָן לֵהּ בְּעִלִּיתֵהּ נֶגֶד יְרוּשְׁלֶם "he (Daniel) had windows in his upper room open toward Jerusalem" Dan 6:11; וְסִפְרִין פְּתִיחוּ "and (the) books were opened" 7:10; כוין פתיחן תמה "there are open windows there" *AP* 25:6; תרעא עלה פתיח לשוק מלכא "the upper gate is opened to King Street" *BMAP* 12:21; אנת שליט למפתח תרעא זך "you have the right to open that gate" *AP* 5:14; [ ] חכים ממלל כי מפתח פם "a sage speaks, for the opening of the mouth . . ." *Aḥ*. 178; פתחה לי ארחא "the road shall be open to me" *Sefire III* 8-9. [Hebr. פָּתַח]. †

פתי , in Qumran texts abs. & cst. often פותי (*puty,* see *LFAA* 79p; cf. עֲפִי "leaf, foliage" & עובי [*'uby*] "thickness"), emph. פְּתָיָא *, w. suff. פותיה & פתיה (*putĕyēh*), פותיהון ; in MT פְּתָי * (*qatāl,* BL 187d); in Jew. Ar. פְּתָאָה; cf. Syr. *pĕtāyā'*), w. suff. פְּתָיֵהּ (read rather פָּתְיֵהּ): **width, breadth.** . . . [בית דרג] פותיה ואורכה משחה חדה "[a staircase] . . . its width and its length are the same dimension" *5QNJ (5Q15)* 2:2-3; כותא רומה אמ[ין] תרתין [ ] [ועובי פותי כותלא "(of) the window, its height two [cu]bits [ ], and (in) thickness (it equals) the width of the wall" *5QNJ (5Q15)* 2:12; פתיה ואו[רכה אמין שת בשת] "its width and [its] leng[th: six cubits by six]" *5QNJ (5Q15)* 2:4; פותיהון ואורכהון [משחה חדה] "their width and their length are the same dimension" *5QNJ (5Q15)* 1:12; פותי תרעיהון קנין תלתה "the width of their gates: three rods" *5QNJ (5Q15)* 1:10; ואזלת ליד טור תורא למדנחא לפותי ארעא "and I moved along Mount Taurus to the east through the breadth of the land" *1QapGen* 21:16; וחזי כמן ארכהא וכמן פתיהא "and see how great is its length and how great is its breadth" *1QapGen* 21:14; בארכא לחד פשכן תלתה . . . ועל פתיא ועביא "in length each three hands . . . and to the width and thickness two fingers" *AP* 26:18; . . . ארכה אמן 13 ופשך 1 פתי . . . אמן 11 "the length of it . . . 13 cubits and 1 hand-breadth, width . . . 11 cubits" *AP* 8:4-5; ותונה הוה מן עליה עד תחתיה אמן בעשתא 11 . . . אמן בעשתא 7 כ 1 בפתי "and the chamber is, from top to bottom, 11 cubits (by the cubit-measure); in width . . . 7 cubits *k* 1 (by the cubit-measure)" *BMAP* 4:6-7; לבש 1 זי קמר [ח]דה לאמן 7 "1 new garment of wool, 7 cubits, 3 hand-breadths (in length), width 4 cubits, R 2" *BMAP* 7:6-7; פשכן 3 פתי אמן 4 ר 2 פְּתָיֵהּ אַמִּין שֵׁת "its breadth: six cubits" Dan 3:1 (read rather פָּתְיֵהּ): Ezra 6:3. †

צ

The letter צ in Old Aramaic designated two primitive sounds:(1) *ṣ;* (2) *ṯ,* later pronounced *ṭ* and written

279

צבה—צבע

by the letter ט : עֵטָה "advice" (Hebr. עֵצָה).

צבה (BL 155q), 3 sg. f. צבית (ṣibyat/ṣibyāt), 2 sg. m. צבית (ṣĕbayt/ṣĕbaytā), 1 sg. צָבִית , 3 pl. m. צבו (ṣĕbô, LFAA 64f); impf. 3 sg. m. יִצְבֶּה & יִצְבֵּא , 2 sg. m. תצבה (tiṣbēh), 2 sg. f. תצבין , 3 pl. m. יצבון ; infin. w. suff. מִצְבְּיֵהּ; ptc. sg. m. צָבֵא : **want, wish, desire.** (1) w. accus.: חזו עליהם מה צבו "look after them, as to what they want" AP 38:5-6; כל זי תצבה שלח לי "send me word about what you desire" Hermopolis 3:7. -- (2) w. לְ & infin.: צָבִית לְיַצָּבָא "I wanted to know all (about the fourth beast)" Dan 7:19; ולמן די צבית למנתן "and to whomever you wish to give (it)" BMAP 3:12; w. infin. understood: לְמַן־דִּי יִצְבֵּא יִתְּנִנַּהּ "He will give it to whomever He wishes" Dan 4:14, 22, 29: 5:19 (4 times), 21; כְּמִצְבְּיֵהּ עָבֵד בְּחֵיל שְׁמַיָּא "He does according to His desire in the host of heaven" 4:32 (cf. Hebr. כִּרְצוֹנוֹ 11:36); למעבד בה כול די תצבה "to do with it whatever you wish" XHev/SeDeedSaleG (XHev/Se 23) 1:3; תהך לה אן זי צבית "she shall go wherever she wants" AP 15:28-29; למן זי צבית תנתן "to whomever you want, you may give (him [a slave])" AP 28:7; [זי] תצבין הבהי "to whomever you wish, give it (the house)" AP 13:16. -- (3) w. complementary finite verb: כען צבית אהנצל המו "now I desire to recover them" BMAP 7:41-42; הן צבה אנת ברי זי תהוה [רם] "if you, my son, wish to be [exalted]" Aḥ. 149. †

צְבוּ , cst. צְבוּת *; f.: **thing, affair, matter** (properly "will," something willed; cf. Hebr. חֵפֶץ). דִּי לָא־תִשְׁנֵא צְבוּ בְּדָנִיֵּאל "that nothing (decided) about Daniel change" Dan 6:18; לא משתמען לי בצבות מראי "they do not obey me in my lord's affair" AD 4:1-2; צבות ביתא זילי "(in) the matter of my house" AD 4:2b. [1]

צבע , **Pa.** ptc. pl. m. מְצַבְּעִין . **Hithpa.,** impf. 3 sg. m. יִצְטַבַּע (BL 55a): **wet, moisten, sprinkle.** מִטַּל שְׁמַיָּא לָךְ מְצַבְּעִין "(they) shall moisten you with heaven's dew" Dan 4:22; בְּטַל

שְׁמַיָּא יִצְטַבַּע "let him be wet with the dew of the heavens" 4:12, 20; מְטַל שְׁמַיָּא גִּשְׁמֵהּ יִצְטַבַּע "his body was wet with the dew of heaven" 4:30; 5:21. [Hebr. cf. noun צֶבַע]. †

צבע as noun: see אֶצְבַּע.

צַד (ṣadd, BL 180n): **side** (cf. גַּב & שְׂטַר). מִלִּין לְצַד עִלָּיָא יְמַלִּל "he shall utter words against the Most High," lit., "to the side of" Dan 7:25; הֲווֹ בָעַיִן עִלָּה לְהַשְׁכָּחָה לְדָנִיֵּאל מִצַּד מַלְכוּתָא "they were seeking to find a fault in Daniel on the side of the kingdom" 6:5. [Hebr. the same]. †

צְדָא * (perh. < verb יצד *, = Arab. *waṣada* "be firm"; cf. BL p. 371): **true, certain.** הַצְדָּא . . . לֵאלָהַי לָא אִיתֵיכוֹן פָּלְחִין "is it true . . . that you do not worship my gods?" Dan 3:14; פלסר [יש]אל הצדא הני מליא אלה . . . וקרא המו שאל המו הצד[א מלי]א אלה "Pilsar ask[s], 'Are these words true?' . . . and call them (and) ask, 'Are these [wor]ds tr[ue]?'" *Assur Letter* 12-13 (*KAI* 233). [1]

צִדְקָה (qatal-at, BL 185s), f.: **justice, righteousness, merit, fidelity.** עד זי אגורא זך יתבנה וצדקה יהוה לך קדם יהו אלה "that that temple be built, and you will have merit before Yaho the god" *AP* 30:27; בצדקתי קדמוה שמני שם טב והארך יומי "for my righteousness before him he has put on me a good name and lengthened my days" *Nerab* 2-3 (*KAI* 226); חֲטָיָךְ בְּצִדְקָה פְרֻק "break off your sins with righteousness" Dan 4:24. Cf. בצדק אבי ובצדקי הושבני "because of the fidelity of my father and because of my fidelity he has settled me" *Barrakib* 4-5 (*KAI* 216); אל תהרכב חטך לצדיק "shoot not your arrow at the righteous" *Aḥ.* 126. [Hebr. צֶדֶק & צְדָקָה]. †

צַוַּאר * (ṣaw'ar, cf. BL 60j, *HGHS* 548z), w. suff. צַוָּארֵהּ צַוָּארָךְ, : **neck.** הַמּוֹנְכָא דִּי־דַהֲבָא עַל־צַוָּארֵהּ "(and have) a chain of gold about his neck" Dan 5:7; 5:16, 29; בצורה יבית תקפה "its strength resides in its neck" *11QtgJob (11Q10)* 36:7. [Hebr. צַוָּאר]. †

צלה , **Pa.**, impf. 3 sg. m. יְצלה (yĕṣallēh); impv. sg. m. צלי (ṣalli); infin. צלָיא (ṣallāyā'); ptc. sg. m. מְצַלֵּא (v.l. מְצַלֵּא), pl. m. מְצַלַּיִן (BL 233g; *GBA* §155): **pray.** . בְּרֵךְ עַל־בִּרְכוֹהִי וּמְצַלֵּא קֳדָם אֱלָהֵהּ . . "(Daniel) knelt upon his knees and prayed . . . before his God" Dan 6:11; לְהֱוֹן . . . מְצַלַּיִן לְחַיֵּי מַלְכָּא "(that) they may . . . pray for the life of the king" Ezra 6:10; הוין . . . מצלין ליהו מרא שמיא "we were . . . praying to Yaho, the Lord of Heaven" *AP* 30:15; נצלה עליך בכל עדן "we shall pray for you at all times" *AP* 30:26; בעא מני די אתה ואצלה על מלכא "he begged me to come and pray over the king" *1QapGen* 20:21; לא יכול אברם דדי לצליא על מלכא "Abram, my uncle, will not be able to pray over the king" *1QapGen* 20:22-23; ויצלה עלוהי ויחה "then (Abram) will pray for him that he may live," i.e., be cured, *1QapGen* 20:23; צלי עלי ועל ביתי "pray for me and for my household" *1QapGen* 20:28. -- Cognate noun: צלות עב[דך] "the prayer of [your] serva[nt]" *4Q-Levi[b] (4Q213a)* 2:8. †

צלח , **Haph./Aph.** 3 sg m. הַצְלַח ; ptc. act. sg. m. מַצְלַח ; pl. m. מַצְלְחִין : (1) trans.: **make someone have success** (wealth, authority). מַלְכָּא הַצְלַח לְשַׁדְרַךְ . . . בִּמְדִינַת בָּבֶל "the king promoted Shadrach . . . in the province of Babylonia" Dan 3:30. -- (2) intrans.: **be successful, prosper.** דָּנִיֵּאל דְּנָה הַצְלַח בְּמַלְכוּת דָּרְיָוֶשׁ "this Daniel prospered during the reign of Darius" 6:29; שָׂבֵי יְהוּדָיֵא בָּנַיִן וּמַצְלְחִין בִּנְבוּאַת חַגַּי . . . וּזְכַרְיָה "the elders of the Jews were building and prospering through the prophesying of Haggai . . . and Zechariah" Ezra 6:14; וַעֲבִידְתָּא דָךְ . . . מַצְלַח בְּיֶדְהֹם "and that work . . . prospers in their hands" 5:8 (impers., m. ptc., BL 330o; or "success [noun, see *AH* I/2. 30] is in their work"). †

צְלֵם (ṣalm, BL 233f, g), cst. צְלֵם & צְלֶם (BL 228f), emph. צַלְמָא , m.: (1) **image, statue.** וַאֲלוּ צְלֵם חַד שַׂגִּיא צַלְמָא דִּכֵּן רַב "and lo, a statue; that statue was very great" Dan 2:31 (put שַׂגִּיא after רַב w. LXX); הוּא צַלְמָא רֵאשֵׁהּ דִּי־דְהַב "the head of that statue was of gold" 2:32 (cf. דִּי I/2b); אֶבֶן . . . מְחָת לְצַלְמָא עַל־רַגְלוֹהִי "a stone . . . struck the statue on its feet" 2:34: 2:35; מַלְכָּא עֲבַד צְלֵם דִּי־דְהַב "the king made a statue of gold" 3:1; לַחֲנֻכַּת צַלְמָא "to the dedication of the statue" 3:2, 3a: 3:3b; תִּסְגְּדוּן לְצֶלֶם דַּהֲבָא "you are to worship the golden statue" 3:5: 3:7, 10, 12, 14, 15, 18; זנה צלמה . . . . צלמה זנה "this is his image . . . this statue" Nerab 3, 6-7 (*KAI* 225). -- צלם m. = statue of a man; צלמה f. = statue of a woman: צלמא די . . . מלכא "the statue of . . . a king" Hatra 1 (*KAI* 243); צלמתא די סמי "the statue of SMY" Hatra 1 (*KAI* 239); + . -- (2) **image, expression** (cf. רו, חֲזוֹת, חֵזוּ, זִיו). צְלֵם אַנְפּוֹהִי אִשְׁתַּנִּי עַל שַׁדְרַךְ "the expression of his face changed against Shadrach" Dan 3:19; כמה . . . שפיר לה צלם אנפיהא "how . . . beautiful (was) the form of her (Sarai's) face" *1QapGen* 20:2. [Hebr. צֶלֶם]. †

צְפִיר * (ṣapīr, BL 188h), cst. pl. צְפִירֵי : **he-goat, kid.** וּצְפִירֵי עִזִּין לְחַטָּיָא עַל־כָּל־יִשְׂרָאֵל תְּרֵי־עֲשַׂר "and as sin-offerings for all Israel twelve he-goats" Ezra 6:17. [Hebr. צָפִיר from Ar. for שָׂעִיר]. [1]

צְפַּר * (perh. ṣippur, BL 191b), pl. צִפְּרִין , cst. צְפָרֵי , emph. צִפְּרַיָּא , f. in Dan 4:18 & 4:9 q. (m. in 4:9 k.): **bird.** וּבְעַנְפוֹהִי יִשְׁכְּנָן צִפְּרֵי שְׁמַיָּא "and in the branches of it (the tree) the birds of the heavens dwell" Dan 4:18: 4:9; וְטִפְרוֹהִי כְּצִפְּרִין "and his nails (became) like (the claws of) birds" 4:30; כי צנפר הי מלה "for a word is (like) a bird" *Aḥ.* 98; צפרי שמיא "birds of the heavens" *11QtgJob (11Q10)* 13:2. [Hebr. צִפּוֹר]. †

קבל

ק

The letter ק designated in Old Aramaic two primitive
sounds: (1) *q;* (2) $\check{\underline{g}}$ (< *ḏ**); later pronounced '
and written as ע : ארק & ארע "land, earth."

קבל , **Pa.** 3 sg. m. קַבֵּל ; impf. 3 pl. m. יְקַבְּלוּן , 2 pl. m.
תְּקַבְּלוּן : **receive.** מַתְּנָן . . . תְּקַבְּלוּן מִן־קֳדָמָי "you will receive . . .
gifts from me" Dan 2:6; דָּרְיָוֶשׁ מָדָי קַבֵּל מַלְכוּתָא "Darius the Mede
received the kingship" 6:1: 7:18. [Hebr. קִבֵּל]. †

קֳבֵל (*qubl,* BL 48a; properly a noun, "that which is in
front of, opposite"; cf. Hebr. נֶגֶד); prep. לָקֳבֵל, קֳבֵל , w. suff.
לְקָבְלָךְ ; כָּל־קֳבֵל , prob. for כְּלָקֳבֵל (BL 262q); cf. כְּ no. 4 &
כלמדנח "to the east" *1QapGen* 21:20; כלצפון "to the north"
4QEnᶜ (4Q204) 1 xii 30. (I) Prep. (1) **before, opposite, in
front of.** אנתם קמו קבלהם "get up before them," i.e., to help
them, *AP* 38:6; קָאֵם לְקָבְלָךְ . . . דִּכֵּן רַב "that statue was great .
. . standing before you" Dan 2:31; קָאֲמִין לָקֳבֵל צַלְמָא "they were
standing in front of the statue" 3:3: 5:1; וְכָתְבָן לָקֳבֵל נֶבְרַשְׁתָּא "and
(the fingers) were writing opposite the lampstand" 5:5; [על] חלא
זי לקבל בירתא "[on] the sand that is in front of the fortress" *AP*
26:6-7; [ע]ב]ד[ו] קרבא . . . לקובלי כדרלע[ומר] "[they f]ought the
battle . . . opposite Chedorla[omer]" *1QapGen* 21:31-32 (for the
pl. form, see BL 257a, 261h). -- (2) **according to.** אנת עבד לקבל
זנה זי המרכריא אמרן "you are to act according to what the accountants say" *AP* 26:22-23; יתי[דע] למראן לקבל זנה זי אנחנה אמרן "it
will be made [known] to our lord (that the matter is) according to
what we are saying" *AP* 27:10; ספרא זנא הנפקי ולקבלה דין עורי עמה
"bring out (f.) this document and according to it bring a court-
case against him" *AP* 8:27; פתפא זנה הבו להם מן פקיד על פקיד לקבל
אדונא זי מן מדינה עד מדינה "give them this provision, from (one) officer to (another) according to the (stages of their) journey from
province to province" *AD* 6:5; עמיר לקבל רכשה "fodder according

284

קבל

to (the number of) his riders' horses" *AD* 6:4. -- (3) **because of,
on account of.** לָקֳבֵל מִלֵּי מַלְכָּא "(the queen entered the banquet-
hall) because of the words of the king" Dan 5:10 (cf. 5:7); לָקֳבֵל
דְּנָה חֲלָק . . . . לָא אִיתַי לָךְ "on account of this . . . you will have no
share" Ezra 4:16; [זי יהבתי לי] לקבל סבול "on account of the
support [which you gave to me]" *AP* 43:4; כָּל־קֳבֵל דְּנָה מַלְכָּא בְּנַס
"because of this the king became angry" Dan 2:12: 2:24; 3:7, 8;
6:10; Ezra 7:17; כָּל־קֳבֵל דְּנָה מִן־דִּי מִלַּת מַלְכָּא מַחְצְפָה "because of
this that the word of the king was severe" Dan 3:22.

לָקֳבֵל דִּי־שְׁלַח (II) W. conj. דִּי : לָקֳבֵל דִּי ,לָקֳבֵל דִּי. כָּל־קֳבֵל דִּי (1) **as.**
דָּרְיָוֶשׁ מַלְכָּא כְּנֵמָא . . . עֲבַדוּ "as Darius the king had sent word, so . .
. they did" Ezra 6:13; לקבל זי בנה הוה קדמין "(let the temple be
rebuilt) as it had been built before" *AP* 30:25; . . . לבונתא יקרבון
לקבל זי לקדמין הוה מתעבד "let them offer incense . . . as it was
done formerly" *AP* 32:9-11; אנת לקבל זי אנה עבדת לך כן אפו עבד לי
"As I did for you, so now do for me" *Aḥ.* 51-52; עבד לקבל זי אנת
עשׂת "do as you think (is right)" *Aḥ.* 68; הלכא לקבל זי קדמן פמון
אבוהי הוה חשל יחשל על ביתא זילי "he must pay the land-tax to my
estate, as Pamun, his father, used to pay formerly" *AD* 8:5-6;
יעבד פתכר סוסה עם רכבה לקבל זי קדמן עבד קדמי "(that) he may make
a sculpture of a horse with its rider as he previously made for
me" *AD* 9:2; זולו מן בתין נכסן ולקבל זי ידכם מה ימנה הבו "sell (?)
property from our houses, and as you can, pay what he assesses,"
lit., "as your hand (permits)" *AP* 38:8-9; כָּל־קֳבֵל דִּי פַרְזְלָא מְהַדֵּק
וְחָשֵׁל כֹּלָּא . . . כָּל־אִלֵּין תַּדֵּק "as iron breaks and shatters everything
. . . (so) will (the fourth kingdom) break up all these (others)"
Dan 2:40: 2:41, 45; 6:11; [כּלקבל זי מן עלא כת[יב] "as is writ[ten]
above" *Mur 72* 1:6. -- (2) **because, since.** עִדָּנָא אַנְתּוּן זָבְנִין
כָּל־קֳבֵל דִּי חֲזֵיתוּן "you are trying to gain time because you see"
Dan 2:8: 3:29; 4:15; 5:12; 6:4, 5, 23; Ezra 7:14; כָּל־קֳבֵל דִּי־מְלַח
הֵיכְלָא מְלַחְנָא . . . עַל־דְּנָה שְׁלַחְנָא "since we eat the salt of the palace .
. . for this reason we have sent word" Ezra 4:14; לקבל זי סבלתני
"because she supported me" *BMAP* 9:17. -- (3) Specifically: לָא

285

הַשְׁפֵּלְתְּ לִבְבָךְ כָּל־קֳבֵל דִּי כָל־דְּנָה יְדַעְתָּ "you did not humble your heart, although you knew all this" Dan 5:22; מִלָּה . . . כָּל־קֳבֵל דִּי כָּל־מֶלֶךְ שָׁאֵל כִּדְנָה לָא "because no king . . . has ever asked for such a thing" 2:10 (cf. כָּל־קֳבֵל דְּנָה no. I 3).

קַדִּישׁ (qattīl, BL 192e), pl. קַדִּישִׁין, cst. קַדִּישֵׁי, adj.: **holy.** רוּחַ אֱלָהִין קַדִּישִׁין "the spirit of the holy gods" Dan 4:5, 6, 18; 5:11 (attract. for קַדִּישָׁה "a holy spirit"); טורא קדישא "the holy mountain" *1QapGen* 19:8. As a noun: יאמיא אנה לך בקדישא רבא "I swear to you by the Great Holy One" *1QapGen* 2:14; וַאֲלוּ עִיר וְקַדִּישׁ מִן־שְׁמַיָּא נָחִת "and lo, a Watcher and a holy one was descending from heaven" Dan 4:10, 20; וּמֵאמַר קַדִּישִׁין שְׁאֵלְתָּא "and the question by a word of holy ones" 4:14; מן קדישין זרעא "the seed was from Holy Ones" *1QapGen* 2:1; קַרְנָא דִכֵּן עָבְדָה קְרָב עִם־קַדִּישִׁין "that horn was doing battle with Holy Ones" Dan 7:21; יְהִיבַת לְעַם קַדִּישֵׁי עֶלְיוֹנִין "(the kingdom shall) be given to the people of the saints of the Most High" 7:27 (attract. for עֶלְיוֹן, BL 202o, 305g): 7:13, 22, 25. [Hebr. קָדוֹשׁ]. †

קֳדָם (qudām), prep. (properly a noun, "face, front," cf. Hebr. פָּנִים); w. suff. (acc. *BHS;* on pl. form, see BL 261h) קָדָמַי קֳדָמַי & (= qŏ-), in pause (BL 23d) קֳדָמָי & קֳדָמָי ; קֳדָמָיךְ, k. & קֳדָמָךְ q. (BL 74w, 77o); קֳדָמוֹהִי & קֳדָמוֹהִי & וּקֳדָמוֹהִי (Dan 7:13); קֳדָמַיה k. & קֳדָמַה q. (BL 79s); קֳדָמֵיהוֹן (qŏdāmêhôn): (1) **before, in front of, in the presence of.** קָדָמוֹהִי יְקוּמוּן "were standing before him" Dan 7:10b; מן הו זי יקום קדמוהי "who is he who can stand before him," i.e., resist a king, *Aḥ.* 107; עדיא אלן זי גזר בר גא]יה קדם אשר[ומלש "(it is) this treaty that Bar Ga'[yah] has concluded [in the presence of (the gods) Asshur] and Mullesh" *Sefire I* A 7-8; קבלת עליך על דברה קדם . . . דיניא "I complained against you about it (the plot of land) before . . . the judges" *AP* 6:5-6. -- (2) **before** (of time). מִן־כָּל־חֵיוָתָא דִּי קֳדָמַיה "from all the beasts that (were) before it" Dan 7:7; בנה הוה מן קדמן קדם כנבוזי

286

"(that temple) was built formerly before Cambyses," came to Egypt, *AP* 32:4-5; קדם שבה "before Sabbath" *IEJ* 11 (1961) 44 (lines 5-6)*; הוית אנת<ת<י מן קדם דה "you were my wife before this" *Mur 19* 1:5 (cf. ה]וי[ת אנתתי מן קדמת דנא *Mur 19* 2:16-17). -- (3) after a verb of saying, etc.: **before, in front of, in the presence of.** עֲנֵה דָנִיֵּאל קֳדָם מַלְכָּא וְאָמַר "Daniel answered in the presence of the king and said" Dan 2:27: 2:10; עֲנֵה דָנִיֵּאל וְאָמַר קֳדָם מַלְכָּא "Daniel spoke up and said before the king" 5:17: 6:14; לממר קדם ארשם על בית מדבחא "(let this be a memento) . . . to speak before Arsames about the altar-house" *AP* 32:2-3; וּפִשְׁרֵהּ נֵאמַר קֳדָם־מַלְכָּא "and we shall utter the interpretation of it (the dream) in front of the king" Dan 2:36: 2:9; 4:5a; 5:17; 6:13, 14 (cf. 6:16); וְחֶלְמָא אָמַר אֲנָה קֳדָמֵיהוֹן "and I recounted the dream in their presence" 4:4: 4:5b; לָא אִיתַי דִּי יְחַוִּנַּהּ קֳדָם מַלְכָּא "there is no one who can show it to the king" 2:11; נִשְׁתְּוָנָא . . . מְפָרַשׁ קֱרִי קָדְמָי "the letter . . . has been plainly read in my presence" Ezra 4:18; קֱרִי קֳדָם־רְחוּם "(the king's reply) was read before Rehum" 4:23; [רז]יך אל תגלי קדם [רח]מיך "do not reveal your [sec]rets in front of your [frien]ds" *Aḥ.* 141; הוּא בָּרֵךְ עַל־בִּרְכוֹהִי . . . וּמוֹדֵא קֳדָם אֱלָהֵהּ "(Daniel) knelt down on his knees . . . and gave thanks in the presence of his God" Dan 6:11: 6:12; אודית תמן קודם אלהא "I gave thanks there before God" *1QapGen* 21:3. -- (4) after a verb of motion: **to, before, into the presence of** (= עַל). עַל קָדָמַי "(Daniel) entered into my (royal) presence" Dan 4:5 (cf. עַל עַל־אַרְיוֹךְ "went in to Arioch" 2:24); הַעֵלְנִי קֳדָם מַלְכָּא "bring me in before the king" 2:24: 2:25; 4:3; 5:13; 6:19; וּלְמָאנַיָּא דִי־בַיְתֵהּ הַיְתִיו קֳדָמָיךְ "and they brought the vessels of His house into your presence" 5:23: 3:13; וּקֳדָמוֹהִי הַקְרְבוּהִי "and they presented him before Him" 7:13; קרבתך קדם סנחאריב מלכא "I brought you into the presence of Sennacherib, the king" *Aḥ.* 50; זי פסמשך יהקרב קדמיך "whom Psamshek will present before you" *AD* 3:7; [לחם ומין] יסתבלון קדם מראי "[bread and water] will be carried into the presence of my lord" *Aḥ.* 72-73; [א]נה קדם מראי שלחת לאמר "I sent word to my lord, saying" *AP* 16:8; גהנת וסגד[ת] לם אחיקר קדם

[אסרח[אדן] "I bowed down and [I] did homage, I, Ahiqar, before Esarhad[don, the king]" *Ah.* 13 (cf. מַלְכָּא . . . לְדָנִיֵּאל סְגִד "the king . . . did homage to Daniel," Dan 2:46); הַשְׁלֵם קֳדָם אֱלָהּ יְרוּשְׁלֶם "deliver (the vessels) before the God of Jerusalem" Ezra 7:19; שמת קדם [אלור] נצבא זנה "I set up this stele before ['Elur (the god)]" *Zkr* B13-14 (*KAI* 202); cf. לאלור . . . בר[ה]דד [נ]צבא זי שם "the [st]ele that Bar Haddad set up . . . for 'Elur" *Zkr* A 1 (*KAI* 202). -- (5) other verbs: **against, by, through,** or as a dative (= לְ, עַל). קֳדָמָיךְ מַלְכָּא חֲבוּלָה לָא עַבְדֵת "against you, O King, I have done no wrong" Dan 6:23 (cf. πάτερ, ἥμαρτον . . . ἐνώπιόν σου "Father, I have sinned . . . against you" Luke 15:18); העדית חטאיך קדמוהי "I took away your offenses against him" *Ah.* 50; מן הו זי יקום קדמוהי להן זי אל עמה "who is the one who can stand against him, if not the one with whom God is?" *Ah.* 107; בזנה קדמי שלם אף תמה קדמ[י]ך שלם יהוי "here there is peace by me, may there also be peace there through you" *AD* 5:1-2 (cf. שלם לן תנה "there is peace for us here" *AP* 37:2; שלם יהוי לך "may there be peace for you" *Ah.* 110); לקבל זי קדמן עבד קדמי "corresponding to that which he formerly made for me" *AD* 9:2; לנקיה קדם אסי אלהתא "as a lamb (offered) to Isis, the goddess" *AP* 72:16 (on נקיה, see *Hermopolis* 2:8); קדם אוסרי בריכה הוי "may you be blessed by Osiris" *Carpentras* 3 (*KAI* 269), (cf. ברכתך לפתח "I bless you through (the god) Ptah" *Hermopolis* 3:1-2). -- (6) **with, in the eyes of, in the opinion of** (= עַל no. 7). שְׁפַר קֳדָמַי "it has seemed good in my eyes" Dan 3:32: 6:2; כָּל־קֳבֵל דִּי קֳדָמוֹהִי זָכוּ הִשְׁתְּכַחַת לִי "because in his opinion I was found innocent," lit., "innocence was found in me" 6:23; a-na-' za-ki-it . . . qu-da-am ra-ab-ra-bi-e "I am innocent in the eyes of those who are great" *Warka* 10-11; לרחמן ישימנך קדם דריוהוש מלכא "may (God) give you favor in the eyes of Darius, the King" *AP* 30:2; לרחמן תהוו קדם אלה שמיא "may you (pl.) find favor with the God of Heaven" *AP* 38:2-3; [לא]שכחה רחמיך קדמיך "[to f]ind favor in your eyes" *4QLevi*[b] (*4Q213a*) 1:15; אגורא זך יתבנה וצדקה יהוה לך קדם יהו אלה "let that temple be rebuilt, and you will have merit in the eyes of the God

[רז]יך אל תגלי קדם [רח]מיך [ו]אל יקל שמך קדמיהם ;AP 30:27 "Yaho"
"do not reveal your [sec]rets before your [frien]ds that your name
be not evil in their eyes" *Aḥ.* 141. -- (7) מִן = מִן־קֳדָם : **from,
before, by.** מַתְּנָן . . . תְּקַבְּלוּן מִן־קֳדָמָי "you will receive . . . gifts
from me" Dan 2:6; עַל־מָה דָתָא מְהַחְצְפָה מִן־קֳדָם מַלְכָּא "why is the
decree from the king so severe?" 2:15 (attributive prep. BL
316h); לֶהֱוֹן . . . דָּחֲלִין מִן־קֳדָם אֱלָהֵהּ דִּי־דָנִיֵּאל "(that people) shall fear
before the God of Daniel" Dan 6:27; 5:19 (cf. Hebr. יָרֵא מִפְּנֵי);
נְהַר דִּי־נוּר . . . נָפֵק מִן־קֳדָמוֹהִי "a stream of fire . . . came out from
before him" 7:10 (cf. Hebr. וַתֵּצֵא אֵשׁ מִלִּפְנֵי יהוה "and fire came
forth from before Yahweh" Lev 9:24); מן קדם אוסרי מין קחי "take
water from Osiris!" *Carpentras* 3 (*KAI* 269); להעדיה ביתא זנה מן
קדמיכי "to take this house away from you" *BMAP* 10:13; מִן־קֳדָם
מַלְכָּא . . . שְׁלִיחַ "(you) are sent . . . by the king" Ezra 7:14; מִן־קֳדָמַי
שִׂים טְעֵם "I make a decree," lit., "a decree is issued by me" Dan
6:27 (otherwise always מִן); אֶתְעֲקַרוּ מִן־קֳדָמַיהּ "(three of the first
horns) were plucked up by it (the little horn)" 7:8; וְאָחֳרִי דִּי סִלְקַת
וּנְפַלוּ מִן־קֳדָמַיהּ תְּלָת "and another (horn) which came up, and
before which three (of the horns) fell" 7:20 (LXX: δι' αὐτοῦ).
[Hebr. קֶדֶם]. †

Cf. קדם, pl. קַדְמִין *, noun, m.: **former time(s)** (cf. אַחֲרִין *).
לקבל זי בנה הוה קדמין "(let that temple be rebuilt) as it was built
(in) former times" *AP* 30:25; לקבל זי לקדמין הוה מתעבד "as it was
done formerly" *AP* 32:10-11; זי . . . בנה הוה מן קדמן "(the temple)
which . . . was built formerly" *AP* 32:4-5; וכעת קדמן כזי מצריא
מרדו "and now, formerly when the Egyptians rebelled" *AD* 7:1.

קָדְמָה *, cst. קָדְמַת (properly that which is before someone or something); in cst. it is a prep.: (1) **before, in the presence of** (like קֶדֶם nos. 1 & 2). ויתלקח קדמתהן בסון "and it will be
recovered (only) in Syene in their presence" *Hermopolis* 1:9; הֲוָא
עָבֵד מִן־קַדְמַת דְּנָה "(as) he had been doing previously," lit., "before
this" Dan 6:11 (cf. מִן no. 4); די הוא מן קדמת דנה "(that place)

which previously belonged (to . . .)" *XHev/Se50+Mur26* d:7;
וּבָנַיִן בַּיְתָא דִּי־הֲוָא בְנֵה מִקַּדְמַת דְּנָה שְׁנִין שַׂגִּיאָן "and we are rebuilding
the house that had been built many years before this" Ezra 5:11;
קדמת זנה בעדן זי זא באישתא עביד לן "before this, at the time when
this evil (f.) was done (m.) to us" *AP* 30:17-18; קדמת יומיא אלן
"before those days" *1QapGen* 21:23. -- (2) **against** (= עַל, like
קֳדָם). חזי קדמתך מנדעם קשה [על א]נפי מ[לך] אל תקום "(if you) see
something hard against you [on the fa]ce of a k[ing], do not rise
up" *Aḥ.* 101; אל תקמי קדמתה "do not rise up against him" *Hermopolis* 2:15.

קַדְמִי * (BL 196d, 2041), m. emph. קַדְמָיָא *, f. emph.
קַדְמָיְתָא; pl. m. emph. קַדְמָיֵא, f. emph. קַדְמָיָתָא, adj.: **first, former.** קַדְמָיְתָא כְאַרְיֵה "the first (beast) was like a lion" Dan 7:4;
תְּלָת מִן־קַרְנַיָּא קַדְמָיָתָא "three of the former horns (were plucked
up)" 7:8; וְהוּא יִשְׁנֵא מִן־קַדְמָיֵא "and he shall be different from the
former (kings)" 7:24; <פ>סמשך פקידא קדמיא "Psamshek, the
former officer" *AD* 7:1; פקידיא [קד]מיא "the former officers" *AD*
7:7-8. [Hebr. קַדְמוֹנִי]. †

קום (see the paradigm, *GBA* pp. 68-69), 3 sg. m. קָם , 3
pl. m. קָמוּ , 1 pl. קָמְנָא & קמן ; impf. 3 sg. m. יְקוּם , 3 sg. f.
תְּקוּם , 2 sg. f. תקומי (*tĕqûmî*); 3 pl. m. יְקֻמוּן & יְקוּמוּן ; impv.
sg. m. קום , sg. f. קוּמִי , pl. m. קמו (*qûmû*); infin. מקם
(*miqām*); ptc. (BL 51h, j, 145m) sg. m. קָאֵם * & קָאֵם , pl. m.
קָאֲמִין (k.) & קָיְמִין (q.), m. emph. קָאֲמַיָּא , pl. f. קימן (*qāyĕmān*).
(1) **rise, get up.** מַלְכָּא . . . יְקוּם . . . וּבְהִתְבְּהָלָה לְגֻבָּא דִי־אַרְיָוָתָא אֲזַל
"the king . . . got up . . . and went in haste to the lions' den" Dan
6:20; וּבָתְרָךְ תְּקוּם מַלְכוּ אָחֳרִי "and after you another kingdom shall
arise" 2:39; אַרְבְּעָה מַלְכִין יְקוּמוּן מִן־אַרְעָא "four kings shall arise
from the earth" 7:17: 7:24a,b. -- Introducing another verb with
some emphasis: וְקָם בְּהִתְבְּהָלָה עָנֵה וְאָמַר לְהַדָּבְרוֹהִי "and (the king)
rose in haste and spoke to his counselors, saying" Dan 3:24; וְכֵן

290

קום

אָמְרִין לַהּ קוּמִי אֲכֻלִי בְּשַׂר שַׂגִּיא "and thus they said to it (the beast), 'Get up, devour much flesh'" 7:5; קום הלך ואזל וחזי "rise, walk about, and go and see" *1QapGen* 21:13-14; אתחלם אברם וקם ובחר מן עבדוהי "Abram summoned up his courage, rose up, and chose from his slaves" *1QapGen* 22:5-6; לא יכלו כול אסיא . . . למקם "none of the physicians were able . . . to rise up and cure him" *1QapGen* 20:20; קָמוּ . . . וְשָׁרִיו לְמִבְנֵא בֵּית אֱלָהָא "they rose .. . and began to rebuild God's house" Ezra 5:2. -- Used in a hostile sense: ו[הן] יקום על מפטחיה לתרכותה מן ביתה "and [if] he rises up against (his wife) Miphṭaḥiah to drive her out of his house" *AP* 15:29-30; זי יקום עליכי "whoever rises up against you (f.)" *BMAP* 5:7; אנחן הן קמן לאמר לא נסבלנך "if we rise up, saying, 'We shall not provide for you'" *BMAP* 5:13. -- (2) **stand (by), remain, resist.** וְקָאֲמִין לְקֳבֵל צַלְמָא "and they were standing in front of the statue" Dan 3:3; צַלְמָא דִכֵּן רַב . . . קָאֵם לְקָבְלָךְ "that great statue . . . was standing before you" 2:31; וְרִבּוֹ רִבְוָן קֳדָמוֹהִי יְקוּמוּן "and myriads upon myriads stood before him" 7:10; קִרְבֵת עַל־חַד "I drew near to one of those standing by" 7:16; וְהִיא מִן קָאֲמַיָּא "and it (God's kingdom) shall remain for ever" 2:44; תְּקוּם לְעָלְמַיָּא "the house . . . the walls of which are ביתא . . . זי אגרוה קימן standing (firm)" *BMAP* 3:4; בעלשמין וקם עמי .[ ] "Be'elshemayin, and he stood by me" *Zkr* A 3 (*KAI* 202); אנתם קמו קבלהם "(as for) you, stand by them!" *AP* 38:6; מן הו זי יקום קדמוהי "who is the one that can stand before him," i.e., resist him? *Aḥ.* 107; אל תקמי קדמתה "do not resist him," lit., "stand against him" *Hermopolis* 2:15; אל תקום חת מנפי לעבק "(when this letter reaches you), do not remain (there); come down at once to Memphis" *AP* 42:7; כספא זי קם יומא הו ביד ידניה "the money that was paid that day into the hand of Yedaniah," lit., "that stood in the" *AP* 22:120-21; א[י]ש זי יזבן ביתא . . . והבה לה בכספא זי יקו[ם] עלוהי "a m[a]n who will buy the house . . . and give it to him for the money at which it is valued," lit., "which stands over it" *AP* 42:6.

Pa. (BL 146r, s), 3 sg. m. קים (*qayyēm/qayyim*), 3 sg. f. קימת (*qayyěmat*), 3 pl. m. קימו (*qayyimû*); infin. קימא & קַיָּמָה : (1) **carry off** (i.e., cause to go up; cf. קום no. 1). ודשיהם קימו וציריהם זי דששיא אלך נחש "and their portals they carried off, and the hinges of those portals were bronze" *AP* 30:10-11. -- (2) **confirm, ratify** (i.e., cause to stand firm; cf. קום no. 2). לְקַיָּמָה קְיָם מַלְכָּא וּלְתַקָּפָה אֱסָר "(his counselors agreed that) the king should confirm an ordinance and enforce an interdict" Dan 6:8 (see 6:9, 13, 16); ידיהם כתבת וקימת קדמי "their hands have written (it) and ratified (it) before me" *Assur Letter* 9 (*KAI* 233); [לקימה זבנה דך קדמך וקדם י[רחך "[to confirm that sale before you and before] your [h]eir" *XHev/SeDeedSaleG (XHev/Se 23)* Recto 5.

Haph./Aph. (BL 147v-148d), 3 sg. m. הֲקֵים & הָקֵים , w. suff. הֲקִימֵהּ & אֲקִימֵהּ , 3 sg. f. הֲקֵימַת , 2 sg. m. הֲקֵימְתָּ , 1 sg. הֲקֵימֵת , 3 pl. m. הֲקִימוּ ; impf. 3 sg. m. יְהָקֵים & יְקִים , 2 sg. m. תְּקִים ; impv. sg. m. w. suff. הֲקִימֵנִי ; infin. הֲקָמָה *, w. suff. הֲקָמוּתֵהּ ; ptc. sg. m. מְהָקֵים : (1) **set up, lift up, erect** (cause to rise; cf. קום no. 1). יְקִים אֱלָהּ שְׁמַיָּא מַלְכוּ דִּי לְעָלְמִין "the God of Heaven will set up a kingdom that (lasts) for ever . . ." Dan 2:44; צַלְמָא דִּי הֲקֵים נְבוּכַדְנֶצַּר "the statue that Nebuchadnezzar had erect-ed" 3:2: 3:1, 5, 7, 12, 14, 18; פתכר זנה הקם ננשת "Nanshet erected this sculpture" *Cilicia* 1 (*KAI* 258). -- (2) **establish, set up** (cause to stand; cf. קום no. 2). הֲקִימוּ כָהֲנַיָּא . . . עַל עֲבִידַת אֱלָהָא "they set up priests . . . for the service of God" Ezra 6:18; מְהָקֵים "(God who) sets up kings" Dan 2:21; מַלְכִין שְׁפַל אֲנָשִׁים יְקִים עֲלַיהּ "(God) sets up over it the lowliest of men" 4:14: 5:21; הֲקֵים עַל־מַלְכוּתָא לַאֲחַשְׁדַּרְפְּנַיָּא "(Darius) established the satraps over the kingdom" 6:2: 6:4; [זי] . . . הקימת בבב היכלא "[whom] . . . I set up in the gate of the palace" *Ah.* 23; הקימני אל בצדיק עמך "set me up, O God, as a righteous man with You" *Ah.* 173 (see בְ no, 7); כְּעַן מַלְכָּא תְּקִים אֱסָרָא "now, O King, establish the prohibition" Dan 6:9: 6:16. -- W. two accus.: הֲקֵימֵהּ . . . רַב חַרְטֻמִּין "(the king) made him . . . chief of the magicians" Dan 5:11; זי הקים לברה "whom he set up as his son," i.e., whom he adopted, *Ah.* 12.

קְטַל

Hoph. (BL 41o, 147b), 3 sg. f. הָקִימַת & הָקְמַת (v.l. הָקֵמַת הָקֵמַת, , cf. BL 149r): **be made to stand, be established, be set up** (be made to stand, rise). וּנְטִילַת מִן־אַרְעָא וְעַל־רַגְלַיִן כֶּאֱנָשׁ הָקִימַת "and (the lion) was lifted up from the ground and made to stand on two feet like a man" Dan 7:4 (cf. *AH* I/1.36: Ginsberg reads הָקֵמַת); לִשְׂטַר־חַד הֳקֵמַת "it (another beast) was raised up on one side" 7:5 (cf. *AH* I/1.37: Ginsberg reads הָקִימַת "raised one side"): a very unclear text.

קְטַל * (& קתל & כטל , BL 33d; *LFAA* 12d), 3 pl. קטלו (qĕṭálû); impf. 3 sg. m. w. suff. יקתלנה (yiqtulinnēh), 3 pl. m. יקתלן (yiqtĕlûn), 1 pl. w. suff. נכטלנהי ; juss. 3 pl. m. w. suff. יכטלוך ; infin. w. suff. מקטלני ; act. ptc. sg. m. קָטֵל ; pass. ptc. sg. m. קטיל , sg. f. קְטִילָה *. **Peil** perf. 3 sg. m. קְטִיל , 3 sg. f. קְטִילַת, 1 sg. קטילת, 3 pl. קטילו . **Hithpe.** impf. יתקטל (yitqĕṭēl); infin. הִתְקְטָלָה : **kill, slay.** דִּי־הֲוָה צָבֵא הֲוָא קָטֵל "(the king) would slay whom he wanted" Dan 5:19; [וישלח יד ב]ברי ויקתלנה "[and should he extend a hand against] my son and kill him" *Sefire I* B 26-27; הן אי[ת] י[ ]ן יקתלן "if they kill me" ('iyyātî Sefire III* 11); [י]קתל מן יקתל "let [him] kill whomever he would kill" *Sefire II* B 9; אל נקטלנהי "let us not slay him" *Aḥ.* 61; [חילא זי]לי קטלו למרדיא "[m]y [troops] killed the rebels" *Bisitun* 13; יכטלוך "may they kill you" *Nerab* 11 (*KAI* 225; cf. *LFAA* 17c-e); די יבעון למקטלני "who will seek to kill me" *1QapGen* 19:19. -- In pass.: אחיקר ספרא זי . . . מלכא קטיל "Aḥiqar, the scribe of . . .the king, has been killed" *Aḥ.* 71; בֵּהּ בְּלֵילְיָא קְטִיל בֵּלְאשַׁצַּר מַלְכָּא "in that night Belshazzar, the king, was slain" Dan 5:30; קְטִילַת חֵיוְתָא "the beast was killed" 7:11; כלא קטילו "all of them were killed" *AP* 31:16; בְּעוֹ דָנִיֵּאל וְחַבְרוֹהִי לְהִתְקְטָלָה "they sought Daniel and his companions, to kill them," lit., "to be killed" Dan 2:13; סריס זילי יתקטל . . . חלף אחיקר זנה "let my eunuch be killed . . . instead of this Aḥiqar" *Aḥ.* 61-62; ולא קטילת "and I was not killed" *1QapGen* 20:10. -- **Pa.** 3 sg. m. קַטֵּל ;

infin. קְטָלָה . -- **Hithpa.** ptc. pl. m. מִתְקַטְּלִין : **kill, slay.** קְטַל
הִמּוֹן שְׁבִיבָא דִּי נוּרָא "the flame of fire killed them" Dan 3:22; דִּי
נְפַק לְקַטָּלָה לְחַכִּימֵי בָבֶל "who had gone out to kill the sages of Babylon" 2:14; דָּתָא נֶפְקַת וְחַכִּימַיָּא מִתְקַטְּלִין "the decree was issued, that
the sages were to be slain" 2:13 (see וְ no. 9). [Hebr. קָטַל]. †

קְטַר * (*Warka* 1 *kiṭar*), pl. קִטְרִין , cst. קִטְרֵי , m.: **joint,
knob; difficulty.** קִטְרֵי חַרְצֵהּ מִשְׁתָּרַיִן "his hip-joints were loosened (because of fear)" Dan 5:6; דִּי־תִכֻּל . . . קִטְרִין לְמִשְׁרֵא "that
you can . . . solve difficulties" 5:16; וּמִשָׁרֵא קִטְרִין הִשְׁתְּכַחַת בֵּהּ
"and solving (ptc.) difficulties has been found in him (Daniel)"
5:12 (read w. Vg. מִשְׁרֵא "the solution of"). †

קַיִט (*qayṭ*), m.: **summer.** וַהֲווֹ כְּעוּר מִן־אִדְּרֵי־קַיִט "and
they became like chaff of the summer threshing-floors" Dan 2:35
(cf. דִּי I/2 a; BL 316h); הא בית שתוא להם והא בית כיצא "that was a
winter-house for them, and that was a summer-house" *Barrakib*
18-19 (*KAI* 216). [Hebr. קַיִץ]. [1]

קְיָם (*qayām*): **covenant, statute.** קְיָם דִּי־מַלְכָּא יְהָקֵים
"(no) statute that the king has established" Dan 6:16; לְקַיָּמָה קְיָם
מַלְכָּא "(the ministers agreed that) the king should establish a statute" 6:8 (cf. דִּי I/2 a); היקים קים עמך "will he contract a covenant
with you?" *11QtgJob (11Q10)* 35:6-7. †

קַיָּם (*qattāl,* BL 191c), sg. f. קַיָּמָה , adj.: **stable, enduring.** הוּא אֱלָהָא חַיָּא וְקַיָּם לְעָלְמִין "He is a living God, enduring for
ever!" Dan 6:27; מַלְכוּתָךְ לָךְ קַיָּמָה מִן־דִּי תִנְדַּע דִּי שַׁלִּטִן שְׁמַיָּא "your
kingdom shall be stable for you from the time that you realize
that Heaven rules" 4:23. †

קתרס, קיתרוס (< Gk. κιθάρα, κίθαρις "lyre"), q. קַתְרֹס ,
k. קִיתָרֹס or קיתָרֹס : **lyre, zither.** קַיתָרוֹס . . . תִּשְׁמְעוּן קָל "(when)

294

you hear the sound of . . . the lyre" Dan 3:5: 3:7, 10, 15 (collect. sg.). †

קָל (qāl, BL 179h), m.: **voice, sound, noise.** לְדָנִיֵּאל בְּקָל עֲצִיב זְעִק "(the king) cried out to Daniel in an anguished voice" Dan 6:21; קָל מִן־שְׁמַיָּא נְפַל "there fell from heaven a voice" 4:28; מִן־קָל מִלַּיָּא רַבְרְבָתָא דִּי קַרְנָא מְמַלֱּלָה "because of the noise of the great words that the horn was uttering" 7:11; . . . קָל תִּשְׁמְעוּן קַיתָרוֹס . . . וְכֹל זְנֵי זְמָרָא "(when) you hear the sound of . . . the lyre . . . and of every sort of musical instrument" 3:5: 3:7, 10, 15; אל יתשמע קל כנר בארפד "may the sound of the lyre not be heard in Arpad" Sefire I A 29; מלך כרחמן אף קלה גבה ה[ן] "a king is like the Merciful One; even his voice i[s] exalted" Aḥ. 107. [Hebr. קֹל ,קָל]. †

קְנָה *, impf. 2 sg. m. תִּקְנֵא : **acquire, get, buy.** תִּקְנֵא בְּכַסְפָּא דְנָה תּוֹרִין "with this money you shall buy bulls" Ezra 7:17; איש זי קנה עבד "the man who buys a slave" Aḥ. 83-84; וכל נכסין זי קנה אבדו "and all (the) goods that he had acquired were lost" AP 30:16. [Hebr. קָנָה]. [1]

קְצַף : **become angry.** מַלְכָּא בְּנַס וּקְצַף שַׂגִּיא "the king became furious and very angry" Dan 2:12. [Hebr. קָצַף]. [1]

קְצַף (qaṣp, BL 183e; LFAA 17c): **anger.** דִּי־לְמָה לֶהֱוֵא קְצַף עַל מַלְכוּת מַלְכָּא "lest (God's) anger come upon the realm of the king" Ezra 7:23; זעיר כצפה מן ברק "swifter is his (a king's) anger than lightning" Aḥ. 101. [Hebr. קֶצֶף]. [1]

קְצַץ , juss. 2 pl. m. תקוצו (tiqqûṣû; cf. יפוק "he will go forth" 1QapGen 22:34); infin. מקץ (miqqaṣ): **cut off, cut down.** בֿ[ני] אנוש אתו ובעין למקץ ולמעקר לא[א]רזא "some men came, seeking to cut down and uproot the [c]edar" 1QapGen 19:15; אל

קצת—קרא

תקוצו ל[א]רזא "do not cut down the [c]edar" *1QapGen* 19:16. --
Pa. impv. pl. m. קֻצּוּ : **cut off.** גֹּדּוּ אִילָנָא וְקַצִּצוּ עַנְפוֹהִי "hew down
the tree and cut off its branches" Dan 4:11. [Hebr. קצץ Qal &
Piel]. [1]

קְצָת (*qaṣawat,* BL 185s, 237f, h; cf. Hebr. קָצָה, "cut
off") cst. (& abs.), f.: (1) **end.** וְלִקְצָת יוֹמַיָּה "and at the end of
(those) days" Dan 4:31: 4:26 (in the same sense Hebr. מִקְצָת
Dan 1:5, 15, 18). -- (2) **part** (everywhere w. pleonastic מִן): (a)
w. partitive מִן (cf. מִן no. 3a): יהבת לכי קצת מן ביתי "I have given
to you part of my house" *BMAP* 9:2-3; . . . קצת מן גורנא זי מלכא
נדשו "they destroyed . . . part of the king's barn" *AP* 27:4-5. --
(b) w. antepositive מִן, quasi nominal, "part of a thing" (see מִן
no. 3a; cf. Brock. II. 360, 397): מִן־קְצָת מַלְכוּתָא תֶּהֱוֵה תַּקִּיפָה וּמִנַּהּ
תֶּהֱוֵה תְבִירָה "part of the kingdom will be solid, and some of it will
be fragile" Dan 2:42 (in the same sense Hebr. מִקְצָת Dan 1:2;
Neh 7:69). -- מִן־קְצָת used predicatively: [זי הוו] עלי מן קצת כסף
[ ] דמי בית מן "[which were] due from me as part of the price of
the value of the house of Mn[ ]" *AP* 29:3-4; איתי לכי עלי כסף ש
מן קצת כספא . . . 2 "you have a claim on me for the sum of 2
sh(ekels) . . . , part of the money (mentioned in your deed)" *AP*
35:3-4; ותושר לכי עמר מן קצתה זי כסף ש 1 "that she send to you
wool as her part of the money (owed) 1 sh(ekel)" *Hermopolis*
2:7. [Hebr. קָצֶה and from Ar. קְצָת]. †

קְרָא * (א"ל > ה"ל, BL 152e), impf. 3 sg. m. יִקְרֵה, 1 sg.
אֶקְרֵא, 3 pl. m. יִקְרוֹן & יִקְרְאוּן * (*Aḥ.* 117; *LFAA* 62a); infin.
מִקְרֵא ; ptc. sg. m. קָרֵא . **Peil** perf. 3 sg. m. קְרִי (BL 156u).
Hithpe. impf. 3 sg. m. יִתְקְרֵי (BL 158k): (1) **call, cry out,
proclaim.** קָרֵא מַלְכָּא בְּחַיִל לְהֶעֳלָה "the king cried out in a loud
voice to bring in (the enchanters)" Dan 5:7 (BL 294r): 4:11;
כְּעַן דָּנִיֵּאל יִתְקְרֵי ;3:4 כָּרוֹזָא קָרֵא בְחָיִל "the herald proclaimed aloud" 3:4;
וּפִשְׁרָה יְהַחֲוֵה "now let Daniel be called, and he will make known

296

the interpretation" 5:12; קרא המו שאל המו "call them; question them!" *Assur Letter* 12 (*KAI* 233); ... אסי מצרין ... ושלח קרא לכול "so he sent (and) called all . . . the physicians of Egypt" *1Qap-Gen* 20:18-19; קרא לי אלו "(the Pharaoh) summoned me," lit., "called me to him" *1QapGen* 20:26; שלחת קרית לממרה "I sent (word and) called Mamre," i.e., I invited, *1QapGen* 21:21; קרית לבני ולבני בני "I called my sons and my grandsons" *1QapGen* 12:16. -- (2) **read** (i.e., aloud): כָּל־אֱנָשׁ דִּי־יִקְרֵה כְּתָבָה דְנָה "anyone who reads this writing" Dan 5:7: 5:15; לָא־כָהֲלִין כְּתָבָא לְמִקְרֵא "they were not able to read the writing" 5:8: 5:16; כְּתָבָא אֶקְרֵא "I shall read the writing for the king" 5:17; קֱרִי ... נִשְׁתְּוָנָא לְמַלְכָּא "the letter . . . has been read before me" Ezra 4:18: 4:23. קֱדָמָי -- (3) **call upon, challenge.** מקריא על אלהן מטא עלי בדינא ... אקרא לך על חרמביתאל "the appeal to our god has been laid on me by the court . . . (that) I should challenge you by (the god) Herembethel" *AP* 7:6-7; והן [אנה] קרית לך בין [נ]קמיא אלה "and if [I] challenge you among these avengers" *AP* 7:10. [Hebr. קָרָא]. †

קְרֵב , 1 sg. קִרְבֵת , 3 pl. קְרִבוּ & קְרִיבוּ (*i* is short!); infin. מקרב (*miqrab*), w. suff. מִקְרְבֵהּ : **draw near, approach.** קְרִבוּ גֻּבְרִין כַּשְׂדָּאִין "Chaldean men drew near (to the king)" Dan 3:8: 6:13; קְרֵב נְבוּכַדְנֶצַּר לִתְרַע אַתּוּן "Nebuchadnezzar approached the door of the furnace" 3:26; כְּמִקְרְבֵהּ לְגֻבָּא "at his approach to the den" 6:21; קִרְבֵת עַל־חַד מִן־קָאֲמַיָּא "I drew near to one of those standing by" 7:16; קרב עלי ואל יאמר לך ר[חי]ק מני "draw near me, and let him not say to you, 'Be f[a]r from me'" *Aḥ.* 194; לא יכל למקרב בהא "he was not able to approach her" *1QapGen* 20:17. -- **Pa.** (BL 130h), 1 sg. w. suff. קרבתה (*qāribtēh*); impf. 2 sg. m. תְּקָרֵב : **bring, offer.** קרבתה קדם אסרחאדן מלך אתור "I brought him before Esarhaddon, the king of Assyria" *Aḥ.* 10; תִקְנֶה ... תּוֹרִין ... "you are to buy . . . bulls . . . and to offer them upon the altar" Ezra 7:17; עלותא יקרבון על מדבחא "they shall offer holocausts on the altar" *AP* 30:25-26; גבר זי יקרב לה עלוה

וּדְבַח "a man who will offer to Him a holocaust and sacrifices"
AP 30:28; על[י מרי וקרבני למהוא לכה [ע]ל[י "[up]on me, my Lord; and
bring me near to be for you . . ." *4QLevi^b (4Q213a)* 1:18. --
Haph./Aph., 3 pl. m. הַקְרִבוּ , w. suff. הַקְרְבוּהִי (BL 53q); ptc.
pl. m. מְהַקְרְבִין : **bring, offer.** עַד־עַתִּיק יוֹמַיָּא מְטָא וּקֳדָמוֹהִי הַקְרְבוּהִי
"he came to the Ancient of Days and was brought before him,"
lit., "they brought him" Dan 7:13; הן גבריא אלך] אהקרב קדמוהי
"[if] I bring [those men] before him" *AD* 3:5-6; דִּי־לֶהֱוֹן מְהַקְרְבִין
נִיחוֹחִין לֶאֱלָהּ שְׁמַיָּא "who may offer pleasing sacrifices to the God
of Heaven" Ezra 6:10: 6:17; אקרבת עלוהי עלואן ומנחה לאל עליון "I
offered on it holocausts and a meal offering to God Most High"
1QapGen 21:2. [Hebr. קרב]. †

קְרָב (*qarāb,* < Akk. infin. *qarābu,* BL 187e): **war,
battle, fight.** קַרְנָא דְכֵן עָבְדָה קְרָב עִם־קַדִּישִׁין "that horn was making
war with (the) saints" Dan 7:21; למעבד קרב] א[חר עבדו קתבא "to
join battle. [T]hen they joined battle" *Bisitun* 12; למעבד קרב
[עבדן קרבא] "[(he came against me) to join battle. We joined
battle]" *Bisitun* 26; עבדו קרב עם ברע מלך סודם "they made war on
Bera, the king of Sodom" *1QapGen* 21:24; כול אלן אזדמנו כחדא
לקרב "all these united together for a battle" *1QapGen* 21:25;
[ומ]ר[בד[ע]ו . . . לקובלי כדרלע[ומר] קרבא "and [they f]ought the battle .
. . against Chedorla[omer]" *1QapGen* 21:31-32. [Hebr. the same,
from Ar.] [1]

קִרְיָה & קַרְיָא (*qatl-at,* BL 182b), emph. קִרְיְתָא , f.: **city,
town.** בָּנַיִן . . . אֲתוֹ לִירוּשְׁלֶם קִרְיְתָא מָרָדְתָּא "they have come to
Jerusalem, the rebellious city . . . (and) are rebuilding (it)" Ezra
4:12: 4:13, 15, 16, 19, 21; הוֹתֵב הִמּוֹ בְּקִרְיָה דִּי שָׁמְרָיִן "he settled
them in (some) towns of Samaria" Ezra 4:10 (indet. collect sg.;
LXX: ἐν πόλεσιν τῆς Σομορων [= Σαμαρείας]; cf. BL 313g);
בקרית אימאם "in the town of 'YM'M" *Sefire I* B 36; הן קריה הא
נכה תכוה בחרב "if it is a city, you must strike it with a sword"

קרן—קשט

Sefire III 12-13; קריב ורחיק בעל דגל וקריה יכלא למחסה "(no)
relative or stranger, soldier or citizen, shall restrain Maḥseh," lit.,
"(no one) near and far, lord of a military detachment and a city"
AP 5:9: 13:10. [Hebr. the same, but also קֶרֶת]. †

קְרֵן (*qarn*), emph. קַרְנָא, du. קַרְנַ֫יִן, pl. קַרְנִין, emph.
קַרְנַיָּא; f.: **horn.** קֶרֶן אָחֳרִי זְעֵירָה "another horn, a small one" Dan
7:8b; עַיְנִין כְּעַיְנֵי אֲנָשָׁא בְּקַרְנָא־דָא "eyes like the eyes of a man in
this horn" 7:8c: 7:11, 21; קַרְנַיִן עֲשַׂר (v.l. קַרְנִין) "ten horns" 7:7;
קַרְנַיָּא עֲשַׂר "the ten horns" 7:20, 24: 7:8a; קָל קַרְנָא "the sound of
the horn (musical instrument)" 3:5, 7, 10, 15. [Hebr. the same]. †

קְרַץ * (*qarṣ*), pl. קַרְצִין *, w. suff. קַרְצֵיהוֹן, קַרְצוֹהִי :
piece, bit, something bitten off; figurative sense: **calumnies**
(אֲכַל/אֲמַר קַרְצֵי) w. gen. "calumniate someone, maliciously accuse
someone"). וַאֲכַלוּ קַרְצֵיהוֹן דִּי יְהוּדָיֵא "and they calumniated the
Jews" Dan 3:8; גֻּבְרַיָּא אִלֵּךְ דִּי־אֲכַלוּ קַרְצוֹהִי דִּי דָנִיֵּאל "those men who
maliciously had accused Daniel" 6:25; וכרצי איש לא אמרת "and
she calumniated no one" *Carpentras* 2 (*KAI* 269). -- The idiom
is borrowed from Akk. *karṣī akālu* "to eat bits" (see *AHW* s.v.
karṣu). †

קְשֹׁט (*qušṭ*, BL 184n, 224j): **truth.** כָּל־מַעֲבָדוֹהִי קְשֹׁט
וְאֹרְחָתֵהּ דִּין "all His deeds are true (i.e., corresponding to prom-
ises) and his ways are just," lit., "truth . . . justice" Dan 4:34;
מִן־קְשֹׁט דִּי אֱלָהֲכוֹן הוּא "truly your God is (God of gods)" 2:47 (see
מִן no. 9); בקושט עמי תמללין ולא בכדבין "that you (f.) are speaking
with me truthfully and without lies" *1QapGen* 2:7; כולא בקושטא
תחוינני "(that) you truthfully make everything known to me"
1QapGen 2:5; ארחת קשט] "paths of truth" *4QLevi^b* (*4Q213a*)
1:12. †

299

ראש

ר

רֵאשׁ (*ri'š*) abs. & cst., emph. רֵאשָׁא * & רֵאשָׁה, w. suff. רֵאשִׁי, רֵאשָׁךְ, רֵאשֵׁהּ, רֵאשָׁהּ (v.l. רֵאשַׁהּ, BL 81z), רֵאשְׁהוֹן ; pl. רֵאשִׁין, w. suff. רֵאשֵׁיהוֹן (= v.l.) & רֵאשֵׁיהֹם (BL 59d, 247f), m.:
(1) **head.** הוּא צַלְמָא רֵאשֵׁהּ דִּי־דְהַב טָב "as for that statue, its head was of fine gold" Dan 2:32; אַנְתְּה־הוּא רֵאשָׁה דִּי דַהֲבָא "you are the head of gold" 2:38; שְׂעַר רֵאשְׁהוֹן לָא הִתְחָרַךְ "the hair of their heads was not singed" 3:27 (v. l. רֵאשֵׁיהוֹן); חֶזְוֵי רֵאשִׁי "the visions of my head" 4:2, 7, 10; 7:15: 2:28; אַרְבְּעָה רֵאשִׁין לְחֵיוְתָא "the beast had four heads" 7:6: 7:20; יבעה ראשי להמתתי "(if) he seeks my head, to kill me" *Sefire III* 11; כסף ... בראשה <הכ>שנא כסף "the divorce money is on his head ... an equal sum shall be on her head" *BMAP* 2:8-9; [דבק]ת לכרמונא נהרא חד מן ראשי נהרא "I [reached} the Carmon River, one of the heads of the (Nile) River" *1QapGen* 19:11-12; [ח]לפת שבעת ראשי נהרא דן "I [cr]ossed the seven heads of this River" *1QapGen* 19:12. -- (2) **beginning.** חֶלְמָא כְתַב רֵאשׁ מִלִּין אֲמַר "he wrote down the dream; he told the beginning of the matter" Dan 7:1 (BL 353f); שנת 21 ראש מלוכתא כזי ארתחששסש מלכא יתב בכרסאה "in the year 21, the beginning of the reign, when King Artaxerxes sat on his throne" *AP* 6:1 (read מלכותא). -- (3) **capital** (in a financial sense). הן מטת מרביתא לרשא ירבה מרביתא כרשא "if the interest is added to the capital, the interest will grow as (does) the capital," lit., "comes to the capital" *AP* 10:6; ירחא זי לא אנתן לך בה מרבית<א> יהוה ראש וירבה "the month in which I do not pay you <the> interest, it will become capital and it will grow," lit., "it will become much" *AP* 11:4-5 (see Cowley's note on line 5). -- (4) בְּרֵאשׁ = prep., **over** (cf. עַל no. 1 c). גֻּבְרַיָּא דִּי בְרָאשֵׁיהֹם "the men who are over them" Ezra 5:10; ואיש חד בראשהו[ם] שלח לערקה] "and [he sent] a man over the[m to meet him]" *Bisitun* 52; ענני בעדה ויאמר שנאת לתמת אנתתי כסף שנא בראשה ינתן לתמת כסף תקלן 7 "if tomorrow or another day Anani rises up on account of her(?) and says, 'I divorce Tamut my wife,' the divorce money is

on his head (i.e. will be owed by him, cf. עַל 1d), he shall give to Tamut in silver 7 shekels" *BMAP* 2:7-8; מחר או יום אחרן תקם תמת "If ותאמר שנאת לבעלי ענני כסף שוה בראשה תנתן לענני כסף שקלן 7 tomorrow or another day Tamut rises up and says, 'I divorce my husband Anani,' a like sum shall be on her head. She shall give to Anani in silver 7 shekels" *BMAP* 2:9-10. [Hebr. רֹאשׁ]. †

רַב (*rabb,* BL 181q, 220a) abs. & cst., emph. רַבָּא , f. רברבי *, emph. רַבָּה ; pl. (BL 221i) רַבְרְבִין , רַבְרְבָן , cst. רברבי (*rabrĕbê*), f. רַבְרְבָן , emph. רַבְרְבָתָא ; adj.: **big, great** (in size, mass). צַלְמָא דְכֵּן רַב "that statue (was) great" Dan 2:31; ... וְאַבְנָא הֲוָת לְטוּר רַב "and the stone ... became a big mountain" 2:35; מַלְכָּא עֲבַד לְחֶם רַב "the king made a great feast" 5:1; אַרְבַּע רוּחֵי שְׁמַיָּא מְגִיחָן לְיַמָּא רַבָּא "the four winds of the heavens were stirring up the great sea" 7:2; מן ימא רבא עד חורן "from the Great Sea (the Mediterranean) to Hauran" *1QapGen* 21:11; כול מדברא רבא "all the Great Desert" *1QapGen* 21:11-12; חֵיוָן רַבְרְבָן "big beasts" Dan 7:3: 7:7, 17; הֲלָא דָא־הִיא בָּבֶל רַבְּתָא "Is not this the great Babylon?" 4:27; אֵ[י]שׁ זי יזבן ביתא [ר]בא "a m[a]n who will buy the [b]ig house" *AP* 42:6; 5 תרען רברבן "5 big gates" *AP* 31:9. -- **great, mighty** (in ability, etc.). אֱלָהּ רַב הוֹדַע לְמַלְכָּא "a great God has made known to the king" Dan 2:45; לְבֵית אֱלָהָא רַבָּא "(we went) ... to the house of the great God" Ezra 5:8; קדם אפתו אלהא רבא "before Apitu, the great god" *AP* 72:15; יתבון לה בעלשמין רבא "may Baal-shamayin, the Great, pay him back" *Cilicia* 3-4 (*KAI* 259); יאמיא אנה לך בקדישא רבא "I swear to you by the Great Holy One" *1QapGen* 2:14; דִּי ... מֶלֶךְ לְיִשְׂרָאֵל רַב בְּנָהִי "which ... a great king of Israel built" Ezra 5:11: Dan 2:10; דִּי הַגְלִי אָסְנַפַּר רַבָּא "(the peoples) that the great Osnappar deported" Ezra 4:10; ועל יהוחנן כהנא רבא "and to Jehohanan, the High Priest" *AP* 30:18; במצעת מלכן רברבן "in the midst of mighty kings" *Bar-rakib* 10 (*KAI* 216); אָתוֹהִי כְּמָה רַבְרְבִין "how great are His signs" Dan 3:33; ואחזי ידך רבתא בה "and show forth your great hand against him" *1QapGen* 20:14-15; וּמַתְּנָן רַבְרְבָן שַׂגִּיאָן יְהַב־לֵהּ "and (the king) gave him many great gifts" Dan 2:48; מִן־קָל מִלַּיָּא רַבְרְבָתָא "because of the sound of the great words" 7:11; וּפֻם מְמַלִּל רַבְרְבָן "and a mouth uttering great things" 7:8: 7:20. -- Substantivized adj.: **great man, chief, noble, commander.** זנה [אחי]קר רב "this [Aḥi]qar (was) a great man" *Aḥ.* 60; כל מלכי ארפד וכל רבוה ועמהם "all the kings of Arpad and all its nobles and their people" *Sefire II* C 15-16; [ארפד] בכל רברבי "among all the nobles of [Arpad]" *Sefire II* A 7; [ן] תלתת גברין מן רברבי מצרי[ן] "three men from the nobles of Egyp[t]" *1QapGen* 19:24; לְאַרְיוֹךְ רַב־טַבָּחַיָּא "to Arioch, the chief of the king's guards" Dan 2:14; וְרַב־סִגְנִין עַל כָּל־חַכִּימֵי בָבֶל "and chief prefect over all the sages of Babylon" 2:48; רב חילא זי סון "commander of the troops of Syene" *AP* 16:7; גברא זך זי רב הוה על[חילא] "that man who was commander o[ver the troops]" *Bisitun* 59. -- Cf. רבה (*rabbēh*) (*LFAA* 77f, g, 71r): [אזל נב]וסמסכן זך רביא "that [Nab]usum-uskin, the officer, [went away]" *Aḥ.* 38; [ח]ד מן רבי אבי "[o]ne of my father's officers" *Aḥ.* 33; ו[ר]בי מאתותהם "and the [of]ficers of their centurions" *AP* 80:3. [Hebr. רַב]. †

רְבָת k. רְבָיְתָ 2 sg. m. רְבַת(ְ), v.l. (1541; רְבָת 3 sg. f. , רְבָה q. (BL 161a); impf. 3 sg. m. ירבה (*yirbēh*): **become great, grow.** רְבָה אִילָנָא וּתְקֵף "the tree grew and became strong" Dan 4:8: 4:17; אַנְתְּה־הוּא מַלְכָּא דִּי רְבַיְתָ "it is you, O King, who have grown" 4:19a (רְבַת q.); רְבוּתָךְ רְבָת "your majesty has grown" 4:19b; עַד דִּי שַׂעֲרֵהּ כְּנִשְׁרִין רְבָה "until his hair grew as long as eagles' (feathers)" 4:30; [ה]א נדן שמה ברי רבא "[l]o, my son, Nadin by name, has grown up" *Aḥ.* 18; במרביתה ירבה עלי כסף חלרן "at interest (which) shall be due from me at the rate of 2 hallurs per shekel per month" *AP* 10:4-5; ירבה עלי כסף חלרן 2 "(interest) shall be due from me at a rate of 2 hallurs," lit., "shall grow against me" *AP* 11:2; ויהוה רבה עלי ירח לירח "and it shall be due from me month by month" *AP* 11:9 (cf. עַל no. 1d;

רבו—רברבן

רֵאשׁ no. 3). -- **Pa.** 3 sg. m. רַבִּי, 1 sg. רבית (*rabbît*): **make great.** מַלְכָּא לְדָנִיֵּאל רַבִּי "the king made Daniel great (with honors)" Dan 2:48; בר אח]תי זי רבית "[the son of] my [sis]ter, whom I had brought up" *Aḥ.* 25. [Hebr. the same]. †

רְבוּ (BL 197g, 23b, 63t), cst. רְבוּת *, emph. רְבוּתָא, w. suff. רְבוּתָךְ, f.: **greatness, majesty.** רְבוּתָךְ רְבָת "your greatness has grown" Dan 4:19; רְבוּ יַתִּירָה הוּסְפַת לִי "extraordinary majesty was awarded me" 4:33; אֱלָהָא עֶלָּיָא מַלְכוּתָא וּרְבוּתָא . . . יְהַב לִנְבֻכַדְנֶצַּר אֲבוּךְ "God Most High gave kingship and greatness . . . to Nebuchadnezzar, your father" 5:18; וּרְבוּתָא דִי מַלְכְוָת תְּחוֹת כָּל־שְׁמַיָּא יְהִיבַת לְעַם קַדִּישֵׁי עֶלְיוֹנִין "and the majesty of kingdoms under the heavens is given to the saintly people of the Most High" 7:27 (BL 310c); בעליא במרה רבותה "by the Most High, by the Majestic Lord" *1QapGen* 2:4; מִן־רְבוּתָא דִי יְהִיב לֵהּ כֹּל עַמְמַיָּא . . . הֲווֹ זָאְעִין "because of the majesty given to him all peoples . . . were trembling (before him)" Dan 5:19. †

רִבּוֹ (BL 196e) cst. (& abs.); pl. רִבְּוָן k. (רִבְבָן q.; BL 251q): **ten thousand, myriad.** רִבּוֹ רִבְבָן קָדָמוֹהִי יְקוּמוּן "myriad of myriads were standing before Him" Dan 7:10 (BL 312i). [Hebr. רְבָבָה, cst. pl. רִבְבֹת]. ¹

רְבִיעָי * (BL 196d, 251u), m. emph. רְבִיעָיָא k. (רְבִיעָאָה q., BL 52k); f. רְבִיעָיָה k. (רְבִיעָאָה q.), emph. רְבִיעָיְתָא : **fourth.** חֵיוָה רְבִיעָיָה "a fourth beast" Dan 7:7: 2:40; 7:23; חֵיוְתָא רְבִיעָיְתָא "the fourth beast" 7:19; וְרֵוַהּ דִי רְבִיעָיָא דָּמֵה לְבַר־אֱלָהִין "and the appearance of the fourth is like a son of (the) gods" 3:25; כוכבאל רביעי לה "Kokab'el fourth to him"*4QEnᶜ (4Q204)* 1 ii 25. [Hebr. רְבִיעִי]. †

רַבְרְבָן * (BL 196b), pl. w. suff. רַבְרְבָנַי, רַבְרְבָנָיִךְ k. (רַבְרְבָנָךְ q., BL 74z, 77o), רַבְרְבָנוֹהִי, substantivized adj.: **a**

303

noble, lord. יִשְׁתּוֹן בְּהוֹן מַלְכָּא וְרַבְרְבָנוֹהִי "(that) the king and his nobles might drink from them" Dan 5:2: 4:33; 5:3, 9, 10, 23; 6:18; מַלְכָּא עֲבַד לְחֶם רַב לְרַבְרְבָנוֹהִי אֲלַף "the king made a great feast for a thousand of his nobles" 5:1. †

רגז , ptc. sg. m. *ra-gi-zu*, i.e., רָגִז * (*Warka* 19): **be angry.** -- **Haph.,** 3 pl. הַרְגִּזוּ : **anger.** מִן־דִּי הַרְגִּזוּ אֲבָהֳתַנָא לֶאֱלָהּ שְׁמַיָּא "because our ancestors angered the God of Heaven" Ezra 5:12. [Hebr. רָגַז]. [1]

רְגַז (*rugz,* BL 184o): **rage.** בִּרְגַז וַחֲמָה אֲמַר "(the king) in rage and fury ordered" Dan 3:13. [Hebr. רֹגֶז]. [1]

רְגַל * (*rigl,* BL 183g, cf. 30a), du. רַגְלַיִן , emph. רַגְלַיָּא , w. suff. רַגְלֹוהִי , רַגְלַיַהּ k. (רַגְלַהּ q., BL 49e, 79s), f.: **foot, leg** (below the knee, with the foot; cf. שָׁק "thigh," upper part of the leg). רַגְלוֹהִי מִנְּהֵן דִּי פַרְזֶל וּמִנְּהֵון דִּי חֲסַף "its feet partly of iron, partly of clay" Dan 2:33; אֶבֶן . . . מְחָת לְצַלְמָא עַל־רַגְלוֹהִי "a stone . . . smote the statue on its feet" 2:34; אֶצְבְּעָת רַגְלַיָּא "the toes of the feet (of the statue)" 2:42: 2:41; נְטִילַת מִן־אַרְעָא וְעַל־רַגְלַיִן כֶּאֱנָשׁ הֳקִימַת "(the beast) was lifted up from the ground and made to stand on two feet like a man" 7:4 (cf. BL 315c): 7:7, 19; לא בידי אנ[ש]א מ[נש]א רגלהם "it is not in the power of human beings to lift up their leg" *Aḥ.* 122; רגליהא כמא שפירן וכמא שלמא להן לה שקיהא "Her feet, how beautiful! How perfect are her legs!" *1QapGen* 20:5-6. -- בתרתי רגליא מרדיא אתכנש[ו] "a second time the rebels gather[ed]," lit., "on two feet" *Bisitun* 11. [Hebr. רֶגֶל]. †

רְגַשׁ *, impf. 3 sg. m. ירגש (*yirguš*): **be excited.** שגיא ירגש מלן שמע "(the king) will be very excited in hearing (words like these)" *Aḥ.* 29. -- **Haph.** 3 pl. m. הַרְגִּשׁוּ : (1) **excite, insist.** הַרְגִּשׁוּ עַל־מַלְכָּא "they insisted with the king (that he should issue

רו—רוח

an order)" Dan 6:7 (see LXX, Theod., Syr.): 6:16. -- (2) **observe, watch.** מצראי מרגשין עלה "the Egyptians were observing her" *Tg. Ps.-Jon.* Exod 2:3; גֻּבְרַיָּא אִלֵּךְ הַרְגִּשׁוּ וְהַשְׁכַּחוּ לְדָנִיֵּאל בָּעֵא "these men were watching Daniel and found him making petition" Dan 6:12 (so LXX, Theod., Vg., Syr.). -- Other meanings of this Ar. verb are derived from Hebr. רָגַשׁ : "throng together" (about the king; to catch Daniel praying). †

רוּ * (ri'w: qitl, BL 184k, l), w. suff. רֵוֵהּ ; m.: **appearance.** צַלְמָא דִּכֵּן רַב . . . . וְרֵוֵהּ דְּחִיל "that statue (was) great . . . and its appearance frightening" Dan 2:31; רֵוֵהּ דִּי רְבִיעָיָא דָּמֵה לְבַר־אֱלָהִין "the appearance of the fourth (man) is like a son of (the) gods" 3:25 (brachylogy). [Hebr. רְאִי]. †

רוּחַ , emph. רוּחָא , w. suff. רוּחֵהּ,רוּחִי ; cst. pl. רוּחֵי , f. m.: (1) **wind, breath.** נְשָׂא הִמּוֹן רוּחָא "the wind (m., BL 333g) carried them (the smashed metals) away," lit., "lifted them up" Dan 2:35; אַרְבַּע רוּחֵי שְׁמַיָּא מְגִיחָן "the four winds of the heavens were stirring up (the Great Sea)" 7:2; מן ארבע . . . רמה עליהון רוחיהון "(Abram) fell upon them . . . from four sides," lit., "from their four winds" *1QapGen* 22:8; זי יבעה רוח אפוה וימלל מלן לחית "who rants and utters evil words," lit., "who causes the breath of his nostrils to boil" *Sefire III* 2. -- (2) **spirit** as the seat of emotion. אֶתְכְּרִיַּת רוּחִי אֲנָה דָנִיֵּאל "as for me, Daniel, my spirit was anguished" Dan 7:15; רוּחֵהּ תִּקְפַת לַהֲזָדָה "his spirit was hardened to act proudly" 5:20; אנסת רוחהא "(Bitenosh) suppressed her emotion" *1QapGen* 2:13; ורוחך כדן עליבא "and (why) is your spirit so depressed?" *1QapGen* 2:17. -- (3) **mind, talent.** רוּחַ יַתִּירָה וּמַנְדַּע . . . הִשְׁתְּכַחַת בֵּהּ "an excellent mind and knowledge . . . were found in him" Dan 5:12: 6:4; רוּחַ אֱלָהִין בָּךְ "(that) a divine talent (is) in you" 5:14; דִּי רוּחַ אֱלָהִין קַדִּישִׁין בֵּהּ "(a man) in whom there is the holy mind of (the) gods" 4:5; 5:11 (attract. for קַדִּישָׁה): 4:6, 15. -- (4) **spirit, demon.** שלח לה אל עליון רוח מכדש למכתשה

305

רום

"God Most High sent him a pestilential spirit to afflict him"
1QapGen 20:16-17; רוחא דא באישתא "that evil spirit" *1QapGen*
20:28; הוא רוחא כתש לכולהון "that spirit afflicted all of them"
1QapGen 20:20. [Hebr. the same]. †

רום , 3 sg. m. רָם (BL 145j): **be high, be puffed up.**
כְּדִי רָם לִבְבֵהּ "when his mind was puffed up" Dan 5:20. --
Haph./Aph., 3 pl. הרמו (*hărîmû*); impf. 2 sg. m. תהרם
(*tĕhārim*); ptc. sg. m. מָרִים (BL 148g): **raise up.** דִּי הֲוָה צָבֵא הֲוָה
מָרִים "whom He would, He raised up" Dan 5:19; מרים אנה ידי
יומא דן לאל עליון "I raise my hand this day to God Most High"
1QapGen 22:20-21; והרמו שר מן שר חזרך והעמקו חרץ מן חר[צה]
"and they raised a wall higher than the wall of Ḥazrak and dug a
trench deeper than [its] tren[ch]" *Zkr* A 10 (*KAI* 202); לתהרם
נבשהם מני "you must not incite them against me," lit., "raise up
their soul higher than me" *Sefire III* 5-6. -- **Hithpe.,** impf. 3 sg.
m. יתרום (*yittĕrûm*): **glory in, boast of.** [זי] לא יתרום בשם אבוהי
"[he who] does not glory in the name of his father" *Aḥ.* 138. --
Polel (BL 146t), ptc. sg. m. מְרוֹמֵם : **extol.** אֲנָה . . . מְשַׁבַּח וּמְרוֹמֵם
וּמְהַדַּר לְמֶלֶךְ שְׁמַיָּא "I . . . praise, extol, and honor the King of Heav-
en" Dan 4:34. -- **Hithpol.** 2 sg. m. הִתְרוֹמַמְתָּ : **extol oneself.** עַל
מָרֵא־שְׁמַיָּא הִתְרוֹמַמְתָּ "you have extolled yourself against the Lord
of Heaven" Dan 5:23. [Hebr. רום]. †

רום * (BL 180m), w. suff. רוּמֵהּ , m.: **height.** מַלְכָּא עֲבַד
צְלֵם דִּי־דְהַב רוּמֵהּ אַמִּין שִׁתִּין "the king made a statue of gold, whose
height was sixty cubits" Dan 3:1 (BL 355a); וַאֲלוּ אִילָן בְּגוֹא אַרְעָא
וְרוּמֵהּ שַׂגִּיא "and lo, a tree in the midst of the earth, and its height
was great" 4:7; וְרוּמֵהּ יִמְטֵא לִשְׁמַיָּא "and its height reached to the
heavens" 4:8; בַּיְתָא יִתְבְּנֵא . . . רוּמֵהּ אַמִּין שִׁתִּין "let the house be
rebuilt . . . its height sixty cubits" Ezra 6:3. [Hebr. the same]. †

306

רז—רחמין

רָז (< Persian), emph. רָזָא & רָזָה; pl. רָזִין, emph. רָזַיָּא,
m.: **secret, mystery.** רַחֲמִין לְמִבְעֵא מִן־קֳדָם אֱלָהּ שְׁמַיָּא עַל־רָזָא דְנָה "to
seek the mercy of the God of Heaven about this mystery" Dan
2:18; רָזָא דְנָה גֱּלִי לִי "this secret has been revealed to me" 2:30:
2:19, 27; 4:6; אִיתַי אֱלָהּ בִּשְׁמַיָּא גָּלֵא רָזִין "there is a God in Heaven
who reveals mysteries" 2:28: 2:29, 47. ; [ע אנתה]די כול רזיא יד
"because [you] kn[ow] all the mysteries" *4QEnGiants^a (4Q203)*
9:3. [Hebr. the same]. †

▲ רְחוּם : **Rehum, Persian commander in Samaria.** רְחוּם
בְּעֵל־טְעֵם "Rehum, the commander" Ezra 4:8, 9, 17: 4:23. †

רַחִיק * (qattīl, BL 192e), pl. רַחִיקִין (v.l. רְחִיקִין), adj.:
far, distant, remote. רַחִיקִין הֱווֹ מִן־תַּמָּה "be far from there!," i.e.,
keep away Ezra 6:6; בר וברה אח ואחה קריב ורחיק "(no) son or
daughter, brother or sister, relative or stranger," lit., "remote one"
AP 5:8-9; רחיקן אנחנה מנך . . . עד עלם "we withdraw from you . . .
for ever," lit., "we are far from" *AP 20:9.* [Hebr. רָחוֹק]. [1]

רַחֲמִין (qatl, BL 182x), only pl. (BL 305e): "entrails,
womb" used figuratively: **mercy, gift, favor.** וְרַחֲמִין לְמִבְעֵא
מִן־קֳדָם אֱלָהּ שְׁמַיָּא "to seek the mercy of the God of Heaven" Dan
2:18 (see וְ no. 9); לרחמן ישימנך קדם . . . מלכא "grant you favor
before . . . the king," lit., "set you for favor" *AP 30:2;* לרחמן תהוו
קדם אלה שמיא "may you be favored before the God of Heaven,"
lit., "may you be for favor" *AP 38:2;* נכסיא וכספא . . . ברחמן יהבת
לכם "I gave you . . . the goods and the money as a gift" *AP 18:2.*
-- Cf. יהבת לך בתיא אלה ברחמה "I have given you these houses as
a gift" *BMAP 6:14;* זי תנתן לה בכסף או רחמת "to whomever you
may give (it) for money or gratis (adv.)" *BMAP 12:26;* [לא]שכחה
רחמיך קדמיך "[to f]ind mercy in your sight," lit., "your mercy"
4QLevi^b (4Q213a) 1:15. [Hebr. רַחֲמִים]. [1]

307

רחץ—רעיון

רחץ , **Hithpe.,** 3 pl. הִתְרְחִׁצוּ : **trust.** דִּי הִתְרְחִצוּ עֲלוֹהִי
"those who trusted in Him" Dan 3:28. [1]

רֵיחַ (< *rawiḥ, prob. < Hebr., BL 186w): **odor.** וְרֵיחַ נוּר
לָא עֲדָת בְּהוֹן "and no odor (prob. m.) had touched (f.) them" Dan
3:27 (or should one read: לָא עֹד בְּהוֹן "was no longer on them"?.
Cf. Theod. 3:94: οὐδὲ ὀσμὴ τοῦ πυρὸς ἦν ἐν αὐτοῖς). [Hebr. the
same]. [1]

רְמָה *, 3 pl. רְמוֹ (BL 154k), 1 pl. רְמֵינָא ; infin. מִרְמֵא .
Peil perf. 3 pl. רְמִיו (BL 156w, 64z). **Hithpe.,** impf. 3 sg. m.
יִתְרְמֵא , 2 pl. m. תִּתְרְמוֹן : (1) **throw, cast.** וּלְגֹב אַרְיָוָתָא רְמוֹ אִנּוּן
"and they threw them into the den of lions" Dan 6:25: 3:20, 24;
6:17; וּרְמִיו לְגוֹא־אַתּוּן נוּרָא "and they were cast into the furnace of
fire" 3:21; יִתְרְמֵא לְגוֹא־אַתּוּן נוּרָא "(whoever does not worship)
shall be thrown into the furnace of fire" 3:6: 3:15; 6:8, 13. -- (2)
fall upon. ורמה עליהון בליליא "and he (Abram) fell upon them
(the kings) by night" 1QapGen 22:8. -- (3) **place, set, impose.**
וַהֲלָךְ לָא שַׁלִּיט "that thrones were placed" Dan 7:9; עַד דִּי כָרְסָוָן רְמִיו
לְמִרְמֵא עֲלֵיהֹם "and it is not lawful to impose a toll on them" Ezra
7:24.

רְעוּ * (BL 197g), cst. רְעוּת , emph. רְעוּתָא *, f.: **judg-**
ment, decision, pleasure. וּרְעוּת מַלְכָּא עַל־דְּנָה יִשְׁלַח עֲלֶינָא "and let
the king send us a decision about this" Ezra 5:17; כִּרְעוּת אֱלָהֲכֹם
תַּעַבְדוּן "you may do, according to the pleasure of your God" Ezra
7:18; רעותה [ ] "[ ] his good pleasure" 1QapGen 2:23; אנה
מן רעותי {יומא דנה} זבנת לך ימה דנה לבתה דילי "I, by my own decision {omit}, have sold to you today my house" XḤev/SeDeed-
SaleC (XḤev/Se 8a) Recto 3.

רַעְיוֹן * (qatalān? BL 195y), cst. pl. רַעְיוֹנֵי , w. suff.
רַעְיוֹנַי , רַעְיוֹנָךְ & רַעְיוֹנָךְ (v.l.) (BL 74z, 77o, for k. רעיונך in Dan

308

רענן—רשם

2:29; 5:10 read רעיוניך , BL 75a), רַעְיֹנֹהִי , m.: **thought, object of thought.** רַעְיֹונָךְ . . . סְלִקוּ מָה דִּי לֶהֱוֵה אַחֲרֵי דְנָה "your thoughts .. . mounted about what would be hereafter" Dan 2:29 (cf. Hebr. form in 2:3); וְרַעְיֹונֵי לִבְבָךְ תִּנְדַּע "that you may understand the thoughts of your mind" 2:30; שַׂגִּיא רַעְיֹונַי יְבַהֲלֻנַּי "my thoughts disturbed me greatly" 7:28: 4:16; 5:6, 10. †

רַעֲנַן (*qatlal*, BL 193k; v.l. רַעֲנָן), adj.: **green, flourishing** (in prosperity, health). אֲנָה . . . וְרַעֲנַן בְּהֵיכְלִי "I, (Nebuchadnezzar) was . . . and flourishing in my palace" Dan 4:1 (cf. 4:17ff.). [Hebr. the same].[1]

רעע , impf. 3 sg. f. תְּרֹעַ (BL 165b). -- **Pa.** ptc. sg. m. מְרָעַע (BL 130h): **crush.** תֶּהֱוֵא תַקִּיפָה כְּפַרְזְלָא . . . דִּי מְרָעַע כָּל־אִלֵּין תַּדִּק וְתֵרֹעַ "(a fourth kingdom) shall be strong as iron . . . which crushes (everything); it shall break and crush all these (others)" Dan 2:40. [Hebr. רעע, רעץ, רצץ]. †

רְפַס *, ptc. sg. f. רָפְסָה : **stamp** (cf. דּוּשׁ). וּשְׁאָרָא בְּרַגְלַיהּ רָפְסָה "and (the fourth beast) stamped the rest with its feet" Dan 7:7, 19. [Hebr. רָפַס, רָפַשׁ]. †

רְשַׁם , 2 sg. m. רְשַׁמְתָּ ; impf. 2 sg. m. תִּרְשֻׁם ; **Peil** perf. 3 sg. m. רְשִׁים : **write, inscribe, sign** (cf. כְּתַב). וּכְתָבָא דְנָה רְשִׁים "and this writing was inscribed (on the wall)" Dan 5:24 (BL 288c): 5:25; תְּקֵים אֱסָרָא וְתִרְשֻׁם כְּתָבָא "establish the prohibition and sign the document" 6:9; דִּי־רְשִׁים כְּתָבָא "(when Daniel knew) that the document had been signed" 6:11 (BL 289d); הֲלָא אֱסָר רְשַׁמְתָּ "did you not sign a prohibition?" 6:13: 6:14; . . . מַלְכָּא רְשַׁם כְּתָבָא וֶאֱסָרָא "the king . . . signed the document (and so confirmed) the prohibition" 6:10; למאל[פה ו]ירשם "to lear[n it and] he will inscribe (it)" *4QPhysHor (4Q561)* 11:14. †

309

שׂגיא–שׁב

שׁ

The letter שׁ in Old Aramaic designated three primitive
sounds: (1) *š;* (2) *ṯ,* later pronounced *t* and written by the
letter ת: שׁוב & תוב "return"; (3) *ś,* later pronounced *s.*

שָׁב * (*qatil,* root *śyb,* BL 186w), cst. pl. שָׂבֵי , emph.
שָׂבַיָּא , adj.: (1) **old.** שב אנה לא אכהל למפלח בבב היכלא "I am old; I
cannot serve in the gate of the palace" *Aḥ.* 17; [אח]יק[ר] זך שבא
"this [Aḥ]iqa[r], the old man" *Aḥ.* 35; סבלתני ואנה ימין סב "she
supported me, when I was old in days" *BMAP* 9:17 (read rather
שב). -- (2) **elder, senior.** שָׂבֵי יְהוּדָיֵא "the elders of the Jews"
Ezra 5:5; 6:7, 8, 14; שְׁאֵלְנָא לְשָׂבַיָּא אִלֵּךְ "we asked those elders"
5:9; [א]דין גבר שב "then an old man" *4QDanSus (4Q551)* 1:2.
[Hebr. שָׂב, ptc. of שׂיב]. †

שַׂבְּכָא & סַבְּכָא (Dan 3:5; cf. שבך, סבך "weave"), emph.
(collect. sg.): **harp** (four-stringed instrument). קָל קַרְנָא . . . סַבְּכָא
"the sound of the horn, . . . the harp" Dan 3:5, 7, 10, 15 [cf. Gk.
σαμβύκη; Hebr. שְׂבָכָה "net"]. †

שְׂגָא * (א"ל > ל"ה, cf. BL 152e), 3 pl. שגיו (*śĕgíw*);
impf. 3 sg. m. יִשְׂגֵּא , 3 pl. m. ישגון (*yiśgôn*): **grow, increase,
be multiplied.** לְמָה יִשְׂגֵּא חֲבָלָא "why should the damage grow?"
Ezra 4:22; שְׁלָמְכוֹן יִשְׂגֵּא "peace be multiplied for you" Dan 3:31;
6:26; וחזי כמן כפלין שגיו "and see how they have doubled and
multiplied," lit., "how many doubles they have been multiplied"
1QapGen 22:29; עתרך ונכסיך ישגון לחדא "your wealth and your
flocks will increase very much" *1QapGen* 22:31. -- **Aph.** impf.
1 sg. אַשְׂגֵּה *:* **multiply.** אשגה זרעך כעפר ארעא "I shall multiply your
descendants as the dust of the earth" *1QapGen* 21:13. [Hebr.
שגה]. †

שַׂגִּיא (*qattīl,* BL 192e), שגי (*śaggî*), f. שגיא (*śaggiyā',*

310

שַׂגִּיא

1QapGen 20:7), pl. m. שגיאין (*śaggî'în*), pl. f. שַׂגִּיאָן . (1) Adj.:
much, abundant, numerous. וִיקָר שַׂגִּיא תְּקַבְּלוּן "and you will receive much honor" Dan 2:6; מַתְּנָן רַבְרְבָן שַׂגִּיאָן יְהַב לֵהּ "(the king)
gave him (Daniel) many great gifts" 2:48; קוּמִי אֲכֻלִי בְּשַׂר שַׂגִּיא
"get up, devour much flesh" 7:5; אִנְבֵּהּ שַׂגִּיא "its (the tree's) fruit
was abundant" 4:9, 18; רוּמֵהּ שַׂגִּיא "its (the tree's) height was
much" 4:7; שְׁנִין שַׂגִּיאָן "many years" Ezra 5:11; ליומן אחרנן שגיאן
"many days later" *Aḥ.* 49-50; בנכסין שגיאין לחדא "with very many
flocks" *1QapGen* 20:33; לבוש שגי די בוץ "many garments of fine
linen" *1QapGen* 20:31; שגי לי עתר ונכסין "my wealth and flocks
are numerous" *1QapGen* 22:32; חכמא שגיא עמהא "(there is)
much wisdom in her" *1QapGen* 20:7; מסרת כול חייא שגיא תהוא
"the opposition of all living beings will be abundant" *4QBirth-
Noahᵃ (4Q534)*1 i 9. -- Substantivized adj.: **much, abundance.**
אף אנה אוספת לה על דילה שגי "I too added much to what he had"
1QapGen 21:6; בשגיא בנן לבבך אל יחדא "in an abundance of
children let not your heart rejoice" *Aḥ.* 106; מה טב שג[יא] כבי[ך]
לזי נ[ג]ע [באנ]ביך "what good is the abundance of your thorns to
him who touches your fruit?" *Aḥ.* 165.
(2) Adv. (BL 337d): **much, very, exceedingly.** After a
verb or word: מַלְכָּא בְּנַס וּקְצַף שַׂגִּיא "the king was angry and very
furious" Dan 2:12; שלם מראן אלה שמיא ישאל שגיא בכל עדן "may
the God of Heaven seek exceedingly the peace of our lord at all
times" *AP* 30:1-2; וַאֲלוּ צְלֵם חַד שַׂגִּיא צַלְמָא דִכֵּן רַב "and lo, a statue;
that statue was very great" Dan 2:31 (put שַׂגִּיא after רַב, as in
LXX: μεγάλη σφόδρα). -- Before a verb or word: שלם ושררת
שגיא הושרת לך "greetings of peace and prosperity I send you in
abundance" *AD* 3:1; מַלְכָּא . . . שַׂגִּיא מִתְבָּהַל "the king . . . was very
alarmed" Dan 5:9: 6:15, 24; אֲנָה דָנִיֵּאל שַׂגִּיא רַעְיוֹנַי יְבַהֲלֻנַּנִי "As for
me, Daniel, my thoughts alarmed me very much" 7:28; אסרחאדן
שגיא ירגש "Esarhaddon will be infuriated" *Aḥ.* 29; שגיא סנחאריב
מלכא רחמני "King Senacherib was very pleased with me" *Aḥ.* 51;
[אלה] שגיא עמ[י] אתנצחו "[these men] were very active with m[e]"

311

Bisitun 75; שׂגי רחמה "he coveted her very much" *1QapGen* 20:8; ושׂגי לבי עלי אדין אשתני "and then my mind was much changed within me" *1QapGen* 2:11. [Hebr. the same]. †

שָׂהֲדוּ * (BL 198g), cst. שָׂהֲדוּת *, emph. שָׂהֲדוּתָא , f.: **testimony.** יְגַר שָׂהֲדוּתָא "mound of testimony" Gen 31:47 (Laban's Ar. name for Jacob's Hebr. גַּלְעֵד). -- Cf. שהד (*śāhid*) "witness": [ה]וה לי שהד חמס "[th]ere was a malicious witness against me" *Aḥ.* 140. [1]

שְׂטַר (*śaṭr*, BL 183e), m.; **side** (cf. גַּב & צַד). לִשְׂטַר־חַד הֳקֵמַת "(the beast) was lifted up on one side" Dan 7:5 (Ginsberg reads הֲקִימַת "lifted up one side"); אגרא זך תדבק לשׂטר ביתי "that portico adjoins the side of my house" *AP* 5:5. -- שְׂטַר מִן * = **except.** שׂטר מן בר וברה זי יזניה "except a son or daughter of Jezaniah" *AP* 25:13; 5 חלכיא אלך שׂטר מן זי יהבו בבבאל "(deliver) those 5 Cilicians except those who were given (to him) in Babylon" *AD* 12:5. [1]

שִׂים , 3 sg. m. שָׂם, w. suff. שָׂמַהּ , שמני , 2 sg. m. שָׂמְתָּ (BL 144h, i), 1 sg. שָׂמֵת , 3 pl. m. שָׂמוּ , w. suff. שמוני (*śāmûnî*); impf. 3 sg. m. ישׂים (*yĕśîm*), w. suff. ישׂימנך (*yĕśîminnāk*), 1 sg. אשים, אשם ('*ăśîm, 'ăśīm*), 3 pl. m. ישׂימון (*yĕśîmûn*), juss. ישׂימו (*yĕśîmû*); impv. sg. m. שׂם (*śīm*), pl. שִׂימוּ . **Peil** perf. 3 sg. m. שׂים , 3 sg. f. שֵׂמַת (Dan 6:18; but read שָׂמַת , BL 145k), 1 sg. שׂימת ; ptc. sg. f. שׂימה, שׂימא (*śîmāh, śîmā'*). **Hithpe.** (BL 145n, p, q) impf. 3 sg. m. & יתשים יִתְּשָׂם , 3 pl. m. יִתְּשָׂמוּן ; ptc. sg. m. מִתְּשָׂם : (1) **put, place, lay, set up.** אֶבֶן . . . שֵׂמַת עַל־פֻּם גֻּבָּא "a stone . . . was placed on the mouth of the den" Dan 6:18; וְאָע יִתְּשָׂם בְּכָתְלַיָּא "and timber is laid in the walls" Ezra 5:8; לשׂמו עמי מאן כסף ונחש עם לבשׂי שׂמוני "they have not put with me (in the grave) silver or bronze vessels; they have laid me (only) with my garments" *Nerab* 6-7 (*KAI* 226); ויתשים ארחא ברגלו[הי] "and on

[his] feet a fetter is put" *Aḥ.* 80; וֹהן רחים אלהן הו ישימון טב בחנכה למאמר "and if he be beloved of (the) gods, they will put some-thing good in his palate to utter" *Aḥ.* 115; בש[מי]ן שימה הי "(wis-dom) is set up in hea[ven]" *Aḥ.* 95; [   ] נצבא זי שם בר[ה]דד בר [   ] מלך ארם למראה למלקרת "the stele that Bar[ha]dad, son of [   ], king of Aram, set up for his lord, Melqart" *Brej* 1-4 (*KAI* 201); שמת קדם [אלור] נצבא זנה "I have set up this stele before [Elur]" *Zkr* B 13-14 (*KAI* 202); ושמו כל מלכיא אל מצר על חזר[ך] "and all these kings laid a siege to Hazra[k]" *Zkr* A 9 (*KAI* 202); לרחמן ישימנך קדם דריוהוש מלכא "may (God) give you favor before Darius the king," lit., "set you for favor" *AP* 30:2; עדי אלהן הם זי שמו אלהן "this is the treaty of gods, which gods have set up" *Sefire I* B 6; לחלבון די שימא על שמאל דרמשק "Helbon which is placed to the north of Damascus," lit., "on the left of" *1QapGen* 22:10; [במ]סגרא שימת "I was put [in pr]ison" *El. Ostr.* A 2 (*HSSD* 54). -- (2) **make** (w. two accus.). שֵׁשְׁבַּצַּר . . . דִּי פֶחָה שָׂמֵהּ "Shesh-bazzar . . . whom he had made governor" *Ezra* 5:14; בֵּהּ בְּדָנִיֵּאל דִּי־מַלְכָּא שָׂם־שְׁמֵהּ בֵּלְטְשַׁאצַּר "in this Daniel, whom the king named Belshazzar," lit., "made his name" *Dan* 5:12; וּבָתֵּכוֹן נְוָלִי יִתְּשָׂמוּן "and your houses shall be made a mound of ruins" 2:5 (cf. his house נְוָלוּ יִתְעֲבֵד *Ezra* 6:11); אהפך טבתא ואשם [לל]לחית "I shall upset the good treaty-relations and make (them) evil" *Sefire I* C 19-20; וישמו תחתיתה [לע]ליתה "and may (the gods) make its lower part its upper part!" *Sefire I* C 23-24. -- (3) **give, pay.** לָא־שָׂם עֲלָיךְ מַלְכָּא טְעֵם "(Daniel) has not paid heed to you, O King" *Dan* 6:14; 3:12; וְעַל דָּנִיֵּאל שָׂם בָּל לְשֵׁיזָבוּתֵהּ "and to Daniel he paid attention, to deliver him" 6:15; שלין לנפשך אל תשים עד [ז]פתא "give no rest to your soul until [you pay off] the [l]oan" *Aḥ.* 130-31; אלהיא שלם ישמו לך "(that) the gods may give you peace" *AD* 13:5; שמני שם טב "he gave me a good name" *Nerab* 3 (*KAI* 226; cf. *Bib* 45 [1964] 227). -- (4) שָׂם טְעֵם = **issue a decree, order** (cf. אֲמַר ; Hebr. צְוָה). מִנִּי שִׂים טְעֵם "a decree has been issued by me" (= "I order"; BL 288b); כּוֹרֶשׁ מַלְכָּא שָׂם טְעֵם בֵּית־אֱלָהָא בִירוּשְׁלֶם בַּיְתָא יִתְבְּנֵא "Cyrus the king issued a decree: As

313

for God's house in Jerusalem, let the house be rebuilt" Ezra 6:3; אֲנָה דָרְיָוֶשׁ שָׂמֶת טְעֵם אֶסְפַּרְנָא יִתְעֲבֵד "I, Darius, have ordered, 'Let it be done diligently'" 6:12 (see דִּי III 5); קִרְיְתָא דָךְ לָא תִתְבְּנֵא עַד־מִנִּי טַעְמָא יִתְּשָׂם "let not this city be rebuilt until the decree is issued by me" 4:21; ולעבק יעבד כזי שים טעם "and let him act at once, as an order is issued" AP 26:22. -- (a) + דִּי w. the impf. (see דִּי III 5): יִסְגֻּד . . . שָׂמְתָּ טְעֵם דִּי "you ordered that . . . one should worship" Dan 3:10; מנך יתשם טעם כזי איש מנדעם באיש לא יעבד "let an order be issued by you that no one should do any harm" AD 5:8; מִנִּי שִׂים טְעֵם דִּי . . . יִתְנְסַח אָע מִן־בַּיְתֵהּ "I have ordered that . . . a beam be torn from his house" Ezra 6:11; מִנִּי שִׂים טְעֵם דִּי כָל־מִתְנַדַּב . . . יְהָךְ "I have ordered that every volunteer . . . may go" 7:13: Dan 3:29; 6:27; . . . מִנִּי אֲנָה אַרְתַּחְשַׁסְתְּא מַלְכָּא שִׂים טְעֵם לְכֹל גִּזַּבְרַיָּא דִּי־כֹל . . . יִתְעֲבֵד "I, Artaxerxes the king, decree that all treasurers (do) . . . let all (that Ezra requires) be done" Ezra 7:21. -- (b) + לְ w. an infin. (see לְ II 2): מִנִּי שִׂים טְעֵם לְהַנְעָלָה . . . לְכֹל חַכִּימֵי בָבֶל "I decreed that one should bring in . . . all the sages of Babylon," lit. decreed to bring in" Dan 4:3; מַלְכָּא שָׂם טְעֵם בֵּית־אֱלָהָא דְנָה לִבְּנֵא "the king decreed that one should rebuild this house of God" Ezra 5:13: 5:3, 9, 17 (cf. Hebr. of Ezra 4:3: צַוָּנוּ "ordered us"); כְּעַן שִׂימוּ טְעֵם לְבַטָּלָא "therefore decree that one stop (those men)" 4:21; סרושיתא זי אנה אשים להם טעם יתעבד להם "the punishment that I shall order (to inflict) be inflicted on them" AD 3:6; אנת שם טעם סרוש[י]ת[א זי פסמשך י[שים] להם טעם למעבד זכי יתעבד להם "issue a decree that that punish[ment], which Psamshek will order to be done to them, be inflicted on them" AD 3:7-8; ויאתה עם גנזא זי מני "and let him come with the treasure that he was ordered to bring to Babylon" AD 10:5 (טעם omitted). -- (c) + וְ (cf. וְ 10): מִנִּי שִׂים טְעֵם . . . וּמִנִּכְסֵי מַלְכָּא . . . נִפְקְתָא תֶּהֱוֵא מִתְיַהֲבָא "I decree . . . that from the king's revenue . . . the expenses are to be paid" Ezra 6:8; מִנִּי שִׂים טְעֵם וּבַקַּרוּ "I decreed, and they have searched" 4:19: 6:1 (cf. לְדָנִיֵּאל אֲמַר לְהַנְסָקָה מִן־גֻּבָּא וְהֻסַּק "(the king) ordered (them) to bring Daniel up from the den, and he was brought up" Dan 6:24). [Hebrew the same]. †

314

שׂכל—שׂנא

שׂכל **Hithpa.** ptc. sg. m. מִשְׂתַּכַּל : **consider.** מִשְׂתַּכַּל הֲוֵית
בְּקַרְנַיָּא "I was considering the horns" Dan 7:8. [Hebr. the same,
in Hiphil]. ¹

שָׂכְלְתָנוּ (< *śuklat-ān-ūt, BL 198g), f.: **intelligence.**
נַהִירוּ וְשָׂכְלְתָנוּ וְחָכְמָה . . . הִשְׁתְּכַחַת בֵּהּ "light and intelligence and
wisdom . . . were found in him" Dan 5:11: 5:12, 14. [Hebr.
שֶׂכַל]. †

שׂנא (ל"א > ל"ה), 1 sg. שׂנאת & שׂנית , w. suff. שׂניתך ;
impf. 3 sg. f. תשׂנא (tiśnā'), w. suff. תשׂנאנך (tiśna'innāk); ptc.
pl. m. w. suff. שׂנאי (śānĕ'ayy), שׂנאיך k. (śānĕ'ayk) & שָׂנְאָךְ
(BL 74z, 77o), שׂנאוה (śānĕ'awih < śānĕ'ayih?); pass. ptc. שׂנאה
(śĕnī'āh): **hate, not love, divorce.** שׂנאת לתמת אנתתי "I divorce
Tamut, my wife" BMAP 2:7 (perf. in marriage contract); שׂנאת
לבעלי עננ[ת] שׂני "I divorce my husband, Anani" BMAP 2:9;
לאנתתי יהוישמע לא תהוה לי אנתת "I divorce my wife, Yehoyishma;
she shall not be a wife for me" BMAP 7:21-22; הן יה[י]ו[שׂ]מע]
תשׂנא לבעלה עניה ותאמר לה שׂני[ת]ך לא אהוה לך אנתת "if Yeh[oyi]sh-
[ma] divorces her husband, Ananiah, and says to him, '[I di]-
vorce you; I shall not be your wife" BMAP 7:24-25; הן . . . ברתי
תשׂנאנך "if . . . my daughter divorces you" AP 9:8; והן תעבד כות
שׂנאה הי "and if she does thus (i.e., cohabits with another man),
she is divorced" BMAP 7:33-34; הן יעבד [כות] . . . [שׂ]נאהי "if he
does [thus], . . . he has divorced her" BMAP 7:37 (or "she is divorced" [= שׂנאה הי, cf. Hermopolis 5:7, מה הי זה = מהידה "what
is this?"]); חֶלְמָא לְשָׂנְאָיךְ "let the dream (that you have had) be for
those who hate you" Dan 4:16; חד מלכן או חד שׂנאי "one of the
kings or one of my enemies," lit., "those hating me" Sefire I B
26; יקם דם ברי מן שׂנאוה "avenge the blood of my son from his
enemies" Sefire III 12; ימותון שׂאני ולא בחרבי "my enemies shall
die, but not by my sword" Aḥ. 174. [Hebr. שָׂנֵא]. ꞌ

315

שְׂעַר (śa'r), w. suff. שַׂעְרֵהּ ; m., only sg. (BL 202m):
hair. שְׂעַר רֵאשֵׁהּ "the hair of his head" Dan 7:9: 3:27; . . . שַׂעְרֵהּ
רְבָה "his hair . . . grew" 4:30. [Hebr. שֵׂעָר]. †

שׁ

שְׁאֵל , 3 sg. m. w. suff. שאלה (śa'lēh), 1 sg. שאלת , 1 pl.
שְׁאֶלְנָא ; impf. 3 sg. m. ישאל (yiš'al), w. suff. יִשְׁאֲלֶנּוּן (BL 123j),
3 pl. juss. ישאלו (yišălû); ptc. sg. m. שָׁאֵל. **Peil** perf. 1 sg.
שאילת (šĕ'îlēt), 2 pl. m. שאילתם. **Hithpe.** impf. 2 sg. m. תשתאל
(tištĕ'ēl), 2 pl. m. תשתאלון. (1) W. accus. of person(s): **ask,
question.** קרא המו שאל המו הצד]א מלי[א אלה "call them, ask them,
'Are these [wor]ds true?'" *Assur Letter* 12-13 (*KAI* 233); שְׁאֶלְנָא
לְשָׂבַיָּא אֵלֶּךְ "we asked those elders" Ezra 5:9; מלכא שאל לגבריא
"the king asked the men" *Aḥ.* 77; שאל לתרוח ודינא על]ל[דנה "ask
TRWḤ and the court abo[ut] this" *AP* 16:9; לה שאל על חרוץ "he
did not ask about Ḥaruṣ" *Hermopolis* 1:6; אנה אתית על [בי]תך
אחתך לאנתו . . . ושאלת מנך לנשן יהוישמע "I came to your [hou]se
and asked for the woman, Yehoyishma, your sister, for marriage"
BMAP 7:3; גברן 5 שאל<ת> מן [נח]תחור ולא יהב לי "I asked for 5
men from Neḥtiḥur, but he did not give (them) to me" *AD* 12:3.
-- Passive (in a forensic sense): שאיל]ת["(you accused me and)
[I] was questioned (by the court)" *AP* 7:6 (restore t instead of ';
cf. *DISO* 287:2); שאילת קד]ם תר[וח ו]דינא "I was questioned
[be]fore TR[WḤ] and the court" *AP* 16:3; אחר שאילתם "then you
were questioned" *AP* 20:8; הן פסמש]ך[אחר קבלת מנך ישלח עלי חסן
תשתאל "if Psamshe[k] later sends me a complaint about you, you
will be strictly questioned" *AD* 4:3: 7:9; למה . . . תשתאל על זנה
"lest . . . you be questioned about this (matter)" *AD* 12:8. -- (2)
W. accus. of thing(s): **seek (after/ out), demand, require.**
מִלְּתָא דִי־מַלְכָּה שָׁאֵל "the thing that the king requires" Dan 2:11:
2:10, 27; שלם מראן אלה שמיא ישאל שגיא בכל עדן "may the God of

Heaven seek the peace of our lord exceedingly at all times!" *AP*
30:1-2 (cf. Hebr. הֲשָׁלוֹם לוֹ "Is it well with him" Gen 29:6);
אלהיא ישאלו שלמך בכל עדן "may the gods seek out your welfare at
all times!" *AP* 56:1. -- (3) W. accus. of person & thing: וחכמה
מ[נדעמתא ז]י שאלה "and (Nadin) told him (the king) wh[atever] he
asked him" *Aḥ.* 10-11; שְׁמָהָתְהֹם שְׁאֵלְנָא לְהֹם "we asked them their
names" Ezra 5:10 (BL 337i); כָּל־דִּי יִשְׁאֲלֶנְכוֹן עֶזְרָא כָהֲנָא "whatever
Ezra, the priest, shall ask of you" 7:21. [Hebr. שָׁאַל]. †

שְׁאֵלָה * (*qatil-at,* BL 186y), emph. שְׁאֵלְתָא (v.l. שְׁאֶלְתָּא,
cf. BL 16z, 22c), f.: **question, matter** (cf. מִלָּה, צְבוּ, טְעֵם).
בִּגְזֵרַת עִירִין פִּתְגָמָא וּמֵאמַר קַדִּישִׁין שְׁאֵלְתָא "the sentence is by a decision of Watchers, and the question by a word of Holy Ones,"
the humiliation of the king, Dan 4:14. [Hebr. the same]. [1]

▲ שְׁאַלְתִּיאֵל : **Shealtiel,** father of Zerubbabel. זְרֻבָּבֶל
בַּר־שְׁאַלְתִּיאֵל "Zerubbabel, son of Shealtiel" Ezra 5:2 (cf. Hebr.). [1]

שְׁאָר (*šu'ār, LFAA* 81d), abs. & cst., emph. שְׁאָרָא,
only sg. (BL 202m), m.: **rest, residue, remainder.** וּשְׁאָרָא
בְּרַגְלַיהּ רָפְסָה "and (the fourth beast devoured and) stamped the
residue with its feet" Dan 7:7, 19; יֵיטַב בִּשְׁאָר כַּסְפָּא . . . מָה דִי עֲלָיךְ
וְדַהֲבָא לְמֶעְבַּד "whatever seems good to you . . . to do with the rest
of the silver and gold" Ezra 7:18; שְׁאָר חַשְׁחוּת בֵּית־אֱלָהָךְ "the rest
that is needed for the house of your God" 7:20; שְׁאָר עֲבַר־נַהֲרָא
"the remainder of (the province) Beyond-the-River" 4:10b, 17b.
-- W. dependent pl.: שְׁאָר חֵיוָתָא הֶעְדִּיו שָׁלְטָנְהוֹן "as for the rest of
the beasts, their dominion was removed," lit., "they removed"
Dan 7:12; שְׁאָר אֻמַּיָּא דִּי הַגְלִי אָסְנַפַּר "the rest of the nations whom
Osnappar deported" Ezra 4:10: 4:9, 17bis; 6:16; Dan 2:18.
[Hebr. the same]. †

317

שבח, **Pa.** 2 sg. m. שַׁבַּחְתְּ, 1 sg. שַׁבְּחֵת (v.l. שַׁבְּחֵת), 3 pl.
שַׁבַּחוּ (Babyl. vocal. שַׁבַּחוּ, BL 133k); ptc. sg. m. מְשַׁבַּח (Babyl.
vocal. *mĕšabbēḥ* BL 133h): **praise.** לָךְ אֱלָהּ אֲבָהָתִי . . . מְשַׁבַּח אֲנָה
"You, O God of my ancestors, I praise" Dan 2:23: 4:31, 34; 5:4,
23. [Hebr. the same]. †

שְׁבַט * (*šibṭ;* < Hebr.), cst. pl. שִׁבְטֵי : **tribe.** לְמִנְיָן שִׁבְטֵי
יִשְׂרָאֵל "for the number of the tribes of Israel" Ezra 6:17. [Hebr.
שֵׁבֶט].[1]

שְׁבִיב * (*šabîb*), emph. שְׁבִיבָא , pl. שְׁבִיבִין : **flame.**
שְׁבִיבָא דִּי נוּרָא "the flame of fire" Dan 3:22; שְׁבִיבִין דִּי נוּר
"flames of fire" 7:9 (cf. דִּי I 2a); [נור ד]י כשביבין "like flames o[f
fire]" *4QEnGiants^c (4Q531)* 12:3. [Hebr. שָׁבִיב]. †

שְׁבַע * (*šabʿ*) m. (used w. f. noun), f. (used w. m. noun)
שִׁבְעָה , cst. שִׁבְעַת : **seven.** שִׁבְעָה עִדָּנִין "seven times (m.)" Dan
4:13, 20, 22, 29; שִׁבְעַת יָעֲטֹהִי "his seven counselors" Ezra 7:14;
לְמֵזֵא לְאַתּוּנָא חַד־שִׁבְעָה עַל דִּי חֲזֵה "to heat the furnace seven times
more than was usual" Dan 3:19; שבע שאן יהינקן אמר "should
seven ewes suckle a lamb" *Sefire I* A 23; שבע שנן יאכל ארבה "for
seven years may the locust devour (Arpad)" *Sefire I* A 27. --
Unchanging pl.: שִׁבְעִין "seventy." [Hebr. שֶׁבַע]. †

שְׁבַק , 2 sg. m. שבקת (*šĕbaqtā*), 1 sg. w. m. suff. שבקתך ,
w. f. suff. שבקתי , 3 pl. w. suff. שבקוהי (*šĕbaqûhī*), 1 pl. שבקן ;
impf. 3 sg. m. ישבק (*yišbuq*); impv. pl. m. שְׁבַקוּ ; infin. מִשְׁבַּק ;
ptc. pl. m. שבקן (*šābĕqīn*). **Peil** perf. 3 sg. m. שביק (*šĕbîq*), 1 sg.
שביקת ; ptc. sg. f. שביקה (*šĕbîqāh*), pl. m. שביקין . **'Ithpe.** impf.
3 sg. f. תשתבק (*tištĕbiq*), 3 pl. juss. ישתבקו . (1) **leave, abandon.** מצריא מרדו אנחנה מנטרתן לא שבקן "(when) the Egyptians
rebelled, we did not abandon our posts" *AP* 27:1; שבקת לרחמיך
"you have left your friends" *Aḥ.* 176; אל <ת>שבקנ[י] "do not

318

שבק

leave me" *Adon Letter* 7 (*KAI* 266); שבק חמר ולא יסבלנהי "the
ass abandoned (its load) and will not carry it" *Aḥ.* 90; חזו כתוני זי
שבקת . . . בית יהה "look for my tunic, which I left . . . in the house
of Yaho" *El. Ostr.* 1-3 (*ASAE* 26 [1926] 27); לה שבק אנה לה 1 "I
am not leaving him alone" *Hermopolis* 3:4; שבקתך בסתר ארזא "I
left you in a hiding place of cedar" *Aḥ.* 175; בית זרע א 30 אשתבק
"a farm of 30 '(ardabs) was abandoned," lit., "a house of seed"
AD 8:2. -- (2) **leave** (= not carry off), **save, spare.** . . . בְּרַם עִקֵּר
בְּאַרְעָא שְׁבֻקוּ "(cut down the tree) but leave the stump . . . in the
ground" Dan 4:12, 20: 4:23; הן יאחדן רשיעא בכנפי לבשך שבק בידה
"if an evil man seizes the edges of your robe, leave (it) in his
hand" *Aḥ.* 171; למשבק זהב בידך [ ] "[ ] to leave gold in your
hand" *Aḥ.* 193; יבעון למקטלני ולכי למשבק "(who) will seek to kill
me and to spare you" *1QapGen* 19:19; שביקת אנה . . . ולא קטילת
"I was saved . . . and not killed"*1QapGen* 20:10. -- (3) **leave**
(to someone), **hand over.** וּמַלְכוּתָה לְעַם אָחֳרָן לָא תִשְׁתְּבִק "and the
sovereignty shall not be left for another people" Dan 2:44 (cf.
יְהַב 5:28; 7:27); ונכסיא כולהון שביקין לך "and all the goods are left
for you" *1QapGen* 22:19-20; והן אשבקן על לבבך [לא תחיה] "(if I
strike you, my son, you will not die), but if I leave (you) to your
own heart, [you will not live]" *Aḥ.* 82. -- (4) **let go, release, set
free.** לא שבקוהי עד "they did not set him free until" *AP* 69:A5;
שבק ושלח כולהון "he set free (the captives) and sent them all a-
way" *1QapGen* 22:25-26; פירמא זך וכנותה ישתבקו "let that Pirma
and his companions be released" *AD* 5:9; אז>כ<ת שבקתכי במותי
"I have gone (and) released you (effective) at my death" *BMAP*
5:4; ואנתי שביקה "and you (f.) have been let go" *BMAP* 5:8-9;
חטאי שבק לה גזר והוא יהודי "a seer, who was a Jew, remitted my
sin for Him" *4QPrNab (4Q242)* 1-3:4. -- (5) **allow, permit, let
alone.** לא שבקן לן למבניה "they do not allow us to build it (the
temple)" *AP* 30:23; שְׁבֻקוּ לַעֲבִידַת בֵּית־אֱלָהָא דֵךְ . . . וּלְשָׂבֵי יְהוּדָיֵא
בֵּית־אֱלָהָא דֵךְ יִבְנוֹן "let the work on that house of God alone; . . .
and the elders of the Jews will rebuild that house of God" Ezra
6:7. †

319

שׁוה—שׁבשׁ

שׁבשׁ , **Hithpa.** ptc. pl. m. מִשְׁתַּבְּשִׁין : **alarm.** וְרַבְרְבָנוֹהִי
מִשְׁתַּבְּשִׁין "and his (the king's) nobles were alarmed" Dan 5:9. [1]

שֵׁגַל * (BL 186a; < Akk. *ša ekalli* CAD 4. 62), pl. w.
suff. שֵׁגְלָתָךְ, שֵׁגְלָתֵהּ : **king's rival wife.** וְרַבְרְבָנוֹהִי שֵׁגְלָתֵהּ וּלְחֵנָתֵהּ
"and his nobles, wives, and concubines" Dan 5:2, 3: 5:23. [Hebr.
שֵׁגַל]. †

שׁדר , **Pa. :** **send word.** [סנ]יא שׁדר לרמנ[א] "the [br]am-
ble sent word to the pomegran[ate]" *Aḥ.* 165. -- **Hithpa./'Ithpa.**
3 pl. m. אשתדרו ; impv. sg. m. התשדר (wt. metathesis; cf. שִׂים
Hithpe.); ptc. sg. m. מִשְׁתַּדַּר : **exert oneself, set one's mind.**
הֲוָא מִשְׁתַּדַּר לְהַצָּלוּתֵהּ "(the king) set his mind to deliver him (Daniel)" Dan 6:15; עד שזבוני . . . אשתדרו עם וידרנג "they exerted
themselves with Widrang . . . until they got me freed" *AP* 38:4-5;
עבד לה והתשדר עמה "(whatever he tells you) do for him, and exert
yourself with him" 3-4 (*IEJ* 11 [1961] 43). †

▲ שַׁדְרַךְ : **Shadrach,** companion of Daniel. שַׁדְרַךְ מֵישַׁךְ
וַעֲבֵד נְגוֹ "Shadrach, Meshach, and Abednego" Dan 2:49; 3:12 + .

שְׁוָה *, ptc. sg. m. שׁוה (*šāwēh*), sg. f. שׁויה (*šāwĕyāh*),
pl. m. שׁוין (*šāwáyin*): **be equal, be worth.** לבש 1 זי עמר שׁוה כסף
שׁקלן 7 מחזי 1 שׁויה כסף חלרן 7 פלג "1 woolen garment worth 7
silver shekels; 1 mirror worth 7 (and) a half hallurs" *BMAP* 2:4-
5; [2] כסן זי נחש 2 שׁוין כסף שקלן "2 bronze cups worth the sum of
[2] shekels" *AP* 15:13-14; כסף שׁוא בראשה "(if Tamut divorces
Anani) an equal sum (of divorce money) shall be on her head,"
i.e., she will owe him *BMAP* 2:8-9. -- **Peil** perf. 3 sg. m. שְׁוִי (or
שֱׁוִי , BL 156s, Dan 5:21 k.): **be made equal.** לְבָבֵהּ עִם־חֵיוְתָא שְׁוִי
"his mind was made like (the mind of) a beast" Dan 5:21 (brachylogy). -- **'Ithpe.** 1 pl. אשתוין (*'ištawîn*): **agree.** אנחנה אשתוין
כחדה ופלגן עלין עבדיה "we have agreed together and have divided

320

the slaves between us" *AP* 28:2-3. -- **Pa.** 3 pl. שַׁוִּיו (Dan 5:21
q.): **make like; make, put, impose.** לְבָבֵהּ עִם־חֵיוָתָא שַׁוִּיו "his
mind was made like (the mind of) a beast" Dan 5:21 q. (imper-
sonal 3 pl.); אנה שוית לך אנתת ל[ב]י "I made you the wife of my
[hea]rt" *Cappadocia* 7-9 (*KAI* 264); ושׁויו עליהון מדא "and they
imposed tribute on them" *1QapGen* 21:26. -- **'Ithpa.,** 3 sg m.
יִשְׁתַּוֵּה (BL 158l): **be made (like).** בַּיְתֵהּ נְוָלִי יִשְׁתַּוֵּה "his house
shall be made a heap of ruins" Dan 3:29 (cf. syn. עֲבַד Ezra 6:11
& שִׂים Dan 2:5). [Hebr. שׁוה]. †

שׁור * (*qūl,* BL 180l), emph. pl. שׁוּרַיָּא & שׁוּרַיָּה (see
below), w. suff. שׁוּרַיַּה * (see BL 49e), m.: **wall.** שׁוּרַיָּא שַׁכְלְלוּ
"they are completing the walls" Ezra 4:12 (see שַׁכְלִל); . . . הֵן
שׁוּרַיָּה יִשְׁתַּכְלְלוּן "if . . . the walls are completed" 4:13, 16 (read
prob. שׁוּרַיַּה "its walls); שׁור חד בנ[ו ב]מנציעת בירת יב וכען שורא זך
בנה "they buil[t] a wall in the midst of the fortress of Yeb; now
that wall is constructed" *AP* 27:5-6; הרמו שר מן שר חזרך . . . ושורא
זנה "they raised a wall higher than the wall of Hazrak . . . and
this wall" *Zkr* A 10-17 (*KAI* 202). [Hebr. the same]. †

▲ שׁוּשַׁנְכָי * (w. Persian suff. *-aka* +perh. Ar. *-āy*), emph
pl. שׁוּשַׁנְכָיֵא : **Susian,** resident of the town Šušan (שׁושׁן). שׁוּשַׁנְכָיֵא
דְּהֲוָא עֵלְמָיֵא "Susians, that is, Elamites" (read דִּי הוּא) Ezra 4:9 (cf.
LXX Σουσαναχαῖοι οἵ εἰσιν Ἡλαμαῖοι). -- Cf. סָוֶנְכָן * (w.
Persian suff. *-aka* + prob. Ar. *-ān, LFAA* 87n): "Syenite,"
resident of Syene (סון). ארמי סונכן "a Syenite Aramean" *AP* 67:3
(cf. ארמי זי סון *AP* 5:2); גברן 5 סונכנן "5 Syenite men" *AP* 33:5-6;
סָוֶנְכָנָי * (perh. + Ar. *-ān* & *-āy*): [י]היב לחילא סונכניא "(what was)
[de]livered to the Syenite garrison" *AP* 24:33. [1]

שְׁחִית *, sg. f. שְׁחִיתָה , adj. (or pass. ptc.): **corrupt, de-**
formed. [למא צלם] אנפיך כדנא עליך שנא ושחת "[why is the expres-
sion] of your face so changed and deformed?" *1QapGen* 2:16-17;

מִלָּה כִדְבָה וּשְׁחִיתָה הִזְדְּמִנְתּוּן לְמֵאמַר "you have agreed to utter a lying and corrupt word (before me)" Dan 2:9; וְכָל־שָׁלוּ. . . וּשְׁחִיתָה וְכָל־עִלָּה "and no pretext or corrupt thing . . . and וּשְׁחִיתָה לָא הִשְׁתְּכַחַת עֲלוֹהִי no negligence or fault was found in him" (Daniel)" 6:5. †

שֵׁיזִב & שֵׁיזִיב (= short *i*), < Akk. *ušēzib*, Šaphel '*zb*, BL 92i; impf. 3 sg. m. יְשֵׁיזִב, w. suff. יְשֵׁיזְבִנְּךְ, יְשֵׁיזְבִנְכוֹן (BL 123j); infin. שֵׁיזָבָה *, w. suff. שֵׁיזָבוּתֵהּ, שֵׁיזָבוּתָנָא, שֵׁיזָבוּתָךְ; ptc. sg. m. מְשֵׁיזִב : **free, deliver** (from a present evil). יָכִל לְשֵׁיזָבוּתָנָא מִן־אַתּוּן נוּרָא "(our God) is able to deliver us from the furnace of fire" Dan 3:17a: 3:28; דִּי שֵׁיזִיב לְדָנִיֵּאל מִן־יַד אַרְיָוָתָא "who has freed Daniel from the power of the lions" 6:28b: 6:17, 21; אשתדרו עם וידרנג . . . עד שזבוני "they exerted themselves with Widrang . . . until they got me freed" *AP* 38:4-5; זי קדמן שזבך מן קטל "who saved you from being killed" *Aḥ.* 46. -- **free, save** (from a future evil). וּמִן־יְדָךְ מַלְכָּא יְשֵׁיזִב "and (God) will save (us) from your power, O King" Dan 3:17b: 3:15; 6:15. Used absolutely: מְשֵׁיזִב וּמַצִּל "(God) saves and delivers" 6:28a. †

שֵׁיצִיא k. (שֵׁיצִי q.), < Akk. *ušēṣī*, Šaphel *yṣ'*, BL 92i, 169j; 3 pl. שֵׁיצִיו *: **finish, complete.** שֵׁיצִיא בַּיְתָא דְנָה "completed this temple" Ezra 6:15 (read prob. pl. w. LXX: שֵׁיצִיו [ἐτέλεσαν, & Vg.: *compleverunt*]). [1]

שכח (BL 132c-n), **Haph./Aph.** 3 sg. m. השכח (*haškaḥ*) & אשכה, 1 sg. הַשְׁכַּחַת (v.l. הַשְׁכְּחִית, הַשְׁכְּחֵת), 3 pl. הַשְׁכַּחוּ, 1 pl. הַשְׁכַּחְנָא; impf. 2 sg. m. תְּהַשְׁכַּח, 1 pl. נְהַשְׁכַּח; infin. הַשְׁכָּחָה & אשכחה; **Hithpe.** 3 sg. m. הִשְׁתְּכַח, 3 sg. f. הִשְׁתְּכַחַת, 2 sg. m. הִשְׁתְּכַחְתְּ : (1) **find, discover.** הַשְׁכַּחַת גְּבַר מִן־בְּנֵי גָלוּתָא דִּי יְהוּד "I have found a man among the exiles of Judah" Dan 2:25; אזלת השכחת לאחיק[ר זך] "I went (and) found [that] Aḥiqa[r]" *Aḥ.* 76; תבעה אתר זי אנת תהשכח [ותקטלנהי] "you are to look for a place where you will find (Aḥiqar) [and you are to kill him]" *Aḥ.* 34-

35; גבריא זי אשתכחו בבבא "the men who were found at the gate" AP 34:4; הִשְׁתְּכַח בְּאַחְמְתָא . . . מְגִלָּה חֲדָה "a scroll . . . was discovered in Ecbatana" Ezra 6:2; תְּהַשְׁכַּח בִּסְפַר דָּכְרָנַיָּא וְתִנְדַּע "you will find in the book of records and you will understand" 4:15; הַשְׁכַּחוּ דִּי קִרְיְתָא דָךְ . . . עַל־מַלְכִין מִתְנַשְּׂאָה "they found that this city . . . has risen against kings" 4:19. -- W. predicative phrase or clause (BL 338k): הַשְׁכַּחוּ לְדָנִיֵּאל בָּעֵה "they found Daniel making petition" Dan 6:12; תְּקִילְתָּה בְמֹאזַנְיָא וְהִשְׁתְּכַחַתְּ חַסִּיר "you have been weighed in the balance, and you have been found lacking" 5:27; כזי כנבוזי על למצרין אגורא זך בנה השכח "when Cambyses came to Egypt, he found that temple constructed" AP 30:13-14; אתית לי לביתי בשלם ואשכחת כול אנשי שלם "I came home safely, and I found all my household safe" 1QapGen 21:19; אשכח אנון שרין בבקעת דן "(Abram) found them encamped in the Valley of Dan" 1QapGen 22:7-8. -- W. prep. לְ : כָּל־אֲתַר לָא־הִשְׁתְּכַח לְהוֹן "no place was found for them (the crushed metals)," i.e., there was no trace of them, Dan 2:35; זי תהשכח לי ביב "what you will find of mine in Yeb" BMAP 11:11; קָדָמוֹהִי זָכוּ הִשְׁתְּכַחַת לִי "before Him I was found innocent," lit., "innocence was found in me" Dan 6:23 (BL 338l); בָּעַיִן עִלָּה לְהַשְׁכָּחָה לְדָנִיֵּאל "they were seeking to find fault in Daniel" 6:5a: 6:5b; וְכָל . . . לָא הִשְׁתְּכַחַת עֲלוֹהִי "and none . . . was found in him" 6:5c; כזי מלה באישה לא יהשכחון לכם "when they will find no fault in you" AP 38:6-7; ומנדעם מחבל [לא] אשתכח לן "and nothing disloyal was found in us" AP 27:2; חָכְמָה כְּחָכְמַת־אֱלָהִין הִשְׁתְּכַחַת בֵּהּ "wisdom like the wisdom of gods was found in him" Dan 5:11: 5:12, 14; 6:24; לָא נְהַשְׁכַּח לְדָנִיֵּאל דְּנָה כָּל־עִלָּה "we shall not find any fault in this Daniel" 6:6a; לָהֵן הַשְׁכַּחְנָא עֲלוֹהִי בְּדָת אֱלָהֵהּ "unless we find (it) against him in the law of his God" 6:6b. -- (2) **find, obtain, come upon; be able.** כֹּל כְּסַף וּדְהַב דִּי תְהַשְׁכַּח בְּכֹל מְדִינַת בָּבֶל "all the silver and gold that you will obtain in the whole province of Babylonia" Ezra 7:16; הן השכחת כסף [ח]ת לעבק "if you come upon (the) money, [come] down at once" AP 42:7: 42:8; לא השכחת כסף ונכסן לשלמה לכי "I did not find money and goods to repay you" AP 13:5; די לא ישכח כול בר אנוש לממניה "which no one can count," lit., "which no human being" *1QapGen* 21:13; קדמיך רחמיך שכחה[לא] "[to f]ind favor in your sight" *4QLevi*^b *(4Q213a)* 1:15. †

שַׁכְלֵל * (< Akk. *ušaklil,* Shaphel of *kll,* BL 92i), 3 sg. m. w. suff. שַׁכְלְלֵהּ , 3 pl. m. שַׁכְלְלוּ ; infin. שַׁכְלָלָה. Pass. **'Ishtaphal**, impf. 3 pl. m. יִשְׁתַּכְלְלוּן : **finish, complete.** . . . שָׂבֵי יְהוּדָיֵא בְּנוֹ וְשַׁכְלְלוּ מִן־טַעַם אֱלָהּ יִשְׂרָאֵל "the elders of the Jews . . . built and completed (the house) at the order of the God of Israel" Ezra 6:14; וּמֶלֶךְ לְיִשְׂרָאֵל רַב בְּנָהִי וְשַׁכְלְלָה "and a great king of Israel built it and finished it (God's house)" 5:11; בַּיְתָא דְנָה לִבְּנֵא וְאֻשַּׁרְנָא דְנָה לְשַׁכְלָלָה "(who authorized you) to build this house and to finish this structure?" Ezra 5:3; 5:9; הֵן קִרְיְתָא דָךְ תִּתְבְּנֵא וְשׁוּרַיָּה יִשְׁתַּכְלְלוּן "if that city is rebuilt and the walls completed" 4:13, 16 (read rather שׁוּרַיָּה "its walls"); אֲתוֹ לִירוּשְׁלֶם . . . בָּנַיִן וְשׁוּרַיָּא שַׁכְלִלוּ וְאֻשַּׁיָּא יַחִיטוּ "(the Jews) have come to Jerusalem . . . and are rebuilding (it); they have completed the walls and repaired the foundations" 4:12 (read rather Pa. perf. יַחִטוּ ; these words are a gloss or corruption, see 4:13, 16, 21).

שְׁכֵן *, impf. 3 pl. f. יִשְׁכְּנָן : **dwell** (cf. דּוּר). בְּעַנְפוֹהִי יִשְׁכְּנָן צִפֲּרֵי שְׁמַיָּא "it its branches dwell the birds of the heavens" Dan 4:18; יהו אלהא שכן יב "Yaho, the god, dwelling in Yeb" *BMAP* 12:2. -- **Pa.** 3 sg. m. שַׁכֵּן : **cause to dwell.** אֱלָהָא דִּי שַׁכֵּן שְׁמֵהּ תַּמָּה "the God who has caused His name to dwell there" Ezr 6:12. [Hebr. שָׁכַן]. †

שְׁלֵה (*šělēh* < *šalī*), adj.: **calm, secure.** אֲנָה . . . שְׁלֵה הֲוֵית בְּבֵיתִי "I . . . was secure in my house" Dan 4:1 (v.l. שָׁלֵה ptc.). [Hebr. שָׁלֵו]. ¹

שלה, q. שָׁלָה = שָׁלוּ "negligence," k. prob. שְׁלָה * (< Akk. *šillatu* "insolence, wicked speech"; cf. *AEDH* 764b: *iqbû šillatu*

שְׁלוּ—שְׁלַח

"they uttered insolence" [against the goddess]; LXX, Theod,
Syr., Vg. *blasphemia*): **insolence, blasphemy.** כָּל־עַם . . . דִּי־יֵאמַר
שָׁלָה עַל אֱלָהֲהוֹן "any people . . . that utters blasphemy against their
God" Dan 3:29. [1]

שָׁלוּ (BL 197g), pl. w. suff. שָׁלְוָתָךְ (v.l. for שָׁלְוָתָךְ), f.:
negligence. וְכָל־שָׁלוּ וּשְׁחִיתָה לָא הִשְׁתְּכַחַת עֲלוֹהִי "and no negligence
or fault was found in him" Dan 6:5; זְהִירִין הֱווֹ שָׁלוּ לְמֶעְבַּד עַל־דְּנָה
"take care lest you commit negligence in this matter" Ezra 4:22;
לֶהֱוֵא מִתְיְהֵב לְהֹם יוֹם בְּיוֹם דִּי־לָא שָׁלוּ "let it be given to them day by
day without negligence" 6:9. †

שְׁלֵוָה * (*qatil-at,* BL 186y), w. suff. שְׁלֵוְתָךְ , f.: **tranquillity.** תֶּהֱוֵא אַרְכָה לִשְׁלֵוְתָךְ "(that) there may be a lengthening of
your tranquillity" Dan 4:24 (wrong v.l.: לִשְׁלֵוָתָךְ "for your neg-
ligences"). [1]

שְׁלַח , 2 sg. m. שלחת , 1 sg. שלחת , 3 pl. שְׁלַחוּ , 2 pl. m.
שְׁלַחְתּוּן , 1 pl. שְׁלַחְנָא & שלחן ; impf. 3 sg. m. יִשְׁלַח ; infin. משלח
(*mišlaḥ*); ptc. pl. m. שלחן (*šālĕḥīn*). **Peil** perf. 3 sg. m. שְׁלִיחַ ;
ptc. sg. m. שְׁלִיחַ . **'Ithpe.** impf. 3 sg. f. תשתלח (*tištĕlaḥ*). -- (1)
send someone, **order to go.** דִּי שְׁלַח מַלְאֲכֵהּ "(God) who sent His
angel" Dan 3:28: 6:23; כל זי רחם הא לי ואשלח מלאכי א[ל]ל[ו]ה לשלם או
. . . ישלח מלאכה אלי "any one who is a friend of mine, when I send
my ambassador to him for peace . . . or he sends his ambassador
to me" *Sefire III* 8; מִן־קֳדָם מַלְכָּא . . . שְׁלִיחַ לְבַקָּרָא עַל־יְהוּד "(you)
are sent by the king . . . to investigate about Judah" Ezra 7:14;
למשלח חיל להצלתי "to send an army to free me" *Adon Letter* 7
(*KAI* 266); אמר למלכא וישלח אנתתה מנה לבעלהא "tell the king that
he should send his wife away from him, (back) to her husband"
1QapGen 20:23; שבק ושלח כולהון "(Abram) released and sent
them (the captives) all away" *1QapGen* 22:25-26. -- **send** a
thing: מִן־קֳדָמוֹהִי שְׁלִיחַ פַּסָּא דִי־יְדָא "from His presence the palm of

325

a hand was sent" Dan 5:24 (perf., BL 289d); שלח לי לבשה זי עליך
"send me the garment that is on you" *El. Ostr.* 4-5 (*RHR* 130
[1945] 20); ישלחן אלהן מן כל מה אכל בארפד "may the gods send
every sort of devourer against Arpad" *Sefire I* A 30; זן זן ירח
בירח הוו שלחן עלי "each item, month by month, they were sending
to me" *AP* 17:3;. לתשלח לשן בביתי "you shall not interfere in my
house," lit., "you shall not send (your) tongue against" *Sefire III*
21. -- **send** a letter, etc.: אִגַּרְתָּא דִּי שְׁלַחוּ עֲלוֹהִי "the letter that they
sent to him," i.e., wrote to him Ezra 4:11: 5:6 (cf. כְּתַבוּ אִגְּרָה חֲדָה
עַל־יְרוּשְׁלֶם לְאַרְתַּחְשַׁשְׁתְּא "they wrote a letter against Jerusalem to
Artaxerxes" 4:8); פִּתְגָמָא שְׁלַח מַלְכָּא עַל־רְחוּם "the king sent a reply:
'To Rehum'" 4:17: 5:7; נִשְׁתְּוָנָא דִּי שְׁלַחְתּוּן עֲלֶינָא "the letter that
you sent to us" 4:18; אגרת מן מראי תשתלח על נחתחור "let a letter
be sent by my lord to Neḥtiḥur" *AD* 10:2; שלח אגרה על דבר כן
לצ<ח>א "he sent a letter about it to Ṣeḥa'" *AP* 40:3 (see 40:2);
אגרת חדה בשלמך לא שלחת עלי "you did not send me a letter about
your welfare" *AP* 41:5; לשלמכי שלחת ספרה זנה "I send this note
for your welfare" *Hermopolis* 1:12-13 (epistolary perf.; see
אִגְּרָה). -- **send** what is written in a letter: רְעוּת מַלְכָּא עַל־דְּנָה יִשְׁלַח
עֲלֶינָא "let the king send us his pleasure about this matter" Ezra
5:17; כלא מליא באגרה חדה שלחן בשמן "the whole affair we have
sent in a letter in our name" *AP* 30:29; הן פסמשך אחר קבלת מנך
ישלח עלי "if Psamshek will send me later a complaint about you"
AD 4:3; הוית אשלח שלמך "I used to send a greeting to you" *AP*
41:3; שלם וחין שלחת לך "I send you (greetings of) health and life"
Hermopolis 3:5 (epistolary perf.). -- שְׁלַח עַל w. an ellipsis =
send (letter, message) **to, write to** someone, **announce, order**:
שלח לי ביד עקבה "write to me through 'Aqbah" *Hermopolis* 3:6;
ספר לה הושרתן לי . . . ולה שלחתן הן חי אנה והן מת אנה "a letter you
have not sent to me . . . and you have not written (asking) whether I am alive or dead" *Hermopolis* 5:7-9; לָקֳבֵל דִּי־שְׁלַח דָּרְיָוֶשׁ
"according to what Darius had sent," i.e., ordered, Ezra 6:13;
שלחי כל טעם זי הוה זי בביתי "send (word about) all that is happening
in my house" *Hermopolis* 1:12; כל זי תצבה שלח לי "write to me

שְׁלֵט

about all that you desire" *Hermopolis* 3:7; קדם מראי שלחת לאמר
"I have sent word to my lord, saying" *AP* 16:8; שלח עלי כן אמר
"he wrote to me, saying thus" *AD* 4:1; מספת שלח גרדא לם זי מראתי
כתש "Maspath sent word, saying, 'He has beaten my lady's
staff'" *AD* 12:8-9; בזך שלח אנה עליכם "on this matter I am
sending word to you" *AP* 38:9; קדמן שלחת עליכם על זנה "I have
previously instructed you about this matter" *AD* 7:5; ישתלח על
ארתונ[ת] "let an order be sent to Artawon[t]" *AD* 3:5; שלחי על תבי
ותושר לכי עמר "write to Tabi and have her send you wool" *Hermopolis* 2:6-7; מני שליח עליהם על זנה "word was sent by me to
them about this matter" *AP* 26:6. -- שְׁלַח + a verb: **order.** מַלְכָּא
שְׁלַח לְמִכְנַשׁ לַאֲחַשְׁדַּרְפְּנַיָּא "the king gave an order to assemble the
satraps" Dan 3:2; שלחת קרית לממרה ולערנם ולאשכול "I sent an
invitation to Mamre, Arnem, and Eshcol," lit., "I sent, I called"
1QapGen 21:21; עַל־דְּנָה שְׁלַחְנָא וְהוֹדַעְנָא לְמַלְכָּא "therefore we sent
and informed the king" Ezra 4:14; על זהב על זנה שלחן והודען "as
for gold, about this we have sent and instructed" *AP* 30:28-29;
שלח לעובע דברהא "he sent off in haste (and) had her brought (to
him)," lit., "(and) led her" *1QapGen* 20:8-9. -- (2) **put forth, extend** a hand (in transferred sense). כָּל־מֶלֶךְ וְעַם דִּי יִשְׁלַח יְדֵהּ לְהַשְׁנָיָה
"every king or people that shall put forth a hand to change" Ezra
6:12; ליכהל ברי [ל/י]שלח יד בבר[ך] "my son shall not be able [to]
extend a hand against [your] son" *Sefire I* B 25; וישלח ידה ויקח
מן ארקי "and should he put forth his hand to take some of my
land" *Sefire I* B 27; לתשלח לשנך בניהם ותאמר לה קתל אחך "you
shall not interfere with them and say to him, 'Kill your brother,'"
lit., "extend your tongue between them" *Sefire III* 17-18. [Hebr.
שָׁלַח]. †

שְׁלֵט , 3 pl. שְׁלֵטוּ ; impf. 3 sg. m. יִשְׁלַט , 3 sg. f. תִּשְׁלַט , 2
sg. m. תִּשְׁלַט : (1) **have authority/ power, rule.** מַלְכוּ . . . דִּי
תִּשְׁלַט בְּכָל־אַרְעָא "a kingdom . . . which will rule over all the
earth" Dan 2:39; וְתַלְתָּא בְמַלְכוּתָא תִּשְׁלַט "and you shall have

327

שְׁלִיט—שִׁלְטוֹן

authority as triumvir in the kingdom" 5:16: 5:7 (cf. שַׁלִּיט לֶהֱוֵא
תַּלְתָּא בְּמַלְכוּתָא 5:29); לָא־שְׁלֵט נוּרָא בְּגֶשְׁמְהוֹן "the fire had no power
over their bodies" 3:27; [ו]אַל תִשְׁלַט בִּי כל שטן "[and] let no satan
have power over me" *4QLevi^b (4Q213a)* 1:17; אִישׁ אחרן לא ישלט
בביתה "no other man shall have power over his house" *BMAP*
4:20 (cf אנת . . . שליט בביתא זך *BMAP* 3:11-12). -- (2) **over-**
power. שְׁלַטוּ בְהוֹן אַרְיָוָתָא "the lions overpowered them" Dan
6:25. -- **Haph.** 3 sg m. הַשְׁלֵט *, w. suff. הַשְׁלְטָךְ , הַשְׁלְטֵהּ :
cause to rule. וְהַשְׁלְטָךְ בְּכָלְהוֹן "and (God) made you ruler over all
of them" Dan 2:38; הַשְׁלְטֵהּ עַל כָּל־מְדִינַת בָּבֶל "(the king) made him
ruler over the whole province of Babylon" 2:48. [Hebr. שָׁלַט]. †

שִׁלְטֹן * (*šulṭān*, BL 196z), cst. pl. שִׁלְטֹנֵי : **official.** וְכֹל
שִׁלְטֹנֵי מְדִינָתָא "and all the officials of the provinces" Dan 3:2. 3.
[Hebr. the same]. †

שָׁלְטָן (*šulṭān*, BL 195z) abs. & cst., emph. שָׁלְטָנָא , w.
suff. שָׁלְטָנָךְ, שָׁלְטָנֵהּ, שָׁלְטָנְהוֹן, emph. pl. שָׁלְטָנַיָּא, m.: **dominion,**
sovereignty. שָׁלְטָנֵהּ שָׁלְטָן עָלַם "His dominion is an everlasting
dominion" Dan 4:31; 7:14b: 3:33; 6:27b; וְלֵהּ יְהִיב שָׁלְטָן "and to
him (son of man) was given sovereignty" 7:14a: 7:6, 27a; שְׁאָר
חֵיוָתָא הֶעְדִּיו שָׁלְטָנְהוֹן "as for the rest of the beasts, their dominion
was removed," lit., "they removed" 7•12; דִּינָא יִתִּב וְשָׁלְטָנֵהּ יְהַעְדּוֹן
"the court shall sit in judgment, and they shall take away his (the
wicked king's) sovereignty" 7:26; מְטָת לִשְׁמַיָּא וְשָׁלְטָנָךְ לְסוֹף אַרְעָא
"(your majesty) reaches to the heavens, and your dominion to the
end of the earth" 4:19. -- Concretely: בְּכָל־שָׁלְטָן מַלְכוּתִי לֶהֱוֹן זָאְעִין
"in all my royal dominion (people) are to tremble" (before Dani-
el's God) Dan 6:27; כֹּל שָׁלְטָנַיָּא לֵהּ יִפְלְחוּן "all dominions shall
serve it," i.e., the kingdom of the saints 7:27b. †

שַׁלִּיט (*qattīl*, BL 192e), emph. שַׁלִּיטָא, pl. & שַׁלִּיטִן
שַׁלִּיטִין, adj.: **powerful, mighty, having power/right over.** מֶלֶךְ

328

שלם

רַב וְשַׁלִּיט "a great and powerful king" Dan 2:10; מִן־דִּי תִנְדַּע דִּי־שַׁלִּטִן שְׁמַיָּא "from the time that you realize that Heaven is powerful" 4:23; מַלְכִין . . . שַׁלִּיטִין בְּכֹל עֲבַר נַהֲרָה "mighty . . . kings in all (the province) Beyond-the-River" Ezra 4:20; שַׁלִּיט עִלָּיָא בְּמַלְכוּת אֲנָשָׁא "the Most High has power over the kingdom of men" Dan 4:14, 22, 29: 5:21; המו שליטן בחלקי "they shall have power over my share" BMAP 4:18-19; ברה שליט יהוה למנשא דשנא "his son shall have the right to take up the gift" AD 2:4; שליטא אנתי בפלג דרגא למסלק ומנחת "you (f.) shall have the right over half of the staircase to go up and to go down" BMAP 9:15; אנון שליטין בחולקהון למנתן לך "they have power over their portions to give you (or not)" 1QapGen 22:24; לֶהֱוֵא שַׁלִּיט תַּלְתָּא בְּמַלְכוּתָא "he shall have power as triumvir in the kingdom" Dan 5:29 (cf. תִּשְׁלַט 5:16); הֲלָךְ לָא שַׁלִּיט לְמִרְמֵא עֲלֵיהֹם "(you) have no right to impose a toll on them" Ezra 7:24. -- As a noun: אַרְיוֹךְ שַׁלִּיטָא דִּי־מַלְכָּא "Arioch, the king's captain" Dan 2:15; אנתה מרה ושליט על כולא "You are Lord and Sovereign over all!: 1QapGen 20:13.

שְׁלֵם, 3 pl. m. שלמו (šĕlímû), 3 pl. f. שלמא (šĕlímā'): be finished, be complete, be perfect. וְעַד־כְּעַן מִתְבְּנֵא וְלָא שְׁלִם "and up till now (the house of God) is being built and is not (yet) finished" Ezra 5:16; עשר שנין שלמא מן יום די נפקתה מן חרן "ten years are complete since the day you departed from Haran" 1QapGen 22:27-28; כמא שלמא להן לה שקיהא "how perfect are her thighs!" 1QapGen 20:6. -- Cf. שלם (šĕlim), adj.: perfect, safe. ואשכחת כול אנשי שלם "and I found all my household safe and sound" 1QapGen 21:19. -- Pa. complete, pay, pay back. מה זי לקחת זיני תשלם "for what you have taken you shall pay the penalty" AD 12:8; עד תשלם בכספך "until you complete your money," i.e., get it back BMAP 11:11; ולא שלמתך בכספך "and I have not paid you your money" AP 10:7; והן לא שלמת לך כל כספך "and if I have not paid you back all your money" AP 11:7-8. -- Haph. 3 sg. m. הַשְׁלֵם *, w. suff. הַשְׁלְמַהּ ; impv. sg. m. הַשְׁלֵם : bring to an end,

329

deliver. מַאנַיָא . . . הַשְׁלֵם קֳדָם אֱלָהּ יְרוּשְׁלֶם "deliver . . . the vessels before the God of Jerusalem" Ezra 7:19 (cf. LXX παράδος); מְנָה־אֱלָהָא מַלְכוּתָךְ וְהַשְׁלְמַהּ "God has numbered (the days of) your kingdom and brought it to an end" Dan 5:26 (cf. LXX, Theod, Vg). [Hebr. שָׁלֵם]. †

שְׁלָם (šalām, BL 187d), emph. שְׁלָמָא, w. suff. שְׁלָמְכוֹן, m.: **peace, safety, welfare, greeting.** שלם לן תנה "there is peace for us here" AP 37:2; בזנה קדמי שלם אף תמה קדמ[י]ךָ שלם יהוי "there is peace here with me; may there also be peace there with you" AD 5:1-2; אגרת חדה בשלמך לא שלחת עלי "you did not send me a letter about your welfare" AP 41:5; שלמך שמעת "I have heard about your safety" AP 41:2; אתית לי לביתי בשלם "I came home safely" 1QapGen 21:19; שלם יהוי לך "Peace be to you!" Aḥ. 110; אלהיא שלם ישׂמו לך "(that) the gods may grant you peace" AD 13:5; שְׁלָמְכוֹן יִשְׂגֵּא "may your peace be multiplied" Dan 3:31; 6:26; לְדָרְיָוֶשׁ מַלְכָּא שְׁלָמָא כֹלָּא "To Darius, the King, all peace!" Ezra 5:7; שְׁלָם "Greeting" 4:17; סָפַר דָּתָא דִּי־אֱלָהּ שְׁמַיָּא <שְׁלָם> גְּמִיר "(to Ezra,) scribe of the law of the God of Heaven, perfect <peace>!" 7:12; שלם מראן אלה שמיא ישׁאל שׂגיא "may the God of Heaven seek exceedingly after the safety of our lord" AP 30:1-2; שלם ביתך ובניך "Peace (be) to your household and your children" AP 34:7; שלם וׁשׁרׁרת שׂגיא הושׁרת ל[ךָ] "I send [you] much peace and prosperity" AD 5:1; שלם וחין שלחת לך "peace and life I send to you" El. Ostr. 2-3 (RHR 130 [1945] 20); הוית לשלמכי אשׁלח שׁלמך "I used to send a greeting to you" AP 41:3; שׁלחת ספרה זנה "for your welfare I send this letter" Hermopolis 1:12-13. [Hebr. שָׁלוֹם]. †

שֵׁם (šim, BL 179f), (abs. &) cst., w. suff. שְׁמֵהּ; pl. (w. augm. -hā-, cf. BL 248g, & s.v. אַב) שְׁמָהָן *, cst. שְׁמָהָת, w. suff. שְׁמָהָתְהֹם, m.: **name.** לֶהֱוֵא שְׁמֵהּ דִּי־אֱלָהָא מְבָרַךְ "blessed be the name of God" Dan 2:20; דָּנִיֵּאל דִּי־שְׁמֵהּ בֵּלְטְשַׁאצַּר כְּשֻׁם אֱלָהִי "Dani-

330

שׁמד

el, whose name, Belteshazzar, is like the name of my god" 4:5: 2:26; 4:16; דִּי־מַלְכָּא שָׁם־שְׁמֵהּ בֵּלְטְשַׁאצַּר "whose name the king made Belteshazzar" 5:12; שמני שם טב "he gave me a good name" *Nerab* 3 (*KAI* 226); אל יקל שמך קדמיהם "(that) your name be not vilified in their sight" *Aḥ.* 141; וִיהִיבוּ לְשֵׁשְׁבַּצַּר שְׁמֵהּ "and they were delivered to one named Sheshbazzar" Ezra 5:14 (BL 358p); נדן שמה ברי רבא "my son, named Nadin, is full-grown" *Aḥ.* 18; למּמטה מדי בכנדור שמה "upon arrival in Media, at (a city) named Kundur" *Bisitun* 25; דִּי נִכְתֵּב . . . שְׁמָהָתְהֹם שְׁאֵלְנָא לְהֹם שֵׁם־גֻּבְרַיָּא "we asked them their names . . . that we might write down the name(s) of the men" Ezra 5:10; מַן־אֲנוּן שְׁמָהָת גֻּבְרַיָּא "what are the names of the men?" 5:4 (cf. Hebr. מִי שְׁמֶךָ Judg 13:17); זנה שמהת נשיא "these are the names of the women" *AP* 34:2. -- Specifically: יסחו שמך . . . מן חין . . . ויהאבדו זרעך "may (the gods) root out your name . . . from life . . . and destroy your posterity!" *Nerab* 9-11 (*KAI* 225); פלאכהל . . . לאבדת אשמהם "then I shall not be able . . . to destroy their name" *Sefire II* B 6-7; וַאֱלָהָא דִּי שַׁכִּן שְׁמֵהּ תַּמָּה "the God who made His name dwell there" Ezra 6:12; בְּשֵׁם אֱלָהּ יִשְׂרָאֵל "(prophesied) in the name of the God of Israel" 5:1; עלותא יקרבון . . . בשמך "they will offer sacrifices . . . on your behalf" *AP* 30:25-26; כלא מליא באגרה חדה שלחן בשמן "the whole matter we have sent in a letter (written) in our name(s)" *AP* 30:29; ספר לה שלחתי בשמה "you have not sent a letter in his name" *Hermopolis* 1:5-6; לא יכהלון יהנפקון עליכי ספר חדת ועתיק בשמי "they will not be able to bring out against you a deed, new or old, in my name" *AP* 8:15-16; ספר חדת ועתיק בשם ביתא זנה "a document, new or old, in the name of this house" *BMAP* 10:15-16. [Hebr. שֵׁם]. †

שׁמד, **Haph.** infin. הַשְׁמָדָה : **destroy.** שָׁלְטָנֵהּ יְהַעְדּוֹן לְהַשְׁמָדָה וּלְהוֹבָדָה עַד־סוֹפָא "they shall take away his dominion, destroying and consuming (it) utterly," lit., "to the end" Dan 7:26. [Hebr. שׁמד]. [1]

331

שׁמין—שׁמם

שְׁמִין (šĕmayn, others šĕmīn, BL 187c, *LFAA* 79o, *GBA* p. 102), emph. שְׁמַיָּא only pl. (BL 305e), m.: **heaven(s).** כל מה לחיה בארק ובשמין "every sort of evil on earth and in heaven" *Sefire I* A 26; בעל שמין "lord of heaven" *Zkr* A 3, 13 (*KAI* 202); כיומי שמין אמין "(as) stable as the days of heaven" *Adon Letter* 3 (*KAI* 266); but see Rosenthal, *JBL* 91 (1972) 552; שמיא וארקא "the heavens and the earth" *Adon Letter* 2 (*KAI* 266); בית מלכת שמין "temple of the queen of heaven" *Hermopolis* 4:1; [חד] בני שמין "[one of] the sons of heaven" *1QapGen* 2:5; אָתִין וְתִמְהִין בִּשְׁמַיָּא וּבְאַרְעָא "signs and wonders in heaven and on earth" Dan 6:28; אֱלָהַיָּא דִּי־שְׁמַיָּא וְאַרְקָא לָא עֲבַדוּ "the gods who did not make the heavens and the earth" Jer 10:11a; מַלְכְוָת תְּחוֹת כָּל־שְׁמַיָּא "kingdoms under the whole heaven" Dan 7:27: Jer 10:11b; צִפֲּרֵי שְׁמַיָּא "birds of the heavens" Dan 4:9, 18; וּבְטַל שְׁמַיָּא יִצְטַבַּע "and let him be wet with heaven's dew" 4:12, 20: 4:22, 30; 5:21; עִם־עֲנָנֵי שְׁמַיָּא "with the clouds of heaven" 7:13; וְרוּמֵהּ יִמְטֵא לִשְׁמַיָּא "and its top reaches heaven" 4:8, 17: 4:19; אַרְבַּע רוּחֵי שְׁמַיָּא "the four winds of heaven" 7:2; אִיתַי אֱלָהּ בִּשְׁמַיָּא "there is a God in heaven" 2:28; עִיר וְקַדִּישׁ מִן־שְׁמַיָּא נָחִת "a Watcher, a holy one, descended from heaven" 4:10: 4:20, 28; כְּמִצְבְּיֵהּ עָבֵד בְּחֵיל שְׁמַיָּא "He acts according to His will in the host of heaven" 4:32; אֱלָהּ שְׁמַיָּא "the God of heaven" 2:18, 19, 37, 44; Ezra 5:11, 12; 6:9, 10; 7:12, 21, 23; אלה שמיא "the God of heaven" *AP* 30:2; מָרֵא שְׁמַיָּא "the Lord of heaven" Dan 5:23; מרא שמיא "the Lord of heaven" *AP* 30:15; מרה שמיא "the Lord of heaven" *1QapGen* 7:7; מֶלֶךְ שְׁמַיָּא "the king of heaven" Dan 4:34; תִּנְדַּע דִּי שַׁלִּטִן שְׁמַיָּא "you realize that heaven rules" 4:23. [Hebr. שָׁמַיִם]. †

שׁמם, **Ithpoal** (BL 166h), 3 sg. m. אֶשְׁתּוֹמַם : **be dismayed.** אֶשְׁתּוֹמַם כְּשָׁעָה חֲדָה "(Daniel) was dismayed for a moment" Dan 4:16. [Hebr. the same]. [1]

שְׁמַע, 1 sg. שִׁמְעֵת ; impf. 3 sg. m. יִשְׁמַע ; ptc. pl. m.
שָׁמְעִין. **Peil** perf. 3 sg. m. שמיע. **Hithpe.** השתמע (*hištěma'*);
impf. 3 sg. m. יתשמע (*Sefire I* A29; wt. metathesis, cf. שִׂים
Hithpe.). **Hithpa.** impf. 3 pl. m. יִשְׁתַּמְּעוּן (BL 275q): **hear, find
out.** בְּעִדָּנָא דִּי־תִשְׁמְעוּן קָל קַרְנָא "at the time that you hear the
sound of the horn" Dan 3:5, 15: 3:7, 10; כְּדִי מִלְתָא שָׁמַע "when
(the king) heard (this) word" 6:15; לָא־חָזַיִן וְלָא שָׁמְעִין "(gods of
silver and gold) see not and hear not," i.e., cannot see or hear,
5:23; אשתמיע במ[דינת אתור] "there was heard in the pr[ovince of
Assyria]" *Aḥ.* 70 (*LFAA* 55d, e); אל ישתמע קל כנר בארפד "may the
sound of the lyre not be heard in Arpad" *Sefire I* A 29; שמעת
כעמלא זי עמלת "I have found out about the trouble that you took"
AP 40:2; שלמך שמעת "I heard about your welfare" *AP* 41:2; כן
שמיע לן לאמר תתפטרן "so we have heard (that) you (pl.) will be
freed" *Padua I* B 6; שמיע לי כזי פקידיא . . . בשוזיא מתנצחן "I hear
that the officers . . . are engaged in the strifes" *AD* 7:3-4; שְׁמַעֵת
עֲלָיךְ דִּי רוּחַ אֱלָהִין בָּךְ "I have heard about you that a spirit of (the)
gods is in you" Dan 5:14: 5:16; שמע מלך סודם די אתיב אברם כול
שביתא "the king of Sodom heard that Abram had brought back
all the captives" *1QapGen* 22:12. -- **listen to, pay attention,
obey.** זי נזר לה ושמע ל[קל[ה "since he made a vow to him, he
listened to his [voice]" *Barhadad* 4-5 (*KAI* 201); הן יאמר [כות]
לא ישתמע לה "if he speaks [thus], no attention will be paid to
him" *BMAP* 7:42; ואמר להם שמעו לי "and he said to them, 'Listen
to me'" *Aḥ.* 59; אשתמעו לה ועבדו "obey him and do (what he
says)" *AD* 4:3; ולישמען בנוה "and (if) his sons will not obey" *Sefire II* B2b; לא משתמען לי "they are not obedient to me" *AD* 4:1;
וְכֹל שָׁלְטָנַיָּא לֵהּ יִפְלְחוּן וְיִשְׁתַּמְּעוּן "and all dominions shall serve and
obey it (the kingdom of the saints)" Dan 7:27. [Hebr. שָׁמַע]. †

▲ שָׁמְרַיִן, שָׁמְרָיִן (cf. BL 23d): **Samaria** a province (Akk.
Samerina, Gk. Σαμάρεια). הוֹתֵב הִמּוֹ בְּקִרְיָה דִּי שָׁמְרָיִן "he settled
them in cities of Samaria" Ezra 4:10 (read rather בְּקִרְיַה ; LXX ἐν

πόλεσιν): 4:17; בני סנאבלט פחת שמרין "the sons of Sanballat, the governor of Samaria" *AP* 30:29. [Hebr. שֹׁמְרוֹן]. †

שׁמשׁ, **Pa.** impf. 3 pl. m. w. suff. יְשַׁמְּשׁוּנֵּהּ (BL 123m): **serve.** אֶלֶף אַלְפִים יְשַׁמְּשׁוּנֵּהּ "a thousand thousands serve him" Dan 7:10. [1]

שֶׁמַשׁ * (*šamš*, BL 225n), emph. שִׁמְשָׁא, m.: **sun.** אל ידנח [עלוהי ש]שמ "let not the su[n] shine [upon him]" *Aḥ.* 138; שפיר מלך למחזה כשמש "glorious is a king to see, like (the) sun" *Aḥ.* 108; וְעַד מֶעָלֵי שִׁמְשָׁא הֲוָא מִשְׁתַּדַּר לְהַצָּלוּתֵהּ "and until the setting of the sun (the king) strove to rescue him (Daniel)" Dan 6:15; [מִן] מערב שמשא "[from] sunset" *AP* 21:8. -- Designating a region: מערב [שמש לה] . . . [מדנח שמש ל[ה "west [of it . . .] east [of] it" *BMAP* 6:7; מן מועה שמש למערב "from east to west," lit., "from the rising of the sun to (its) setting" *BMAP* 12:15. [Hebr. שֶׁמֶשׁ]. [1]

▲ שִׁמְשַׁי : **Shimshai**, scribe of the prefect of Samaria. שִׁמְשַׁי סָפְרָא "Shimshai, the scribe" Ezra 4:8, 9, 17, 23. †

שֵׁן * (*šinn*), du. שִׁנַּיִן, w. suff. שִׁנַּיהּ k., שִׁנַּהּ q. (BL 49e, 75c, 79s): **tooth.** וּתְלָת עִלְעִין בְּפֻמַּהּ בֵּין שִׁנַּיהּ "and (it had) three ribs in its mouth, between two (rows of) teeth" Dan 7:5; וְשִׁנַּיִן דִּי־פַרְזֶל "it had great iron teeth" 7:7; שִׁנַּיהּ דִּי־פַרְזֶל "its teeth were of iron" 7:19; שנוהי שוין "his teeth (will be) even" *4QPhys-Hor (4Q561)* 1 i 3. [Hebr. the same]. †

שְׁנָה *, 3 pl. שְׁנוֹ (BL 154n), w. suff. שְׁנוֹהִי ; impf. 3 sg. m. יִשְׁנֵא (BL 153h), 3 sg. f. תִּשְׁנֵא ; ptc. sg. f. שָׁנְיָה, pl. m. שָׁנַיִן (BL 233g), pl. f. שָׁנְיָן : (1) **be different.** דִּי תִשְׁנֵא מִן־כָּל־מַלְכְוָתָא "which will be different from all the kingdoms" Dan 7:23: 7:24; אַרְבַּע חֵיוָן . . . שָׁנְיָן דָּא מִן־דָּא "four beasts . . . different one from the other" 7:3 (v.l. שָׁנְיָן pass. ptc., BL 157j); חֵיוְתָא רְבִיעָיְתָא דִּי־הֲוָת

שְׁנָיָה מִן־כָּלְּהוֹן "the fourth beast which was different from all of them" 7:19 (v.l. שַׁנְיָה pass. ptc.). -- (2) **make different, be changed** (for worse). סָרְבָּלֵיהוֹן לָא שְׁנוֹ "their cloaks were not changed," i.e., singed, Dan 3:27; דִּי לָא־תִשְׁנֵא צְבוּ בְּדָנִיֵּאל "that nothing might be changed about Daniel" 6:18; זִיוֹהִי שְׁנַיִן עֲלוֹהִי "his appearance became different" 5:9; מַלְכָּא זִיוֹהִי שְׁנוֹהִי "as for the king, his appearance became different" 5:6 (cf. *Bib* 45 [1964] 227); [למא צלם] אנפיך כדנא עליך שנא "[why] has [the appearance of] your face so changed?" *1QapGen* 2:16-17. -- **Pa.** שַׁנִּי *, 3 pl. שַׁנִּיו (BL 160s); impf. 3 pl. m. יְשַׁנּוֹן (BL 158n); pass. ptc. sg. f. מְשַׁנְּיָה (BL 160v). -- **Haph.** impf. 3 sg. m. יְהַשְׁנֵא ; infin. הַשְׁנָיָה ; ptc. sg. m. מְהַשְׁנֵא . -- (1) **change.** וְהוּא מְהַשְׁנֵא עִדָּנַיָּא "and He changes the times" Dan 2:21; יִסְבַּר לְהַשְׁנָיָה זִמְנִין וְדָת "(the evil king) plots to change times and (the) law" 7:25; הִיא מְשַׁנְּיָה מִן־כָּל־חֵיוָתָא "it changed from all the (other) beasts" 7:7; לִבְבֵהּ מִן־אֲנָשָׁא יְשַׁנּוֹן "let his mind be changed from a man's," lit., "let them change" 4:13 (see אֱנָשׁ no. 3); כָּל־אֱסָר . . . לָא לְהַשְׁנָיָה "(so that) no interdict . . .is to be changed," lit., "no one (can) change any interdict" 6:9 (see לְ II 5); דִּי לָא לְהַשְׁנָיָה כְּדָת־מָדַי וּפָרַס "so that one (is unable) to change (it) according to the law of the Medes and the Persians" 6:9. -- (2) **transgress, violate.** דִּי . . . שַׁנִּיו מִלַּת מַלְכָּא "who . . . have violated the king's word" Dan 3:28; דִּי יְהַשְׁנֵא פִּתְגָמָא דְנָה "whoever will transgress this decree" Ezra 6:11; דִּי יִשְׁלַח יְדֵהּ לְהַשְׁנָיָה "who will dare to transgress," lit., "will put forth his hand" 6:12. -- **Ithpa.** 3 sg. m. אֶשְׁתַּנִּי Dan 3:19 q., 3 pl. m. אֶשְׁתַּנּוּ k. (BL 159s, 165g); impf. 3 sg. m. יִשְׁתַּנֵּא , 3 pl. m. יִשְׁתַּנּוֹן (BL 158n), juss. יִשְׁתַּנּוּ (BL 89d): **be changed.** צְלֵם אַנְפּוֹהִי אֶשְׁתַּנִּי "the expression of his face was changed" Dan 3:19 (q., the pl. אֶשְׁתַּנּוּ k. agrees w. אַנְפּוֹהִי BL 334m); זִיוָיִךְ אַל־יִשְׁתַּנּוֹ "let not your appearance be changed" 5:10: 7:28; אשתני אנפי עלי "(that) my expression had changed" *1QapGen* 2:12; עַד דִּי עִדָּנָא יִשְׁתַּנֵּא "till the time will be changed" Dan 2:9. [Hebr. שָׁנָה]. †

שָׁנָה[1] * (qal-at, BL 178d), cst. שְׁנַת, emph. שנתא
(šantā'); pl. שְׁנִין, emph. שׁניא (šěnayyā'), f.: **year.** כְּבַר שְׁנִין
שִׁתִּין וְתַרְתֵּין "(Darius became king), being about sixty-two years
old," lit., "like a son of sixty-two years" Dan 6:1 (cf. כְּ no. 5);
ברת שנן 100 . . . בר שנן 100 "(if you die) at the age of 100 . . . (if I
die) at the age of 100" BMAP 4:17-18; מִקַּדְמַת דְּנָה שְׁנִין שַׂגִּיאָן
"many years ago," lit., "before this" Ezra 5:11; שבע שנן יאכל ארבה
"for seven years may the locust devour (Arpad)" Sefire I A 27;
בזא שנתא "in this year" AP 71:14; שנתא זא "this year" AP 81:39;
שנה בשנה "year by year" Tema A 20 (KAI 228); כל ירחן ושנן "all
months and years" AP 45:8; הן מטא תנין שנה "if there comes a
second year (and I have not paid you)" AP 10:7; שניאלסוף חמש
אלן "at the end of those five years" 1QapGen 19:23; ולשנין ארבע
שגיא "and in the fourth year it produced much wine עבד לי חמר
for me" 1QapGen 12:13-14; ביום חד לשתא חמישיתא [מן בתר מב]ולא
"on the first day of the fifth year [after] the [fl]ood" 1QapGen
12:15-16; תרתין שנין בתר מבולא "two years after the flood" 1Qap-
Gen 12:10. Used of the year of a reign (BL 252y; always cst.
שְׁנַת w. a cardinal number; the name of the king w. or wt. לְ):
בִּשְׁנַת חֲדָה לְכֹרֶשׁ "in the first year of Cyrus" Ezra 5:13; 6:3: Dan
7:1; עַד שְׁנַת תַּרְתֵּין לְמַלְכוּת דָּרְיָוֶשׁ "until the second year of the reign
of Darius" Ezra 4:24; דִּי־הִיא שְׁנַת שֵׁת לְמַלְכוּת דָּרְיָוֶשׁ "which is the
sixth year of the reign of Darius" 6:15; 2 לְי[ום] 2 ל[י]רח אפף שנת 27
לדריוש מלכא "on the 2d day of the [m]onth Epiphi, of the 27th
year of Darius, the King" AP 1:1; שנתא זא שנת 5 דריוהוש "this
year is the 5th year of Darius" AP 21:3; בשנת 14 דריוהוש [מל]כא
"in the 14th year of [Ki]ng Darius" AP 27:2; שנת 1 ארתחשסס[ש]
מלכא "the 1st year of King Artaxerxes" BMAP 9:1; ב 28 לירח
פאפי שנת 2 חשירש [מל]כ[א] "on the 28th of the month of Paophi in
the 2d year of King Xerxes" AP 2:1; בשנת 34 [נ]בוכדרצר מלך
[בב]ל "in the 34th year of Nebuchadnezzar, king of [Baby]lon]"
Sefire (?) A 4-6 (KAI 227). [Hebr. שָׁנָה]. †

שְׁנָה 2 * (qil-at, BL 179g), w. suff. שְׁנָתֵּהּ (v.l. שִׁנְתֵּהּ, BL 199d, 241t, u), f.: **sleep.** שְׁנָתֵּהּ נַדַּת עֲלוֹהִי "his sleep fled from him" Dan 6:19; [אתעירת אנה] נוח מן שנתי "[I], Noah, [awoke from my sleep" *1QapGen (1Q20)* 15:21. [Hebr. שֵׁנָה]. [1]

שָׁעָה (qāl-at, but cf. BL 179i, 241v), emph. & שָׁעֲתָה שַׁעֲתָא (v.l. שָׁעֲתָא), f.: **hour, moment.** אֶשְׁתּוֹמַם כְּשָׁעָה חֲדָה "(Daniel) was dismayed for a moment" Dan 4:16 (cf. כְּ no. 4); בַּהּ־שַׁעֲתָה נְפַקָה אֶצְבְּעָן דִּי יַד־אֱנָשׁ "at that moment the fingers of a man's hand came out" 5:5 (בְּ w. dem. suff.; see בְּ no. 3); מַן־דִּי־לָא יִפֵּל וְיִסְגֻּד בַּהּ־שַׁעֲתָא יִתְרְמֵא "whoever does not fall down and worship shall be cast at that moment (into the furnace)" 3:6.: 3:15; 4:30. †

שְׁפַט * (< Can., Hebr., GBA §18), ptc. pl. m. שָׁפְטִין : **judge.** מֶנִּי שָׁפְטִין וְדַיָּנִין "appoint judges and magistrates" Ezra 7:25 (to the Hebr. title is added the Ar. title); [לְמָ]ה ישפטון עקן עם אשה "why should logs strive with fire?" *Aḥ.* 104. [Hebr. שָׁפַט]. [1]

שַׁפִּיר (qattīl, BL 192e), adj.: **beautiful, handsome.** עָפְיֵהּ שַׁפִּיר "its (the tree's) foliage was beautiful" Dan 4:9, 18; שפיר מלך למחזה כשמש "handsome is a king to look at, like the sun" *Aḥ.* 108; שפיר לה צלם אנפיהא "(how) beautiful the form of her face" *1QapGen* 20:2; דשפיר ודטב קדמיך "that which is beautiful and good in your sight" *4QLevi[b] (4Q213a)* 1:16. †

שפל **Haph./Aph.** 2 sg m. הַשְׁפֵּלְתְּ (v.l. הַשְׁפֵּלְתָ, BL 101e); impf. 3 sg. m. יְהַשְׁפֵּל ; infin. הַשְׁפָּלָה ; pts. sg. m. מַשְׁפֵּל (BHS מַשְׁפִּיל, BL 115q): **abase, put down, humiliate.** דִּי מַהְלְכִין בְּגֵוָה יָכִל לְהַשְׁפָּלָה "He is able to abase those who walk in pride" Dan 4:34: 5:19; לָא הַשְׁפֵּלְתְּ לִבְבָךְ "you have not humbled your mind" 5:22; וּתְלָתָה מַלְכִין יְהַשְׁפִּל "and he shall put down three kings" 7:24; זי יהשפל לאיש רם "(God) who humbles the tall man" *Aḥ.* 150. [Hebr. שָׁפֵל]. †

שְׁפַל (šapal), adj.: **humble, lowly.** וּשְׁפַל אֲנָשִׁים יְקִים עֲלַיַּהּ
"and He sets over it (the kingdom) the lowly of men" Dan 4:14
(read rather אֲנָשָׁא ; BL 320i). [Hebr. שָׁפָל]. ⌐

שְׁפַר, impf. 3 sg. m. יִשְׁפַּר , 3 pl. f. ישפרן (yišpĕrān): **be
beautiful, please** (cf. טָאֵב). וכל בתולן . . . לא ישפרן מנהא "and no
virgins . . . are more beautiful than she" 1QapGen 20:6; מִלְכִּי
יִשְׁפַּר עֲלָיךְ "may my counsel be pleasing to you" Dan 4:24; שְׁפַר
קֳדָמַי לְהַחֲוָיָה "it pleased me to show" 3:32; שְׁפַר קֳדָם דָּרְיָוֶשׁ וַהֲקִים
"it pleased Darius to set up" 6:2 (cf. וְ no. 10). [Hebr. שָׁפַר]. †

שְׁפַרְפָּר (qataltāl, BL 193j), emph. שְׁפַרְפָּרָא : **dawn.**
בִּשְׁפַרְפָּרָא יְקוּם בְּנָגְהָא "at dawn (the king) arose, at daybreak" (last
word is a gloss) Dan 6:20. [Hebr. שִׁפְרָה "calm"]. ¹

שָׁק * (qāl, BL 179h), du. w. suff. שָׁקוֹהִי, f.: **thigh** (cf.
חֲרַף, רְגַל, יַרְכָה). דִּי חֲסַף . . . שָׁקוֹהִי דִּי פַרְזֶל רַגְלוֹהִי "its thighs were of
iron, its feet . . . of clay" Dan 2:33; רגליהא כמא שפירן וכמא שלמא להן
לה שקיהא "her feet, how beautiful! how perfect are her thighs!"
1QapGen 20:5-6. [Hebr. שׁוֹק]. ¹

שָׂרה *, infin. מִשְׁרֵא ; ptc. sg. m. שָׁרֵא ; pass. ptc. sg. m.
שְׁרֵא, pl. m. שָׁרַיִן (BL 233g): (1) **solve, free, explain.** קִטְרִין
לְמִשְׁרֵא "(you are able) to solve difficulties" Dan 5:16 (instead of
Pa. ptc. מְשָׁרֵא in 5:12, read מִשְׁרֵא); אֲנָה חָזֵה גֻּבְרִין אַרְבְּעָה שְׁרַיִן
"I see four men, freed, walking about" 3:25; קתל אחך או מַהְלְכִין
אסרה ו[אל] תשריה "kill your brother or imprison him, but do [not]
free him" Sefire III 18. -- (2) **divest** (travelling gear in order
to), **(en)camp, dwell.** אברם שרא בעמק שוא "Abram was encamped in the Valley of Shaveh" 1QapGen 22:13-14; הוית שרא
[עמה ב]כל אתר משריאתי "I (Abram) camped [with him (Lot) at]
every place of my (former) encampments" 1QapGen 20:34-21:1.
-- pass. ptc. שְׁרֵא "divested": נְהִירָא עִמֵּהּ שְׁרֵא "the light dwells

שרש—שת

with Him" Dan 2:22; אשכח אנון שרין בבקעת דן "he found them encamped in the Valley of Dan" *1QapGen* 22:7-8. -- **Hithpe.** ptc. sg. m. משתרה (*mištĕrēh*): **eat lunch.** כזי צידא עבד אנה תנה ובאתרא זנה משתרה אנה "whenever I go hunting here, I eat lunch in this place" *Cilicia* 4-6 (*KAI* 261). -- **Pa.** 3 pl. שָׁרִיו; ptc. sg. m. מְשָׁרֵא (Dan 5:12; see above): **begin.** שָׁרִיו לְמִבְנֵא בֵית אֱלָהָא "they began to rebuild the house of God" Ezra 5:2; למפלח . . . אנה שרית "I began . . . to cultivate the earth" *1QapGen* 12:13; שרית בארעא למשתיה ביום חד לשתא חמישיתא "I began to drink it (the wine) on the first day of the fifth year" *1QapGen* 12:15. -- **Hithpa.** ptc. pl. m. מִשְׁתָּרֵין (BL 233g, *GBA* §155): **be loosened.** קִטְרֵי חַרְצֵהּ מִשְׁתָּרֵין "the joints of his hips were loosened" Dan 5:6. †

שְׁרֹשׁ * (*šurš*), pl. w. suff. שָׁרְשׁוֹהִי : **root, scion.** עִקַּר שָׁרְשׁוֹהִי בְּאַרְעָא שְׁבֻקוּ "leave the stump of its roots in the earth" Dan 4:12, 20: 4:23; אל ירת שר[ש]ה אשם "May his sci[on] inherit no name" *Sefire I* C 24-25. [Hebr. שֹׁרֶשׁ]. †

שְׁרֹשִׁי q. (שרשו k.), (< Persian *sranšyā, AD* p. 47), emph. *: **punishment** (Gk. παιδεία). הֵן לְמוֹת הֵן לְשָׁרֹשׁוּ "whether for death or for punishment" Ezra 7:26; . . . סרושיתא יתעבד "the punishment . . . will be inflicted on them" *AD* 3:6. [1]

▲ שֵׁשְׁבַּצַּר : **Sheshbazzar, governor of Judah.** וִיהִיבוּ לְשֵׁשְׁבַּצַּר שְׁמֵהּ "and they were delivered to one named Shezhbazzar" Ezra 5:14; 5:16 (see Hebr. 1:8, 11). †

שֵׁת & שִׁת (*šidt*, BL 183h, 250j), f. שִׁתָּה *: **six.** פְּתָיֵהּ דִּי־הִיא אַמִּין שֵׁת "its (the statue's) width was six cubits" Dan 3:1; שְׁנַת־שֵׁת לְמַלְכוּת דָּרְיָוֶשׁ "which is the sixth regnal year of Darius" Ezra 6:15. [Hebr. שֵׁשׁ]. †

339

שתה—תבר

שתה (BL 155q), 3 sg. m. אִשְׁתִּי * (w. prosthetic א), 1 sg. אִשְׁתִּית *, 3 pl. אִשְׁתִּיו ; impf. 3 sg. m. יִשְׁתֶּה *, 3 pl. m. יִשְׁתּוֹן ; infin. w. suff. מִשְׁתְּיֵהּ *; ptc. sg. m. שָׁתֵה, pl. m. שָׁתַיִן (BL 233g): **drink.** חַמְרָא שָׁתֵה . . . מַלְכָּא "the king . . . was drinking wine" Dan 5:1: 5:4; וְיִשְׁתּוֹן בְּהוֹן "that they might drink from them" 5:2 (see וְ no. 9; BL 352g): 5:3, 23; זי ישתה חמרא "who drinks wine" *Aḥ.* 93; תהך ותשתה "you will go and drink" *AP* 71:22; יהוון בב[רא ז]ך שתין מיא "they would be drinking water from [th]at w[ell]" *AP* 27:7-8; ואכלת ואשתית תמן "and I ate and drank there" *1QapGen* 21:20; שרית למשתיה "I began to drink it" *1QapGen* 12:15. [Hebr. שָׁתָה]. †

שְׁתִּין (invar.): **sixty.** רוּמֵהּ אַמִּין שְׁתִּין "its (the statue's) height was sixty cubits" Dan 3:1; שְׁתִּין < > אַמִּין רוּמֵהּ "its height < > (will be) sixty cubits" Ezra 6:3 (LXX: ὕψος πήχεις ἑξή-κοντα πλάτος αὐτοῦ πήχεων ἑξήκοντα); כְּבַר שְׁנִין שְׁתִּין וְתַרְתֵּין "being about sixty-two years of age" Dan 6:1; לשוק חד אמין [ו]שתין ושבע "for a street (of) sixty-seven cub[its]" *5QNJ (5Q15)* 1 i 5. [Hebr. שִׁשִּׁים]. †

▲ שְׁתַר בּוֹזְנַי : **Shethar-bozenai,** Persian governor of Sa-maria. אֲתָא . . . שְׁתַר בּוֹזְנַי וּכְנָוָתְהוֹן "there came . . . Shethar-bozenai and their colleagues" Ezra 5:3: 5:6; 6:6, 13 (cf. שתברזן "Sati-barzan" *AP* 5:16). †

ת

The letter ת in Old Aramaic designated only the primitive sound *t*, but later it also designated the sound *t*, derived from primitive *ṭ*, written earlier as שׁ.

תְּבַר * (*t* < *ṭ*), pass. ptc. sg. f. תְּבִירָה : **break.** עמודיא זי אבנא זי הוו תמה תברו המו "the pillars of stone that were there they

תדיר—תוב

broke" *AP* 30:9; עלעי תנין יתבר "(a king's tongue) breaks the ribs
of a dragon" *Aḥ.* 106; ותבר אנון והוא רדף להון "(Abram) routed
them (his enemies), and he pursued them"*1QapGen* 22:9; כן
ישבר אנרת והדד [קשת מתעאל] וקשת רבוה "so may Inurta and Hadad
break [the bow of Mati'el], and the bow of his nobles!" *Sefire I*
A 38-39; מאן טב כס[ה] מלה בלבבה ו[הו זי] תביר הנפקה ברא "a good
vessel hid[es] a thing within itself, but [one that is] broken pours
(it) out" *Aḥ.* 109; מִן־קְצָת מַלְכוּתָא תֶּהֱוֵה תַקִּיפָה וּמִנַּהּ תֶּהֱוֵה תְבִירָה "the
kingdom will be partly strong and partly broken" Dan 2:42 (BL
297c). [Hebr. שָׁבַר]. [1]

תְּדִיר * (root *dūr,* prefix *ta-*), emph. תְּדִירָא : **continuation.**
אֱלָהָךְ דִּי אַנְתְּה פָּלַח־לֵהּ בִּתְדִירָא הוּא יְשֵׁיזְבִנָּךְ "may your God, whom
you serve continually, deliver you" Dan 6:17; 6:21. †

תוב (*t* < *ṯ*), 3 sg. m. תָּב *, 3 sg. f. תבת (*tā̆bat*), 2 sg. m.
תבת (*tā̆btā*), 1 sg. תבת ; impf. 3 sg. m. יתוב , 1 sg. אתוב (*'ă̆tûb*):
return, come back. עֵינַי לִשְׁמַיָּא נִטְלֵת וּמַנְדְּעִי עֲלַי יְתוּב "I raised my
eyes to heaven, and my understanding came back to me" Dan
4:31: 4:33; אתוב "I shall come back" *AP* 45:5; ותבת ואתית לי
לביתי בשלם "then I returned and came home safely" *1QapGen*
21:19; מן די תבת מן מצרין "since you returned from Egypt" *1Qap-
Gen* 22:29; ושבת תלאים ל[בר גא]ה ולברה "and (the city) Tal'ayim
has returned to [Bar Ga'y]ah and his son," i.e., into their possession *Sefire III* 25. -- **Haph./Aph.** 3 sg. m. הֲתִיב ,התב (*hă̆tīb*),
אתיב, w. suff. אתיבני , 3 pl. השבו (*hă̆tī̆bû*) , אתבו , w. suff.
הֲתִיבוּנָא ; impf. 3 sg. m. יהתב (*yĕhā̆tīb*), 2 sg. m. w. suff. תהשבהם
(*tĕhā̆tī̆bhōm*), 3 pl. m. יְהָתִיבוּן , יְתִיבוּן ; impv. sg, m. התב
(*hă̆tīb*); infin. w. suff. הֲתָבוּתָךְ : (1) **restore, return.** מָאנֵי בֵית־אֱלָהָא
יְהָתִיבוּן . . . "let them restore . . . the vessels of God's house" Ezra
6:5; זי לקחת כלא התב הב למספת "restore to Maspat all of what you
have taken" *AD* 12:7; החסן ולא התיב לה "he kept (them) and did
not return (them) to him" *AP* 20:7; נכסיא זי לקחו אתבו . . . על מריהם

341

"the goods that they have taken they have restored . . . to the owners of them" *AP* 34:6; [נרביל]יהתב המו לאפק "let him return them to Upaqa[narbayil]" *Assur Letter* 11 (*KAI* 233); הן השב זי [זי לה] לי אהשב "if he has restored my (fugitives), I shall return [his]" *Sefire III* 20; תהשבהם לי "you must return them to me" *Sefire III* 6; [ת אבי]השבו אלהן שיבת בי "the gods have restored [my father's] hou[se]" *Sefire III* 24-25 (cf. Hebr. בְּשׁוּב יְהֹוָה אֶת־שִׁיבַת צִיּוֹן "when the LORD restored the fortunes of Zion" Ps 126:1). -- (2) **bring back, turn back.** די אתיבני לארעא דא בשלם "because He had brought me back to this land safely" *1QapGen* 21:3-4; אתיב אברם כול שביתא "Abram had brought back all the captives" *1QapGen* 22:12; למה אלהיא . . . יהתיבנהי עליך "lest God . . . turn it (the arrow) back on you" *Aḥ.* 126; וֶאֱדַיִן יְתִיבוּן נִשְׁתְּוָנָא עַל־דְּנָה "and then they bring back the letter about this matter" Ezra 5:5. -- (3) **give.** הֲתִיב עֵטָה וּטְעֵם לְאַרְיוֹךְ "(Daniel) gave prudent advice to Arioch" Dan 2:14; לָא־הַשְׁחִין אֲנַחְנָה עַל־דְּנָה פִּתְגָם לַהֲתָבוּתָךְ "we have no need to give you an answer in this matter" 3:16; פִּתְגָמָה הֲתִיבוּנָא לְמֵמַר "they gave us (this) response, saying" Ezra 5:11. [Hebr. שׁוּב]. †

תְּוַהּ (BL 151v): **be astonished.** מַלְכָּא תְּוַהּ וְקָם "the king was astonished and got up" Dan 3:24. [Hebr. תָּמַהּ]. [1]

תּוֹר * (*tawr*), pl. תּוֹרִין : **ox, bull.** עִשְׂבָּא כְתוֹרִין יֵאכֻל "(the king) shall eat grass like oxen" Dan 4:30: 4:22, 29; 5:21; . . . תְּקַנֵּא תּוֹרִין . . . וּתְקָרֵב הִמּוֹ עַל־מַדְבְּחָה "you shall buy . . . bulls . . . and offer them on the altar" Ezra 7:17; וּבְנֵי תוֹרִין . . . לַעֲלָוָן "and young bulls . . . for holocausts" 6:9; הַקְרִבוּ לַחֲנֻכַּת בֵּית־אֱלָהָא דְנָה תּוֹרִין מְאָה "they offered at the dedication of this house of God one hundred bulls" 6:17; וקן תור ענז מקלו [ל]א יתעבד תמה "and no sheep, oxen, goats are made a sacrifice there" *AP* 33:10 (collect. sg.); דבקת לטור תורא "I reached Mount Taurus," lit. "the mount of the ox" *1QapGen* 21:16. Cf. שורה יהינקן עגל [שבע] "[should seven] cows give suck to a calf" *Sefire I* A 22-23. [Hebr. שׁוֹר]. †

תחת—תחתי

תְּחַת * (*taḥt*) & תְּחוֹת (*tuḥāt*, w. assimilation to *u*; cf. אֱנוֹשׁ, *GBA* §22, *ti-ḫú-u-tú Warka* 3), w. suff. תַּחְתּוֹהִי & תְּחֹתוֹהִי: as a noun, **place under, lower part**; as a prep. **under, beneath, below.** עֲלֵי אֲרָם וּתְחִתָּה כֹל "all Upper-Aram and Lower-Aram," lit., "and its lower part" *Sefire I* A 6; שבו לתחתכ[ם] "stay where yo[u] are," lit., "in a place under you" *Sefire III* 7; יֵאבַדוּ מֵאַרְעָא וּמִן־תְּחוֹת שְׁמַיָא אֵלֶּה "(false gods) shall perish from the earth and from under these heavens" Jer 10:11; תְּנֻד חֵיוְתָא מִן־תַּחְתּוֹהִי "let the beast flee from beneath it (the tree)" Dan 4:11 (v.l. תְּחוֹתוֹהִי); לא אכל אנצל לפלטי מן תחת לבבך "I shall not be able to take away Palṭi from (a place) under your heart," i.e., as long as you love him (= מנך 2:14b) *BMAP* 2:13-14a; תְּחֹתוֹהִי תְּדוּר חֵיוַת בָּרָא "under it dwells the beast of the field" Dan 4:18: 4:9; מַלְכְוָת תְּחוֹת כָּל־שְׁמַיָא "the kingdoms under all the heavens" 7:27; תחת מנה בית פרסא "and below it is the house of Parsa" *BMAP* 9:4 (see מן no. 8; and תַּחְתִּי *); כתיבן בספרא מן תחת ומ[נעל] "(its boundaries) are written in (this) document, from below and a[bove]" *BMAP* 6:9. [Hebr. תַּחַת]. †

תַּחְתִּי *, f. תחתיה (*taḥtāyāh*), emph. תחתיתא (*taḥtāytā'*), w. suff. תחתיתה (*taḥtāytēh*); as adj.: **lower, inferior** (opp. עֶלָי); as f. noun: **lower part.** וישמו תחתיתה [לע]ליתה "and may (the gods) make its lower part its [up]per part!" *Sefire I* C 23-24; פקידא זי במצרין בתחתיתא "the officer who is in Lower Egypt," lit., "in Egypt, in its lower part" *AD* 7:1*; בגיא זילי זי בעליתא ותחתיתא "my estates which are in Upper and Lower (Egypt)" *AD* 5:5-6. -- Specifically: תַּחְתִּיָה * f.: **lower part, south** (or) **north.** משחתה ארכה מן תחתיה לעליה אמן 13 . . . מן מועא למערב "its dimensions: its length from south to north . . . from east to west" *AP* 8:4-5; בתחתיה ומנעלא כוין פתיחן "at the lower end and above there are open windows" *AP* 25:6 (= לתחתיה *AP* 6:10; = תחתיה [accus.] *AP* 8:6 = "to the south"); תחתיא מנה אגר דרגא "to the south of it is the wall of the stairway" *BMAP* 9:10. [Hebr. תַּחְתּוֹן].

343

תְּלַג (*talg*): **snow.** לְבוּשֵׁהּ כִּתְלַג חִוָּר "His garment was as white as snow" Dan 7:9; עליהון תלגא [נ]חת "the snow [was com]ing down on them" *4QEnastr^b (4Q209)* 23:10. [1]

תְּלִיתָי * (BL 251v), f. תְּלִיתָיָא k. & תְּלִיתָאָה q. (BL 51k): **third.** מַלְכוּ תְלִיתָיָא אָחֳרִי דִּי נְחָשָׁא "(there will arise) another, a third kingdom of bronze" Dan 2:39. [Hebr. שְׁלִישִׁי]. [1]

תְּלָת (*talāt*) m.; f. תְּלָתָה & תְּלָתָא , cst. תְּלָת *, w. suff. תְּלָתְהוֹן (> תְּלָתֵּהוֹן *, BL 67s, 249h): **three.** וּתְלָת עִלְעִין בְּפֻמַּהּ "and three ribs in its mouth" Dan 7:5; תְּלָת מִן־קַרְנַיָּא קַדְמָיָתָא אֶתְעֲקַרוּ "three of the first horns were plucked" 7:8: 7:20; בשנת תלת עשרה "in the thirteenth year they rebelled" *1QapGen* 21:27; גברין מרדו "three hundred and eighteen . . . men" תלת מאא ותמניאת עשר . . . *1QapGen* 22:6; הֲלָא גֻבְרִין תְּלָתָא רְמֵינָא לְגוֹא־נוּרָא "did we not cast three men into the fire?" Dan 3:24: 6:3, 11, 14; עַד יוֹם תְּלָתָה לִירַח אֲדָר "on the third day of the month Adar" Ezra 6:15; וּתְלָתָה מַלְכִין יְהַשְׁפִּל "and he shall put down three kings" Dan 7:24; אחר לי[ו]מן "then after three more d[a]ys" *Ah.* 39; פשכן תלתה אחרנן תלתה "three hand-breadths by three hand-breadths" *AP* 26:15; גֻבְרַיָּא "all three my servants" כל תלתה עלימן זילי *AD* 6:4; אִלֵּךְ תְּלָתֵהוֹן "those three men" Dan 3:23; די פם חד תלתהון ממללין "for the three of them were speaking as one man," lit., "(with) one mouth" *1QapGen* 20:8; [אתו] לי תלתת גברין מן רברבי מצרי[ן] "three men from the nobles of Egyp[t came] to me" *1QapGen* 19:24; תלתת שרשוהי "its three roots" *6QpapGiants (6Q 8)* 2:1 (DJD 36.80). [Hebr. שָׁלוֹשׁ]. †

תְּלָת * (BL 252w), emph. תְּלִתָּא , w. suff. (*GBA* §71) תַּלְתִּי : **third, triumvir** (cf. Akk. *šalšu* "third part," magistrate's title). תַּלְתָּא בְמַלְכוּתָא תִּשְׁלַט "you will rule as triumvir in the king-dom" Dan 5:16: 5:29; תַּלְתִּי בְמַלְכוּתָא יִשְׁלַט "he shall rule as my triumvir in the kingdom" 5:7 (v.l. תַּלְתָּא "as triumvir"). [Hebr. cf. שָׁלִישׁ]. †

תלתין—תנין

תְּלָתִין (invar.): **thirty.** יוֹמִין תְּלָתִין "thirty days" Dan 6:8, 13; כרשן תלתין "thirty karsh" *BMAP* 8:8; [אמין תלתין וחנש] "thirty-five cubits" *5QNJ (5Q15)* 1 i 13. [Hebr. שְׁלֹשִׁים]. ¹

תַּמָּה (BL 205b, 253b), adv.: **there.** אֱלָהָא דִּי שַׁכֵּן שְׁמֵהּ תַּמָּה "the God who caused His name to dwell there" Ezra 6:12; בְּבֵית גִּנְזַיָּא דִּי־מַלְכָּא תַּמָּה דִּי בְּבָבֶל "in the king's archives there in Babylon" 5:17; דִּי גִנְזַיָּא מְהַחֲתִין תַּמָּה בְּבָבֶל "where they (also) store the treasures in Babylon" 6:1; רַחִיקִין הֲווֹ מִן־תַּמָּה "stay far away from there" 6:6; מנדעם מן תמה לא מהיתין עלי "they are not bringing me anything from there" *AD* 10:2; כוין פתיהן תמה "windows are open there" *AP* 25:6; אתין תמה עליכם "they are coming there to you" *AP* 38:5; אגורא . . . יהעדו מן תמה "let them remove from there . . . the temple" *AP* 30:6; מן תמה תנפק ותנעל ביתא זנה "from there you will go out and go in to this house" *BMAP* 12:22; בזנה קדמי שלם אף תמה קדמ[י]ך שלם "(there is) peace here with me; (may there be) peace there too with you" *AD* 5:1-2. *תַּמָּן (cf. כְּמָן for כְּמָה, s.v. מָה): בנית תמן מדבח . . . ואכלת ואשתית תמן "I built an altar there . . . I ate and drank there" *1QapGen* 21:20.-- Cf. תְּנָה *: **here, hither** (*LFAA* 118a). שלם לן תנה "(it is) well with us here" *AP* 37:2; [מ]טאת ספינתא תנה עלין "the boat has [re]ached us here" *BMAP* 13:7; עד תנה תחום דנל "up to here (stretches) the area of DNL" *Cilicia* 1 (*KAI* 259). [Hebr. שָׁם, שָׁמָּה]. †

תִּמַהּ * (timh), pl. תִּמְהִין, emph. תִּמְהַיָּא, w. suff. תִּמְהוֹהִי, m.: **wonder.** אָתַיָּא וְתִמְהַיָּא דִּי עֲבַד עִמִּי אֱלָהָא "the signs and wonders that God has done for me" Dan 3:22: 6:28; תִּמְהוֹהִי כְּמָה תַּקִּיפִין "how mighty His wonders" 3:33; תמהא אחד לי "wonder seized me" *11QtgJob (11Q10)* 4:5. [Hebr. תֵּמַהּ]. †

תִּנְיָן * (tinay + ān, for *tinay-āy, cf. קַדְמָי * "first," תְּלִיתָי * "third," BL 196a), f. תִּנְיָנָה : **second.** חֵיוָה אָחֳרִי תִנְיָנָה דָּמְיָה לְדֹב "another beast, a second one, like a bear" Dan 7:5; הן מטא

345

תנינות—תקל

תנין שנה ולא שלמתך "if a second year comes and I have not paid you" *AP* 10:7; ובניתה תניאני "and I built it (the altar) a second time" *1QapGen* 21:1; [ואחריתא] י[היבת לתנינה די קאם פנבד "and the other (loaf) was [g]iven to his second who was standing nearby" *2QNJ (2Q24)* 4:16. [Hebr, שֵׁנִי]. [1]

תִּנְיָנוּת , adv. (BL 254o, cf. *LFAA* 119i; cf. תִּנְיָנֵי s.v. תִּנְיָן): **a second time, again.** עֲנוֹ תִנְיָנוּת וְאָמְרִין "they spoke up a second time and said" Dan 2:7. [1]

תִּפְתֵּי (< Persian), emph. pl. תִּפְתָּיֵא : **magistrate** (prob. protector of public order). מַלְכָּא שְׁלַח לְמִכְנַשׁ . . . תִּפְתָּיֵא "the king sent to assemble . . . the magistrates" Dan 3:2; 3:3; הן אזד יתעבד מן דיניא תיפתיא "if an inquiry be made of the judges, magistrates" *AP* 27:8-9. †

תַּקִּיף * (*qattīl*, BL 192e), f. תַּקִּיפָה & תַּקִּיפָא , pl. תַּקִּיפִין , adj.: **strong, mighty.** מַלְכוּ רְבִיעָיָה תֶּהֱוֵא תַקִּיפָה כְּפַרְזְלָא "there shall be a fourth kingdom, strong as iron" Dan 2:40; 2:42; מַלְכִין תַּקִּיפִין "mighty kings" Ezra 4:20; תִּמְהוֹהִי כְּמָה תַקִּיפִין "how mighty are His wonders" Dan 3:33; חֵיוָה רְבִיעָיָה . . . תַּקִּיפָא יַתִּירָא "a fourth beast . . . exceedingly strong" 7:7; אנתתי בחלץ תקיף עמי מללת "my wife spoke to me with mighty vehemence" *1QapGen* 2:8; ובכית אנה אברם בכי תקיף "and I, Abram, wept mightily," lit., "wept a mighty weeping" *1QapGen* 20:10-11; ואנה . . . אסתרך לך לתקיף "and I (shall be) a buckler for you against anyone stronger than you" *1QapGen* 22:30-31. [Hebr. the same]. †

תְּקַל *, **Peil** perf. 2 sg. m. תְּקִילְתָּה (v.l. תְּקֵילְתָּא, תְּקִילְתָּא): **weigh.** תְּקִילְתָּה בְמֹאזַנְיָא "you have been weighed on the scale" Dan 5:27; תתב על מוזנא ותתקל ל[אס]חור כסף שקלן 7 "she shall return to the scale and weigh out for [As]hor the sum of 7 shekels" *AP* 15:23-24. [1]

346

תקל—תקף

תְּקֵל (_tiql_), m.: **weight, shekel** (a unit of weight, = 10 hallurs; cf. Akk. *šiqlu*). מְנֵא תְּקֵל וּפַרְסִין "MENE, TEQEL, and PARSIN," lit., "a mina, a shekel, and two half-minas" Dan 5:25: 5:27 (see מְנֵא); 7 כסף תקלן "a sum of 7 shekels" *BMAP* 2:8 (cf. שקלן 2:10); 7 תתקל ל[אס]חור כסף שקלן "she shall weigh out for [As]hor the sum of 7 shekels" *AP* 15:24. [Hebr. שֶׁקֶל]. †

תקן, **Hoph.** 3 sg. f. הָתְקְנַת, 1 sg. הָתְקְנֵת (v.l.): עַל־מַלְכוּתִי הָתְקְנֵת "I was restored to my kingdom" Dan 4:33 (read rather הָתְקְנַת, but see LXX ἀποκατεστάθη ἡ βασιλεία μου ἐμοί, which = עֲלַי, "my kingdom was restored to me" BL 115u, v). [Hebr. the same]. †

תְּקֵף, 3 sg. f. תֶּקְפַּת (BL 46m, 30z), 2 sg. m. תְּקֵפְתְּ (BL 101e): **become strong/severe, prevail, be hardened.** רְבָה אִילָנָא וּתְקֵף "the tree grew and became strong" Dan 4:8: 4:17, 19; רוּחֵהּ תֶּקְפַּת לַהֲזָדָה "his spirit was hardened to act proudly" 5:20 (Theod. ἐκραταιώθη); תקף מלך עילם ומלכיא די עמה למלך סודם "the king of Elam and the kings who were with him prevailed over the king of Sodom" *1QapGen* 21:25-26; עלוהי . . . לסוף תרתין שנין תקפו מכתשיא ונגדיא "at the end of two years . . . the plagues and afflictions became (more) severe for him" *1QapGen* 20:18. -- **Pa.** infin. תַּקָּפָה : **enforce.** לְקַיָּמָה קְיָם מַלְכָּא וּלְתַקָּפָה אֱסָר "that the king should set up an ordinance and enforce an interdict" Dan 6:8 (cf. דִּי I 2a at the end). †

תְּקֹף (_tuqp_), cst. תְּקָף (read perh. תְּקָף־ or w. v.l. תְּקֹף, BL 187d), emph. תָּקְפָּא : **strength, power, might, force.** אֱלָהּ שְׁמַיָּא מַלְכוּתָא חִסְנָא וְתָקְפָּא וִיקָרָא יְהַב־לָךְ "the God of Heaven has given you the kingdom, the power, the might, and the glory" Dan 2:37; בֱנַיְתַהּ לְבֵית מַלְכוּ בִּתְקָף חִסְנִי "I have built it with my mighty power as a royal residence" 4:27; דברת אנתתי מני בתוקף "my wife has been taken away from me by force" *1QapGen* 20:14; אהוה לך

347

סעד ותקף "I shall be to you both support and strength" *1QapGen* 22:30-31. [Hebr. תְּקֶף]. †

תְּרֵין * m. (du., *tirayn* < *tinayn*, BL 249f; *r* perh. < f.), cst. תְּרֵי; תַּרְתֵּין f. (*tirtayn* < *tintayn*, dissim. *n* > *r;* cf. ¹בַּר), cst. תרתי : **two** (cf. תִּנְיָן). שְׁנִין שִׁתִּין וְתַרְתֵּין "sixty-two years" Dan 6:1; גבריא אלך תרין זי עמה "those two men who were with him" *Aḥ*. 56; תרתין מלן שפירה "two things are fair" *Aḥ*. 92; כל [ו] פסמסנית תרין נופתיא זי כרכיא "Psamsaneith and [ ], both boatmen of the fortifications" *AP* 26:7-8; עַד שְׁנַת תַּרְתֵּין לְמַלְכוּת דָּרְיָוֶשׁ "until the second year of Darius' reign" Ezra 4:24; בתרתי רגליא מרדיא אתכנש[ו] "the rebels rall[ied] a second time"*Bisitun* 11; ומלי תרין חברוהי "and (the king heard) the words of his two companions" *1QapGen* 20:8; תרתין שנין בתר מבולא "two years after the flood" *1QapGen* 12:10; והיא עמה תרתין שנין "and she was with him for two years" *1QapGen* 20:18. -- לְקְצָת יַרְחִין תְּרֵי־עֲשַׂר "at the end of twelve months" Dan 4:26; בגי סגנן אמן עשרה ותרין "within ribs(?) (of) twelve cubits" *AP* 26:10-11; שִׁבְטֵי . . . תְּרֵי־עֲשַׂר עַל־כָּל־יִשְׂרָאֵל "for all Israel, the twelve tribes of Israel" Ezra 6:17; תרתי עשרה שנין הוא יהבין "for twelve years they kept paying (their tribute)" *1QapGen* 21:26-27 (s.v. עֲשַׂר). [Hebr. שְׁנַיִם]. †

תְּרַע (*tar'*), (abs. &) cst., emph. תרעא (*tar'ā'*), m.: **gate, door.** קְרֵב . . . לִתְרַע אַתּוּן "(the king) came near . . . to the door of the furnace" Dan 3:26; יהבת לי תרע ביתא זילך למבנה אגר 1 תמה "you have given me the gateway of your house to build there 1 wall" *AP* 5:3-4; אנת שליט למפתח תרעא זך "you have the right to open that gate" *AP* 5:14; ותרעא עלה פתיח לשוק מלכא "and the gate above opens to the king's street" *BMAP* 12:21; . . . 5 תרען זי אבן "5 gates of stone . . . they destroyed; and they lifted off their portals, and the hinges of those portals were bronze" *AP* 30:9-11; [סלקין עד] תרעי שמי[ה] "[were mounting up to] the gates of heav[en]" *4QEnᵃ (4Q201)* 1 iv 9-10. -- Specifically: וְדָנִיֵּאל בִּתְרַע מַלְכָּא "but Daniel (remained) at the king's gate," i.e., his court Dan 2:49; זי הקימת בתרע היכלא "(the son) whom you set in the gate of the palace" *Ah.* 44; אנה נוח הוית בתרע תיבותא "I, Noah, was at the door of the ark" *1QapGen (1Q20)* 11:1. [Hebr. שַׁעַר]. †

תְּרָע * (*tarrāʿ,* BL 191c), emph. pl. תָּרָעַיָּא , m.: **door-keeper.** תָּרָעַיָּא . . . וּפָלְחֵי בֵּית אֱלָהּ שְׁמַיָּא "the doorkeepers . . . and servants of the house of the God of Heaven" Ezra 7:24. [Hebr. שׁוֹעֵר].[1]

תַּרְתֵּין : see תְּרֵין .

▲ תַּתְּנַי : **Tattenai,** governor. אֲתָא עֲלֵיהוֹן תַּתְּנַי פַּחַת עֲבַר־נַהֲרָה "Tattenai, the governor of (the province) Beyond-the-River, came to them" Ezra 5:3: 5:6; 6:6, 13. †

Printed on May 2011
by Arti Grafiche Srl - Pomezia, Rome (IT)
[0.5]